Historical Archaeology:
A Guide to Substantive and Theoretical Contributions

Historical Archaeology:
A Guide to Substantive and Theoretical Contributions

Edited by

Robert L. Schuyler

Department of Anthropology
City College and Graduate Center
City University of New York

Baywood Publishing Company, Inc.
Farmingdale, New York 11735

Copyright © 1978 by Baywood Publishing Company, Inc.
120 Marine Street, Farmingdale, New York 11735.
All rights reserved.

Printed in the United States of America

International Standard Book Number 0-89503-008-X
Library of Congress Catalog Card Number 77-94409

Library of Congress Cataloging in Publication Data
Main entry under title:

Historical archaeology.

    Includes bibliographies.
    1. Archaeology and history--United States--
Addresses, essays, lectures. I. Schuyler,
Robert L., 1947-
CC77.H5H57   930'.1   77-94409
ISBN 0-89503-008-X

*Historical Archaeology: A Guide to Substantive
and Theoretical Contributions*
is dedicated to
J.C. Harrington
and
John L. Cotter
two pioneers in the founding of the discipline
in America

All editorial royalties from this volume will be used, in varying proportions,
to support the publication programs of the

Society for Historical Archaeology
Conference on Historic Site Archaeology
Society for Post Medieval Archaeology
Society for Industrial Archaeology
and the
Australian Society for Historical Archaeology

Robert L. Schuyler is Assistant Professor of Anthropology at the City College and Graduate Center of the City University of New York. As a highschool student he received his first introduction to archaeology as a member of the Archaeological Society of Connecticut excavations on Grannis Island, New Haven. At the University of Arizona he majored in anthropology graduating " Magna Cum Laude " in 1964. His MA and PhD are from the University of California, Santa Barbara. Concerned primarily with historical archaeology, Dr. Schuyler has directed projects on a 17th-18th century Piscataway Indian site in the Potomac River Valley, a 19th century Black oystering town on Staten Island, and most recently at Lowell, Massachusetts, the first major industrial city in America. Presently he is establishing a long term research design on the urban archaeology of the New York metropolitan area. With special interests in Historic Sites Archaeology and Industrial Archaeology, he has published several articles on these topics. Some recent items include, "The Supply Mill on Content Brook, an Example of the Excavation of Recent Historic Sites" (*Journal of Field Archaeology*, with Christopher Mills, 1976, Vol. 3, No. 1), "Images of America: the Contribution of Historical Archaeology to National Identity" (*Southwestern Lore*, 1976, Vol. 42, No. 4), and "Euroamerican Indian Interaction, Evidence from Historic Sites" (Chapter 7 in the California Volume of the *Handbook of North American Indians*). Schuyler has also served as the Archaeology Editor for the *Abstracts In Anthropology* and since 1972 has compiled the section on international research for the *Newsletter* of the Society for Historical Archaeology. He is currently Deputy Chairman of the CCNY Department of Anthropology.

CONTENTS

Preface

Since World War II archaeology in America has seen the emergence of an entirely new area of scholarly research and public concern. Paralleling a continued growth of prehistoric studies has been the awareness that the development of American culture itself has left a rich and varied archaeological record. A similar evolution has occurred in England and other parts of Europe. In 1967, for example, both the (American) Society for Historical Archaeology, now with over 1,000 members, and the (English) Society for Post-Medieval Archaeology organized. This major establishment has been followed in America by the creation of the Society for Industrial Archaeology, which was predicated on a longer tradition of industrial archaeology in Great Britain, as is seen in the large number of regional surveys of that country. Outside of Europe and North America the growth of the field is seen in the 1970 founding of the Australian Society for Historical Archaeology which has also stimulated work in other parts of Oceania.

Work in this country by the National Park Service, and more recently groups like the National Register for Historic Sites, has been followed by the formal recognition of Historical Archaeology on the college and university level. Presently Historical Archaeology is offered as a separate course in several American and Canadian institutions. It is normally housed in departments of anthropology and is also supported by a growing number of field schools concentrating on historic sites.

Instructors wishing to teach Historical Archaeology or people wishing to gain an informal understanding of the field have a plethora of published materials to draw upon; however, the recent and rapid rise of the discipline has created a widely scattered literature frequently of limited and hard to find editions. A number of the better known site reports and articles are already out of print. Except for volumes concerned with methodology, no general synthesis or reference book exists that can serve as an introduction for either the student or the general reader.

Historical Archaeology: A Guide to Substantive and Theoretical Contributions is an attempt to create the first source book for the field. It is inclusive and should serve as a text or supplementary text on both the undergraduate and graduate levels while it also presents an ingress for the general reader or professional archaeologist who is entering the subject for the first time. It surveys both the subject matter of Historical Archaeology and the theoretical interpretation of those data by bringing together 35 reprinted items, including two full site reports, which are structured into five major sections.

The first two parts introduce the reader to the discipline by reprinting a number of early classic papers and more recent statements that define the subject matter, purpose, and orientation of all the potential subfields of Historical Archaeology. Although there is a brief global review in Part 2, the remainder of the volume concentrates on fieldwork and theory as practiced in North America.

Part 3 offers a number of examples of the end product of two decades of research on historic sites and analysis of historic artifacts and assemblages. These selections are arranged in a hierarchical sequence moving from the more fundamental levels of ecology and economics through social and political organization to ideology.

With Parts 4 and 5 the emphasis of the volume shifts from substantive results to theory. The "historicalist"-anthropological debate on the purpose and intrinsic nature of Historical Archaeology is summarized in a number of famous encounters between Iain Walker, Clyde Dollar, and a number of anthropologists including Lewis R. Binford. The implications of an anthropological orientation, which has come to dominate the field, are seen in the final section of the book that discusses very recent innovations in method and a set of continuing theoretical problems that are far from solution.

Contributors

JIM ALLEN is a Fellow of the Department of Prehistory in the Research School of Pacific Studies at the Australian National University.

K.J. BARTON is Director of the Hampshire County Museum Service at Chilcomb House in Winchester, England.

LEWIS R. BINFORD is Professor of Anthropology at the University of New Mexico.

JOANNE BOWEN is a graduate student in the Department of Anthropology at Brown University.

MARLEY R. BROWN III is a graduate student in the Department of Anthropology at Brown University and is teaching in the Department of History at Boston University.

R.A. BUCHANAN is Director of the Center for the Study of the History of Technology at the University of Bath, England.

CHARLES E. CLELAND is Professor and Curator of Anthropology at the Museum of Michigan State University.

JOHN L. COTTER is Associate Curator of North American Historical Archaeology at the University Museum, University of Pennsylvania.

JAMES F. DEETZ is Associate Director of Plimouth Plantation and Professor of Anthropology at Brown University.

EDWIN S. DETHLEFSEN is Professor of Anthropology at Franklin Pierce College in Rindge, New Hampshire.

CLYDE D. DOLLAR is a member of the Department of History at the University of Arkansas, Fayetteville.

JAMES E. FITTING is Manager of the Human Resources Planning Department, Environmental System Division, of Gilbert Commonwealth, Jackson, Michigan.

CARL RUSSELL FISH (1876–1932) was Professor of History at the University of Wisconsin.

BERNARD L. FONTANA was for many years an Ethnologist at the Arizona State Museum and is presently a member of the administration of the University of Arizona.

OLEG GRABAR is Professor of Fine Arts at Harvard University.

JOHN W. GRIFFIN is a Southeastern Archaeologist who has worked on several historic sites for the National Park Service and the State of Florida.

D.B. HARDEN is one of the founding members of the Society for Medieval Archaeology. He has recently retired as Director of the London Museum.

J.C. HARRINGTON is one of the founders of Historical Archaeology in the United States. He is now retired from a long career with the National Park Service and lives in Richmond, Virginia.

IVOR NOËL HUME is Director of the Department of Archaeology at Colonial Williamsburg.

MARK P. LEONE is Associate Professor of Anthropology at the University of Maryland.

JOHN HOWLAND ROWE is Professor of Anthropology at the University of California, Berkeley.

CARL P. RUSSELL (1894–1967) held many positions in the National Park Service and was a leading historian of the American West.

ROBERT L. SCHUYLER is Assistant Professor of Anthropology at the City College and Graduate Center of the City University of New York.

STANLEY SOUTH is a member of the Institute of Archaeology and Anthropology at the University of South Carolina and the founder of the Conference on Historic Sites Archaeology.

IAIN C. WALKER has been active in Historical Archaeology in both North America and Great Britain and is a leading expert on clay pipes.

ARTHUR WOODWARD is one of the early pioneers in American Historical Archaeology. He now lives in Patagonia, Arizona.

Acknowledgements and Sources

A very large number of individuals, both within and outside of the archaeological profession, helped to make this volume a reality. Baywood Publishing Company and its President, Norman Cohen, recognized the need for such a book and gave support to the project at all stages. Paula Horan and Mary Rogan successfully oversaw all the technical aspects in the production of the text, while Sheona Downie did a superlative job on promotion. Frederick Gardner, adviser to Baywood, also provided continuing encouragement.

All thirty-five chapters are reprinted items having originally been published between 1910 and 1977. The following list of sources gives full original bibliographic data and permission-statements for each article.

Chapter 1. Archaeology as an Auxiliary Science to American History by J.C. Harrington is reprinted from *American Anthropologist*, Vol. 57, No. 6 (December 1955), pp. 1121–1130 by permission of the author and the American Anthropological Association.

Chapter 2. Relation of Archaeology and History by Carl Russell Fish is reprinted from the *Proceedings of the Wisconsin State Historical Society*, Vol. 57 (1910), pp. 146–152 by permission of the State Historical Society of Wisconsin.

Chapter 3. Historic Objects as Sources of History by Carl P. Russell is reprinted from Appendix A, pp. 387–401 of *Firearms, Traps, and Tools of the Mountain Men* by Carl P. Russell. Copyright © 1967 by Betty W. Russell. Reprinted by permission of Alfred A. Knopf, Inc.

Chapter 4. The Study of Historic Archaeology in America by Arthur Woodward is reprinted from *Boletin Bibliografico de Antropologia Americana*, Vol. 1 (1937), pp. 101–103 by permission of the author.

Chapter 5. Symposium on Role of Archaeology in Historical Research, Summary and Analysis by John L. Cotter is reprinted from the mimeographed paper, *Symposium on Role of Archaeology in Historical Research*, Ed. John L. Cotter, 1958, pp. 1–3 by permission of the author.

Chapter 6. End Products of Historic Sites Archaeology by John W. Griffin is reprinted from *Symposium on Role of Archaeology in Historical Research*, Ed. John L. Cotter, 1958, pp. 1–6 by permission of the author and the editor.

Chapter 7. On the Meaning of Historic Sites Archaeology by Bernard L. Fontana is reprinted from *American Antiquity*, Vol. 31, No. 1 (1965), pp. 61–65 by permission of the author and the Society for American Archaeology.

Chapter 8. Historical and Historic Sites Archaeology as Anthropology: Basic Definitions and Relationships by Robert L. Schuyler is reprinted from *Historical Archaeology*, Vol. 4 (1970), pp. 83–89 by permission of the Society for Historical Archaeology.

Chapter 9. The Renaissance Foundations of Anthropology by John Howland Rowe is reprinted from *American Anthropologist*, Vol. 67, No. 1 (February 1965), pp. 1–20 by permission of the author and the American Anthropological Association.

Chapter 10. The Society for Medieval Archaeology by D.B. Harden is reprinted from *Medieval Archaeology*, Vol. 1 (1957), pp. 1–3 by permission of the author and the Society for Medieval Archaeology.

Chapter 11. The Origins of the Society for Post-Medieval Archaeology by K.J. Barton is reprinted from *Post-Medieval Archaeology*, Vol. 1 (1967), pp. 102–103 by permission of the author and the Society for Post-Medieval Archaeology.

Chapter 12. Late Man in North America: Archaeology of European Americans by James Deetz is reprinted from *Anthropological Archeology in the Americas*, Ed. Betty J. Meggers, 1968, pp. 121–130 by permission of the author and the Anthropological Society of Washington.

Chapter 13. Industrial Archaeology: Retrospect and Prospect by R.A. Buchanan is reprinted from *Antiquity*, Vol. XLIV, 1970, pp. 281–287 by permission of the author and the Antiquity Trust.

Chapter 14. Islamic Archaeology, an Introduction by Oleg Grabar is reprinted from *Archaeology*, Vol. 24, No. 3 (June 1971), pp. 197–199, Copyright 1971, Archaeological Institute of America, by permission of the author and the Archaeological Institute of America.

Chapter 15. Dating Stem Fragments of Seventeenth and Eighteenth Century Clay Tobacco Pipes by J.C. Harrington is reprinted from the *Quarterly Bulletin of the Archaeological Society of Virginia*, Vol. 9, No. 1 (September 1954), pp. 9–13 by permission of the author and the Archaeological Society of Virginia.

Chapter 16. A New Method of Calculating Dates From Kaolin Pipe Stem Samples by Lewis R. Binford is reprinted from the *Southeastern Archaeological Conference Newsletter*, Vol. 9, No. 1 (1961), pp. 19–21 by permission of the author and the Southeastern Archaeological Conference.

Chapter 17. Evolution and Horizon as Revealed in Ceramic Analysis in Historical Archaeology by Stanley South is reprinted from *The Conference on Historic Site Archaeology Papers 1971*, Vol. 6, Pt. 2, pp. 71–106 by permission of the author.

Chapter 18. Death's Head, Cherub, Urn and Willow by James F. Deetz and Edwin S. Dethlefsen is reprinted from *Natural History*, Vol. 76, No. 3 (March 1967), pp. 29–37 by permission of the authors and the publisher. Copyright © the American Museum of Natural History, 1967. Redrawn illustrations by permission of Mark P. Leone.

Chapter 19. *New Light on Washington's Fort Necessity* by J.C. Harrington. Originally published in 1957 (reprinted 1970) by the Eastern National Park and Monument Association, Richmond, Virginia. Reprinted from the 1970 edition by permission of the author and the publisher.

Chapter 20. The Archaeology of Nineteenth-Century British Imperialism: An Australian Case Study by Jim Allen is reprinted from *World Archaeology*, Vol. 5, No. 1 (June 1973), pp. 44–59 by permission of the author and the publisher.

Chapter 21. Probate Inventories: an Evaluation from the Perspective of Zooarchaeology and Agricultural History at Mott Farm by Joanne Bowen is reprinted from *Historical Archaeology*, Vol. 9 (1975), pp. 11–25 by permission of the author and the Society for Historical Archaeology.

Chapter 22. Archaeological Investigations at La Purísima Mission by James F. Deetz is reprinted from the *UCLA Archaeological Survey Annual Report 1962–1963*, pp. 163–208 by permission of the author and the UCLA Archaeological Survey.

Chapter 23. Archaeology as the Science of Technology: Mormon Town Plans and Fences by Mark P. Leone is reprinted from *Research and Theory in Current Archaeology*, Ed. Charles Redman, pp. 125–150. Copyright © John Wiley & Sons, Inc., 1973. By permission of the author and the publisher.

Chapter 24. The Why, What, and Who of Historical Archaeology by Ivor Noël Hume is reprinted from Ivor Noël Hume, *Historical Archaeology* (New York: Alfred A. Knopf, 1969, pp. 7–20) by permission of the author and Curtis Brown, Ltd. Copyright © by Ivor Noël Hume, 1968.

Chapter 25. Historic Archaeology—Methods and Principles by Iain C. Walker is reprinted from *Historical Archaeology*, Vol. 1 (1967), pp. 23–34 by permission of the author and the Society for Historical Archaeology.

Chapter 26. Some Thoughts on Theory and Method in Historical Archaeology by Clyde D. Dollar is reprinted from *The Conference on Historic Site Archaeology Papers*, Vol. 2, Pt. 2 (1968), pp. 3–30 by permission of the author and the editor, Stanley South.

Chapter 27. Binford, Science, and History: the Probabilistic Variability of Explicated Epistemology and Nomothetic Paradigms in Historical Archaeology by Iain C. Walker is reprinted from *The Conference on Historic Site Archaeology Papers*, Vol. 7, Pt. 3 (1972), pp. 159–201 by permission of the author and the editor.

Chapter 28. A Reply to 'Some Thoughts on Theory and Method in Historical Archaeology' by Bernard L. Fontana is reprinted from *The Conference on Historic Site Archaeology Papers*, Vol. 2, Pt. 2 (1968), pp. 75–78 by permission of the author and the editor.

Chapter 29. The Crisis of Identity: Theory in Historic Sites Archaeology by Charles E. Cleland and James E. Fitting is reprinted from *The Conference on Historic Site Archaeology Papers*, Vol. 2, Pt. 2 (1968), pp. 124–138 by permission of the authors and the editor.

Chapter 30. 'Evolution and Horizon as Revealed in Ceramic Analysis in Historical Archaeology'—a Step Toward the Development of Archaeological Science by Lewis R. Binford is reprinted from *The Conference on Historic Site Archaeology Papers*, Vol. 6 (1972), pp. 117–125 by permission of the author and the editor.

Chapter 31. Exploring Analytical Techniques by Stanley South is reprinted from Stanley South, *Method and Theory in Historical Archaeology* (New York: Academic Press, 1977, Chapter 6, pp. 167–199) by permission of the author and the publisher. Copyright © 1977, Academic Press, Inc. Original illustrations on pages 173, 181, 185, 186, and 190 have been deleted.

Chapter 32. A Discussion of the Contrasts in the Developments of the Settlement at Fort Michilimackinac Under British and French Rule by Lewis R. Binford is reprinted from the *Southeastern Archaeological Conference Newsletter*, Vol. 9, No. 1 (1962), pp. 50–52 by permission of the author and the Southeastern Archaeological Conference.

Chapter 33. The Spoken Word, the Written Word, Observed Behavior and Preserved Behavior; the Contexts Available to the Archaeologist by Robert L. Schuyler is reprinted from *The Conference on Historic Site Archaeology Papers*, Vol. 10, Pt. 2 (1977), pp. 99–120 by permission of the editor, Stanley South.

Chapter 34. The Use of Oral and Documentary Sources in Historical Archaeology: Ethnohistory at the Mott Farm by Marley Brown III is reprinted from *Ethnohistory*, Vol. 20, No. 4 (1974), pp. 347–360 by permission of the author and the American Society for Ethnohistory.

Chapter 35. A Cognitive Historical Model for American Culture: 1620–1835 by James Deetz is reprinted from *Reconstructing Complex Societies*, Ed. Charlotte Moore, Chapter 2 (1974), pp. 21–24 by permission of the author and the American Schools of Oriental Research.

part 1

Emergence and Definition
of a New Discipline

INTRODUCTION

In 1620 a Pilgrim exploratory party discovered several Indian mounds on Cape Cod. Surface deposits of mats and corn indicated that the burials were recent but when one of the more elaborate graves was opened an unexpected collection of artifacts was revealed. Grave goods had been buried with the dead but aboriginal items were intermixed with European objects — white glass beads, an iron knife, even a pair of breeches (Young 1841:109-110). Thus one of the first recorded excavations in America could equally serve as one of the earliest examples of either prehistoric or historical archaeology. There were a number of similar excavations, including work at European colonial sites, during the 18th and 19th centuries, but, unlike prehistoric studies, Historical Archaeology as an organized and accepted scholarly discipline is a mid-20th century phenomenon.

There could be no archaeology of Europeans in the New World until historic remains and monuments were perceived as artifacts and potential archaeological sites. Such recognition depended on cultural differentiation. A rapid succession of different European cultures in one region could produce the needed variation and a number of the isolated, early instances of archaeological excavations were encouraged by English and Spanish occupation of former French colonies. More generally, however, the passage of time was the essential stimulus. Normal stylistic and technological change within Angloamerican, or other European derived, material culture enabled scholars to view the recent historic past as an archaeological subject.

Recognition did not immediately produce a scholarly discipline. In fact, the very context of the recognition erected several obstacles that impeded the growth of the field. These fundamental problems are seen as three themes that run through the seven essays in Part I. The first three selections represent an earlier historicalist answer to these basic questions, while the last four articles, in contrast, propose an anthropological solution.

1. Why excavate sites dating from periods that have a full documentary record?

Harrington, in his classic statement, Fish, and Russell all represent the historicalist position. They tended to avoid or circumvent the question by concentrating on the weakest segments of the archival record — frontier situations or other circumstances that produced a dearth of written accounts. The value of archaeology was enhanced only by default. Their approach was influenced in part by their theoretical position but equally important was the social and economic context of their work. The first thirty years of the emergence of Historical Archaeology was simultaneously spurred and held back by a desire to preserve or reconstruct famous historic sites such as Williamsburg, Jamestown, Fort Vancouver, and the various Spanish missions in the West. Even Fish, who was certainly precocious in his 1910 statement, foreshadowed the pattern when he limited all his examples to non-excavated materials and architecture. This powerful preservation-restoration influence elevated practical and political objectives over purely scholarly goals (Schuyler 1976) and reduced archaeology to a supplemental technique in the service of architecture, narrow, specific historical questions, and the National Park Service. In contrast, Cotter, Fontana, and Griffin see archaeology as primarily concerned with the creation of cultural images of the past that are more complete and to some degree different than those generated from documentary history alone. Indeed Fontana and Griffin clearly expose the negative impact of preservation and restoration on the growth of a field that should have scholarly and not technical, specific goals as its *raison d'être*.

2. What potential does Historical Archaeology have for advancing general scholarship?

This question is still a point of debate among archaeologists. The essays outline the evolution of this debate by splitting into a conservative and a more optimistic group. The historicalist approach, particularly as seen in Harrington, views archaeology as basically providing only data. The anthropologists see archaeology as an equal *partner* with traditional history in creating more replete culture histories or cultural reconstructions. Cotter's essay is of interest (beyond the fact that he correctly predicts the name of the Society for Historical Archaeology and its journal) in that its 1958 date puts him in the transitional position of endorsing both sides of the debate. It should also be noted that most of the authors, irrespective of their orientations, do not discuss the explanation of past cultural patterns, only the scholarly creation of those patterns. A processual perspective is not evident except in the last two articles. My own emphasis on comparative studies, which John Griffin also noted in some of his early writings, will be returned to in Part 5. My advocacy for the retention of Harrington's term "Historic Sites Archaeology" proved to be ineffective. "Historical Archaeology" has triumphed as both a general and specific appellation in America.

3. Is Historical Archaeology a subfield of American history or anthropology?

Some researchers consider this question to be artificial but its significance is clearly seen in all the essays. Fish, Russell, and Harrington saw archaeology as a natural handmaiden to history. On the practical level they urged the training of historical archaeologists in academic departments of history. Nevertheless, they were all frustrated by the repeated indifference or open hostility of historians toward archaeology. Examination of Woodward's article, written in the 1930's, indicates the actual future course for the discipline. Because archaeologists in America, with the exception of Classicists, were anthropologists, the first historical archaeologists had to come from an anthropological background. They were drawn into Historical Archaeology along two routes. An interest in American Indians moved some of them, like Woodward, toward the study of historic trade goods found on native sites. A larger group became involved more artifically when the Great Depression created

a large number of jobs for archaeologists at historic monuments under the National Park Service. Oddly it took another 30 years for anthropological archaeologists to bring their theoretical perspective to bear on historic assemblages and sites. In part this lag was related to the fact that most prehistoric archaeologists were doing pre*history* until the rise of processual archaeology in the 1960's.

In 1977 Historical Archaeology is a recognized and established field of research in the United States and Canada. It is a subfield of general anthropology with almost all its practitioners trained in that science. With a few exceptions professional historians are not involved in the discipline and they tend to ignore the findings produced by hundreds of excavations (cf. Wilderston 1975).

The question of disciplinary affiliation is concerned not only with the fortuitous historical events that influenced the rise of Historical Archaeology but also with important points of theory. Part 4 will detail these debates.

REFERENCES CITED

SCHUYLER, ROBERT L.
    1976 Images of America: the Contribution of Historical Archaeology to National Identity. *Southwestern Lore,* Vol. 42, No. 4, pp. 27-39.
WILDERSTON, PAUL W.
    1975 Archaeology and the American Historian: an Interdisciplinary Challenge. *American Quarterly,* Vol. XXVII, No. 2, pp. 115-132.
YOUNG, ALEXANDER
    1841 *Chronicles of the Pilgrim Fathers.* Boston.

CHAPTER 1

Archaeology as an Auxiliary Science to American History

J. C. HARRINGTON

When starting to assemble material for this paper, I intended to review the accomplishments of so-called "colonial" or "historical" archaeology in this country and to furnish specific annotated references to all major contributions in this field. Such an approach would have been possible ten years ago. In fact, at that time it would have been essential to intelligent participation in any discussion of the subject by either anthropologists or historians. But the situation has changed considerably since the end of World War II, for a great deal of digging has been done during the last few years at sites associated with the history of white men in North America. A bibliography of published reports alone would consume the space allowed for this paper; and the many important projects for which published reports have not yet appeared would deserve mention in any such list. The two summaries of activities in this field, published in *American Antiquity* (17:78–81; 18:287–88), although not all-inclusive, cover the subject quite adequately through 1952. (See also Preface by Heizer and McCown in Bennyhoff and Elsasser 1954.)

So comprehensive a title for a paper of this length calls for some delimitation. The discussion will be limited to the employment of archaeological methods in the study of the history of peoples of European origin in the area of the United States and Canada, from the time of the earliest explorations to the present day. Of course, the broad and proper concept of American history would not exclude the aborigine, for the historian, as well as the anthropologist, is concerned with the meeting of two such disparate racial and ethnic groups and in the cultural processes resulting from such contacts. The importance of archaeology in ethnohistorical studies has been convincingly demonstrated by the work of the Amerind Foundation at contact sites in Arizona and New Mexico (DiPeso 1953). This line of investigation, however, important as it can be to anthropologists as well as to historians, is not what I am concerned with here; nor will I include the related but more limited interest of the archaeologist who uses data secured from white sites for help in establishing chronology at Indian sites occupied during historic times.

It will probably be most useful if we consider the projects in respect to objectives, or the use to which the data have been put, because the objectives of most historic site excavations have had a definite bearing on the contributions of these projects. Objectives have, on the whole, been rather limited, and the effects of those objectives are reflected in the selection of sites to be explored, in the scope of the projects, in the nature of the interpretations, and in the publication of

reports. Objectives have also, to a limited extent, affected field methods.

By far the majority of archaeological projects undertaken at historic sites have had as their primary, and often sole, purpose the securing of data for use in interpreting the sites to visitors. In a few cases the goal has been a full-scale reconstruction of the entire scene. The best known, as well as the most ambitious, project of this kind is Colonial Williamsburg (Wertenbaker 1954). As at most historic sites, the archaeological evidence, although extensive, served largely to supplement the documentary. But archaeology did permit more authentic reconstruction, and it furnished considerable data which contributed directly to a more accurate and a more realistic interpretation of conditions in eighteenth-century colonial Virginia.

Results of archaeological investigations at many other sites have been employed in a more limited manner than at Williamsburg although for the same purpose, namely, "to make the past live again" or, as Williamsburg more wistfully expresses it, "so that the future may learn from the past." Partial or full reconstruction is planned for other sites, but the development has seldom been carried to completion. Examples are the iron-making communities at Saugus in Massachusetts and Hopewell Village in Pennsylvania; the Yorktown battlefield in Virginia; the Sonoma Mission in California; the mid-nineteenth-century village of Appomattox Courthouse in Virginia; and Fort Necessity in Pennsylvania, scene of the first battle in the French and Indian War.

Excavations were carried on at Fort Necessity by the National Park Service in 1952-53. Although the data were subsequently used in reconstructing the fort, the project was initiated for the purpose of determining the exact location and shape of the 1754 structure. Historical research and earlier excavating had presented evidence interpreted as showing a rather large fort of peculiar shape. The recent explorations produced quite positive evidence for a much smaller fort, with outlying entrenchments, and provided many details of the fort's construction (Harrington 1954).

In some cases reconstruction is not contemplated at present. The data have been, or are to be, used along with documentary evidence to interpret the site or event through museum exhibits, books and pamphlets, dramatizations, and other devices. Many of the historic sites administered by the National Park Service fall in this category, such as Jamestown in Virginia, Fort Frederica in Georgia, and Fort Vancouver in Washington. At the latter site, center of the Hudson's Bay Company's nineteenth-century fur trade activity in the Pacific Northwest, excavations were carried on under the direction of Louis R. Caywood in 1947 for the express purpose of locating the fort site. Not only was the site located, but considerable information came to light regarding its original appearance, as well as the activities that centered there for a quarter of a century (Caywood 1955).

Although most digging at historic sites has been done with on-site interpretive development in mind, there have been a few projects in which development of the site for visitors has not been anticipated. One group includes "salvage" excavating, such as the emergency work at sites of nineteenth-century frontier settlements and army posts which are endangered by construction or flooding incident to water control projects. These excavations have provided considerable information on the physical histories of the sites themselves, as well as data which should contribute directly to broader historical studies. In view of their unique position in respect to Indian cultures, such sites should also provide data of use in acculturation studies. To my knowledge, however, no attempt has been made to use the data from these projects in research of this type, either in respect to the white culture involved or that of adjacent Indian tribes.

Other projects in this general class are some in which attempts have been made to supply information for specific and limited historical reasons. A good example is the work at the old stone tower in Newport, Rhode Island. This ruin has been a favorite, and often heated, subject of discussion for many years. Although there is very little documentary evidence relating to its origin and use, there have been some very firm contentions concerning it—a Viking structure, an English colonial windmill, a colonial watchtower, a church, and an office building! Excavations carried out by William S. Godfrey in 1948 and 1949 were not conclusive, but they furnished data which not only fairly well dispose of a Norse origin but make the English colonial watchtower-mill theory much more convincing (Brøndsted 1954:382–91; Godfrey 1951).

A slightly different problem was involved in the search by the University of California Archaeological Survey for the site associated with Sir Francis Drake's explorations along the California coast in 1579. Work on this project has been carried on intermittently over the last several years at Drake's Bay, Marin County, California, beginning with Robert F. Heizer's excavations in 1940. Thus far seven sites have been explored (Heizer 1950; Meighan 1950). The problem here was to locate the exact site, although the dating of these shell mounds would be extremely valuable in the study of the Indian culture of the late period in central California. Thus far, no positive evidence has been found which would identify Drake's landfall, although sufficient artifact material of the period has been recovered to support the earlier conclusion that the site is in the general locality of Drake's Bay.

The third kind of nondevelopment project I have in mind is that which has been undertaken primarily for the purpose of extending other fields of research but which has involved excavation of historic sites and has resulted in definite contributions to American history. Important examples are the Peabody Museum's Awatovi expedition (Montgomery, Smith and Brew 1949), the Spanish mission projects in Florida (Boyd, Smith and Griffin 1951), and the work at Ste. Marie I in Ontario (Kidd 1949; Jury 1954).

I realize that the interest of anthropologists in the results of excavations at mission sites lies in the contribution such projects can make in acculturation and other anthropological

studies, to which I referred briefly in connection with the work of DiPeso. Our interest in them here, however, is in their contribution to the more conventional approach to American history. Acculturation, of course, works both ways, for the effects of Indian cultures on Europeans is, or should be, considered in any historical study in which such contacts are involved.

Although the Awatovi report is more detailed and carries the reconstruction of buildings and of mission life further than the others, each of the projects cited above succeeds in presenting a graphic picture of an important facet of American history, based upon both archaeological and documentary evidence. Brew, in the Awatovi report, comments on this objective as follows (Montgomery, Smith and Brew 1949:xx):

> *One of the primary aims of archaeology is to reconstruct conjecturally not only the buildings and industries and arts of bygone time but also the way of life of the builders of those buildings and the practicers of those arts.*

In so far as this objective is achieved, the fundamental difference between Franciscan Awatovi and Colonial Williamsburg is in the method of presenting the conjectural reconstructions. Colonial Williamsburg does not publish technical accounts of the methods used in obtaining the archaeological data, nor does it publish detailed descriptions of the excavated artifacts and ruins. Except for limited exhibits of archaeological specimens and a few displays of especially important records, "documentation" for the reconstructions is largely implied. Although not adequate for the inquisitive scholar, some information concerning reconstruction methods, including archaeological explorations, architectural research, and use of historical documents, is provided through the visitor audiovisual orientation program. For that matter, the evidence that archaeologists clamor for—detailed descriptions of all artifact material—is also missing for Awatovi, as well as for most projects. Some writers promise more detailed artifact descriptions in later publications; a few have obliged fairly adequately in their first reports, such as Forman in his study of Jamestown architecture (1938) and Kidd in his report on Ste. Marie I (1949). I will have more to say later regarding the content and publication of reports.

Although the question and some of the answers have been anticipated in the previous remarks, it is time we ask specifically what these excavations at historic sites have contributed to American history. Briefly, it is my contention that their contributions to *historical data* are considerable; to *history*, relatively little. In making this appraisal I recognize that everyone would not accept my implied definition of history. If we ask, in line with the general topic of this group of papers, what these excavations have contributed to a better understanding of our own culture, my answer would be that, aside from a very limited number of acculturation studies, there have been no direct contributions to date. Certainly the data are there for historical studies and possibly for certain kinds of anthropological research, but these data have not yet been applied to historical or anthropological problems in such a manner that we can point to conspicuous contributions. The really important thing is whether this situation represents limitations inherent in the subject matter or is due to controllable factors. I am not prepared to give a final answer, but I contend that no conclusion is warranted until more and better data have been made available and until attempts have been made to use these data in relevant studies. I believe it would be worthwhile, however, to consider some of the factors which may have a bearing on this problem.

A very important factor in the course this "discipline" has taken is the kind of people who have directed the research. Almost invariably they have been anthropologists, which has been both good and bad. This was probably inevitable, for students of American history were neither especially interested in these projects nor trained to carry them out. The archaeologists who were available had been trained in departments of anthropology and, on the whole, were not trained as historians. Some were just in need of employment; some saw these projects as contributing to American Indian studies. Few had any real familiarity with the cultures involved or with the intricacies of historical research. There have been some benefits from this situation. First of all, these excavators have been good technicians—possibly too good in some cases. Second, they presumably brought to the projects an anthropological approach, although I must admit that the effects of this are not obvious in the published reports. Another benefit has been the familiarity gained by these people in the use of documentary source material, which should stand them in good stead in any American Indian research they might subsequently pursue.

The experience at Awatovi, although not typical, is revealing. Brew (Montgomery, Smith and Brew 1949:xx) relates with feeling how, after the first season's work, it was realized that they must have the assistance of specialists in two fields—ecclesiastical architecture and Spanish-American history. Most fortunately this was realized in one man, Ross Montgomery, of whom Brew writes: "In his inspired descriptions the bones take on flesh and we follow the working of minds as well as the flash of the axe and the track of the trowel."

Few, if any, other projects have been so fortunate, nor have funds been available to employ a battery of specialists. This points up what is possibly the greatest shortcoming in this field—properly trained supervisors. How can the condition be overcome? The obvious, although immediately unattainable, answer is to train people especially for it. Even so, we cannot expect a single individual to be qualified to excavate and interpret cultural remains so varied and so complex as those represented in this country any more than we would consider an Egyptologist qualified to excavate in the Roman Forum. Yet we send out an archaeologist to investigate a seventeenth-century English plantation site, a Civil War fort site, or a Hudson's Bay post, naïvely assuming he can do the job because he has successfully excavated prehistoric Indian sites. Admittedly, the choice is better than sending out a historian with no archaeological training or experience, but obviously something must be done to meet this basic training problem if we are to make real contributions to American history through the excavation of historic sites. Until such time as special departments or curricula can be set up, I suggest that anthropology departments encourage students to acquire some acquaintance with historical research methods as well as with the principles of historiography.

In his article on trade goods research, Kidd (1954) outlines the specialized training needed by the person who is dealing with such materials. Although his specifications, on the whole, are somewhat impracticable, he does make some very worthwhile suggestions. Those who read his paper will at least realize why there are no "experts" in this field. As Kidd points out, rather than trying to become a specialist in a number of subjects, any one of which would require a lifetime to master, it would seem more practicable for each to supplement his general training and experience by specialization along a particular line. On the whole, I would recommend specializing in periods and national backgrounds rather than in classes of objects—for example English colonial or French colonial rather than ceramics, weapons, architecture, and the like for all groups and periods.

Inadequate training of the directors of these projects has certainly had something to do with the fact that significant contributions to American history have not been forthcoming, but the real reason for this, as well as for the fact that the work has had little appeal to historians, lies in the limited objectives of these projects. It is true that the data furnished are of a different sort from those with which historians customarily deal, but the really basic fault lies in the fact that the results of the digging and the correlated documentary studies have not been oriented to specific historical problems of the sort that appeal to historians. By and large, the archaeologists who have conducted the projects have had neither the incentive nor the necessary training in historical research methods to undertake studies beyond the immediate objectives of site interpretation. They have recovered a great store of data which should be of use in historical studies, but, with rare exceptions, they have not taken the next step—analysis and synthesis; nor have the data been made sufficiently appealing and palatable to historians.

Recognition and admission of these shortcomings do not absolve the archaeologist from the responsibility of making the results of the excavations more available through detailed descriptive reports. But even if the results of all the digging at historic sites were to be put in the hands of historians, the data would probably be insufficient for the kinds of studies historians would be interested in pursuing. This again is due to the limited and specific objectives of the excavations, for seldom, if ever, has a site been selected in reference to lacunae in historical data. Confronted with one-sided and incomplete source material, the historian loses interest, for he is not in a position to initiate archaeological projects designed to furnish the desired data, nor can he wait for the excavation of a site or a series of sites which, by pure accident, might furnish the missing material. In other words, the results of excavations at historic sites will not be of really major value to historians until historians who themselves have formulated specific research problems become archaeologists or have a hand in selecting sites to be excavated.

As already indicated, the preparation and publication of reports in this field are unquestionably a real problem. Concern has been expressed, and rightly, over the lack of published reports; but just meeting the clamor for publications is not enough, for an inadequate publication is not much better than none at all except that it helps call attention to the project. Here, as with the conduct of the projects themselves, the reports have suffered from the fact that they have been written by people whose main reporting experience has had to do with Indian archaeology. Unfamiliar as he is with the cultural material encountered, the reporter on historic site excavations feels that he must describe and illustrate every object. This procedure was often necessary with his Indian materials, for he had not been privileged to work with ceramic types which could be neatly characterized by such simple phrases as, for example, "Wedgewood creamware" or "Lambeth delftware." He is inclined, therefore, to devote unnecessary space in his report to lengthy objective descriptions when a single word or phrase would suffice. In some cases, however, careful descriptions are needed, as of, for example, the products of local craftsmen. Here, as in field methods, the necessary judgment and selectivity can be acquired only from training and experience.

One of the main obstacles to adequate publication is the complexity of the subject matter. Whereas a full report on an Indian site might cover a very limited group of objects and relatively simple structures, a report on a colonial site would be infinitely more complex. Adequate discussion of the architecture alone might well consume a full volume. Seldom are funds available to meet such extensive publication needs, even if qualified people are found to carry out the research and prepare the manuscripts.

In addition to the problems of cost and personnel, the apparent apathy toward publication of reports on excavations at historic sites goes right back to the objectives of the projects themselves. Often, when the results of an excavation are employed primarily in interpretation at the site, publication of detailed technical reports is not considered necessary, for the obligation of making the results available is considered to have been met through the interpretive development. An argument could be advanced in support of this view, although it does not meet the objection of the scholar who wants to know about every potsherd and every gunlock; nor does it serve the student who cannot visit the site. Such a view, too, loses sight of the possibilities of improving the interpretation through a broader knowledge of the social history of the period that would come by comparative analyses of contemporary colonizing situations.

Although adequate publications are scarce, it is true that reports have been written in most cases. They were prepared, however, for the guidance of site developers and are usually not in a form suitable for publication. This does not meet the need of the archaeologist working at related sites, nor does it help the historian who wishes to use such material in his historical research. What will probably prove of greater value than narrative accounts of the digging are well-illustrated descriptions of excavated materials. They will be used, and to advantage, by historians, archaeologists, and ethnologists, but they must be recognized for what they are— historical data. They contribute an important body and a special kind of historical record, but in themselves they do not constitute *history*.

The need for making this specialized information available has been recognized from the first. Attempts have been made to meet this need by preparation of short articles for magazines and journals. Some of a general nature have appeared in publications of state and local history societies, but editors of historical journals on the whole are not interested in detailed artifact descriptions and tedious accounts of excavating procedures and, if they were, could not publish them because of the illustrations required. This has resulted in many specialized studies being published in nonprofessional magazines. Some on Jamestown subjects, for example, have appeared in the most unexpected places, from the house organ of an iron foundry to a magazine published by a horsemen's association. This has the obvious drawback of the material being widely scattered and difficult to find and use. However, since it is obvious that this situation will continue under any circumstance, the least we can do is to make available to interested workers a complete annotated bibliography of all such sources.

In addition to published and unpublished reports, there is a vast amount of pertinent reference material that should be made known and made available to workers in this field. As Kidd points out (1954:6), there should be a clearing house where photographs and other data could be filed for reference or loan. This, and other developments that would advance the discipline, will probably not come about until a professional organization or suborganization is formed. It is a little soon, however, to talk about an organization, when the discipline, if it can be called that, has not even settled on what to call itself.

In spite of all the digging that has been done, there has not been much concern in the past over what the activity should be labeled. Now that they have demonstrated to most people's satisfaction, however, that what they have been doing is in fact archaeology, diggers of sites of white occupation have finally begun to feel the need for group recognition and status and have been casting about for an adequate term for what they are doing. To distinguish between history and prehistory the term "historical archaeology" has been used extensively, although this fails to deal with the matter of Indian sites showing white contacts. "Colonial archaeology" is also popular but has obvious deficiencies, for "colonial" varies with different groups and in different parts of the country, and it does not provide for sites of postcolonial times. "Historic site archaeology," first suggested in 1947 (Harrington 1952), has not caught on, and where it has, it has been altered, probably for the better, to "historic sites archaeology." My objection to this term, although I first suggested its use, is that it implies a narrowness of interest which unfortunately also characterizes the projects themselves. The matter cannot be settled here, but I bring it up to show something of the status of this field of research.

With the growing diversification and specialization in both the anthropological and historical professions, neither at present is looking for a stray waif. In spite of the strong anthropological flavor of its formative stage, due primarily to fortuitous circumstances, I feel that the discipline properly belongs to American history and that the future development of special curricula along this line in universities should be in the history departments. When we are able to convince historians generally that archaeology really has something to contribute to the study of American history, progress will, I am hopeful, be made in this direction. However, the acceptance of archaeology as an auxiliary science to American history depends not just upon the archaeologists but on the historians themselves. There are encouraging signs in this direction in the recognition among historians that the reduction of history to a "social science" has sometimes resulted in losing sight of the actors and the properties on the historical stage.

In the preceding pages I have discussed what I believe to be the more important factors affecting the contributions made to the study of American history through the excavation of historic sites. They are, on the whole, controllable factors. Awareness of them and possible changes in them may, in time, make it possible for archaeology to make a more imposing contribution. But there are still inherent limitations in its use as a tool for studying American history that should be recognized by both historians and archaeologists.

Dealing as they do with a field on the whole well documented and intensively and extensively researched, archaeological findings will seldom make any real alteration in the nistorical account. No one supposes that the archaeologist working around Independence Hall will prove that the Declaration of Independence was signed in some year other than 1776. Archaeology may be able to verify or confirm a questionable or uncertain historical fact, as, for example, the exact location of Fort Raleigh, the 1585 English settlement in North Carolina (Harrington 1953). Or it may provide useful negative evidence, as in the case of the Newport Tower (Brøndsted 1954). But it is unrealistic to expect much more, especially in respect to the relatively recent past.

As pointed out earlier, archaeology can provide historical data even though its contributions to the broader history or to social processes may not be conspicuous. It can flesh out the bones of chronology and social trend and make them more understandable. A historian writing on the Virginia Declaration of Rights will gain a better appreciation of his subject by visiting Colonial Williamsburg. As a picture is reputed to be worth a thousand words, so the interpretation of the historical scene through the use of objects and archaeological data contributes insight, even though it often is intangible and hard to acknowledge specifically. This is being recognized by historians, as can be seen from an increasing use of site studies, in conjunction with documentary research, by graduate students of American history in some universities. The value of site studies as an aid to the teaching of history has long been recognized and put to good use.

Actually, outstanding historians are already championing the cause of archaeology as an important historical tool. For example, Wertenbaker, eminent scholar in the field of colonial history, in commenting on the opportunities offered American historians in this field of research (1954:454), writes:

> Hitherto they have depended too much upon manuscript evidences.... Perhaps the day is not distant when the social historian, whether he is writing about the New England Puritans, or the Pennsylvania Germans, or the rice planters of Southern Carolina, will look underground, as well as in the archives, for his evidence.

SELECTED BIBLIOGRAPHY

BENNYHOFF, J. A. and A. B. ELSASSER
1954 Sonoma Mission—an historical and archaeological study of primary constructions, 1823–1913. Reports of the University of California Archaeological Survey, No. 27. Berkeley.

BOYD, MARK F., HALE G. SMITH and JOHN W. GRIFFIN
1951 Here they once stood—the tragic end of the Apalachee Missions. Gainesville, University of Florida Press.

BRØNDSTED, JOHANNES
1954 Norsemen in North America before Columbus. Annual Report of the Smithsonian Institution for 1953, pp. 367–405. Washington, D.C.

CAYWOOD, LOUIS R.
1955 Final report, Fort Vancouver excavations. National Park Service, San Francisco.

DiPESO, CHARLES C.
1953 The Sobaipuri Indians of the upper San Pedro river valley, southeastern Arizona. Amerind Foundation, No. 6. Dragoon, Arizona.

FORMAN, HENRY C.
1938 Jamestown and St. Mary's—buried cities of romance. Baltimore, The Johns Hopkins Press.

GODFREY, WILLIAM S.
1951 The archaeology of the Old Stone Mill in Newport, Rhode Island. American Antiquity 17:120–29, Salt Lake City.

HARRINGTON, J. C.
1952 Historic site archeology in the United States. In Archeology of Eastern United States, ed. J. B. Griffin, pp. 295–315. Chicago, University of Chicago Press.

1953 Archeology and local history. Indiana Magazine of History 49:157–67.

1954 Fort Necessity—scene of George Washington's first battle. Journal of the Society of Architectural Historians 13:25–27.

HEIZER, R. F.
1950 Observations on historic sites and archaeology in California. Reports of the University of California Archaeological Survey, No. 6. Berkeley.

JURY, WILFRID and E. M. JURY
1954 Sainte-Marie among the Hurons. Toronto, Oxford University Press.

KIDD, KENNETH E.
1949 The excavation of Ste. Marie I. Toronto, University of Toronto Press.

1954 Trade goods research techniques. American Antiquity 20:1–8. Salt Lake City.

MEIGHAN, W. W.
1950 Excavations in sixteenth century shellmounds at Drake's Bay, Marin county. Reports of the University of California Archaeological Survey, No. 9. Berkeley.

MONTGOMERY, ROSS, WATSON SMITH and J. O. BREW
1949 Franciscan Awatovi. Papers of the Peabody Museum of American Archaeology and Ethnology, Harvard University 36. Cambridge, Mass.

WERTENBAKER, T. J.
1954 The archeology of Colonial Williamsburg. Annual Report of the Smithsonian Institution for 1953, pp. 447–54. Washington, D.C.

CHAPTER 2

Relation of Archaeology and History*

CARL RUSSELL FISH

The derivation of the word *archaeology* gives little idea of its present use. "The study of antiquity" is at once too broad in scope and too limited in time—for the followers of a dozen other "ologies" are studying antiquity, while the archaeologist does not confine himself to that period. The definition of the word in the *New English Dictionary* corrects the first of these errors, but emphasizes the second, for it describes it as, "The scientific study of remains and monuments of the prehistoric period." This obviously will not bear examination, for the bulk of archaeological endeavor falls within the period which is considered historical; I cannot conceive any period prehistoric, about which archaeology, or any other science, can give us information. Actually, time has nothing whatever to do with the limitations of archaeology; to think of it as leaving off where history begins, is to misconceive them both. The only proper limitation upon archaeology lies in its subject matter. I conceive that it cannot further be defined than as, "The scientific study of human remains and monuments."

In considering the relations of the science to history, I do not wish to enter into any war of words as to the claims of "sociology," "anthropology," and "history" to be the inclusive word, covering the totality of man's past, but simply to use history as it is generally understood at present, and as its professors act upon it. Certainly we are no longer at the stage where history could be defined as "past politics"; it is equally certain that there are fields of human activity which are not actually treated in any adequate way by the historian. The relations of the two do not depend on the definition of history; the more broadly it is interpreted, the more intimate their relationship becomes. The sources of history are three-fold: written, spoken, and that which is neither written nor spoken.

To preserve and prepare the first, is the business of the philologist, the archivist, the paleographer, the editor, and experts in a dozen subsidiary sciences. The historian devotes so much the larger part of his time to this class of material, that the period for which written materials exists is sometimes spoken of as the "historical period," and the erroneous ideas of archaeology which I have quoted, become common.

Least important of the three, is the spoken or traditional; although if we include all the material that was passed down for centuries by word of mouth before being reduced to writing, such as the Homeric poems or the Norse sagas, it includes some of the most interesting things we know of the past. In American history, such material deals chiefly with

the Indian civilizations, and its collection is carried on chiefly by the anthropologists. In addition, nearly every family preserves a mass of oral traditions running back for about a hundred years; and there is a small body of general information, bounded by about the same limit, which has never yet been put into permanent form. The winnowing of this material, to secure the occasional kernels of historic truth that it yields, is as yet a neglected function.

The material that is neither written nor oral, falls to the geologist and the archaeologist. Between these two sciences there is striking similarity, but their boundaries are clear: the geologist deals with natural phenomena, the archaeologist with that which is human, and which may, for convenience, be called monumental. The first duty of the archaeologist is to discover such material and to verify it; the next is to secure its preservation, preferably its actual tangible preservation—but if that is not possible, by description. Then comes the task of studying it, classifying and arranging it, and making it ready for use. At this point the function of the archaeologist ceases, and the duty of the historian begins—to interpret it, and to bring it into harmony with the recognized body of information regarding the past. It is not necessary in every case, that different individuals do these different things. We must not press specialization too far. Nearly every historian should be something of an archaeologist, and every archaeologist should be something of an historian. When the archaeologist ceases from the preparation of his material, and begins the reconstruction of the past, he commences to act as an historian; he has to call up a new range of equipment, a new set of qualifications.

The fields in which the services of archaeology are most appreciated, are those to which written and oral records do not reach. Its contributions in pressing back the frontier of knowledge are incalculable, and are growing increasingly so with every passing year. To say nothing of what it has told us of the civilizations of Egypt and Assyria, it has given to history within the last few years the whole great empire of the Hittites. We have learned more of Mycenaean civilization from archaeology, than from Homer. Practically all we know of the Romanization of Britain is from such sources, and that process, not long ago regarded almost as a myth, is now a well-articulated bit of history. In America, within the last thirty-five years, by the joint work of the archaeologist and the anthropologist, many of the points long disputed concerning the Indians have been set at rest; more knowledge of them has been recovered than was ever before supposed possible; new questions have been raised, which incite renewed activity. From all over the world, moreover, remains of the past, amounting to many times those now known, call

*First read before the Wisconsin Archaeological Society at Madison, July 29, 1910.

for investigation. It is safe to say that within the next fifty years more sensational discoveries will be made by following material, rather than written, records.

It is, however, not only in the periods void of written sources, that archaeology can perform its services. It is in the period of classical antiquity that we find the combination happiest. There, indeed, it is difficult to find an historian who does not lay archaeology under tribute, or an archaeologist who is not lively to the historical bearing of his work. When we come to the medieval period, the situation is less ideal; the historian tends to pay less attention to monuments, and the archaeologist becomes an antiquarian, intent upon minutia, and losing sight of his ultimate duty. In the modern period, the historian, self-satisfied with the richness of his written sources, ignores all others; and the archaeologist, always with a lingering love for the unusual and for the rust of time, considers himself absolved from further work.

As one working in this last period, I wish to call the attention of American archaeologists to some possibilities that it offers. Abundant as are our sources, they do not tell the whole story of the last couple of centuries, even in America: we have monuments which are worthy of preservation, and which can add to our knowledge of our American ancestors, as well as of our Indian predecessors. Even in Wisconsin, something may be obtained from such sources.

The most interesting of our monumental remains are, of course, the architectural. Everybody is familiar with the log cabin, although something might yet be gathered as to the sites selected for them, and minor differences in construction. Less familiar is the cropping out of the porch in front, the spreading of the ell behind, and the two lean-to wings, then the sheathing with clap-boards, the evolution of the posts into Greek columns, and the clothing of the whole with white paint, all representing stages in the prosperity of the occupants. In nearly every older Wisconsin township may be found buildings representing every one of these stages—the older ones indicating poor land or unthrifty occupants, and being generally remote from the township centre, or else serving as minor farm buildings, in the rear of more pretentious frame or brick structures. In the same way the stump fence, the snake fence, and the wire fence, denote either advance or retardation of progress. Other studies of economic value may be made from the use of different kinds of building materials. The early use of local stone is one of the features of Madison; its subsequent disuse was due not so much to the difficulty of quarrying as to the decreased cost of transportation, making other materials cheaper, and was coincident with the arrival of the railroads. Very interesting material could be obtained from the abandoned river towns, which still preserve the appearance of fifty years ago, and furnish us with genuine American ruins.

On the whole, the primitive log cabins were necessarily much alike; but when the log came to be superseded by more flexible material, the settler's first idea was to reproduce the home or the ideal of his childhood, and the house tends to reveal the nationality of its builder. Just about Madison, there are farm houses as unmistakably of New England as if found in the "Old Colony," and others as distinctly of Pennsylvania or the South. I am told of a settlement of Cornishmen, which they have made absolutely characteristic; even the automobilist may often distinguish the first Wisconsin home of the German, the Englishman, or the Dutchman. Where have our carpenters, our masons, and finishers come from, and what tricks of the trade have each contributed?

Such studies reveal something also of the soul of the people. Not so much in America, to be sure, as in Europe, where national and individual aspirations find as legitimate expression in architecture, as in poetry; and less here in the West, which copied its fashions, than in the East, which imported them. Still, we have a few of the Greek-porticoed buildings which were in part a reflection of the influence of the first French Republic, and in part represented the admiration of the Jeffersonian democracy for the republics of Greece; but before Wisconsin was settled, that style had almost passed away. We have a number of the composite porticoed and domed buildings, which succeeded and represented perhaps the kinship between the cruder democracy of Jackson and that of Rome. We have many buildings, both public and private—some, extremely beautiful—which reflect the days in the middle of the nineteenth century, when the best minds in America drew inspiration from the Italy of the Renaissance, when Story and Crawford, and Hawthorne and Margaret Fuller lived and worked in Rome. The succeeding period is everywhere illustrated, when the French mansard stands for the dominating influence on things artistic (or rather, inartistic) of the Second Empire. The revival of English influence is indicated in the Queen Anne style; the beginning of general interest in American history, in the colonial; the influence of the War with Spain, in the square cement. Many other waves of thought and interest, can be pointed out in almost any town. A careful study of its architecture will nearly always reveal the approximate date of its foundation, the periods of prosperity and depression, the origin of the inhabitants, and many other facts of real importance.

I have thus far spoken of the contribution of archaeology to the science of history. Fully as great, are its possibilities along the lines of popularization and illustration. The work of neither archaeology nor history can proceed without popular support, and the local appeal is one of the strongest that can be made. Not every town has an interesting history; but almost every one, however ugly, can be made historically interesting to its inhabitants if its streets can be made to tell its history, and by reflection something of the history of the country; this may be done merely by opening their eyes to their chirography. It should be part of the hope of the local archaeologist to make his neighbors and his neighbor's children see history in everything about them. If this is accomplished, we may hope gradually to arouse a deeper and more scientific interest, and a willingness to encourage that research into the whole past, in which historian and archaeologist are jointly interested.

On a recent visit to Lake Koshkonong, I found my interest much stimulated by a certain admirable map, and some plates illustrating the Indian life about its shores. It has occurred to me that one extremely valuable way of arousing general interest and of arranging our archaeological data, would be in a series of such minute maps. For instance, the first in the series would give purely the physical features; the next, on the same scale, would add our Indian data— mounds, village sites, cultivated fields, arrow factories, battlefields, trails, and any other indications that might appear; then, one on the entrance of the white men, with trading posts, garrisons, first settlements and roads; the next would begin with the schoolhouse and end with the railroad; and one or two others would complete the set. Such studies of the material changes of a locality, would not form an embellishment, but the basis of its history.

Another work might be undertaken through the local high

school. The pupils might be encouraged to take photographs of houses, fences, bridges, and other objects—interesting for the reasons I have pointed out—as well as all objects of aboriginal interest. These should always be dated, and the place where they were taken noted. In fact, a map should be used, and by numbers or some such device, the pictures localized. These photographs, properly classified and arranged, would give such a picture of the whole life of the community in terms of tangible remains, as could not fail to interest its inhabitants as well as serve the student. In the newer portions of the State, particularly in the north, it would be possible to take pictures of the first clearing, and then file these away; a few years later, one could take another picture of the farmstead, with its improvements— and so on, until it reached a condition of stability. Thus to project into the future the work of a science whose name suggests antiquity, may seem fantastic, but even the future will ultimately become antiquity. We have still in Wisconsin, some remnants of a frontier stage of civilization which is passing and cannot be reproduced, and it cannot be held superfluous to provide materials to express it to the future. If we may imagine the joy that it would give to us to find a photograph of the site of Rome before that city was built, or of one of the great Indian villages of Wisconsin before the coming of the white man, we may form a conception of the value to the future student of the civilization of our own day of such an ordered and scientific collection as I have suggested.

CHAPTER 3

Historic Objects as Sources of History

CARL P. RUSSELL

ADVENT AND GROWTH OF THE HISTORIAN—ARCHAEOLOGIST PROGRAM

For convenience, I shall be arbitrary in recognizing three stages in the development of the historian-archaeologist program in America:

1. The day of the Wisconsin School, early 1900's.
2. The period of Arthur C. Parker, Clark Wissler, and the concurrent "New Deal" activities, 1930's and 1940's.
3. The postwar period, which I choose to regard as continuing, currently.

I am confident there are workers who feel that the above chronology is poorly conceived, but perhaps it will suffice for present purposes.

In my view, Carl Russell Fish (not a relative of the writer) was among the first to urge historians to embrace three-dimensional objects as "documents" among historical records. His essay "Relation of Archaeology and History" was first read before the Wisconsin Archaeological Society at Madison on July 29, 1910. In referring to then-neglected historic objects, Dr. Fish said:

> *The first duty of the archaeologist is to discover such material and to verify it; the next is to secure its preservation.... Then comes the task of studying it; classifying it and arranging it, and making it ready for use. At this point the function of the archaeologist ceases and the duty of the historian begins; i.e., to interpret it, and to bring it into harmony with the recognized body of information regarding the past. It is not necessary that different individuals in every case do these different things ... nearly every historian should be something of an archaeologist and every archaeologist should be something of an historian.... When the archaeologist ceases from the preparation of his material, and begins the reconstruction of the past, he commences to act as an historian and has to call up* <u>a new range of equipment, and a new set of qualifications</u>
[emphasis mine].

Thus it seems apparent that the astute Dr. Fish anticipated the disciplines of the historian-archaeologist more than half a century ago, but most of his colleagues remained passive. Nothing effective was done by either the universities or the museums of this country to set up the "new range of equipment," nor did they recognize any need for the "new set of qualifications." Such research and identification as was done in the field of historic objects was undertaken by men and women having an antiquarian turn of mind. Seldom were their findings taken seriously by the profession. I think there is fair evidence of the truth of this assertion in various papers published by competent investigators who focused upon the prehistoric or aboriginal artifacts from their digs but tossed aside or evaded the "contact junk" encountered.[1] Sometimes these archaeologists included a few historic objects in the plates accompanying their published papers but made no comment in their texts regarding the significance of the historic objects. One gets the impression that generally the anthropologist shunned historic objects. Some of the trade objects recovered by unsympathetic archaeologists found their way into museum collections, where they are still to be seen, but often the meager data that accompanies them lend but little to any definitive understanding. Yet it must be said that these orphan artifacts are valued by certain present-day workers who have the initiative to study and the resourcefulness to "put two and two together." Shining examples of constructive work done with long neglected Western collections appear in T. M. Hamilton's "Indian Trade Guns."[2] Here is a work that really challenges the historian-archaeologist to begin studying the accumulated artifacts piled up but never identified by our predecessors.

But, getting back to the chronology for the movement to recognize historic objects as sources of history, in 1938 our well-loved American Indian, Dr. Arthur C. Parker, made a plea for better use of three-dimensional "documents" in presenting history through museum exhibits. He wrote:

> *History can be written by piecing together the evidences of man's thought as revealed by his handiwork. But this history cannot be reconstructed by haphazard methods. Visible storage in museum cases of miscellaneous articles is not history. It is confusion. Order and sequence are necessary ... and to attain this order the student must be able to classify and assign his material culture objects to their proper places. [Dioramas and life-size groups are good] but if we are unable to have such presentations, we may still show the horizontal stratification of our culture by exhibiting representa-*

---

[1] *Arthur Woodward: "Archeology—The Scrap Book of History,"* Regional Review, Nat'l Park Serv., Richmond, Va., I:2 (August 1938), pp. 8–10. *Mr. Woodward is a senior member within the current generation of archaeologist-historians. Inasmuch as he worked with Reginald P. Bolton during the 1920's, he constitutes something of a link with the earlier generation. In that pioneer group, besides Bolton and Fish, were such workers as William M. Beauchamp, W. L. Calver, Charles E. Brown, Henry C. Mercer, David L. Bushnell, W. Holmes, and George A. West. Each of these men is to be credited with publications that are milestones in historic-site archaeology.*

[2] *In* The Missouri Archeologist *(December 1960), pp. vii–226.*

tive utensils, implements, etc., of each stage of our historical development, so "writing" a record of cultural progress comparable to the better types of ethnological exhibits.

. . . When our workers are able to understand the ethnology of the whiteman . . . museums of history will take on a new and more significant meaning.

I do not know whether Parker was at all conscious of the admonitions voiced by Dr. Fish thirty years earlier, but his thinking had entered the same channels. Fish had said: "Where have our carpenters, our stonemasons, our iron workers, our woodsmen, our miners, our boatmakers, our millers, and our gun manufacturers come from, and what tricks of the trade have each contributed? Studies of these things reveal something of the soul of the people."

At the time that Dr. Parker was perfecting his history exhibits at Rochester, New York, the National Park Service obtained funds with which to develop museums in a number of the nation's most important historic places. Without much prior notice the bureau found it necessary to locate and employ a staff of curators, museum planners, and preparators who could begin work immediately, without the benefits of special training for the special jobs in hand. Of the thirteen curators on that early staff, most were trained anthropologists recently out of college. They went to work in such field areas as Colonial National Historic Park, Virginia; Morristown, New Jersey; Fort McHenry National Monument, Maryland; Ocmulgee, Georgia; Chickamauga and Chattanooga National Military Park, Georgia and Tennessee; Guilford Courthouse, North Carolina; Shiloh, Tennessee; and Vicksburg, Mississippi. Extensive collections of historic objects already were on hand in all of the areas, and in some instances notable additions to the collections were acquired through excavations after the museum program was started. The curators did their best as they shaped exhibit plans to utilize the rich cultural materials at their command but, with four exceptions, they confessed to their overwhelming difficulties in discerning the significance of the "relics" to which they had had no previous introduction. The park historians, fellow workers with the curators on the field jobs, in most cases were unable to give much assistance in handling the three-dimensional objects.

I mention these circumstances without any intention of disparaging the individuals. I have been in touch with these same pioneer curators during the thirty or more years that have elapsed. With the exception of two who have died, these men are enjoying successful careers in the National Park Service or in leading universities and museums, and a couple of them are now expert in the field of historic objects. But the point I would make is that in 1935–6 neither the history nor the anthropology departments in colleges and universities provided training in the handling of history materials having three-dimensional characteristics.

With a thought to publicizing the unfavorable situation, the American Association of Museums scheduled a paper, "The Use of Historic Objects as Sources of History," for the History Museums Section at its annual meeting in Detroit in 1940. This paper[3] advocated that the association take steps to establish trial courses at the university level for the purpose of training historians, archaeologists, and curators to use artifacts as research and interpretive materials in

history. Consistent with the views of the day regarding student preparation for museum work, the speaker urged that the educational phase of training be offered in the university and that the training phase be given in selected museums.

There was no direct response to the paper from the organization, but among the officers were men active in the American Council of Learned Societies, a group then headed by Dr. Waldo Leland with headquarters in Washington. Presently Dr. Leland asked the National Park Service to delegate someone to discuss the history-archaeology problem with his council at a regular meeting. The Service complied, and the story was presented to this panel of philosophers and educators very much as it had been given to the museum people. The subject was accorded rather full discussion, but the consensus was that historic objects belonged in the museum realm not in the university curriculum; "anyhow, where could a professor be found who is prepared to teach this subject?"

Apparently only Dr. Leland of the Learned Societies visualized the practicability of adding historic objects to the teaching materials in a university history department. He suggested that a foundation might be induced to provide funds with which to establish a chair at William and Mary as a start in launching the desired courses of training. He expressed intention of carrying the matter to other congresses but advised that it might be politic to "sell" the idea of such curricular expansion first to some of the regularly employed historians and archaeologists already in the National Park Service. Since the leaders in the National Park Service Branch of Historic Sites were already "sold," there was no problem in arranging pertinent staff meetings.

The fact that a specialized job was to be done in so many different parks and monuments with few or no employees available who might be equal to the task engendered a certain determination. In March 1940 several interbranch conferences were held in the National Park Service Director's Office, Washington, in order that staff historians, archaeologists, and museum workers might air their views regarding the impasse. Four two-hour meetings were held. Detailed minutes of the sessions are still available for reference.[4] The conferees were experienced in various aspects of interpretive work in the field; at this late date it is interesting to note, in the record of the discussions, the maturity and directness of their approach to a discipline that at the time did not even have a name.

In effect, these men confessed to inadequacy in meeting obligations in handling cultural objects, but they recognized clearly enough that because of the basic values—"historic objects have a statement to make just as do written sources"—someone would have to master these three-dimensional materials. In their own words:

The historic objects now in possession, or destined to come into the ownership of the National Park Service henceforth shall receive the best care, study, and interpretive use possible under existing limitations imposed by lack of knowledge and experience.

. . . Every effort is to be made to bring about establishment of courses of training in colleges and universities designed to prepare historians, anthropologists, and museum curators to work with historic objects. Pend-

[3]By C. P. Russell. MS in National Park Service Museums Library, Washington, D.C.

[4]R. F. Lee and C. P. Russell, eds.: Historic Objects; Their Place in Research and Interpretation (Washington, D.C.: Nat'l. Park Serv.; 1940), 56 pp. (mimeographed).

ing the day when especially prepared employees may be recruited from the universities, the National Park Service must utilize its existing staff leadership in conducting in-service training designed to increase the capacity of presently employed field men to work more effectively in the realm of historic objects.

World War II brought disruption and near disaster to many plans projected by the National Park Service; the anticipated plans of the interpreters for in-service training collapsed because of the drastic cuts in personnel and appropriations. One notable triumph was gained before the blow fell; Ned J. Burns's *Field Manual for Museums* was published by the Government Printing Office in 1941. This book became an important instrument in advancing the parks museum program. The National Park Service outlook upon its responsibilities in the field of historic objects is given on pages 22–3 and 105–7 of that volume.

The five-year interruption of normal progress in National Park Service programs brought about by war caused serious setbacks, but fortunately most of the Service personnel concerned with historic sites and historic objects returned to their jobs. Dr. Leland, as a member of the Advisory Board, remembered his earlier explorations in the matter of training specialists in history-archaeology. In May 1946 an important conclave of Service officials and numerous educators, historians, and anthropologists from universities and museums of the eastern United States was called in Colonial National Historical Park, Virginia. Dr. Leland's American Council met the travel expenses of those not employed by the government.

Dr. J. C. Harrington of the National Park Service managed the meeting; R. F. Lee, Chief of the History Branch, National Park Service, sounded the keynote: "How can the existing body of physical sources of history within NPS areas best be utilized in writing American history? How are students to be trained to approach physical sources as part of their schooling?"

Potentially it was a high-powered conference. Participating in the discussions were well-known anthropologists, historians, and educators from Johns Hopkins, Harvard, Duke, William and Mary, the University of Virginia, the University of North Carolina, Louisiana State University, Williamsburg Restoration, Inc., the Philadelphia Museum of Art, and the United States National Museum. The idea of training students to become proficient in using historical objects seemed to set some of the university professors back on their heels. A number of them spoke with some regrets about the "yawning gap between historians and the sites and artifacts of history," but a general doubt was expressed regarding the practicability of detaching students from their campuses for long-enough assignments on archaeological digs.

Universities have done little or nothing about such student training because they cannot afford to spend money and time on it, at the same time that presently-prescribed programs of teaching are in progress. In any event, average graduate students would have great difficulty in mastering the intricacies of identification of cultural materials even in the laboratory, not to mention the added difficulties of identifying artifacts as they come from the ground. In other words, students who have signed up for history have not planned to be archaeologists. Today graduate students in history seldom are given enough training in handling manuscripts. The proposed additional training in handling three-dimensional objects would strain a university

history department and its average student beyond established limits.

No one professor uttered all of these comments, but the connotation of several short speeches added up to the above pessimistic outlook.

J. O. Brew of Harvard sounded a more optimistic note as he made a plea for recognition by the panel of the pressing need for historian-archaeologists. He quoted Dr. Harrington's assertion that the National Park Service had immediate need for one hundred specialists in this field. He remarked that in his own fieldwork at Concord he found much pottery in the form of sherds that could not be dated. "The hardware encountered offered a similar problem. Digs in Arizona recovered 17th century Spanish objects about which full information could not be obtained." He urged that a clearinghouse for the identification of historic objects be established even though definitive descriptions might be impossible in some instances. He also urged that publication of finds be a regular procedure, although interpretation may of necessity be imperfect.

Dr. Frank Setzler of the National Museum asked for the establishment of standards in identifying historic objects.

In museums, workers are constantly confronted with problems of identifying objects. This panel should not limit its thinking to the Colonial period; we face the broad field of historic objects and we should recognize the need to improve the knowledge imparted to any and all students of history. The National Museum needs able men at this moment to enter the field of cultural objects. The museum staff cannot take time to teach, and, presently, universities do not have professors who are equal to the task. There is occasion for this conference to perform a broad public service, as well as a service to the National Park Service.

Fiske Kimball, Philadelphia Museum of Art, observed:

Probably universities are not as well prepared to meet the problems described as are the great museums which own large collections. Men prepared to teach any part of the subject, cultural materials, are snatched up by museums. Even the museums do not have trained personnel capable of handling all problems of identification. I subscribe to J. O. Brew's plea for publication. Field reports should not be held secret; the National Park Service should publish its reports; Williamsburg should make known its finds, even though interpretation may not be perfect. Workers in the museums of the country will find it possible to contribute to understanding of three-dimensional objects if they can study published reports. Everybody can benefit if the reports get distribution.

Kendrow of Williamsburg expressed intention of making better progress in publishing, but he explained that major efforts were still directed upon the study of the physical remains requiring exposition, and that the editors in his organization were hesitant. To this Dr. Kimball said: "The mistake in the past grows out of striving for perfection. Publish in the raw, but publish without delay. Even pictures of the physical materials will serve an important purpose if they are distributed."

Here Harrington spoke of the example of Lambeth Delft found at Jamestown: "The American Wing was about to publish a definitive paper on delftware without knowing of the major collection at Jamestown." R. F. Lee of the National Park Service outlined the scope of the historic sites under the administration of the Service and advocated that a practicable scheme for shaping and maintaining a cumulative record of cultural materials be set up, "starting now." Dr. Charles Porter, also of the National Park Service, proposed the "organization of a society of antiquarians, not in the old sense of antiquarianism, for the exchange of knowledge and for joint study of objects." Marshall gave a warm second to this proposal. "In Great Britain it is dignified to be an antiquarian. The United States should breed some." (It is of more than slight significance that Williamsburg ultimately imported one of the English antiquarians as Chief Archaeologist.)

Dr. Leland concluded the discussions with an admonition to the National Park Service to establish and publicize a practical guide to the physical remains (cultural objects) in its possession.

During the twenty years that have elapsed since Dr. Leland's Jamestown meeting, the ranks of the historian-archaeologists have grown considerably. The reasons are not far to seek.

1. Many of the states of the Union and numerous historical societies, museums, universities, and other organized groups have established state parks, memorials, and similar reservations upon sites where historic events transpired. In order that these sites may be protected, managed, and interpreted it is necessary often to practice the best possible historic-site archaeology. Historian-archaeologists (or potential historian-archaeologists) are searched out, cultivated, and hired by the state and private agencies concerned. Currently they continue in this employment.

2. The responsibilities of the National Park Service have not diminished since 1946; on the contrary, additional historic sites have been acquired, and investigative work has been intensified at some of the earlier reserves. Under the authority of the Historic Sites Act of 1935, the Park, Parkway and Recreation Area Study Act of 1936, and the Flood Control Act of 1944, the National Park Service cooperates with and obtains assistance from federal (the Smithsonian Institution, especially) and state agencies in conducting archaeological surveys and salvage on numerous sites, some of which are threatened by the widespread program of dams and reservoirs now in progress throughout much of the country. In this extensive salvage work, historic sites as well as the prehistoric centers are precisely located and excavated in order that historical data and historic objects may be saved. Here, at the moment, is the larger realm of the historian-archaeologist.[5]

3. Among the miscellaneous programs that demand the attention of the historian-archaeologist is the relatively new underwater archaeology. In this field lies the opportunity to link certain historic sites in such a way as to clarify the history of some international relationships; also, through the recovery and comparison of artifacts to contribute importantly to the long-wanted standardization of identification. Obviously a great new realm is opened by this expansion of the frontiers of exploration and discovery. In truth, underwater archaeology may well constitute a new dimension of the historian-archaeologist's discipline needed to round out the profession and to perfect the organizational scheme visualized in 1946.

It would be satisfying to say that the objectives set forth at the Leland-Harrington forum in Colonial National Historical Park twenty years ago are close to attainment, but no such good report is given. In the words of one of the leaders who has busied himself continuously in historic-site archaeology:

Thinking back on the Jamestown conference [1946], I regret to say that nearly every one of the problems and concerns we talked about then are still with us—acceptance by historians, training for this kind of archaeology, access to specialized data, publishing results, etc. There has been progress in each, but it is slow. . . . One of the more encouraging advances is the contributions forthcoming from continued conferences such as those organized by Stanley South. A host of people are now in or on the fringes of this new field. Some are making real contributions, but our basic problem is the same as it was 25 years ago—we still have to turn to "Indian" archaeologists to dig historic sites.[6] . . . In regard to examples of published reports in this field the list is becoming extensive, but we still have the same old problem of finding publication outlets; the reports get into weird places.

A significant move was made in 1949 when the military-minded element among the historian-archaeologists established their own society, The Company of Military Collectors and Historians, in Washington, D.C. They created the journal Military Collector and Historian, thus providing the quarterly outlet for a wealth of original material on one class of historic objects. This classified literature so created, assembled, and integrated through a quarter of a century exceeds in interest and value anything created and released by other antiquarians in America. The Company hews to its line, never boasting of its unique accomplishment, but in its success, I think, is encouragement for the establishment of the much-needed all-inclusive society of historian-archaeologists.

A variety of reasons have been advanced for the failure of the academic historians to give hearty support to "antiquarianism." To me the reasons do not seem valid, but the fact remains that no real union has been attained. Perhaps it is worthwhile to review the steps taken during the past decade looking toward the all-important coalition.

In the 1950 American Heritage William S. Powell adopted Dr. J. C. Harrington's appellation "Historic Site Archaeology" and summarized the projects then in work. Included was a Florida underwater job, but no reference was made to it as "underwater archaeology." Generally the release constituted applause for the successful birth of a new discipline and a new national interest in history. Understandably Mr. Powell conceived of the main objective as being principally "rebuilding" and he therefore advanced the descriptive term "restoration archaeology." Also in 1950, The New-York Historical Society published Calver and Bolton's important History Written with Pick and Shovel, designed to encourage and guide the growing fraternity of military specialists and other fieldworkers. Heizer's Manual of Field Methods also appeared in 1950.

During the 1950's fieldwork in Virginia continued, and numerous historic sites in Arizona, California, Canada, Florida, Michigan, Pennsylvania, Rhode Island, and Washington were excavated. At least one of the resulting reports, Harrington's New Light on Washington's Fort Necessity, published in 1957, stands as a classic. By 1957 the professional concern with historic-site archaeology was such as to prompt the American Association for State and Local History to schedule a panel discussion, "The Artifact in History," at its annual meeting in Columbus, Ohio. Here for the first time the usefulness of the historic object was discussed pro and con in the light of a considerable body of data derived through

---

[5]Archaeological work on pipelines and highways adds two significant salvage activities to the National Park Service archaeology program.

[6]Regarding this matter, Ivor Noël Hume observes: "Even today fine archaeologists trained to excavate and study the cultures of the Southwestern Indians are sent to work on colonial sites in Virginia" (Here Lies Virginia. An Archaeological View of Colonial Life and History. [New York: Alfred A. Knopf, 1963], p. 97). Mr. Noël Hume fails to point to a source of trained historian-archaeologists who might be recruited for the colonial digs.

practical experience. Probably the most constructive offering was made by Harrington, who at the close of his recounting of examples persuaded his listeners:

> *Artifacts can be employed as nondocumentary sources by historians; they not only fill in missing details, but may even furnish extremely critical information . . . . Their value to the historian is in proportion to how much is known of their cultural context in a given historical situation. A rusty fragment of a matchlock firing mechanism found at Jamestown, with pertinent archaeological data available to the scholar, constitutes a unique and valuable bit of historical source material. Depending upon the particular historical problem under consideration, this artifact might well be more valuable than a complete gun of the period, bought from a collector [for exhibit purposes].*

Patent though this reasoning be, the number of professional historians who hear it (or read it) is infinitesimal. The historians' doubts expressed in 1946 still prevail—"Universities cannot afford to spend money and time on historic objects, and yet conduct their presently prescribed programs." A greater and more deplorable circumstance is seen in the academic historian's seeming adherence to the Hogarthian belief voiced so long ago, "the artifact stops short of any possibility of truly reconstituting the picture of the human past; to that end the literary documents are all-essential, now and in the future." The works of two historians, Bloch (1953) and Hockett (1955), offer hope that the profession ultimately will take a more searching look at the three-dimensional source materials.

It seems pertinent to refer here to the *Bulletin* and to the new "Technical Leaflet" series published by the American Association for State and Local History. The editorial outlook is sympathetic to the cause of the historian-archaeologist, and sometimes the printed subject matter constitutes argument for a wedding of the laboratory and the historians' classroom. Potentially the American Association for State and Local History offers liaison.

At the annual meeting of the American Anthropological Society in Washington in 1958, there was featured an important "Symposium on the Role of Archaeology in Historical Research." Techniques at the dig, collaboration between specialists, "intellectualization" of the results of the dig, and cultural reconstruction and publicizing finds were narrated by five "kingpins" of the profession, and their papers were discussed by five equally distinguished members. The record of this meeting provides the most sophisticated expressions extant of the philosophy of the historian-archaeologist. I like the words of the speaker who closed the meeting: "The historian-archaeologist must be competent in historical research as well as in archaeology. He must have a basic knowledge of architecture. Finally, he must be an anthropologist, for *it is the study of cultures and the physical entity of man himself that gives to him insight in human perspective.*"

Among the speakers at this 1958 meeting, only J. O. Brew referred to training: "The universities are still not providing their students with concepts, much less training in this growing field."

Since 1958 Harvard has shaped a course of training, and Professor Anthony Garvan of the University of Pennsylvania initiated one on material culture. At Pennsylvania also, Dr. John L. Cotter conducted a field school in historic-site archaeology during the summer of 1963.

At the University of Arizona in February 1964, Arthur Woodward launched a prescribed college course, "Historical Archaeology," under the joint aegis of the departments of anthropology and history. His course has lapsed, however.

Instruction not of college level, but deserving of mention, is given at Cooperstown, New York, where the New York State Historical Association has conducted sessions on "Managing Small Museum Collections," including historic objects. This is a part of the Annual Seminars on American Culture offered to amateurs and professionals. Since 1947 twenty of the seminars have been held.

The Museum Division of the National Park Service, Washington, conducts an annual museum methods training course. "Historical objects receive attention in this training, and the responsibility for care of historic objects is written into the job description of Regional Curators. We stress the need for research on our historical collections and try to pave the way for such research."

By way of recapitulation I would say that two or three of the goals defined by the conferees at Jamestown in 1946 have not been attained:

1. There is no central clearing house for the identification of historic objects; no established standards useful in identifying and comparing historic objects; and no step has been taken toward the creation and maintenance of a cumulative record of America's cultural materials.[7]
2. The desired "Society of Antiquarians" has been advocated by one or more speakers whenever historian-archaeologists gather, but until recently nothing practical had been done toward the founding of a society. Just as this book was to go to press we received the welcome news that the Society for Historical Archaeology has been established under the presidency of John L. Cotter. It is proposed that the society shall publish an annual journal, *Historical Archaeology*, and *Current Year*, a report on field activities.

To be somewhat less negative in ending this work, I say that very constructive steps have been taken under the pioneering efforts of Harrington and the later contributions of South, Noël Hume, Goggin, Cotter, and others to give definition to the discipline of the historian-archaeologist. At least a beginning has been made in establishing university courses designed to prepare future historian-archaeologists. One course is in a department of history, one in archaeology, and a third receives the blessings of both a department of anthropology and a department of history. It is too early to say whether or not the future development of the special curriculum will reside generally in American history (as I think it should), but it is not too early to predict that presently the training will be available in one or another department in numerous institutions and, eventually, there will come the full-fledged "school" of historic-site archaeology.

The dramatic qualities of recovered weapons and of certain Indian trade pieces appeal to the curiosity of almost every citizen; public interest is good. So far as dedicated collectors are concerned, interest is lively, and the educated concern they show usually is helpful to the historian-archaeologist and to his broad program of research. This book is directed to the average reader and to the collector as well as to the professional curator of history. May it testify to the fact that even now a certain continuity and an all-important partnership prevail in the efforts exerted by the dirt-encrusted digger and the researcher among the documents.

[7] *In 1963 Harper & Row published* Soldier and Brave, *"a record of Indian-connected sites without parallel in our historical literature." This is the first major publication of the National Survey of Historic Sites and Buildings, National Park Service. In 1964* Colonials and Patriots, *in the same series, was produced by the Government Printing Office. These books do for two classes of historic sites the service that should be done for historic objects.*

CHAPTER 4

The Study of Historic Archaeology in America

ARTHUR WOODWARD

During the past eleven years I have concentrated upon the study of historic archaeology in North America. Very little attention has been paid to the study of the historic period, i.e., the immediate contact and post-European contact periods extending from the 15th to the 20th centuries. Students of American archaeology, when encountering European materials in burials and village sites, have usually minimized the importance of such specimens, without seriously attempting to place them in the chronological scale. This has resulted in many erroneous beliefs concerning the period of occupation on various sites. In certain areas discoveries of European trade items have been glibly called "post contact" but no attempts have been made to actually learn whether the specimens were distributed in the 16th or 18th centuries, and an erroneous estimate embracing a period of 200 years is enough to mislead the archaeologist in his final deduction—and it will likewise mislead students who continue the work in such areas. Hence, my task has been to make a beginning in the first contact periods. Of course the period of contacts varies in different sections. That fact is naturally taken into consideration. However, such items as glass beads, for example, are common denominators and they vary with the different centuries and through tribal preferences. To that end I am trying to assemble a type collection of glass beads from known historic sites or from sites where corroborative material capable of being dated has been discovered. The approximate date of the site is usually determined by the latest type of European material encountered. Among other factors, such as quantity, condition of artifacts, location of the site, character of the soil, age of the individual (in case of burials), associated artifacts are taken into consideration. At present I am continuing this study of glass beads.

In addition to the beads, I am also constantly checking up on silver ornaments distributed by the European Colonials in North America, c. 1740–1850. Clay pipes, glass bottles, sword and gun, furniture, pewter, brass and silver spoons, knives, kettles, axes, in brief, any object of European manufacture capable of withstanding the ravages of time are chronological criteria in this study.

There is a need for more specialists in this field. The establishment of an accurate chronological scale for the historic ethnology of the tribes north of Mexico, particularly in reference to the origins of costume and the possible influence of the European culture upon all sections of the country during the past four hundred years. Eventually, I hope to collaborate with Mr. M. R. Harrington in the publication of a book on Indian costume, arranged to indicate the Chronological evolution.

Bibliographical notes: My latest contribution in the field of American archaeology is—"A Shell Bracelet Manufactory"; *American Antiquity*, Vol. 2, October, 1936.

Articles concerning the study of historic archaeology are relatively scarce. The following items, some of which are recent, others not so recent, are useful to the students in this field:

REFERENCES

BRANNON, PETER A.
1935 "The Southern Indian Trade", 87p. The Paragon Press, Montgomery, Alabama. (Note: This item is well illustrated with types of historic specimens found on historic Indian sites in Alabama and contains localized information necessary to a student working in the general field of comparative historic archaeology and ethnology.)

A Series of articles:

BRANNON, PETER A.
1934 "Trading Paths in the Gulf Country". Alabama Highways, July-August. Nos. 3 and 4, pp. 3-10-11-12; illustrated with three maps.
"Indian Traders in the Alabama Country". Alabama Highways, Sep.-Oct., 1934; pp. 3-7-10-11-12-13-14; illustrated.
"Pocket Knives and Looking Glasses". Alabama Highways, Nov.-Dec., 1934; pp. 3-7-10-11-12-13-14; illustrated.

GILLINGHAM, HAROLD. E.
1934 "Indian Silver Ornaments". The Pennsylvania Magazine of History and Biography, Vol. 58; pp. 97–126; illustrated. Published by The Historical Society of Pennsylvania, Philadelphia, Pa. (Note: This item concerns local Philadelphia silversmiths and is not a treatise on the evolution or general distribution of such wares. No analysis of either the specimens themselves or an indication of widespread usage of these objects).

WOODWARD, ARTHUR.
1932 "The Value of Indian Trade Goods in the Study of Archaeology". The Pennsylvania Archaeologist, Vol. 3, No. 1; illustrated.
1933 "Wampum and Its Uses". Pennsylvania Archaeologist, Vol. 3, No. 5.
1927 "Those Green River Knives". Indian Notes, Vol. 4, No. 4, Museum of the American Indian Heye Foundation.
1926 "Indian Use of the Silver Gorget". Indian Notes, Vol. 3, No. 4.

Other items which are useful to students in the study of historic archaeology, but not of recent date:

BROWN, CHARLES E.
1918 "Indian Trade Implements and Ornaments". The Wisconsin Archaeologist, Vol. 17, No. 3.

BEAUCHAMP, WM. M.
1902 "Metalic Implements of the New York Indians". Bulletin 55, New York State Museum, Albany, N. Y.
"Metalic Ornaments of the New York Indians". Bulletin 73, Albany, N. Y., 1903.

THE COLLINS CO. COLLINSVILLE, CONNECTICUT.
1926 "Cien Años de Existencia". Relato conciso del Desenvolvimiento de la Compañía Collins en la Fabricación de Hachas, Machetes y Herramientas de filo, en Conmemoración de su centenario, 1826–1926. Collinsville. (Note: This item pertains to the manufacture of certain implements and tools widely distributed over North America during the past 111 years and affords a check on axes and weapons stamped with the Collins trade mark).

CHAPTER 5

Symposium on Role of Archaeology in Historical Research, Summary and Analysis

JOHN L. COTTER

Let us neither kid ourselves nor misrepresent the contribution of archaeology to historical research. It isn't earth shaking or such as to transform the whole mode of historical and architectural research. In fact, we may even admit it is a contribution of modest but definitely useful substance. At this symposium, however, we have intimated that the archaeologist can and should transcend his contribution as a technician.

W. H. Holmes said, "Archaeology is the great retriever of history . . . it reads and interprets that which was never meant to be read or interpreted . . . revealer of vast resources of history of which no man had previously taken heed." And Grahame Clark put it this way: "To see big things whole they must be seen from a distance, and that is precisely what archaeology enables one to do." This is really the crux of the matter; namely, the ability of archaeological evidence to add a third dimension to historical research which will bring into clearer focus the familiar, everyday life of the past, no matter in what period.

In this sense, Clyde Kluckhohn has pointed out in his *Mirror for Man* "The historical anthropologists have performed a great service in emphasizing the concrete and the historically unique. The facts of chance, of historical accident, must be understood as well as the universals of socio-cultural process . . . ." Kluckhohn agrees with Lancelot Hogben that archaeology is "a powerful intellectual vitamin."

In this seminar John Griffin stated a necessary premise; namely, that we are first anthropologists; second, archaeologists; and third—for those of us who go that far—historians. Archaeology for the anthropologist is a technique. So it may be for the historian—only few historians are equipped to use these techniques, and so the anthropological archaeologist is called in. Griffin then went on to ask "What is the relation of the anthropological archaeologist to a project dedicated to historical ends?" He envisioned these ends to be strictly limited, and pointed out that to him, both historian and archaeologist act merely as technicians applying techniques to a particularly restricted problem. In this view Griffin and Harrington are in agreement. Then Griffin has proceeded to go a step further and confess his view that the one to compile the facts amassed by the historical and archaeological technician should be the archaeologist who then steps out of his technical chrysalis and spreads his wings as an anthropologist, thus taking the research, as it were, off the ground, and out of the fact file. Griffin refuses to allow the archaeologist to be merely a technician. I suspect any historian of cultural perception and high professional standing would likewise refuse to let the historian be a technician. There is a point at which one eye gazing at history and the other eye at culture

manages to focus on a remarkably enlightening, three-dimensional image of the past. Viewers from both disciplines have too often been cross-eyed or walleyed. I suspect the trick can be accomplished by anyone of sufficient scholarly information and understanding of man and his past, be he historian or anthropologist. The focusing takes practice, and needs to be done more often.

Ivor Noël Hume has viewed the status and problems of the archaeologist as historical investigator with the detachment of one entering the field in America from England. And he has done this with considerable wit and wisdom. I hope he is discovering in the New World that there is a visible compulsion toward ancestor veneration securely tied to a fancy for antiques. All of which gives the archaeologist the green light (provides money for the gas, too!) But—just when we are on the threshold of enticing successfully the interest and support of individuals and of private and public institutions for the archaeological investigation and salvage of our national heritage, we are drawn up short with the reminder that we know too little about details of historical arts, crafts and custom. In fact, for sites as little as a hundred years old we, as archaeologists, are often not competent to assist the historian and architect. The simple, closely-dated trash pit, ever the piece de resistance of the archaeologist, must once more be sought to give us diagnostic objects, even while whole houses and villages remain untouched. Then Noël Hume has mentioned the most salient point: When the data on life, artifacts, customs, houses and so on are ready for use, how can they be described for publication?

Here, then, is an immediate need for organizing a society which will galvanize the efforts of antiquarian, historian, architect, archaeologist and local and national patriotic groups. What, indeed, are we waiting for? A name? The Society for Historical Archaeology? A journal? The journal of the Society, called, say, *Historical Archaeology*—probably a slick paper affair publishing summaries of projects and achievements, with illustrations. Don't forget, the American Heritage syndrome is solidly in back of us. So much for possibility—I might venture to add, inevitability.

Dr. Brew added an important fourth to the triumvirate of archaeologist, historian and architect; namely, the engineer, whose assistance is vital to large-scale salvage operations in river valleys, drainage projects, highway construction and any area clearing or excavating for foundations and pipelines. To this add the technician who can teach us photogrammetry for recording—a most significant aid to architect, engineer, historian and archaeologist alike.

Both Kenneth Kidd and Hubert Smith have pointed to the perspective which the archaeologist can give to the culture of the European immigrants, beginning with the Age of Discovery and exploration and ultimately colonization. As Smith reminded us, nothing in human history is foreign to the humanist or—as we might add more specifically—the anthropologist. Here I might add the importance of a clear view on the part of the archaeologist working at contact and frontier sites to note carefully evidence of acculturation flowing from traits of the Indian into white culture—a social factor noted by Hallowell but often neglected.

Archaeology, then, is a technique of investigation that can be used not only by anthropologists but by historians and architects. For the purposes of historical and architectural investigations, it requires of the archaeologist knowledge and skills far beyond the normal demands of the prehistoric village or campsite, cave or accidental deposition. Thus, the archaeologist who devotes his efforts toward the historical field must, in effect, become competent in historical research and know its methods. Above all, he must know specifically and in detail the culture and times which characterize his field of operations, be it an 18th century American Colonial house or an 11th century Japanese temple. And, if the archaeologist is aiding in the assembling of data for restoring a Romanesque church in Normandy or a Franciscan monastery at an Indian pueblo in the southwest, he must have a basic knowledge of the architecture involved.

But first of all, and also finally, the archaeologist, in order to fill a need wherever investigations in his legitimate field are attempted, must be an anthropologist. For it is the broad background of the study of cultures and the physical entity of man himself that gives the archaeologist a training in human perspective that exceeds the scope of the historian, architect or engineer.

To those who inquire how an archaeologist who undertakes to assist historians and architects can afford to devote the many patient years of study required to qualify him as an anthropologist, let historians and architects understand clearly that the archaeologist cannot be merely a technician able to direct laborers and record objects found in the ground. He must be much more than this, and, if he is worthy of his hire, he is worthy of considerable respect. And, to conclude on a dynamic and vital note, let me add that the archaeologist so qualified is worthy of substantial pay as a scientific researcher.

CHAPTER 6
End Products of Historic Sites Archaeology

JOHN W. GRIFFIN

As originally suggested, my topic read, "Problems of the Historian's Attitude toward Archaeology and the Archaeologist's Attitude toward History." Quite apart from the cumbersome nature of the title, I felt it to be misleading. It implied for one thing that historians and archaeologists had a particular and unified way of looking at one another, and it further implied that history and archaeology were disciplines on the same level.

Now I, for one, am convinced that there is no such thing as a science of archaeology—no separate and distinct discipline in any true sense of the word. Archaeology, to me, is nothing more than a body of techniques for assembling data on Man's past. The decision of what data to assemble, and what to do with it once assembled, leads one beyond archaeology itself. It leads to more basic fields—history and anthropology for example.

I feel that unless it is a field man who knows only how to dig, there is no such thing as an archaeologist apart from his membership in some other field of scholarly or scientific endeavor.

Most of us in this room are anthropological archaeologists. We took our training in departments of anthropology; we are in symposium at a meeting of the American Anthropological Association. The tendency is for the word archaeology, for us, to suggest the study of human prehistory—as a defined subfield of anthropology. Yet, is not any competent archaeologist with this background attempting at the least to do prehistoric ethnography, by the application of a certain body of techniques in the field and laboratory? Is he not concerned, perhaps, with the broader ramifications of prehistoric ethnology or cultural anthropology? Is he not, in effect, a cultural anthropologist dealing with a particular portion of the data of culture, with techniques appropriate to that segment? There are specialists in this type of anthropology, and for convenience we call them archaeologists.

But it is well to remember that there are other kinds of archaeologists. There are persons who are basically classicists, art historians, and historians specializing in such fields as the ancient Near East, or the Far East. Insofar as they employ a body of techniques to recover data from the ground, these people, too, are archaeologists. We are not here interested in quibbling about whose techniques are the best, but only in separating the techniques from the basic discipline for which they are applied.

It follows, then, that it would be possible for historic sites archaeology to be done by historians who have learned or developed the requisite techniques. I would see no problem in calling such investigators archaeologists even though they were not anthropological archaeologists.

But, as a matter of fact, there has been very little movement in this direction. Most historic sites work in this country has been done by anthropological archaeologists, and the vast majority of us participating in this symposium are of that breed. And here lies the crux of the problem, if there is a problem. What is the relation of the anthropological archaeologist to a project dedicated to historical ends?

We should immediately point out that the ends, toward which most historic sites archaeology is conducted, are strictly limited. Harrington has convincingly pointed this out in an earlier paper. The most usual end is the gathering of data for use in interpretive development, an aspect which will be dealt with by the following speaker.

As an example of an archaeological project with strictly limited objectives, I may mention a recent small scale excavation which I conducted in the sally port of the Castillo de San Marcos in St. Augustine, Florida. The objective of this work was simply to locate the level of the original Spanish floors in this section of the fort. The purpose was to provide information for regrading this section to its original level, and was tied in with the project of reconstructing the drawbridge of the fort, which obviously had to meet the floor.

Now a project of this sort utilizes archaeological techniques. The archaeologist acts as a reader of physical evidence; he combines his experience in excavation with whatever he has managed to pick up in the way of architectural knowledge.

Such a project also utilizes historical techniques. The historian associated with the project employs his knowledge of documentary research and historiography to assemble what material he can bearing on the project at hand.

Actually, both historian and archaeologist are acting merely as technicians. They are both applying techniques to the elucidation of a particularly restricted problem. In the example used, the result could not conceivably change the history of the Castillo, or its historical significance. Nor could it conceivably add to our knowledge of culture and its processes. In short, the product was not history or anthropology. It was data to be used in interpretive development.

We may liken such a project to work in the preparation room of a museum, where pots are glued together and repaired so that the public may better visualize them. In this case, the artifact is the complete fort. How it is to be interpreted is another matter, and one which infringes on Hubert Smith's topic.

It should be clear by now that such projects *can* be frustrating to both archaeologists and historians dedicated to pure research, and that alone. Unless the professional interests of these scholars are tempered with the conviction that interpretation to the public—which is to say education—is a worthwhile objective, we will have dissatisfied workers. But this is not a problem which is unique to historic sites archaeology. It is found in varying degrees in any museum which combines research and exhibit functions. We all know curators who resent every moment they have to spend on exhibit planning and consultation. For that matter, we all know university professors who resent having to teach.

But there are projects on historic sites which have, or should have, broader objectives. Some are organized to discover in more detail than given by the documents the way of life at a particular time and place. Some are, in fact, undertaken with strictly anthropological objectives in mind. The question arises, are any undertaken for strictly historical ends?

The answer depends upon how one defines historical ends. Traditionally, historians have aimed at the writing of a narrative record of past events, nothing more. Conservatively, this has meant no explanations or interpretations of the observed facts. Or, it has meant explanation in terms of "common sense," which, as Historian Marc Bloch has said, "usually turns out to be nothing more than a compound of irrational postulates and hastily generalized experiences."

This type of history generally has little regard for physical objects as an aid in its aims. As recently as 1955 in a highly regarded book on historical method Homer Carey Hockett wrote: "The sources of his (the historian's) knowledge are primarily written documents, although he may sometimes supplement these by utilizing various kinds of unwritten matter, such as structures, utensils, weapons, artifacts, drawings, fragments of bone, and other evidences of human life antedating the invention of writing. These, however, are properly the materials for writers who deal with the prehistoric period. We distinguish them from the historians by calling them archaeologists, anthropologists, or ethnologists."

Note particularly that upon the invention of writing, to Hockett, archaeological materials cease to have significance. Under such a concept of history it is clear that historic sites archaeology has little to contribute, except perhaps in the identification or validation of particular sites, and the provision of illustrative materials.

This is not, however, the only view that historians take of their field. If we turn again to the French historian Marc Bloch we find him saying:

"The past is, by definition, a datum which nothing in the future will change. But the knowledge of the past is something progressive which is constantly transforming and perfecting itself . . . . the ingenuity of the scholars in further ransacking the libraries or in opening new excavations on ancient sites is neither the sole nor, perhaps, even the most effective means of enriching our picture of the past. Hitherto unknown techniques to investigation have also come to light. We are more skillful than our predecessors in examining language for the evidence of customs, and tools for the evidence of techniques. Above all, we have learned how to probe more deeply in the analysis of social developments."

Bloch has done more than wed the artifact to the document in the sentences quoted above. He has expressed a view of history which involves the analysis of social developments utilizing all available conceptual tools. In short, he is speaking a language which we as anthropologists can understand. His ends become virtually indistinguishable from anthropological ends.

I do not think that Bloch is an isolated example by any means. He marks a trend in the field of history. Just as we in anthropology have liberally borrowed concepts from wherev-er they might be found, our colleagues in the other social sciences are borrowing from us. Our treasured concept of culture is on the move, and we should not be dismayed to find it obeying the laws of cultural process.

As this trend develops, it will become purely academic to try to determine whether a particular project is aimed at historical or anthropological ends.

We come now to the form of the final result of historic sites archaeology. Here I am not speaking of the form in the sense of a restoration, onsite development, museum exhibit or other interpretive device, but in the customary form of a published report, presumably written to further scholarship and science.

It is immediately obvious that many of the limited projects will not result in a publication, since any publication would do little more than record a physical situation without any particular historical or cultural significance.

Other excavations, however, will reveal to greater or lesser degree information which should be analyzed and presented in printed form. In many instances a fairly standard archaeological report will suffice, but there are other instances, particularly on larger sites, that call for a different approach.

An ideal publication of an historic site, to my mind, would be in the form of an ethnographic monograph. In such a work, the information from written documents, field excavation, and analysis of artifacts would be presented in an integrated form rather than in the form of a standard archaeological site report.

Obviously, such a report would call for cooperative effort. It should probably rest on a series of other reports, which would not necessarily be published, any more than the ethnographer would publish his field notebooks.

Documentary sources should be culled and organized by the historian. A cross-referenced card file might be more useful than the traditional documentary narrative. The evidence of structure and association from the excavations should be put in usable form by the archaeologist. The analysis of artifacts should be carried as far as possible, which in the realm of historic objects usually means the consultation of a number of authorities.

Someone should then put all of this together. Who? I may be prejudiced, but I feel it should be the archaeologist, who at this stage of the game steps into his broader self and becomes an anthropologist.

But, despite the fact that most archaeologists have been reared in anthropology departments, many of them are incapable of, or are disinterested in, undertaking such a task. They have taken courses in cultural anthropology, but their professional experience has seldom gone beyond the counting of potsherds and the erection of time-space frameworks. They have rarely come to grips with cultural reconstruction.

Is the historian any better qualified? Usually not. He has probably had a rather traditional historical training, knows his documentary sources, is a qualified historiographer, is aware of the broad historical background of which the site is a part; but unless he has picked it up on his own, he has had little experience with actual physical objects and the reconstruction of a way of life.

But someone should make an effort to do such work. Let us not pass the buck as the Near Eastern archaeologists used to do—and still do for all I know—to non-existent culture historians who are supposed to derive meaning from the purely descriptive archaeological reports.

What I am suggesting is a kind of culture history, or cultural anthropology, or social history, or historical ethnography—I'm not concerned with what it is called—which will adequately describe and interpret the way of life at a historic community in much the same way as a good ethnography records the way of life of a particular living community.

Unless the archaeologist takes some such task to himself, he is very apt to find that in historic sites work he has become a mere technician—a digging foreman with a developed sense of what to look for in the ground. His results will be utilized, insofar as they fit, by architects in restoration, by historians to a limited degree as illustrative material, and by museum men and interpretive workers as tangible devices for instructing the public.

But I would venture to say that these various persons could use the information better if it were consolidated into an anthropological framework of cultural reconstruction, which at the same time would constitute a genuine contribution to knowledge.

LITERATURE CITED

Marc Bloch
    1953   *The Historian's Craft.* Knopf, New York.
J. C. Harrington
    1955   "Archaeology as an Auxiliary Science to American History," *American Anthropologist,* vol. 57, no. 6.
Homer Carey Hockett
    1955   *The Critical Method in Historical Research and Writing.* Macmillan, New York.

CHAPTER 7

On the Meaning of Historic Sites Archaeology*

BERNARD L. FONTANA

Historic sites archaeology apparently means many things to American archaeologists. It is not, however, that American archaeologists disagree on a definition; it is rather that definitions have not been forthcoming. Workers have labored in "historic" sites and have assumed that there is general accord on what these sites are and that historic sites archaeology is a commonly understood term. Such, unfortunately, is not the case, and the present remarks are offered as an attempt to arrive at a definition of the term and at a useful classification of historic sites.

It should first of all be said that this discussion is confined to the New World. Although the notion of historic sites archaeology may have validity for other parts of the world, its major utility is in the Americas and not elsewhere. Why this is so will be explained below.

DEFINITION OF HISTORIC SITES ARCHAEOLOGY

It has been suggested in discussions among archaeologists, and probably in print as well, that historic archaeology is that carried out in sites which were in existence in historic times—that is, in sites in use when the area in which they occurred began to be mentioned in writing. But the crucial distinction between historic and prehistoric is not one that involves writing alone. Sites occupied after the arrival of the first Europeans in a given locale, and which therefore are posthistoric but which contain no material evidence of non-Indian culture and which were not mentioned by Europeans, we would not call historic sites. Moreover, it is probably safe to say that we would not include Mayan sites within the pale of historic sites archaeology even should we eventually decipher Mayan writing. Writing, the presence or absence of documentary evidence, is not the touchstone.

There does seem to be agreement among archaeologists that the existence of non-Indian artifactual material in New World archaeological sites qualifies such sites as "historic." What this means in most cases is the presence of European or European-derived material culture. Other instances occur in which the evidence may be Asiatic or even African in origin, but the American nonaboriginal population is overwhelmingly European.

The conception of non-Indian material culture *in* a site

This paper was inspired largely by discussions held among participants in the symposium on "The Meaning of Historic Sites Archaeology" at the 1963 annual meeting of the Society for American Archaeology, Boulder, Colorado. The panelists were Bernard L. Fontana (chairman), Lewis R. Binford, Louis R. Caywood, John L. Cotter, Stephen L. Glass, Henry Hornblower II, Kenneth E. Kidd, Edward Larrabee, Carlyle Smith, and Arthur Woodward.

should be extended to include non-Indian evidence *about* a site. In other words, if we have written mention or description of a site by nonaborigines, such a site should be called historic whether it contained foreign material culture or not. This treats documentary evidence as if it were another artifact, not in situ, perhaps, but an artifact associated with the site nonetheless. It is clear that such evidence requires different handling and analysis than that of material culture.

Historic sites archaeology may be defined as *archaeology carried out in sites which contain material evidence of non-Indian culture or concerning which there is contemporary non-Indian documentary record.* "Indian" in this definition refers to the American Indian, that is, to the New World aboriginal population.

Classification of Historic Sites

If we can agree on the above definition, we can then classify historic sites into five major types. Involved in this classification is the degree to which a site is "Indian" or not. The sequential arrangement of types also parallels New World historical development: from Indian to non-Indian.

It must be understood that this taxonomic system is underlain by a developmental continuum and that, as in most taxonomic schemes, the units chosen for naming are somewhat arbitrary. There will be particular situations which are not neatly accommodated by these types, and there will be many sites which could as well be assigned to one type as to another. But such difficulties are largely academic and should not detract from the utility of the classification of historic sites presented here. I have illustrated the types with Arizona examples because these are excavations with which I am most familiar.

Protohistoric. These are aboriginal sites in which there is evidence of nonaboriginal culture but which were occupied before the arrival of nonaborigines on the immediate scene. Such sites are post-Columbian (after A.D. 1492) but pre-date either the actual physical presence of non-Indians at the site or their documentary description of the location. Normally one would expect the non-native tool assemblage in such ruins to be scanty and to be characterized by ornamental objects, household utensils, simple tools, and bones, especially of horses and cattle.

The best-known such sites in the United States are found in the Plains, where elaborate trading systems among Indians introduced the horse, knives, kettles, guns, glass beads, and innumerable other objects before their European originators introduced themselves.

In Arizona there are three rather well-known sites over

which arguments have arisen whether they are prehistoric, protohistoric, contact, or later. One of these is the University Indian Ruin, where the reported presence of a majolica bowl would make at least a portion of the site protohistoric or later (Hayden 1957: 178).

The second of these locations is that called by Charles C. DiPeso (1956) San Cayetano del Tumacacori, where two "wrought iron objects" were associated with burials; one majolica sherd was found on the floor of a house; and three pieces of Spanish glass, two Spanish glaze sherds, and the bronze handle of a spoon occurred in the fill of a borrow pit. DiPeso interprets the architecture of three structures in the site as the result of Spanish influence, and of 177 animal bones identified, three are believed to be from horse (*Equus caballus*) and four from cow (*Bos taurus*). This evidence, combined with documentary data which could also be used to show that the site is not that of San Cayetano del Tumacacori of the 1690's, is all we have to show that the site is historic (DiPeso 1956: 123, 190, 532, Plate 7, and Fig. 65). Albert Schroeder (n.d.) has pointed out some of the weaknesses in DiPeso's arguments bearing on the identification of this excavated ruin. He has suggested that it may be historic and postcontact but that contact was with Spaniards in 1542 rather than as late as 1691.

It may be that when we learn more about the nature of protohistoric sites generally, in the Great Plains and elsewhere, we shall be better able to identify them as such when we find them. Much of the evidence presented by DiPeso hints that "San Cayetano" may be a protohistoric location instead of a contact site.

Finally, the Babocomari Village site in southeastern Arizona, also excavated by DiPeso (1951), yielded some "*Bison* (could be cow, but probably not)" bones. DiPeso (1956: 1) later wrote: "Should they prove to be cow, Spanish contact at the Babocomari Village is proved." Again, it is suggested that the presence of cow bones may indicate nothing more than a protohistoric site, as do the presence of horse bones in many sites on the Plains.

Contact. These are aboriginal sites actually visited by non-Indians and which were present earlier. Such contact may have been casual and made little or no impression on the natives, or it may have marked the opening of an era of continuing and growing conjunction with nonaborigines. Unlike protohistoric sites, contact sites are likely to be described in writing; that is, there are usually documentary data about them as well as artifactual evidence *in* them. Contact sites have been of particular interest to prehistorians who have wanted to use the direct historic approach in trying to link prehistoric remains with remains of Indians who were living when Europeans and others first saw and described them. DiPeso's (1953) work at Quiburi is an outstanding example of the use of the direct historic approach. Quiburi is indubitably a Spanish and Indian *contact* site that was in existence in prehistoric times.

Postcontact. These are aboriginal sites which originated after their native populations had been visited by non-Indians and which did not exist prehistorically or protohistorically. Such sites would include recent Indian settlements as well as modern ones with a long history. In Arizona the only such ruin thus far excavated has been a portion of the Sobaipuri-Papago Indian village of Bac, a village segment dating from the Franciscan period rather than from the earlier Jesuit period. It has not yet been reported in the literature.

Frontier. These are sites essentially nonaboriginal in nature, in that they were founded and administered by non-Indians. Here we find military posts, missions, trading posts, and some colonial settlements. Such sites are characterized by a great deal of interaction with Indians, and their artifact assemblages or documentary data concerning them should give evidence of mixed Indian and non-Indian culture. Frontier sites exemplify the institutional arrangements specifically established by nonaborigines to deal with the natives. Viewed in another way, these are the non-Indian sites equivalent to Indian contact and postcontact sites described above. Excavations in Arizona at Fort Lowell and Camp Grant—yet to be published—and work at Mission San Xavier del Bac (Robinson 1964) and at Franciscan-period Mission Tumacacori (Beaubien 1937) are Arizona examples of investigations in such sites.

Nonaboriginal. These are sites that involve Indians only in a minor way or not at all. The artifact assemblages are wholly or almost wholly non-Indian. The culture history derived from the analysis of such sites is our own (that is, nonaboriginal) history.

Nonaboriginal ruins may contain Indian artifacts, and their documentary histories may tell of involvement with Indians. The important distinction, however, is that such sites were not established specifically to deal with the native population and would have existed regardless of natives. Among such sites we can list non-Indian ranches, mining towns, villages, cities, manufacturing centers, military establishments whose reasons for being do not relate to Indians and, in short, the panoply of sites characterizing nonaboriginal civilization in the New World. To date, only two nonaboriginal locations have been dug in Arizona. These are the Gila Bend Stage Station (unpublished) and Johnny Ward's Ranch (Fontana and others 1962).

Type versus Phase

It is obvious that many historic sites contain components of various types, in which instances the types become phases. In fact, if we were dealing with prehistoric units, we might label these types as phases. There would probably be opposition to calling a place like the Saugus Iron Works (Robbins and Jones 1959) a "nonaboriginal phase" site. For one thing, nonaboriginal sites as types are not like phases, ". . . spatially limited to the order of magnitude of a locality or region and chronologically limited to a relatively brief interval of time" (Willey and Phillips 1958:22). It is only when we are dealing with sequences of events in a specific historic site that the phase concept has real utility in historic archaeology.

Ventana Cave in southern Arizona is simultaneously a prehistoric and a historic site. Its prehistoric remains, which constitute by far the greater part, illustrate several different phases (Haury and others 1950); its historic remains exemplify a postcontact phase. Protohistoric and contact phases may be represented as well, although the available evidence does not justify such a conclusion.

Innumerable other instances could be cited in which the names here applied to types of historic sites could also be applied to phases within a site. This is in fact the case for many of our illustrative examples. The point, however, need not be belabored.

USEFULNESS OF THE
HISTORIC SITE CONCEPT

One could raise dozens of questions concerning specific sites and their "correct" placement within this typological scheme. What about pre-Columbian Viking sites, for example? What about colonial Spanish ranches and farms established as *encomiendas* and of which the *repartimiento* system was an integral part? Are these frontier or nonaboriginal sites? What about Spanish *presidios* which doubled as colonial settlements?

To put aside such questions for now, let us refer to the dictum of John O. Brew (1946: 65):

The main value of a published description of a given system is that it may then be adapted by another student to his problems, not that he should force his material into it . . .

. . . As archaeologists we must classify our material in all ways that will produce for us useful information. I repeat, we need more rather than fewer classifications, different classifications, always new classifications, to meet new needs.

It is precisely in this spirit that the above definition of historic sites archaeology and the classification of historic sites are proposed.

And have we here served any useful purpose? I will mention some ways in which I think we have.

First of all, it is obvious that for communication and clear understanding alone it is useful to agree on what we mean by historic sites archaeology and to recognize that there are different types of historic sites. Secondly, much is to be gained in distinguishing, for example, between protohistoric and contact sites. We should some day be able to make good guesses for many sites as to whether they are one or the other solely on the basis of their artifactual assemblages. We readily recognize that the presence of horse bones in an excavation need not make the place a contact site. What about cow bones? How long can cattle survive in the wild, and how far ahead of their European introducers might they get? And what about domestic sheep? Is it fair to suggest that the presence of domestic sheep bones argues less for protohistoric than it does for contact, or later; and that cow, and especially horse, could be evidence of either?

For later types we are forced to make critical and minute analyses of our artifactual materials in order to identify and date them and to determine whether we have, say, a contact or post-contact site, using such analyses in conjunction with interpretation of documentary evidence. Too many instances can be cited in which archaeologists have failed to give non-Indian artifacts in aboriginal sites the same kind of treatment they accord Indian artifacts, dismissing the former simply as "European," "American," or "Spanish."

And this brings us to another point that is minor in the minds of some archaeologists but major in the minds of others. Unfortunately, invidious distinctions are sometimes made concerning historic sites archaeology. Perhaps when we analyze the situation, and if we are honest with ourselves, we will agree that among American archaeologists prehistoric archaeology carries more status than historic archaeology. The problem, however, is not one of time; it is

one of type. It has to do with whether the artifacts are Indian or non-Indian and whether the site is aboriginal or otherwise. In this, American archaeologists share with many of their anthropological brethren a learned dislike for studies of anything not Indian or not involving nonliterate peoples. Such is the historical heritage, if not the very focus, of our profession.

No prehistorian objects to work in contact sites when the aim is to relate the findings to the prehistoric period, especially if he is not asked to read the documentary history and to analyze the non-Indian artifacts himself. Few prehistorians would look askance at work in any kind of Indian historic site, particularly if the aim is to discover analogies which might help them to interpret prehistoric ruins. Let the archaeologist interest himself in frontier and nonaboriginal sites, and he will be asked if he might not as well be a historian trained in archaeological techniques. And, indeed, he might. Anthropologists, however, should be able to ask questions of archaeological data never dreamed of by academically trained historians, and anthropologists should be capable of interpreting the findings of archaeology in ways in which historians could not, whether the sites be aboriginal or otherwise.

And we come to the final point: the varying uses of historic sites archaeology itself. Probably when the first work was done in historic sites in the Southwest, as at Pecos, Hawikuh, and Awatovi, the conception of historic sites archaeology as such had occurred to no one. Only in more recent years, with work in ruins that were to be preserved and restored as public parks and monuments, has the distinction arisen. Most such sites have been frontier and nonaboriginal, and money to support this work has come largely from the public. In these instances, the chief use to which archaeology is put is to aid in preservation or accurate restoration in such a manner that the site is properly interpreted for the public.

When the sole or principal aim of archaeological work is preservation or restoration for this purpose, it is archaeological technique as opposed to archaeological methodology (that is, anthropology) which is essential. In wholly nonaboriginal sites and in many frontier sites a historian trained in archaeological techniques may do a better job of restoration than an anthropologically trained archaeologist. "Interpretation" here is on the level of reproducing accurately the physical appearance of the site at a given point in time or of showing how tools were used, glass was made, butter churned, and knives forged. As often as not, most data will come from documentary sources, and a good job requires someone trained in historiographic techniques as well as in other skills. Many archaeologists are poor historiographers.

In to-be-restored sites that involve Indians, there is little question that the talents of anthropologists are called for, whether they be archaeologists, ethnologists, or ethnohistorians, or combine the training of all three. On the other hand, historic sites archaeology has been and could be put to many uses that have nothing whatsoever to do with site preservation and restoration. It shares most of these uses with prehistoric archaeology except that there are even more uses. Such uses are made possible by the availability of added evidence from written sources.

If one is interested in understanding the impact of European culture upon American Indian villages, he can choose a contact or postcontact site in which to dig. If one is interested in knowing what happened to Indians who developed a symbiotic relationship with non-Indians (as on a folk-urban continuum), he can pick a frontier site for excavation. If the objective is to study the impact of European material culture on villages of a specific tribe and compare this with subsequent impact brought about by the actual presence of Europeans themselves, then the archaeologist should look for both protohistoric and contact sites and dig both.

Other questions involving rates, kinds, and amounts of culture change, levels of sociocultural integration, and many more—all in terms of their relation to material culture—may best be examined in historic sites if they are to be examined archaeologically at all. This is because we have artifactual data and data from documentary sources, often both historic and ethnographic.

Many archaeological concepts can be rigorously tested in historic sites: type, phase, tradition, focus, horizon, horizon style, component, period, stage, culture, and others. This is once more the case because of added evidence available from written records. The theoretical problems formulated for testing should largely determine the type of historic site selected for excavation. Contrariwise, the formulation of site typology should help in sharpening theoretical formulations. Uses to which historic sites archaeology may be put are not, of course, mutually exclusive. A historic site dug for purposes of preservation, restoration, and presentation to the public can serve quite another purpose in a professional report. It often has.

CONCLUSION

If the definition of historic sites archaeology and the classification of historic sites proposed in this paper do no more than suggest to archaeologists new hypotheses, new means of answering old questions, and new ways of looking at old data, they will have accomplished their purpose. If communication among archaeologists on this subject has been enhanced by these remarks on the meaning of historic sites archaeology, our purpose in committing them to print will have been doubly served.

ACKNOWLEDGEMENTS

I wish to acknowledge with thanks the helpful criticisms of Roderick Sprague and William Robinson, both of whom read an early draft of this paper.

REFERENCES

BEAUBIEN, PAUL
　1937　Excavations at Tumacacori—1934. *Southwestern Monuments Special Report*, No. 15. National Park Service, Coolidge, Arizona.
BREW, JOHN O.
　1946　Archaeology of Alkalai Ridge, Southeastern Utah. *Papers of the Peabody Museum of American Archaeology and Ethnology,* Vol. 21. Cambridge.
DiPESO, CHARLES C.
　1951　The Babocomari Village Site on the Babocomari River, Southeastern Arizona. *The Amerind Foundation, Inc.,* No. 5. Dragoon, Arizona.
　1953　The Sobaipuri Indians of the Upper San Pedro Valley, Southeastern Arizona. *The Amerind Foundation, Inc.,* No. 6. Dragoon, Arizona.
　1956　The Upper Pima of San Cayetano del Tumacacori. *The Amerind Foundation, Inc.,* No. 7. Dragoon, Arizona.
FONTANA, BERNARD L., JOHN C. GREENLEAF, CHARLES W. FERGUSON, ROBERT A. WRIGHT, AND DORIS FREDERICK
　1962　Johnny Ward's Ranch: A Study in Historic Sites Archaeology. *The Kiva,* Vol. 28, Nos. 1 and 2. Arizona Archaeological and Historical Society, Tucson.
HAURY, EMIL W., KIRK BRYAN, EDWIN H. COLBERT, NORMAN GABEL, CLARA L. TANNER, AND T. E. BUEHRER
　1950　*The Stratigraphy and Archaeology of Ventana Cave, Arizona.* University of Arizona Press and University of New Mexico Press, Tucson and Albuquerque.
HAYDEN, JULIAN D.
　1957　Excavations, 1940, at University Indian Ruin, Tucson, Arizona. *Southwestern Monuments Association, Technical Series,* Vol. 5. Gila Pueblo, Globe, Arizona.
ROBBINS, ROLAND W. AND EVAN JONES
　1959　*Hidden America.* Alfred A. Knopf, New York.
ROBINSON, WILLIAM J.
　1964　Excavations at San Xavier del Bac, 1958. *The Kiva,* Vol. 29, No. 2, pp. 35-37. Arizona Archaeological and Historical Society, Tucson.
SCHROEDER, ALBERT H.
　n.d.　Comments on San Cayetano del Tumacacori. Mimeographed. Santa Fe.
WILLEY, GORDON R. AND PHILIP PHILLIPS
　1958　*Method and Theory in American Archaeology.* University of Chicago Press, Chicago.

CHAPTER 8

Historical and Historic Sites Archaeology as Anthropology: Basic Definitions and Relationships

ROBERT L. SCHUYLER

Normally a discipline either inherits its title from its subject matter, witness for example Egyptology, Classical Archaeology, or more vaguely Prehistoric Archaeology, or it inherits it from its basic approach to its subject matter. In the latter category would fall such neologisms as "new archaeology" and "processual archaeology."Since there is little evidence of anything particularly new about the techniques used in studying materials from historic periods from either an anthropological or historical point of view, it is obvious that such studies in the main must follow the normal pattern and be named after their subject matter.

Considering even the nature and boundaries of this subject matter is apparently no easy task. Among the various titles proffered for the field are found: Historical Archaeology, Historic Archaeology, Historic Site Archaeology, Historic Sites Archaeology, Post-Medieval Archaeology, and a list of more specific terms ranging from Restoration and Colonial to Tin Can Archaeology.

Of course a number of the different terms listed above devolve to sterile points of grammar, euphonics, or at best bare-bones semantics. Nowhere was this clearer than at the 1967 founding meeting of the Society for Historical Archaeology at Southern Methodist University in Dallas (Pilling 1967:3−4). Debate on the naming of the society, its journal, and its subject matter revolved as much around such semantic questions as around truly substantive points. Noël Hume pointed out at that meeting and elsewhere that the word *site* seemed to exclude artifacts, while *historic* (Hume 1969:5−6) in the minds of many, including politicians, refers to a site on which an event of significant historical impact occurred. Such a stand is incorrect in reflecting a narrow, archaic view of history (which it is true some government agencies still hold). I do not want to argue on this level of meaning, however, and it is readily admitted that the terminological relationship advanced, or more accurately endorsed, in this article is not completely logical or consistent. Periclean Athens is a historic site both in that it dates from a period with historical documentation and in that important events transpired there.

What is proposed is that, putting such minor problems aside, there are presently in the literature two terms which already carry a historical precedent for use. The actual problem is that the terms will be interchanged randomly or one, Historical Archaeology, will crowd the other into extinction and there is already evidence that this is happening. More importantly underlying this terminological tangle is a subject matter, Historic Sites Archaeology, that is vital to both history and anthropology and to which our contribution

may be badly curtailed by the imposition of unnecessary limitations.

When and where the two terms in question first appeared in the literature is not clear although as early as 1910 the famous Wisconsin historian, Carl Russell Fish, was discussing the problems involved but without coining any labels. The tradition he represents, however, runs to the present in the writings of such scholars as Carl P. Russell who has adopted and proposed the term "historian-archaeologist."

Apparently Historical Archaeology as a name has been in existence for decades and predates Harrington's "Historic Site Archaeology." In the 1930s Woodward (1937:101) was using "Historic Archaeology" and contemporarily or slightly later Frank Setzler (1943:211, 217−18) put in print "Historical-Archaeology" as a hyphenated word. Interestingly Setzler already realized the terminological problems and offered "Colonial Archaeology" as an alternative but with the understanding of its obvious limitations.

Historical Archaeology therefore has been in use for quite some time although its resurgence in popularity is certainly the product of its adoption by the new Society for Historical Archaeology and more publicly by the appearance of Noël Hume's book (1969) carrying that title.

Historical Archaeology has never been tightly defined except when it has subsumed the meaning of Historic Sites Archaeology. It is a general and inclusive term and therein lies its usefulness. It is proposed that Historical Archaeology be defined as: *the study of the material remains from any historic period.*

Such a definition does not equate Historical Archaeology with the presence or absence of writing, although there is a vague correlation between level of cultural complexity and the appearance or acceptance of writing. "Historic period" means a period in which the cultures in question have a documentary record and that writing is having a full impact both on the cultures being studied and on the scholarship of the investigation. When records are capable of altering the basic methods and techniques of studying past societies then we are dealing with Historical Archaeology.

For example, all pre-contact New World civilizations would be excluded by this definition. Even if Maya glyphs are deciphered it is extremely unlikely that Maya archaeology will be radically altered by the scanty data they seem to contain.

Historical Archaeology is proposed as a general term, equivalent in many ways to "prehistoric archaeology," because as new areas and time periods began to be studied with a combined archaeological and documentary approach, the same technical problems of how to handle the data will appear that are presently facing historical archaeologists in Europe and America and which certainly were encountered much earlier by Classical Archaeologists. In fact, a comparison of the rise of Classical Archaeology on a technical level with our own field might prove very enlightening.

The chronologies, cultural and historical specifics may vary tremendously, but methodologically such fields are (at least in theory) connected. At this moment in its development, however, the field is in truth named for its subject matter, as vague as that may be, more than methodology as that has yet to be spelled out.

More specifically such a covering term includes fields ranging from Colonial to Industrial Archaeology in America and from Classical to Industrial in Europe. The Society for Historical Archaeology and its journal are aptly named in that they are already serving not only scholars dealing with 16th to 18th Century materials, but also as vehicles for the emergence of American Industrial Archaeology. Even the Vikings can be allowed entrance under this definition, with or without the Newport Tower.

Turning to the second term, Historic Sites Archaeology, although it may have its ultimate origin in the Historic Sites Act of 1935 or earlier sources, it was initially defined in 1947 by J. C. Harrington (1952:336; 1955:1128) and redefined from a somewhat different point of view in 1965 by Bernard Fontana.

Harrington emphasized Euro-American remains in his definition of Historic Sites Archaeology although he did not exclude Indian contact sites, while Fontana was certainly working from the reverse perspective as his definition demonstrates (1965:61):

> . . . archaeology carried out in sites which contain material evidence of non-Indian culture or concerning which there is contemporary non-Indian documentary record.

Drawing on Harrington and Fontana it is proposed that Historic Sites Archaeology be defined as:

> The study of the material manifestation of the expansion of European culture into the non-European world starting in the 15th century and ending with industrialization or the present depending on local conditions.

Historical Archaeology is viewed as covering a subject matter which in no sense is a unified historical entity, although, as already mentioned, there is a developmental relationship. The unity of Historical Archaeology is, or at least should be, primarily technical and involves the methodology of investigation more than the subject matter under investigation. Historic Sites Archaeology in contradistinction deals with a specific historical subject that has temporal, spatial, and cultural boundaries.

Chronologically it would see its inception in the 15th Century perhaps with 1415, the date of the fall of Ceuta signalling initial Portuguese penetration of Africa, as an arbitrary but generally agreed upon point (Parry 1961: 7–12). Geographically its boundaries fluctuated from decade to decade but are fairly well documented. Culturally a more complex problem arises because involved are not only the European cultures in question but also the degree of acculturation on indigenous societies. When is a North American Indian site a historic site? Is the key factor the presence or absence of trade artifacts, the moment of initial contact, or the point of continuous contact?

Many have discussed this problem and Fontana has advanced a typology running from Proto-Contact through Contact, Post-Contact, and Frontier to Non-Aboriginal. As Larrabee (1965:10–11) has pointed out, Fontana's typology is confusing and perhaps too simplistic. Its main shortcoming, however, is its perspective. Fontana seems to be concentrating on the contact situation rather than the ultimate causes and processes involved. For example, he defines (1965:62) Post-Contact sites as:

> . . . aboriginal sites which originated after their native populations had been visited by non-Indians and which did not exist prehistorically.

In many cases such a classification has no meaning in that such contact had no influence on basic cultural patterns. Drake's 1579 possible landing and Cermeno's 1595 landing at what today is called Drake's Bay in California may help to date middens there by intrusive artifacts (Heizer 1942), but the sites are still prehistoric both in that the aboriginal cultural patterns seem unaffected, at least the archaeological data does not demonstrate the contrary, and in that the basic research approach is still that of prehistoric archaeology.

Historic Sites Archaeology has temporal, geographical, and cultural boundaries because a complex of fundamental underlying patterns and processes creates the historical entity it is studying. These are European in origin and include such factors as the rise of mercantile capitalism, the emergence of national monarchies, and major technological innovations and the impact of these factors outside of Europe. Indigenous sites become historic sites, and thus the subject matter of our discipline, only when their basic cultural and ecological patterns have been altered by contact and when this is displayed in the archaeological data. Such a relationship will frequently correspond to a simultaneous appearance of documentation, as, for example, California Mission records on neophyte villages. Even if such data are lacking for a specific site it is still possible to move from general documentary knowledge to interpret the situation.

Of course direct contact with Europeans is not necessarily a prerequisite for such far reaching changes. Was the rise of the Iroquoian League or the Powhatan Confederacy indigenous or the product of contact, or both? Even if only stimulus diffusion and indirect acculturation are the prime movers, such situations, assuming they can be recognized, are at least in part the subject matter of Historic Sites Archaeology.

Defining Historic Sites Archaeology and its relationship to contact situations as has been done in this article is valid for the New World, all of Oceania, and much of Africa. However, when we turn to Asia a different situation appears. Not only were Europeans observing the natives and recording their observations, but the natives were looking back and also recording. Perhaps such contacts should be called Historic Sites Archaeology to the second power.

More seriously, such a statement is not meant as ethnocentrism, but merely to point out the possible interplay between the various subfields of Historical Archaeology: Historic Sites Archaeology and whatever scholarship has developed around the archaeological and documentary record of the local development of Asian, and for that matter North African, societies. One of the major problems on a global level is our lack of knowledge about what is transpiring in

Historical and Historic Sites Archaeology outside of Europe and North America. Are Japanese archaeologists studying those periods of their national emergence that postdate written records including those which reflect European contact? Are the Indian archaeologists trained under Wheeler excavating Anglo-Indian sites from the 18th and 19th Centuries? The vital importance of such knowledge involves the relationship of these fields to general anthropology.

Turning from this attempt to define Historical and Historic Sites Archaeology and their interrelationship to their relationship to anthropology one finds an even more complex debate. This question has created considerable interest as is seen in Clyde Dollar's recent (1968) essay. Anthropologists tend not to be keenly interested in idiosyncratic behavior and Dollar's use of terminology and concepts was certainly idiosyncratic on occasion. However, what was surprising about the 1968 *Historical Archaeology Forum* was not Dollar's arguments, some of which exposed key problems and questions, but the very poor defense put up by anthropological archaeologists. The papers by Foley (1968) and especially that by Cleland and Fitting (1968) were exceptions.

Harrington in 1955 (:1125) pointed out that although an anthropologically trained archaeologist should bring his theoretical training to bear on the excavation of a historic site there was little evidence for this happening. This is still true and in part is related to the claim of the "new archaeologists" (Binford and Binford 1968) that most American archaeologists, although supposedly trained in anthropology, have not until recently been at all anthropological in their research.

It is not my purpose to go into a detailed discussion of history and anthropology in this article, however, Harrington's sentiments that history is not nor should it attempt to be a social science are fully endorsed. If an archaeologist or anthropologist is trained in the fundamentals of historiography this will not make him a historian any more than a historian with knowledge of surveying and seriation becomes an archaeologist. There is, however, a corollary to this statement which is not true. Anthropologists can use archival data in their research; in fact, such sources can be the basis for their research. Harrington claimed that Historic Sites Archaeology might make contributions to historical data but not to broader history (1955:1124, 1129):

No one supposes that the archaeologist working around Independence Hall will prove that the Declaration of Independence was signed in some year other than 1776.

This example is indisputable but although it is certainly not implied that Harrington, or indeed Fish (cf. 1910:93–94) fifty years earlier, were advocates of a narrow view of history, a few cases, especially the work of Deetz (Dethlefsen and Deetz 1966) and Fontana (Fontana, Greenleaf et al. 1962), have already brought the spirit of such a statement into dispute. Historic Sites Archaeology can correct documentary error, fill in lacunae in the record, certainly, but can it make a major contribution to our understanding of the past? The answer is patently becoming more and more a strong affirmative. How much does a culture record about its basic economic, political, social and ecological structure when frequently the individuals that compose the society in question are only superficially aware of or at least take for granted such patterns and processes?

However the crucial problem is not how much information

is excluded or only indirectly reflected in the records, but our habit of thinking of material objects and archival data as separate entities. On a methodological level such a dichotomy is a given, but this unfortunately tends to carry over onto the synthetic and interpretative levels. In the 1920s Arthur Woodwood (1932,1937) had already recognized the importance of historic artifacts, now archaeologists are extending his recognition into a full-blown discipline, but usually in the process making reference to historical documents only for chronological or specific, limited data. Even fewer historians are seen either using or advocating the use (Whitehill 1968:253–63) of such findings to check or supplement their research. The future development of our field, however, does not lie in such attempts to gain specific data, although such data may certainly be useful, nor in an attempt to fuse archaeology and the discipline of American History, but in making Historic Sites Archaeology, including artifacts and documents, an integral part of anthropology.

As previously mentioned, anthropologists, once they have been trained in the use of documentary sources, can use these in their research but from a different point of view than *most* historians. Why can not Historic Sites Archaeologists, as anthropologists, investigate the broadest and most significant questions involved in American history, or any historic record for that matter? Why not redo much of American, or other, history but from an anthropological point of view? Historic Sites Archaeologists conceived their field as an encounter with artifacts and are only now moving into an appreciation of and more than passing interest in primary written sources. The future may well hold a continuing disciplinary evolution that will witness a much more extensive, if not complete, absorption of the documentary record by archaeologists as anthropologists and at the same time a continuing and intensified utilization of material data.

Dollar has discussed the duo-disciplinary nature of our field, but he and Harrington have also hit upon what will terminate this phase. If Historic Sites Archaeology is only a footnote producer for historians, which perhaps it is, it can be much more for anthropologists. A certain amount of research may remain and perhaps should remain in the historian's camp, especially where very specific data are an end goal as with limited excavation in restoration projects, but hopefully problem oriented research free of the impediment of restoration will emerge.

Implied in the above discussion is that anthropology is more holistic than history, and in some ways it may well be. Nevertheless we must not forget that certain schools of historical thought and certain historians also very much take economic, social, political, environmental and ideological processes into account as well as the impact of individuals or specific "key" events. What really distinguishes the two fields, and would distinguish their use of the same documentary or artifactual data, is that anthropology as a social science is ultimately searching for underlying patterns, processes, "laws" (call them what you will) to explain cultural reality.

Specifically how is Historic Sites Archaeology tied into such an approach? The connection is on both a technical and theoretical level, which do, however, merge. Technically Historic Sites Archaeology is a testing ground for methods and approaches used in general archaeology and which on occasion, as in the "new archaeology," arise in part out of anthropological theory. This has been pointed out many times but frequently is viewed as a passing and low level potential. Already specific techniques such as seriation have been checked in historical context (e.g. Barka 1965; Deetz and Dethlefsen 1966), but more importantly major problems of social, economic, and ideological interpretation such as are being debated in the "new archaeology" can be settled in part by Historical and Historic Sites Archaeology as well as Ethnoarchaeology. How is social organization or economic structure reflected in the material inventory of a community? Longacre (1966) or Hill (1966) can only indirectly infer this at a prehistoric site in the Southwest but a ghost town in the same region (Fontana 1968: 179–180; Schuyler 1969:2), or better a Classical Greek site where no question of industrialization would intrude, with records on the demographic, social, and ethnic structure would be much more enlightening.

On a theoretical level, besides the holistic perspective, another of the distinguishing traits of anthropology is the comparative approach. Deetz and Larrabee have mentioned this in regard to Historic Sites Archaeology, but in a limited sense. Deetz (1968:122–23) in reference to assemblage differences between Jamestown and Plymouth and their significance, and Larrabee (1966:5–6; 14) on a more general level although his example is a narrow comparison of specific historic artifacts of a common source in different geographic and cultural areas.

Prehistoric archaeologists have repeatedly pointed out that the New World on a pre-contact level has because of its isolation importance not in its impact on world history, but as a comparative laboratory for the social sciences. The publication of Robert M. Adams's (1966) *The Evolution of Urban Society* is ample evidence of this potential.

Historic Sites Archaeology has the same potential but for opposite reasons. Just as the lack of diffusion and contact created the situation outlined above so its overpowering and global presence in the Age of Exploration and Colonization creates another laboratory for the anthropologist. There are situations where the same European culture was in contact at the same period, thus giving us a control, with indigenous cultures ranging from the band level to civilization. There were dissimilar European cultures in contact simultaneously with the same native culture. These are built in situations for testing and formulation of hypotheses.

Earlier in this article the complexity of contact situations was discussed and it is natural for anthropologists to immediately notice acculturation potential in Historic Sites Archaeology. However the possibilities on a comparative basis are much broader for anthropology. What of a comparison of European cultures themselves in acculturation situations as in Canada and the Southeastern United States? What of situations where during colonization the same European culture was intruded into radically different environments and the resulting ecological adaptation, or dissimilar cultures into the same ecological zone? What of the selective processes of migration and colonization as Foster (1960) studied in *Culture and Conquest*.

Modern anthropology is rapidly undertaking more research on complex societies and processes and just as Kathleen G. Aberle (1967) has called upon ethnography to study not only conquered non-Western cultures but also the process of imperialism itself, so Historic Sites Archaeology can make a major contribution to modern anthropology by studying the processes of European expansion, exploration, and colonization as well as those of culture contact and imperialism, that underlie one of the most dynamic periods of world history and which are reflected in both artifactual and documentary data.

Methodologically Historic Sites Archaeology, and other branches of Historical Archaeology, should be the most sophisticated archaeology. It is the least sophisticated. Historic Sites Archaeology should be highly productive on a theoretical level but in many ways is inferior theoretically to American prehistoric archaeology. Historic Sites Archaeology should be making major contributions to our understanding of the expansion of Europe and the world wide impact of that expansion, rather than adding marginal footnotes to historical research.

The criticism may be raised that this will all come in good time, that Historic Sites Archaeology is a new field. This attitude, which might be called the "not ready yet hypothesis" has a parallel in the so-called "jigsaw hypothesis" of an earlier generation of American prehistorians: if proper control of the raw data is gained and facts are piled up, they will speak for themselves. Of course the end result was a large number of prehistoric junk piles still housed in American museums. It will indeed be unfortunate if Historic Sites Archaeology, as well as other branches of Historical Archaeology, must blindly repeat the mistakes seen in the rise of prehistoric archaeology.

Specific hypotheses must be applied to the data, artifactual and written, and these hypotheses must be in a broad theoretical structure which will come mainly from anthropology and other social sciences. As Historic Sites Archaeology becomes more and more an integral part of anthropology, and less related to restoration, it will evolve as a valid and relevant field of research and help to maintain general archaeology as a productive part of modern anthropology.

BIBLIOGRAPHY

ABERLE, KATHLEEN GOUGH
1967 Anthropology and Imperialism. Paper presented at the 1967 Southwestern Anthropological Association meetings. Reissued by the Radical Education Project, Ann Arbor.

ADAMS, ROBERT McC.
1966 The Evolution of Urban Society. Aldine, Chicago.

BARKA, NORMAN
1965 Historic Sites Archaeology at Portland Point, New Brunswick, Canada 1631 - c. 1850 A.D. Phd Dissertation, Department of Anthropology, Harvard University, Cambridge.

BINFORD, SALLY and LEWIS R. BINFORD
1968 New Perspectives in Archaeology. Aldine, Chicago.

CLELAND, CHARLES E. and JAMES FITTING
1968 The Crisis of Identity: Theory in Historic Sites Archaeology. Papers of the Conference on Historic Sites Archaeology, 1967, (ed.) Stanley South, Vol.2, Pt.2, pp.124–38. Raleigh, N.C.

DEETZ, JAMES
1968 Late Man in North America: Archaeology of European Americans. Anthropological Archaeology in the Americas, (ed.) Betty J. Meggers, pp. 121–130. Washington Anthropological Society, Washington, D.C.

DEETZ, JAMES and EDWIN DETHLEFSEN
1966 Deaths Heads, Cherubs and Willow Trees: Experimental Archaeology in Colonial America. American Antiquity, Vol.31, pp.502–10. Salt Lake City.

DOLLAR, CLYDE D.
1968 Some Thoughts on Theory and Method in Historical Archaeology. Papers of the Conference on Historic Sites Archaeology, 1967, (ed.) Stanley South, Vol.2, Pt.2, pp.3–34. Raleigh, N.C.

FISH, CARL RUSSELL
1910 The Relation of Archaeology and History. The Wisconsin Archaeologist, Vol.9, No.4, pp.93–100. Milwaukee.

FOLEY, VINCENT P.
1968 'Some Thoughts on Theory and Method in Historical Archaeology' a Critique. Papers of the Conference on His-

toric Sites Archaeology, 1967, (ed.) Stanley South, Vol.2, Pt.2, pp.142–157. Raleigh, N.C.

FONTANA, BERNARD L.
1965 On the Meaning of Historic Sites Archaeology. American Antiquity, Vol.31, No.1, pp.61–65. Salt Lake City.
1968 Bottles, Buckets, and Horseshoes: the Unrespectable in American Archaeology, Keystone Folklore Quarterly, Fall Issue, pp.171–184. Pennsylvania Folklore Society, Harrisburg.

FONTANA, BERNARD L, J. CAMERON GREENLEAF, et al.
1962 Johnny Ward's Ranch: a Study in Historic Archaeology. The Kiva, Vol.28, Nos.1 & 2. Arizona Historical and Archaeological Society, Tucson.

FOSTER, GEORGE M.
1960 Culture and Conquest. Viking Fund Publications in Anthropology No.27, Chicago.

HARRINGTON, J. C.
1952 Historic Sites Archaeology in the United States. Archaeology of the Eastern United States, (ed.) James B. Griffin, pp.335–344. Chicago.
1955 Archaeology as an Auxiliary Science in American History. American Anthropologist, Vol.57, No.6, pp.1121–1130. Menasha.

HEIZER, ROBERT F.
1942 (1951) Archaeological Evidence of Sebastian Rodriguez Cermeno's California Visit in 1595. California Historical Society Quarterly. Vol.20, pp.5–22. Sacramento.

HILL, JAMES N.
1966 A Prehistoric Community in Eastern Arizona. Southwestern Journal of Anthropology, Vol.22, No.1, pp.9–30. Albuquerque.

HUME, IVOR NOËL
1969 Historical Archaeology. Alfred Knopf, New York.

LARRABEE, EDWARD McC.
1965 Historic Sites Archaeology in Relation to Other Archae-

ology. Paper delivered at the Society for American Archaeology meetings, May 1966 and published in Historical Archaeology 1969, pp.67–75.

LONGACRE, WILLIAM A.
1966 Changing Patterns of Social Integration: a Prehistoric Example from the American Southwest. American Anthropologist, Vol.68, No.1, pp.94–102. Menasha.

PARRY, J. H.
1961 The Establishment of the European Hegemony. Harper & Row, New York.

RUSSELL, CARL P.
1967 Firearms, Traps, and Tools of the Mountain Men. Alfred A. Knopf, New York.

SCHUYLER, ROBERT L.
1969 Historic Sites Archaeology and Its Relevancy to the Question of Professional and Amateur Archaeology. Newsletter of the Archaeological Survey Association of Southern California. Vol.16, No.1, pp.1–2. Los Angeles.

SETZLER, FRANK M.
1943 Archaeological Explorations in the United States, 1930–1942. Acta Americana, Vol.1, pp.206–220. Mexico, D.F.

WHITEHILL, WALTER MUIR
1968 Historic Sites Archaeology in the Study of Early American History. The Reinterpretation of Early American History, (ed.) Ray Allen Billington, pp.253–263. Norton & Co., New York.

WOODWARD, ARTHUR
1932 The Value of Indian Trade Goods in the Study of Archaeology. Pennsylvania Archaeologist, Vol.3, No.1, pp.8,9,16–19. Harrisburg.
1937 The Study of Historic Archaeology in North America. Boletin Bibliografico de Anthropologia Americana, Vol.1, pp.101–103. Mexico City.

part 2

Subfields of
Historical Archaeology

INTRODUCTION

If Historical Archaeology is defined as the study of the material remains of any society with a full documentary record then all specialties, whether they are concerned with Assyria, Han China, or 19th century New Orleans, are subfields of this broader discipline. Although this volume is primarily concerned with Historic Sites Archaeology and Industrial Archaeology as they are practiced in North America, Section 2 presents in brief outline the complete spectrum of Historical Archaeology.

Rowe's essay presents a startling interpretation on the relationship between archaeology and anthropology. Of equal importance is the fact that the earliest archaeology was not concerned with prehistory but with the literate civilizations of Greece and Rome. Historical Archaeology was the first archaeology. The later rise of prehistoric studies in the 19th century fragmented archaeological scholarship into specialized camps. This subfield isolation was particularly pronounced in America where experts on Indian prehistory had little in common with their colleagues in classics and history departments.

With the exception of Classical Archaeology, Assyriology, and Egyptology, all other branches of Historical Archaeology are 20th century developments. Fields emerged, more or less in a logical chronological sequence, in Europe and North America that correlated with the major historic periods between A.D. 1000 and 1900. The Society for Medieval Archaeology, as D. B. Harden relates, was founded in 1957. A decade later the investigation of structures and deposits postdating A.D. 1450 commenced. In fact, both the Society for Post-Medieval Archaeology in England and its counterpart in the United States, the Society for Historical Archaeology, were established in 1966-1967. Deetz' paper serves as a good example of research on the European colonization of America, one of the subjects of Historic Sites Archaeology.

Buchanan traces the roots of Industrial Archaeology in England back to the 1950's. As an organized, scholarly endeavor, however, the excavation and archaeological study of the Industrial Revolution is an affair of the 1970's. In America the Society for Industrial Archaeology was not founded until 1972.

Several patterns are highlighted in these six essays. The logical chronological sequence for the appearance of different subfields is explained, in part, by historical linkage. Post-Medieval Archaeology arose from the examination of medie-val-post-medieval ceramics in England. Medieval Archaeology, in turn, had its institutional roots in such associations as the Society for the Promotion of Roman Studies. Archaeologists digging on classical sites in England, and other parts of Europe, could not avoid encountering more recent deposits.

The degree of isolation and splintering of these areas of research is surprising. Part of the explanation lies in the lack of any unifying discipline or theoretical structure (which in America is supplied by anthropology) in Europe. Only the "Underwater" or "Nautical" archaeologists have maintained a unity that transcends geography and historic period. This one case of unity is purely technical. Most archaeologists, classical to industrial, can not dive (swim ?). The limited number who can are therefore called upon to explore wrecks and marine sites ranging from the Bronze Age to the 19th century.

Of major significance to anthropology is the possibility for comparative studies inherent in the various subfields in Historical Archaeology. European culture history is, of course, well established archaeologically but the deep historic records of Asian and North African societies should not be overlooked. That the proliferation of subfields related to these subjects is starting is seen in Grabar's "Islamic Archaeology, an Introduction". Parallels to Islamic Archaeology already exist, if not clearly defined, in India, China, Japan, and Southeast Asia. The more recent periods of Asian history are or soon will be explored with trowels and shovels. European exploration and colonization between 1500 and 1900 tie such scholarship into Historic Sites Archaeology in the New World. Grabar in his final comments espouses an anthropological, or general social scientific, position when he proposes comparative surveys of urbanism, and other macro-processes, in different parts of the Islamic world. It is this possibility, reenforced by common methodological concerns, that will eventually reunify all of Historical Archaeology. A small advance in that direction has already been achieved with the establishment of the Association for Field Archaeology (1974) and its publication of the *Journal of Field Archaeology.* All aspects of archaeology, prehistoric and historical, are covered. Readers interested in current developments in Historical Archaeology should join one or more of the following societies.

SOCIETY FOR HISTORICAL ARCHAEOLOGY
(Issues an annual, *Historical Archaeology,* and a quarterly *Newsletter.* Excellent annual national meetings open to all

members. Meetings rotate throughout the United States and Canada; have been held in Virginia, Arizona, Pennsylvania, Minnesota, California, South Carolina, Ontario, and Texas. Membership $10.00 ($20.00 institutions) per year; SHA, Secretary, J. Rodeffer, Ninety Six Historic Site, Ninety Six, South Carolina 29666).

CONFERENCE ON HISTORIC SITE ARCHAEOLOGY
(Issues an annual *Papers* and holds a joint yearly meeting with the Southeastern Archaeological Conference. Membership $8.00; CHSA, Institute of Archaeology and Anthropology, University of South Carolina, Columbia 29208).

SOCIETY FOR INDUSTRIAL ARCHAEOLOGY
(Issues a semiannual, *IA,* and a *Newsletter.* Membership $8.00; S.I.A., National Museum of History and Technology, Room 5020, Smithsonian Institution, Washington, D.C. 20560).

SOCIETY FOR POST-MEDIEVAL ARCHAEOLOGY
(Issues an annual, *Post-Medieval Archaeology,* and a news sheet. Membership $8.00 ($12.00 institutions); SPMA, Secretary, Passmore Edwards Museum, Ronford Road, Stratford, London E15 4LZ, England).

AUSTRALIAN SOCIETY FOR HISTORICAL ARCHAEOLOGY
(Issues a *Newsletter* and occasional special publications. Membership $A4.00 ($A10.00 institutions); ASHA, Department of Archaeology, University of Sydney, NSW 2006, Australia).

CHAPTER 9

The Renaissance Foundations of Anthropology

JOHN HOWLAND ROWE

The comparative point of view of anthropology rests on a recognition that there are physical and cultural differences among human populations which must be taken into account in any attempt to generalize about mankind. It is anthropology's recognition of the scientific importance of such differences which chiefly distinguishes it from other disciplines concerned with man and human behavior. The history of this idea is therefore a particularly important part of the history of anthropology.[1]

It is the thesis of this paper that the anthropological tradition of interest in differences among men had its beginnings in the Italian Renaissance of the 14th and 15th centuries and specifically in Renaissance archaeology. The first differences which were recognized as significant to a general understanding of mankind were the cultural and linguistic differences between Classical antiquity and what was then the present. It was only after the beginnings of an archaeological perspective had been established that the interest in differences was extended to contemporary contrasts.

Renaissance studies of Classical antiquity not only stimulated a general interest in differences among men, they also provided models for describing such differences. When the problem of describing contemporary non-Western cultures arose, there were Renaissance studies of Roman customs and institutions to serve as precedents. Similarly, Renaissance grammars and dictionaries of Classical Latin and Greek became models for the description of spoken languages in all parts of the world, and the study of the ancient monuments of Italy and Greece became the basis for archaeological reporting elsewhere. The beginnings of physical anthropology were delayed, because the study of Classical antiquity in this case offered little precedent.

In order to demonstrate the Renaissance origin of the comparative point of view of anthropology, it is necessary to show first that there was no continuous anthropological tradition of comparative studies stretching back through the Middle Ages to Classical antiquity, and second that the interest in differences of custom and language and in local antiquities, characteristic of some writers of the period of the voyages of discovery, was related to a fundamental change in men's attitude toward Classical antiquity which was the essence of the Italian Renaissance.

I

It is a fact that there was no continuous anthropological tradition of comparative studies in Classical antiquity and the Middle Ages. There were, however, a number of individual writers in both periods who displayed some interest in cultural differences. The number of such writers was not large, and their anthropological interests made little impression on their contemporaries; if they were respected it was for other qualities. Such ancient writings of an anthropological nature as still survived were discovered with great enthusiasm by Renaissance scholars and only then began to influence effectively the development of anthropology.

The essence of the anthropological point of view is that in order to understand ourselves we need to study others. In contrast, the ancient Greeks for the most part held that the way to understand ourselves is to study ourselves, while what others do is irrelevant. This was the view taken by such influential thinkers as Thucydides and Socrates, for example. It was congenial to Greek ethnocentrism and contributed to the lack of any sustained interest in the customs and languages of "the barbarians," i.e., all non-Greeks. The Romans acknowledged the natural superiority which the Greeks liked to claim and therefore endeavored to identify themselves with the Greeks as far as possible. Instead of studying the differences between the Greeks and themselves, a procedure which would have implied an acceptance of their barbarian status, the Romans traced their ancestry to the heroes of Greek legend, identified their gods with Greek ones, imitated Greek manners, and used the grammatical categories of Greek to describe the Latin language.

In this context of general indifference the few writers of Classical antiquity who took an interest in anthropological comparison are conspicuous exceptions. The earliest and most important of such writers was Herodotus, whose *History* was written about the middle of the 5th century B.C. Herodotus displays as much interest in the customs of the Egyptians, Scythians, and other "barbarian" peoples as he does in Greek and Persian political history, and it has been said on this account that he is "the father of anthropology" as well as "the father of history."[2] The epithet is misleading, as will be seen from the discussion which follows.

How did Herodotus happen to develop an interest so foreign to the main current of Greek thought? A good case can be made that he learned it from Persian sources. There is no question that Herodotus had access to such sources. He was born a Persian subject in Halicarnassus, a cosmopolitan Greek city on the coast of Asia Minor. In his youth he travelled extensively in the western provinces of the Persian Empire, collecting information which he later used in his *History* (1921-38). Some of the Persian historical traditions which he incorporated in the *History* were evidently derived from sources in the Persian nobility.[3]

The Persians had no less national pride than the Greeks did, but they managed to combine it with a respect for the customs and languages of others which was unique in the ancient world.[4] Herodotus illustrates the Persian attitude by telling how the Persian king, Darius the Great, rebuked the Greeks who were present at his court for their intolerance toward "barbarian" customs. Herodotus says:

> If it were proposed to all nations to choose which of all customs seemed best, each, after examination, would place its own first, so strongly is each persuaded that its own are by far the best.... That all men have this feeling about their customs may be concluded from many proofs, among them this. When Darius was king he summoned the Greeks who were with him and asked them for how much money they would be willing to eat the dead bodies of their fathers. They answered that there was no price for which they would do it. Then he summoned those Indians who are called Callatians, who eat their parents, and asked them, with the Greeks present and understanding what was said through an interpreter, what price they would accept to burn their dead at death [i.e., follow the Greek custom]. The Indians cried aloud and begged him to avoid such sacrilegious speech. Such is the nature of custom, and I think it is rightly said in Pindar's poem that custom is lord of all (Bk 3 ch. 38; 1921-38, 2:50).

Darius had evidently taken the trouble to inform himself about some of the differences in custom among his subjects.

It was this same Darius who had his deeds recorded on the cliff at Bisitun in Old Persian, Babylonian, and Elamite, the three languages most likely to be understood by educated travellers in this area. The Bisitun inscriptions are famous today because they provided the basis for the decipherment of the cuneiform script, but the cultural significance of the repetition of the king's message in three languages is rarely noted. Earlier ancient rulers simply expected any subject who was interested in reading royal inscriptions to learn the official language.

The Jews, who benefited greatly from the Persian policy of toleration, perserved its memory long after the Persian Empire had fallen. The Book of Esther in the Old Testament, written in the second half of the 2nd century B.C., is a historical romance laid at the court of the Persian king Xerxes, the son of Darius, who ruled from 485 to 465 B.C. Part of the local color which is provided to authenticate the story is a statement that royal dispatches were issued "to every province in its own script and to every people in its own language." This phraseology is repeated each time the issue of a royal order is mentioned.[5]

The Persian royal tradition appeared again in the 1st century B.C. exemplified by Mithridates the Great, king of Pontus, who claimed descent from one of the companions of Darius. Mithridates is said to have spoken fluently the languages of the 25 peoples who were under his rule: "quinque et viginti gentium quas sub dicione habuit linguas percalluit."[6]

If the ancient Persian interest in differences of culture and language led to the formation of a body of written literature of a more or less anthropological character, however, the *History* of Herodotus is its principal and perhaps only surviving document. Almost the whole of Old Persian literature perished after the conquest of the Persian Empire by Alexander the Great in the 4th century B.C.

No tradition of comparative cultural study developed in antiquity out of Herodotus' work. On the contrary, Herodotus was attacked time and again as a liar, and it was his statements about the unfamiliar customs of the "barbarians"

which his Greek and Roman readers found particularly difficult to believe. As Arnaldo Momigliano has pointed out, Herodotus had many admirers in antiquity who praised his work as a model of literary style and an inspiring account of the heroic deeds of the Persian war, but none of them ever went so far as to defend him from the charge of being a liar. Herodotus' credit for veracity was not restored until 1566, when Henri Estienne argued that the information on differences in custom available in his day demonstrated the credibility of Herodotus' data on cultural variation (Momigliano 1960; Estienne 1566:xxix–xxxii; see also Legrand 1932; Spiegelberg 1927; Burn 1962:1–17).

The only lasting effect which Herodotus' ethnographic information had on Greek and Roman thought was that it inspired a tenuous thread of interest among philosophers in the fact that customs are different in different areas. As early as the end of the 5th century B.C. some of the teachers of rhetoric and ethics were asking whether there was in fact any absolute standard by which to distinguish between what is honorable and what is shameful, since the same act may be honorable in one place and shameful in another (Diels 1959:405–416; Taylor 1911:102–105; Untersteiner 1954:304–310). This debating problem became part of the standard repertory of Greek philosophers, and every teacher needed a few handy examples of contrasts in custom to which he could refer. As a very minor part of his comprehensive effort to organize knowledge and provide materials for teaching, Aristotle made a collection of examples of odd customs, only a few fragments of which have come down to us (Heitz 1869:297–299; Moraux 1951:130–131). A similar collection was made in the 1st century B.C. by Nicholas of Damascus, a later member of Aristotle's school (Jacoby 1926–30, A:384–390, C:255–261; Reimann 1895; Wacholder 1962: 70–88). The examples in these collections were compiled from the works of earlier writers on history and geography, including Herodotus. The philosophers did not make fresh ethnographic observations of their own.

The closest approach to an anthropological study in Greek after Herodotus appears to have been the description of India and its peoples by Megasthenes, written in the 3rd century B.C. (Müller 1874-83, 2:397–429; McCrindle 1877; Stein 1931). Megasthenes was ambassador of the Greek ruler of western Asia, Seleucus Nicator, at the court of Chandragupta, where he had excellent opportunities to see Indian life at first hand and to question informants. He was active only about 20 years after the Persian monarchy had been overthrown, and he represented the state which had inherited the lion's share of the former Persian territory. It is not unlikely that the Persian tradition of tolerant awareness of cultural differences influenced him, as it had influenced Herodotus. Only fragments of Megasthenes' work have been preserved, but it evidently contained substantial sections on Indian customs and beliefs as well as descriptions of the country and of Indian plants and animals. Like Herodotus, Megasthenes was branded as a liar by later Classical writers. The charge was inaccurate; Megasthenes' weakness was not mendacity but an innocent inability to distinguish the circumstantial narratives of Indian mythology from factual reports of areas he had not visited personally.

In Latin literature the only work of Classical antiquity which resembles an ethnographic report is a treatise entitled *On the origin, location, customs and peoples of the Germans*, written by Cornelius Tacitus in A.D. 98 (Tacitus 1938; Norden 1922; Walser 1951; Syme 1958:46–48; 126–128). This work is better known by the short title *Germania*, but the longer one gives a clearer idea of its contents. The whole treatise is not much longer than a modern journal article, and it conveys rather less ethnographic information than does Herodotus' description of the Scythians. Nevertheless, the fact that a Roman should write any separate work on a foreign people is notable in itself.

Tacitus was a Roman lawyer and civil servant, and it is not at all certain that he was ever in Germany. At the time he wrote his essay on the Germans, the Roman emperor Trajan was on the left bank of the Rhine, and the timing suggests that Tacitus was motivated by a desire to persuade the emperor to undertake an invasion of Germany. The *Germania* certainly reads like an article of the sort written by the political commentators of today to explain the background of current events and perhaps influence public policy at the same time. The author took advantage of the opportunity to read his fellow citizens a moral lesson by praising the Germans for maintaining certain values which Tacitus identified as part of the older Roman tradition and which he felt that his contemporaries were neglecting. In discussing those German customs which conflicted with Roman values, however, Tacitus' attitude was one of marked disapproval.

The *Germania* failed to influence Trajan's foreign policy, and it inspired no interest among the Romans in making more detailed studies of the Germans or of other foreign peoples. In fact, it had little effect on anyone's thinking until after its rediscovery in the Renaissance, when a new tradition of interest in cultural differences had developed on a different basis. In this new context the Germania was read with enthusiasm and attention for the ethnographic information it contained. It was hailed as a "golden book," and it had a considerable influence on pioneer ethnographic writings.

There is a certain amount of information on human differences scattered through the rest of ancient literature, particularly in works on geography, such as that of Strabo, and in more encyclopaedic works, of which the *Natural History* of the elder Pliny is the chief example that has come down to us (Strabo 1917–32; Plinius Secundus 1938–63). The information provided by the geographers consists of brief references to foreign customs which the author considered sufficiently peculiar to amuse his readers. It is present only as incidental detail, the main emphasis being on physical geography, the location of cities, and varieties of animals and plants. The complete lack of an anthropological perspective is particularly striking in Pliny's *Natural History,* a work which includes four books on geography (Books III–IV) and one on man (Book VII). There is a section at the beginning of the book on man in which Pliny provides a catalogue of the fabulous anatomical freaks with which the imagination of the ancients peopled the more remote parts of the earth; thereafter, he discusses human variation only in terms of Greek and Roman examples.

Such information on foreign customs as we find in ancient literature is greatly reduced in value by the tendency of ancient writers to copy well-turned phrases from one another and show greater concern with form than with content. In discussing barbarians, men felt free to transfer an interesting statement of a peculiar custom from one people to another. Thus, statements made by Greek writers about Scythian customs were applied by Tacitus to the Germans. Evidently differences among barbarians were not considered important enough to require accurate reporting by historians and encyclopaedists. The result was the development of a series of ethnographic commonplaces such as that barbarians use neither images nor temples in their worship; that they

live by war and pillage; that they do not appreciate the value of precious metals; and so forth.[7]

During the Middle Ages some Arabic writers showed more interest in cultural differences than was common in Classical antiquity, but their work failed to influence the European tradition of the time. A certain number of Arabic works were translated into Latin and circulated in Mediaeval Europe, but these were chiefly mathematical and medical works. No significant influence of Moslem interest in cultural differences can be traced in Europe until the time of Giovanni Leone Granatino ("Leo the African") who completed the Italian version of his *Description of Africa* in 1526 (Granatino 1957). Renaissance scholars of the 14th and 15th centuries were, on the whole, hostile to Arabic learning, which they compared unfavorably with that of the ancient Greeks.

The intellectual climate of Mediaeval Europe was not favorable to comparative studies. European Christians were much concerned about religious differences but only for the purpose of suppressing them. Other cultural differences were assigned little importance; it was differences in character and morality among individuals which were considered significant. At the same time, there was a literary interest in monsters and marvels, derived from the Classical literary tradition represented by the elder Pliny, which biased the expectations of travellers to distant lands. Thus, Mediaeval writers added little new information on differences among men to the stock which they had inherited from the geographical compilations of Classical antiquity.

In the 13th century, however, the Europeans had their attention forcibly attracted to the Mongols, a strange people from the eastern end of the world about whom the European literary tradition provided no information. Jenghiz Khan defeated the Russians at the Kalka River in 1223; Batu overran Russia between 1237 and 1240, and in 1241 he destroyed the armies of Poland and Hungary, supported by French and German contingents. In 1259 Berke invaded Poland again and defeated a crusade sent against him from the west. Here were "barbarians" whom the Europeans obviously could not afford to ignore. Many emissaries were sent to the new rulers of Asia with orders to collect information while conducting their official business. Respect for the military power of the Mongols led to some sober and factual reporting.

The most informative of the European envoys to the Mongol courts were the Franciscan friars Giovanni da Pian del Carpini, who travelled in Asia between 1245 and 1247, and Willem van Rubroek, who made his trip in 1253 and 1254. These men wrote accounts of their experiences among the Mongols which were intended primarily as military intelligence reports but included a certain amount of information on Mongol customs. Pian del Carpini's *History of the Mongols* fills 68 small pages in English translation; a little over one quarter of it is devoted to presenting ethnographic information. Rubroek's *Itinerary* is nearly twice as long (130 of the same size pages) and about one fifth of it deals with Mongol customs (Wyngaert 1929:1–130, 145–332; Dawson 1955).

A few years later (1275–1292) Marco Polo, the son of a Venetian merchant, spent 17 years in the service of Kublai Khan as an official of his imperial administration, eventually returning to Italy with many marvellous tales to tell. He was taken prisoner by the Genoese in a sea fight in 1296 and spent two or three years in a Genoese prison. There, in 1298, his story was written down in rough French by a fellow prisoner, Rusticiano of Pisa. Marco Polo's narrative is very different in tone from the earlier Franciscan reports. It is, in a sense, propaganda for Kublai Khan, whom Marco served loyally and greatly admired; it also reflects a personal interest in cultural differences which Marco says he learned from the Great Khan himself (Polo, ch. 16; 1938, 1:86). However, the ethnographic information in Marco Polo's book is neither very extensive nor very accurate. It is intermingled with much fabulous material on the "wonders of the east" which reflects a characteristically Mediaeval attitude (Polo 1938; Olschki 1960:138–146).

The influence of the works of Giovanni da Pian del Carpini, Willem van Rubroek, and Marco Polo on European thought was not proportional to the value of the information they provided. Pian del Carpini's brief account of the Mongols was reproduced in the *Speculum historiale* of Vincent of Beauvais, compiled between 1256 and 1259 as part of Vincent's great encyclopaedia, the *Speculum maius,* a popular Mediaeval work of reference. Marco Polo's picturesque narrative was also widely read. The more detailed and informative work of Willem van Rubroek was used by Roger Bacon, who met the author, and through Bacon's influence it had a modest circulation in England. It was unknown to continental scholars, however, until it was printed in the 16th century (Dawson 1955:2, 88; Bacon 1900, 1:305).

Roger Bacon, who lived from about 1214 to about 1292, was one of the most original thinkers of his time. He had a vision of a comprehensive science in the service of religion which he expounded to Pope Clement IV in his *Opus maius* of 1267 (Easton 1952). Part Four of this work contains a description of the world, occupying more than 70 pages, in which the reports of Pian del Carpini and Rubroek are both utilized. Here, if anywhere in Mediaeval literature, we might expect to find a foreshadowing of the comparative point of view of anthropology. Bacon does, indeed, stress the fact that the customs of men are different in different regions, but he goes on to explain that the differences are determined by the astrological influence of the planets, so that the way to study them is to determine the precise latitude and longitude of every place. There is no suggestion that direct observation of human behavior might be useful.[8] Bacon derived this theory of astrological determination from the pseudo-Aristotelian *Secret of secrets*, a work which profoundly influenced his thinking (Easton 1952:73).

Our review of pre-Renaissance writings by Europeans concerned with cultural differences can be summed up by saying that works of this sort were not numerous, and that the best ones were neglected or disbelieved. The intellectual climate of Europe was not favorable to a native development of anthropology either in Classical antiquity or in the Middle Ages, and the European tradition successfully resisted Persian and Mongol influence in this direction.

II

When a broader perspective was finally developed, it did not originate with observations of contemporary differences but with the study of Greek and Roman antiquity. The first cultural contrast to be recognized was that between the present and the past. This recognition was an achievement of the Italian Renaissance and, in fact, was the new idea which generated the greater part of the Renaissance movement. Only when men had learned to see differences by studying the past were they able to observe contemporary differences in the world around them in any systematic fashion.[9]

Before the Renaissance, Europeans were no more sensitive to differences in time than they were to differences in space. The only remote past which the Greeks and Romans recognized as different enough to form a contrast with the present was a realm of mythological fantasy, and when the myths ceased to be acceptable in their literal sense they were reinterpreted as allegories. The Christians transferred the allegorical method to the interpretation of biblical texts, thus destroying the documentary value of these texts as records of a non-Classical culture.

In the Middle Ages Europeans recognized no significant difference between themselves and the ancients. The distinction between a Classical and a Mediaeval period was an invention of the Renaissance which would have been incomprehensible to the people of earlier times. The fact is that the cultural tradition of Greece and Rome continued unbroken into the Middle Ages. Latin was everywhere the language of education and continued to be the common written language of Europe. Educated people were therefore not entirely cut off from ancient literature, although books became very scarce. Some ancient writers continued to be read, chiefly the later ones of Christian Rome. Stories from ancient literature and history were retold and illustrated in art. The fact that some changes had taken place was recognized, but the changes were regarded as isolated discrepancies, not sufficiently significant to establish a systematic contrast between antiquity and the present. Where their attention was not called to a specific difference, people simply assumed that the ancients behaved in familiar ways; thus Alexander the Great appeared in Mediaeval romances as a feudal monarch, and the heroes of ancient Rome were depicted in Mediaeval dress in paintings and book illustrations. As Erwin Panofsky puts it, "For want of a 'perspective distance' classical civilization could not be viewed as a coherent cultural system within which all things belonged together" (1960:111). The Renaissance has done its work so well that it now requires some effort to understand this Mediaeval point of view.

In the 13th century, with the rise of scholasticism and the High Gothic style in art, there was a general abandonment of the Classical tradition in philosophy, literary style, architecture and sculpture, the change being particularly marked in France. In architecture, for example, Classical ornament was almost systematically eliminated. The Latin language was not abandoned, but it was modified in syntax and vocabulary to fit the new patterns of scholastic thinking, and Classical writers were no longer taken as models of literary style.[10]

The Renaissance began in the 14th century as a reaction against the new ideals of the 13th. The founders of the Renaissance wanted to turn again to Classical models and restore the old tradition. Their attack on the work of their immediate predecessors, however, led them to emphasize the differences between current practice and Classical values, so that the cultural contrast between antiquity and the present gradually came to be recognized. The Renaissance learned to see antiquity at the "perspective distance" stipulated by Panofsky.

The man who was most influential in starting the Renaissance movement was Petrarch (Francesco Petrarca, 1304–1374), and his interests shaped its development.[11] Petrarch was a poet and essayist, an artist with language who was more concerned with literary form than with content. He collected the works of ancient writers, particularly the Roman poets and orators, modelled his Latin style after theirs, imitated their literary forms, and wrote on subjects which they suggested to him. Antiquity for Petrarch represented an ideal of perfection in every department of life, an ideal to be imitated as faithfully as possible. In order to imitate Classical antiquity, however, it was first necessary to study it. Petrarch's own studies of Roman literature were too personal and unsystematic to initiate a tradition of scholarship, and for this step we must look to his friend and admirer, Giovanni Boccaccio (1313–1375), who wrote treatises on Classical mythology and topography as well as the prose stories for which he is now more famous (Voigt 1894:159–180; Hortis 1879; Wilkins 1927). The first systematic observations of archaeological monuments were made about 1375 by another friend of Petrarch's, the physician and mechanical engineer Giovanni Dondi (1318–1389) [Sarton 1948:1676–1677; Rossi 1871 and 1888:330–334; Bormann and Henzen 1876:xxvii-xxviii; Panofsky 1960:208–210].

Petrarch particularly admired the poetry of Virgil and Cicero's prose, but he knew also the works of perhaps 15 to 20 other ancient Roman writers from manuscripts which were more or less readily accessible in northern Italy. He studied Greek, though only with limited success, and owned a manuscript of Homer and several of the works of Plato. The selection of ancient literature available gradually increased as Petrarch's followers became more numerous and began to exchange copies of the manuscripts they found. The search for manuscripts was carried on chiefly in Italy at first, but shortly after 1400 Italian scholars discovered the riches of the monastery libraries north of the Alps and began purchasing manuscripts in Greece and at Constantinople. The greater part of ancient Greek and Latin literature which has survived was known in Italy by about 1430.[12] By this time also a tradition of teaching ancient literature was well established. The effective beginning of Greek studies in Italy dates from the appointment in 1396 of the Byzantine scholar Manuel Chrysoloras to teach Greek at Florence (Symonds 1888:108–113; Voigt 1894:219–228).

The discovery, reproduction, and teaching of ancient literature occupied the energy of Renaissance intellectual leaders until well into the 15th century, allowing little opportunity for the development of systematic study. Then, with many new resources available, the foundations of modern scholarship were laid by three remarkable men, Ciriaco de' Pizzicolli of Ancona (1391–1452), Lorenzo Valla (1406–1457), and Biondo Flavio of Forlì (1392–1463).

Ciriaco de' Pizzicolli founded the discipline of archaeology.[13] In 1421 he had occasion to study the Latin inscription on the triumphal arch of Trajan at Ancona and was inspired by the idea that archaeological monuments could provide a more direct testimony of antiquity than the literary tradition. He devoted the rest of his life to studying ancient monuments in the field, copying inscriptions and recording ancient sculpture and architecture in Italy, Dalmatia, Greece, Turkey, and even Egypt. Once, at Vercelli in northern Italy, an ignorant priest asked Ciriaco his business, and the archaeologist replied, "Restoring the dead to life" (Pizzicolli 1742:55). The remark is still a good statement of the business of archaeology.

Ciriaco's concern with ancient monuments implied no rejection of the literary tradition of antiquity; he regarded the two kinds of evidence as complementing one another. He was himself an enthusiastic student of ancient literature and collected many important Greek manuscripts on his eastern travels. Some of his field notes were made in the margins of a copy of Strabo's *Geography* which was his guide to the identification of many ancient sites.

Little of Ciriaco's work has come down to us in the form it left his hands. Only a few pages of his voluminous original field notes *(Commentaria)* have survived, and we know his work chiefly from copies of extracts made by contemporaries who were interested in the evidence he provided. He wrote no work of synthesis of his own. Nevertheless, his influence on posterity was considerable.

Lorenzo Valla was the founder of the Renaissance tradition of linguistics (Mancini 1891; Gaeta 1955; Valla 1962). His major linguistic work was a manual of literary style entitled *Elegances of the Latin language* which was begun before 1435 and finished in 1444 (Valla 1962, 1:1–235; Mancini 1891:261–275). It is a descriptive study of Classical usage based on specific examples from ancient texts. Valla's perspective view of ancient Latin enabled him to recognize that linguistic change had occurred, and his descriptive method made study of such change possible. The *Elegances* was first printed in 1471 and went through 26 editions before 1500.

Valla also stimulated Renaissance interest in cultural differences by translating Herodotus into Latin. He is probably best known, however, as the founder of historical criticism. He earned this title by an attack, written in 1440, on the authenticity of the so-called "Donation of Constantine," a forgery of the time of Charlemagne on which the popes had, for several centuries, based their claims to temporal power (Valla 1922 and 1962, 1:761–795). Valla's attack on the "Donation" includes such explicit criticism of abuses in the church that he has been hailed as a forerunner of Luther. He had the further audacity to criticize St. Jerome's Latin translation of the New Testament, which he proposed to correct by comparison with the original Greek. A comparable degree of intellectual independence had brought Jan Hus to the stake only a few years earlier, but the triumph of the Renaissance in Italy introduced an interlude of toleration which not only saved Valla from persecution but made it possible for him to be appointed a papal secretary.

Valla was a versatile scholar who wrote philosophical and devotional essays, current history, polemics, and verse as well and the linguistic and critical works mentioned. In addition, he was one of the discoverers of manuscripts of ancient literature.

Biondo Flavio also made important contributions to Renaissance linguistics and archaeology, and he was the first to undertake a systematic study of ancient Roman culture.[14] His first work was an essay on the language spoken by the ancient Romans, written in 1435.[15] Leonardo Bruni and others had suggested that Latin was only the literary language of ancient Rome, while the spoken language was like the Italian of their own day. This theory in effect projected the 15th century situation into the past, in Mediaeval fashion, and blurred the new perspective view of antiquity. Biondo defended the Renaissance position by presenting evidence that the spoken language of the ancient Romans was a form of Latin. In doing so, he displayed an essentially modern view of dialect differences.

Between 1444 and 1446 Biondo wrote the first archaeological monograph intended for publication. It was entitled *Rome restored* and was a study of the topography and monuments of the ancient city based on a combination of literary evidence and observations of surviving remains. Printing was introduced into Italy in 1464, and Biondo's *Rome restored* became the first archaeological work to be published by the new process, appearing in 1471. It had a profound influence on later work. Biondo followed up his study of ancient Rome with another one which provided similar topographic treatment of the antiquities of other parts of Italy. *Italy illustrated*, as this work was called, was written between 1448 and 1453 and printed in 1474.

Biondo's study of ancient Roman culture was written between 1457 and 1459 and was first printed about 1473. It was entitled *Rome triumphant* and included sections on religion, government, military organization, life and customs, dwellings and transportation, and public honors. There were also frequent comparisons with customs and institutions of the author's own time which reflect the beginnings of an anthropological point of view.

Biondo was also a historian concerned with more recent events. His *Decades of history from the decline of the Romans,* written between 1438 and 1453, is a general history of Italy from the end of the 4th century to the year 1441, the first survey of the Middle Ages from the Renaissance point of view and a work which had a great influence on later scholarship in the Mediaeval field. It ends with an account of the arrival of envoys from Ethiopia at the papal court.

The Renaissance scholars whose work we have discussed treated antiquity as a different world from the one they knew, remote but accessible to all through its literature and its monuments. The Renaissance education of their time spread the view that the ancients were both different and worthy of study. Men trained in this tradition were better prepared than any of their predecessors to observe and record contemporary cultural differences when the opportunity presented itself.

The importance of the Renaissance point of view in making men sensitive to cultural differences is clearly seen in the records of early Portuguese and Spanish explorations in Africa and the Atlantic. The accounts of most of the early explorers are limited to relating their own adventures, discussing problems of navigation, and indicating the physical characteristics of the new lands and the opportunities for trade which they presented. The rare writers who devoted some attention to the natives and their customs in the early days of the great voyages of discovery were all either educated Italians or men who had been exposed to Italian Renaissance influence.

The first great program of western voyages, that of Prince Henry the Navigator of Portugal, took place in the 15th century and was contemporary with the first flowering of Renaissance scholarship in Italy. After sending ships to explore Madeira and the Azores, Prince Henry turned his attention in 1434 to the west coast of Africa, looking for slaves and gold. In 1441 his captains reached the Senegal at the northern edge of black Africa, and Europeans stood at the threshold of their first contemporary new world. Thereafter, voyages along the West African coast for trade and further exploration were frequent. Although a number of the captains who participated in these voyages wrote reports which have come down to us, only one made a systematic attempt to provide some ethnographic information on the peoples he visited. He was an Italian merchant, Alvise Ca' da Mosto (1432–1483), member of the Venetian nobility, who made two voyages to West Africa for Prince Henry, one in 1455 and the other in 1456. His account of what he saw in Rio de Oro, the Canary Islands, Senegal and Gambia was printed in 1507 (Ca' da Mosto 1937:1–84).

The Renaissance tradition of scholarship was taken to Spain in the late 15th century by Elio Antonio de Lebrija (1444–1522), an Andalusian educated at Bologna, and Pietro Martire d'Anghiera (1457–1526), an Italian scholar attached to the court of Ferdinand and Isabella. Lebrija was a notable pioneer in linguistics. His Latin-Spanish and Spanish-Latin dictionary, published in 1492–95, was the first bilingual dictionary to include a modern spoken language, and his Spanish grammar, published in 1492, was the first grammar of a spoken language inspired by Renaissance scholarship (Lebrija 1926, 1946, 1951). While based on a Latin grammar which Lebrija had written earlier, the Spanish grammar is by no means a mechanical application of the rules of Latin to Spanish. Where differences between Latin and Spanish struck his attention, Lebrija attempted to describe the Spanish constructions in their own terms. He was especially interested in pronunciation and proposed a reform of Spanish spelling to bring it more into line with the results of his analysis of the sounds of the language. Lebrija's work set a precedent for the later efforts of missionaries, many of them Spanish or Spanish trained, to describe the native languages of America.

Pietro Martire considered the discovery of America to be the most interesting event of his time. Although he never visited the New World himself, he became its first systematic reporter, beginning at once, with the return of Columbus in 1493, to collect information on American explorations from the men who were participating in them. His position at court enabled him to keep in close touch with events, and he entertained and questioned many of the explorers on their return to Spain. He saw the objects they brought with them and examined the captives they exhibited to the king. The information he collected was communicated immediately in elegant Latin to the popes and the community of Renaissance scholarship. A small volume in Italian based on his letters was published in Venice without the author's name in 1505. Pietro Martire's own Latin version of his reports was published in parts, the first in 1511, the first three in 1516, and the entire work in eight parts in 1530, after the author's death. It was entitled *New World decades* (Salas 1959:13–60 and references; Wagner 1947; Anghiera 1892 and 1912).

Pietro Martire took a special interest in ethnographic and linguistic information about the natives of the newly discovered lands. His letter of November, 1493, to Cardinal Ascanio Sforza, which became Book 1 of the first *Decade,* includes a brief vocabulary of Taino words recorded from the natives of Hispaniola whom Columbus brought back from his first voyage. This vocabulary is our earliest European record of any New World language. Pietro Martire's ethnographic information is relatively abundant and is presented in a notably objective fashion, the only American customs which he feels called upon to condemn outright being cannibalism and human sacrifice. The fairness of his attitude toward both cultural and physical differences is well illustrated by a passage in which he gives his reactions to the sight of the lip plugs worn by some Mexicans whom Cortés had sent to the Spanish court:

> *I do not remember ever having seen anything more repulsive; they, however, consider that there is nothing more elegant under the orb of the moon, an example which teaches us how absurdly the human race is sunk in its own blindness, and how much we are all mistaken. The Ethiopian considers that black is a more beautiful color than white, while the white man thinks otherwise. The hairless man thinks he looks better than the hairy one, and the bearded man better than the beardless. It is clearly a reaction of the emotions and not a reasoned conclusion that leads the human*

race into such absurdities, and every district is swayed by its own taste (Decade 4, bk. 7; Anghiera 1892, 2:41-42).

Darius the Great would have approved this statement.

The anthropological importance of Pietro Martire rests on more than his own objective reports on American ethnography, however. It was he who inspired the actual explorers of the New World to make notes on native customs. He provided a focus of interest in such matters at the Spanish court, questioning returning travellers, demanding reports, distributing information, and over the years creating a public interest which stimulated others to publish the information they had collected in far countries. To give only one specific example of his influence, a good case can be made on circumstantial evidence that Gonzalo Fernández de Oviedo y Valdés was stimulated to write his *General and natural history of the Indies* by the visit he paid to Pietro Martire in January, 1516, and by reading the first three *Decades* published in the same year. There is no doubt that Fernández de Oviedo came to regard himself as Pietro Martire's great rival as an expert on New World matters. Once started on his American research, however, Fernández de Oviedo drew on a Renaissance background of his own. He had travelled in Italy between 1497 and 1502 and had read extensively in Classical literature. He utilized this background to compare New World customs with those of antiquity in a much more systematic fashion than Pietro Martire had done (Salas 1959: 122–125).

No one who makes a general survey of the literature bearing on historical ethnology which has come down to us from 16th century Europe can fail to be struck by the fact that it provides better and more detailed information on New World cultures than on those of the other parts of the world which the Europeans were exploring at the same time. The difference can be credited very largely to Pietro Martire's influence.

III

The significance of the Renaissance to the history of anthropology is that it created a "perspective distance" at which antiquity or any more recent culture might be seen whole and observed with a respect that would make it an acceptable object of study. The perspective of anthropology owes much to the experience of Europeans in the great voyages of discovery, but it did not originate in the observation of contemporary differences. Travellers see only what they are prepared to see, and men's eyes had first to be opened by the study of Classical antiquity in a framework which contrasted it with their own times.

It is paradoxical in a sense that Renaissance admiration for Classical antiquity should have made men more ready to study linguistic and cultural differences in the world around them. Why did they not concentrate exclusively on the study of Classical antiquity? Many, of course, were content to do so. But the Renaissance movement was more than a nostalgic return to the past. It was a dynamic reform movement which asked the advice of the past in order to handle the problems of the present, and it was born in comparison. There were always many Renaissance thinkers for whom the present had to be part of the equation.

The enthusiasm of the Renaissance for Classical antiquity had the further effect of cracking the shell of ethnocentric prejudice which had traditionally isolated the men of the west. If the Greeks and Romans were the great masters, never rivalled since, it was ridiculous for any modern people to claim an exclusive excellence. A touch of humility toward the great past made possible the impartial curiosity of men like Pietro Martire d'Anghiera.

NOTES

[1] This paper is a by-product of research on the early history of archaeology. Its central idea is the result of thinking about the history of anthropology in the framework provided by Arnaldo Momigliano's Sather Lectures of 1962, "The Classical foundations of modern historiography," and Erwin Panofsky's work on the significance of the Renaissance (Panofsky 1960, 1962). Momigliano's Sather Lectures have not yet been published, but key portions of his argument are available in earlier articles (Momigliano 1955, 1960).

My argument, inspired by Momigliano, that there was no continuous anthropological tradition in Classical antiquity, is intended to challenge the notion common among anthropologists interested in the history of their discipline that anthropology begins with Herodotus and has had a more or less continuous development since. This notion is derived from such earlier studies as Myres 1908, Sikes 1914, and Trüdinger 1918, where its presence reflects the influence of the idea of progress.

A shorter version of this paper was read at the Seventh Annual Meeting of the Kroeber Anthropological Society, Berkeley, April 6, 1963. It is a pleasure to express my appreciation to William C. Sturtevant, John F. Freeman, Dell H. Hymes, Luís Monguió, Gene M. Schramm, Dorothy Menzel, and Margaret T. J. Rowe for encouragement and suggestions. Except as specifically noted, all translations were made by me from the original texts.

[2] It was Cicero who called Herodotus "the father of history" (see Momigliano 1960:29) and J. L. Myres (1908:125) who called him "the father of anthropology." Momigliano (1960:44) concludes that "Herodotus has really become the father of history only in modern times."

[3] Wells 1923; Glover 1924:60–61; Myres 1953: 159–160.

[4] The best general account of Persian imperial policy is still that of Eduard Meyer (1953–56, 4. Band, 1:20–89). Meyer contributed a summary of this account in English to the eleventh edition of the *Encyclopaedia Britannica* (article Persia). A detailed study of Persian toleration is badly needed.

[5] Esther 1:22, 3:12, 8:9, quoted from the Revised Standard Version.

[6] Gellius (mid 2nd century A.D.), *Noctes Atticae*, Bk. XVII, ch. xvii; 1927–28, 3:262–263.

[7] Schroeder 1921; compare John George Clark Anderson's review of the influence of commonplaces in the *Germania* in Tacitus 1938:xxvii–xxxvii.

[8] Bacon 1900, 1:300–301. Bacon took most of his geographical and ethnological information from Pliny.

[9] There is an immense literature on the Italian Renaissance. For present purposes the most useful research guides to this literature are Stark 1880 and Cosenza 1962. Novices in the Renaissance field should be warned that there has been much controversy among historians in recent years regarding the differences between the Renaissance and the Middle Ages (see Ferguson 1948 and Helton 1961). In this controversy I follow Panofsky, because I find his arguments

convincing. The neo-Burckhardtian approach of this paper therefore represents a deliberate and reasoned choice among the alternatives.

[10]This paragraph is based on Panofsky 1960:101–103.

[11]On Petrarch see especially Voigt 1894; Essling and Müntz 1902; Nolhac 1907; Venturi 1929; and Mommsen 1957.

[12]On the recovery of Latin and Greek manuscripts see Symonds 1888:127–142; Voigt 1894:229–259; and Sabbadini 1905–14.

[13]Bodnar 1960:8–15 gives an extensive bibliography of works relating to Ciriaco; to it should be added Essen 1958. The basic source on Ciriaco's life is Scalamonti 1792. On the value of his field records see Lehmann-Hartleben 1943 and Ashmole 1956.

[14]Biondo Flavio 1927:xix–cxciii (by Bartolomeo Nogara), and notes kindly provided by Margaret T. J. Rowe. Biondo, of course, wrote in Latin, although the titles of his works are given in English in the text of this paper.

[15]*De verbis Romanae locutionis;* Biondo Flavio 1927:115–130.

REFERENCES CITED

ANGHIERA, PIETRO MARTIRE D'
1892 De orbe novo Petri Martyris Anglerii . . . decades octo quas scripsit ab anno 1493 ad 1526 . . . cura et studio D. Joachim Torres Asensio. Madrid, Typis Viduae et Filiae Gomez Fuentenebro. 2 vols.
1912 De orbe novo; the eight Decades of Peter Martyr d'Anghera, translated from the Latin with notes and introduction by Francis Augustus MacNutt. New York and London, G. P. Putnam's Sons. 2 vols.

ASHMOLE, BERNARD
1956 Cyriac of Ancona and the Temple of Hadrian at Cyzicus. Journal of the Warburg and Courtauld Institutes XIX, nos. 3–4, July to December, pp. 179–191. London.

BACON, ROGER
1900 The Opus majus of Roger Bacon, edited, with introduction and analytical table by John Henry Bridges. London, Edinburgh, Oxford, Williams and Norgate. 3 vols.

BIONDO FLAVIO
1927 Scritti inediti e rari di Biondo Flavio, con introduzione di Bartolomeo Nogara. Studi e Testi 48. Roma, Tipografia Poliglotta Vaticana.

BODNAR, EDWARD W.
1960 Cyriacus of Ancona and Athens. Collection Latomus vol. XLIII. Bruxelles-Berchem.

BORMANN, EUGEN, and WILHELM HENZEN
1876 Inscriptiones urbis Romae Latinae. Pars prima. Corpus Inscriptionum Latinarum 6:1. Berlin, Georg Reimer.

BURN, ANDREW ROBERT
1962 Persia and the Greeks; the defence of the west, c. 546–478 B.C. New York, St. Martin's Press.

CA' DA MOSTO, ALVISE
1937 The voyages of Cadamosto and other documents on western Africa in the second half of the fifteenth century, translated and edited by G. R. Crone. Works issued by the Hakluyt Society, second series, no. LXXX. London.

COSENZA, MARIO EMILIO
1962 Biographical and bibliographical dictionary of the Italian humanists and of the world of Classical scholarship in Italy, 1300–1800. Boston, G. K. Hall & Co. 5 vols.

DAWSON, CHRISTOPHER HENRY
1955 The Mongol mission. Narratives and letters of the Franciscan missionaries in Mongolia and China in the thirteenth and fourteenth centuries, translated by a nun of Stanbrook Abbey, edited with an introduction by Christopher Dawson. London and New York, Sheed and Ward.

DIELS, HERMANN
1959 Die Fragmente der Vorsokratiker. Neunte Auflage herausgegeben von Walther Kranz. Berlin-Charlottenburg, Weidmannsche Verlagsbuchhandlung. 2 vols.

EASTON, STEWART C.
1952 Roger Bacon and his search for a universal science; a reconsideration of the life and work of Roger Bacon in the light of his own stated purposes. New York, Columbia University Press.

ESSEN, CAREL CLAUDIUS VAN
1958 I Commentaria di Ciriaco d'Ancona. Il mondo antico nel Rinascimento; atti del V Convegno Internazionale di Studi sul Rinascimento, Firenze—Palazzo Strozzi, 2–6 Settembre 1956, pp. 191–194. Firenze, Istituto Nazionale di Studi sul Rinascimento.

ESSLING, VICTOR MASSENA, PRINCE D', and EUGÈNE MÜNTZ
1902 Pétrarque; ses études d'art; son influence sur les artistes; ses portraits et ceux de Laure; l'illustration de ses écrits. Paris, Gazette des Beaux-Arts.

ESTIENNE, HENRI
1566 Apologia pro Herodoto, siue Herodoti historia fabulositatis accusata. Herodoti Halicarnassei Historiae lib. IX, & De vita Homeri libellus . . . ab Henr. Stephano.

FERGUSON, WALLACE KLIPPERT
1948 The Renaissance in historical thought; five centuries of interpretation. Cambridge, Houghton Mifflin Company, The Riverside Press.

FERNÁNDEZ DE OVIEDO Y VALDÉS, GONZALO
1851-55 Historia general y natural de las Indias, islas y tierrafirme del Mar Océano. Madrid, Real Academia de la Historia. 4 vols.

GAETA, FRANCO
1955 Lorenzo Valla; filologia e storia nell' umanesimo italiano. Istituto Italiano per gli Studi Storici, Pubblicazione 8. Napoli.

GELLIUS, AULUS
1927–28 The Attic nights of Aulus Gellius, with an English translation by John C. Rolfe. Loeb Classical Library. London, William Heinemann; New York, G. P. Putman's Sons. 3 vols.

GLOVER, TERROT REAVELEY
1924 Herodotus. Sather Classical Lectures, vol. 3. Berkeley, University of California Press.

GRANATINO, GIOVANNI LEONE
1957 Jean-Léon l'Africain. Description de l'Afrique. Nouvelle édition traduite de l'italien par A. Epaulard et annotée par A. Epaulard, Th. Monod, H. Lhote et R. Mauny. Institut des Hautes-Etudes Marocaines, Publication 61. Paris, Librairie d'Amérique et d'Orient Adrien Maisonneuve. 2 vols.

HEITZ, EMIL
1869 Fragmenta Aristotelis. Paris, Editore Ambrosio Firmin-Didot.

HELTON, TINSLEY
1961 The Renaissance; a reconsideration of the theories and interpretations of the age. Edited by Tinsley Helton. Madison, University of Wisconsin Press.

HERODOTUS
1921–38 Herodotus, with an English translation by A. D. Godley. Loeb Classical Library. London, William Heinemann Ltd.; Cambridge, Harvard University Press. 4 vols.

HORTIS, ATTILIO
1879 Studi sulle opere latine del Boccaccio, con particolare riguardo alla storia della erudizione nel Medio Evo e alle letterature straniere. Trieste, Libreria Julius Dase Editrice.

JACOBY, FELIX
1926–30 Die Fragmente der Griechischen Historiker (F Gr Hist); zweiter Teil, Zeitgeschichte. Berlin, Weidmannsche Buchhandlung. 2 vols. in 6 parts.

LEBRIJA, ELIO ANTONIO DE
1926 Nebrija, Grammatica de la lengua castellana (Salamanca, 1492), Muestra de la istoria de las antiguedades de España, Reglas de orthographia en la lengua castellana, edited with an introduction and notes by Ig. González-Llubera. London, Humphrey Milford, Oxford University Press.
1946 Grammatica castellana. Texto establecido sobre la ed. "princeps" de 1492 por Pascual Galindo Romeo y Luis Ortiz Muñoz, con una introducción, notas y facsímil. Madrid, Junta del Centenario. 2 vols.
1951 Vocabulario español-latino por Elio Antonio de Nebrija (Salamanca ¿1495?). Real Academia Española, Facsímiles, serie II, no. IV. Madrid.

LEGRAND, PHILIPPE ERNEST
1932 De la "malignité" d'Hérodote. Mélanges Gustave Glotz, 2:535–575. Paris, Les Presses Universitaires de France.

LEHMANN-HARTLEBEN, KARL
1943 Cyriacus of Ancona, Aristotle, and Teiresias in Samothrace. Hesperia, XII, no. 2, April–June, pp. 115–134. Baltimore.

McCRINDLE, JOHN WATSON
1877 Ancient India as described by Megasthenes and Arrian . . . with introduction, notes, and map of Ancient India . . . Calcutta, Thacker, Spink & Co.; Bombay, Thacker & Co.; London, Trübner & Co.

MANCINI, GIROLAMO
1891 Vita di Lorenzo Valla. Firenze, G. C. Sansoni, Editore.

MEYER, EDUARD
1953–56 Geschichte des Altertums. Fünfte Auflage. Basel, Benno Schwabe & Co. Verlag. 4 vols. in 7 (first published 1884–1902).

MOMIGLIANO, ARNALDO
1955 Ancient history and the antiquarian. Contributo alla storia degli studi classici, Storia e Letteratura 47, pp. 67–106. Roma.
1960 The place of Herodotus in the history of historiography. Secondo contributo alla storia degli studi classici, Storia e Letteratura 77, pp. 29–44. Roma.

MOMMSEN, THEODOR ERNST
1957 Petrarch's testament, edited and translated, with an introduction. Ithaca, Cornell University Press.

MORAUX, PAUL
1951 Les listes anciennes des ouvrages d'Aristote. Préface par Augustin Mansion. Aristote; Traductions et Etudes, collection publiée par l'Institut Supérieur de Philosophie de l'Université de Louvain. Louvain.

MULLER, CARL WILHELM LUDWIG
1874–83 Fragmenta historicorum Graecorum. Paris, Editore Ambrosio Firmin-Didot.

MYRES. JOHN LINTON
1908 Herodotus and anthropology. Anthropology and the classics; six lectures delivered before the University of Oxford . . . edited by R. R. Marett, pp. 121–168. Oxford, Clarendon Press.
1953 Herodotus, father of history. Oxford, Clarendon Press.

NOLHAC, PIERRE DE
1907 Pétrarque et l'humanisme. Nouvelle édition, remaniée et augmentée. Bibliotheque Littéraire de la Renaissance, n.s., tome I–II. Paris, Librairie Honoré Champion, Editeur. 2 vols.

NORDEN, EDUARD
1922 Die Germanische Urgeschichte in Tacitus Germania. Zweiter Abdruck mit Ergänzungen. Leipzig, Berlin, Verlag von B. G. Teubner.

OLSCHKI, LEONARDO
1960 Marco Polo's Asia; an introduction to his "Description of the World" called "Il milione." Berkeley and Los Angeles, University of California Press.

PANOFSKY, ERWIN
1960 Renaissance and renascences in western art. The Gottesman Lectures, Uppsala University, VII. Stockholm, Almqvist & Wiksell. 2 vols.
1962 Artist, scientist, genius: notes on the "Renaissance-Dämmerung." The Renaissance; six essays. Harper Torchbooks, The Academy Library, pp. 123–182, TB 1084. New York and Evanston, Harper & Row, Publishers.

PIZZICOLLI, CIRIACO DE'
1742 Kyriaci Anconitani Itinerarium nunc primum ex ms. cod. in lucem erutum . . . Editionem recensuit . . . nonnullisque ejusdem Kyriaci epistolis . . . locupletavit Laurentius Mehus. Firenze, Giovanni Paolo Giovannelli.

PLINIUS SECUNDUS, CAIUS
1938–63 Pliny, Natural history, with an English translation . . . by H. Rackham, W. H. S. Jones, and D. E. Eichholz. Loeb Classical Library. London, William Heinemann; Cambridge, Harvard University Press. 10 vols.

POLO, MARCO
1938 Marco Polo, The description of the world. A. C. Moule & Paul Pelliot. London, George Routledge & Sons Limited. 2 vols.

REIMANN, EUGEN
1895 Quo ex fonte fluxerit Nicolai Damasceni paradoxon ethon synagoge. Philologus, 54. Band (n.F., 8. Band), no. 4, 654–709. Göttingen.

ROSSI, GIOVANNI BATTISTA DE
1871 Sull' archeologia nel secolo decimo quarto. Bulletino dell' Instituto di Correspondenza Archeologica per l'anno 1871, nos. I, II, Gennaio è Febbraio, 3–17. Roma.
1888 Inscriptiones Christianae urbis Romae septimo saeculo antiquiores, edidit Ioannes Bapt. de Rossi. Vol. 2, pt. 1. Roma, Libreria Filippo Cuggiani.

SABBADINI, REMIGIO
1905–14 Le scoperte dei codici latini e greci ne' secoli XIV e XV. Firenze, G. C. Sansoni, Editore. 2 vols.

SALAS, ALBERTO MARIO
1959 Tres cronistas de Indias; Pedro Mártir de Angleria, Gonzalo Fernández de Oviedo, Fray Bartolomé de las Casas. México, Fondo de Cultura Económica.

SARTON, GEORGE
1948 Introduction to the history of science. Carnegie Institution of Washington, Publication 376, vol. III, Science and learning in the fourteenth century, part II. Baltimore, The Williams & Wilkins Company. (reprinted 1953).

SCALAMONTI, FRANCESCO
1792 Vita di Ciriaco Anconitano. Della antichita Picene dell' Abate Giuseppe Colucci, 15:i–clv. Fermo, dai torche dell' autore. (text in Latin).

SCHROEDER, WALTER ALFRED
1921 De ethnographiae antiquae locis quibusdam communibus observationes. Dissertatio inauguralis . . . in Academia Fridericiana Halensi . . . Halle, Karras, Kroeber & Nietschmann.

SIKES, EDWARD ERNEST
1914 The anthropology of the Greeks. London, David Nutt.

SPIEGELBERG, WILHELM
1927 The credibility of Herodotus' account of Egypt in the light of the Egyptian monuments . . . with a few additional notes by the translator Aylward M. Blackman. Oxford, Basil Blackwell.

STARK, KARL BERNHARD
1880 Systematik und Geschichte der Archäologie der Kunst. Handbuch der Archäologie der Kunst, erste Abteilung. Leipzig, Verlag von Wilhelm Engelmann.

STEIN, OTTO
1931 Megasthenes 2) Griechischer Ethnograph Indiens, im 4./3. Jhdt. v. Chr. Paulys Real-Encyclopädie der Classischen Altertumswissenschaft, neue Bearbeitung begonnen von Georg Wissowa, 29. Halbband, pp. 230–326. Stuttgart, J. B. Metzlersche Verlagsbuchhandlung.

STRABO
1917–32 The Geography of Strabo, with an English translation by Horace Leonard Jones. Loeb Classical Library. London, William Heinemann Ltd., Cambridge, Harvard University Press. 8 vols.

SYME, RONALD
1958 Tacitus. Oxford, Clarendon Press, 2 vols., paged continuously.

SYMONDS, JOHN ADDINGTON
1888 Renaissance in Italy; the revival of learning. New York, Henry Holt and Company. (first ed., 1877).

TACITUS, CORNELIUS
1938 De origine et situ Germanorum, edited by J. G C. Anderson. Oxford, Clarendon Press.

TAYLOR, ALFRED EDWARD
1911 The Dissoi logoi. Varia Socratica, first series, St. Andrews University Publications 9:91–128. Oxford, James Parker & Co.

TRÜDINGER, KARL
1918 Studien zur Geschichte der griechisch-römischen Ethnographie. Inaugural-Dissertation . . . Basel. Basel, E. Birkhauser.

UNTERSTEINER, MARIO
1954 The sophists. Translated from the Italian by Kathleen Freeman. Oxford, Basil Blackwell.

VALLA, LORENZO
1922 The treatise of Lorenzo Valla on the Donation of Constantine; text and translation into English, by Christopher B. Coleman. New Haven, Yale University Press.
1962 Laurentius Valla, Opera omnia, con una premesa di

Eugenio Garin. Monumenta Politica et Philosophica Rariora, series I, nos. 5–6. Torino, Bottega d'Erasmo. 2 vols.

VENTURI, LIONELLO

1929 La critica d'arte e Francesco Petrarca. Pretesti di critica, pp. 37–51. Milano, Ulrico Hoepli Editore.

VOIGT, GEORG

1894 Pétrarque, Boccace et les débuts de l'humanisme en Italie, d'apres la Wiederbelebung des classischen Alterthums de George Voigt. Traduit sur la 3e édition allemande par M. A. Le Monnier. Paris, H. Welter, Editeur.

WACHOLDER, BEN ZION

1962 Nicolaus of Damascus. University of California Publications in History, vol. 75. Berkeley and Los Angeles, University of California Press.

WAGNER, HENRY RAUP

1947 Peter Martyr and his works. Proceedings of the American Antiquarian Society, 56, pt. 2:239–288. Worcester.

WALSER, GEROLD

1951 Rom, das Reich und die fremden Völker in der Geschichtsschreibung der früher Kaiserzeit; Studien zur Glaubwürdigkeit des Tacitus. Baden-Baden, Verlag für Kunst und Wissenschaft.

WELLS, JOSEPH

1923 The Persian friends of Herodotus. Studies in Herodotus, pp. 95–111. Oxford, Basil Blackwell.

WILKINS, ERNEST HATCH

1927 The University of Chicago manuscript of the Genealogia deorum gentilium of Boccacio. Chicago, University of Chicago Press.

WYNGAERT, ANASTAAS VAN DEN

1929 Itinera et relationes fratrum minorum saeculi XIII et XIV, collegit, ad fidem codicum redigit et adnotavit P. Anastasius van den Wyngaert, O.F.M. Sinica Franciscana, vol. I. Quaracchi-Firenze.

CHAPTER 10

The Society for Medieval Archaeology

D. B. HARDEN

Launching a new society and journal devoted to archaeological matters, especially a society and journal of national standing, is not to be undertaken lightly, and those who took part in the initiation of this present venture were fully seized of the difficulty of their project and the hard work it would entail. That they were prepared to undertake it at all is some measure of their profound belief in the need for such a society and in the existence of a sufficient measure of support for it, both in this country and abroad, to ensure that success would ultimately crown their efforts.

At the time of writing these words, when barely twelve months have elapsed since the Society was formally launched, the Society has already attained a membership of 387 (294 individuals, 93 libraries). This number is not yet sufficient to ensure the continuance, let alone the prosperity of the Society and of its journal, but it is, we believe, a promising start, and if those who are already members will help to make the Society's existence known and bring in others, there need be no risk that the necessary support will not be forthcoming to enable future annual volumes of the journal to be even larger than this present one. It is the expressed hope of the Officers and Council, speaking for the Society, that an annual volume of at least 200 text pages can ultimately be maintained, perhaps appearing in two parts of 100 pages each.

The first moves towards founding the Society took place in 1956 and by the end of the year it was already clear to the principal sponsors that there existed an appreciable measure of support for such a venture. The Officers of the Society of Antiquaries of London, the Royal Archaeological Institute, the British Archaeological Association, the Society for the Promotion of Roman Studies and the Prehistoric Society were approached and they one and all expressed approval of the plan and a welcome for the venture. The President of the Society of Antiquaries, Sir Mortimer Wheeler, was particularly helpful and kindly disposed toward it, and readily agreed to take the chair at the first public meeting, which took place in his Society's apartments in Burlington House, freely lent for the occasion, on 16 April, 1957. At that meeting, which was attended by upwards of 85 people, it was decided, with only one dissentient, to appoint a steering committee of six to prepare a draft constitution. That committee's proposals were duly laid before a second public meeting, at which Sir Mortimer Wheeler again took the chair, on 13 June, 1957, and were approved without dissentient voice. This second meeting also appointed officers and a committee, and the Society was thereupon in being.

The Constitution then adopted is printed at the end of this volume, together with the names of the Society's Officers and Committees for 1957–58. The Society's financial year runs from 1 April–31 March and the initial subscriptions of founder members cover the year 1 April, 1957–31 March, 1958, as does this volume of its journal. That the volume appears after the end of that twelvemonth period is greatly regretted by the Council, but it is intended that the second volume shall be produced within its appropriate financial year ending 31 March, 1959, and further volumes annually thereafter, provided the necessary financial support continues to exist.

At the two public meetings on 16 April and 13 June, 1957, much discussion took place about the aims which the Society should set itself to attain, and the decisions were ultimately embodied in paragraph 3 of the Constitution. But it is well to elaborate these aims here so that all can recognize their intent and implications. The Society's prime purpose is to encourage the study of the archaeology of the period of the growth of the English nation. Since 1936, when the Prehistoric Society was refounded as a national body based on the former Prehistoric Society of East Anglia, it has covered the archaeology of these islands (and beyond) up to the Roman conquest, and since 1911 the period of the Roman domination has been well covered by the Society for the Promotion of Roman Studies, which has always paid special attention to Roman Britain. Agreement was therefore unanimous that any new Society should take as its sphere of influence the period following the official departure of the Roman armies from our shores and should cover the whole of the dark-age and medieval periods, as they are generally understood in these islands. That the term 'dark-age' is excluded from the Society's title is due in part to an attempt to attain brevity and in part also to an attempt to fit in with the generally-accepted terminology of historians in this country and on the continent.

Though this journal is essentially an archaeological one and will not as a rule include articles that are primarily historical or philological, it is hoped that it will attract the support of exponents of those allied studies by using such studies, where it is proper or desirable, to elucidate the archaeological evidence, and *vice versa*. The day is past when the historian, the philologist, the art-historian and the archaeologist could ignore each other—not, perhaps, with impunity (for that never was so)—but without attracting adverse criticism for such action. Today all four disciplines and many others too, including the more purely scientific ones, must work together even more closely if they are to make significant progress. This first volume of our journal includes an article on '*Beowulf* and Archaeology' by a Lecturer in Anglo-Saxon studies and one on 'Tree-ring analysis as an aid to medieval studies,' written jointly by a meteorologist and an archaeologist. Future volumes will continue this attempt to show the interaction of one discipline upon another, and to open out new avenues for coordinated research on medieval antiquities.

THE ANNUAL GENERAL MEETING, 1957

The First Annual General Meeting of the Society was held in the rooms of the Society of Antiquaries of London at Burlington House on 6 December, 1957. The appointment of the honorary vice-presidents was confirmed and the election of the vice-presidents was approved. Mr. R. L. S. Bruce-Mitford delivered his Presidential Address entitled 'Some comments on the Miniatures and Ornaments of the Lindisfarne Gospels'.

THE SHEFFIELD CONFERENCE

The first Annual Spring Conference of the Society was held at Sheffield from Friday, 28, to Sunday, 30 March, 1958, its theme being 'The Relationship of Archaeology and History in the Study of the Medieval Period'. The conference opened on the Friday evening with three short talks on aspects of medieval archaeology in the Peak district, Mr. J. Bartlett discussing the Anglian settlement, Mr. Forest Scott (the local Secretary) the pre-Norman Christian remains and Mr. L. H. Butcher, Cruck Barns. After these talks, which took place in the Museum, there was a reception given by the Lord Mayor of Sheffield and the Museum galleries were thrown open for inspection by the delegates. On Saturday the meetings took place in the lecture theatre of the new chemistry building of the University. After delegates had been welcomed by the Vice-Chancellor, Mr. Brian Hope-Taylor gave a talk on his excavations during 1953–1958 at the Anglo-Saxon Royal Palaces at Yeavering, Northumberland. He was followed by Mr. J. Hurst and Mr. M. Beresford, with a joint paper on the excavations at the deserted medieval village of Wharram Percy. After lunch Mr. W. A. Pantin in a paper entitled 'Monuments or Muniments', discussed the interrelation of material remains and documentary sources and this was followed by a symposium on the same theme in which Mr. C. E. Blunt, Mr. W. A. G. Doyle-Davidson, Mr. G. C. Dunning, Dr. H. P. R. Finberg, Dr. N. B. Lewis and Mr. A. J. Taylor took part. On the Sunday delegates visited Cartledge Hall, Holmesfield, and its cruck barn; the Tudor manor-house at Wingfield; the Anglian carvings at Wirksworth and Bakewell; and a Norman ring-motte at Camp Green, Hathersage.

More than a hundred and twenty people participated in this most successful conference, and great credit is due to Mr. Scott and his helpers who undertook the local organization.

CHAPTER 11

The Origins of the Society for Post-Medieval Archaeology

K. J. BARTON

The publication of the first Journal of the Society, 12 months after its inaugural meeting, is an appropriate moment to chronicle the events leading up to its foundation.

In the Spring of 1963 I was asked by Dr. Graham Webster of the University of Birmingham Extra-Mural Department to run a week-end school at Shrewsbury on the subject of Post-Medieval Ceramics. I invited Mr. John Hurst, F.S.A., to assist with the course as he has made an intensive study of the subject with particular reference to the imported ceramics in this period. The response to the course exceeded our expectations; thirty-eight people attended and the discussion was lively, culminating in the demand that some sort of group activity should be organized. After much discussion Mr. Hurst and I decided to launch the Post-Medieval Ceramics Research Group to study those ceramics made or used in England during the period 1450–1750. These two dates were carefully selected: by 1450 medieval influence in pottery was in rapid decline and imported wares were having noticeable effects on home products, and 1750 is the accepted date for the commencement of the manufacture of porcelain in England and its subsequent effects on traditional products.

The new group was to be a loosely formed body without a hierarchy, having only a Secretary and an Adviser. Its formation, with a membership subscription of 10/- and bi-annual meetings, was announced through the publications of the C.B.A. and the Museums Association. Information was also sent out to people thought to be interested. Circulation was financed by the Extra-Mural Department of Birmingham University. The response of eighty interested persons was most encouraging and on this basis it was felt that an inaugural meeting could be held in the Autumn of 1963.

This was held at Bristol City Museum under the auspices of the Bristol Archaeological Research Group and through the kindness of Mr. Alan Warhurst, the Museum Director, who provided free facilities and the use of the Museum Lecture Theatre. There was an attendance of 100 people which exceeded our hopes.

The Group, thus launched, issued its first Broadsheet in the Spring of 1964, a typed booklet with stiff covers containing short articles, notes and news. Four such Broadsheets were issued between Spring, 1964, and Autumn, 1966.

The main function of the group was to meet at carefully-chosen centres and, by examining the regional products, to gain a picture of the ceramic variations. Following the Bristol Conference meetings were held at Leeds University Extra-Mural Department; Colchester Museum; Hanley Museum, Stoke-on-Trent; Plymouth Museum; London (British Museum and Cuming House, Southwark); and Grosvenor Museum, Chester. To the Curators of these Museums, their staffs and Committees we extend our thanks for the facilities so kindly and freely provided. The meetings were always lively and informal; discussion and argument continued into the small hours and much of considerable value was gained, from the museum collections and especially from the practice of members in exhibiting exhibit material found during the previous 6 months, so that new light was continually being shed on to the subject.

During 1964 Mr. Hurst and I invited Mr. R. J. Charleston of the Victoria and Albert Museum and Mr. Hugh Tait of the British Museum to form a small committee. Mr. Charleston became Chairman, I was Secretary/Treasurer and Editor, Mr. Hurst and Mr. Tait were nominated advisers. The membership of the Group grew apace with many enquiries from overseas until by the end of 1966 the membership was nearly 200.

The administration of the Group became too much for one man and at the Hanley meeting I stepped down from my three-fold position and it was split—Mr. P. Mayes becoming Secretary, Mr. J. Ashdown Treasurer, and myself remaining Editor. Also during 1965 it was also becoming apparent that the Broadsheet was not a suitable vehicle for more than rough notes and news, and that there was need to provide a journal of quality to take the rapidly growing number of excavation reports that could not be placed in existing Journals. Further, amongst our members were those active in fields akin to our own, such as metal working, glassmaking, early industry, and building who also wished to publish their research. Throughout 1965 efforts were made to determine the support in the Group for an enlargement of its scope. Support gradually increased with a vote of confidence passed at Southwark in the spring of 1966, and this confidence grew into the acceptance of a Constitution for the Society for Post-Medieval Archaeology at the Chester meeting, autumn 1966, at which the founding body, the Post-Medieval Ceramic Research Group was dissolved, and its assets and goodwill transferred to the new Society.

CHAPTER 12

Late Man in North America:
Archaeology of European Americans

JAMES F. DEETZ

Most laymen think of archaeology as concerned with the old, the buried and the exotic. From this identification comes a *de facto* definition of archaeology as the study of excavated remains of ancient cultures quite different from our own. Until recently, such a definition would not have encountered serious criticism, even from members of the anthropological profession. However, a developing interest in the archaeology of European culture in North America has brought us to reject all three of the above criteria, and has even led to some fundamental reconsiderations of the basic structure of archaeology.

Although a specific designation has not yet been applied to such studies—historic, colonial, or historic site archaeology all have been suggested and used—they have developed to a point where a new national organization has been founded to coordinate their results. Annual meetings of the Society for American Archaeology also now regularly include sessions on historic studies, and a large body of literature on the subject has accumulated over the past several years.

This paper will consider various applications of the archaeological study of European Colonial culture in North America through numerous examples. These applications range from the direct use of results in the development of outdoor museums to quite sophisticated refinements in the method and theory of modern archaeology and anthropology, and include results of historical and ethnological value as well.

Archaeological investigations of seventeenth and early eighteenth century house sites in southeastern Massachusetts have been of considerable value to the reconstruction of Colonial Plymouth by Plimoth Plantation, an educational organization which is devoted to educating the public in Colonial culture through outdoor museum exhibits and research and publication. Many complex problems of detailed reconstruction of early seventeenth century households are solved through the study of documentary evidence, contemporary paintings, museum collections and excavation. Archaeological studies in the Plymouth area represent a long tradition. What is almost certainly the earliest example of controlled scientific archaeological excavation was done in 1853 by James Hall, who exposed the foundations of Miles Standish's home in Duxbury, Massachusetts. The records and artifacts from this remarkable project come to light only in 1963, when they were sent from Mexico to the Pilgrim Society of Plymouth by a descendant of Hall's. Included was a detailed scale plan of the excavations and a portion of what had been a complete, well-catalogued collection of artifacts. The plan showed the location of each artifact, indicated its *in situ* position, and notes included statements of the stratigraphic relationships of deposits within the house foundation. The excavations were tied to *two* datum points. Cataloging was meticulous, each artifact bearing a tag identifying it and relating it to the plan.

Later work included the excavation of the Aptucxet trading post by Lombard in the 1920's (Lombard, 1933), of an early seventeenth century house site in Kingston by Strickland in the 1930's, Hornblower's work at the Winslow site in Marshfield and the R.M. Site in Plymouth in 1940 and 1941 (Hornblower, 1943, 1950), and Deetz's excavations of the Bartlett site in Plymouth, and the Bradford and Howland sites in Kingston from 1959 through 1966 (Deetz, 1960a, b). The collections from most of these excavations are stored at Plimoth Plantation where they function as a valuable corpus of data on which to base details of architectural reconstruction and house furnishing. Whether the problem involves hinges, nails, window cames, pottery, glass or cutlery, there is usually a series of artifacts on which to base one's reconstruction or corroborate evidence from other sources. The collections are not only of the usual material culture inventory, but include extensive faunal samples, which will be of great value to the reconstruction of a mid-seventeenth century farm complex soon to be built on the plantation site. While it might be argued that one need not excavate so many sites just to determine the general form of seventeenth century colonial culture, since documentary evidence is in fact rather rich, the latter approach only tells us what was available to the early settlers and not what was actually used. There are significant differences between the archaeological collections from Jamestown and Plymouth, although both colonies were drawing from the same larger pool of European materials. One striking difference is seen in the occurrence of forks and Chinese porcelain in a seventeenth century context at Jamestown, while both artifact types are totally lacking from contemporary Plymouth, a difference which probably reflects the difference between the socioeconomic backgrounds of the settlers in each case, with the Plymouth plantation deriving from a more humble background than that of the Jamestown planters. There are also similarities in domestic crafts between both colonies which seem to transcend their common cultural heritage. In both colonies, bricks used in construction exhibit the same trends in dimensional changes through the seventeenth century, even though there was little contact between the colonies of a type which would account for the similarity. In each case, bricks become shorter, wider and thicker (Deetz, 1960b), changing from an earlier presumably common set of dimensions shared by both groups in England prior to their removal to the New World. A possible explanation of this pattern is found in an additional shared feature, mortar prepared from shells, oysters in Jamestown and clams in Plymouth. Shell mortar is inferior to that made from commercial lime, and as a result, wider brick would provide a better bearing surface. Thickening the bricks would permit fewer courses to obtain a wall of the same height. These two changes would then make the bricks heavier, but shortening them would be one way to retain the same volume. In Plymouth, even though all three dimensions change through the century, the cubic content remains unchanged. This pattern of identical change from a common form after isolation, brought about by a similar set of external factors, is reminiscent of the process of drift as it has been perceived in language, and may well be a legitimate analogy.

The archaeological program at Plymouth has applications of a broader nature than simply aiding in restoration and reconstruction. It has frequently been said that archaeology can serve as a valuable supplement to history, since each discipline has a quite different emphasis. As the number of excavated sites in the Plymouth area increases over the coming years, the pattern of settlement and expansion of the colony will be made clear in a way not available from other sources. Since the dating of these early house sites is quite accurate, we can confidently expect to obtain a detailed pattern not only of the location but duration of various farmsteads. Many of these are now located in wooded areas, although they certainly occupied cleared and cultivated land at the time of their use. Another advantage gained from the Plymouth sites results from their relatively brief occupation. The cellars of most of these early houses are sealed samples of twenty to thirty years duration. Since they are rarely stratified, and are isolated in areas which even today have seldom been plowed, very accurate dates can be assigned to various artifact types within them. At a recent meeting of the Society for Post-Medieval Archaeology in London, it was apparent that the occurrence of certain pottery types in closely dated contexts in Plymouth serves as a source of refinement of the chronology of ceramic manufacture in England, since English sites seldom if ever have such clear temporal limits.

In addition to supplementing the historical record, archaeological study of European sites in this country frequently sheds light on the process of acculturation of the aboriginal population. An excellent case in point is provided by recent work at La Purisima Mission in Lompoc, California, fifty miles north of Santa Barbara (Deetz, 1963). Following the destruction of the original mission, Purisima Vieja, in 1812 by severe earthquake, the fathers moved to a new site and rebuilt. By 1814 they had constructed a long barracks building formed of contiguous two-room units to house the neophytes, each unit occupied by a nuclear family group. The only Indians not housed in this structure were unmarried adolescent girls, who were confined to separate quarters. Brief mention of this Indian barracks was made by the resident *padre*, but it was not until the Civilian Conservation Corps restorations of the 1930's that it was discovered archaeologically. A portion of it was excavated at that time, and the remainder by Norman Gabel in 1950 and by James Deetz in 1962. Final mapping of the feature showed it to have been 540 feet long, of heavy adobe brick construction with a tile roof. The artifact content of this structure was extremely rich, consisting of both aboriginal materials and European trade objects.

Careful analysis and comparison of the inventory from the barracks with assemblages from contemporary aboriginal village sites in the same area produced a striking pattern. Aboriginal artifacts from the barracks were divided into two categories; those reflecting male activity and those representative of female activities. Artifacts of male association were extremely rare; only a scant handful of stone knives, points and scrapers were encountered in the entire structure. Furthermore, waste flakes which would have resulted from the on-the-spot manufacture of stone tools were virtually absent. Female-associated artifacts on the other hand were just as common as in contemporary aboriginal village sites. Bowls, mortars, pestles, baskets, manos, and metates form the vast majority of the aboriginal assemblage from the barracks. Since we know from the historical record that adults of both sexes occupied the barracks, and since the walls and floors of the structure provided close spatial control, the explanation of the differential rate of material culture loss could be made with confidence. Indian males underwent a rather profound change in roles, with herding, farming and crafts replacing the older hunting and fishing pattern. Females on the other hand probably continued to perform domestic tasks not too different from those of pre-contact days. The result is seen in the assemblage from the barracks, with almost total loss of material culture reflecting aboriginal male roles and little if any change or loss in the female-associated sub-assemblage. In fact, in comparison to contemporary village sites near the mission, female industries almost seem elaborated, possibly the result of a more sedentary life-way in the mission compound. A final support of this explanation is provided by a small measure of chronological control within the boundaries of the structure, since it could be shown that the majority of the few male-associated artifacts recovered was from the older portion of the barracks.

The examples thus far cited indicate that there is considerable anthropological and historical value to the archaeological study of European sites in North America. Although recent and not particularly exotic, such sites are as relevant as older or less familiar cultural remains. Another kind of research that can be legitimately included in historic archaeology is the work currently being done on Colonial mortuary art in New England (Deetz and Dethlefsen, 1965, 1967; Dethlefsen and Deetz, 1966). In this case, we are not dealing with excavated evidence; all of the artifacts are on the surface, and field equipment is limited to pencil, paper and camera. In a one hundred mile square area centering on Boston, there are over 100,000 gravestones of the late seventeenth, eighteenth, and early nineteenth centuries. These artifacts constitute a unique and powerfully controlled context in which to refine and develop archaeological method and elaborate archaeological theory. They are particularly suited to this purpose since they were the products of a folk culture, and their spatial, temporal, and formal dimensions can be controlled to a very high degree. Each stone has a date inscribed, the location of manufacture is known, and relationships between styles can be clearly delineated through our knowledge of their carvers. With such control on the primary dimensions of archaeological variation, it is possible to measure diffusion rates (Deetz and Dethlefsen, 1965), to relate stylistic change as it reflects social differences (Deetz and Dethlefsen, 1966), to measure religious change in time and space (Dethlefsen and Deetz, 1966), and to postulate and test a host of other aspects of variation in a class of artifacts as it reflects changes in the producing culture. Although a complete description of the results of this study is far beyond the scope of this paper, an example will serve to emphasize its relevance to archaeological method (Earle, 1966).

In eastern Massachusetts, between 1700 and 1820, three styles of mortuary design were popular in gravestone art, each during a particular period. Earliest was the winged death's head, and its gradual decline and ultimate disappearance has been shown to be a function of the decline of orthodox Puritanism in Massachusetts Bay Colony. This motif is replaced during the eighteenth century by a cherub design, and cherubs dominate the mortuary art of the middle and late eighteenth century until they are replaced by a third design, the urn and willow motif, which rapidly becomes universal in the early years of the nineteenth century. Graphs showing stylistic sequence and replacement in each cemetery studied provide solid support to the traditional "battleship" shaped curve of seriation method. Although the rates and times of replacement vary considerably from community to community, the overall sequence is repeated in practically every cemetery in the study area.

One area provides a notable exception, and in this case, the death's head design, when plotted against time, forms a wasp-waisted curve that violates the general assumptions underlying proper seriation (Figure 1). However, since our controls are so rigorous, there is no question that the hourglass form is indeed an accurate reflection of the popularity career of the death's head design in this case. One must then ask why this distortion occurs, and what one might learn from attempting to explain its existence.

The area where this divergent style curve is seen is Cape Cod, and in those communities further out on the Cape the effect is more pronounced. The degree of construction of the curve is thus a function of the distance from the point of attachment of the Cape to southeastern Massachusetts. A study of stylistic sequences in other communities of eastern Massachusetts provides us with a clear and convincing explanation of this pattern. Before considering why the death's head has such a peculiar temporal distribution on the Cape, we must first examine the differences in its rate of disappearance elsewhere.

The death's head motif has its longest duration in and around Boston, where it did not vanish completely until the first decades of the nineteenth century. This is probably a function of the strength of residual Puritan values and their accompanying symbols in the conservative folk element of urban Boston. Communities further removed from Boston show a progressively earlier date of final death's head disappearance, and in the Plymouth area, fifty miles south of Boston, they had vanished completely by the 1750's. This rapid disappearance was a function of a change in religion and mortuary symbolism generated by the great awakenings of the mid-eighteenth century combined with a differential in the date of appearance of the first locally produced cherub motifs in the area. Cherub designs, strongly correlated with the more cosmopolitan elements of the population in Boston and especially in Cambridge, diffuse slowly into the surrounding countryside at a rate of roughly one mile per year, reaching the Plymouth area in the late 1750's. A time space line marking the last use of death's head designs would slope downwards (earlier) as it moved outward from Boston in any direction on a spatial axis.

Cape Cod, with its sandy soils and absence of good quarries, had no resident stone carvers, and all gravestones were imported to the Cape from elsewhere in eastern Massachusetts. By the mid-eighteenth century, the soils of the Cape had lost much of their agricultural potential, and popula-

tions were increasing. Communities began to turn to fishing as a primary means of subsistence and economy. The further out on the Cape a community was located, the more pronounced was the change from an agrarian to a marine economy. Communities such as Sandwich, almost on the mainland portion of southeastern Massachusetts, were hardly affected by soil exhaustion.

When the distorted style curves for the death's head motif are examined closely, the date of maximum constriction coincides with the time of establishment of the first fishing fleets on the Cape. This in turn provides us with an understanding of the reasons for the distortion. When the communities turned to a maritime occupation, they also changed their market orientation. While farming was the primary occupation, all Cape communities participated in the Plymouth market area, a pattern which probably reflects an earlier political grouping of the Cape with Plymouth Colony until its absorption by Massachusetts Bay Colony under the New Charter in 1692. This shift from agrarian to marine economy meant a shift from the Plymouth market sphere to that of Boston. Gravestones, being entirely imported, were a commodity brought in along the lines of broader market trade, and the change of orientation simply meant that they were being brought in from Boston rather than Plymouth after the mid-century market change. However, while the death's head design was no longer being produced in Plymouth by the time this change occurred, stones with death's heads were still nearly universal in Boston. The final result was a style curve for the type marked by a near disappearance and then a sudden return to popularity, which in such communities as Truro and Eastham on the outer Cape approaches 100 per cent in the years after 1760, and does not return to the earlier popularity low point until ca. 1800.

Operating on purely formal criteria of classification, there is relatively little difference between the death's heads of Plymouth and those of Boston. What is important in this consideration is that local preferences were overshadowed by availability. Had there been resident stone cutters in the Cape communities, a normal distribution of the style across time almost certainly would have occurred. But since all preferences were ultimately primarily a function of those held elsewhere, a distortion is introduced which in less rigorously controlled circumstances would almost certainly be the source of controversy and possible improper ordering of individual samples in time.

If analysis such as that just described are essentially archaeological, and I would insist that they are, then the last of the three criteria cited in the introduction of this paper has been disposed of. We are now dealing with recent and familiar objects that are not even buried. Such a study in turn suggests that perhaps the role of archaeology in the broader framework of anthropology be re-examined.

The precise relevance of the archaeology of Colonial America to anthropology is that it is an area in which a certain unification of data can be brought about to the desirable end of making more powerful our various integrative methods and inferential theories. The twin aims of archaeology are the writing of culture history and the explanation of extinct cultures in a synchronic sense. The former is dependent on the latter, much in the way that historical linguistics must ultimately be based on sound structural linguistic theory. The essence of sophisticated theoretical treatment of past cultures in order to derive meaningful inferences lies in our understanding of the manner in which the patterning of cultural behavior is reflected in that part of his physical

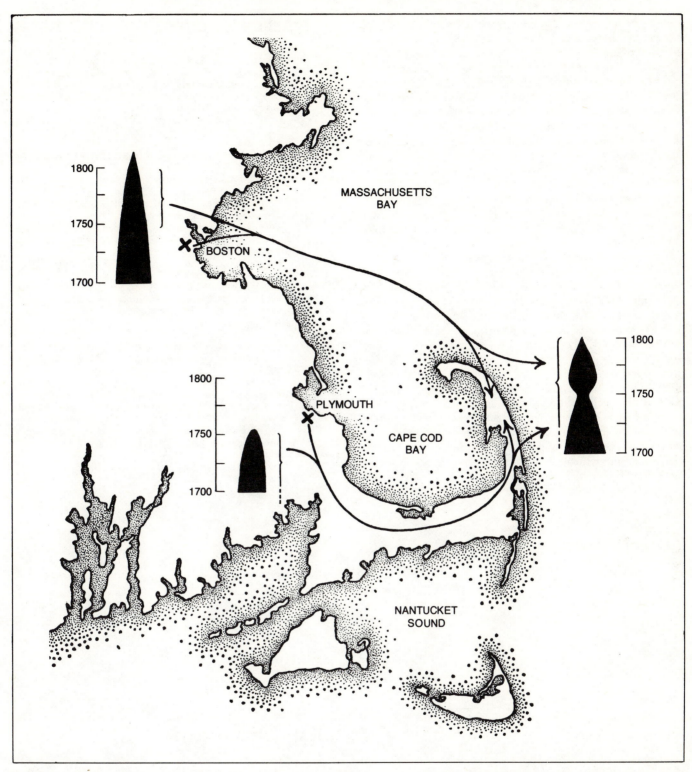

FIGURE 1.   Changes in Tombstone Style in Eastern Massachusetts During the 18th Century. This Abnormal Double Climax in the Popularity of the Death's Head Style on Cape Cod, which Contrasts with the Normal Frequency Curves of its Popularity at Plymouth and Boston, is Explainable by a Mid-18th Century Transfer of Trade Relations and Consequently of Tombstone Importation from Plymouth (Where the Style was Nearly Extinct) to Boston (Where it Still Remained Popular).

environment which man manipulates, forms and modifies. From this it follows that archaeology must concern itself with material culture regardless of provenience, be it archaeological in the excavated sense or ethnographic in terms of present use. Colonial archaeology, in the broadest of terms as defined here, bridges the gap between these extremes, and because of its documentary support, gives the archaeologist an area in which to develop general theory treating the relationships between culture and its tangible products.

Once such a position is taken by the archaeologist—if he still thinks of himself as such—other avenues of approach become readily apparent. Recent activity in the areas of transformational grammar as it applies to style and the basic structural aspects of material assemblages based on structural linguistic theory can be and are applied to all of material culture regardless of provenience (Deetz 1967). Freeing oneself from reliance solely on imperfect excavated data but not rejecting it, and adding to it from areas of more rigorous control is certain to advance the area of archaeology far more significantly than digging alone ever would. The term "New Archaeology" is very much in fashion at present, but perhaps it is an unfortunate choice, in that much of what is old in this sense is quite significant. Instead of the emphasis on "new" versus "old," with the implication of one replacing the other, it would seem a wiser course to expand the field to include certain subject areas, in this way stressing additive rather than replacive change. This problem might seem to be simply a matter of semantic quibbling, but as anthropologists we are all aware of how our labels tend to shape our world.

In a semi-serious vein, I would suggest the formal area of "Late Man" in this connection, since it derives from the precedent of the formal reified concept of "Early Man." In fact, Late Man studies are more sharply bounded in a temporal sense, with their earlier limit coinciding with the first written records in North America. By comparison the limiting date of Early Man studies lies somewhere in a five century limbo.

By whatever term it is known, the area of historical archaeology holds promise for the refinement and advancement of archaeology and anthropology. Only recently have anthropologists developed a broad and lively interest in this field, and as they work more and more in the expanding horizons of the recent and familiar, buried or not, deeper understandings which can only sharpen our theoretical tools are bound to result.

REFERENCES CITED

DEETZ, JAMES
1960a   Excavations at the Joseph Howland Site (C-5), Rocky Nook, Kingston, Massachusetts, 1959: A Preliminary Report. Howland Quarterly, vol. 24, no. 2–3.
1960b   The Howlands at Rocky Nook: An Archaeological and Historical Study. Howland Quarterly, vol. 24, no. 4.
1963   Archaeological Investigations at La Purisima Mission. UCLA Archaeological Survey, Annual Report for 1962–63, pp. 165–241.
1967   Invitation to Archaeology. Natural History Press, New York.

DEETZ, JAMES and EDWIN DETHLEFSEN
1965   The Doppler Effect and Archaeology: A Consideration of the Spatial Aspects of Seriation. Southwestern Journal of Anthropology, vol. 21, pp. 196–206.
1966   Some Social Aspects of New England Colonial Mortuary Art. Paper delivered at 65th Annual Meeting, American Anthropological Assn., Pittsburgh, Pa.
1967   Death's Head, Cherub, Urn and Willow. Natural History, vol. 76, no. 3, pp. 29–37.

DETHLEFSEN, EWIN and JAMES DEETZ
1966   Death's Heads, Cherubs and Willow Trees: Experimental Archaeology in Colonial Cemeteries. American Antiquity, vol. 31, pp. 502–510.

EARLE, TIMOTHY
1966   Chatham, Massachusetts: A Study in Death. Unpublished paper prepared for Anthropology 112, Harvard University.

HORNBLOWER II, HENRY
1943   The Status of Colonial Archaeology in Massachusetts in 1941. Massachusetts Archaeological Society Bulletin, vol. 4, p. 41.
1950   Pilgrim Sites in the Old Colony Area. Eastern States Archaeological Federation Bulletin, no. pp. 9–10.

LOMBARD, PERCIVAL
1953   The Aptucxet Trading Post. Bourne Historical Society, Bourne, Mass.

CHAPTER 13

Industrial Archaeology: Retrospect and Prospect

R. A. BUCHANAN

There is no agreed definition of industrial archaeology. My own preference is that it is a field of study concerned with investigating, surveying, recording, and, in some cases, with preserving industrial monuments. An 'industrial monument' in this context is any relic of an obsolete phase of an industry or transport system, but in practice it is useful to confine attention to the monuments of the last 200 years, both because earlier periods are dealt with by more conventional archaeological or historical techniques, and because of the sheer mass of material dating from the beginning of the Industrial Revolution. The study is 'archaeological' in so far as it deals with physical objects and requires field-work, even if the excavatory techniques of the classical archaeologist are not often applicable. Professor Hoskins has said that the primary article of equipment of the local historian is a strong pair of walking shoes, and Michael Rix has capped this with the remark that the industrial archaeologist requires gum boots. It is by the success and validity of its practical techniques that the claim of industrial archaeology to academic attention must, in the last resort, be judged.

Whatever shade of meaning is given to industrial archaeology in theory, there is little disagreement in practice amongst its practitioners. The term was coined in the mid-1950s in response to an urgently felt need to do something to prevent the apparently thoughtless wastage of the industrial heritage of Britain. The particular forces which have then and since loomed large as the potential destroyers have been the processes of modernization in industry and transport, and the acceleration of urban redevelopment and suburban expansion. Let it be said at once that industrial archaeologists are rarely opposed to such processes themselves, but only in so far as they may lead to the loss of significant artifacts without even an opportunity to record them adequately for posterity. The first great *casus belli* was the Doric Portico at Euston Station which was finally pulled down by British Railways in 1962 despite strong protests from amenity bodies and other organizations. The last decade has seen many similar confrontations and some successes, such as the preservation of Telford's suspension bridge at Conway. The mounting efficiency with which the case for the preservation of significant industrial monuments has been presented in these years reflects the vigorous development of local industrial archaeological societies throughout the country. Even though the subject has not established itself in the undergraduate syllabus of any university, industrial archaeology has become a popular choice amongst adult educational groups in the last ten years, and has succeeded in generating much extra-mural discussion about its objectives and methods.

Any short survey of the development of industrial archae-ology tends to exaggerate the role of preserving industrial monuments. In fact, only a small minority of the artifacts threatened at any time can be preserved, and the conscientious industrial archaeologist is aware of this and seeks only to ensure that the proper criteria are observed in selecting monuments for preservation. Apart from this, he is concerned with 'investigating', 'surveying', and 'recording' industrial monuments in the words of the definition suggested above, to make as certain as is humanly possible that all the available information about past phases of industrial development is put into a permanent and readily available record. To this end the Research Committee appointed by the CBA launched a National Survey of Industrial Monuments, preparing a standardized record card for the purpose in the hope that field workers would complete them and return them to its Consultant on Industrial Archaeology, Mr Rex Wailes. After a shaky start this recording service began to grow steadily in 1965, when it was made the responsibility of the Centre for the Study of the History of Technology at Bath University of Technology, under the title of the National Record of Industrial Monuments. In May 1968 there were 5089 entries in this Record which, although far from complete and showing great unevenness in the quality of the entries, is beginning to assume the character of a national archive.

There are thus two complementary incentives to the study of industrial archaeology. On the one hand, there is the cultural incentive to preserve a representative selection of the obsolete industrial artifacts of the country as a significant aspect of its heritage. Old churches and castles have long been given such attention, and industrial archaeologists seek to extend this protection, as cultural assets, to select industrial monuments. On the other hand, there is the historical incentive, with which we are primarily concerned here. This is the incentive to preserve as much information as possible about the physical remains of the industrial past. To the historian, all information is, potentially at least, good information. But there are four distinct ways in which industrial archaeological information can provide useful evidence for the social and economic historian.

In the first place, it is capable of giving a practical dimension to historical studies which become so easily second-hand and devoid of imaginative depth. How many authors of the standard textbooks, one wonders, know how a set of fulling stocks work? Or a spinning jenny or Watt's separate condenser? Even when the authors have mastered such elementary technical detail, they rarely manage to convey it to their students. Economic historians often lack a geographical consciousness, using such terms as 'Flanders' with bewildering diversity of meaning. Even the Cambridge

Economic History could be improved with some more maps. To add to this weakness a lack of technical consciousness is to remove their subject one stage further from reality and to make it so much the less significant and understandable. This is not to say, of course, that all economic historians suffer from such blind-spots, but only to maintain that the identification of such a blind-spot is an admission of the importance of the practical dimension to the subject. At this level, industrial archaeology is a new way of looking at economic, social, industrial, and technological history. It opens the imaginative eye of the student to new perspectives, in much the same way as a knowledge of architecture enables one to see more in an urban landscape than one would see without it.

Secondly, there is the value of possessing a comprehensive archive of industrial monuments such as has already been described. The utility of this to economic historians, human geographers, and even to city planners, should be clear enough. It promises to make available information about the siting, distribution, and size of industries to supplement and correct the picture available from other sources. The lack of such evidence can occasionally have a serious practical result, as when the desirable properties erected by suburban developers in ancient coal mining areas like that of Kingswood to the east of Bristol subside into old mine workings. Of more consequence to the economic historian, perhaps, the example of the lead industry on the Mendips may be mentioned. This was the subject of an excellent study in 1930 by Dr. J. W. Gough, then Lecturer in History at Bristol University. The work was compiled largely from the Waldegrave papers, however, and gave little attention to the technical details or to the precise location of particular workings. This weakness was reflected in the inadequate maps, one of which, an antique representation of the various mineries, can only be regarded as a documentary curiosity. The important point about this case is that subsequent fieldwork by industrial archaeologists is bringing to light much new evidence about the location of the industry and about the techniques employed in it. This is the sort of evidence which will eventually find its way into local and national archives, providing future historians with richer sources of material than those which have normally been hitherto at their disposal.

A third source of value of industrial archaeological evidence is an extension of this point regarding archival records. It is the provision of technical information on specific aspects of now obsolete processes which would be virtually unobtainable from other sources. The diligence with which some industrial archaeologists have taped the reminiscences of elderly workers who were once engaged in industries which have since disappeared, has proved to be a rewarding exercise. In some cases, the details of processes have been recovered and recorded, while in others problems of specialized terminology, inexplicable by any other method, have been resolved. Although the distorting qualities of old men's recollections must be taken into account, there is thus a useful source of information available here. A similar service is available from old film, although the task of assembling collections of industrial film has hardly been begun and the wastage of old film is extraordinarily high. Another source of technical information which has been exploited by industrial archaeologists is that of photographs. A single example of this medium being skillfully used is the collection of Mr. George Watkins's photographs of stationary steam engines. His book *The Stationary Steam Engine* covers all the main types of reciprocating steam engine used in industry and illustrates them with a wealth of technical detail. As most of the engines illustrated have now been scrapped, the photographs provide the best remaining source of information about them. A final source of technical information which should be mentioned here is that of written material when the writing is in the form of ephemeral semi-technical literature which does not normally find its way into library collections. Such are the voluminous trade catalogues put out by firms, which are often valuable sources of information about equipment and about commodities on the market. Such, also, are pamphlets like *The Mine under the Sea*, in which the pseudonymous author Jack Penhale describes the monstrous 'man engine' which lowered its human load into the depth of the Levant Mine in Cornwall until a disastrous accident in 1919 led to its prohibition.

The fourth value of industrial archaeological evidence is that it can supply a useful measuring rod of economic growth and social change. Classical archaeology has long made use of pottery shards for fixing dates, and there is an interesting extension of this technique into modern times in the utilization of fragments of clay tobacco pipes for dating sites, particularly in North America where there is often a dearth of documentary evidence about early settlements. Admittedly, there is little opportunity to exercise this technique in Europe, but in other ways industrial archaeological material may reflect the successive stages of industrial development. The development of a port, for example, can frequently be interpreted from the physical remains of docks, wharves, cranes, locks, bridges, warehouses, and workshops. Similarly, the changes which have overtaken the metallurgical industries in Britain can be unravelled by a careful study of the mass of industrial monuments which they have left, and an investigation of the transport relics of a region can show how one means of transport has been superseded by another. Such remains contribute to the 'palimpsest' quality of the British landscape, whereby successive generations have modified the environment without completely destroying the artifacts of their predecessors, so that a discerning eye can read the current face of a city and reconstruct the significant phases of its development. While economic growth can be assessed by the nature and distribution of the industries of a region over a period of time, social change can be judged from the ancillary features of the industrial landscape—the homes of the workers, their public houses, parks, and chapels. It is fashionable now to look for psychological changes in response to the early stages of rapid industrialization in Britain, but it may also be relevant to look for physiological changes, and the surviving evidence of workers' houses in a model community like Robert Owen's New Lanark does suggest a marked change in this respect.

Taken together, these indications of the possible value of industrial archaeological material to historical scholarship show that it deserves to be taken seriously in the academic world. Economic historians, in particular, would be wise to keep a close eye on industrial archaeological literature, which is increasing rapidly. With such an interdisciplinary subject it is difficult to draw the bibliographical boundaries. Even if the classics of technological history from Agricola's *De Re Metallica* to the five volume *Oxford History of Technology* are excluded from consideration, together with the standard works on economic and social history including the 'Vista Books' series and the Faber series 'Technology Today and Tomorrow', the number of books and articles on specifically industrial archaeological subjects has undergone a remarkable rate of multiplication since 1963. That year saw the appearance of E. R. R. Green: *The Industrial Archaeology of County Down*, Belfast, HMSO, the first use of the term in a full-length publication. It was also the first systematic survey of a region from an industrial archaeological point of view, and it is still a model of scholarly thoroughness in this field. In the same year was published K. Hudson: *Industrial Archaeology*, John Baker, 1963, and now available in University Paperback. This assembled material collected in the first place for the CBA and presented it in a brisk journalistic manner. The book has proved to be a useful popularizer for the subject. Hudson followed it up with the much slighter and less valuable book: *Handbook for Industrial Archaeologists*, John Baker, 1967. This should not be confused with the *Industrial Archaeologists' Guide* 1969–70, edited by N. Cossons and K. Hudson and published by David & Charles of Newton Abbot in 1969, which contains useful essays and lists on a wide range of industrial archaeological subjects.

Kenneth Hudson also pioneered the *Journal of Industrial Archaeology* which began in 1964 and of which he was Editor until 1968. At the end of its second year, in the autumn of 1965, the *Journal* experienced a publishing crisis from which it was rescued by the intervention of David & Charles of Newton Abbot. From the start of its third year it has appeared under the modified title: *Industrial Archaeology* (with the sub-title 'The Journal of the History of Industry and Technology'), published by David & Charles. The contents of the *Journal* reflected the piecemeal and random nature of the subject during these early years, and little attempt was made to impose any editorial direction upon the material. The Editorship has now passed to Dr. John Butt of the University of Strathclyde.

The enterprising firm of David & Charles now has a list which itself reads like a bibliography of industrial archaeology. Apart from extensive series of canal and railway histories, the firm is publishing a series devoted specifically to industrial archaeology, designed mainly on a regional basis but with a number of associated topics. The first of these to appear (1965) was again by K. Hudson: *The Industrial Archaeology of Southern England*, written with verve but with a strange disregard for detailed accuracy. However, the book has already run to a second edition (1968), which has provided an opportunity for removing some of the worst discrepancies. This book has been followed by David M. Smith: *The Industrial Archaeology of the East Midlands* (1965), a careful scholarly account written by a geographer; Frank Booker: *The Industrial Archaeology of the Tamar Valley* (1967), with a brisk narrative by a local man who knows his subject intimately; and John Butt: *The Industrial Archaeology of Scotland* (1967), a useful analysis by an economic historian which attempts to cover too much ground to do justice to the industrial archaeological detail. The associated volumes in the series so far have been—J. P. M. Pannell: *The Techniques of Industrial Archaeology* (1966), which made the mistake of regarding the subject primarily as a study requiring professional surveying and drawing techniques; Bertram Baxter: *Stone Blocks and Iron Rails* (1966), a detailed chronicle of the early tramroad systems of Britain; and Jennifer Tann: *Gloucestershire Woollen Mills* (1967), a comprehensive survey of the cloth businesses of the Stroud valleys and their buildings. Taken together, these books represent a very creditable achievement for a single publishing house over four years, but this stream has become a torrent with further publications on—*The Industrial Archaeology of Dartmoor* (by Helen Harris—this volume actu-

ally appeared early in 1969); *The Industrial Archaeology of Derbyshire* (by Frank Nixon); *The Industrial Archaeology of the Bristol Region* (by R. A. Buchanan and Neil Cossons); and *The Industrial Archaeology of Lancashire* (by Owen Ashmore).

Other publications by David & Charles are animated by a strong sense of industrial archaeology. The series which includes—Robin Atthill: *Old Mendip* (1964); W. G. Hoskins: *Old Devon* (1966); and Arthur Raistrick: *Old Yorkshire Dales* (1967)—contains a wealth of material for students of industrial relics. A series of *Illustrated Histories*, moreover, is intended to supplement the industrial archaeology series— so far only two have appeared, those by John Butt, Ian L. Donnachie, and John R. Hume: *Industrial History in Pictures—Scotland* (1968), and the volume on *Bristol*, by R. A. Buchanan and Neil Cossons (May 1970). In this line also two other picture books by David & Charles should be mentioned—Aubrey Wilson: *London's Industrial Heritage* (1968); and the remarkable work by George Watkins: *The Stationary Steam Engine* (1968), to which attention has already been drawn. Another parallel series of volumes by the same firm is that on industrial histories, which so far includes the masterly technical survey by W. K. V. Gale: *The British Iron & Steel Industry* (1967); and Stanley D. Chapman: *The Early Factory Masters* (1967), on the first generation of factory owners in the Midlands textile industry. Yet another publishing venture by David & Charles is the republication of books which have become industrial archaeological classics, such as Samuel Smiles: *Lives of the Engineers*, 3 vols, first published 1862 (D & C edition 1969) with introduction by L. T. C. Rolt. Even *Bradshaw's Railway Guide* for April 1910 and for August 1887 has been reissued, and a complete set of the First Edition of the One Inch Ordnance Survey, issued between 1805 and 1873, is being produced.

Of course, other republications of works with industrial archaeological interest have already appeared, notably those published by Frank Cass which include H. W. Dickinson: *A Short History of the Steam Engine*, first published in 1938, Cass edition 1963 with a new introduction by A. E. Musson— but the competition from David & Charles is having a salutary effect on the price of such volumes. Lest the impression be formed, however, that David & Charles have a virtual monopoly of industrial archaeological publications, let us look at the work of other publishers in this field. Early in 1969 Longmans published the first three volumes in their long-awaited industrial archaeological series, under the general Editorship of L. T. C. Rolt. These are, first, a contribution by Mr. Rolt himself: *Navigable Waterways*; secondly, W. K. V. Gale: *Iron and Steel*; and thirdly, Anthony Bird: *Roads and Vehicles*. At least eleven more volumes are envisaged, covering a wide range of industries and transport systems. Incidentally, it is worth recording that Rolt's own 'Lives of the Engineers'—his series of biographical studies beginning with *Isambard Kingdom Brunel* (Longmans, 1957)—has been one of the most important literary influences stimulating a widespread interest in industrial archaeology.

Another publisher who has established a reputation in industrial archaeology is D. B. Barton of Truro, who writes and publishes books and sells them in his own bookshop. His fine study: *The Cornish Beam Engine* (1965), has been widely acclaimed, and he has followed it up with: *A History of Copper Mining in Cornwall and Devon* (1967) and: *A History of Tin Mining and Smelting in Cornwall* (1967). His wife has participated in the enterprise by writing—R. M.

Barton: *A History of the Cornish China-clay Industry* (1966), and the firm now publishes books by other people such as—Nellie Kirkham: *Derbyshire Lead Mining through the centuries* (1968). D. B. Barton's early interest in the tin and copper mining relics of the South West was expressed in a series of pamphlets such as: *A Guide to the Mines of West Cornwall* (1963). These were poorly bound with glued spines, but this criticism cannot be applied to the later full-length books by the firm, which are all excellently produced.

Amongst several books which have become, retrospectively, works on industrial archaeology, at least two are worth mentioning—Rex Wailes: *The English Windmill* (Routledge, 1954), and J. W. Gough: *Mines of Mendip* (Oxford, 1930), and new edition (David & Charles, 1967). Rex Wailes has become, as Consultant on Industrial Archaeology to the Council for British Archaeology, one of the few 'professional' industrial archaeologists and a pioneer propagandist for the subject. Windmills have been the specialist interest of his life, and he writes about them with authority. Something has already been said about Gough's work, but despite its weakness on the physical remains, it has become a valuable source of information about Mendip lead mining. The lead industry has received careful attention at the hands of industrial archaeologists to whom, in addition to the books by Gough and Kirkham, the following works have proved useful—W. J. Lewis: *Lead Mining in Wales* (University of Wales, 1967); A. Raistrick and B. Jennings: *A History of Lead Mining in the Pennines* (Longmans, 1966); and Robert T. Clough: *The Lead Smelting Mills of the Yorkshire Dales*, published privately by the author in 1962. Watermills have not yet been so well treated as windmills—Leslie Syson: *British Watermills* (Batsford, 1965), is a fair introduction, but does less than justice to the complexity and variety of water power. Amongst books in preparation which bear directly on industrial archaeology, Batsford have a *Gazetter* on the outstanding sites in England and Wales (by Neil Cossons), and Penguin have a general survey under way (by R. A. Buchanan). HMSO, which showed an early interest in the subject with Green's work on *County Down*, has published a study of *Mines, Mills and Furnaces, an Introduction to Industrial Archaeology in Wales* (by D. Morgan Rees).

Turning briefly to the pamphlet and periodical literature, the growing interest in industrial archaeology is evident in a spate of publications of which only a brief selection can be conveniently given here. These may be divided roughly into general accounts and particular surveys. In the first category stand Michael Rix: *Industrial Archaeology*, Historical Association pamphlet, 1967; R. A. Buchanan (ed.): *The Theory and Practice of Industrial Archaeology* (Bath University Press, 1968; contains papers by R. A. Buchanan, Frank Atkinson, Michael Rix, and Kenneth Hudson, given to the Bath Conference on Industrial Archaeology in 1967); and K. Hudson (ed.): *The Industrial Past and the Industrial Present* (Bath University Press, 1967, contains papers delivered to the Conference in Bristol under this title in 1965); and 'Today's Junk: Tomorrow's Treasure', *Esso Magazine*, Winter 1968–9. In the category of particular surveys, some hard fieldwork by local industrial archaeological societies and keen individuals has produced valuable results. See, for instance—W. Branch Johnson: *Industrial Monuments in Hertfordshire* (Hertfordshire County Council, 1967); Peter Laws and Geoffrey Sands: *Industrial Archaeology in Bedfordshire* (Bedfordshire County Council, 1967); W. E. Minchinton: *Industrial Archaeology in Devon* (Dartington Amenity Research Trust, 1968); R. A. Buchanan: *The Indus-trial Archaeology of Bristol* (Bristol Branch of the Historical Association, 1967); Neil Cossons: *Industrial Monuments in the Mendip, South Cotswold and Bristol Region* (Bristol Archaeological Research Group, 1967); Frank Atkinson: *The Great Northern Coalfield* 1700–1900 (Durham County Local History Society, 1966); and W. A. McCutcheon: 'The Use of Documentary Source Material in the Northern Ireland Survey of Industrial Archaeology', *Economic History Review*, 2nd series, vol. xix, no. 2, August 1966.

Many of the thriving industrial archaeological societies are now producing ambitious periodicals of their own. Good examples are those of the Gloucestershire Industrial Archaeological Society, the South East Wales Industrial Archaeological Society, The Teesside Industrial Archaeological Society, the Industrial Archaeological Society of Portsmouth College of Technology, *Search*—the Bulletin of the Salisbury and South Wiltshire Industrial Archaeology Group, the *Bulletin* of the North East Industrial Archaeology Group, and *BIAS Journal*—the publication of the Bristol Industrial Archaeological Society. Finally, it need hardly be added that much industrial archaeological material is published in the columns of these journals and those of *Industrial Archaeology, Transport History, Transactions of the Newcomen Society,* and the publications of local historical and archaeological societies, which it would be impractical to particularize here, even though a detailed analysis of this proliferating literature would certainly be useful.

To conclude: industrial archaeology is still a new study, and its literature shows some of the brashness and superficiality which is inevitable wherever a new discipline is evolving. The very word 'discipline' is enough to rouse the suspicions of some of its most able practitioners, for the subject is experiencing in an acute form the tension between the 'amateur' and the 'professional' which has long bedevilled classical archaeology. Like classical archaeology, it is a subject which invites the participation of the enthusiastic laymen because many different sorts of expertise are relevant to its methodology. But such amateur experts are liable to resent the intrusion of 'professionals'—which usually means academics, though wrongly so in this context, because the academic historians, geographers, archaeologists, and engineers who are showing an interest in the subject have more of a 'lay' status than most of the self-styled 'amateurs'. The real distinction, however, which needs treating with sympathy, is between those who participate in industrial archaeology as an enjoyable leisure activity only, and those who seek its systematic organization and study in universities and elsewhere. However desirable the latter, it is essential that the continuing role of the former as active fieldworkers should remain.

Even though the scope of the subject needs keeping in proportion—some of its enthusiastic supporters occasionally make exaggerated claims for it—and it must be admitted that its primary function is to fill-out and give greater depth to orthodox modes of historical research rather than to replace them, industrial archaeology does have a significant contribution to make to historical scholarship. In addition, it should be remembered that it deserves attention also on other grounds: for its contribution to the preservation of a vital part of the cultural heritage of the community; as a powerful teaching aid for a range of studies in schools, colleges, and universities; and as a very important means of enriching the experience of life of its practitioners. At the end of the day, one can say no more for any pursuit than that those who do it do it because they enjoy it.

CHAPTER 14

Islamic Archaeology, an Introduction

OLEG GRABAR

There is at first glance something incongruous about the very notion of an "Islamic" archaeology. The vast world which extends from Morocco through Pakistan and from south of the Sahara to the steppes of Siberia is not now and was hardly ever united except insofar as it accepted the faith and the precepts of Islam. Neither the piety nor the law of Islam had developed—at least in theory—a system of visual forms which, like the temple or the statue of a divinity, could be considered characteristic of a culture. Although defined, like the Classical world, in terms of a way of life and system of values, the Muslim world did not possess an ideal physical setting in which its own "good life" could grow. Furthermore, although there are a number of geographical and political features which are shared by almost all Muslim lands, they lack the physical cohesion provided by the Mediterranean to Greece and Rome or the administrative unity provided by the Church in the Christian Middle Ages. Thus, it may be more appropriate to see Islam as a moment in the growth of a vast number of disparate regions: North Africa, Egypt, the Fertile Crescent, Anatolia, Iran, Central Asia, the Indian subcontinent. Even though something may be shared by these moments wherever they occurred, the predominant cultural forces remained regional and ethnic and we must think in terms of traditional areas or peoples. Such, in fact, has been the thrust of some contemporary scholarship, notably in Turkey, Iran and Central Asia. If valid, this approach denies, in large part, the likelihood of an Islamic world and thus of an Islamic archaeology.

There is yet another difficulty in dealing with Islamic archaeology: it is that Islam, created out of Arabia in the seventh century after Christ, is still a living force in almost all the areas which had, at one time or another, become Muslim. We are not dealing here with a "dead" culture but with an actual continuum which, however modified by history and circumstances, has existed from the moment of its appearance until today. In part, this is a practical difficulty, for past and present are inextricably mixed in much of the Muslim world and the recovery of the former is complicated, especially when, as happens only too often, the greedy and uncontrolled present moves over and destroys ancient vestiges. Another practical difficulty is the consistently confused stratigraphy which occurs in sites of continuous or recent habitation. The difficulty is also a theoretical one, for the historian and the archaeologist are not always equipped to separate past from present. It is often dangerous to interpret discoveries of old through practices of today, just as the maintenance of traditional ways today makes it, at times, difficult to appreciate the complex nuances which actually explain the past. As the last layer of the rich archaeology of the Near East, the Islamic or mediaeval level is often the

most damaged. All of us have tales of lamentable disregard of these levels by archaeologists.

Finally, Islamic archaeology shares with a number of other archaeological efforts the problem of concerning itself with a highly literate culture, whose history, thought and institutions are easily available through texts. Archaeology becomes all too easily the provider of objects for museums and collectors, the source of supplies for art historical research. And the very quality of much of traditional Islamic art has led, especially in Iran, to frightening destruction of superb sites by clandestine diggers. Even if we disregard the ethical problems connected with such "excavations," the purely scientific loss is immense. The general lack of concern for the loss is due in no small part to the feeling that the results of archaeology are but the gathering of "pretty things."

Uncertainty about the very validity of a notion of Islamic archaeology, difficulty of separating past from present, unclarity in the nature of the remains and their proper sequence, a particularly weak record of publications, apparent duplication when related to literary evidence, clandestine destructions of sites—these are characteristics hardly suited to give any sort of respectability to the field. One could argue, of course, that it is a very young field. It is only during the last decade of the nineteenth century that the great epigraphist Max van Berchem saw the need for the development of Islamic archaeology and only a handful of specifically Islamic excavations took place before World War II, many still unpublished. The considerably greater activities which followed the war were technically superior to the earlier ones. The results of some are found in the articles which follow. From these as well as from the mass of practical and theoretical problems just outlined, it is possible to draw a sort of profile of the tasks, purposes and expectations of Islamic archaeology.

Let us begin at the simplest level. From Morocco to India there are some thirty thousand monuments of Islamic architecture still standing in varying degrees of preservation. Perhaps four times as many objects in ceramics, glass, metal or wood have remained and are scattered in the museums of the world. The monuments of architecture, like the great mosques of Cairo or of Isfahan, are being constantly repaired or are deteriorated. The first task of Islamic archaeology is then to record and explain standing monuments, to show the complex history of most of them, and to seek or preserve such information as can demonstrate their meanings and construction or decoration. This task is often the responsibility of national departments of antiquities and a special expression of gratitude must be extended to the often tedious and rarely rewarded job of repairing and consolidating carried out by devoted teams of architects, draftsmen and archaeologists in all Middle Eastern and North African countries. It is unfortunate that so much of their work remains unpublished. Some steps must be found to change this state of affairs, so that, for instance, the extraordinary citadel of Aleppo may be better known to visitors, or the large scale restorations carried out in Turkey, Egypt, Iran and Central Asia are properly explained. Most of these activities have led to major discoveries which, more often than not, have been lost. Few local departments are financially or technically equipped to accomplish all the necessary tasks and in many instances a collective international effort will probably be required.

Matters are somewhat different when we consider objects. The uniquely Islamic technique of luster had been known for many decades before excavations at Samarra and at Fustat made it possible to suggest a ninth century date for the technique's formation. New excavations in Egypt and in Iraq seem to indicate an even earlier date for its invention. The point of importance is that only careful excavations can explain the development of the major artistic forms typical of the first centuries of Islam, as has been amply demonstrated by the Metropolitan Museum's work at Nishapur, there is much which is still unknown. We have no clear idea as to when and where major ceramic types of Iran—known in books as Rayy, Kashan or Gurgan—first appeared. There are some seven hundred objects of silver—known generally as Sassanian—which will remain unexplained and whose authenticity will be suspected as long as their archaeological setting is not discovered. The uniquely Islamic technique of silver inlaid bronzes is insufficiently dated or localized.

Such examples can easily be multiplied and we may thus define the first objective of Islamic archaeology as providing, as accurately as can be done, the exact features of standing monuments and the chronological and spatial setting of objects. Archaeology in this sense is at the service of the history of art. It is an indispensable tool for the authentication, the dating, the localization and the explanation of works of art. In this sense Islamic archaeology is not different from classical or western mediaeval archaeology but far less work has been accomplished in it than in the latter two fields, and the need for study is heightened by the importance in Islamic culture of the work of the urban artisan as opposed to the ecclesiastical or royal artist. For there occurred in the Muslim world a multiplicity of creative centers the peculiarities of which—as well as their inter-relationships—can only be made known through minute descriptions and studies.

A second objective of Islamic archaeology consists of formal excavations, i.e. of systematic searches for new evidence. It is through a series of excavations in Syria and Palestine that the understanding of early Islamic aristocratic life was revolutionized and that a totally new chapter in the history of early mediaeval art was made possible. Excavations in Afghanistan and in Soviet Central Asia have brought to light the first royal art of the Turkic dynasties which dominated the Muslim world from the eleventh century onward, while almost contemporary palaces were discovered in North Africa. It is not an accident that so many excavations brought to light princely establishments, for those were often situated outside of the main centers of inhabitation and were abandoned after the rule of one or two individuals.

A more challenging task of Islamic archaeology is that of trying to describe and explain the actual physical setting in which this unique culture developed. Much of this setting was urban and thus the most exciting aspect of Islamic archaeology lies in the study of cities. Some investigations such as Sauvaget's on Aleppo or Le Tourneau's on Fez have provided monographs on individual towns in two key provinces. They tended, however, to be limited to literary sources and to such monuments as had been accidentally or willfully preserved over the centuries. Excavations at Siraf in Iran or at Qasr al-Hayr Sharqi in Syria are exploring abandoned cities whose role no longer is meaningful today, but which were developed because they corresponded to unique needs of classical Islamic times. Through them much is being learned about the characteristics of the greatest periods in Islamic history. The exploration of Fustat in Egypt by G. Scanlon brought to light a moment in the growth of a huge metropolis, while R. Adams' exploration, of the area around Baghdad illuminated the physical nature of the urban-agricultural continuum over several centuries. Since Barthold, Soviet archaeologists have devoted much effort to a definition of the Central Asian town. But all these scattered examples are mere scratches when one considers the immensity of the task and its urgency, for the expansion of the modern world will not wait for the archaeologist and more than one site has already been ruined beyond repair.

The investigation of Muslim cities requires an extraordinary combination of talents. Archaeologists, historians, philologists and ecologists must combine their various expertises to provide that particular balance between the uniqueness of any one city and its typological value to understand all cities. The rewards are likely to be great, for a concerted scholarly effort may succeed in solving the general problems of a culture far better than the haphazard efforts which have occurred until now. In fact, because of its youth, Islamic archaeology is in the enviable position of being able to set forth the kind of problems it ought to solve. It is unfettered by tradition and enough work has been done by philologists, historians and art historians to define what can only be known through archaeological exploration.

Finally there is a third level of significance attached to Islamic archaeology. It is a level which extends its importance beyond Islamic culture alone. One aspect of it is methodological. Since much of the Muslim world is located in the Middle East, the area where some of the most important theoretical developments in Old World archaeology have taken place, Islamic archaeology is in a unique position to formulate and solve some of the nagging practical and theoretical problems posed by the differences in purpose and method between prehistoric, ancient and mediaeval archaeology.

But another aspect of Islamic archaeology at this level, perhaps more interesting, is that the peculiar history and location of the Muslim world makes its physical setting an illustration of far more than itself. Its cities are typical of Islam but also of urban life. Comprising as it does fertile valleys, near deserts, mountains, landlocked areas and seaports, the world of Islam, especially in its early centuries, can serve to illustrate the nature of the balance between local conditions and traditions and a presumably unified mode of behavior and way of life. In intellectual significance, it can be compared to Hellenistic or to Gothic archaeology and its evidence can help in refining the crucial question of the relationship between man's ideas and his physical setting. Located between the Far East and Western Europe, the Muslim world was affected by both and in turn influenced both. Its evidence has been of major importance in explaining a number of features of Chinese pottery, but there is far more than the mere question of dating a ceramic series. In reality a mass of problems pertaining to international trade and relations can be illuminated by the archaeological investigation of this area which had been for centuries the middle man between Asia, Europe and Africa.

These are only some of the questions posed by the very fact of an Islamic world. They extend beyond the explanation of individual monuments or localized problems, and archaeology alone holds solutions to these problems. Whether answers will ever be reached and problems solved no longer depends on the setting down of the problems but on the willingness of scholars and institutions to engage in actual archaeological work and to make results available rapidly and efficiently. Much is being done and a few of the results are presented in this issue of ARCHAEOLOGY and previous issues have occasionally mentioned other pertinent activities. An immense amount still remains to be done.

part 3

Substantive Contributions

INTRODUCTION

J. C. Harrington's pronouncement that excavators were recovering data but not history was an accurate assessment in 1955. Nevertheless, a small number of current projects have shown that this limitation was temporary and not inherent in the subject matter. Part 3 is a selection of several short artifact and fieldwork accounts and two full site reports that demonstrate the unique worth of archaeology in illuminating the recent past.

If the three major goals of archaeology are the outlining of sequences of local events (culture history), the creation of images of specific periods and cultures (reconstruction of past lifeways), and the explanation of past cultural variation (processual studies), then, at the same time, it must be admitted that the successes of Historical Archaeology have been confined to the first two. In fact, most historial archaeologists have concerned themselves with the most basic level of culture history—the time-space framework. Quite early in the history of the discipline it was realized that historical assemblages possessed two contradictory characteristics. First, scholars knew less about historic artifacts than they did about prehistoric assemblages. Second, the technical and stylistic evolution of historic objects, unlike their prehistoric counterparts, changed rapidly within a known and controlled setting. Whether prehistoric and historic assemblages are qualitatively different is not yet understood, but the context of historic artifacts makes them the basis of new and innovative dating techniques. As a corollary this situation can also be reversed allowing general archaeological methodology to be tested under controlled, almost laboratory, conditions.

One of the first chronological breakthroughs, reviewed in the articles by Harrington and Binford, was the discovery that the diameters of the holes in clay pipe stems decreased systematically between 1600 and 1760. Such patterned changes, and statistical techniques based on them, have more recently been applied to other artifact categories. Stanley South has advanced and successfully tested a "Mean Ceramic Formula" for the dating of the most intensive occupation of a site rather than just the extremes of initial settlement and abandonment. That such techniques have more than just temporal and spatial relevancy is also seen in South's findings on diffusion rates and in the paper by Deetz and Dethlefsen in this volume. Rates of evolution and spread of New England colonial gravestone styles allow the authors to test the assumptions underlying seriation. These chronological indicators also reflect past cultural behavior.

Harrington's "New Light on Washington's Fort Necessity" is considered a classic site report within the culture history genre. It highlights both the negative and positive nature of the preservation-restoration movement and is an impressive, if small, contribution to 18th century colonial history. I believe that even Harrington has underestimated the scholarly importance of his monograph. An accurate plan of an 18th century frontier fort may be of little import to a historian studying the French-British struggle for North America. It may also signify little to a biographer of Washington. But to a social scientist researching frontier adaptations and settlement patterns it is an important piece of data.

The remaining four papers signify a meaningful shift in approach and emphasis. They do not attempt to merely outline history but offer a much fuller reconstruction of specific aspects of culture. It is expectable, of course, that acculturation situations would draw the attention of an anthropologist like Deetz, but the other essays reveal an equal attention given to Euroamerican cultures. Because many anthropologists tend to view culture as a set of interconnected subsystems—technoeconomic, sociopolitical, and ideological—the four papers were chosen for their varying emphasis on one or more of these subsystems.

Allen's survey of Port Essington in Australia covers several factors but his discussion of ecological adaptation, especially as seen in architecture, is most interesting. More generally, Bowen's analysis of faunal remains from the Mott Farm Site in Rhode Island convincingly demonstrates that archaeology is equal in importance to written sources in the reconstruction of colonial economic behavior. In fact, the projects that Deetz and his students at Brown University have been running at the Mott Farm and at Plimouth Plantation, which in the main are still unpublished, will be the first major cultural reconstruction of New England society based on archaeology.

Finally Leone's essay, although it is concerned with technological items and general settlement patterns, approaches these features as reflections of Mormon religion. It is thus one of the very few examples of archaeological research on the ideological subsystem of historic America.

CHAPTER 15

Dating Stem Fragments of Seventeenth and Eighteenth Century Clay Tobacco Pipes*

J. C. HARRINGTON

Studies carried on over the past decade have established certain fairly definite dating criteria for clay tobacco pipes, particularly those made in England during the seventeenth century, but almost without exception these criteria relate to the pipe bowl.[1] The few definable differences in pipe stems, for which development sequences have been noted, such as increase in stem length, must be used with caution, even when it is feasible to use them at all.

It might be possible to work out a stem thickness sequence extending from the light stems of the very early (c. 1600) pipes, through a period of fatter stems, followed by a long period over which the stems became thinner and thinner. Even if such a sequence could be demonstrated, the dating of a small fragment by this means would necessitate knowing from what point along the tapering stem the fragment came; obviously impossible in most cases.

The length of the stem seems to bear a very definite relationship to the period of manufacture, and has always been recognized as a more reliable dating criteria than any other stem characteristic. Generally speaking, the stem increased from a relatively short length of possibly 6 to 8 inches during the early seventeenth century, up to the long "church warden" pipes of the early eighteenth century. There apparently was little change in pipe styles after that until the stems started to be shortened again toward the end of that century; and, with the short-stemmed nineteenth century types, we are finally back where we started.

However, the stem length is seldom applicable as a dating device, since whole stems, or even long sections, are rarely found in an excavation or when making a surface collection. In the Jamestown collection, for example, there are approximately 5,000 bowls or major portions of bowls, an estimated 50,000 stem fragments, but only three or four complete stems. Then, too, there are certain exceptions to this general rule that the stem length increased gradually throughout the seventeenth century. Although stems had become relatively long by 1700, short-stemmed pipes were also made during the last quarter of the century. In Ireland they were known as the "Dhudeen", and in Scotland as a "cutty-pipe", or simply a "cutty".[2]

Once sufficient studies have been made, stem decoration will possibly be of value in dating stem fragments. At the present time, however, this is not of too much value, even though certain types of ornamentation appear to belong to given periods. The principal difficulty is that plain stems far outnumber decorated ones at any given time, and even a fairly large collection is likely to contain no decorated stems.

Even though it is now possible to date pipe bowls within relatively limited periods, whole, or nearly whole, bowls are usually required for dating purposes. Far too often, however, a site will yield nothing but short stem fragments, or pieces of bowls too small to date. Just recently I was shown a cigar box full of stem fragments from a site in Virginia in which there was not a single bowl or even a large bowl fragment. The usual comment when confronted with such a collection is something like this: "If there were only a few bowls, we could probably date the material; but there is not much you can do when you have nothing but stem fragments".

In working with the Jamestown pipe collection I had observed that the early pipes have relatively large holes through the stems, while the holes in later specimens are much smaller. If this represented a definite and consistent trend, then it might possibly be useful as a dating criterion. Presumably the stem hole was of constant diameter throughout, and this was determined to be the case, with one major exception, upon examining a number of relatively long fragments. The exception occurs at the mouth end of the stem, where the hole had been enlarged in the process of removing the wire which had been inserted in the clay when the pipe was moulded.

Following up this lead, stem hole diameters were secured for a series of datable pipes. In taking these measurements, only those specimens were used which could be dated within relatively limited time periods, and which had sufficient stems remaining to permit an accurate measurement to be made of the stem hole diameter. These limitations somewhat restricted the number of specimens available for measurement, particularly for the eighteenth century, since many of the characteristic bowl shapes of that period changed very little during much of the century. In all, some 330 specimens were measured, or an average of 66 for each of 5 periods. Those used for the seventeenth century periods were largely from the Jamestown collection, while the eighteenth century examples came from the collections at Colonial Williamsburg and Fort Frederica National Monument. To the statistically minded, this will probably seem like too small a sampling on which to base definite conclusions. I am quite confident, however, that the validity of the observations would not be altered through use of a much larger sampling. Although it is

---

This is the second in a series of articles on clay pipes by Mr. Harrington. The first one appeared in the June, 1951, Vol. 5, No. 4 issue of this Bulletin, under the issue of this Bulletin, under the title "Tobacco Pipes from Jamestown."

[1] *For the best discussion, see Adrian Oswald, "English Clay Tobacco Pipes," in* The Archaeological News Letter, *London, April, 1951.*

[2] Quarterly Notes, *Belfast Municipal Art Gallery and Museum,* September, 1914, p. 5.

quite possible that the percentages might differ slightly with a larger number of measurements, this is really of no concern, in view of the very marked "modal" distribution for each time period.

The particular periods used in the study were chosen, not to produce attractive distributions, but because these were the periods for which I was able to select an adequate sampling of datable specimens. It is quite true that many bowls could be dated more closely than the time spans used for the study. For example, several of those in the first group (1620–1650) are quite definitely earlier than 1640, and some can be placed without much hesitation at around 1620. But the majority of the specimens could not be dated within such narrow limits, so the only practical approach was to use the longer periods.

It will also be noted that the time spans are not of equal length. This is due solely to my inability to date the pipes from these longer periods within narrower limits. This is particularly true of certain bowl shapes which remained relatively unchanged over much of the eighteenth century.

In taking the measurements, I used the most practical and inexpensive equipment I could find—a set of steel drills. A set suitable for this purpose, containing 6 drills in 1/64th steps, from 1/16 to 9/64 of an inch, can be purchased at most "dime stores" for 39 cents.[3] Results of the measurements of the 330 specimens are shown in the accompanying chart (Figure 1).

I want to make it quite clear that this study is not in the same class with a statistical analysis of a million army inductees, or a study of ten thousand college entrance candidates. Nor is it in a class, statistically or otherwise, with certain well-known sexual behavior studies. In my opinion, it would be quite ridiculous in the present instance to employ the customary statistical procedures, such as standard deviation, coefficient of correlation, et cetera.

USE OF THE CHART

In making use of this dating device, the first requirement is a 39-cent set of drills; the second is common sense.

Before discussing the application of the chart, I should warn that it is based entirely upon pipes of English make. Although I have not had an opportunity to study a large number of Dutch pipes, it would seem that for comparable periods, many of the Dutch pipes had smaller stems and smaller stem holes than English pipes. The bowls of these Dutch pipes are usually quite easily recognized, but if stem fragments only are available, they are not so readily identifiable.

As mentioned earlier, the finished end of the stem presents a problem, in that the hole at the very end was usually enlarged when the wire was withdrawn from the freshly moulded clay. However, such a fragment will usually be long enough to provide a normal hole measurement at the broken end.

It would be unwise, on the whole, as well as statistically unthinkable, to apply the data on the chart to a single stem fragment. Even so, it will be seen that a single specimen can be assigned to a period of not over 100 years, although this is

[3]*All stem holes, of course, are not an even 64th of an inch. However, after measuring a test series using diameters of 128ths of an inch, I found that the final results were as accurate and quite as useable if the measurements were limited to the more convenient 64ths.*

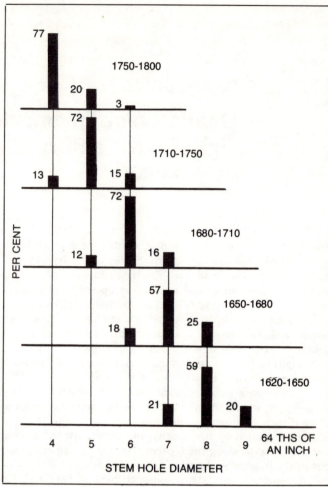

FIGURE 1.

too long a period to be of much use in most instances. For example, a specimen with a 7/64 hole could be assigned with considerable certainty to the period of 1620 to 1710. However, there is a very good chance that it would date from 1650 to 1680, and, even though one would not date a site on such meager evidence, it would serve as a clue, or as corroborative dating evidence. On the other hand, if one were considering a collection of 10 stem fragments, one with a hole diameter of 8/64, but 9 with a diameter of 7/64, a date of 1650 to 1680 would certainly not be statistically offensive.

We might take an actual situation in which a few stem fragments, but no bowls, were found. In the excavations at Fort Necessity in western Pennsylvania, 9 stem fragments were recovered. From the strata in which they were found, and from the very definite historical information available, these specimens could only have been deposited there in 1754. Of the 9 specimens, 5 have a hole size of 4/64 and 4 are 5/64. If one did not know the date of the site, and had to go to the chart for a dating clue, the resulting estimate would probably be 1730 to 1780.

A second example will serve to illustrate the soundness and the limitations of this method of dating. A deposit of material of European origin was recently uncovered in a military reservation on the James River a few miles down stream from Jamestown. The material, much of which can be dated within relatively narrow limits, all falls within the period of 1620 to 1640, or possibly as late as 1650 in some instances. I am under the impression that there were additional small pipe fragments in the deposit, but apparently only the longer stem pieces were saved. A tabulation of the hole diameters of the stem fragments, numbering 17, is shown below, including a comparison with the distribution of hole sized from the 1620–1650 period as shown on the chart.

Hole Diameter	James River Site	Chart
7/64	11%	21%
8/64	60	59
9/64	29	20

This quite definitely places the collection in the 1620–1650 zone. The sample is too small to permit a more limited estimate, but if a larger sampling were to present the same percentages, one would be justified in advancing the dates somewhat. In any event, the dating determined from the chart coincides very satisfactorily with the evidence from other artifacts.

As stated before, common sense will always have to be used in applying this dating device to a series of stem fragments. It has its limitations, but it does appear to be useful in those all-too frequent instances when the only clay pipe fragments available from a site are short pieces of stems.

CHAPTER 16

A New Method of Calculating Dates
from Kaolin Pipe Stem Samples

LEWIS R. BINFORD

In 1954 Harrington published an article on the study of metrical changes in kaolin pipe stem hole diameters through time. He found that there was a general and regular reduction in the hole diameters as you go from 1620 to 1800. In attempting to use this correlation to date Indian occupations in the Virginia-North Carolina area in 1954-55, I found that Harrington's method of data presentation was rather clumsy when attempting to compare archaeological samples of pipe stems to the control data or basic data on which the correlation was originally determined. Harrington had presented the observed correlation as a series of percentages for the occurrence of various hole diameters by forty year time periods. Very seldom is an archaeological sample likely to correspond to the forty year time periods set up by Harrington, so that when comparing observed percentages with the basic chart it was very difficult to arrive at an accurate age estimate. While attempting to eliminate this cumbersome difficulty it became quite obvious that Harrington's observed correlation of a metrical attribute with time was ideal for regression analysis. I computed from Harrington's percentages a straight line regression and arrived at a formula which would allow me to substitute values from any archaeological sample into the formula and determine an absolute date which would be the mean date for the period of sample accumulation. This I was able to do by using Harrington's original percentages and converting them to mean hole diameters for the given time period. This allowed me to calculate a straight line regression formula using years and mean hole diameters. The resulting formula is: $Y = 1931.85 - 38.26X$, Y being the date you are attempting to determine, 1931.85 being the theoretical date, if we project this correlation, at which the stem hole diameters would reach zero, and 38.26 being the slope of the line, that is, the interval of years between a mean of any one of the various metrical categories 5, 6, 7, 8, or 9/64 of an inch. If you had a sample with a mean of 5/64ths, and another with a mean of 6/64ths, there is an interval of 38.26 years between them according to Harrington's correlation. X in the formula is the mean pipe stem diameter for the sample you are attempting to date, and this is determined simply by measuring the hole diameters of the pipe stems in the sample and computing the arithmetic mean for the sample. The formula then gives you the mean date of the pipe stem sample, and is the mean date for the period of accumulation.

The first set of data on which I used this particular formula was the historic Nottoway and Meherrin Indian sites in the Virginia area. I had very good data as to the period of occupancy for at least four documented sites, and in all cases

(this was the first application of the formula as such) I was amazed. I couldn't believe the results could be so close to the known dates. On one particular site, a Warrasqueoc occupation of 1675-1702, the mean pipe stem date determined by this formula was 1683, and with the other sites I found equally good results. In conversing with Carol Erwin, who is writing up the historic material from the Macon Trading Post, I learned that she had found, in using the formula, that the mean pipe stem dates fall between the known estimated periods of occupation for the site. H. Geiger Omwake, who is one of our better authorities on pipe makers' marks, originally analyzed five fairly well dated historic sites, using Harrington's method in an attempt to demonstrate that the correlation was in fact valid. I have reapplied my formula to his data and was able to make more refined temporal estimates for the sites which were actually closer to the known dates. The other cases of application of the formula are Fort Michilimackinac and Brunswick Town. For the former site we have excellent documentation on the date of abandonment although its date of establishment is in dispute, being somewhere between 1700 and 1720. In addition to the documented span of the site, we have documented dates for the period of use of various structures, one of which was a soldiers' barracks built in 1769 and torn down in 1781. From the fireplace and a small closet that was adjacent to the fireplace of this structure a large sample of kaolin pipe stems were recovered yielding a mean pipe stem date of 1776, right in the middle of the known period of occupancy. These cases of application have convinced me and others that Harrington's correlation and this method is valid and quite useful for dating historic sites.

There are certain limitations to the method. When I applied the formula in the analysis of a sample from Mackinac Island, occupied from 1780 until the present, I found that the correlation fell to pieces. Known samples of pipe stems derived from hearths dated 1805 yielded pipe stem dates of 1732. In other cases of the application of the technique to late materials the results were equally disturbing. In the way of explanation it is quite obvious that with the influx of pipes manufactured in Montreal and at other seats of American pipe making there is a corresponding reoccurrence of certain "early" styles, in addition to the appearance of a new style of elements. This break in the traditional direction of stylistic change is responsible, I feel quite sure, for the breakdown in the correlation after roughly 1780.

I will mention certain sampling problems which also will affect the validity of any mean date determined by this technique. First, it must be kept in mind that you must have an *adequate sample*, that is, a large enough sample to be representative of the population being dated. The next major caution was brought forcibly to my attention by the material from Fort Michilimackinac. Early in the analysis of the Fort material it was obvious that throughout the span of the fort there had been an increasing logistics efficiency as well as an increase in population. The factors taken together resulted in there being many more pipes in use during the late period as contrasted with the early period. Thus, the increased rates of accumulation for the late period tend to skew the total sample from the site in favor of a later date. This brings us to the point that the accuracy of the date depends upon the possession of a random sample of a population which was stable with regard to rates of deposition through the period of sample accumulation. If either one of these conditions are not met, then you can expect less accuracy in dating.

I might briefly mention that by calculating the standard deviations of the means of samples, you have a rough estimate of the length of time over which the sample was accumulating.

In summary the regression formula presented here allows you to estimate from the variation observed in the hole diameters of kaolin pipes, a mean date for the period of sample accumulation and by using standard deviations estimate the length of time involved in accumulating the sample. The accuracy of the date depends upon (1) derivation of the sample from a population deposited prior to 1780, (2) randomness of the sample, (3) representativeness of the sample, and (4) a constant rate of accumulation throughout the period of sample building. I might mention that these limitations apply whether using Harrington's percentage technique or my regression formula.

CHAPTER 17

Evolution and Horizon as Revealed in Ceramic Analysis in Historical Archaeology

STANLEY SOUTH

INTRODUCTION

In this paper we will examine the relationship between the manufacture period of ceramic types found on British American sites and the occupation period for the sites on which type fragments are found. We will present data indicating that on eighteenth century sites there is a high correlation between the ceramic manufacture dates and the site occupation period. We will also look at the effectiveness of ceramic analysis based on presence and absence as compared to quantification of fragments of ceramic types. The process of evolution and horizon as reflected in analysis of ceramics from historic sites will also be examined.

Terms

Attributes are those observable criteria by which a ceramic type has been defined, including shape, paste, hardness, design, decoration, color, glaze, etc. A *type* is a term used to refer to pottery defined by one or more key attributes. With historic ceramics a type is often distinguished on the basis of a single attribute.[1] *Shape* is used to the physical form of an object, such as a teapot shape, or a teacup shape. *Form* is a generalized term which includes shape, as well as those other attributes from which types are defined. Thus the *evolutionary* process is seen in the change of *form* through time.

Quantification

In 1960 I urged historical archaeologists to utilize quantification of historic pottery based on frequency distribution, and illustrated the validity of statistically dealing with ceramics from colonial American sites (South 1962:1; Appendix I, this chapter). The point made at that time was that quantification of European ceramics from eighteenth century British American sites would allow the archaeologist to date the occupation period of a ruin. An assumption was that a comparison of the percentage relationships from enough historically dated ruins would allow a prediction to be made as to the occupation of ruins of unknown dates based on the frequency distribution of ceramic types.

[1] *See Clark 1968:134 for a discussion of attribute and artifact systems.*

The percentage relationships of ceramic types from various ruins in the mid-eighteenth century colonial English town of Brunswick, North Carolina were compared. The bar graphs of ceramic types frequencies were found to be similar when similar occupation periods for the ruins were involved (Appendix I). Ruins having a beginning historical date in the 1760's could be separated from those having a beginning date in the 1730's based on the frequency occurence of creamware, a separation not possible when using presence-absence alone. Historical archaeologists were urged to use frequency occurrence in ceramic studies to further test the possibilities of this approach with historic site data.

As can be seen from the historic site literature since that admonition there has been no general rush toward frequency analysis of historic ceramics. There even seems to be an attitude held by some that quantification of pottery fragments on the historic site level will not reveal information of any significance beyond that gained from presence or absence of the ceramic types. In this paper we will present quantification data that tend to demonstrate that there are advantages to be gained through use of type fragment frequency in conjunction with certain analysis tools.

Type Manufacture Date and Deposition Date

In historical archaeology the period during which artifacts were manufactured can be arrived at through documents, paintings, patent records, etc. The beginning date for the manufacture of a type may depend on the innovative action of one individual acting to introduce an additional attribute which is subsequently used to establish a type. The green glaze of the Whieldon-Wedgwood partnership developed in 1759, for instance, (Noël Hume 1970:124−25) which quickly went out of production, provides us with a known beginning manufacture date, and an end manufacture date probably no later than 1775. In many cases the end manufacture date cannot be fixed with the degree of accuracy of that of the beginning date. The point midway between the beginning and end manufacture date would be the median manufacture date, an important date for the purpose of this study. As Noël Hume points out, "The trick is to be able to date the artifacts . . ." (1970:11). The knowledge of manufacture dates for artifacts is an invaluable aid in the determination of occupation dates for historic sites. This is not to say that the manufacture date and the occupation date are the same, but rather that there is a connection between the two in that the manufacture date provides a *terminus post quem*, "a date after which the object must have found its way into the ground." (Noël Hume 1970:11). This is, as Noël Hume points out, "the cornerstone of all archaeological reasoning." However, there are those who believe there is such a slight connection between the date of manufacture and the date of deposition of ceramic type specimens on historic sites that they view as error any attempts to fix the occupation of sites by association of ceramics with the known date of manufacture (Dollar 1968:41–45). A major concern of this paper is to present data revolving around the artifact-manufacture-date and the artifact-deposition-date.

Evolution

Another major consideration here is the evolutionary concept of changing ceramic form through time as a dating tool as seen in fragments recovered from historic sites. Sixteen years ago this writer emphasized the necessarily intimate relationship between the process of archaeology and evolutionary theory as a basic framework of archaeology (South 1955). This paper also is anchored in the assumption that evolution of form is basic to the culture process and is the foundation for the "cornerstone of all archaeological reasoning" of which Noël Hume speaks in his discussion of *terminus post quem*.

Horizon

Through the excavation of a variety of eighteenth century historic sites I have become increasingly convinced that groups of ceramic types from different ruins of the same time period are similar enough to allow them to be used as dating tools for determining site occupation periods. This seems to be so regardless of whether the site is a remote frontier fort, a Cherokee village, a congested port town house, or a mansion. This has resulted in the development of analytical tools for use in determining the occupation dates for eighteenth century British American sites. These tools are useful and reliable when used on sites of varying functions over a broad area (Maryland, North Carolina, South Carolina). The explanation of this can be suggested in terms of the horizon concept (Willey and Phillips 1958:31–34), where the horizon is defined as:

> ... *a primarily spatial continuity represented by cultural traits and assemblages whose nature and mode of occurrence permit the assumption of a broad and rapid spread.*
> *The archaeological units linked by a horizon are thus assumed to be approximately contemporaneous (Willey and Phillips 1958:31–34).*

This concept of a broad and rapid spread of groups of contemporaneous ceramic types in the eighteenth century is examined through the tools described in this paper.

The Unimodal Curve

The ceramic types are seen to represent a unimodal curve that had an inception (beginning manfacture date), a rise to popularity, and a decrease in popularity to extinction (end manufacture date). This basic assumption is expressed by Dunnell based on concepts outlined by Rouse, Ford, Phillips, and Griffin:

> *The distribution of any historical or temporal class exhibits the form of a unimodal curve through time. The rationale for this assumption is that any idea or manifestation of an idea has an inception, a rise in popularity to a peak, and then a decrease in popularity to extinction (Dunnell 1970:309).*

An example of this concept is seen in Mayer-Oakes' study of illumination methods used in Pennsylvania between 1850 and 1950 as cited by James A. Ford in *A Quantitative Method for Deriving Cultural Chronology*. Washington 1962, Figure 6.

THE PROBLEM

In the seventeenth century, British American settlements were relatively few and far between compared with those of the eighteenth century, and population density was considerably less. As a result there are fewer seventeenth century sites for archaeologists to examine. This, plus fewer historical references to the manufacture dates of ceramics, combine to limit our knowledge of seventeenth century ceramics. We do know that the lower class seventeenth century household had a much greater dependence on pewter, leather and wooden trenchers, and other vessel forms and less daily use of ceramics than did the gentry. From the ruins of the mansions of the seventeenth century we would therefore expect to find ceramics more abundantly represented than from ruins of the lower class homes (Noël Hume 1970:24; personal communication on October 26, 1971). This status difference is *not* seen to be reflected in ceramics from archaeological sites in the eighteenth century.

Also to be considered is the fact that the limits of our present knowledge of seventeenth century ceramic manufacture dates and the temporally significant attributes within certain wares, results in a broader manufacture time span being assigned in comparison with the eighteenth century where short manufacture periods can be assigned to a number of marker types. As a result of this lack of refinement of our knowledge of seventeenth century ceramic types a comparison of manufacture dates with site occupation may well reveal less correlation than such a comparison made with data from eighteenth century sites. We might at first be inclined to interpret this as a time lag phenomenon, and indeed some time lag may well be involved in that with less use of ceramics in the lower class seventeenth century homes less breakage would naturally be expected to occur, resulting perhaps in a greater percentage of older ceramic types finding their way into the midden deposits. In the upper class homes, however, we would expect more ceramics and a closer correlation between manufacture dates and site occupation dates due to more frequent use in the home. However, as far as the time it took barrels of ceramics to make the trip from Britain to America aboard a vessel, there would be no appreciable difference between the seventeenth and the eighteenth century, in either case it was a relatively rapid process.

An hypothesis can also be constructed regarding a ceramic chronology model. Ceramic types found on colonial sites are well enough known from documents and kiln site excavations that an approximate beginning and end manufacture date can be assigned to ceramic types within certain limits of variability. Each of these ceramic types is seen to represent a unimodal curve through time as the type was introduced, reached a peak of popularity and then was discontinued. The median date for the ceramic types is the point mid-way through the duration of its period of manufacture. When the median date for a group of ceramic types is known, the types can be arranged so as to represent a chronology based on the median dates. Since such a chronology is based on document-ed duration periods of manufacture it is seen as an historical chronology, not a relative one such as those derived from stratigraphy and seriation on prehistoric sites. In construct-ing such a chronology, ceramic types such as locally made wares of *unknown* manufacture duration periods, or coarse English earthenwares of *unknown* periods of manufacture are not included for the obvious reason that they will contribute nothing to the chronology. If coarse earthenware and local wares of *known* periods of manufacture are present, they are most certainly to be used as valuable additions to the chronology model. From these postulates we can state that British ceramic types can be arranged in an historical chronology on the basis of the median known manufacture date, and this chronology reflects the evolutionary develop-ment of the ceramic forms through time. Colonial French and Spanish ceramics could also be arranged in a similar histori-cal chronology provided the manufacture dates are known for the ceramic types. Once the approximate beginning and end manufacture dates of groups of historic artifact types such as wine bottles, wine glass, tobacco pipes, buttons, etc., are established, these too can be used to construct historical chronologies representing the evolution of form through time that in turn can be used to arrive at the duration of occupation of historic sites.

We can also state an hypothesis involving the horizon concept as defined by Willey and Phillips (1958:31–34). Eighteenth century English ceramics were manufactured in groups of several types at any one point in time, with some types having a shorter manufacture span than others. They were available in several types at the factories and groups of types were exported to British American ports. A limited number of these ceramic types were available on order through agents in Britain or through American outlets. Among those types available to the colonist was Chinese porcelain which took its place along with British ceramic types in the colonial American home. The purchasers of these ceramic types were no farther than a few days or weeks at the most from the remote frontier of the colonies, thus the possibility was present for the rapid distribution of ceramic types over a broad area (Noël Hume 1970:25). This broad and rapid spread of a limited number of ceramic types at any one point in time can be described as a horizon in which the cultural traits are approximately contemporaneous (Willey and Phillips 1958:31–34). Thus eighteenth century historic sites ceramics can be seen to represent a series of horizons in sequence.

Ceramic types of short manufacture duration are excellent temporal markers for determining the approximate brackets for the accumulation of the sample, allowing an interpreta-tion to be made regarding the occupation period of the historic site. Such short-manufacture period types can be used effectively on a presence and absence basis as clues to sample accumulation. An important consideration here is that a ceramic type specimen cannot appear on a site prior to the beginning manufacture date for the type, thus creating a temporal relationship between the manufacture date and the occupation of the site by those who used and broke the ceramic objects.

Regarding broken ceramics we can state a final hypothesis based on several postulates. The cultural use-patterns of the eighteenth century were such that not long after ceramic types arrived in the home in a town or frontier fort, breakage began to occur. The broken ceramic types were discarded and older types broken along with the most recent acquisitions resulted in a number of types becoming associated in the midden deposits. Although a few heirloom pieces would be broken along with a few of the most recent acquisitions, the *majority* of the fragments would represent those *most in use* during the occupation of the site. Those few most recent acquisitions would provide the clue for placing the end date on the deposit using presence-absence. From these postulates we can state that an approximate mean date for the ceramic sample representing occupation of an eighteenth century British American site can be determined through the median manufacture dates for the ceramic types and the frequency of the types in the sample. With these problems in mind we will construct tools for use in ceramic analysis to examine the data.

THE TOOLS

The Chronological Model for Constructing the Analysis Tools

The first step in constructing ceramic analysis tools is to build a chronological model upon which the tools can be based. An excellent example of the potential of historic site data in this regard is the use of hole measurement of tobacco pipestems by Harrington (1954) for arriving at an approxi-mate date of the accumulation of the sample, and the expression of this by Binford (1961) in terms of a regression line formula. The pipestem analysis tool as well as our ceramic analysis tools and other constructions built on a chronological framework are based on the evolution of form through time.

Any unique combination of attributes, constituting a type that becomes extinct, represents a time capsule having a median date that can be fixed as an approximate point in time, provided the beginning and ending dates can be reason-ably determined. If a series of overlapping ceramic types with known median dates can be determined historically and refined archaeologically, we have a temporal scale by which we can fix a collection of ceramic types in time. If this scale is established through occurrence or frequency seriation, as is the case with prehistoric artifact types and classes, the seriation can be viewed as a gross chronology, verifiable only through carefully controlled stratigraphic studies designed to accompany the seriation, or through radiocarbon dating (Dunnell 1970:315). However, if previously dated groups of attributes representing historical stylistic types are used, such as Deetz and Dethlefsen (1966) have done with dated New England gravestones, there is a positive historical chronology involved that provides a more direct rather than a gross framework with which to work. In their study Deetz and Dethlefsen demonstrated variation in time and space because they were dealing with an artifact form that was a locally manufactured folk object. With the present ceramic study, however, a standardized factory product with a known manufacture period is involved, thus eliminating local variation. Therefore, with known historically based typologies such as those found in historical archaeology, a specific chronology can be constructed in a manner not possible on the prehistoric level. Historical archaeologists are only beginning to explore the possibilities offered by this unique quality of their historic site data toward the examination of cultural problems.

Historic site archaeologists have constructed typologies of ceramics based on the references available to them and on their own observation, and these have been dealt with in temporal terms with varying degrees of success. Some have seen the numerous historic types and the accompanying documents as a confusing situation, and one not to be improved by attempts at typology and seriation of historic artifacts (Dollar 1968:14). Meanwhile, others have continued to define the diagnostic criteria for recognition of ceramic types in time and space with emphasis on those attributes of color, surface finish, design, decoration, form, etc., by means of which delineation of types can be accomplished. One of the leaders in the field of English ceramics has been Ivor Noël Hume, Chief Archaeologist at Colonial Williamsburg. Before the publication of his book *A Guide to Artifacts in Colonial America* (1970), he and others were exposed to some criticism for what was seen as a lack of concern for artifact description based on specific criteria (Cleland and Fitting 1968). With the publication of this book, however, it is clear that Noël Hume is concerned with the determination of specific ceramic attributes that have significance in time and space. A book incorporating a definitive typology for English ceramics is still to be written. Meanwhile this book along with basic ceramic references can be used by the archaeologist to acquire an acquaintance with the ceramic types found on British American sites. Noël Hume does not use quantification based on ceramic fragments from archaeological sites, but prefers to use vessel shape along with presence and absence in his analysis. Some of us, on the other hand, have utilized specific attributes of ceramic types as Noël Hume has done, but have added the ingredient of frequency occurrence of the fragments as well as presence and absence.

With the present availability of information regarding ceramic types, both descriptive and temporal, the historical archaeologist should be able to explore the next step. For years to come we will continue to be concerned with description in historical archaeology, as we should be, but we should not lose sight of the fact that this is not the goal, only the means toward attaining the goal. Lewis Binford has quoted Sherwood L. Washburn, a physical anthropologist, in regard to this point:

> The assumption seems to have been that description (whether morphological or metrical), if accurate enough and in sufficient quantity, could solve problems of process, pattern, and interpretation . . . But all that can be done with the initial descriptive information is to gain a first understanding, a sense of problem, and a preliminary classification. To get further requires an elaboration of theory and method along different lines (Binford and Binford 1968:26; after Washburn 1953:714–15).

It is time we began to construct hypotheses and tools with which to deal with historic site data. Descriptive typology, temporally anchored in history is available for a number of classes of historic site artifacts. This descriptive base will be refined as more information becomes available. However, for illustrating the analytical tools in this paper we have confined ourselves to Noël Hume's criteria as seen in *A Guide to Artifacts in Colonial America*, and through personal communication with him and Audrey Noël Hume.

The procedure used to construct the model was to select seventy-eight ceramic types based on attributes of form, decoration, surface finish, hardness, etc., with the temporal dates assigned by Noël Hume for each type. These were given type numbers and classified according to the type of ware (Figure 1), with page numbers following the types discussed in Noël Hume's book. Since Noël Hume has spent a lifetime attempting to define and delimit the attributes and temporal brackets for the manufacture of English ceramic types, his manufacture dates can be assumed to be based on the historical and archaeological documents available to him at the time the book was written. These dates were recently updated in a conference with him. It should be emphasized that in arriving at the median manufacture date Noël Hume's generalized "1770's", was expressed as 1775 for the model, and that he frequently uses "about" and "around" and "c." to indicate that he is generalizing. The variation introduced by our conversion of these qualifying statements as definite dates is seen to be a relatively minor one when we consider the scale of the model we are building. In this study we are dealing with the ceramic types often seen on colonial sites in the English tradition, and comparable chronological models need to be constructed for sites reflecting French or Spanish tradition. This is illustrated by debased Rouen faience (Type 21) which is found on French sites to date around 1755, whereas on English sites it dates some twenty years later (Noël Hume 1970:141), clearly demonstrating the need for separate models for different cultural traditions.

Type 49, decorated delftware, is seen to have a time span of two hundred years (Figure 1). Because of this a median manufacture date of 1650 was assigned for use when the site is obviously of the seventeenth century, and a date of 1750 for use when associated types are from the eighteenth century. This is the only deviation from the true median manufacture date that was used in this study, however, if other types having manufacture duration periods of from 140 to 160 years could be separated into more than one type having shorter temporal brackets the chronology would be considerably refined from that presently known for those types as presently defined. These types are "catch-all" in nature, such as types 26, 39, 49, and 65, and therefore reflect less sensitive temporal data.

The chronology might be extended through the nineteenth century by anyone interested in testing it during those decades, but our study only includes a few nineteenth century types. It should also be kept in mind that additional types can be added by the archaeologist who knows the manufacture dates for such types, and it may well be found that some of the longer time span types can be eliminated from consideration until such time that diagnostic temporal attributes can be determined. Thus the degree of refinement of the model is dependent upon the degree of sophistication of the archaeologist's ceramic knowledge. Because of this it might be argued that the more knowledgeable archaeologist may find he has little use for the analysis tools outlined in this paper. The extent of usefulness of the tools presented here is yet to be determined, but we have found them useful. The archaeologist may well be able to distinguish white salt-glazed stoneware from creamware, pearlware, and "clouded" ware, but not be well acquainted with the manufacture brackets for the types. For such an archaeologist the tools presented in this paper may well assist him in interpreting the occupation period of his historic sites.

A. The Ceramic Types Used to Construct the Analysis Tools

from *A Guide to Artifacts of Colonial America,* (1970) by Ivor Noël Hume

PORCELAIN

TYPE NUMBER	DATE RANGE	MEDIAN DATE	CERAMIC TYPE NAME AND PAGE REFERENCE
5.	c.1800-1830	1815	CANTON PORCELAIN (262).
7.	c.1790-1825	1808	OVERGLAZE ENAMELED CHINA TRADE PORCELAIN (258 and 261).
26.	c.1660-1800	1730	OVERGLAZE ENAMELLED CHINESE EXPORT PORCELAIN (261).
31.	c.1745-1795	1770	ENGLISH PORCELAIN (137).
39.	c.1660-1880	1730	UNDERGLAZE BLUE CHINESE PORCELAIN (257).
41.	c.1750-1765	1758	"LITTLER'S BLUE" (119-23) (ON WHITE SALT-GLAZED STONEWARE, PORCELAIN, AND CREAMWARE).
69.	c.1574-1644	1609	CHINESE PORCELAIN, UNDERGLAZE BLUE, LATE MING (257 and 264).

STONEWARE

BROWN

TYPE NUMBER	DATE RANGE	MEDIAN DATE	CERAMIC TYPE NAME AND PAGE REFERENCE
1.	c.1820-1900+	1860	BROWN STONEWARE BOTTLES FOR INK, BEER, ETC. (78-79).
46.	c.1700-1810	1755	NOTTINGHAM STONEWARE (LUSTERED) (114).
52.	c.1700-1775	1738	BURSLEM "CROUCH" PALE BROWN STONEWARE MUGS.
53.	c.1690-1775	1733	BROWN SALT-GLAZED MUGS (FULHAM) (111-13).
54.	c.1690-1775	1733	BRITISH STONEWARE (EXCLUDING 1, 52, 53) (112-14).
66.	c.1620-1700	1660	DETERIORATED BELLARMINE FACE BOTTLES (ONE DATE EXAMPLE TO THE 1760'S) (56-57).
74.	c.1550-1625	1588	BELLARMINE, BROWN SALT-GLAZED STONEWARE, WELL-MOLDED HUMAN FACE (55-57).
75.	c.1540-1600	1570	RHENISH BROWN-GLAZED SPRIGGED MOULD-DECORATED, COLOGNE TYPE STONEWARE (277-79).

BLUE, GRAY

TYPE NUMBER	DATE RANGE	MEDIAN DATE	CERAMIC TYPE NAME AND PAGE REFERENCE
44.	c.1700-1775	1738	WESTERWALD, STAMPED BLUE FLORAL DEVICES, GEOMETRIC DESIGNS (284-85).
58.	c.1650-1725	1668	SPRIG MOLDING, COMBED LINES, BLUE AND MANGANESE DECORATED RHENISH STONEWARE (280-81).
59.	c.1690-1710	1700	EMBELLISHED HOHR GRAY RHENISH STONEWARE (284).
77.	c.1700-1775	1738	WESTERWALD CHAMBER POTS (148, 281).

WHITE

TYPE NUMBER	DATE RANGE	MEDIAN DATE	CERAMIC TYPE NAME AND PAGE REFERENCE
16.	c.1740-1765	1753	MOULDED WHITE SALT-GLAZED STONEWARE (115).
24.	c.1765-1795	1780	DEBASED "SCRATCH BLUE" WHITE SALT-GLAZED STONEWARE (118).
30.	c.1755-1765	1760	TRANSFER PRINTED WHITE SALT-GLAZED STONEWARE (128).
34.	c.1744-1775	1760	"SCRATCH BLUE" WHITE SALT-GLAZED STONEWARE (117).
40.	c.1720-1805	1763	WHITE SALT-GLAZED STONEWARE (EXCLUDING PLATES AND MOULDED) (115-17).
41.	c.1750-1765	1758	"LITTLER'S BLUE" (119-23) (ON WHITE SALT-GLAZED STONEWARE, PORCELAIN, AND CREAMWARE).
43.	c.1740-1775	1758	WHITE SALT-GLAZED STONEWARE PLATES (115-117).
48.	c.1715-1775	1745	SLIP-DIPPED WHITE SALT-GLAZED STONEWARE (114-15).
55.	c.1720-1730	1725	"SCRATCH BROWN OR TRAILED" WHITE SALT-GLAZED STONEWARE (117).

OTHER

TYPE NUMBER	DATE RANGE	MEDIAN DATE	CERAMIC TYPE NAME AND PAGE REFERENCE
3.	c.1813-1900	1857	IRONSTONE AND GRANITE CHINA (131).
27.	c.1750-1820	1785	"BLACK BASALTES" STONEWARE (121-22).
28.	c.1763-1775	1769	ENGINE-TURNED UNGLAZED RED STONEWARE, (121).
37.	c.1690-1775	1733	REFINED RED STONEWARE, UNGLAZED SPRIGGED (120-21).
50.	c.1732-1750	1741	RALPH SHAW, BROWN, SLIPPED STONEWARE (118-19).

EARTHENWARE

SLIPWARE

TYPE NUMBER	DATE RANGE	MEDIAN DATE	CERAMIC TYPE NAME AND PAGE REFERENCE
56.	c.1670-1795	1733	LEAD GLAZED SLIPWARE (COMBED YELLOW) (107,
63.	c.1650-1710	1680	NORTH DEVON SGRAFFITO.SLIPWARE (104-05).
67.	c.1612-1700	1656	WROTHAM SLIPWARE (103-04).
68.	c.1630-1660	1645	"METROPOLITAN" SLIPWARE (103).
70.	c.1610-1660	1635	RED MARBELIZED SLIPWARE (NORTH ITALIAN (77).
73.	c.1580-1625	1603	WANFRIED SLIPWARE (139).

REFINED

TYPE NUMBER	DATE RANGE	MEDIAN DATE	CERAMIC TYPE NAME AND PAGE REFERENCE
2.	c.1820-1900+	1860	WHITEWARE (130-31).
6.	c.1795-1890	1843	MOCHA (131).
29.	c.1740-1780	1760	"JACKFIELD" WARE (123).
33.	c.1759-1775	1767	GREEN GLAZED CREAM-BODIED WARE (124-25).
36.	c.1740-1770	1755	"CLOUDED" WARES, TORTOISE SHELL, MOTTLED GLAZED CREAM-COLORED WARE (123).
42.	c.1740-1775	1758	REFINED AGATE WARE (132).
51.	c.1725-1750	1738	"ASTBURY" WARE, WHITE SPRIGGED AND TRAILED (123).
78.	c.1790-1840	1815	LUSTER DECORATED WARES.

COARSE

TYPE NUMBER	DATE RANGE	MEDIAN DATE	CERAMIC TYPE NAME AND PAGE REFERENCE
35.	c.1750-1810	1780	COARSE AGATE WARE (EXCLUDING DOOR-KNOBS) (132).
38.	c.1745-1780	1763	IBERIAN STORAGE JARS (143).
47.	c.1720-1775	1746	BUCKLEY WARE (132-33, 135).
61.	c.1650-1775	1713	NORTH DEVON GRAVEL TEMPERED WARE (133).

TIN ENAMELED

TYPE NUMBER	DATE RANGE	MEDIAN DATE	CERAMIC TYPE NAME AND PAGE REFERENCE
21.	c.1775-1800	1788	DEBASED ROUEN FAIENCE (141-42) (c.1755 ON FRENCH SITES).
32.	c.1730-1830	1780	PEDESTAL-FOOTED TYPE DELFT OINTMENT POT (204-05).
45.	c.1700-1800	1750	EVERTED RIM, PLAIN DELFT OINTMENT POT (204-05).
49.	c.1600-1802	(1650) (17th CENT.) (1750) (18th CENT.)	DECORATED DELFTWARE (105-11).
57.	c.1750-1800	1775	PLAIN DELFT WASH BASIN.
60.	c.1710-1740	1725	MIMOSA PATTERN DELFT (108-11).
62.	c.1620-1720	1670	ENGLISH DELFTWARE (BLUE DASH CHARGERS) (108-09).
64.	c.1630-1700	1665	CYLINDRICAL DELFT OINTMENT POTS (109, 203-10).
65.	c.1640-1800	1720	PLAIN WHITE DELFTWARE (109).
71.	c.1620-1775	1698	DELFT APOTHECARY JARS (MONOCHROME).
72.	c.1580-1640	1610	DELFT APOTHECARY JARS AND POTS (POLYCHROME) (203).
76.	c.1660-1800	1730	DELFT CHAMBER POTS (146-47).

CREAMWARE

TYPE NUMBER	DATE RANGE	MEDIAN DATE	CERAMIC TYPE NAME AND PAGE REFERENCE
8.	c.1790-1820	1805	"FINGER PAINTED" WARES (POLYCHROME SLIP ON CREAMWARE OR PEARLWARE) (132).
14.	c.1780-1815	1798	"ANNULAR WARES" CREAMWARE (131).
15.	c.1775-1820	1798	LIGHTER YELLOW CREAMWARE (126-28).
18.	c.1765-1810	1788	OVERGLAZE ENAMELLED HAND PAINTED CREAMWARE.
22.	c.1762-1820	1791	CREAMWARE (125-26).
23.	c.1765-1815	1790	TRANSFER PRINTED CREAMWARE (126-28).
25.	c.1762-1780	1771	DEEPER YELLOW CREAMWARE (126-28).
41.	c.1750-1765	1758	"LITTLER'S BLUE" (119-23) (ON WHITE SALT-GLAZED STONEWARE, PORCELAIN, AND CREAMWARE).

PEARLWARE

TYPE NUMBER	DATE RANGE	MEDIAN DATE	CERAMIC TYPE NAME AND PAGE REFERENCE
4.	c.1820-1840	1830	UNDERGLAZE POLYCHROME PEARLWARE, DIRECTLY STENCILED FLORAL PATTERNS, BRIGHT BLUE, ORANGE, GREEN, PINKISH RED (129).
6.	c.1795-1890	1843	MOCHA (131).
8.	c.1790-1820	1805	"FINGER-PAINTED" WARES (POLYCHROME SLIP ON CREAMWARE OR PEARLWARE) (132).
9.	c.1800-1820	1810	EMBOSSED FEATHERS, FISH SCALES, ETC. ON PEARLWARE (131).
10.	c.1795-1840	1818	"WILLOW" TRANSFER-PATTERN ON PEARLWARE (130).
11.	c.1795-1840	1818	TRANSFER-PRINTED PEARLWARE (128-130).
12.	c.1795-1815	1805	UNDERGLAZE POLYCHROME PEARLWARE (129).
13.	c.1790-1820	1805	"ANNULAR WARES" PEARLWARE (131).
17.	c.1780-1820	1800	UNDERGLAZE BLUE HAND PAINTED PEARLWARE (128-29).
19.	c.1780-1830	1805	BLUE AND GREEN EDGE PEARLWARE (137).
20.	c.1780-1830	1805	UNDERCOATED PEARLWARE.

B. An Application of the Analysis Tools

THE MEAN CERAMIC DATE FORMULA USING PRESENCE—ABSENCE AND FREQUENCY

THE MEAN MANUFACTURE DATE FOR THE GROUP OF COLONIAL ENGLISH CERAMIC TYPES FROM AN HISTORIC SITE TAKING INTO CONSIDERATION THE FREQUENCY OF OCCURRENCE OF FRAGMENTS OF THE TYPES, CAN BE DETERMINED BY A MEAN CERAMIC DATE-FREQUENCY FORMULA AS FOLLOWS:

where the mean ceramic date, Y, is expressed:

$$ Y = \frac{\sum\limits_{t=1}^{n} x_i \cdot f_i}{\sum\limits_{t=1}^{n} f_i} $$

where
- x_i = the median date for the manufacture of each ceramic type
- f_i = the frequency of each ceramic type
- n = the number of ceramic types in the sample

BRUNSWICK TOWN, NORTH CAROLINA RUIN 57

CERAMIC TYPE	TYPE MEDIAN (x_i)	SHERD COUNT (f_i)	PRODUCT ($x_i \cdot f_i$)
22	1791	483	43953
33	1767	25	1675
26	1730	62	1860
34	1760	32	1920
36	1755	55	3025
37	1733	40	1320
43	1758	327	18966
49	(1750)	583	29150
44	1738	40	1520
47	1748	28	1344
39	1730	241	7230
53, 54	1733	52	1716
56	1733	286	9438
29	1760	9	540
		2263	123657 ÷ 2263 (+ 1700) = 1754.6

HISTORIC DATES: 1734-1776   MEAN CERAMIC DATE: 1754.6
HISTORIC MEDIAN DATES: 1755   PIPESTEMDATE: 1756

NOTE: SINCE THIS CHART WAS PREPARED IT HAS BEEN FOUND THAT A MORE ACCURATE DATE CAN BE OBTAINED BY NOT USING TYPES 26 AND 39 WITH THE FORMULA.

C. The Marker-Type Model

THROUGH PRESENCE AND ABSENCE OF MARKER TYPES ON APPROXIMATE BEGINNING AND END, DATA CAN BE ASSIGNED TO THE ARCHAEOLOGICAL SAMPLE.

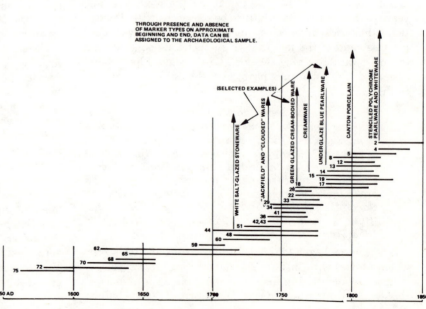

FIGURE 1. Ceramic Analysis Tools for Eighteenth Century Colonial English Sites

D. Application of the Analysis Tools

The Ceramic Analysis Data from Eleven Sites Using Interpretive Occupation Brackets, Presence and Absence, and the Mean Ceramic Data Formula Compared to the Documented Site Occupation Period.

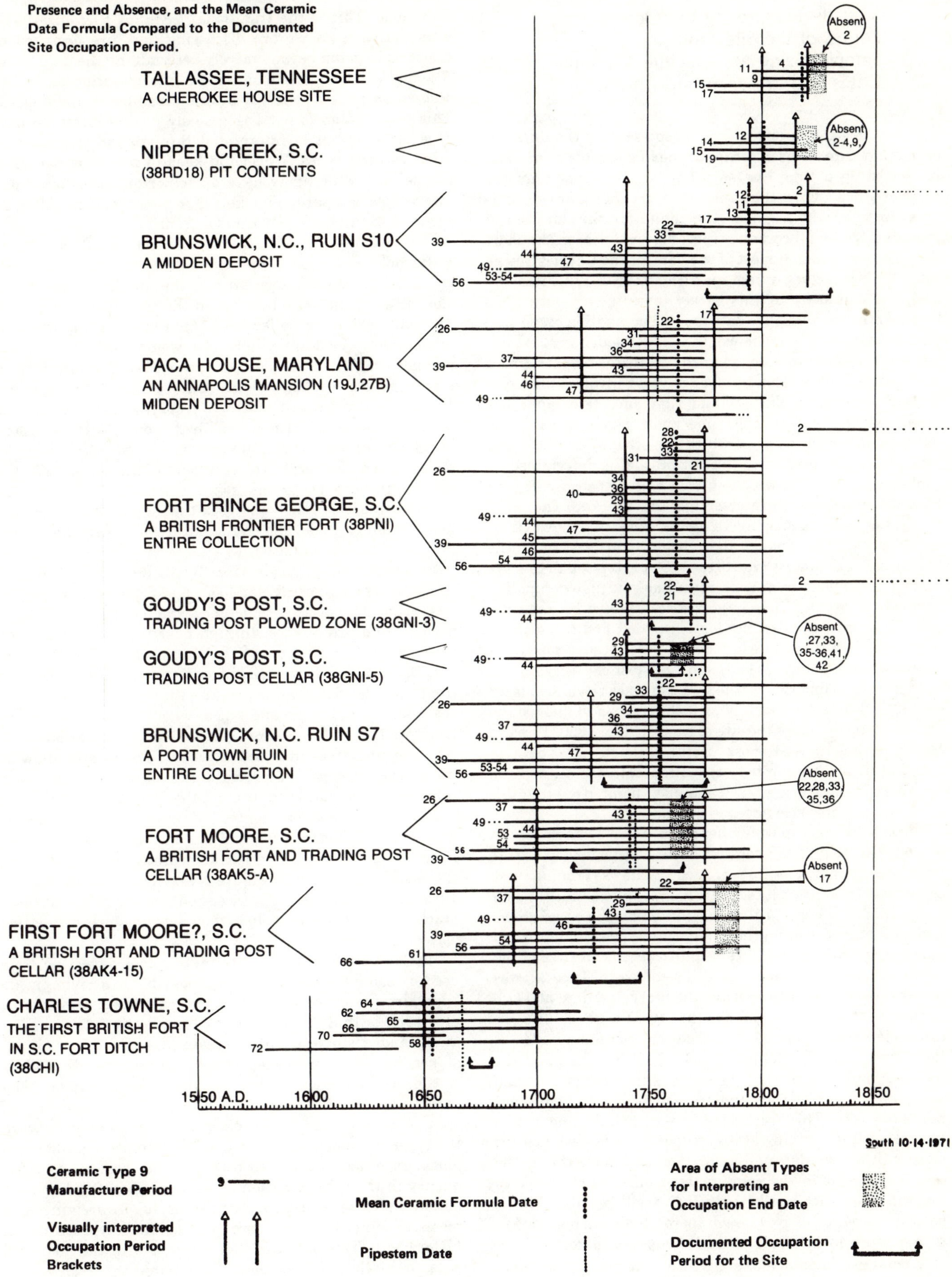

TALLASSEE, TENNESSEE
A CHEROKEE HOUSE SITE
NIPPER CREEK, S.C.
(38RD18) PIT CONTENTS
BRUNSWICK, N.C., RUIN S10
A MIDDEN DEPOSIT
PACA HOUSE, MARYLAND
AN ANNAPOLIS MANSION (19J,27B)
MIDDEN DEPOSIT
FORT PRINCE GEORGE, S.C.
A BRITISH FRONTIER FORT (38PNI)
ENTIRE COLLECTION
GOUDY'S POST, S.C.
TRADING POST PLOWED ZONE (38GNI-3)
GOUDY'S POST, S.C.
TRADING POST CELLAR (38GNI-5)
BRUNSWICK, N.C. RUIN S7
A PORT TOWN RUIN
ENTIRE COLLECTION
FORT MOORE, S.C.
A BRITISH FORT AND TRADING POST
CELLAR (38AK5-A)
FIRST FORT MOORE?, S.C.
A BRITISH FORT AND TRADING POST
CELLAR (38AK4-15)
CHARLES TOWNE, S.C.
THE FIRST BRITISH FORT
IN S.C. FORT DITCH
(38CHI)
Absent 2
Absent 2-4,9,
Absent ,27,33, 35-36,41, 42
Absent 22,28,33, 35,36
Absent 17
1550 A.D.
1600
1650
1700
1750
1800
1850
South 10-14-1971
Ceramic Type 9 Manufacture Period
Visually interpreted Occupation Period Brackets
Mean Ceramic Formula Date
Pipestem Date
Area of Absent Types for Interpreting an Occupation End Date
Documented Occupation Period for the Site

FIGURE 1. Continued

Visually Interpreting the Occupation Period of the Site From a Sample Using Manufacture Duration Dates and Presence and Absence.

Once the unimodal curve representing the duration of manufacture for each ceramic type in a sample from a site is plotted on a time line as a bar, and the type bars are arranged one above the other in a graphic manner, it is possible to see at a glance the limits for the duration of manufacture for all ceramic types. For instance, on the chart (Figure 1) we see that most of the bars for the Charles Towne Site (38CH1) include a time span from 1580 to 1725. Immediately we can see that this surely indicates a relationship between the manufacture date and the occupation of the site. To demonstrate otherwise would take some doing. However, we are interested in narrowing the temporal bracket, and a method used by us for a number of years involves placing a vertical bracket to the left and right on the ceramic bar graph, with the resulting time span between being the *interpreted* period inside of which the occupation of the site took place. The placing of the left bracket is determined by choosing the point at which at least half of the ceramic type bars are touching or intersecting the bracket. The right bracket is placed generally using the same rule, however, it must be placed far enough to the right to at least touch the beginning of the latest type present. An exception to this are surface collections from sites revealing multiple occupation periods as revealed in a gap or discontinuity between the ceramic bars of the first occupation period and those of the later period. In such cases brackets for both occupations must be placed (see Goudy's, GN3, and Fort Prince George, PN1, in Figure 1). Using this method we can place the brackets for site 38CH1 at 1650 and 1700, which happens to include the known historic date of the site of from 1670 to 1680. This is a tool that has proved most useful through the years in arriving at an interpreted occupation date for a site from ceramics from historic sites. It should be pointed out that this is entirely a presence-absence approach.

The time period can be further narrowed in some instances by consideration of the ceramic types conspicuously *absent* from the sample. For instance, the Goudy's Trading Post cellar hole from site 38GN1−5 (Figure 1) has a bracket date range from 1740 to 1775, which can be narrowed when we realize that absent from the sample are types manufactured during the 1750's and 1760's usually present on sites of the 1760's (Types 27, 33−36, 41, 42). If creamware (Type 22) was present, we would have to leave the bracketed date at 1775. In the absence of it as well as other types of the 1760's, we can assign an occupation date from approximately 1740 to the early 1760's for the cellar hole. This matches well the historical information that the site was occupied in 1751 and was attacked by Cherokee Indians and most of the buildings burned in 1760. This bracketing from ceramics alone is seen to work well in arriving at an occupation period for historic sites with known dates of occupation, and since this is the case we have it in the same manner on sites of unknown historic dates, such as Cherokee Indian village sites. This is basically a *terminus post quem* approach also using marker type *absence* to interpret an end occupation date.

A point we should make clear here is that in a sealed archaeological deposit the beginning manufacture date for the latest type present gives us a date after which the deposit was made. This is the traditional *terminus post quem*. The interpretive tools we are discussing here are designed to assist us in going beyond merely determining the date of the fill, and allowing us to make an interpretation as to the *occupation period* reflected by the ceramics in the deposit. This information is not based solely on the latest ceramic type present, but is interpreted through the frequency of other ceramic types. We should keep in mind the nature of the deposit, which may have an important bearing on our interpreted occupation brackets. For instance, if the fill is an accumulation of midden thrown from a house over a long period of time we would expect a different result than if the cellar hole was filled at one moment in time using soil and refuse collected from other areas of the site. In the latter case the fill would have no bearing on the structure represented by that particular cellar hole. However, our interpreted occupation period in either case would be based on the ceramic fragments in hand, and whether they are from a single feature, a combination of features, a cellar hole, or are the sum of every sherd recovered from the ruin site (such as is the case with the Brunswick Town and Fort Prince George samples), an *interpreted* occupation period *represented by the sample* will emerge. The judgment of the archaeologist is important here as to the significance of the interpreted occupation period. The validity of the interpreted occupation period would still depend on the nature of the archaeological data on which it is based.

On sites such as Brunswick Town, Fort Prince George, Goudy's Trading Post, Fort Moore and Charles Towne there has been little occupation since the eighteenth century period use of these sites. In high density urban occupation areas there may well be continuous occupation to the present. Because of this it would be necessary to isolate features from high density sites and deal with these so as to reduce the effect of later ceramic types, whereas on sites such as Brunswick, Fort Moore, Fort Prince George, etc., every sherd from the site can be included in our sample and still allow an interpreted occupation period relative to the eighteenth century. We should keep in mind the fact that in discussing *occupation periods* represented by ceramics we are dealing with cultural generalities and not historical specifics. For instance our occupation periods interpreted from ceramics as revealed on the chart in Figure 1 vary from fifteen years in duration to eighty years, but we should also notice that these brackets most often *do* include the known historic occupation period for the sites.

Similar versions of this interpretive tool have long been used by some historic site archaeologists for arriving at an approximate occupation period for their sites. However, a drawback is that it does not take frequency into consideration, and a single sherd of creamware (Type 22), for instance, has the same weight as five hundred sherds of white salt-glazed stoneware in determining the approximate temporal range for the sample. Consideration of frequency of occurrence would certainly place the relationship between the types in a more valid perspective than presence-absence alone. In order to consider both presence-absence and frequency in the determination of our approximate occupation period we have devised a formula useful in arriving at a mean ceramic date for a group of ceramic types from an historic site. This date can then be used with the historical data, or with *terminus post quem* dates to arrive at an interpreted occupation period represented by the sample. This date can also be compared with mean pipestem dates, as well as with other artifact data to arrive at an interpretation of the site occupation period.

The Mean Ceramic Date Formula Using Presence-Absence and Frequency.

The mean manufacture date for the group of British ceramic types from an eighteenth century historic site taking into consideration the frequency of occurrence of fragments of the types, can be determined by a mean ceramic date-frequency formula as follows:

The mean ceramic date, Y, is expressed:

$$Y = \frac{\sum\limits_{i=1}^{n} X_i \cdot f_i}{\sum\limits_{i=1}^{n} f_i}$$

Where X_i = the median date for the manufacture of each ceramic type

f_i = the frequency of each ceramic type

n = the number of ceramic types in the sample

The median manufacture date for each ceramic type in the sample is determined from the documents, and in this study we have derived this from the book by Noël Hume (1970), and through personal communication with him. This information is seen in the list of ceramic types in Figure 1. In order to use the formula the sherd count for each type is placed in a column beside the median date and these are multiplied, producing a third column, which is a product of the median date times the frequency of occurrence. The sum of the frequency column is divided into the sum of the product column, producing the mean ceramic date for the sample. Although this frequency-adjusted manufacture date might be assumed not to have anything to do with the occupation date for an historic site, we will see that there is a remarkable degree of similarity between the mean ceramic date derived from use of the formula and the historically known median occupation date of the eighteenth century historic sites on which it has been used.

Note: Before proceeding to use the formula the reader should also read my later paper in this forum in which it is recommended that Types 26 and 39, Chinese Porcelain, not be included. By eliminating these types from use in the formula a more accurate mean ceramic date is obtained.

APPLICATION OF THE TOOLS

Applicability

The beauty of the Binford (1961) and the Hanson (1971) formulas for dating tobacco pipestems is the fact that anyone can pick up a set of drills and proceed to measure a sample and arrive at a mean pipestem bore size from which a mean date for the accumulation of the sample can be deter-

mined. The mean ceramic date formula is not as easily applied since the user must know something about British ceramic types before he can determine a mean ceramic date from a group of types. If he has little understanding of the attributes for separating the seventy-eight types used in the model he will not get far in arriving at a meaningful mean ceramic date from the formula. For the formula to be used, therefore, a knowledge of ceramic types is necessary, which can be learned from the many references available. This reference work must be combined with a familiarity with the archaeological specimens. A knowledge of the ceramic type attributes cannot be overemphasized for there are far too many meaningless descriptions appearing in the historic site literature now in spite of the availability of numerous excellent sources to act as guides for learning. It is totally meaningless to describe a ceramic type as being "Whieldon-ware or Rockingham ware" (Harris 1971:67), types with a source of origin separated by the Atlantic Ocean and one hundred years in time. Historical archaeology is plagued by reports revealing no interpretation of any kind, historical, anthropological, cultural, or archaeological to justify a catalog type publication of objects. To use the mean ceramic date formula, therefore, there is no easy way out. The archaeologist should have more than a passing knowledge of the ceramic types with which he deals. Some archaeologists may prefer to deal primarily with a *terminus post quem* date for a deposit, and feel they have no need for a median date such as the formula provides. Others may find it useful in the interpretation of site occupation periods.

The Sample

The size of the sample cannot always be controlled by the archaeologist due to the fact that only seven sherds may be recovered from a feature from which he wishes to apply his ceramic analysis tools. He should remember, however, that a sample of that size would be somewhat less reliable than one of a much larger size. The nature of the sample would most certainly also have a bearing on the date that results from any interpretive analysis of the ceramics. For instance, a sloppily excavated cellar hole where poor contextual control was maintained by the archaeologist might contain fragments of creamware or ironstone that fell into the hole during excavation from layers outside the actual contents of the cellar fill, or were carelessly thrown into the bag by an irresponsible worker. These fragments would require a much later date to be assigned to the feature than would have been the case had these one or two fragments been allowed to intrude upon the sample from the context of the cellar. The importance of tight provenience control in the field cannot be overemphasized (unless the reasons for the control are not understood by the practitioner and an unnecessarily expensive and fruitless nit-picking approach is used to no effectual end, as is too frequently witnessed on historic sites). A large, tightly controlled sample is desirable, regardless of the length of time a site was occupied. In the absence of a large sample, however, the tools described here can still be used by the reliability might naturally be expected to be less.

Instead of the frequency occurrence based on individual sherds by ceramic type as we have done in this study, quantification by type and shape could as well be used, and in some instances where shape is a sensitive attribute, a more refined temporal bracket may result. It is through an analysis of shape (teacups, saucers, plates, platters, mugs, etc.) that this writer feels that certain sensitive cultural differences may be reflected. Our present study is concerned, however, with ceramic type analysis as a reflector of the occupation period of historic sites.

Noël Hume has provided us with a frequency tabulation for the ceramic types from the Trebell Site Cellar (TS 807C) by object and by sherd count. With a cellar fill date of c.1810, and a construction date of c.1769, based on creamware, the median date should be around 1790. The documents indicate a probable occupation period from 1768 to 1826, with a median date of 1797. Using both sets of data with the formula we obtain a mean ceramic date of 1780.5 using the object count and 1788.9 using the sherd count. This would tend to point to a more accurate formula date using sherd count than when an object count is used.

The Technique of Application

The Visual Bracketing Tool to Historic Site Ceramic Samples. In Figure 1 eleven sites have been plotted with the following information graphically shown. The duration of manufacture of each ceramic type has been plotted as a bar against a time line. The known historic occupation period is plotted as a heavy horizontal bar with arrows indicating the approximate beginning and end dates as determined from the documents. The visual bracket for the interpretive occupation period of the site is plotted as two vertical lines that touch at least half of the ceramic type bars on both ends. The mean ceramic date for the site sample derived from the use of the ceramic date formula is plotted as a vertical line of large dots, with the pipestem date represented as a vertical line of small dots. The influence of absent ceramic types within a zone where they are usually found on historic sites is plotted as a shaded area of dots. This allows the interpreted occupation date to be narrowed in some cases.

The Mean Ceramic Date Formula to Historic Site Ceramic Samples. An example of this process is illustrated by unit S7 in the ruined town of Brunswick, North Carolina. This ruin was a stone-lined cellar located on lot 71 in Brunswick (South 1959). The records reveal that the structure was probably standing by 1734, and was burned in 1776. The collection of ceramic material from the entire ruin was used as the sample. The historic date would bracket the period from 1734 to 1776, with a median historic date of 1755.

(Coded by subtracting 1700 from the Type Median)

Ceramic Type	Type Median	(X_i) (X_i-1700)	Sherd Count (f_i)	Product
22	1791	91	483	43953
33	1767	67	25	1675
26	1730	30	62	1860
34	1760	60	32	1920
36	1755	55	55	3025
37	1733	33	40	1320
43	1758	58	327	18966
49	(1750)	50	583	29150
44	1738	38	40	1520
47	1748	48	28	1344
39	1730	30	241	7230
53,54	1733	33	52	1716
56	1733	33	286	9438
29	1760	60	9	540
			2263	123657

$$= \sum_{i=1}^{n} X_i \cdot f_i$$

This mean ceramic date formula

$$Y = \frac{\sum\limits_{i=1}^{n} X_i \cdot f_i}{\sum\limits_{i=1}^{n} f_i}$$

$$Y = \frac{123657}{2263} + 1700 = 1754.6$$

It is interesting to note that the mean ceramic date derived from the formula is the same as the known median historic date for the ruin. As we will see, this appears to be more than a coincidence. The pipestem date for this ruin using the Binford formula (1961) is 1756, revealing an interesting correlation between historic, ceramic, and pipestem dates.

Ceramic Analysis of Samples from Historic Sites

Charles Towne (38CH1): The First English Fortification in South Carolina. Each of the eleven sites on the chart Figure 1(D) can be discussed to reveal various aspects seen in refining a temporal bracket for the occupation of a site through ceramics using the methods outlined here. Our discussion will follow the chronological chart from bottom to top Figure 1(D), beginning with the fortification ditch dug by the first Charles Towne settlers in South Carolina in 1670, and abandoned by 1680, provided a median historic date of 1675. The bracketing tool reveals a date from 1650 to 1700, which includes the historic occupation period. Attempting to narrow this date by means of the mean ceramic date formula produces a date of 1654.4 some twenty-one years prior to the known historic median date. This difference may well reflect our present knowledge of the ceramic types from which the mean date was derived. It may also reflect a time lag by the latest items not being present in the households at Charles Towne when the first settlers arrived in 1670. This gap may also relate to the fact that far more references are available to leather and wooden trenchers being in the town than ceramics revealing, perhaps, less daily use of ceramic items and thus less breakage (South 1971 MS). In this case the breakage that did occur would reveal a greater time lag than is seen on eighteenth century sites where ceramics came into more daily use and breakage. This hypothesis needs to be checked by the use of the mean ceramic date formula on more seventeenth century sites of known occupation dates. This time lag may well be found to be a factor present on any seventeenth century site, in which case the formula can be altered to take this into consideration once enough data is at hand from seventeenth century sites. The pipestem date from this feature is also too early, being 1667 (Hanson 1971:2), again possibly reflecting a true time-lag situation with artifacts in the seventeenth century. From this site we see an exception to the high reliability seen in the use of the mean ceramic date formula on sites of the eighteenth century. Noël Hume has pointed out that on seventeenth century sites of the wealthy class he has found many ceramic types represented, with little time lag being evident, whereas on the ruins of the less affluent there are definitely fewer ceramic types present, thus revealing a socioeconomic distinction not seen to exist on sites of the eighteenth century (Noël Hume personal communication).

The First Fort Moore? (38AK4−15): An Eighteenth Century Frontier Fort and Trading Post. The second site is a cellar hole of a timber and clay structure with a clay chimney, located on the bank of the Savannah River at the historic site of Fort Moore, South Carolina. The first Fort Moore was built in 1716, and a second one was ordered built in 1747 with the site going into private hands in 1766. This site was excavated during the summer of 1971 by Richard Polhemus, Assistant Archaeologist of the Institute of Archaeology and Anthropology at the University of South Carolina. Using the bracketing method we can see that the site was likely occupied between 1700 and 1775. The mean ceramic date formula produces a date of 1726.1, not far from the historic median date for the first Fort Moore of 1732. The presence of creamware (Type 22) (two sherds in the top layer of the cellar), but the absence of pearlware (Type 17), does not allow us to narrow the date bracket using absence (shaded area of the graph). The Hanson pipestem formula produces a date of 1730.9. These early dates within the known historic range for the occupation of the first Fort Moore allow us to interpret this cellar and this area of the site as likely that for the first Fort Moore. Even though creamware is present in the top layer of fill, providing us with a *terminus post quem* date for the final *filling of the cellar*, the frequency of types of the earlier period is such that a first Fort Moore *period of occupation* is interpreted as being represented by the ceramic sample.

Fort Moore (38AK5−A): An Eighteenth Century Frontier Fort and Trading Post. One hundred yards away from the cellar just discussed another cellar of the same type of construction was excavated some years ago, and the material from this cellar is stored at the Institute of Archaeology and Anthropology at the University of South Carolina. The bottom two feet of this cellar fill was used in the ceramic analysis, which contained the large majority of the ceramics present. The bracketing bars reveal a likely date of 1700 to 1775 for the occupation of the site. However, the fact that there is an absence of types 22, 28, 33, 35, and 36, usually seen on sites of the 1760's and 70's, this range can be narrowed to include the period from 1700 to the early 1760's. The mean ceramic date formula produced a date of 1741.7 and the pipestem date was 1744.16. The mean ceramic date is virtually the same as the known median historic date of 1741 for the occupation of Fort Moore from 1716 to 1766.

From the use of the bracketing and mean ceramic date tools on the Fort Moore site it was possible to separate a ceramic sample from a cellar likely representing the entire occupation of Fort Moore, from a cellar with a ceramic sample interpreted as representing the occupation period of the first Fort Moore. An interesting point here is that the cellar having the earliest mean ceramic date has creamware present in the fill, whereas the cellar without creamware has a later mean ceramic date, the reverse of what one might interpret from presence-absence alone. This illustrates the potential value of the mean ceramic date in such instances, particularly when supported by the same relationship between the pipestem dates as seen here. This does not mean we ignore the *terminus post quem* date indicated by creamware for the final *fill of the cellar*. It does mean that we are giving consideration to the *mass* of the ceramics rather than to the latest type on the sample (perhaps represented by a single sherd), when it comes to interpreting the major *occupation period* represented by the collection.

Brunswick Town, North Carolina (S7): A Colonial English Port Town. We have discussed this ruin previously and found the historic median to be 1755, the mean ceramic date to be 1754.6, and the mean pipestem date to be 1756. Other Brunswick Town ruins demonstrate the following comparison between the historic median and the ceramic formula mean:

S15	historic median date	1751.0
	ceramic formula date	1746.4
	pipestem date	1748.9
N1	historic median date	1754.0
	ceramic formula date	1750.1
S2	historic median date	1754.0
	ceramic formula date	1749.0
	pipestem date	1748.0
S18	historic median date	1769.5
	ceramic formula date	1776.2
	pipestem date	1756

Large samples, such as those from Brunswick Town are particularly desirable for use with the mean ceramic date formula (see tables in Appendix).

Goudy's Trading Post at Fort Ninety Six, South Carolina (38GN1−3 and 38GN1−5). Goudy's Trading Post at Ninety Six, South Carolina, was begun in 1751 and was attacked and burned in 1760. Preliminary excavation revealed a small cellar hole with some eighteenth century objects in the top surface of the fill. The cellar is yet to be excavated. Only four ceramic types and a total of seven sherds were recovered, but these were used to attempt to date the deposit using the tools under discussion here. The median historic date is 1756, with a mean ceramic date of 1754.6, an impressive match using only seven sherds. However, without the known historic date we can establish a duration using our bracketing tool of from around 1740 to 1775. In the absence of types 27, 33−36, 41, 42 (representing the types likely to be present if the sample dated from the 1760's), and also using the mean ceramic formula date of 1754.6, we could say that the deposit represents an approximate date range of from around 1744 to the early 1760's, impressively close to our 1751 to 1760 historic data. We have arrived at this date using the ceramic analysis tools here under discussion, and not our historic data.

The surface layer and plowed soil zone of Goudy's Trading Post site revealed creamware, which was absent from the cellar hole sample. This sample was designated 38GN1−3, and has an historic occupation date of unknown length after the first occupation of 1751 and the fire of 1760. From the mean ceramic date formula we determine a date of 1769.3, and with this and our known beginning date of 1751 as half of our date range, we can conjecture a date from 1751 to around 1787 for the period represented by the sample, since *if we know the mean date and one end* we can interpret the approximate position of the opposite bracket. It should be noted that one sherd of whiteware was found on the site in the plowed soil (Type 2), and because of the absence of pearlwares, this clearly reveals a disconformity between it and the other ceramic types, reflecting a post 1820 occupation and not a continuous one.

Fort Prince George, South Carolina (38PN1): A British Military Post on the Cherokee Frontier. Fort Prince George was built by Governor Glen of South Carolina in 1753, and the last reference to it is in 1768 when it was abandoned. The median historic date is 1761. The site was dug by John Combes, Assistant Director of the Institute of Archaeology and Anthropology, University of South Carolina. The ceramic sample includes all sherds recovered from the entire site. From the bracketing technique of the ceramic type bars we arrive at a date of around 1745 to 1775 for the site. The mean ceramic date formula reveals a mean date of 1763.0, and the pipestem date is 1750.14 (Hanson 1971:2). In this case the mean ceramic formula date is much closer to the median date for the site than is the pipestem date. Without the known historic date we might take our interpreted end date of 1775 and the mean ceramic formula date of 1763, and conjecture a date bracket of from 1751 to 1775, again not far removed from the known occupation of 1753 to 1768.

The Paca House, Annapolis, Maryland (19J,27B): A Town House Mansion. The Paca House was built in 1763 by William Paca, signer of the Declaration of Independence, and is still standing and in the process of being restored. Archaeological work was carried out there in 1967 by this writer (through a contract with Contract Archaeology, Inc.) and two eighteenth century midden deposits were discovered still relatively undisturbed (South 1967 MS). These were combined for this analysis. The median historic date for the sample is not known, but the context in which the midden was found indicates that it was among the earliest midden thrown from the house after it was constructed in 1763. The presence of creamware and one piece of pearlware, however, indicate that the midden received material at least as late as the 1780's. The mean ceramic formula date for the deposit is 1763.1. The left and right bracketing lines fall at 1720 and 1780, and using the mean ceramic date of 1763, we can narrow our interpreted date range to 1748 to 1780.

The Dump at Brunswick Town (S10). Nath Moore's Front in Brunswick Town (ruin S10) was burned in 1776 (South 1958) and the interior of the stone foundation wall for the cellar was used as a garbage dump for some years afterward, in fact, judging from the whiteware present it was used into the 1830's. The last reference to anyone living in Brunswick was in the early 1830's. The median historic date for the dump would be 1803. Using the vertical brackets we arrive at a date of from 1740 to 1820. The mean ceramic date is found to be 1794.0, not too far from the historic median date of 1803. An interesting feature of this ceramic profile is the continuation of the overlapping ceramic type-bars throughout the period of the Revolution into the early decades of the nineteenth century.

The Nipper Creek Site (38RD18). No historical information is available on this pit, which was located in a bulldozed area of an Archaic Indian site. The brackets point to a short time span from 1795 to 1815, with a mean ceramic formula date of 1801.3. The absence of types of the 1815–35 period indicate that this ceramic sample can be interpreted as representing an occupation period from around 1795 to about 1810.

Tallassee A Nineteenth Century Cherokee Indian?: House Site in Tennessee. The historic information available on this site indicates that it was transferred from Indian to White hands in the early nineteenth century. Other than this no information is available, except that a quantity of Cherokee ceramic types were found associated with the house ruin, suggesting possible Indian occupants.

The mean ceramic formula date was found to be 1818.1. In

Table 1. COMPARATIVE TABLE OF CERAMIC ANALYSIS DATA

Site	Historical Date Range	Bar Graph Date Range	Historical Median Date	Mean Ceramic Formula Date	Years Away From Historical Median With Quantification	Pipestem Date	Formula Date Without Quantification	Years Away From Historical Median Without Quantification	Site Name
38CH1	1670–1680	1650–1685	1675	1654	(21)	1667	1661	(14)	Charles Towne
38AK4-15	1716–1747	1725–1775	1732	1726	(6)	1731	1736	(4)	1st Ft. Moore
38AK5-A	1716–1766	1725–1775	1741	1742	(1)	1744	1738	(3)	Ft. Moore
S7	1734–1776	1740–1775	1755	1755	(0)	1756	1749	(6)	Brunswick
38GN1-5	1751–1760	1745–1775	1756	1755	(1)	—	1752	(4)	Goudy's Post
38GN1-3	1751– ?	1740–1775	—	1769		—			Goudy's Post
38PN1	1753–1768	1740–1775	1761	1763	(2)	1750	1755	(6)	Ft. Prince (George)
Paca (19J,28B)	1763– ?	1750–1780	—	1763		1753			Paca House
S10	1776–1830	1740–1820	1803	1794	(9)	—	1773	(30)	Bruns. Dump
38RD18	?	1795–1805	?	1801		—			Nipper Creek
Tallassee	c.1800–?	1800–1815	?	1818		—			Tallassee
S18	1763–1776	1740–1775	1770	1776	(6)	1751	1753	(17)	Brunswick
S15	1726?–1776	1740–1775	1751?	1746	(5)	1748	1755	(4)	Brunswick
N1	1731–1776	1740–1775	1754	1750	(4)	—	1746	(8)	Brunswick
S2	1731–1776	1740–1775	1754	1749	(5)	1748	1757	(3)	Brunswick
38PN4	18th Cent.	1750–1775	?	1750		1748			Rock Turtle
38OC3	18th Cent.	1725–1780	?	1736		—			Toxaway
					(39)			(85)	

Average Years From Historical Median With Quantification   (4)

Average Years From Historical Median Without Quantification   (8) the absence of type 2 we would interpret a date bracket of from 1800 to 1820 as the likely range for the occupation represented by the sample.

Additional Cherokee Indian Village Sites Not Shown in Figure 1 The Rock Turtle Site (38PN4): An Eighteenth Century Indian Village Site. One hundred yards from the site of Fort Prince George a Cherokee Indian village site (38PN4) was tested, and revealed ceramic types producing a mean ceramic formula date of 1749.7, and a Hanson pipestem date of 1756.36. There is no historic data associated with the site other than its close association with Fort Prince George and the eighteenth century Cherokee Town site of Keowee.

Toxaway (38OC3): An Eighteenth Century Cherokee Indian Village Site. This Indian village site was excavated by John Combes some years ago. The absence of creamware, and the presence of pearlware and nineteenth century stoneware clearly reveal a nineteenth century occupation distinct from the eighteenth century occupation represented by white salt-glazed stoneware and combed yellow slipware. For this reason two dates were determined for this site. This is an excellent example of two occupation periods clearly revealed through the absence of a major ceramic type, in this case, creamware. If creamware were present there would be no archaeological justification for separation the ceramic groups for obtaining separate mean ceramic dates since there would be a continuous sequence of types represented.

A Discussion of the Reliability of the Ceramic Analysis Tools. The measure of the reliability of the temporal bracketing and mean ceramic formula analysis tools is the degree of correlation between the interpreted dates and the known historic dates for the particular site. Prehistorians do not have such a readily available check on their chronologies and seriations. As we have seen with the individual samples from various historic sites the bracketing and mean ceramic tools, along with presence-absence consideration, allows a relatively high percentage of correlation between the interpreted and the historically known dates. Table 1 illustrates the comparison between the *historical bracket* and *median date*, and the *visual bracketing tool* and the *mean ceramic formula date* for those sites in this study, with a detailed tabulation in the Appendix. The correlation between the historical median date for a site and the mean ceramic formula date is seen to be quite high in most instances. What is needed now is more application of the tools to determine the limits of reliability on a broader time and space frame of reference.

To judge the role of quantification in the mean ceramic date formula between the known historical median date and the formula date, we substituted the frequency of one for each of the ceramic types and thereby nullified the effect of quantification on the date derived from the formula. This reduced the formula to a presence-absence tool, and by comparing the date thus determined with the ceramic formula date, we can see which is closer to the historical median. This comparison can be seen on the chart in Table 1. This reveals a slight advantage in reliability when using quantification as opposed to presence-absence along. This advantage can be seen by comparing the number of years away from the historical median are the formula dates *with* frequency and *without* frequency being considered. Using frequency only one date is as much as nine years from the known historical median for the occupation of the site, whereas without considering frequency two of the ten sites are seventeen and thirty years distant from the known historical median. The average deviation from the historical median date using frequency is only four years, whereas the average deviation

without consideration of frequency is eight years, or twice that when frequency is considered. Our conclusion from this is that frequency consideration appears to have a refinement advantage over presence-absence when used with the mean ceramic date formula.

From this average four years variation from the known historic median occupation for the ten eighteenth century sites in this study we can make an additional refinement of our mean ceramic date. We can now state that when frequency is considered, the mean ceramic date derived can be followed by an average deviation of *plus or minus four years* on sites of the eighteenth century. As the ceramic collection from a larger number of sites are examined with this formula, this plus or minus factor can be refined as the data indicates. Without using frequency by type, thus utilizing the formula strictly on a presence-absence basis, a plus or minus eight years should be added to the mean ceramic date thus derived. The number of plus or minus years may well be found to vary by area as groups of sites are tested using this formula. Such variation may be found to reflect areal cultural variation within the broader cultural horizon.

We will now look at the one seventeenth century site represented in this study, the Charles Towne fortification ditch (38CH1). The deviation here between the known median date of 1675 and the ceramic formula dates with and without frequency considered is 21 and 14 years respectively. This is a dramatic contrast to the ten eighteenth century sites for which the median historical manufacture dates are known. At present this gap seems to be a result of possibly two factors, lack of knowledge of seventeenth century ceramic types and manufacture dates, and a possible status factor. Noël Hume has found seventeenth century upper class mansions have more ceramics represented than do the lower class homes of that period, but has not found this to be so in the eighteenth century (Noël Hume 1970:25; and personal communication). This writer thinks that the lower class seventeenth century homes may well have had a greater time lag represented in ceramics than there was in the mansions. This is not seen, however, as a lag resulting from less "broad and rapid spread" of ceramic types but from the greater nonfunctional status role played by ceramics within the lower class seventeenth century household. The rapid distribution of ceramics from factory to British American ports, and the subsequent journey to the frontier is seen to result in the horizon phenomenon in both the seventeenth and eighteenth century periods. This will probably best be demonstrated through analysis of ceramics from the more affluent seventeenth century homes, but such a status difference is yet to be demonstrated through ceramics from eighteenth century British American sites. On the eighteenth century sites included in this study the high percentage of correlation between the mean ceramic manufacture date derived from the formula and the historic median date for the occupation of the site is seen as a clear demonstration of the horizon phenomenon.

In instances where we might have wanted more precision in our tool we can sometimes see a possible explanation in terms of a small sample. The Paca House midden for example had only 46 sherds, and a probable historical range for the deposit of from 1763 to around 1780 when the house was sold to a new owner, producing a median date of around 1771, some eight years later than the formula date of 1763 plus or minus four years. However, if no historical date were available our slightly "too early" mean ceramic date would still be only eight years away from the actual date.

It is hoped that more such formulas will be forthcoming with which to deal with historic site data, with buttons, beads, wine bottles and glasses all contributing their individual chronologies and mean artifact dates suitable for comparison with the mean ceramic date and brackets, pipestems, and coins, but this only as introduction to the examination of questions of broader scope.

The apparent success of the tools discussed here is thought to be due to the fact that with colonial artifacts we are dealing with a historical chronology reflecting cultural process, just as we would be doing with a study of motifs from a collection of dated coins from the same cultural tradition. The coins are indicators of the historical as well as the cultural process as well as reflecting the temporal occupation span for a site just as we have seen ceramics to be. For instance, at Brunswick Town the documented duration of the site was from 1725 until it was burned in 1776. The coins from the ruins of houses burned at that time date from 1696 to 1775. The coins from all ruins including those occupied after the Revolution into the 1830's date to 1820. Thus coins are used along with ceramics to help fix dates for historic site occupation. However, they are not often found in quantity sufficient for them to be a major tool. They can provide auxiliary data as historically fixed documents, just as we have seen ceramics utilized in this study.

In order to help understand what the use of the mean ceramic date formula does we might visualize each sherd as having imprinted on it the median manufacture date, equivalent to finding a dated coin for each sherd. Thus Type 61, North Devon Gravel Tempered Ware sherds found in the amount of 45 sherds would equate with 45 coins having the date 1713 clearly remaining on each. The formula allows us to deal with this wealth of dates represented by each sherd found on the site, and arrive at an interpreted date representing the mean of all the median dates represented by the sherds.

INTERPRETIVE SUMMARY

In this study we have concentrated on the *similarity* between groups of eighteenth century ceramic types as found on colonial English historic sites over a wide area and of varying functions. We have suggested that this can be done due to the horizon nature of the ceramic groups in the eighteenth century, and the fact that the ceramic types reflect culture change through time. We have not dealt with the important *differences* between ceramic forms as reflectors of functional or socioeconomic factors at work within the culture. The potential of such a study has been pointed out by Stone (1970) and others regarding porcelain as an index of status. Miller and Stone (1970) have also indicated that ceramic analysis offers great potential in studies of sociocultural change, status and social level, and functional interpretations. The study of ceramic *types* as we have done in this paper as indicators of site occupation periods reflecting the cultural horizon concept does not negate the study of ceramic *shapes* as more sensitive indicators of status and function within the culture. Although ceramic analysis by *type* can be demonstrated to vary but relatively little from a port town such as Brunswick and the frontier forts of the same period, thus providing us with a valuable temporal tool for use on eighteenth century sites, an analysis of the same ceramic fragments using *shape* might well reflect status or cultural pattern of a different sort. Garry Stone at the 1970 meeting of

the Society for Historical Archaeology presented a paper illustrating the use of a number of ceramic shapes dealing with the tea ceremony at the frontier outpost of Fort Dobbs, North Carolina. In the present study of the nineteen ceramic types present at the frontier site of Fort Prince George, ten were represented by the presence of teapots, teacups or saucers, tending to support the observations made by Stone in North Carolina regarding the extension of the tea ceremony to the far corners of the colonial frontier (see Roth 1961). The emphasis on *shape* as opposed to *type*, reflecting perhaps an emphasis on *function* as compared to *time* can be seen in the manner in which archaeologists approach their data. Noël Hume, for instance, classifies and catalogs his ceramics by quantification of the *shape* of various types present, whereas this archaeologist has always used quantification by fragments of ceramic *types* present. Analysis by shape would seem to be a more sensitive indicator of *function* and possible socioeconomic level, whereas that by type is useful for discovering the kind of cultural information dealt with in this present study. Thus the manner in which we classify our data has a bearing on our interpretations.

Other points dealing with this subject should be mentioned. Ceramic analysis should consider such factors as absence, which may well correlate with documents, such as the period from about 1640 to 1680 when the English were barred from Chinese ports, thus having a definite effect on the import of Chinese porcelain during this period (Noël Hume 1970:257). The absence of porcelain in the collection from the Charles Towne deposits of 1670–1680 is therefore no surprise. Another point is that from the first Fort Moore of the early eighteenth century fewer ceramic shapes were present dealing with the tea ceremony than were found on the later frontier forts in the area. This difference in ceramic shape between these eighteenth century forts may reflect the greater popularity of the tea ceremony from the mid-eighteenth century on as opposed to its popularity in the early part of the century (Roth 1961).

Although Stone (1970) found an association between porcelain and the more affluent in the inventories he studied, we surely need more data before we can say that this is reflected in archaeological collections. Miller and Stone (1970:100) have also suggested that archaeologists "should be able to establish the relative socioeconomic level of a population and define any major status differences which existed at a site by means of the distributional analysis of ceramics." Archaeologists often give lip service to this view, but we have yet to see the demonstration of this milking process archaeologically demonstrated. Comparison of French with English ceramics at Michilimackinac was done by Miller and Stone with interesting differences observed, but whether status or socioeconomic differences can be witnessed within the context of an *eighteenth century* British American site is yet to be demonstrated. Cleland (1970:122) has mentioned differences in ceramics from two row houses being interpreted as reflecting social status of the occupants, and suggests that this interpretation can validly be made in the absence of specific historical data for the row houses themselves. I suggest that this is only one of the possibilities, but one yet to be validly demonstrated. I do not think interpretations based on a single comparison can be considered to be valid. We need several such ceramic differences in comparisons made between a number of archaeologically examined historic ruins. I would suggest that we need a *pattern* of such differences before we could archaeologically demonstrate that a status situation is indeed responsible. Another approach to this problem could come through the excavation of ruins of homes of historically known affluent people at one particular point in time and comparison of the ceramics recovered from ruins of historically known non-affluent individuals at the *same period in time*. This would provide a control against which the archaeological data could be examined. At such a time we might begin to be able to make statements regarding status as reflected by the ceramics from the sites we excavate. Meanwhile status appears to be a goal we all think we should somehow milk from our ceramics, but as yet we have not discovered the proper grip for producing this stream of cultural knowledge from our archaeological data from eighteenth century British American sites.

Functional interpretations from historic site ruins are also often frustratingly unproductive. With kiln sites, furnaces, and other specialized structures the interpretation becomes obvious as the data is revealed. However, with the town ruins of Bethabara, North Carolina, for instance, maps of 1760 and 1766 revealed the functional use for each structure at that time, the tailor shop, kitchen, pottery shop, business manager's house, the doctor's laboratory, the apothecary shop, the blacksmith shop, the millwright's house, the gunsmith shop, and the tavern, but when excavation was complete not a single structure could be interpreted from the archaeological data as to its correct function except the pottery shop of Gottfried Aust, identifiable from the clay wedging floor and the kiln waster dump. We should be cautious, therefore, and anchor our research goals in something more productive than a consideration of the function of the structure we are examining. Fortunately, there are other questions that can be asked about historic site data, such as those examined in this paper.

In this study we have seen that eighteenth century British American sites of varied functions, from port town ruins, to town house mansions to frontier forts and Indian villages have similar groups of ceramic types present at similar periods of time. This has been interpreted in terms of the horizon concept (Willey and Phillips 1958:31–34). The time required for the spread of the cultural material representing the horizon is a factor to be considered, as Willey and Phillips point out. Therefore, an *approximate* contemporaneity is involved. With our historic ceramics used in this study we are dealing with a class of objects that originated, for the most part, in England and were brought into America aboard vessels to ports such as Charleston, Savannah, Boston, New York, and Philadelphia, and from these centers were distributed to inland sites. This distribution was often quite rapid, being only as long as it took a man on horseback to ride the distance from the port town where the limited collection of ceramic types was available, to his frontier destination at Fort Prince George, Goudy's Trading Post, or Fort Moore. A few months at the most might have been involved, so that within a few weeks after a ship arrived in a port town, teacups, teapots, and saucers of white salt-glazed stoneware or "clouded" polychrome painted cream-colored ware could easily have been used by an Indian to pour a cup of the "black drink" at the Cherokee town of Keowee opposite Fort Prince George. Such ceramic types and forms are found in Cherokee midden deposits, and whether they reached the Cherokee nation by way of Philadelphia or Charleston is immaterial when we consider that in either case the journey would take but a few weeks at the most. Thus the argument that considerable time lag must have been involved for English ceramic types to reach the various remote corners of the colonial frontier is a more difficult position to support than

that dispersal of goods was a relatively rapid process. If this was so then we can understand why a great deal of uniformity would exist among ceramic types from sites of the same time period, regardless of the fort, port, or Indian village function of the site on which the ceramics were used.

Documents from port records may well reveal that certain colonial ports received ceramic goods from different English ports, thus theoretically introducing another variable into the picture. However, as Cleland has said (1970:122), "These are historic facts that are really irrelevant to the interpretation of the archaeological data." For example, if the historical documents were to reveal that Charleston did not receive any Oriental porcelain in the eighteenth century this would not alter the percentage relationships of this type from the sites in this study, or the applicability of the mean ceramic date formula, or the interpretation of the data in terms of the horizon concept. It would point to questions centering around transportation and supply routes relative to the sites in this study merely as additional historical information.

From this examination of our hypotheses we can see that the bracketing and mean ceramic date formula tools have proved of value in producing a time bracket for eighteenth century sites that correlates well with the historically known occupation periods. From this correlation the validity of our hypotheses has tended to be demonstrated to the limits of our present data. More use of these and similar tools on a broader scope should now be undertaken by historic site archaeologists in similar studies if we are to interpret the most from our historic site data.

The construction of tools such as pipestem and ceramic analysis formulas, however, is only a first step toward discovering answers to the larger questions of culture process. This paper has attempted to address itself to some of these questions. Historical archaeology data particularly lends itself to analysis in a controlled and specific manner not possible on the prehistoric level. For this reason it offers an ideal arena for the examination of cultural concepts long explored on prehistoric sites. Historical archaeology has now matured to the point where we should begin to explore this potential rather than continuing to crowd our bookshelves with descriptive catalogs of our systematized relic collecting devoid of any redeeming analytical or interpretive value. Historical archaeologists have a challenge and a responsibility to abstract order through analysis and meaning through interpretation of their data. "From the pages of the earth, the historical archaeologist gathers bits and pieces representing past human activity and relates these to the shreds and patches surviving as the worn documents and faded words of history. From this collection of essentially meaningless, unique fragments of the past, he abstracts the order, and strives to press a meaning" (South 1969). Too often we stop with description of the bits and pieces and the relation of these to the documentary shreds and patches without attempting to abstract the order and discover the meaning. We historical archaeologists should more frequenty take that next step from data to theory, a step so clearly stated by Hempel (1966:15):

> *The transition from data to theory requires creative imagination. Scientific hypotheses and theories are not derived from observed facts, but invented in order to account for them. They constitute guesses at the connections that might obtain between the phenomena under study, at uniformities and patterns that might underlie their occurrence.*

In this paper we have made guesses at some of the connections and uniformities we have observed from historic site ceramics. If our guesses prove valid we have sharpened our theoretical tools (Deetz 1968:130), and revealed the cultural "treasure from earthen vessels", a goal of archaeology.

ACKNOWLEDGEMENT

I would like to thank John and Joan Combes, George Teague, Robert L. Stephenson, and Audrey and Ivor Noël Hume for discussing this paper with me and helping to clarify some of the concepts.

BIBLIOGRAPHY

BINFORD, LEWIS, H. and MOREAU S. MAXWELL
   1961   *Excavation at Fort Michilimackinac, Mackinac City, Michigan, 1959 Season.* Stone Printing Co., Lansing.
BINFORD, SALLY R. and LEWIS R. BINFORD
   1968   *New Perspectives in Archeology.* Aldine Publishing Co., Chicago.
CLARK, DAVID L.
   1968   *Analytical Archaeology.* Methuen & Co., Ltd., London.
CLELAND, CHARLES E.
   1970   Diverse Comments and Sundry Suggestions Concerning Ceramics in Suffolk County, Massachusetts, Inventories 1680–1775—A Preliminary Study with Diverse Comments Thereon, and Sundry Suggestions, *Conference on Historic Site Archaeology Papers,* Historical Archaeology Forum 3, Part 2.
CLELAND, CHARLES E. and JAMES E. FITTING
   1968   The Crisis of Identity: Theory in Historic Site Archaeology. *Conference on Historic Site Archaeology Papers,* Historical Archaeology Forum 2, Part 2.
DEETZ, JAMES
   1968   Late Man in North America: Archeology of European Americans. *The Anthropological Society of Washington.* Washington, D.C.
DEETZ, JAMES and EDWIN DETHLEFSEN
   1966   Death's Heads, Cherubs, and Willow Trees: Experimental Archaeology in Colonial Cemeteries. *American Antiquity* 31, No. 4.
DOLLAR, CLYDE D.
   1968   Some Thoughts on Theory and Method in Historical Archaeology. *Conference on Historic Site Archaeology Papers,* Historical Archaeology Forum 2, Part 2.
DUNNEL, ROBERT C.
   1970   Seriation Method and Its Evaluation. *American Antiquity* 35, No. 3.
FORD, JAMES A.
   1961   *A Quantitative Method for Deriving Cultural Chronology.* Technical Publications and Documents, Dept. of Social Affairs, Pan American Union.
HANSON, LEE H., JR.
   1971   Kaolin Pipe Stems—Boring in on a Fallacy. *Conference on Historic Site Archaeology* 4, Part 1.

HARRINGTON, J. C.
   1954   Dating Stem Fragments of Seventeenth and Eighteenth Century Clay Tobacco Pipes. *Quarterly Bulletin of the Archaeological Society of Virginia* 9, No. 1.
HEMPEL, CARL G.
   1966   *Philosophy of Natural Science.* Prentice-Hall, Inc., Englewood Cliffs, N. J.
MAYER-OAKES, WILLIAM J.
   1955   Prehistory of the Upper Ohio Valley. *Annals of the Carnegie Museum* 34, (Anthropological Series, No. 2). Pittsburgh, Pa.
MILLER, J. JEFFERSON and LYLE M. STONE
   1970   *Eighteenth-Century Ceramics from Fort Michilimackinac.* Smithsonian Institution Press, Washington, D.C.
NOËL HUME, IVOR
   1970   *A Guide to Artifacts of Colonial America.* Alfred A. Knopf, New York.
ROTH, RODRIS
   1961   Tea Drinking in 18th-Century America: Its Etiquette and Equipage. *Contributions from the Museum of History and Technology, Paper* 14. Smithsonian Institution, Washington, D.C.
SOUTH, STANLEY
   1955   Evolutionary Theory in Archaeology. *Southern Indian Studies* 7.
   1958   Nath Moore's Front, Unit S10, 1728–1776. MS on file at State Department of Archives and History, N. C. and at the Institute of Archaeology and Anthropology, University of South Carolina, Columbia.
   1959a   The McCorkall-Fergus House, Unit S18, c.1760–1775. MS on file at State Department of Archives and History, N. C. and at the Institute of Archaeology and Anthropology, University of South Carolina, Columbia.
   1959b   The Hepburn-Reonalds House, Unit S7, 1734–1776. MS on file at State Department of Archives and History, N. C. and at the Institute of Archaeology and Anthropology, University of South Carolina, Columbia.
   1962   The Ceramic Types at Brunswick Town, North Carolina. *Southeastern Archaeological Conference Newsletter* 9, No. 1.
   1967   The Paca House, Annapolis, Maryland. MS on file at the Institute of Archaeology and Anthropology, University of South Carolina, Columbia.
SOUTH, STANLEY
   1971   Archaeology at the Charles Towne Site (38CH1) on Albemarle Point in South Carolina. MS on file at the Institute of Archeology and Anthropology, University of South Carolina, Columbia.
STONE, GARRY WHEELER
   1970   Ceramics in Suffolk County, Massachusetts, Inventories 1680–1775—A Preliminary Study with Diverse Comments Thereon, and Sundry Suggestions, *Conference on Historic Site Archaeology, Historical Archaeology Forum* 3, Part 2.
WASHBURN, S. L.
   1953   The Strategy of Physical Anthropology. In A. L. Knoeber, (Ed.), *Anthropology Today.* Chicago: University of Chicago Press.
WILLEY, GORDON R. and PHILIP PHILLIPS
   1958   *Method and Theory in American Archaeology.* University of Chicago Press, Chicago.

CHAPTER 18

Death's Head, Cherub, Urn and Willow

JAMES F. DEETZ and EDWIN S. DETHLEFSON

Enter almost any cemetery in eastern Massachusetts that was in use during the seventeenth and eighteenth centuries. Inspect the stones and the designs carved at their tops, and you will discover that three motifs are present. These motifs have distinctive periods of popularity, each replacing the other in a sequence that is repeated time and time again in all cemeteries between Worcester and the Atlantic, and from New Hampshire to Cape Cod.

The earliest of the three is a winged death's head, with blank eyes and a grinning visage. Earlier versions are quite ornate, but as time passes, they become less elaborate. Sometime during the eighteenth century—the time varies according to location—the grim death's head designs are replaced, more or less quickly, by winged cherubs. This design also goes through a gradual simplification of form with time. By the late 1700s or early 1800s, again depending on where you are observing, the cherubs are replaced by stones decorated with a willow tree overhanging a pedestaled urn. If the cemetery you are visiting is in a rural area, the chances are quite good that you will also find other designs, which may even completely replace one or more of the three primary designs at certain periods. If you were to search cemeteries in the same area, you would find that these other designs have a much more local distribution. In and around Boston, however, only the three primary designs would be present.

If you were to prepare a graph showing how the designs change in popularity through time, the finished product might look something like three battleships viewed from above, the lower one with the bow showing, the center one in full view, and the third visible only in the stern. This shape, frequently called a "battleship-shaped" curve, is thought by archaeologists to typify the popularity career of any cultural trait across time. Prepared from controlled data taken from the Stoneham cemetery, north of Boston, where the style sequence is typical of the area around this eighteenth-century urban center of eastern Massachusetts, the graph following shows such a curve. (See Figure 1).

It is appropriate here to interrupt and pose the question: why would an archaeologist study gravestones from a historic period?

Whether archaeology can be considered a science in the strict sense of the word is much debated. One of the hallmarks of scientific method is the use of controls in experimentation that enable the investigator to calibrate his results. Since archaeology deals largely with the unrecorded past, the problem of rigorous control is a difficult one. Much of modern archaeological method and theory has been developed in contexts that lack the necessary controls for precise checking of accuracy and predictive value. For this reason, any set of archaeological data in which such controls are available is potentially of great importance to the development and testing of explanatory models, which can then be used in uncontrolled contexts.

For a number of reasons, colonial New England grave markers may be unique in providing the archaeologist with a laboratory situation in which to measure cultural change in time and space and relate such measurements to the main body of archaeological method. All archaeological data—artifacts, structures, sites—can be said to possess three inherent dimensions. A clay pot, for example, has a location in space. Its date of manufacture and use is fixed in time, and it has certain physical attributes of form. In a sense, much of archaeological method is concerned with the nature and causes of variation along these dimensions, as shown by excavated remains of past cultures.

The spatial aspect of gravestones is constant. We know from historical sources that nearly all of the stones in New England cemeteries of this period were produced locally, probably no more than fifteen or twenty miles away; an insignificant number of them came from long distances. This pattern is so reliable that it is possible to detect those few stones in every cemetery that were made at a more remote town. Once placed over the dead, the stones were unlikely to have been moved, except perhaps within the cemetery limits.

Needless to say, the dimension of time is neatly and tightly controlled. Every stone bears the date of death of the individual whose grave it marks, and most stones were erected shortly after death. Like the spatial regularity, this temporal precision makes it possible to single out most of the stones that were erected at some later date.

Control over the formal dimension of gravestone data derives from our knowledge of the carvers, who, in many instances, are known by name and period of production, and who, even if anonymous, can be identified by their product with the help of spatial and temporal control. Thus, in most cases stones of similar type can be seen to be the product of a single person, and they reflect his ideas regarding their proper form.

Furthermore, it is known that the carvers of the stones were not full-time specialists, but rather workers at other trades who made stones for the immediate population as they were needed. We are dealing, then, with folk products, as is often the case in prehistoric archaeology.

Other cultural dimensions can also be controlled in the gravestone data with equal precision, and with the addition of these, the full power of these artifacts as controls becomes apparent: probate research often tells the price of individual stones; status indication occurs frequently on the stones, as well as the age of each individual. Since death is related to religion, formal variations in the written material can be analyzed to see how they reflect religious variations. Epi-

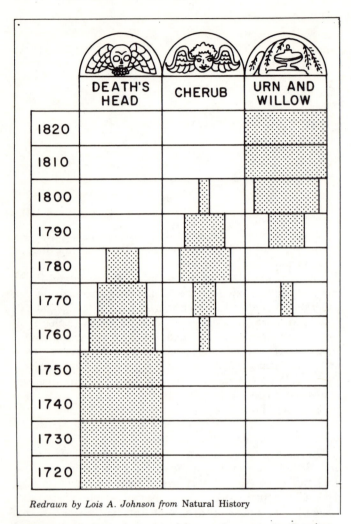

	DEATH'S HEAD	CHERUB	URN AND WILLOW
1820			░░░
1810			░░░
1800		░	░░░
1790		░░	░░
1780	░	░░░	
1770	░	░░░░	░
1760	░░	░	
1750	░░░		
1740	░░░		
1730	░░░		
1720	░░░		

Redrawn by Lois A. Johnson from Natural History

FIGURE 1. Stylistic Sequence from a Cemetery in Stoneham, Massachusetts.

taphs provide a unique literary and psychological dimension. Spatial distributions can be measured against political divisions. In short, the full historical background of the seventeenth, eighteenth, and nineteenth centuries permits both primary and secondary control of the material, and with the resulting precision, explanations become quite reliable.

With such controls available to the archaeologist, the pattern of change in colonial gravestone design and style can be used with great effect to sharpen our understanding of cultural process in general.

To return to the battleship-shaped curves in this essay, what does this mean in terms of culture change? Why should death's heads be popular at all, and what cultural factors were responsible for their disappearance and the subsequent rise of the cherub design? The most obvious answer is found in the ecclesiastical history of New England. The period of decline of death's heads coincides with the decline of orthodox Puritanism. In the late seventeenth century, Puritanism was universal in the area, and so were death's head gravestones. The early part of the eighteenth century saw the beginnings of change in orthodoxy, culminating in the great awakenings of the mid-century. In his recent, excellent book on the symbolism of New England gravestones, *Graven Images*, Allan Ludwig points out that the "iconophobic" Puritans found the carving of gravestones a compromise. While the use of cherubs might have verged on heresy, since they are heavenly beings whose portrayal might lead to idolatry, the use of a more mortal and neutral symbol—a

death's head—would have served as a graphic reminder of death and resurrection.

Given the more liberal views concerning symbolism and personal involvement preached by Jonathan Edwards and others later in the eighteenth century, the idolatrous and heretical aspects of cherubs would have been more fitting to express the sentiment of the period.

It is at this point that available literary controls become valuable. Each stone begins by describing the state of the deceased: "Here lies" or "Here lies buried" being typical early examples. Slowly these are replaced by "Here lies [buried] |the body [corruptible, what was mortal] of." This slightly, but significantly, different statement might well reflect a more explicit tendency to stress that only a part of the deceased remains, while the soul, the incorruptible or immortal portion, has gone to its eternal reward. Cherubs reflect a stress on resurrection, while death's heads emphasize the mortality of man. The epitaphs that appear on the bottoms of many stones also add credence to this explanation of change in form over time. Early epitaphs, with death's head designs, stress either decay and life's brevity:

> My Youthful mates both small and great
> Come here and you may see
> An awful sight, which is a type of which
>   you soon must be

or a Calvinistic emphasis on hard work and exemplary behavior on the part of the predestined:

> He was a useful man in his generation, a lover of
> learning, a faithful servant of Harvard College above
> forty years.

On the other hand, epitaphs with cherub stones tend to stress resurrection and later heavenly reward:

> Here cease thy tears, suppress thy fruitless
>   mourn
> his soul—the immortal part—has upward
>   flown
> On wings he soars his rapid way
> To yon bright regions of eternal day.

The final change seen in gravestone style is the radical shift to the urn and willow design. It is usually accompanied by a change in stone shape; while earlier stones have a round-shouldered outline, the later stones have square shoulders. "Here lies the body of" is replaced by "In memory of," or "Sacred to the memory of," quite different from all earlier forms. The earlier stones are markers, designating the location of the deceased or at least a portion of him. In contrast, "In memory of" is simply a memorial statement, and stones of this later type could logically be erected elsewhere and still make sense. In fact, many of the late urn and willow stones are cenotaphs, erected to commemorate those actually buried elsewhere, as far away as Africa, Batavia, and in one case—in the Kingston, Massachusetts, cemetery—"drowned at sea, lat. 39 degrees N., long. 70 degrees W." The cultural changes that accompany the shift to urn and willow designs are seen in the rise of less emotional, more intellectual religions, such as Unitarianism and Methodism. Epitaphs change with design and in the early nineteenth century tend more to sentiment combined with eulogy.

This sequence of change did not occur in a vacuum,

unrelated to any cultural change elsewhere; indeed, the sequence of three major types also takes place in England, the cultural parent of the Massachusetts colony, but about a half century earlier. Thus cherubs have become modal by the beginning of the Georgian period (1715), and urns and willows make their appearance, as a part of the neoclassical tradition, in the 1760s. In fact, the entire urn and willow pattern is a part of the larger Greek Revival, which might explain the squared shoulders on the stones—a severer classical outline.

Thus far we have been discussing formal change through time, and some of the fundamental causes. We have seen that New England is changing in harmony with England, with an expectable time interval separating the sequences. But we have not identified the relationship of all of this to archaeological method.

The battleship-shaped curve assumption is basic to many considerations of culture process in general and to such dating methods as seriation. Seriation is a method whereby archaeological sites are arranged in relative chronological order based on the popularity of the different types of artifacts found in them. The approach assumes that any cultural item, be it a style of pottery or a way of making an arrowhead, has a particular popularity period, and as it grows and wanes in popularity, its prevalence as time passes can be represented graphically by a single peaked curve. Small beginnings grow to a high frequency of occurrence, followed in turn by a gradual disappearance. If such an assumption is true, it follows that a series of sites can be arranged so that all artifact types within them form single peaked curves of popularity over time. Such an arrangement is chronological, and tells the archaeologist how his sites relate to one another in time.

By plotting style sequences in this manner in a number of cemeteries, we find that the assumption, not previously measured with such a degree of precision, is a sound one: styles do form single peaked popularity curves through time. By adding the control of the spatial to the form-time pattern explained above, we gain a number of understandings regarding diffusion—the spread of ideas through time and space and how this, in turn, affects internal change in style. In looking now at the three dimensions we will see that all of the secondary cultural controls become even more important.

The style sequence of death's head, cherub, and urn and willow design is to be found in almost every cemetery in eastern Massachusetts. However, when we inspect the time at which each change takes place, and the degree of overlap between styles from cemetery to cemetery, it becomes apparent that this sequence was occurring at a widely varying rate from place to place. The earliest occurrence of cherubs is in the Boston-Cambridge area, where they begin to appear as early as the end of the seventeenth century. Occasional early cherubs might be found in more distant rural cemeteries, but in every case we find them to have been carved in the Boston area and to be rare imports from there. The farther we move away from the Boston center, the later locally manufactured cherubs make their appearance in numbers. The rate at which the cherub style spread outward has even been approximately measured, and shown to be about a mile per year. It is not common in archaeology to make such precise measurements of diffusion rate—the usual measurements are cruder, such as hundreds of miles in millenniums.

We can view Boston and, more significantly, nearby Cambridge as the focus of emphasis of Puritan religion with its accompanying values, and inquire what factors might contribute to the initial appearance of cherubs and the change in religious values in this central area. We have noted that the change had already been accomplished in England by the early eighteenth century, so that when the first cherubs begin to appear in numbers in Cambridge, they were already the standard modal style in England. While cherubs occur in Boston, they never make a major impression, and as many death's heads as cherubs are replaced by the urn and willow influx.

On the other hand, in Cambridge cherubs make an early start and attain a respectable frequency by the late eighteenth century. Although they never attain a full 100 percent level there, as they do in most rural areas, they do at least enjoy a simple majority. When the cherub stones in Cambridge are inspected more closely, we find that roughly 70 percent of them mark the graves of high status individuals: college presidents, graduates of Harvard, governors and their families, high church officials, and in one case, even a "Gentleman from London." From what we know of innovation in culture, it is often the more cosmopolitan, urban stratum of society that brings in new ideas, to be followed later by the folk stratum. If this is true, then the differences between Boston and Cambridge indicate a more liberal element within the population of Cambridge, reflected in the greater frequency of cherub stones there. This is probably the case, with the influence of the Harvard intellectual community being reflected in the cemetery. It would appear that even in the early eighteenth century, the university was a place for innovation and liberal thinking. Cambridge intellectuals were more likely to be responsive to English styles, feelings, and tastes, and this could well be what we are seeing in the high number of cherub stones marking high-status graves.

Introduced into Cambridge and Boston by a distinct social class, the cherub design slowly begins its diffusion into the surrounding countryside. Carvers in towns farther removed from Cambridge and Boston—as far as fourteen miles west in Concord—begin to change their gravestone styles away from the popular death's head as early as the 1730s, but fifty miles to the south, in Plymouth, styles do not change until the fifties and sixties and then in a somewhat different cultural context. We find, however, that the farther the cemetery is from Boston, and the later the cherubs begin to be locally manufactured, the more rapidly they reach a high level of popularity. The pattern is one of a long period of coexistence between cherubs and death's heads in the Boston center, and an increasingly more rapid eclipsing of death's heads by cherubs in direct proportion to distance, with a much shorter period of overlap. One explanation is that in towns farther removed from the diffusion center, enforcement of Puritan ethics and values would lessen, and resistance to change would not be so strong. Furthermore, revivalism and the modification of orthodox Puritanism was widespread from the late thirties through the sixties in rural New England, although this movement never penetrated Boston. Such activity certainly must have conditioned the rural populace for a change to new designs.

We have, then, a picture of the introduction of a change in the highly specific aspect of mortuary art, an aspect reflecting much of the culture producing it. We see the subsequent spread of this idea, through space and time, as a function of social class and religious values. Now we are in a position to examine internal change in form through time, while maintaining relatively tight control on the spatial dimension.

One significant result of the use of gravestone data with its

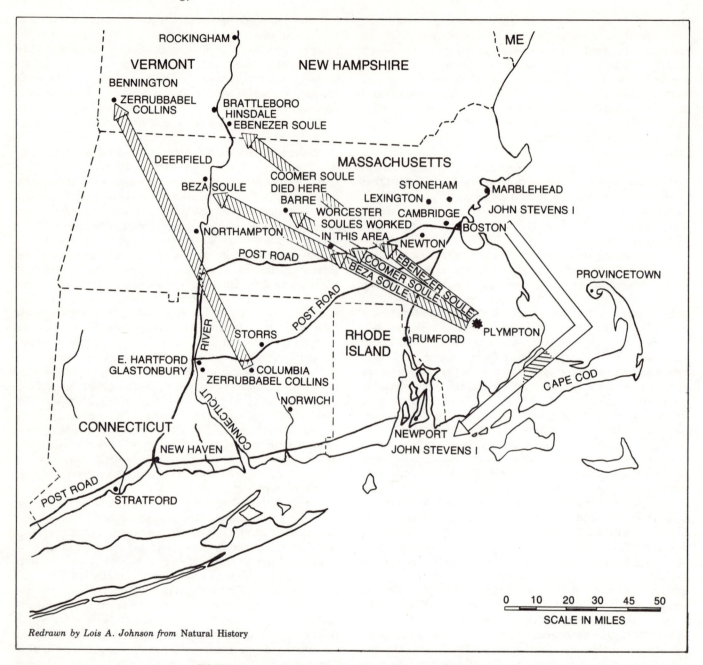

FIGURE 2. Some Gravestone Locations and Movements of Carvers.

accompanying controls is the insight it provides in matters of stylistic evolution. The product of a single carver can be studied over a long period of time, and the change in his patterns considered as they reflect both ongoing culture change and his particular manner of handling design elements. The spatial axis extending outward from Boston shows not only systematic change in major style replacement rates but also a striking pattern of difference in style change. We find that in many cases, the farther removed we become from Boston, the more rapid and radical is change within a given single design. This has been observed in at least five separate cases, involving a number of the styles of more local distribution; we can inspect one of these cases closely, and attempt to determine some of the processes and causes of stylistic evolution.

The design in question is found in Plymouth County, centering on the town of Plympton. Its development spans a period of some seventy years, and the changes effected from beginning to end are truly profound. Death's heads occur in rural Plymouth County, as they do elsewhere in the late seventeenth century. However, in the opening decade of the eighteenth century the carver(s) in Plympton made certain basic changes in the general death's head motif. The first step in this modification involved the reduction of the lower portion of the face, and the addition of a heart-shaped element between nose and teeth. The resulting pattern was one with a heartlike mouth, with the teeth shrunken to a simple band along the bottom. The teeth soon disappear entirely, leaving the heart as the sole mouth element. This change is rapidly followed by a curious change in the feathering of the wings.

While early examples show all feather ends as regular scallops crossing the lines separating individual feathers, shortly after the first changes in the face were made, every other row of feather ends had their direction of curvature reversed. The resulting design produces the effect of undulat-

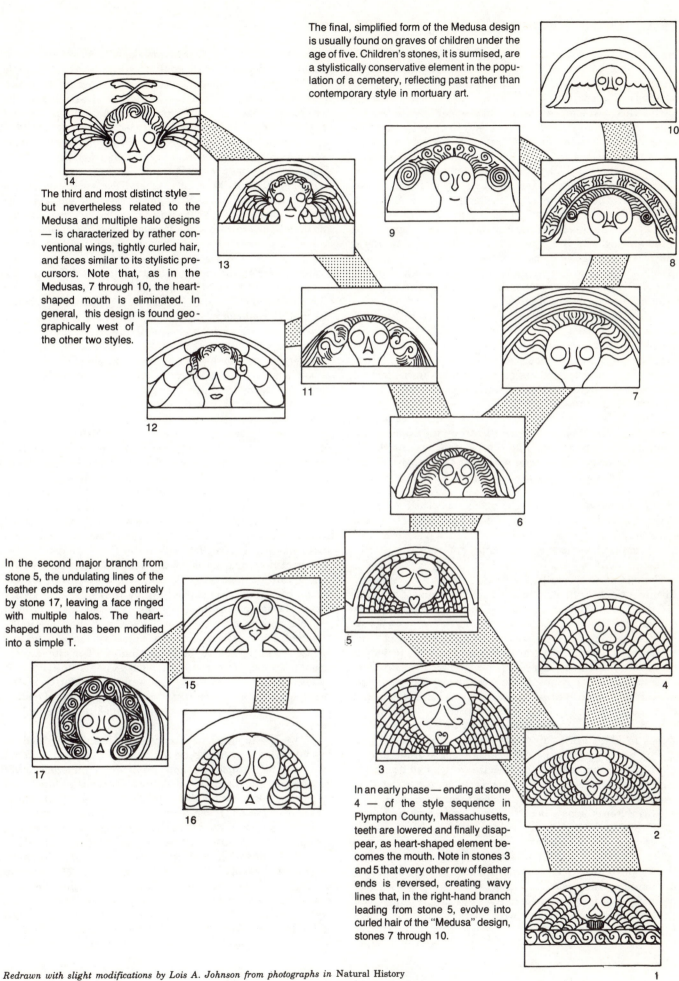

The final, simplified form of the Medusa design is usually found on graves of children under the age of five. Children's stones, it is surmised, are a stylistically conservative element in the population of a cemetery, reflecting past rather than contemporary style in mortuary art.

The third and most distinct style — but nevertheless related to the Medusa and multiple halo designs — is characterized by rather conventional wings, tightly curled hair, and faces similar to its stylistic precursors. Note that, as in the Medusas, 7 through 10, the heart-shaped mouth is eliminated. In general, this design is found geographically west of the other two styles.

In the second major branch from stone 5, the undulating lines of the feather ends are removed entirely by stone 17, leaving a face ringed with multiple halos. The heart-shaped mouth has been modified into a simple T.

In an early phase — ending at stone 4 — of the style sequence in Plympton County, Massachusetts, teeth are lowered and finally disappear, as heart-shaped element becomes the mouth. Note in stones 3 and 5 that every other row of feather ends is reversed, creating wavy lines that, in the right-hand branch leading from stone 5, evolve into curled hair of the "Medusa" design, stones 7 through 10.

Redrawn with slight modifications by Lois A. Johnson from photographs in Natural History

FIGURE 3. Evolution of Styles in a Plympton Cemetery.

ing lines radiating from the head, almost suggesting hair, at right angles to curved lines that still mark the feather separation. These two changes, in face and wing form, occupy a period of 35 years from 1710 through 1745. During the later forties this development, which has so far been a single sequence, splits into two branches, each the result of further modification of wings. In the first case, the arcs marking feather separations are omitted, leaving only the undulating radial lines. Rapid change then takes place, and soon we are confronted with a face surmounted by wavy and, later, quite curly hair. The heart mouth has been omitted. We have dubbed this style "Medusa." In the second case, the separating lines are retained, and the undulating lines removed; the result in this case is a face with multiple halos. At times, space between these halos is filled with spiral elements, giving the appearance of hair, or the halos are omitted entirely. The heart-shaped mouth is retained in this case and modified into a T-shaped element.

Both of these styles enjoy great popularity in the fifties and sixties, and have slightly different spatial distributions, suggesting that they might be the work of two carvers, both modifying the earlier heart-mouthed design in different ways. Yet a third related design also appears in the forties, this time with tightly curled hair, conventional wings, and a face similar to the other two. Although this third design seems to be a more direct derivative of the earlier death's head motif, it is clearly inspired in part by the Medusa and multiple halo designs. This tight-haired style has a markedly different spatial distribution, occurring to the west of the other two, but overlapping them in a part of its range. Of the three, only the Medusa lasts into the seventies, and in doing so presents us with something of an enigma. The final form, clearly evolved from the earlier types, is quite simple. It has a specific association with small children, and has never been found marking the grave of an adult, and rarely of a child over age five.

The carver of the fully developed Medusa was probably Ebenezer Soule of Plympton; a definitive sample of his style is found in the Plympton cemetery. Normal Medusas, except for the late, simple ones marking children's graves, disappear abruptly in the late sixties. In 1769, and lasting until the eighties, stones identical to Soule's Medusas, including the simple, late ones, appear in granite around Hinsdale, New Hampshire. Fortunately, a local history has identified the carver of some of these stones as "Ebenezer Soule, late of Plympton." This alone is of great interest, but if Soule did move to Hinsdale in 1769, who carved the later children's stones in Plymouth County? As yet, no answer is known.

This development raises two interesting considerations. First, we see that a style, the Medusa, which had been used for the general populace, ends its existence restricted to small children. This pattern has been observed elsewhere, with children's burials being marked by designs that were somewhat more popular earlier in time. In other words, children are a stylistically conservative element in the population of a cemetery. While no clear answer can be given to this problem, it may well be that small children, not having developed a strong, personal impact on the society, would not be thought of in quite the same way as adults, and would have their graves marked with more conservative, less explicitly descriptive stones.

The second problem raised by the Medusas is their reappearance in Hinsdale. If, as archaeologists, we were confronted with the degree of style similarity seen between Hinsdale and Plympton in mortuary art, might we not infer a much greater influence than a single individual arriving in the community? After all, mortuary art would be about the only distinctively variable element in material culture over eighteenth-century New England, and such a close parallel could well be said to represent a migration from Plympton to Hinsdale. One man moved.

Placing this striking case of stylistic evolution in the broader context of culture change and style change in eastern Massachusetts, we find that it is paralleled by other internal modifications of death's head designs in other remote rural areas. The closer we move toward Boston, the less change takes place within the death's head design, and in Boston proper, death's heads from 1810 are not that different from those from 1710. Yet 1710 death's heads in Plympton and elsewhere had changed so radically by 1750 that it is doubtful that we could supply the derivation of one from the other in the absence of such an excellently dated set of intermediate forms. This difference in rate of change can be explained by referring back to the long, parallel courses of development of both death's head and cherub in the diffusion area's Boston center. However, culture change in the area of religion, marked by a shift of emphasis from mortality to immortality, probably generated a desire for less realistic and less grim designs on stones. Given this basic change in religious attitudes, what were the alternatives facing carvers in Boston as opposed to the Ebenezer Soules of rural New England? In Boston it was simply a matter of carving more cherub stones and fewer death's head stones; neither had to be altered to suit the new tastes. The choice between cherub and death's head in Boston has been seen as ultimately a social one, and if there was a folk culture component within Boston, there was nothing but folk culture in the more democratic, less-stratified rural areas. With no one to introduce cherubs and to call for them with regularity in the country, carvers set to work modifying the only thing they had—the death's head. The more remote the community, the later the local cherubs appear, diffusing from Boston, and the more likely the tendency to rework the common folk symbol of skull and wings. Thus we get Medusas and haloed T-mouthed faces populating the cemeteries of Plymouth County until cherubs finally appear. Even then, the waning popularity of the death's head in this area might be more the result of Soule's exit than their unsatisfactory appearance compared to the new cherubs.

Only a few applications of gravestone design analysis have been detailed here. A three-year program is presently under way, through which we hope to pursue numerous other aspects of this fascinating study. There is a large and important demographic dimension to these data; since precise date of death is given, as well as age at death, patterns of mortality and life expectance through time and space can be detailed. The results of this work, in turn, will add a biological dimension of style to the cultural one described above. Studies of diffusion rate, and its relationship to dating by seriation will be continued. Relationships between political units—counties, townships, and colonies—and style spheres will be investigated to determine how such units affect the distribution of a carver's products. Finally, a happy byproduct will be the preservation on film of over

25,000 gravestones, a vital consideration in view of the slow but steady deterioration these informative artifacts are undergoing.

Aside from the value of this work to archaeology and anthropology in general, one final comment must be made. Compared to the usual field work experienced by the archae-ologist, with all of its dust and heavy shoveling under a hot sun, this type of archaeology certainly is most attractive. All of the artifacts are on top of the ground, the sites are close to civilization, and almost all cemeteries have lovely, shady trees.

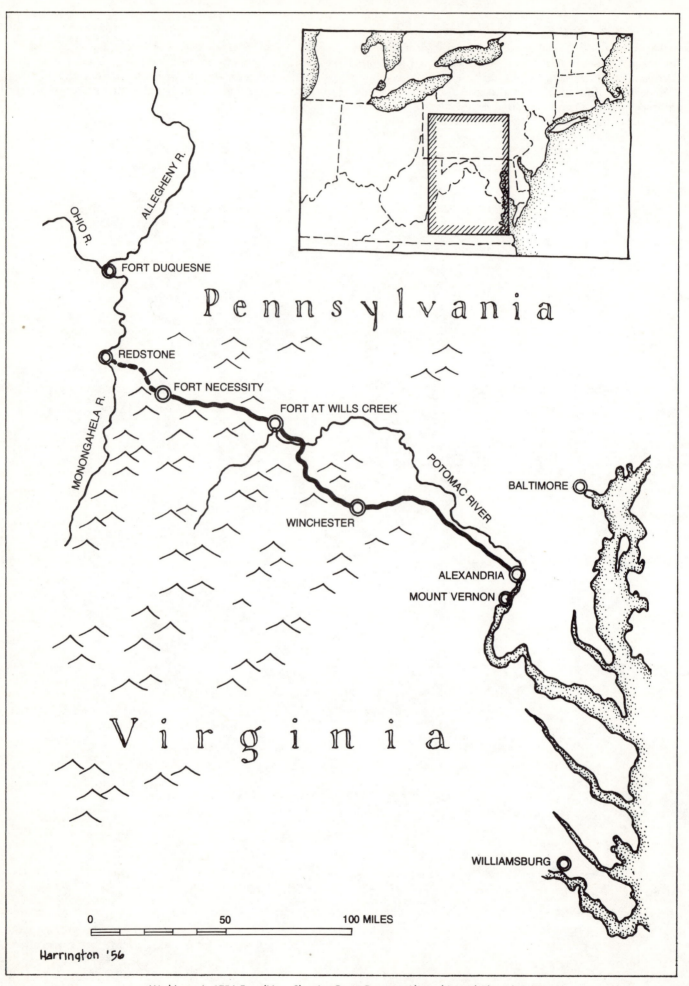

OHIO R.

ALLEGHENY R.

FORT DUQUESNE

MONONGAHELA R.

REDSTONE

FORT NECESSITY

FORT AT WILLS CREEK

Pennsylvania

POTOMAC RIVER

BALTIMORE

WINCHESTER

ALEXANDRIA

MOUNT VERNON

Virginia

WILLIAMSBURG

| 0 | 50 | 100 MILES |

Harrington '56

Washington's 1754 Expedition, Showing Route Between Alexandria and The Ohio Country.

CHAPTER 19

New Light on Washington's Fort Necessity

J. C. HARRINGTON

PREFACE

On July 3, 1754, in an open meadow between two mountain ridges in southwestern Pennsylvania, was fought the first battle of the long struggle between France and England for control of North America. The English colonial troops occupied a little makeshift fortification known as Fort Necessity. The larger French army, which finally won the engagement and forced the English to withdraw temporarily from the disputed "Ohio Country", was fighting from the cover of woods that bordered the meadow.

The scene of this important, but little-known opening battle of the French and Indian War, is now a national shrine. As Fort Necessity National Battlefield Site, it has been administered by the National Park Service, U.S. Department of the Interior, since 1933. It is located in Fayette County, Pennsylvania, on U.S. Route 40, 55 miles west of Cumberland, Maryland, and 11 miles east of Uniontown.

To more adequately interpret the site to the visiting public, the National Park Service found it necessary to supplement the scanty documentary information by archaeological exploration. Excavating began in August, 1952, under the author's supervision, with little expectation of finding more than a few "relics" and possibly the remains of certain entrenchments, which, according to the records, lay outside a stockade erected by the English just a month before the battle. The chance of discovering any remnant of the original stockade seemed very slight, in view of the extensive excavations carried on in connection with the earlier development and the project offered little challenge as an archaeological problem.

As it turned out, however, the archaeological explorations of 1952 and 1953 proved to be both exciting and productive. Assumptions as to the fort's location, size, and shape, which, through more than a century of repetition, had come to be accepted as established facts, were found to be in error. Most important was the recovery of relatively complete information on the original fort, including both the stockade and the outer entrenchments, permitting an authentic reconstruction on the exact original site. Reconstruction, as a matter of fact, was not a major concern when the work began, as the reproduction constructed in 1932 was believed to be on the original site and, on the whole, correct as to details.

The present report describes the archaeological explorations and interprets the discoveries in the light of available recorded information. I would have preferred giving only a general narrative account of the digging, with emphasis on interpreting the data. However, it is widely held, and undoubtedly with justification, that the digger should first of all make available the complete record so that others may use the data as they see fit, or can better appraise the archaeolo-

gist's interpretations. Unfortunately the bald record is not particularly interesting. I even considered relegating it to an appendix, but even this seemed to be too much of a departure from accepted reporting practice.

It may seem that I have included more background material than would be required for the reader to follow the account of the excavating and the subsequent interpretations. I have elaborated on certain incidents prior to 1952, not just to set the stage for the archaeological project, but, as I will point out in the Introduction, because this project is such a clear demonstration of the rewards that come from the historian and the archaeologist joining hands in a cooperative venture. It is also an excellent example of faulty criticism of historical data, brought out so clearly in the controversy, which went on for over a century, as to whether the fort was triangular or diamond shaped.

The usual archaeological report takes up at an early point the geography of the site and the flora and fauna. The natural environment certainly played a part in the historical events that we are dealing with here, but the situation is not exactly comparable to the excavation of an Indian shell midden. Rather than devoting a separate section to the geography of the site, data of this sort will be presented in appropriate places along with the description of the excavations and analysis of the findings.

Acknowledgments are not easy because so many people had a hand in the project in one way or another. The neighbors of the Battlefield Site, as well as people in surrounding communities, were genuinely interested in the excavating and reconstruction and helped in many ways, from furnishing historical information to seeing that I had proper nourishment and shelter. The following are singled out, not because they were any more cooperative than the many who are not listed, but because they rendered some particular service or assistance. Mr. Melvin J. Thorpe, Superintendent of Fort Necessity National Battlefield Site, took care of all the time-consuming and irksome administrative details, as well as helping directly with the field work and looking after the project in my absence. Dr. Frederick Tilberg, Historian at Gettysburg National Military Park, assembled documentary materials prior to the excavating, and conferred with me throughout the project in the relating of archaeological discoveries to the historical evidence. Exhibits in the reconstructed storehouse were planned and executed by the Branch of Museums, National Park Service, under Mr. Ralph Lewis' direction. Mrs. Preston Martin, Custodian of the Mount Washington Tavern Museum, helped in innumerable ways, as did Mr. Martin, then Superintendent of Fort Necessity State Park. Dr. William Blake Hindman of Uniontown gave us the benefit of his long and scholarly study of the historical records and his intimate knowledge of the site. Mr. Harry Blackford, Civil Engineer, who mapped and excavated the site in 1931, turned over all of his notes and records and cooperated unstintingly, even though our more extensive explorations brought out evidence contrary to his earlier findings. Walter J. (Buzz) Storey, Jr., Staff Writer for the *Uniontown Evening Standard* performed a service that is difficult to appraise. Through his lively, timely, and accurate news stories and his daily column, he kept local interest alive and did much to keep up the morale of all of us on the job. Technical advice and related assistance was furnished by Dr. J. H. Easterby, Director of the South Carolina Archives Department; Mr. Minor Wine Thomas, then of Colonial Williamsburg; Dr. Charles W. Porter, III, Mr. Harold Peterson, Mr. Frank Barnes, Dr. J. Walter Coleman, and a host of others in the National Park Service. Identification of stockade specimens was furnished by the Forest Products Laboratory, Forest Service, U.S. Department of Agriculture. Mr. James Holland lent a willing and valuable hand in reviewing the manuscript, advising on references, and in many other ways. Mrs. Virginia Harris did all of the typing, including the final duplicating copy, and much of the editorial work.

J. C. Harrington
National Park Service
Richmond, Virginia

December 1, 1955

Later note: The reader will wonder, and rightly, why Hugh Cleland's work, George Washington in the Ohio Valley, *is not cited extensively in this report. Unfortunately, my manuscript, with the exception of Appendix 1, had been completed and typed for publication before I had seen Professor Cleland's book, which contains many of the contemporary accounts quoted and referred to here. However, some of the accounts, such as the Shaw document, are not quoted in full by Professor Cleland, and are, therefore, retained in the present work. Moreover, it will be more convenient for the reader of this report to include them here.*

INTRODUCTION

Archaeology has been referred to as the "handmaiden of history", but only within the past twenty years or so has it come to be accepted generally by students of American history. Even so, the acceptance has not been without reservation, although the increasing number of spectacular demonstrations of archaeology's contribution—Jamestown, Williamsburg, Saugus, and many others—are beginning to bear fruit.

There are several explanations for the reticence on the part of the "American" historian to take up with this newcomer, even though archaeology has long been accepted by students of the Near East and other areas as a valuable historical tool. Foremost is the fact that the historian has for so long been interested in different problems and different approaches from those of concern to the archaeologist. Probably of almost equal importance is the fact that the historian has utilized a different kind of raw material. Usually he has at hand such a wealth of recorded source material that the data provided through archaeology, in comparison, seems pitifully meager and, at times, inconsequential. Then too, the archaeologist has often been concerned entirely with objects, which makes

him, in the eyes of the historian, an antiquarian of sorts. But excavations at a great many historic sites during the past two decades have shown that archaeology can provide significant historical data. With increasing evidence that archaeological studies can be set in a framework acceptable to historians, and that archaeological data are of value to historians, students of the American scene are showing more interest in archaeology as a useful accessory.[1]

The Fort Necessity project not only brings out the value of archaeology as a historical tool but clearly demonstrates the importance of the archaeologist and historian working as a team from the outset, checking and interpreting each bit of evidence as it comes to light. By no means is this the first archaeological exploration at a historic site in this country to have demonstrated the value of the historian and archaeologist joining hands in the study of the physical and cultural history of a buried site. The Fort Necessity project, however, shows more clearly than almost any other the importance of conducting documentary research and excavations with the problems and progress of each being known and considered at every step by both the historian and the archaeologist. In this case the excavating would certainly have terminated before the original remains had even been found had the archaeologist not reanalyzed and reappraised the documentary information in relation to the results of the excavating from the first season's field work. The point should be evident from the present report, even though attention is not called to it explicitly.

The Fort Necessity project offers also an excellent lesson in historiography. For over a century, qualified scholars had had their say as to what the fort looked like on the day of the battle in 1754. Had they confined their ruminations to evidence from written records, they probably would not have gone so far astray. But quite properly they took into account the physical evidence observable at the site; some even resorting to archaeology. Unfortunately, this led to two distinct and irreconcilable interpretations—neither, as it ironically turned out, being correct.

Even the most conscientious scholar would probably admit that the precise location and appearance of Fort Necessity is of no great consequence to American history. The most detailed account of the battle at Great Meadows is not affected particularly by whether the fort was round or square; whether it was 50 feet or 65 feet across; or whether the storehouse within the fort faced south or east. On the other hand, these data, if known, can make the narrative more realistic, even though they may have little effect on the historian's final conclusions. Moreover, a fact is a fact, and it is the responsibility of the historian, as well as his firm intention, to avail himself of as many facts as he can, even though his particular interest or approach does not exploit equally every fact available to him.

For the development of the site as an educational exhibit, knowledge of the most minute details of the fort's construction was important. Whether such an exhibit should take the form of a full-scale reconstruction or a museum diorama, the closer the reproduction can be to the original, the more intelligible it will be to the viewer. Normally, the relative amount known about the original structure determines whether a reconstruction can be undertaken. Other practical and theoretical considerations enter into the decision, but a reconstruction would not even be contemplated

[1] *See J. C. Harrington, "Archaeology as an Auxilliary Science to American History".*

unless enough were known to make the final product highly authentic.

In the present instance, the archaeological explorations were initiated with no real expectation of uncovering enough information to warrant a reconstruction. There was little hope, in fact, of determining the original size and shape of the fort, let alone sufficient construction details to permit the construction of a defensible reproduction. This fact, however, did not affect the research procedure, although there is no denying that it dampened the enthusiasm of the archaeologist, particularly when the results of the first season's work were completely negative.

In this account, I will treat the historical background as briefly as feasible, since I have nothing new to offer and since it serves only as orientation for the archaeological report. I will include a section on the century-long controversy over the shape of the fort, partly because it had a definite bearing on the archaeological program, and partly because it is of interest as an object lesson in the critical use of historical data. Primarily, however, I will fulfill the researcher's professional obligation of entering for the record a detailed account of the excavations and the interpretations derived from the archaeological and historical data. Finally, I believe it will be of interest to describe briefly the way the site was developed as an educational exhibit, since the interpretive development was, in fact, the primary justification for the excavating.

BACKGROUND: CONSTRUCTION OF FORT NECESSITY AND EVENTS LEADING UP TO THE BATTLE AT GREAT MEADOWS

The story of Washington's first military venture, culminating in the battle at Great Meadows on July 3, 1754, has been recounted so many times and in such detail that there seems little need to go into it here, other than to provide a very general summary and to emphasize the points that relate directly to the archaeological project.[2] Nor does it seem necessary to support every statement in this summary with footnotes, since the many published accounts are adequately documented. If, in this brief account, the more important historical aspects of the story are slighted and less important ones are given more than summary treatment, it is either because the former have been fully covered in readily available sources, or because the latter are more directly related to the interpretation of the archaeological discoveries. There are several concise and vivid contemporary accounts of the battle, some of which are included as appendixes to this report (1 through 5). The present historical summary, therefore, will treat the actual battle more briefly than would be called for otherwise.

Lt. Col. George Washington, in command of about 160 Virginia volunteers, arrived at Great Meadows on May 24, 1754. For nearly two months this untrained, poorly pro-

visioned army had been hauling supplies and heavy equipment all the way from Alexandria, Virginia, much of the way over narrow mountain trails. There had been desertions; the men were hungry, tired, and dissatisfied. Little wonder that the broad, open expanse of this meadow, with ample pasture for horses and cattle, appealed to Washington and that he decided at once to make it his main base of operations. The winding streams running through the meadow provided natural entrenchments, and, after bushes along the stream banks had been cut, he wrote Governor Dinwiddie that he had here "a charming field for an encounter".[3]

This was not Washington's first visit to these parts. Earlier that year, as a special emissary of the Virginia governor, he had carried a message to the French warning them that they were encroaching on land "notoriously known to be the property of the Crown of Great Britain".[4] But the warning was defied by the French, who looked upon the English as the encroachers. Governor Dinwiddie had then sent an expedition to the Ohio Country to build a fort at "The forks", site of the present City of Pittsburgh. Washington's detail was the vanguard of an army being recruited by Dinwiddie, with Col. Joshua Fry in command, which was to assist and support the little garrison at the forks. Washington, then only 22 years old, and with his new commission of Lieutenant Colonel, had set out on April 2 with the advance party from Alexandria.[5] The main body was to follow as soon as men could be recruited and supplies and equipment assembled. The nature of the entire expedition was altered, however, when word was received along the way that the partially completed fort at the forks had been surrendered to the French.

To understand why the little fort at Great Meadows, later named Fort Necessity, was built as it was, it is important to keep in mind exactly what Washington's objectives were after the French drove the English from their partially completed fort at the forks and began construction of Fort Duquesne. Although Governor Dinwiddie had specifically instructed Washington to resort to force, if necessary, the intent of the advance detachment had been to reinforce the garrison at the forks. On the way, they were also to improve the trail over which the main army would march, but the principal objective was to strengthen the garrison and help complete the fort.

Learning, however, that the French were established at that strategic point, the original plans had to be altered, and, in addition to constructing a road, Washington was now to build a fort on the Monongahela River at the mount of Redstone Creek.[6] With the way thus prepared, the main

---

[2]Most of the references cited hereafter, which deal specifically with Fort Necessity and the 1754 expedition, contain good discussions of events leading up to the battle at Great Meadows, as well as the battle itself. For good brief accounts, see A. A. Salley, The Independent Company from South Carolina at Great Meadows, Frederick Tilberg, Fort Necessity, and John P. Cowan, "George Washington at Fort Necessity". Two of the fullest accounts were written more than a century apart: Jared Sparks, The Writings of George Washington, and Douglas S. Freeman, George Washington.

[3]Of the site of the future Fort Necessity, Washington wrote soon after arriving at Great Meadows: "We have, with Nature's assistance, made a good Intrenchment, and, by clearing the Bushes out of these Meadows, prepar'd a charming field for an Encounter". (Letter to Robert Dinwiddie, May 27, 1754, in John C. Fitzpatrick, ed., The Writings of George Washington, I, 54. This work will be cited hereafter as Fitzpatrick, Writings.) Even before preparing the first temporary entrenchments, the natural terrain offered some protection, for Washington wrote in his journal that upon arriving at the Meadows on May 24, he "placed Troops behind two natural Intrenchments, and had our wagons put there also". (John C. Fitzpatrick, ed., Diaries of George Washington, I, 85, This work will be cited hereafter as Frederick, Diaries.) The "natural Intrenchments" undoubtedly were the creek beds of Great Meadow Run and a small branch, later known as "Indian Run". (See Figure 1.)

[4]Freeman, George Washington, I, 309.

[5]Ibid., 343–344.

[6]Later in the French and Indian War, after the capture of Fort Duquesne, Fort Burd was built at this same point, and became an important British outpost. It is now the site of the city of Brownsville.

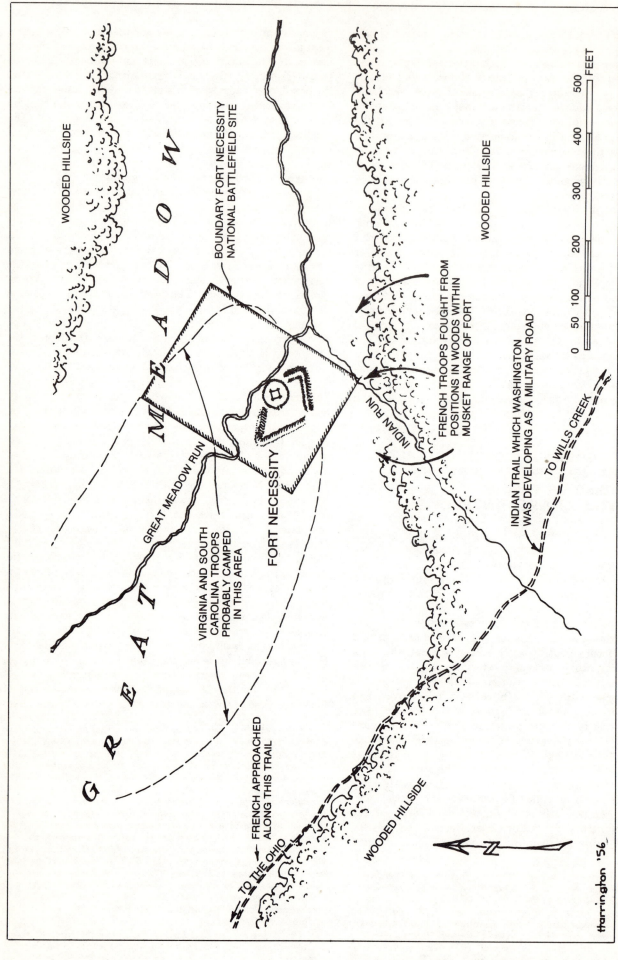

WOODED HILLSIDE

WOODED HILLSIDE

WOODED HILLSIDE

G R E A T   M E A D O W

GREAT MEADOW RUN

BOUNDARY FORT NECESSITY
NATIONAL BATTLEFIELD SITE

VIRGINIA AND SOUTH
CAROLINA TROOPS
PROBABLY CAMPED
IN THIS AREA

FORT NECESSITY

FRENCH APPROACHED
ALONG THIS TRAIL

TO THE OHIO

FRENCH TROOPS FOUGHT FROM
POSITIONS IN WOODS WITHIN
MUSKET RANGE OF FORT

INDIAN RUN

INDIAN TRAIL WHICH WASHINGTON
WAS DEVELOPING AS A MILITARY ROAD

TO WILLS CREEK

N

0   50 100   200   300   400   500

FEET

Harrington '56

FIGURE 1. Conjectural Plan of Great Meadows in 1754 as Reconstructed from Historical and Archaeological Evidence, Shown in Relation to Fort Necessity National Battle-field Site. In 1962 the Entire Historic Area Became Part of Fort Necessity National Battlefield.

94

army would be assembled at the new base on the Monongahela, from which it would be in position to launch an attack against Fort Duquesne. In advising Governor Dinwiddie of the new plans, Washington wrote: "We will endeavour to make the road sufficiently good for the heaviest artillery to pass, and when we arrive at Red-stone Creek fortify ourselves as strongly as the short time will allow."[7]

It was important that this road over the mountains (which, on the whole, followed the Nemacolin Trail) should be adequate for use by horse and wagon, as well as mounted cannon.[8] The base at Great Meadows was intended simply as a station along this road between the main base at Wills Creek (later Fort Cumberland) and the new advance post on the Monongahela. Subsequent events, it is true, necessitated construction of a defensible fort at Great Meadows. But its situation with reference to the overall plan of the expedition, as well as the circumstances of its construction, must be recognized to understand its small size and unusual design. Expediency, not lack of military sophistication, accounts for the plan of Fort Necessity, even though Washington admittedly was a novice in military affairs at this time. Even so, he, as well as his officers, had some familiarity with frontier forts of conventional design. He had observed, among others, the stockaded fort at Wills Creek and even the more elaborate Fort Le Boeuf of the French, where he had delivered Dinwiddie's ultimatum the preceding winter. In addition, as evidenced by various statements found in his writings during this period, he was sufficiently versed in military arts to have definite opinions as to the suitability of sites for forts.

The important point to keep in mind is that the site of Fort Necessity was selected originally for an operating base, where supplies could be stored and the expedition temporarily headquartered. Washington had no intention of building any kind of a fort whatever at Great Meadows when his band of road-builders first stopped there on May 24. At such an advanced position, however, and with rumors continuously coming to him of French and Indian activities in the vicinity, he knew there was always a possibility that he might be attacked at any point along the way. Washington was not planning to become involved in a major engagement at this stage. But the possibility could not be ignored, and it is easy to understand why this place appealed to him as a "charming field for an encounter".

After setting up camp at Great Meadows, word came that a party of French soldiers was in the vicinity. With a force of 40 men, Washington, early in the morning of May 28, surprised the French at their campsite a few miles from Great Meadows. In the skirmish that followed, in which the French were quickly and decisively defeated, their leader, Sieur de Jumonville, was killed.[9] One Frenchman escaped, the rest being killed or taken prisoner. Fearing reprisal by the main

French army, Washington quickly returned to Great Meadows and hastily began building a stockade with some earth entrenchments.[10] It would appear, however, that work stopped on the fortification as soon as it seemed the French did not intend to retaliate.

During the month of June, Washington worked on the road westward toward the Monongahela, continuing to use Great Meadows as the main camp and supply base. His force had been increased by the remainder of the Virginia regiment and by a South Carolina Independent Company of regular troops, bringing it to around 400 officers and men. Word had come that Colonel Fry had been fatally wounded in an accident and Col. James Innes, who had arrived at Wills Creek with a North Carolina regiment, had been placed in command of the entire expedition. Washington, now commissioned a full colonel, was given command of the Virginia regiment, with Captain James Mackay in charge of the British regulars from South Carolina.

Toward the end of June, word came that a large body of French and Indians was advancing from Fort Duquesne. The Virginia troops, who then were working on the western section of the road to Redstone Creek, first considered making a stand at Gists' Plantation, several miles northwest of Great Meadows, where they had thrown up a temporary fortification. But they decided to fall back to Great Meadows, which they reached on July 1, and set to work strengthening their position. There was little time to do much, for the French attacked on the morning of July 3. The fighting lasted throughout the day, in a pouring rain, and at eight o'clock that night the French Commander, Villiers, requested a parley. After several hours of negotiating, an agreement was reached that was satisfactory to both Villiers and Washington. It called for the English to give up Fort Necessity, although they were accorded honors of war and allowed to keep their small arms and supplies. The following morning, July 4, they marched out of the fort, making their way as best they could to Wills Creek. The French destroyed the fort and returned to Fort Duquesne. Thus ended the opening battle of the French and Indian War.[11]

HOW FORT NECESSITY GOT ITS NAME

The term "Fort Necessity" is found only once in the contemporary records dating from the period prior to the

---

[7]*Letter to Governor Dinwiddie, April 25, 1754, in Fitzpatrick, Writings, I, 41.*

[8]*This trail had been laid out by the Delaware Indian, Nemacolin, in 1750 at the request of Capt. Thomas Cresap. (See Archer B. Hulbert, Washington's Road, 96.) Cresap, one of the earliest of the Virginia settlers in this section, had been employed by the Ohio Company in 1748 to mark out a route to the Ohio.*

[9]*Probably more pages have been written about this skirmish, often referred to as "The Jumonville Incident", than to the remainder of the expedition, including the Battle of Fort Necessity. Some writers call this engagement the opening "battle" of the French and Indian War. However, it quite definitely was not a battle in the military sense, but only a skirmish between two scouting parties. Its importance lay more in the way it was exploited for propaganda purposes by the French to show that the English were the real aggressors in the disputed Ohio Country. The incident was magnified immeasurably by its unfortunate inclusion in the terms of capitulation at Fort Necessity, in which Washington, misadvised by*

the interpreter, admitted that Jumonville had been assassinated. (For Washington's account of the Jumonville skirmish, see Fitzpatrick, Writings, I, 55–58 and 64–65. For a short account, see Tilberg, Fort Necessity, 8–10.) Washington very ably refuted the French claim of Jumonville's assassination, which first came to his attention through the translation back into English of his Journal, which had been translated into French and published for propaganda purposes soon after it was captured at the Battle of Fort Necessity. (See Fitzpatrick, Writings, I, 36–37.)

[10]*There seems to be no consistent application of the terms "palisade" and "stockade" at the time of Fort Necessity's construction, although later military usage definitely distinguishes between them. Washington always used some form of the word "palisade", e.g., "palisado'd Fort". Governor Dinwiddie, on the other hand, called Fort Necessity a "Pallisadoed Ford" when writing to Washington, probably out of politeness, (Official Records of Robert Dinwiddie, I, 230), but when writing to his superiors in England, he referred to it as a "Stockade Fort". (Ibid., 206.) Shaw, describing the fort soon after the battle, referred to a "stockade". (See page 26.) Colonel Burd, who stopped at the site in 1759, also called it a "stockade". (See page 28.) Since "stockade" was used more commonly in contemporary references, that term, rather than "palisade", will be used in this report.*

[11]*See Appendixes 1 through 5 for contemporary accounts of the battle.*

battle, and very infrequently in such records thereafter. The battle is referred to invariably as "The Battle at the Great Meadows"—never "The Battle of Fort Necessity".[12] The earliest known reference to "Fort Necessity" is in an entry in Washington's journal on June 25, 1954, which reads as follows: "I thought it proper to send Captain Montour to Fort Necessity in order to try if he could persuade the Indians to come to us (to where the Virginia volunteers were working on the road some distance to the west)".[13]

Although Washington mentions the Great Meadows many times in his diary and in letters, I know of only one subsequent use of the term "Fort Necessity" in any of his writings. Many years after the battle, in describing the 1754 expedition, he referred to "a small stockade in the middle of the entrenchment called Fort Necessity".[14] Nor does the name appear in any of the contemporary official records dealing with the battle. Even so, the name "Fort Necessity" almost certainly was widely known and used. It is so designated on maps drawn a year later in connection with the Braddock Campaign.[15]

The earliest explanation of the origin of the name is in a letter dated May 12, 1755, written by John Banister, Jr., a participant in the battle. He wrote: ". . . we built a fort called 'Necessity', from the great difficulty of procuring necessaries for subsistence when our soldiers were there employed".[16] Even though this contemporary account has the ring of authenticity, slightly different origins for the name have been suggested. Douglas Freeman, for example, accounts for it as follows: "The whole and the parts were not a design of engineering art but of frontier necessity. Wherefore, George gave it the name, Fort Necessity".[17] I would be more willing to accept Freeman's explanation if he had said "military necessity" rather than "frontier necessity".

It has also been suggested that the name originated with the necessity of having to erect makeshift defenses at Great Meadows (following the Jumonville incident), at a time when Washington quite clearly was intent only on building a road to the Monongahela. The fort at Great Meadows was not planned, as was the proposed fort at the mouth of Redstone Creek, but was built out of necessity when Washington expected to be attacked momentarily by a superior force.

In all probability, an entirely satisfactory explanation for the name will never be found, unless we accept Banister's. We can be reasonably sure, however, that it had to do with the difficulties and hardships associated with the fort's construction and use.

THE TRIANGLE VERSUS DIAMOND-SHAPED CONTROVERSY

In 1816, Freeman Lewis, a professional surveyor, visited Great Meadows and mapped the surface remains of Fort Necessity, still quite conspicuous at that time. Inexplicably to those who later visited the site, he recorded the remains as triangular in plan, with a small, semi-hexagonal bulge extending out from the base of the triangle (Figure 2). Lewis' map was not published at the time, and was not generally available to scholars, nor widely known, until it was published in Lowdermilk's History of Cumberland in 1878.[18] To my knowledge, the first published drawing purporting to be a plan for the fort based upon field observations and measurements, appeared in Jared Sparks' work of 1837 (Figure 3).[19] Sparks, whose field inspection was made in 1830, was the first to show the fort as diamond-shaped, although it is quite evident that he had not seen the Lewis drawing, nor did he realize that he was to start a century-long argument; an argument that could have been settled quite easily by an inspection of the remains. The resulting discussion over the shape of the fort, which Douglas Freeman characterizes as "almost amusingly heated"[20], was finally brought to a close, and, it is hoped, incontestably, by the recent archaeological discoveries. Further discussion of the subject might seem superfluous at this stage. However, it is of interest not only from the standpoint of historical criticism, but also relevant to the present discussion of the archaeological explorations of 1952 and 1953, as well as the earlier excavations in 1931.[21] It explains, in part, why the only really pertinent documentary evidence relating to the original appearance of the fort was ignored; why the stockade was incorrectly reconstructed in 1932; and how the correct location of the stockade and entrenchments came very close to never being discovered.

Strangely enough, in spite of all the discussion through the years as the plan of the surface traces, no really detailed topographic survey was made until 1931, when Harry Blackford accurately mapped the site prior to archaeological excavations and reconstruction.[22] Since Lewis was reputed to have been a competent surveyor, and since there had been so much discussion by writers over the years, the National Park Service, in preparation for extensive repairs, was practically

---

[12]Although most contemporary accounts call it "The Battle at the Great Meadows", in his note of appreciation to the Virginia House of Burgesses, dated October 23, 1754, for their commendation of his conduct at the battle, Washington referred to "the late unsuccessful Engagement with the French at the Great Meadows". (Fitzpatrick, Writings, I, 103.)

[13]Fitzpatrick, Diaries, I, 101.

[14]Fitzpatrick, Writings, I, 40.

[15]See page 27.

[16]Letter to Robert Bolling, cited in William and Mary College Quarterly, old series, X, 104.

[17]Freeman, George Washington, I, 402. There is no basis for giving Washington credit for naming the fort, although presumably he had the right to do so, since it was built under his command. Some writers state that Major Stobo laid out the fort and directed its construction.

[18]The original Lewis map is now (1955) in the possession of Mrs. J. A. Batton, 136 Belmont Circle, Uniontown, Pennsylvania. It was first published, as a facsimile (redrawn from the original by D. S. Stewart), in W. H. Lowdermilk, History of Cumberland, opp. 76. Later reproductions, all of which vary from the original Lewis manuscript map in various details, may have been copied from Lowdermilk. The Lewis document, but with interlineal "translations" of the descriptive notes, was published as a broadside of the Westmoreland Fayette Branch of the Historical Society of Western Pennsylvania, presumably at the time of the Washington Bicentennial. (The broadside carries no publication date.)

[19]Jared Sparks, ed., The Writings of George Washington, I, opp. 56. A description of the remains, but without the map, is also found in Sparks' later work, The Life of George Washington, 51.

[20]Freeman, George Washington, I, 402.

[21]For a more complete review of the history of this controversy, see, in addition to other references cited in this chapter, Frederick Tilberg, The Location and Structure of Fort Necessity. I apologize for referring frequently to unpublished reports, but they cover important points in the discussions and must be noted, even though they are not readily accessible. Pertinent sections of the unpublished report on the 1931 excavations are furnished in the Appendix. The several manuscripts by Frederick Tilberg and J. C. Harrington, all relevant to the present report, are too detailed to be included as appendixes, but can be consulted, if desired, at the sources indicated in the Bibliography.

[22]In addition to the map furnished by Blackford, as reproduced in Figure 9, I was also furnished the original field notes made by Mr. Blackford in 1931, from which additional information, not shown on his map, was obtained. Blackford's material proved particularly valuable in working out the final solution to the fort problem. His map was first published in Frederick Tilberg, "Washington's Stockade at Fort Necessity", 253.

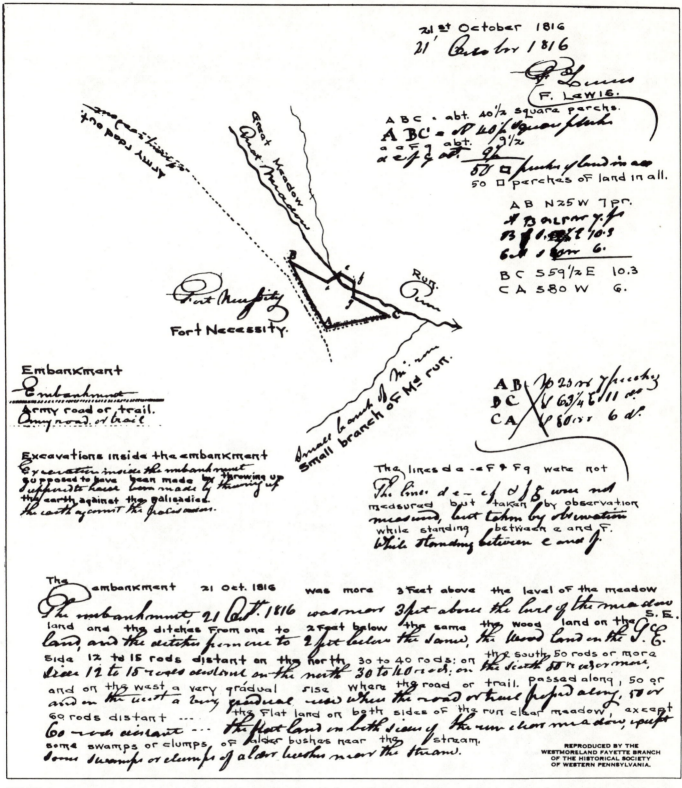

FIGURE 2. Freeman Lewis Survey Made in 1816. Interlineation Made on Photo-Reproduction of Original Map for Broadside, Published by Westmoreland Fayette Branch, Historical Society of Western Pennsylvania, Circa 1932.

compelled to do a little exploring to settle, if possible, this old argument, even though the results of the 1931 explorations seemed at the time to be conclusive.

It is now quite apparent that there would have been no argument over the plan of the existing surface remains if those who objected to Sparks' layout had taken the trouble to return to the site and check the earlier survey. Actually, however, this disagreement as to the plan of the fort was not the real reason why it took so long to arrive at the correct solution. Basically, the trouble did not lie in the shape of the surface remains, but in their interpretation. It all started with a note on Lewis' map to the effect that the ridges and depressions were the result of earth having been piled against the stockade posts, and that the ridge, therefore, represented the line of the original stockade. Later writers, whether or not they followed Lewis' triangular plan, invariably gave the same interpretation to these surface ridges.

A single example from the many that might be cited, is

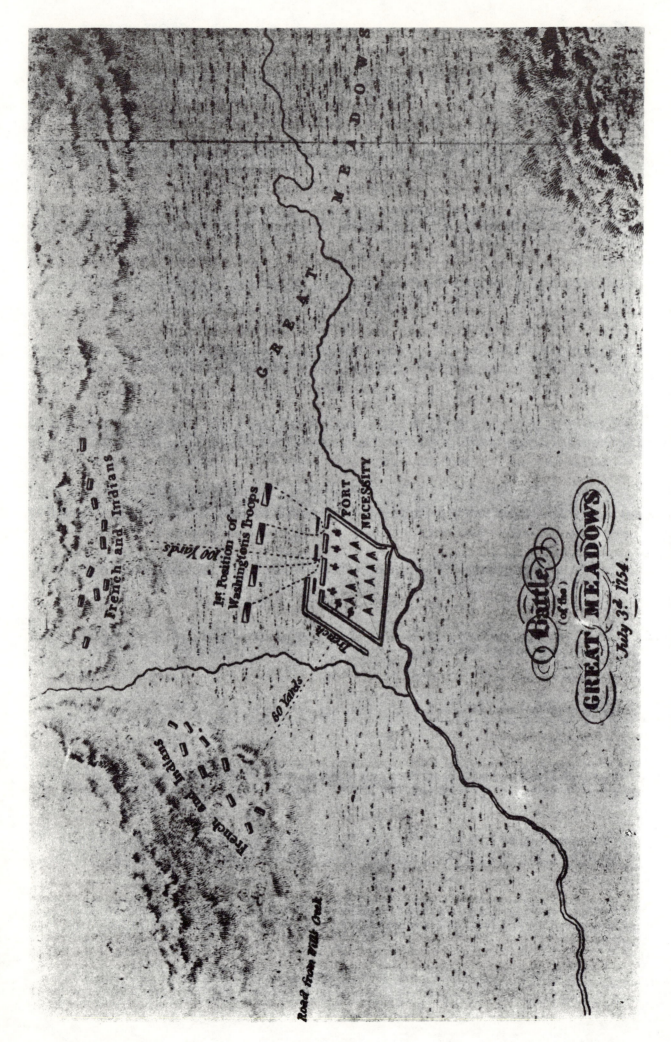

FIGURE 3. Map Published in Jared Sparks, *The Writings of George Washington,* 1837.

sufficient to show how this interpretation, possibly only a tentative suggestion on Lewis' part, was accepted as an established fact. In a discussion of the Great Meadows tract, describing the site as it appeared about 1881, a local writer referred to "the ruins of the fort or *embanked stockade*, which it really was . . . "[23] (italics added). Even Douglas Freeman, as late as 1948, after a most exhaustive study of the source materials, implicitly followed this interpretation when he sided with the Lewis opponents as to the shape of the fort.[24] In fact, this interpretation was still accepted without question when archaeological explorations were carried out in 1952.

Some twenty years after Sparks' work was published, James Veech, a local attorney who had worked with Lewis, came out quite vigorously, almost emotionally, in support of the triangular plan.[25]

In referring to Sparks' drawing and description of Fort Necessity, Veech wrote: "It may have presented that diamond shape, in 1830. But in 1816, the senior author of these sketches (Freeman Lewis) made a regular survey of it with compass and chain . . . As thereby shown, it was in the form of an obtuse angled triangle . . . "[26] Veech then goes on to present a good case for the triangular plan, and having dealt with Sparks, he turns to Colonel Burd, who had innocently described the ruins as he saw them in 1759.[27] "A more inexplicable, and much more inexcusable error than that in Mr. Sparks' great work, is the statement of Colonel Burd, in the Journal of his expedition to Redstone in 1759. He says the fort was round! with a house in it! That Washington may have had some sort of a log, bark-covered cabin erected within his lines, is not improbable; but how the good Carlisle Colonel could metamorphose the lines into a circular form is a mystery which we cannot solve".[28]

On this matter of a round fort, even Hulbert agreed with Lewis and Veech. As an argument against the Lewis triangular shape, Hulbert wrote: "He (Burd) described its remains as circular in shape. If it was originally a triangle it is improbable that it could have appeared round five years later. If, however, it was originally an irregular square, it is not improbable that the rains and frosts of five winters, combined with the demolition of the fort by the French, would have given the mounds a circular appearance".[29] Even Freeman accepted this explanation,[30] as did Tilberg, in reviewing the subject in 1952.[31] The interesting thing is that not one of these students considered the possibility that Lewis and Burd were describing two entirely different features of the fort.

Partly because Veech was a convincing writer, partly because Lewis was an experienced surveyor, and partly because Veech's dissertation was not available to most scholars until 1892, no champion of the Sparks diamond shape appeared on the scene until 1901 when Archer Hulbert carefully examined the site and found, to his amazement, that the old Lewis survey did not fit the existing remains.[32] It is not too surprising that Lowdermilk, in 1878, should have reproduced the Lewis map (Figure 4), but it is surprising that no one on the Pennsylvania State Commission on Frontier Forts inspected the site before their report was published in 1896.[33] In that report, the Lewis map is improved upon by adding entrenchments outside the stockade, possibly inspired by Sparks (Figure 5). The shape of the little bulge at the back of the fort was also changed, as well as the location of Meadow Run. Other topographic features were added, all very reminiscent of the Sparks map (See Figure 6).

Hulbert presented a most detailed explanation, or rationalization, as to how Lewis could have made so conspicuous an error. The error, of course, would have been obvious to anyone taking the trouble to inspect the site, as Blackford found in 1931, or as Thwaite observed when he visited the site in 1903 and made a rough check of the surface remains.[34] Hulbert's review of the evidence was so thorough, and his arguments so convincing, that the case would seem to have been closed once and for all. Douglas Freeman, whose research and analysis was as thorough as any ever done on the 1754 expedition, was satisfied with the explanation and wrote that Hulbert's "conclusions are accepted".[35]

The Hulbert discussion was reviewed in the report of the 1931—1932 project, results of which appeared to provide added proof of Hulbert's basic interpretation, with certain refinements provided through archaeological exploration.[36] Later, in Frederick Tilberg's "orientation report" prepared as a guide for the 1952 explorations, the Hulbert discussion was again presented, along with an appraisal of the added evidence from the 1931 explorations.[37] Hulbert, with certain modifications, was still accepted as the final word at the close of the 1952 explorations, when, in my brief preliminary report, I wrote that "on the basis of existing evidence, the present reconstruction is probably located very close to the

[23] The Frontier Forts of Western Pennsylvania, *II*, 38, *citing Evert, History of Fayette County.*

[24] *Freeman, George Washington, I, 402.*

[25] *James Veech, The Monongahela of Old. The work was started by Freeman Lewis in 1850. He turned it over to Veech, who had not completed it at the time of his death. A few copies, with one chapter unfinished, were made up from the printed sheets, and privately distributed in 1859. The chapter was completed by Veech's daughter and limited edition published in 1892. It was reissued in 1910.*

[26] *Veech, The Monongahela of Old, 53.*

[27] *Sherman Day, Historical Collections of the State of Pennsylvania, 336. (See page 28 for further information on Colonel Burd and his visit to Great Meadows.)*

[28] *Veech, The Monongahela of Old, 53–54.*

[29] *Hulbert, Washington's Road, 182.*

[30] *Freeman, George Washington, I, 402, F.N. 113.*

[31] *Tilberg, Fort Necessity Stockade—A Preliminary Study. He paraphrased Hulbert as follows: "It is probable, if the original fort were an irregular square or parallelogram, that the action of rain and snows over the five years since it was erected, as well as the demolition of the fort by the French, may well have left an appearance of circular mounds".*

[32] *Hulbert, Washington's Road, 177.*

[33] *George D. Albert, ed., The Frontier Forts of Western Pennsylvania, (map between pp. 32 and 33.)*

[34] *R. G. Thwaite, How George Rogers Clark Won the Northwest, 290–292. Thwaite's observations are of interest. He wrote: "It was surprising to find the remains of Fort Necessity so well preserved. Great Meadow Run, originally a lazy, weedgrown stream some ten feet wide, has been straightened by the present proprietor into a drainage ditch, but its ancient windings are readily distinguishable. (They still were in 1931, and fortunately Blackford mapped them at that time.) The change in the course of the run destroyed an outlying work, but the embankment of the fort itself is traceable through the greater part of its length. The line of earthwork is still some eight or ten inches above the surrounding level; while on the inner side, counting the excavation ditch, it has a height of about fifteen inches . . . There are of course no remaining evidences of the palisade, on top of the embankment, for this was at the time destroyed by the French . . . In the centre of the fort still rests, although upheaved by frost, a hewn block of limestone, two feet square, the only surviving memento of a movement . . . for the erection here of a Washington monument (in 1854) . . ."*

[35] *Freeman, George Washington, I, 402.*

[36] *Harry Blackford, Record and Description of the Reconstruction of Fort Necessity. (Cited hereafter as Blackford, Record).*

[37] *Frederick Tilberg, Fort Necessity Stockade—A Preliminary Study. Tilberg repeated this discussion in his later report, The Location and Structure of Fort Necessity.*

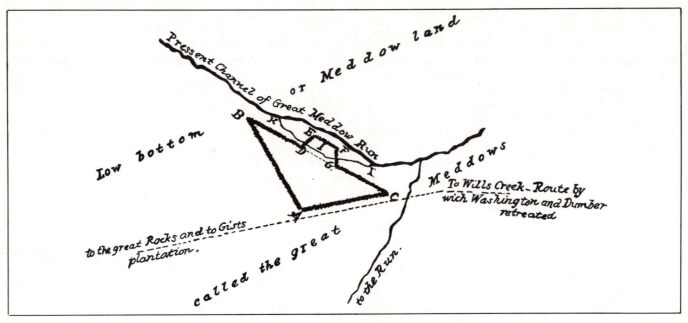

FIGURE 4. Map Published in W. H. Lowdermilk, *History of Cumberland,* 1878.

FIGURE 5. Map Published in George D. Albert, *The Frontier Forts of Western Pennsylvania,* 1896.

original lines of the fort".[38] Through all of the years of discussion of these surface traces, there had never been any question raised as to the validity of their interpretation as remnants of the earth piled against the stockade. The sole point of all the discussions, some rather heated, had been whether the fort was triangular or diamond-shaped in plan.

In view of the uncritical adherence to Lewis' original interpretation on the part of serious students, it is interesting to observe that a few people had visited the site and had naively reported what they saw, just as Burd did in 1759, unprejudiced by the unfortunate notation on Lewis' map. A canal surveyor, for example, passed the site in 1825 and wrote that he had seen "the mud walls of Fort Necessity . . . Its shape and extent are still to be traced by the

remains of the embankments . . . The embankments of the Fort I have said are still visible . . .".[39] Obviously, this visitor had not read about Washington having built a stockade, and he visualized the fort as a typical earthwork. Townsend Ward visited the site in 1854 and wrote: "A faint outline of the breastwork and a trace of the ditch are yet visible".[40] Ward, apparently, was one of the few who saw the remains in their true light, and very likely was the last writer to describe just what he saw, unprejudiced by the later arguments.

Now that the clouds have cleared away, it is difficult to see how anyone could have brushed aside Colonel Burd's observation, and it is rather surprising that almost everyone

---

[38]*J. C. Harrington,* Preliminary Report, Archaeological Explorations, Fort Necessity National Battlefield Site, *August–September, 1952.*

[39]*Tilberg,* The Location and Structure of Fort Necessity, *etc.,* 20, *citing the* Daily National Intelligencer, *Oct. 18, 1825.*

[40]*Quoted in Tilberg,* ibid., *citing* Pennsylvania Archives, *XII, 423.*

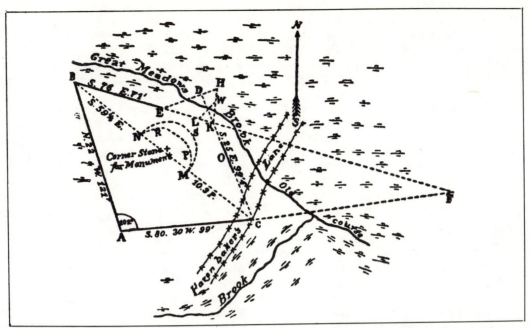

FIGURE 6. Survey Made by Robert McCracken and Published in Archer B. Hulbert, *Washington's Road,* 1903.

accepted Lewis' interpretation of the surface remains, or arrived at the same conclusions independently, especially since those interpretations are not particularly logical from the standpoint of military precedent. Unfortunately, almost any interpretation gains prestige by repetition and especially by publication, no matter what the qualifications of the author may be. It can gain so much prestige, in fact, that even new evidence will not be given proper consideration.

Such was the case when the Shaw document came to light some fifteen years ago.[41] The document is a deposition made only two months after the battle by a certain John Shaw, presumably a participant in the battle, and contains the following statement: "There was At this Place a Small Stocado Fort made in a Circular form round a Small House . . .". No one gave credence to this new evidence when it was discovered, and even as late as 1952, when preparing for archaeological explorations, it was summarily brushed aside, along with Colonel Burd's note, because it was counter to the traditional and accepted interpretation. After all, if one could see with his own eyes that the fort was diamond-shaped, why pay any attention to these people who said it was round?

A brief "case history" of this century-long controversy has been included, here, not to excuse, but to explain what now looms up as an unwarranted reluctance on everyone's part to analyze critically the available evidence. It explains also why, even with the Shaw document at hand, we saw the main objectives of the preliminary archaeological explorations as (1) locating the "lost" entrenchments, and (2) settling once and for all, the triangle versus diamond-shape controversy. In the detailed description of the excavations, I will show how this stubborn resistance to accepting perfectly good documentary evidence, which originated innocently with a note on a surveyor's map, finally was overcome.

GREAT MEADOWS SINCE THE BATTLE[42]

What happened at the site of Fort Necessity after the 1754 episode is of no great importance historically, but it could be important in the interpretation of archaeological findings. For that reason, the archaeologist needs to know how the land was used, what structures were built on it, and any other occurrences that might leave some record in the ground.

Great Meadows apparently played no important part in the Braddock Campaign just a year after the burning of Fort Necessity. The old trail that Washington had struggled so hard to make into a serviceable road had been improved for use by a much larger army, which passed by the ruins of Fort Necessity on June 25, 1755, on its march toward Fort Duquesne. By coincidence, Braddock was buried only a mile to the west of the site during the retreat of the British following their disastrous defeat by the French on July 9.[43] Fort Necessity, however, is indicated on several maps relating to the Braddock Campaign. For example, a British map dated 1755 shows "Great Meadow-Fort Necessity"[44], and a French map of the same year indicates the site as "F. de Necessite".[45]

The next we hear of Fort Necessity is in the accounts connected with the Forbes expedition. In a letter to Col. Henry Bouquet, dated August 2, 1758, Washington recom-

---

[41]*Deposition made by John B. W. Shaw before Governor James Glen of South Carolina on August 27, 1754. Original document in British Public Record Office; photostatic copy furnished by Historical Commission of South Carolina from microfilm negative. See Appendix 4 for transcript of this document and a note on the identification of Shaw. The manuscript will be cited hereafter as Shaw Deposition.*

[42]*The long controversy as to the size and shape of Fort Necessity, which began with the survey by Freeman Lewis in 1816, has been covered in the preceding section, and incidents relating thereto will not be repeated in this section.*

[43]*The site believed to be the spot where Braddock was buried is near the point where the Old National Pike (U.S. 40) crosses the Braddock Road about one mile west of the Mount Washington Tavern. A 23-acre tract surrounding the presumed burial site was acquired by the Braddock Park Association in 1909 and a monument erected in 1913. In 1932 the plot was transferred to the Pennsylvania Department of Forests and Waters, and in 1962 became a part of Fort Necessity National Battlefield.*

[44]*Tilberg, The Location and Structure of Fort Necessity, Exhibit IV.*

[45]*Ibid., Exhibit VI.*

mended Great Meadows as the best site in that vicinity for a post because of the forage available for horses and cattle.[46] The following year, Col. James Burd, the Scotch road builder was sent out to repair and improve the Braddock Road between Cumberland and Redstone. Reporting to Colonel Bouquet, Burd wrote of his stop at Great Meadows on September 10, 1759: "...saw Colonel Washington's Fort which was called Fort Necessity. It is a small circular stockade with a small house in the center; on the outside there is a small ditch goes around it, about eight yards from the stockade. It is situated in a narrow part of the meadows commanded by three points of woods. There is a small run of water just by it. We saw two iron swivels."[47]

Reference to the property first appears in official land records when a patent conveying the property to Washington was issued by the Commonwealth of Pennsylvania in 1771.[48] In spite of his earlier unfortunate experiences in this locality, Washington seemed to have had a fondness for Great Meadows, and although he held it throughout the remainder of his life, the property was always a liability. In 1786 he wrote that the tract "sometimes has, and at other times has not a tenant (though no rent has ever yet been paid me for it)..."[49] Washington had visited the place on a trip west in 1784, writing in his diary for September 12, "....stopped awhile at the Great Meadows and viewed a tenement I have there".[50]

Washington never succeeded in renting the land, and finally in 1794 he attempted to dispose of it.[51] He failed even to sell it, and we find the tract listed among his holdings when his estate was settled. In this list of properties owned by Washington when he died, the Great Meadows tract is appraised at $1,404, quite an increase over the "30 pistoles" that he paid for it 30 years before.[52] In 1807, executors of the estate sold the property to Andrew Parks, whose wife was a relative and legatee of Washington. Parks sold it to

Archibald Henderson and Joshua Longstreet in 1809, and during the next fifty years or so it was owned in turn by General Thomas Mason, Joseph Huston, Nathanial Ewing, James Sampey, Ellis Beggs, and Godfrey Fazenbaker.[53] During the years that Washington owned the property, the Braddock Road, which gradually assumed greater importance as pioneers began settling the West, was widened and improved. Taverns, mostly log buildings, sprang up along the road, but the Great Meadow tract remained unimproved and undeveloped. Washington's claim that the place offered excellent possibilities as a stand for a public house was not put to the test until the Braddock Road was replaced by the new National Road early in the nineteenth century. The new toll road which, in this vicinity, roughly followed the Braddock Road, was started in 1811, and passed over the hill some 300 yards to the northeast of the old fort site in the meadow. The present highway, U.S. 40, follows fairly closely the line of the National Road.

About 1828, after this section of the National Road was completed, Judge Ewing built a large brick house on the new highway, which he named Mount Washington Tavern. Washington's appraisal of the site for use by a publican was more than borne out, for the operator of the tavern reported a profit of $4,000 during a single year in the 1840's.[54]

The tavern was closed when Beggs acquired the property, and never functioned again as an inn. The Fazenbakers, who purchased the land in 1856, were farmers and stock raisers. They added a frame wing to the brick tavern and used it as their residence. They built a large barn and several frame farm buildings along the highway near the old tavern.[55] The Fazenbakers were probably the first to put the meadow to use, but according to tradition that portion on which Fort Necessity had been built was employed strictly for grazing. They always claimed with pride that the fort site had never been disturbed by the plow. Fences were built across the meadow, the channel of Great Meadow Run was straightened, and an "all weather" lane was built across the bottom land near the old fort site (Figure 9).

The first known disturbance of the fort site was the laying of the corner stone for a proposed memorial at the centennial celebration in 1854. Fortunately, the memorial was never built and apparently the corner stone subsequently was removed.[56] The next activity was in 1931 in connection with the Washington Bicentennial, when plans were made for a rather ambitious development, including a reproduction of the original fort and construction of an elaborate memorial.[57]

Although the final development was less pretentious than originally proposed, considerable work was accomplished, largely during the spring of 1932. Included was the construction of a stockade, walks and drives, bridges over the creek,

[46]Fitzpatrick, Writings, II, 258–259.

[47]J. W. Abraham, "Redstone Old Fort", in Fort Necessity and Historic Shrines of the Redstone Country, 31.

[48]Umble (R. E. Umble, "Mt. Washington, Fort Necessity, Park and Shrine", in Fort Necessity and Historic Shrines of the Redstone Country, 36) furnishes the following pertinent information: " 'By virtue of an original order on Application No. 3383 entered June 13, 1769 by William Brooks, who, by Deed dated October 17, 1771 conveyed the said tract with appurtenances unto George Washington in fee simple and a warrant for the acceptance of the survey issued to him February 14, 1782 and on February 28, 1782 the Commonwealth of Pennsylvania granted to His Excellency, George Washington, Esq., a patent for the same in consideration of 35 pounds, 15 shillings and 8 pence, the said land situate on the East side of Laurel Hill where Braddocks Road crosses the Great Meadows'. Enrolled at Harrisburg, Pa., in Patent Book 6, Volume 1, page 136 and recorded in the Recorder's Office of Fayette County, Pa., in Deed Book 507 page 458".

[49]Fitzpatrick, Writings, XXXIX, 97. Through the years Washington was unsuccessful in renting the tract, and the records contain several letters to his agent on this subject, of which the following to Thomas Freeman, dated September 23, 1784, is typical: "My tract at the Great Meadows may be rented for the most you can get, for the term of ten years: there is a house on the premises, arable land in culture, and meadow inclosed; much of the latter may be reclaimed at a very moderate expence; which, and its being an excellent stand for an Innkeeper, must render it valuable". (Fitzpatrick, Writings, XXVII, 469.) There seems to be no record as to when, or by whom, the house was built, or its location within the tract.

[50]Fitzpatrick, Diaries, II, 288.

[51]In a letter to his agent in 1794, Washington wrote that the tract "consists chiefly of Meadow, and is very valuable though unimproved ... an excellent stand for a Publican", and instructed that the property be sold. (Fitzpatrick, Writings, XXXIII, 379.)

[52]E. E. Prussing, The Estate of George Washington, Deceased,

301–302. A "pistole" varied in value, but was equivalent roughly to $4.00 in present day currency. Another source gives the cost as 35 pounds, 15 shillings, 8 pence (f.n. 47, page 28).

[53]Albert, The Frontier Forts of Western Pennsylvania, 331. (See also Thomas B. Searight, The Old Pike: A History of the National Road.)

[54]Searight, The Old Pike, 228.

[55]All of these later structures have been removed. The brick tavern has been restored and is used as a museum.

[56]The memorial was to consist of a monument of "hollow iron, about 4 feet square at the base, composed of plates, and about 50 feet high..." (R. E. Umble, "Mount Washington, Fort Necessity and Shrine", in Fort Necessity and Historic Shrines of the Redstone Country.

[57]A Young Colonel from Virginia (no author). This was a brochure put out by the Fort Necessity Memorial Association describing the proposed developments.

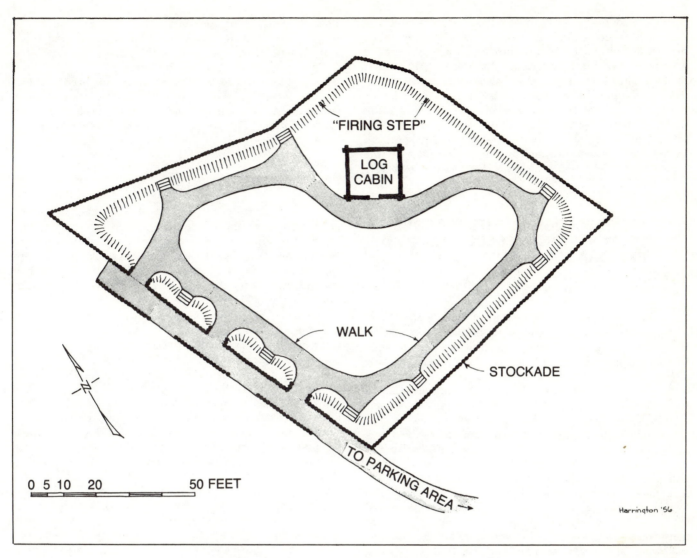

FIGURE 7. Plan of Fort Necessity as Developed in 1932.

and a large parking area across the creek from the fort site.[58]

Before starting this development, a careful survey was made of the surface remains of the fort and the trace of the original creek channel by Harry Blackford, registered Civil Engineer (Figure 9). An archaeological exploration of the site was begun in November 1931, under Mr. Blackford's supervision.[59] Based upon the location of the surface traces and results of the excavating, a stockade was constructed the following spring. Locust logs, 12 feet long and squared on two sides, were set in the archaeological trench and imbedded in concrete. A firing step was built around the inside of the stockade, subsurface drainage lines were installed, the adjacent ground was filled to a depth up to 2.5 feet, a log cabin was constructed, a flag pole was erected, bronze historical markers were put up on the stockade, and the area made ready for the celebration on July 3 and 4 (Figure 7).

The 2-acre tract on which the fort site is located, and on which the Washington Bicentennial developments were carried out, was deeded to the Federal Government on March

21, 1932.[60] This is the area now comprising Fort Necessity National Battlefield Site. It was first administered by the War Department, then transferred to the National Park Service in 1933. The 311-acre State Park surrounding the Battlefield Site was purchased by the Commonwealth of Pennsylvania in 1932 and developed for recreational use, largely under the Civilian Conservation Corps program between 1935 and 1938.[61] The principal work affecting the battlefield proper, accomplished during this period and later, was the planting of trees. The plan was to restore the surrounding hillsides to their wooded condition as of 1754. Unfortunately, much of the reforestation has been in pine, whereas the forest at the time of the battle was hardwood, predominately oak.

In September, 1953, following the exploratory excavating of the preceding spring when the original stockade remains were discovered, the entire 1932 stockade and related structures were demolished. Later that fall, and during the spring of 1954, the circular stockade and entrenchments were

[58]*The work was carried out by the Fort Necessity Memorial Association under the sponsorship of the Fort Necessity Chapter, Pennsylvania, Society of the Sons of the American Revolution. (See introductory chapter Fort Necessity and Historic Shrines).*

[59]*See later discussion of 1931 archaeological project and Appendix 6.*

[60]*Deed Book 512, page 480, Fayette County Records, Uniontown, Pa.*

[61]*Other Federal relief agencies also had a part in the site development, particularly in the historical and research program and restoration of the Mount Washington Tavern. Included were the Works Progress Administration and the National Youth Administration.*

reconstructed, the bronze plaques reinstalled on the stockade wall, a log storehouse built, and a new system of walks constructed within the area (Figure 8). To keep the ground drier under foot, the fill placed over the area in 1932 was left in place. Thus the reconstruction, although properly located in plan, is approximately a foot higher in elevation than the original structures. The channel of Meadow Run was left in its straightened course, rather than restoring the original meandering course. Some clearing of young volunteer growth in the meadow was accomplished in preparation for the bicentennial celebration, which was observed with elaborate ceremonies on July 3 and 4, 1954.

ARCHAEOLOGICAL EXPLORATIONS: PREVIOUS ARCHAEOLOGICAL EXPLORATIONS

The 1901 Project

The first careful examination of the site after Freeman Lewis' visit in 1816 took place in 1901 when Archer Hulbert went to Great Meadows to secure firsthand information for his account of the Braddock Road in the "Historic Highways of America" series. He was familiar with the controversy over the shape of the remains, and states that he went there convinced that Lewis, rather than Sparks was correct.[62] The owner of the land, however, pointed out that the visible surface remains did not conform to the Lewis survey. Robert McCracken, a surveyor, was in the Hulbert party and he soon discovered that two sides of the Lewis triangle were correctly mapped, but that the base of Lewis' triangle was not represented by visible traces.[63] They also found a third ridge, as distinct as the two correctly mapped by Lewis, but not shown on his map. In addition to these more conspicuous ridges and depressions, Mr. Fazenbaker, the owner, also called attention to a very faint trace of an isolated ridge along the fourth side near the Run, marked "O" on McCracken's map (Figure 6).

Hulbert did enough digging to convince him that the main ridges were man-made, but what seemed more important to him was finding in "Mound O" what he believed to be remains of the original stockade.[64] Here, in two cross trenches (location unknown) at a depth of "about four and one-half feet", a considerable amount of bark was encountered. He interpreted this bark to be remains of the original stockade posts, and made quite a point of the alleged fact that bark is more durable than wood. This bark, which turned out to have no connection with Fort Necessity (see page 128), was encountered also in the 1931 excavations, and again interpreted as remains of Washington's "palisado'd Fort". It was simply a case of wishful thinking, but it seemed to Hulbert, as it did to later excavators, that this discovery furnished final proof that Lewis' triangular plan was in error.[65] It would almost seem that Hulbert was more interested in disposing of Lewis and Veech than in finding the remains of Fort Necessity, although I may be doing him an injustice. But in spite of his concern with Lewis' mistake, his major contribution was in noting and recording "Mound O", since the slight trace of this ridge had completely disappeared by

1931. As pointed out later in this report, the presence of a ridge at this location was a major factor in arriving at an entirely new interpretation of all the ridges, thus leading to the discovery of the original fort remains.

Hulbert refers to certain "relics" as having been found at the site, including "the barrel of an old flint-lock musket, a few grape shot, a bullet mould and ladle, leaden and iron musket balls".[66] The present location of these objects is not known.

The 1931 Project

Only a brief summary of the 1931 excavations will be given here, since the excavator's account is appended to this report. The explorations carried out in preparation for the Washington Bicentennial Celebration developments were supervised by Harry Blackford, a Civil Engineer, who had mapped the site for the Memorial Committee in August of the same year (Figure 9).[67]

The first step in the archaeological excavating, which began on November 17, was to dig "exploratory trenches at right angles to the existing embankments to determine, if possible, the location of the old stockade with reference to the embankments".[68] Finding no evidence of stockade remains in these cross trenches, the next step was to put down a continuous trench, approximately 3 feet wide and 2 to 3 feet deep along the crest of each of the three ridges. Where remains of embankments were no longer visible, these lineal exploratory trenches followed the general location of the fort outline shown on McCracken's map. Finally, at one point in this trench, at the northernmost section, near the Run, several post ends were found in what appeared to be a straight line. Using the new evidence, which departed at this point from the McCracken (Hulbert) map, the trench was continued in a straight line toward the point where the surface traces played out. Only one additional post fragment was found along these assumed lines of the fort, but the same bark reported by Hulbert was encountered, and again erroneously interpreted as remains of the stockade posts.

No plan was made showing the location of the 1931 explorations, but the lineal trenches were marked imperishably when they were filled with concrete as an anchor for the new posts of the reconstruction. Nor was a map made showing the exact position of the few post ends encountered, but, from the narrative account, it would appear that a short, continuous section was uncovered, as well as at least one isolated post.

Although the first exploratory cross trenches would have intersected the original ditches of the entrenchments, these remains were not recognized. Nor was the line of the original circular stockade noted when it was crossed, except at those points where post remains occurred, and even there it was observed as a straight line rather than curved. The stockade line was later intersected at several points in digging the trenches for the drain tiles, and several post ends were encountered, but they were not recognized as being significant since they were not found along the traditional or

---

[62]Hulbert, Washington's Road, 177.

[63]Although McCracken was a surveyor and presumably mapped the site, the only record of his survey is a very simple map at small scale reproduced in Hulbert's published work (ibid., 179).

[64]Ibid., 184–185.

[65]Hulbert, Washington's Road, 185–187.

[66]Ibid., 187.

[67]Mr. Blackford worked under the immediate direction of Dr. W. Blake Hindman, Chairman of the Fort Necessity Memorial Committee. Both Mr. Blackford and Dr. Hindman visited the site while work was in progress in 1952 and 1953, and supplemented and confirmed Blackford's earlier report.

[68]Blackford Report, Appendix 6.

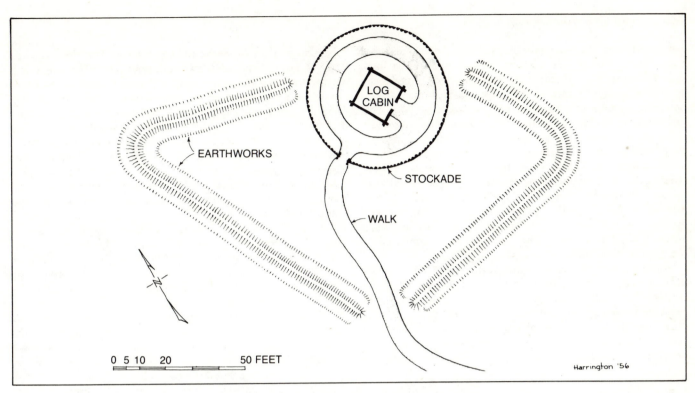

LOG CABIN

EARTHWORKS

STOCKADE

WALK

0 5 10 20   50 FEET

Harrington '56

FIGURE 8. Plan of Fort Necessity as Developed in 1954.

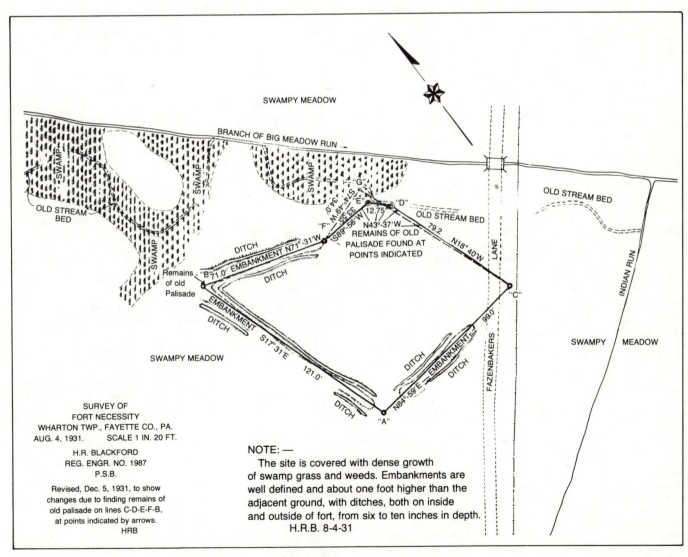

SWAMPY MEADOW

BRANCH OF BIG MEADOW RUN

SWAMP

OLD STREAM BED

SWAMP

SWAMP

SWAMP

OLD STREAM BED

OLD STREAM BED

INDIAN RUN

LANE

FAZENBAKERS

"G"

"E"

"D"

"F"

12.75

N43°-37'W

79.2

REMAINS OF OLD PALISADE FOUND AT POINTS INDICATED

N18°-40'W

"C"

DITCH

EMBANKMENT N71°-31'W

"B" 71.0"

Remains of old Palisade

DITCH

EMBANKMENT

DITCH

S17° 31'E

121.0'

DITCH

DITCH

EMBANKMENT

99.0

DITCH

N84°-59'E

DITCH

"A"

SWAMPY MEADOW

SWAMPY MEADOW

SURVEY OF
FORT NECESSITY
WHARTON TWP., FAYETTE CO., PA.
AUG. 4, 1931.   SCALE 1 IN. 20 FT.

H.R. BLACKFORD
REG. ENGR. NO. 1987
P.S.B.

Revised, Dec. 5, 1931, to show
changes due to finding remains of
old palisade on lines C-D-E-F-B,
at points indicated by arrows.
HRB

NOTE: —

The site is covered with dense growth
of swamp grass and weeds. Embankments are
well defined and about one foot higher than the
adjacent ground, with ditches, both on inside
and outside of fort, from six to ten inches in depth.
H.R.B. 8-4-31

FIGURE 9. Survey Made by Harry R. Blackford, 1931.

105

assumed line of the stockade. (Fragments of post ends were found during the 1953 excavating that had been thrown back into the drain tile ditches near where they crossed the original stockade.) A section of the stockade remains was also encountered when digging the hole for the flag pole, but, again, the wood fragments had no business being there, and so were dismissed as of no possible importance, if, in fact, they were noticed. Failure to note evidence of the original entrenchments or the stockade trench where post ends were missing is not at all surprising, since the people who did the excavating were not experienced in distinguishing subtle soil differences. Moreover, they were looking strictly for stockade evidence in the form of wood remains, and such remains, according to the accepted theory, lay in straight lines, mostly represented by visible surface ridges.

Quite a few "relics" were found during the 1931 excavating, as well as during the site development the following spring. They include lead and iron balls, a concentration of swan shot in one of the drain tile trenches, a few fragments of glass and china, and bits of rusty iron. This material is described, along with that found in the 1952–1953 explorations, in a later section.

The Setting

Although I promised in the Preface not to give a detailed description of the geography of the site and its flora and fauna, some mention of the physical setting is needed. Winding irregularly between low bordering hills for a distance of 1½ to 2 miles is a typical upland meadow, called "Great Meadows" even before Washington's first visit. Some 200 to 300 yards wide, it is traversed by a small meandering stream known as Meadow Run.[69] Except for certain areas which have been altered in recent years, the meadow is marshy, with typical marsh vegetation—grasses generally, with alders and small bushes along the stream banks.[70] During spring floods, and possibly at times of heavy rains, the stream has overflowed its banks and over the years has gradually built up the floor of the plain. Archaeological evidence shows that the meadow was 2 to 3 feet lower in relatively recent geological times, with indications of a heavier growth of vegetation, but the geological history of the area is really of no concern to us here.

The present meadow is relatively level, with an elevation of around 1840 feet above sea level. The ground slopes up from the edges of the flat bottom land, rather gradually at first, then more sharply to irregular ridges and hills, which reach an elevation of 1900 to 2100 feet. In 1754 a hardwood forest apparently began at the edge of the meadow (Figure 1). These woods furnished logs for the stockade, and also provided shelter for the attacking French soldiers. Contemporary accounts of the battle indicate that the woods came to within 60 yards of the fort on the southeast side, but were

beyond musket range on the other sides. The old trails and roads skirted the meadow, running just inside the woods line, presumably to stay on drier ground (Figure 1). The area selected by Washington for his camp, and later for the fort, apparently was a slightly elevated knoll or tongue of higher ground extending into the meadow.[71] It was bounded on one side by a small tributary of Meadow Run, known as Indian Run. The presence of this second stream, which, with the meandering bed of the main stream, provided natural defenses for the troops until they could build their own, probably was the primary reason for selecting this particular site for the camp.

Today the scene has changed in many respects, although as noted previously, the terrain within the Battlefield has been restored to its earlier wooded condition. It has been reforested with pine, however, rather than oak. Outside the Battlefield most of the sloping land adjoining the meadow is under cultivation. Also, the meadow itself in the immediate vicinity of the fort site has been altered considerably. First of all, about 100 years ago a straight channel was dug for the portion of the Run adjacent to the fort. In 1932 the grading operations in the 2-acre memorial tract raised the ground level as much as 2 feet or more in places. Other work carried out at that time and during the later development of the Battlefield, such as the entrance road and parking area, has changed considerably the appearance of the meadow. Even more recently an earth dam has been built just upstream from the fort site, forming a small reservoir. Actually, none of these alterations had any real effect on the archaeological explorations, other than the additional digging necessitated by the 1932 fill.

Nature, however, was more successful in confusing the archaeologist through the activities of crayfish. Even though the site allegedly had never been cultivated, the ground had been worked over quite thoroughly by these industrious creatures, making it very difficult to distinguish soil differences at the upper levels. Moreover, these innumerable crayfish holes, some bigger than a shovel handle, were responsible for finding lead musket balls and other objects at a much lower level than they should have been.

Objectives

The program of archaeological exploration at Fort Necessity can be divided into two distinct phases having quite different objectives. The first corresponds with the opening season's field work (August-September, 1952), and the second with the two periods of field work in 1953 (April and September).

Before excavating began in 1952, an "orientation" report was prepared, in which pertinent documentary materials were synthesized and interpreted as a guide to the archaeologist in planning and reporting on the excavations.[72] The conclusions as to the physical appearance of Fort Necessity

[69]Also referred to as "Great Meadow Run" and "Great Meadows Run".

[70]Freeman Lewis described the site as it appeared in 1816 by brief notation on his map: "The flat land on both sides of the run clear meadow, except some swamps or clumps of alder bushes near the stream". (Note on original Lewis map, Figure 2.) Jared Sparks, who was there a few years later, describes it as follows: "Fort Necessity was situate in a level meadow, about two hundred and fifty yards broad, and covered with long grass and low bushes. The foot of the nearest hills came to within one hundred yards of the fort, and at one place within sixty yards. The space between the fort and hills was open and smooth, the bushes having been cleared away". (The Writings of George Washington, I, 54.)

[71]There is no known topographic map of the site showing grades prior to the 1932 grading operations. I was told that the War Department had mapped the site when it was first acquired, but no such map has been located.

[72]Frederick Tilberg, Fort Necessity Stockade—A Preliminary Study. This report was revised and enlarged by Dr. Tilberg (The Location and Structure of Fort Necessity and the Physical Features of Great Meadows), making use of the findings of the preliminary explorations and the report on these excavations (J. C. Harrington, Report on 1952 Archeological Explorations at Fort Necessity National Battlefield Site).

presented in this pre-excavation report followed those generally accepted over the years. The report, on the whole, dealt with the controversy as to whether the original stockade had been triangular in plan, or more square-shaped, a discussion that had been going on for over a hundred years. Even after assembling and reviewing all the documentary evidence, none of us seriously considered the third alternative of a small, round stockade—actually the only one of the three alternatives supported by contemporary documentary evidence. It was still assumed that both Shaw and Burd had actually observed an irregular, but straight-sided stockade, which appeared superficially to them to be round.

In the preliminary explorations, the primary concern was to locate the entrenchments presumably lying outside the stockade erected in 1932. It was thought that the restoration of this feature would be an interesting and valuable supplement to the reconstructed stockade, and would fill out the setting so that the story of the battle would be more intelligible to visitors. Secondary objectives were

1. to settle, once and for all, the "triangle versus square" controversy,
2. to establish the 1754 location of the stream bed, and
3. to secure additional objects for museum display.

It was taken for granted that the excavating and construction carried on in 1931 and 1932 would have destroyed all remains of the original stockade. Recovery of additional information on this feature, therefore, seemed quite unlikely.

The second phase of the archaeological explorations was concerned with locating the circular stockade and securing as full information as possible on the entire fort. Such a project, however, was quite unforeseen when the first season's field work was started.

Excavating Procedure

Three factors limited the extent of the preliminary explorations, and, to some extent, the later more extensive excavations. These were

1. the fill made in connection with the 1932 developments,
2. existing features, such as walks and lawn, and
3. limited funds.

In the area explored, fills up to over a foot in depth had been made in 1932 for the purpose of providing a less marshy condition around the reconstructed fort, and to lessen the danger of inundation during spring floods. Ideally, this earth fill might better have been removed entirely, with power equipment, before starting the archaeological work, but, for obvious reasons, such a plan was not practicable. Even though additional digging caused by this foot or so of fill limited the extent of testing that could be accomplished with the funds available, it is doubtful whether any more exploring would have been done in any event, for the only foreseeable result at that time was the recovery of more relics. Since it was assumed that the surface of the ground had been examined thoroughly before the fill was made, it seemed unlikely that any sizable objects would be found. Although it eventually became necessary to remove the 1932 stockade, as well as the paved walks, nothing so drastic was anticipated when the field work started.

When the excavating began in 1952, it was expected that only a few exploratory trenches would be dug. It did not seem necessary, therefore, to lay out the site on a grid system, particularly since the trenches could not be oriented with the grid lines in any event. The trenches, therefore, were designated "A", "B", etc., and were tied into the permanent boundary markers at the corners of the 2-acre tract. The same system was continued at the outset of the second season, for even at that time it was not yet known whether the modern structures would have to be removed. As soon as archaeological evidence made it quite clear that the 1932 reconstruction was incorrect and would have to be replaced, the area was staked out on a regular coordinate system and subsequent trenches laid out in reference to this grid. For convenience, the 252-foot "south" side of the 2-acre rectangular tract was assumed to run east and west, with the southwest property marker designated as the zero point on the grid.

The top of the northeast corner marker, recorded in Blackford's field notes as elevation 1845.62 feet above sea level, was used as the datum for all vertical measurements. In some instances, features, soil levels, and artifacts were recorded by surface depth, without reference to the datum. Such figures, however, can be transposed to actual elevation, or vice versa, since surface elevations were recorded at each stake and at intermediate points as indicated by irregularities in the topography.

Exploratory trenches were either 3 or 5 feet wide, depending upon the nature of the anticipated feature. When an important feature was encountered, the trench was widened, as required.

Field records for the project consist of detailed notes in engineers' bound field notebooks; field drawings on 18 x 23 inch cross-section paper; and photographs, both black and white and colored. All objects were numbered in a continuous series (1 through 243). Wood fragments, consisting mostly of water-preserved post ends, were treated in different ways to assure preservation of typical examples. On most of the larger pieces, no preservative was used, the wood being allowed to dry out very slowly. After two years, the wood appeared to be quite sound, and further proof that this is a satisfactory method is offered by the untreated pieces excavated in 1931, which are in excellent condition. A few sample specimens of wood were dried out by the alum-glycerine treatment and then impregnated with a solution of linseed oil, turpentine, and acetone. Iron objects were preserved by the standard treatment of mechanical and chemical rust removal, with final paraffin coating. All objects, including those recovered in 1931 and 1932, are on display at the Fort or in the Tavern, or are in storage at the Tavern.

1952 PRELIMINARY EXPLORATIONS

Plan of Attack

Archaeological explorations were started in August, 1952, for the express purpose of locating the entrenchments which presumably would be found just outside the stockade. At this time there was no inclination on anyone's part to question the correctness of the 1932 reconstruction, particularly as to the location of the stockade. There is no contemporary description of these entrenchments, and none of the later visitors to the site, with the exception of Jared Sparks, makes any mention of them.[73] Colonel James Burd, however, almost certainly was referring to the entrenchments when he noted after his visit in 1759 that "there is a small ditch goes around it (the stockade) about 8 yards from the stockade."[74] Whereas Burd left no drawing, Sparks provides us with a map purporting to be an accurate record of what he claimed to have observed at Great Meadows when he visited the area in 1830 (Figure 3).

Several things in Sparks' drawing, however, raised doubts as to its reliability. Although the plan of the stockade appeared to conform, in general, to the plan established by Hulbert and by the 1931 explorations certain details, such as the three entrances, did not quite ring true. There were other reasons for questioning Sparks' map, notwithstanding its superficial appearance of authenticity. Although it showed many features in considerable detail, the few that can be checked—such as the "Road from Wills Creek" and the two streams—were seen to be inaccurately drawn. We could not overlook completely, however, the entrenchments, which Sparks showed approximately 20 feet from the line of the stockade, particularly when this conforms so closely to Burd's "8 yards". On the other hand, it was recalled that Lewis and Veech, who made a detailed survey of the site several years before Sparks' visit, had not been able to find any trace of entrenchments, although they searched the ground for them. However, we had no clear-cut evidence that Sparks had not seen and correctly recorded the entrenchments, and there was no good reason for not using his convincingly delineated map as a starting point for laying out the first test trenches. It was assumed that evidence of the entrenchments would be found within a reasonable distance of the stockade, and it seemed most likely that they would have been located on the south and west sides of the stockade, as shown by Sparks.

Two exploratory trenches were dug on the outside of the reconstructed stockade specifically in search of these entrenchments (Trenches "A" and "C", Figure 10). A third trench, "B", was dug at the southeast corner for the purpose of checking original topography and soil conditions in the vicinity of the Run. We even considered the possibility of finding evidence of conventional pointed bastions at the corners, so convinced were we at that time that the original stockade corresponded in general with the 1932 reconstruction.

The nature of the earth made it rather difficult to detect old soil disturbances, largely because of its wet, marshy character, and because of the great number of crayfish holes that extended from the surface to a depth of two to three feet. The farm road (Fazenbaker lane) also confused things in Trench "A". Although its location was known (mapped by Blackford in 1931), it was assumed that the lane was relatively superficial and would not extend deep enough to obliterate remains of the original entrenchment.

Not finding evidence of a ditch at a likely distance from the stockade, the first two exploratory trenches were extended as far as there seemed any possibility of the entrenchments having been located (80 feet for "A" and 70 for "C"). Although some interesting information came to light, no evi-

[73]Sparks wrote: "The fort itself was an irregular square, each side measuring. thirty-five yards, with a trench partly finished on two sides. The entrances were guarded by three bastions". (The Writings of George Washington, I, 56.) Entrenchments similarly located to those on Sparks' map are indicated on the map in Frontier Forts of Pennsylvania, but it is almost certain that the draftsman copied this feature from Sparks.

[74]Sherman, Historical Collections, 336.

dence of the ditch of the 1754 entrenchments was found in either trench. It was recognized that the shallow remains of the old ditch could have been obliterated by the lane, or made indistinguishable through years of crayfish activities. It was also realized by this time that the exploratory trenches had not been too well located, at least not for the purpose of checking Sparks' plan. Excavation of other test trenches outside the stockade was considered, but it was decided that this would have to wait until it was possible to carry out a more extensive program of explorations. Funds for the first season's tests were quite limited, and there was still the matter of looking for the base of the Lewis-Veech triangle.

Trench "A"

The principal results from the excavation of this 80-foot trench were

1. negative evidence on the entrenchments (although not too satisfactory because of the deep disturbance of the lane),
2. exact location and certain construction details of the lane,
3. information concerning the natural soil conditions and the grading accomplished in 1932, and
4. location and depth of the shallow ditch along the outside of the ridge (confirming Blackford's 1931 survey).

The remains of Fazenbaker's lane, although found in the location shown on Blackford's map, were much more extensive than anticipated. But even though the ground had been disturbed to a depth of over a foot below the 1754 grade, some evidence of the entrenchment ditch should have been found if it had been in this location. In the vicinity of the fort, where the ground was low and marshy, earth and stones had been added to the roadbed of the lane from time to time. Where Trench "A" cuts the lane, this fill was more than a foot thick, and spread over a width of some 20 feet (Figures 10 and 11). Before the stone fill was made, there had been a ditch along the southeast side of the lane (Feat. 2, Figure 11).

A full description and analysis of the various soil layers adjacent to the lane would require specialized geological study. Moreover, it is irrelevant to the present discussion, since all but the layer added in 1932 are natural deposits, and presumably date from well before 1754. Of interest to the present study, however, is the deep clay layer in which were found remains of tree roots, branches and grass. These remains of an ancient marsh vegetation were preserved by having been below the normal water table, and thus continuously wet. This buried plant zone obviously has no connection with the history of Fort Necessity, but its discovery in the exploratory trenches quite definitely contributed to the discovery of the original stockade, as later discussions will show. The soil above this zone appears to be a combination of natural humus development and flood deposits.

In the short distance between the lane and the existing stockade, the situation was confused and it was not possible to determine the 1754 ground line with any certainty. The trench profile did confirm the recent known history of the site beginning with the excavations of 1931. A trench had been dug along the crest of the still visible ridge, about 3 feet wide and 2.5 to 3.0 feet deep. (See description of 1931 excavations, Appendix 6.) When the stockade was reconstructed the following spring, a six-inch layer of crushed rock was laid in the bottom of this trench, on which was poured a thin layer of concrete. The stockade posts were then set on the concrete-stone footing and the entire space around the posts filled with concrete. Extensive grading followed, in which a wide, shallow depression was formed along the outside of the reconstructed stockade, and a firing step formed on the inside. A

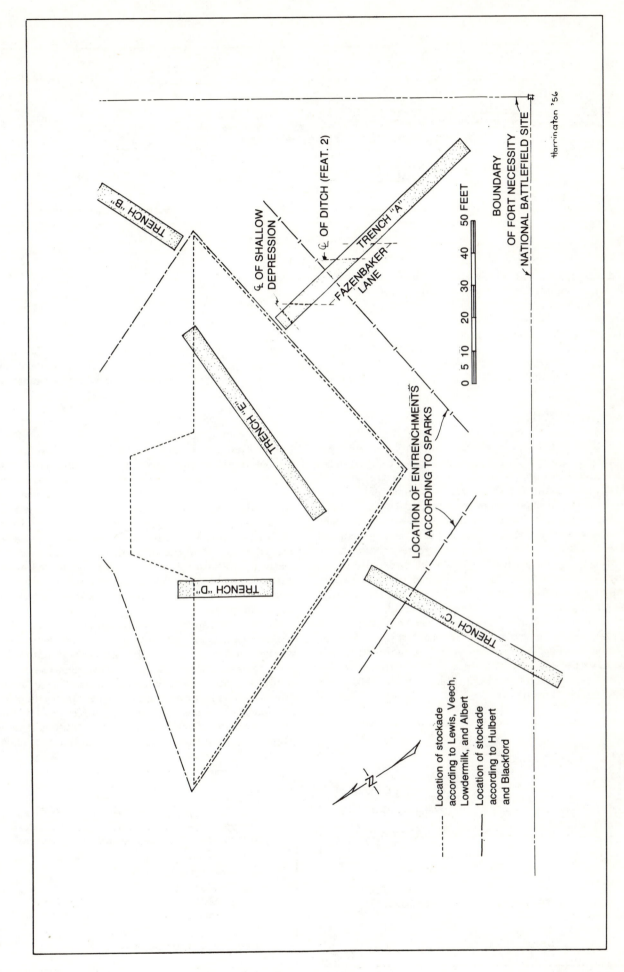

FIGURE 10. 1952 Exploratory Trenches in Relation to Various Theories as to Location of Original Stockade and Entrenchments.

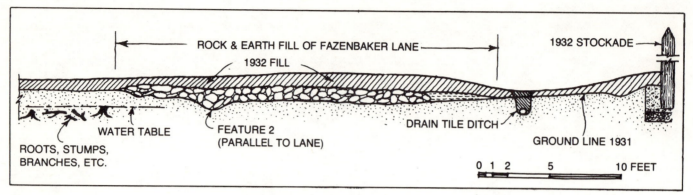

FIGURE 11. Simplified Profile—Trench "A".

tile drain, placed under the outside depression, further confused the soil picture. But in spite of these disturbances, it was possible to determine the pre-1931 surface, except along the crest of the ridge. A slight depression was noted in the Trench "A" profile, 3.5 feet from the centerline of the earlier excavation trench. This checks with Blackford's survey and undoubtedly represents the depression mapped by Lewis in 1816 and still faintly visible in 1931.

Trench "B"

This 30-foot trench was dug primarily to observe soil conditions in the vicinity of the original creek bed, and to see if the natural soil profile, as already noted in Trenches "A" and "C", also obtained in this area. No evidence of the "lost" entrenchments or extension of the stockade was found here. The most important observation was the presence of the deep clay layer containing remains of vegetation, exactly as found in Trench "A", although it was slightly deeper than in the first trench; not surprising in view of the proximity of the stream bed (Figure 12). The 1754 ground line was readily apparent, with the thin edge of the Fazenbaker lane deposits lying directly on it. Above this was the 1932 fill, here a little more than a foot thick. The trench was not extended far enough to reach the original stream bed, but the soil conditions and the slope of the old ground line indicated that it must have been just beyond the end of the trench, which confirms the location recorded by Blackford in 1931 from surface traces. (Figure 13).

Trench "C"

This trench, dug expressly in search of the original entrenchments, produced nothing of importance. It showed the normal soil conditions better than Trench "A", since the only post-1754 disturbances revealed in its 70-foot length were a superficial road fill (part of the 1932 developments) and the grading done in connection with the reconstruction.

Trenches "D" and "E"

The purpose of these two trenches was to check on the possibility of there having been some feature here to account for the base of Lewis' triangle (Figures 14 and 15). The surface of the ground had been examined here by Blackford when he mapped the site in 1931, and he had found no surface traces of any sort. In 1901, Hulbert and McCracken also had looked for evidences. However, no one had checked below the surface, and it was felt that the century-old argument could possibly be settled even more convincingly by some archaeological testing. The two exploratory trenches were so located that they would cross the line in question.

Absolutely no subsurface disturbance, other than the drain tile ditches dug in 1932, was found in either trench. What was believed to be the 1754 ground line was quite evident in both trenches, although later evidence raised some question as to the accuracy of this interpretation. The situation was this. A humus layer, averaging about 3 inches in thickness, was found along each profile, lying directly below the 1932 fill (Figure 13). Below this thin upper humus layer was a more normal natural humus zone. The line of demarcation

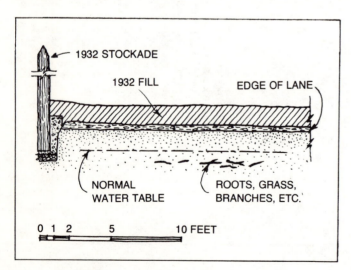

FIGURE 12. Simplified Profile—Trench "B".

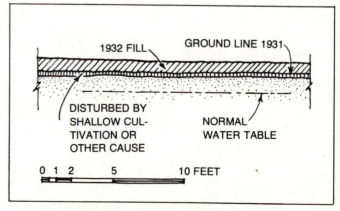

FIGURE 13. Simplified Profile—Trench "E".

between the two was quite indistinct, but nevertheless was there. At first this upper portion of the humus zone was thought to have been caused from intensive use of the site in 1754—men and animals tramping over the ground when it was wet. This, however, would probably not have disturbed the ground to so uniform a depth. The only other conclusion is that the site had been subjected to relatively shallow cultivation. Further evidence for the latter interpretation came from subsequent excavating, and one is forced to the conclusion that Mr. Fazenbaker's claim that the site had never been under cultivation was in error (see pages 119–121.)

The few artifacts found in the excavating came from this upper disturbed zone (except those that had fallen into crayfish holes). They consisted mostly of lead musket balls, gun flints, and small iron cannon balls, and will be described along with the objects from the 1953 excavating.

Summary

Although the location for the three exploratory trenches outside the stockade had not been selected ideally, the evidence from them indicated that there had been no entrenchments in the area explored. Nor had the explorations thrown any new light on the function of the ridges and depressions along which the 1932 reconstruction had been erected. The discovery of roots, branches, and bark in Trenches "A" and "B" at approximately the same depth as the bark reported from the 1931 excavating was very revealing. Blackford had found "pieces of charred wood and lumps of charcoal" at a depth of "about three feet" (Appendix 6), and interpreted them as remains of the original stockade. Finding these remains of vegetation in 1931 was one of the principal arguments advanced at that time for the stockade plan as reconstructed the following year. It now appeared probable that the bark and "charcoal" encountered by Blackford was the ancient buried vegetation and had been misinterpreted as remains of the original stockade posts.

Discovery of the nature and extent of the Fazenbaker lane also proved valuable in working out a new theory for the location of the original stockade. A section of ridge had been noted by Hulbert early in the nineteenth century, and was shown on the sketch map prepared for Hulbert by Robert McCracken ("Mound O", Figure 6). Blackford was unable to find any trace of this ridge when he mapped the site in 1931. Noting that the ridge and depressions mapped by Blackford between points "A" and "C" (Figure 9) stopped at the edge of the lane, it was considered likely that the ridge noted by Hulbert might also have stopped at the lane. Plotting this ridge accordingly on the base map suggested that it, too, stopped at the edge of the lane. It was quite obvious now that the ridges near point "C" had not been obliterated by flood action, as all writers had contended previously, but by construction of the lane. Blackford undoubtedly was correct when he assumed that the ridges originally had continued to "C".

The preliminary explorations left certain questions unanswered, and raised others. Why had we not found those well-documented entrenchments? Was it because we had not dug in the right places, or was it because the evidence had been obliterated or confused by later disturbances, such as the Fazenbaker lane? Should the search be continued in other directions from the fort, and possibly at a greater distance? It was also possible, although we were reluctant to press the

point, that remains of the entrenchments were present but had not been recognized. Each of these problems were considered, for we knew that the entrenchments had been some place in this vicinity, and almost certainly not very far from the line of the stockade.

A New Stockade Theory

It has already become legend that the discovery of a previously unknown document (the Shaw Deposition) was responsible for the new theory that the stockade had been circular, rather than squarish or triangular in plan. The truth is that this document was looked upon with favor only after the theory of a circular stockade was advanced in the archaeological report for the 1952 preliminary explorations, and was, in fact, not exploited in publicity until after the circular stockade was found. The document had been known, however, long before the new theory was worked out, and had, in fact, been dismissed by everyone concerned, as unreliable evidence. When the exploratory excavations were started in 1952, there still seemed to be too much evidence in favor of a straight-sided stockade, and everyone was content with the existing reconstruction, or, at least, with its location.

The three main factors that brought a reappraisal of the evidence, resulting in a new theory as to the location and shape of the stockade and location of the entrenchments were

1. the absence of remains of the entrenchments in the exploratory trenches,
2. the absence of ridges and depressions in *one area only* (their absence at the lane had now been accounted for, and erosion by the creek, when it overflowed its banks, could no longer be credited with the total obliteration of the traces in the single vacant space), and
3. the fact that stockades were not usually constructed by piling up earth against the posts.

A minor factor that also had to be considered was the bulge shown at the north side of the fort on all early maps of the site, particularly those prepared by Lewis and Sparks, both of whom had visited the area before it had been disturbed. Later writers rationalized this bulge as representing an extension of the stockade over the creek for access to drinking water, but the early visitors to Fort Necessity must have observed some evidence on the ground to have caused them to map this extension. The interesting point was that this bulge lay exactly in the space where the ridges and depressions, always assumed to be remnants of the stockade, were missing.

In regard to the method of constructing the stockade, even if earth had been piled against the posts to strengthen them, there would have been no need to have set them 3 feet in the ground, the depth at which the few posts ends were found in 1931. The 1952 explorations showed that at this depth the bottom ends of the posts would have been preserved by ground water. Why, then, had no post ends been found along the ridges, and corollarially, why were the ones that were found all from the section where there was no ridge? These are some of the questions that arose when the results of the preliminary explorations were appraised in the light of all other evidence; questions that could not be answered satisfactorily by the currently accepted theory that the stockade had originally been located along the ridges.

Once these questions had been raised, and other inconsis-

FIGURE 14. Exploratory Trench "D" Inside 1932 Stockade.

FIGURE 15. Exploratory Trench "E" Inside 1932 Stockade.

tencies considered, it was quite natural that the discarded documentary evidence for a small, circular stockade should be looked at again with a less prejudiced view. After weighing all the evidence very carefully, and, at first, rather hesitantly, a report was submitted suggesting that the ridges and depressions were not the remains of the earth banked against a stockade, but rather the remains of the entrenchments. Working on this thesis, it was a natural step to the theory that the stockade had, in fact, been small and circular, and had been located in the space where the ridges were lacking. In the report presenting this new idea, which also

outlined plans for future explorations, a circular stockade, roughly 54 feet in diameter, was proposed.[75]

[75] *A pertinent portion of the report reads as follows: "If we . . . accept the possibility of the ridge and depressions being the remains of the original outer entrenchments, where, then was the stockade? This brings the 'round' fort back into the picture". The report then goes on to present a number of arguments in favor of a small, circular fort. The report concludes the discussion as follows: "In presenting this radical hypothesis of a small, round . . . fort, I am definitely not suggesting that the present plan has nothing in its favor, or that it should be discarded. I am only attempting to arrive*

1953 EXPLORATIONS

Summary of Procedure and Results

Excavating was resumed in the spring of 1953 with quite definite objectives based upon conclusions and recommendations presented in the report on the previous year's preliminary explorations.[76] These objectives were:

1. to check the circular stockade theory, and, if found to be correct, to obtain as much information as possible on the stockade's original construction; and
2. to look for evidence of the outer entrenchments, which, according to the newly developed theory, would be found under the reconstructed "firing step" just inside the 1932 stockade.

We started by laying out three test trenches across the calculated line of the circular stockade (Trenches "G", "H" and "I", Figure 16). The presence of paved walks, the log cabin, and the high "firing step" along the reconstructed stockade limited the area that could be explored and still keep the site open to the public. Before the removal of these features could be justified, it was necessary to demonstrate clearly the validity of the circular stockade thesis.

After removing the 1932 fill and a post-1754 accumulation or disturbance from shallow cultivation, an intrusive band of earth was noted in each of the three test trenches. This band of differently colored earth varied in width in each of the three trenches, but was roughly a foot and a half wide. It was quite evident that these bands represented an old ditch or trench, and their position conformed almost exactly to the pre-exploration calculation of the circular stockade location. There could be little doubt about this being the line of the original stockade but even more conclusive evidence was soon to be found as we went deeper. Charcoal and burned earth was found in two of the three trenches (Figure 17), and, at the level of normal ground water, remains of wood posts were encountered in the same two trenches in which charcoal and burned earth had been noted at a higher point (Figures 18, 19, and 20). These water-preserved post ends averaged from one to one and a half feet in length, and were found standing in a vertical position. The lower ends rested on the bottom of the original stockade trench, which had been dug to a depth of 2.0 to 2.3 feet below the 1754 ground line. There was no doubt now that the original stockade had been found, and almost exactly according to the estimated location.

The stockade was then checked at a fourth point on the circle, permitting its outline to be plotted with considerable accuracy. It was found to be almost exactly circular, with a diameter of roughly 53 feet. Very little more digging was done in the vicinity of the stockade during the spring of 1953, since it was now evident that the walks, as well as the entire 1932 stockade and log cabin, would have to be removed before the area could be excavated systematically. Quite obviously we would now have to give up entirely any idea of revising the earlier reconstruction; it would have to be removed and rebuilt completely.

The principal thing left to be done at this time was to check under the reconstructed "firing step" for evidence of the

at a solution that most nearly fits all of the evidence available at this time. The round . . . fort seems to be to offer an explanation for certain facts and situations which are not satisfactorily met in the present reconstruction". (Harrington, Report on 1952 Archeological Explorations at Fort Necessity National Battlefield Site.)

[76]Harrington, J. C., Preliminary Report, Archeological Explorations, Fort Necessity National Battlefield Site, August-September, 1952.

original outer entrenchments, which we were now more confident than ever would be found just inside the line of the reconstructed stockade. Excavating soon showed the validity of this thesis. Not only was the inner ditch of the original entrenchments found in each of the three test trenches (Trenches "M", "R", and "S"), but their exact size and shape could be determined. Fortunately, the 1931–1932 excavating had followed along the center of the ridges (the remains of the original parapet), leaving the ditches unmolested. Work was terminated at this point, postponing fuller excavation and the demolition of modern features until after the summer travel season.

Excavating was resumed in September, the first operation being the removal of the 1932 stockade, "firing step", log cabin, and paved walks. It was then possible to follow out the entire length of the circular stockade, or that portion which had not been destroyed by the 1932 developments. Because of the fill placed over the entire area in 1932, averaging nearly a foot in depth, it was not feasible to excavate as much of the site as desired. For example, instead of following out the entire length of the entrenchment ditch, it was checked only at intervals by a series of cross trenches (Figure 16). About half the area inside the original stockade was explored, although we soon discovered that the ground here had been disturbed considerably in 1932 in laying a network of underground drains and in constructing the log cabin. No excavating was done beyond the limits of the line of the original entrenchments, except to locate the earlier course of the stream where it had come closest to the circular stockade.

In the following detailed discussions of the principal archaeological features, identification and interpretation will be presented along with the discussion of evidence found in the excavating. Description and interpretation of objects found in the excavations will be discussed under functional groups (cannon, small arms, uniforms, other military equipment, etc.).

The Circular Stockade

Approximately one-fourth of the stockade had been destroyed in the course of the 1932 work, but there was enough left to determine quite accurately its original plan and method of construction. Equally interesting was the clear evidence of how the stockade had been destroyed by the French the day after the battle. It had been almost exactly circular in plan, varying in overall diameter from 53.0 to 53.5 feet (Figure 21). The stockade trench varied in cross-section from point to point, but its general character was the same throughout, as shown in Figure 22. In digging this trench, the men had worked from the inside of the circle, since the vertical face of the trench was always on the outside and the sloping face on the inside. The trench varied from 2.2 to 2.5 feet in width at a point just below the thin pre-1932 plowed or disturbed zone. Although post remains were missing completely along much of the stockade trench, there was no difficulty in locating it, as the trench fill contrasted quite definitely with the natural yellow clay subsoil into which the trench had been dug.

Careful examination revealed no irregularities at the 1931 ground line which would mark in any way the presence of the stockade trench. If there ever had been anything of this sort, such as earth thrown out when the trench was dug originally, or a depression from removal of the posts, such evidence had been obliterated, either through cultivation or by natural processes.

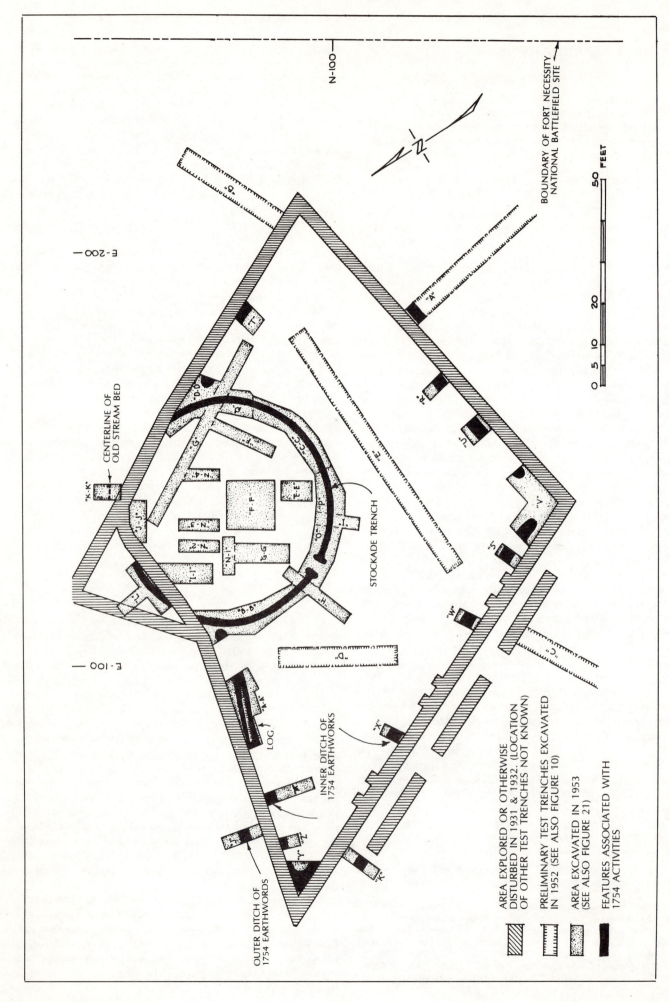

N-100

E-200

E-100

N

CENTERLINE OF
OLD STREAM BED

STOCKADE TRENCH

LOG

INNER DITCH OF
1754 EARTHWORKS

OUTER DITCH OF
1754 EARTHWORDS

BOUNDARY OF FORT NECESSITY
NATIONAL BATTLEFIELD SITE

"K-K"   "J-J"   "I-I"   "H"   "G-G"   "N-I"   "N-2"   "N-3"   "F-F"   "E-E"   "D-D"   "P"   "G"   "F"   "N-4"   "C-C"   "B-B"   "O"   "T"   "R"   "A"   "U"   "V"   "S"   "W"   "O"   "K"   "Z"   "Y"   "A-A"   "D"

0   5   10   20   50 FEET

AREA EXPLORED OR OTHERWISE
DISTURBED IN 1931 & 1932. (LOCATION
OF OTHER TEST TRENCHES NOT KNOWN)

PRELIMINARY TEST TRENCHES EXCAVATED
IN 1952 (SEE ALSO FIGURE 10)

AREA EXCAVATED IN 1953
(SEE ALSO FIGURE 21)

FEATURES ASSOCIATED WITH
1754 ACTIVITIES

FIGURE 16. Location of Excavations of 1931, 1952, and 1953 Showing Archaeological Features Associated with Fort Necessity.

114

FIGURE 17. Charred Remains of Stockade Posts Lying just below 1931 Ground Line (Trench "O-I-P").

FIGURE 18. Second Section of Water-Preserved Post Ends (Trench "D-D").

Most of the stockade posts were missing, and those found were largely in two continuous, but separate sections. Although no record was made of the post ends found in 1931, Blackford's description of their discovery furnishes a rough idea of their position, and it would now seem that they stood in a more-or-less continuous line, thus making in all three such sections of post ends (Figure 21).

At the top of the stockade trench, and directly over the two sections of post ends uncovered in 1953, were found charcoal and burned earth. The charcoal was in very poor condition, but it definitely constituted the remains of vertical wood members of the same size and shape as the lower water-preserved post ends (Figure 17). The earth in the vicinity of this charcoal was burned hard and red, showing that the posts at these points had been burned while still in place. In addition to the charred remains of the standing posts, charcoal was also found scattered out a short distance from the stockade trench. This might have been interpreted as charcoal scattered from the charred posts through cultivation, except for the fact that the earth under this scattered charcoal showed evidence of exposure to heat. In addition to the burned sections above the preserved post ends, charcoal and burned earth were observed also along the top of the stockade trench at another point where no post remains were found (Feature 13). The charcoal in this instance, however, was lying with the grain of the wood horizontal. In every

FIGURE 19. First Section of Water-Preserved Post Ends (Trench "O-I-P"), with Round Gate Post in Foreground.

FIGURE 20. Close-Up of Portion of First Section of Water-Preserved Post Ends.

instance, the 3-inch cultivated or disturbed zone at the 1931 ground line extended unbroken over the stockade trench and over these burned areas.

The evidence is quite clear, therefore, that the French destroyed the stockade by pulling up about three-fourths of the posts, stacking them against the three standing sections of the stockade, and then burning them. In addition, some logs were burned in separate piles, such as represented by Feature 13. Almost certainly the posts would not have been consumed entirely, and this would account for the fact that Col. Burd could still see the remains of a circular stockade when he visited the site five years after the battle. Gradually

the above-ground remains disappeared (which they apparently had by the time of Lewis' visit in 1816), leaving about 2.0 to 2.5 feet of post in the ground, the upper few inches of which had been charred by the fire. Some of the charred section lasted through the years, along with the lower ends that were below the ground water line, while the portion between gradually rotted way. This was the condition discovered in the excavations, as shown in Figure 22. Since the charcoal and burned earth did not show up in the 3-inch surface zone, it would appear that this layer had been disturbed after the fort was burned. The only explanation is that the area had been cultivated, but probably no more than

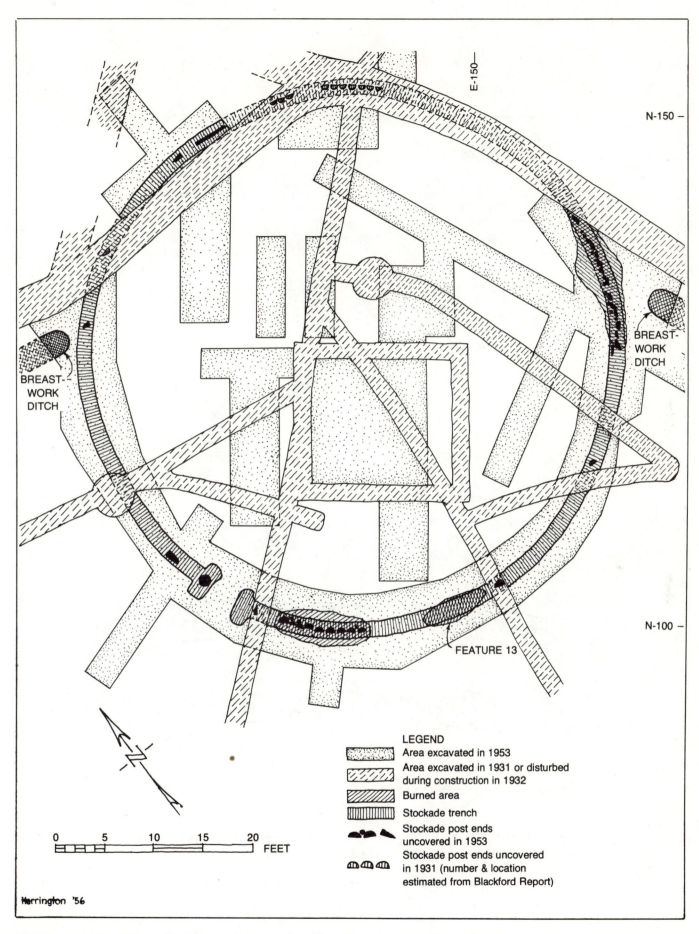

FIGURE 21. Detailed Plan of Explorations in Vicinity of Circular Stockade, Showing 1931—1932 and 1952—1953 Excavations and Principal Archaeological Features.

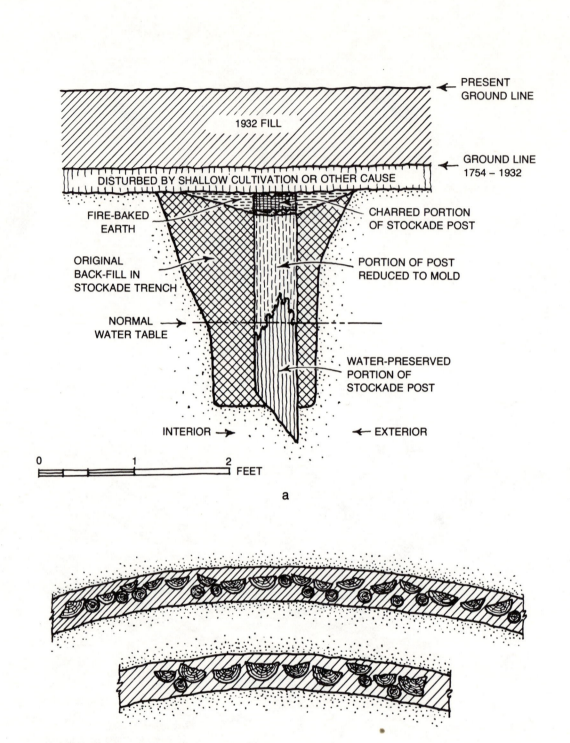

PRESENT GROUND LINE

1932 FILL

GROUND LINE 1754 – 1932

DISTURBED BY SHALLOW CULTIVATION OR OTHER CAUSE

FIRE-BAKED EARTH

CHARRED PORTION OF STOCKADE POST

ORIGINAL BACK-FILL IN STOCKADE TRENCH

PORTION OF POST REDUCED TO MOLD

NORMAL WATER TABLE

WATER-PRESERVED PORTION OF STOCKADE POST

INTERIOR →

← EXTERIOR

0   1   2 FEET

a

0   1   2   5 FEET

b

a.   Typical cross-section at point where posts were burned in place.

b.   Plans of two sections of stockade where posts were burned in place. A third similar section was probably encountered in 1931.

FIGURE 22.   Cross-Section and Plan of Stockade Trench.

118

a disking to improve the pasture. In his claim that the fort site had never been cultivated, Mr. Fazenbaker apparently meant that it had never been plowed and planted to crops, and the archaeological evidence seems to bear this out.

Scattered along the stockade trench were a few ends of posts, lying horizontally or at an angle, not vertically, with the exception of a single large gate post, described later. Six such fragments were found, and presumably represent posts that had broken off when the stockade was torn down, or isolated posts that were partly pushed over, but not removed and burned with the majority. As with the vertical remains, these odd pieces rotted away, except for the portion below the ground water level.

The stockade had been built with logs of white oak (*Quercus alba* L.), split in two, with the split, or flat, side facing out. The original logs ranged from 7 to 13 inches in diameter; the majority 9 or 10 inches. The lower ends show the original ax cuts, some cut nearly at right angles to the log, and some quite slanted (Figure 23). Some bark remained on most of the posts, and there is no reason to assume that any of the logs were peeled before they were split and set in the stockade trench.

In addition to the large split posts, small unsplit logs were used along the inside of the stockade wall. These were mostly about 5 inches in diameter, and seemed to have been distributed quite at random. They probably were used largely as fillers behind large cracks, although shorter ones possibly served as gun rests at the bottom of loopholes. Judging from the number of posts found in the two undisturbed sections, it is estimated that approximately 150 split posts and 50 to 75 small round posts were used in the original structure.

It was a distinct surprise to find split posts in the stockade, for such a practice, to my knowledge, was not common, and, in fact, its use at Fort Necessity may be unique. It is easy to rationalize that a flat surface would be better than a round one as protection from musket fire, and it is obvious that if split posts were used, the flat side would be faced outward. Even though this sounds quite plausible, it is possible that defense against enemy fire was not the full reason for the logs having been split. When the stockade was erected Washington had only about 160 men to cut and carry the logs to the fort site, dig the stockade trench, erect the posts, and build entrenchments, all within a period of less than five days.[77] In fact, there must have been considerably fewer than 160 men available to work on the fort, for some were out on scouting parties, some were taking the French prisoners from the Jumonville skirmish back to Wills Creek, and some undoubtedly were indisposed for one reason or another. Thus, the number of able bodied men available, as well as the need for great haste, accounts for the small size of the stockade and possibly, too, for the use of split logs. It was quicker and easier to split a log than to chop down another tree and cut off a log of the right length. Moreover, a full oak log of this size would weigh at least 300 pounds, whereas a split one could be carried from the woods and erected quite easily by two men. Even the archaeological evidence, there-fore, or at least the interpretation of that evidence, bears witness to the appropriateness of the name "Fort Necessity".

Only one break was found in the stockade trench. At a point on the west side there was a space exactly 3 feet wide where the trench had not been dug. At each side of this break the trench had been extended out in the form of a T (Figure 21). The preserved end of an 11-inch round post was found at the center of one of these T's (Figure 19), but all other stockade members were missing in this vicinity. The shape of the trench, however, suggests that there had been three round posts at each side of the opening, which almost certainly formed a gateway.

Every writer on Fort Necessity, and everyone who has drawn a map of the surface remains, real or imaginary, assumed that the stockade had been built partly over Great Meadow Run to provide a ready source of water for the men stationed within the fort. Blackford's record of the trace of the original channel, still partly visible in 1931, suggests that the stream had been very close to the stockade, but possibly did not extend into it. To check this, a test trench was excavated at the side of the circle nearest the stream. Archaeological evidence here showed quite clearly that the circular stockade had been erected right up to the stream, but had not extended over it.

It is possible that a second gate was located at the rear of the stockade to provide access to the stream, or a surface well may have been dug against the inner side of the stockade wall at the closest point to the stream. But what provision, if any, was made for a water supply inside the fort will never be known, since the ground in this vicinity was disturbed to a depth of over 3 feet during the earlier excavating. Of course, if every square foot of the site had been excavated, evidence of a well—if one had existed within the fort—would have been found.

Although the 1953 excavations produced considerable evidence as to the method of constructing the stockade, there is no way of determining the length of the posts. Large, permanent stockade structures, such as Washington saw at Fort Le Boeuf, made use of whole, squared logs, pointed at the top, and often extending as much as 12 feet above the ground. The makeshift structure at Great Meadows would certainly have been lower, but that is about all we can say as to its height. Loopholes would probably have been provided by separating adjacent split logs and placing a short round log behind this opening, with the top of the filler log about 4 feet above the ground. This would account for some of the round poles, while others approximately the length of the main posts would have served to fill normal cracks. Except for the use of split logs, this method of constructing a stockade is shown in military manuals of that period.

The Storehouse

According to Shaw, there was a crudely built storehouse, covered with bark and hides, in the center of the stockade. Presumably it was made of logs or split planks, as he states that men were wounded during the battle by splinters knocked from this structure. Although built for the storage of provisions and ammunition, it is said that the storehouse was used during the battle as a first aid station.[78] Shaw said that this building "might be 14 feet square" but he

[77] *Some historians have contended that the stockade was constructed just prior to the battle, when a last hurried effort was made to improve the fortifications. (For example, see Cowan, "George Washington . . .", 173). It seems quite clear from the documentary evidence, however, that the entire circular stockade was built during the three or four day period immediately following the Jumonville incident. Washington stated quite clearly that a palisaded fort was built at that time. The last-minute improvements early in July must have comprised work on the entrenchments, rather than on the stockade.*

[78] *Although the bronze plaque placed on the reconstructed storehouse in 1932 states that the original structure was so used, I have been unable to find any documentation to support the claim.*

FIGURE 23.   Typical Water-Preserved Stockade Post Ends. Split Post on Left, Unsplit "Filler" Post on Right.

FIGURE 24.   Log, 13 Feet Long, Found in Bottom of Inner Ditch of Earthworks.

said also that it was 8 feet from the stockade wall.[79] One of these figures obviously is wrong, since the stockade is known to have been 53 feet across. The 8-foot dimension is less reasonable than the 14-foot storehouse, as 14 feet would seem to be about the maximum size for a small storage shed. It is quite possible that an error was made in recording Shaw's deposition, and that he had said 18 feet, rather than 8. This figure would fit the requirements very nicely.

Even though the space within the stockade circle had been disturbed considerably in 1932, much of this area was explored in 1953, primarily in search of some indication of the storehouse size and orientation. No positive evidence was found, but this is not surprising, as the structure must have rested directly on the ground. In one of the exploratory trenches a change in the character of the original upper soil layer was noted. Although the edge of this soil change could be followed but a short distance because of recent ground disturbances, its location and orientation was suggestive. It was at right angles to the line of the gate and 8 feet from the exact center of the stockade, thus coinciding rather closely with 14-foot dimension for the storehouse. Suggestive as this is, it is really too vague to consider as acceptable evidence for the location and size of the original structure.

One discovery outside the stockade may have some relation to the storehouse. This was a log found at the bottom of the entrenchment ditch (Figure 24). The log has a diameter of nearly 9 inches at the butt, and is exactly 13 feet long, with ax cuts on both ends. Being a whole log, it obviously was not used in the stockade, unless as one of the gate posts. It might have been a wall or roof log from the storehouse or a log reinforcement along the top of the entrenchment. The former probably should be ruled out, since this log, although of approximately the right length, is not notched or shaped in any way.

Lacking archaeological evidence, we can only surmise that the storehouse was probably a very crude log structure. Since it was intended as a storehouse for powder and provisions, it would have been of fairly solid construction, even though hurriedly and crudely built. It may well have had a relatively flat, shed roof, as suggested in the conjectural reconstruction shown in Figure 31. The bark and skins mentioned by Shaw would have been laid on small branches placed close together across the sloping roof logs. The building would have had a fairly rugged door, probably of split planks. It would have been windowless, with a dirt floor.

Other Features Associated with the Stockade

No features that can be associated with the construction of the fort, or with its occupancy, were discovered inside the stockade. The only evidences of fires were the burned areas along the line of the stockade, and these can only be explained as incident to the final destruction of the fort. Since ammunition was stored in the storehouse, remains of campfires would not be expected in, or near, this structure, although it would seem quite probable that the men, clustered inside the stockade on the day of the battle, might have built small fires close to the stockade wall.

No metal objects were recovered which definitely can be identified as having been used in the fort structures. An iron bolt was found just above the remains of the large round gate post, and may have been used in some manner in framing or

hanging the gate. On the other hand, it is more likely that this bolt came from one of the wagons which were destroyed, with the fort, by the French. Both the stockade gate and the storehouse door probably were supported on wooden pins and secured with wooden bars and other improvised fasteners.

A few iron nails were found scattered about the area, but there certainly were not enough in the vicinity of the storehouse to suggest that nails or spikes were used in its construction. Those that were found very likely came from wagons, chests and boxes that were destroyed with the fort.

The Entrenchments

No less important than the discovery of the stockade remains was that of the entrenchments. Limitations of time and funds prohibited the exploration of the entire length of the trenches, and probably the only value of their complete excavation would have been the recovery of additional objects, particularly musket balls. The first exploratory trenches crossing the line of the entrenchments revealed that the original ditch lay inside the 1932 concrete footing. Fortunately, the reconstructed stockade was placed along the crest of the original parapet or breastwork.

After the ditch as disclosed in the first three cross trenches had been carefully plotted, it was apparent that Blackford's survey provided an accurate record of the entire ditch location, except for the missing section on the east side. Cross trenches were dug at points where Blackford's map showed a change in course of the ditch, as well as at the ends adjacent to the circular stockade. No attempt was made to locate the ditch at Corner "C", since evidence from the previous season's work indicated that the rock fill of Fazenbaker's lane would have destroyed all remains of the entrenchment.

The various cross trenches showed that the ditch was fairly uniform in section. It had been dug about 2 feet below the 1754 grade, which took it down to the level of the normal water table (Figure 25). In spite of the 1932 disturbances, it was possible to determine the exact shape of the original ditch, which, in turn, permitted an accurate reconstruction of the entire entrenchment.

Observations at the site through the years indicated quite definitely that there had also been a ditch along the outside of the parapet, but probably not as deep as the main ditch.[80] Previous excavating and grading on the outside of the ridges made it difficult to obtain a clear picture of what the original situation had been. Apparently a relatively shallow ditch had also been dug adjacent to the toe of the parapet along certain portions of the entrenchment. Customarily, such a ditch was not dug in constructing a simple shelter trench, but there are obvious reasons for its use at Fort Necessity, which will be discussed later.

The ends of the ditches adjacent to the circular stockade were found, as well as a gap at one corner, this opening obviously providing the main entrance into the entrenched area. There is a possibility that some sort of a detached breastwork or even a palisade was placed outside this opening, but it was not feasible to explore this area during the

[79]Shaw Deposition.

[80]Lewis stated that in 1816 the ditches were "from one to two feet below" the level of the meadow (Figure 2). Thwaite, who visited the site in 1903, mentions only the inner depressions, which he says were about 15 inches below the top of the ridge. (R.G. Thwaite, How George Rogers Clark Won the Northwest, 290–292). Blackford, on the other hand, states that in 1931 the ditches on the outside were 6 to 12 inches below the level of the ground, while those on the inside were 6 to 10 inches deep. (Blackford's original survey notes.)

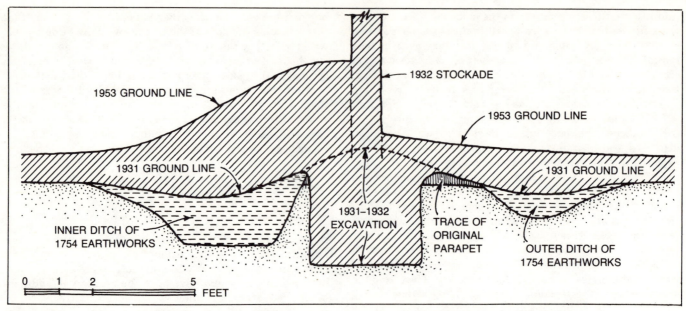

FIGURE 25. Typical Cross-Section through 1932 Stockade and across Line of 1754 Earthworks.

1953 field season. Except for the opening at one corner, the evidence from previous surveys and archaeological excavations shows that the earthworks formed a continuous line of defenses protecting the side of the stockade facing the road, or trail, some 180 yards distant. It had been calculated correctly that any enemy attack would come from this side due, presumably, to the proximity of both the trail and the woods.

Quite a few lead musket balls were found in the back slope of the inner ditch; otherwise relatively few objects were recovered from exploration of the entrenchments. The 13-foot log, previously mentioned, was found near the stockade end of the north ditch, with a small round post, 3.4 feet long, lying beside it. In the earth adjacent to these logs were found fragments of clay tobacco pipe stems, several lead musket balls, and four gun flints.

With the location and width of the parapet delimited by the outer and inner ditches, and the amount of earth used to form the parapet determined by the cross-section of these ditches, the original shape was not difficult to reconstruct (Figure 26). The inner slope would have been relatively steep, probably approximately the slope of the ditch wall immedi-

ately below it. Many writers have stated, or suggested, that the breastwork was reinforced with logs. It is not improbable that logs were imbedded in the parapet near the top of the outer slope, particularly in view of finding the 13-foot log in the bottom of the ditch, although one log was insufficient evidence from which to conclude that logs were used along the entire breastwork. Moreover, there seemed to have been enough earth from the two ditches to form a parapet high enough to conform to requirements for a simple shelter trench. Although relatively little exploring was done on the outside of the original parapet line, no evidence was found of palisades in the outer ditch or of fraises at the other toe of the parapet.

In constructing the breastworks, digging in the inner ditch would have stopped when ground water was reached. Since, upon reaching the water table, additional earth would be needed to bring the parapet up to the required height, either the ditch would have to be widened or earth supplied from the outside. Simple shelter, or field, trenches varied considerably in design, often depending upon the time available to build them. A good height for the parapet was 4.5 feet above the bottom of the ditch, which would provide protection for

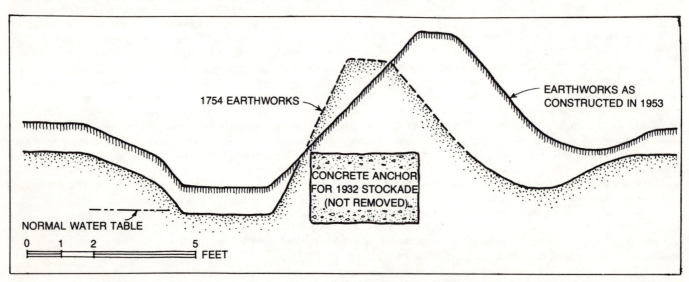

FIGURE 26. Cross-Section (parapet conjectural) of 1754 Earthworks and Earthworks Constructed in 1953.

reloading by stooping down, and the proper height for resting the barrel of the gun when firing. A parapet six feet high was even more desirable, but this would have required a firing step. Such a design would not be expected in a simple, hastily constructed work, nor was there sufficient room as the ditch did not have width enough for even a narrow firing step. Assuming, too, that the main ditch did not provide enough earth to bring the parapet up to the required height, additional earth could have been secured most easily from the topsoil layer just outside the parapet.

There is good evidence that an attempt was being made to improve or extend the fortifications on the morning of the French attack. Washington reported that "as our Numbers were so unequal, we prepared for our Defence in the best manner we could, by throwing up a small Intrenchment, which we had not Time to perfect..."[81] It might seem from this reference that the "small Intrenchment" was distinct from the major earthworks constructed a month earlier. Almost certainly Washington was referring to the completed, larger works when he stated that his troops "drew up in Order before our Trenches" when the French approached.[82]

The archaeological explorations throw no light on the problem of how much, or which part, of the entrenchments were built during the first period of construction, or the portion which may have been built just before the battle. Nor did the explorations reveal any supplementary works, either outside or inside the main line of entrenchments, although it is possible that this last-minute effort was so scattered, or so superficial, that evidence of it was missed in the test trenches.

There can be no question but that entrenchments were constructed during the first flurry of activity immediately after the Jumonville incident. Washington stated quite definitely that the entrenchments had been completed early in June, and that they were considered suitable for defense against any conceivable attacking force.[83] These entrenchments, with the stockade, were built in great haste, and for a specific emergency. They were designed to accommodate the force at Great Meadows, at the time less than 160 men. With the coming of additional troops during the following few weeks, bringing the total force to around 400, no thought apparently was given to enlarging the fortifications. Since Washington considered the first entrenchments properly constructed for defensive purposes, although by a smaller garrison, it would seem that the activities interrupted by the attack on July 3 most likely consisted in extending, rather than modifying, the existing entrenchments. It is reasonable to conclude, therefore, that the system of earthworks represented by the ridges and depressions, and more definitely delimited through archaeological explorations, is the final enlarged line of entrenchments.

Another troublesome problem is accounting for the disposition of some 400 men during the battle. The main camp area,

possibly located in the meadow upstream from the fort, would have been abandoned with the first warning of the French approach. We know that the horses and cattle were left outside the fort, for it is recorded that one of the first things the French did was to kill these animals.[84] If the fighting strength was only about 300 men, as Washington claimed, the rest of the troops, many of whom were sick, must have been packed within the circular stockade.[85] Some may have huddled outside the stockade on the side away from the line of fire, or in sheltered spots along the stream bed. The main fighting strength was stationed in the entrenchments, but, at best, not over half the force could have fought effectively from the earthworks. The stockade might have served some 50 fighters, and a number of men, of course, were involved in various other activities, such as caring for the wounded. It is quite obvious, therefore, that the defenses at Fort Necessity were badly designed for use by an army of 400 men, and that undoubtedly the fort could have been defended more easily with half that force.

Great Meadows Run

One of the main objectives listed in the plans for the first season's explorations was to determine the exact location of the pre-Fazenbaker channel of Great Meadows Run. However, as we learned more about the physical conditions at the site, and when Blackford's original survey records were made available, this phase of the project was given up. Moreover, one of the principal reasons for determining the original stream location was to have just that much more information on which to interpret the documentary data and to appraise the previous interpretations.

It had been said by several writers that spring floods caused frequent changes in the stream's channel. This claim apparently had been advanced in support of certain theories as to the fort's original shape and to explain the absence of the ridge and depressions near the Run. Once the true situation had been determined, the exact position of the stream in 1754 was no longer of any great concern.

One trench was excavated at the back of the original stockade, as mentioned in the discussion of the stockade's location in reference to the Run. Evidence here showed that the banks of the stream channel prior to its straightening were not particularly steep, and presented a profile which one could assume would have withstood normal flooding conditions. It would also seem a reasonable assumption that Blackford's survey shows correctly the stream bed location prior to its straightening by Fazenbaker (Figures 9 and 16). The channel change by Fazenbaker took place only about 100 years after the battle, and there is no strong reason to believe that the old trace mapped by Blackford is too different from its 1754 course.

FURNISHINGS AND EQUIPMENT

General Comments

Very little can be learned from the records as to the military equipment, tools, or personal furnishings of the

---

[81] Virginia Gazette, *July 19, 1754, (Appendix 2). Shaw's account is similar to Washington's. He stated that "in the Morning before the Engagem^t they Endeavour'd to throw up a little Entrenchm^t round them about two feet deep, But could not finish it..." (Shaw Deposition, Appendix 4).*

[82] Virginia Gazette, *July 19, 1754.*

[83] Washington wrote Governor Dinwiddie on June 3 as follows: *"We have just finish'd a small palisado'd Fort, in which, with my small numbers, I shall not fear the attack of 500 men". (Fitzpatrick, Writings, I, 71.) Almost certainly he was referring to the combined entrenchments and stockade, for a letter of the same day to his brother stated that the entrenchments were completed. (ibid., 70.)*

[84] *In his description of the battle, Washington wrote: "The enemy had deprived us of all our Creatures; by killing, in the Beginning of the Engagement, our Horses, Cattle, and every living Thing they could, even to the very Dogs" (Virginia Gazette, July 19, 1754.)*

[85] *"...our whole Force not exceeding 300...". (Virginia Gazette, July 19, 1754.)*

armies at Great Meadows. Archaeology adds some information, but not a great deal. Accounts by early travelers passing the site speak of seeing swivel guns lying about, but even these were finally carried away.[86] Undoubtedly the Indians, as well as emigrants traveling the Braddock Road, salvaged all usable objects and picked up other things simply as trinkets or souvenirs. Owners of the property and later visitors probably recovered an occasional relic and a number of items exhibited in the Tavern are said to have been picked up on the fort site or in the surrounding meadow or woods.

From some of Dinwiddie's letters written just before Washington set out from Alexandria, we might formulate a list of things considered desirable or essential for such an expedition. There is no evidence, however, that these items were assembled, and, in fact, one might judge from Washington's numerous complaints, that many of them were never furnished. Except for the officers, the Virginia Regiment undoubtedly was poorly equipped, although the South Carolina company would surely have been in regular army uniforms and properly armed. From scattered references, as well as from inference, we can be reasonably certain that there were wagons, horses and riding gear, axes and shovels, pickaxes and spades, and other tools needed in felling trees, erecting structures, and building roads. There would have been medical supplies and equipment, utensils for storing, preparing and eating food, tents and blankets, casks for the rum, and personal items, such as tobacco pipes.

For the present report to be complete, I probably should analyze all documentary references and describe in detail the most likely tools, equipment, and furnishings that would have been used or stored at Fort Necessity. However, I am leaving for some future student with special interests and knowledge of the subject the task of providing such inventory and description. I will confine my discussion of artifacts to those found in the excavating, relating them, where possible, to documentary references.

Weapons

Small Arms. Small arms, in contrast to cannon, would have been taken for granted, whereas powder and shot would have to have been provided in considerable quantity and issued to the men as needed. That is why the latter appear more frequently in the records. A man's musket posed no problem of transportation and would have been the last thing he would have relinquished. In various letters written in connection with preparing for the expedition, Governor Dinwiddie mentions equipment required, including "300 small arms, powder and shott".[87]

There are other indirect references to powder, but no mention of arms. Probably almost every man carried a musket, and some of them, if not all, were equipped with bayonets.[88] The officers would have carried swords and, in some instances, pistols.

[86] A letter by Townsend Ward, printed in the North American, July 3, 1754, and quoted in Albert, Frontier Forts, page 34, reads: "The artillery which Washington was unable to remove, remained a number of years, and it is said to have been the custom of emigrants who encamped at the fort to use it in firing salutes. At length the pieces, one by one, were carried to Kentucky by some of the emigrants who crossed the mountains".

[87] Dinwiddie Papers, I, 121.

[88] Detailed descriptions of the battle, such as that published in the Williamsburg Gazette, tell how the Virginia and South Carolina troops fixed their bayonets for a last desperate stand after their powder became too wet to use.

Of the objects found in the excavating, very few relate to small arms. One interesting item is the brass tip of a sword scabbard of the type used with a typical British infantry sword of the period (Figure 27). Probably the most common items in this category are the numerous lead balls and shot. These are of several sizes and, of course, include both French and English ammunition.

On the whole, the lead balls fall into two size groups, the larger ranging from 66 to 73 caliber, the smaller from 52 to 60, as shown in Table 1. Measurements, of course, are not true indications of original sizes, since there is considerable corrosion and often slight deformation. Because of the corrosion and irregularity of the balls, measurements were made only to the nearest 0.02 of an inch. Balls flattened from impact with a hard object are not included in the table.

Table 1. LEAD MUSKET BALLS

		Caliber (approximate)	Average Weight (ounces)	Number of Specimens
Group A —	1	52	0.47	9
	2	54	0.52	12
	3	56	0.56	10
	4	58	0.61	9
	5	60	0.66	3
Group B —	1	66	0.92	19
	2	68	1.00	27
	3	70	1.05	20
	4	72	1.25	2

There were probably at least three different caliber muskets represented, 54 or 55, 69, and 75. The smallest balls (A-1 and A-2) could have been intended for either rifles or pistols.

All flattened balls (29 in number) fall in the small group, their weight being around 0.50 ounces. They were found mostly along the stockade trench, where they apparently had dropped after striking the stockade. This is in agreement with other evidence that the French muskets of that period were a smaller caliber than the British.

Several musket balls were found imbedded in the back slope of the entrenchment ditches, and a great many undoubtedly would have been recovered if more of the ditch had been excavated. The British troops must have left fairly large quantities of ammunition at the fort, and we know that they broke the powder casks and scattered the powder about so that it could not be used by the French and Indians. This would account for a greater number of larger size balls being found, although if the entire fort site had been dug, and the earth carefully screened, it is possible that the smaller French sizes would have predominated.

Several blobs of lead, found in the stockade area, showed evidence of having been in a fire. Since the weight of each of these is about that of an average musket ball, they are probably balls that were imbedded in the logs of the stockade or cabin, and melted when the logs were burned by the French.

A "cache" of small lead shot was found in 1932 when digging a drain tile trench in the vicinity of the reconstructed cabin. This deposit totaled 610 shot, ranging in size from 0.08 to 0.22 of an inch in diameter, the majority falling between 0.14 to 0.18. These "bird shot" may well have been for hunting birds and other small game. In the same deposit were 10 larger shot measuring 0.24 to 0.36 of an inch, which

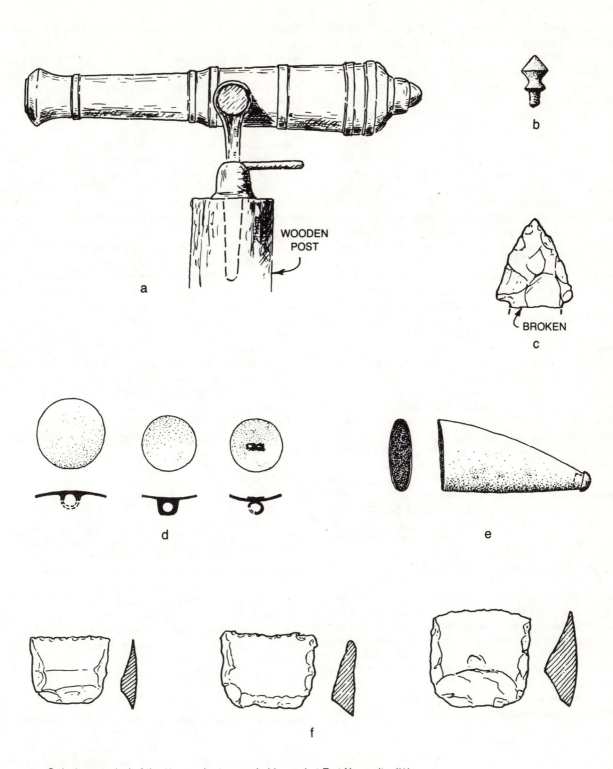

a. Swivel gun typical of the ½ pounder type probably used at Fort Necessity. (⅛)
b. Brass fastener.
c. Indian arrow head.
d. Brass buttons.
e. Brass tip of sword scabbard.
f. Typical gun flints.
Objects b through f were recovered in the excavations. All are ¾ life size.

FIGURE 27. Military Specimens.

is in the "buck shot" range. Except for this single concentration, relatively few shot of these smaller sizes were found.

Of the guns themselves, not a single fragment was found. Sixteen gun flints, however, were recovered, although they tell us less about the guns than do the lead balls (Figure 27). Since they mostly came from within the stockade area, or from the entrenchments, we can assume that they were from muskets of the Virginia or Carolina troops, rather than the French.

Cannon. Not until June 9, with the arrival of reinforcements bringing 9 swivel guns, did Washington have any weapons other than the small arms carried by the troops.[89] These small cannon, however, are mentioned more often in the records than all other military equipment combined. Washington quite obviously looked upon this armament as important in the defense of Fort Necessity, should the need arise to make a stand there. This is reflected, for example, in preparations made on June 12 for an anticipated attack. Through a misunderstanding of intelligence from a scout that a large force of French was approaching, Washington "ordered Major Muse to repair into the fort, and erect the small swivels for the defence of the place, which he could do in an hour's time".[90]

There is other evidence that great stock was put in these cannon, although they turned out to be a distinct liability. They were lugged over the mountain trail during the late June expedition, and then carried back to Fort Necessity when the pack horses could better have been used for transporting the sick and tired troops.

When the French attack finally came on July 3, these "small swivels", on which Washington had relied so heavily, proved quite ineffectual. According to the French commander's report, the swivel guns were used only at the outset of the battle, and then with little effect. He described the action as follows: "As we had no knowledge of the locality we presented our flank to the fort whence they began to fire cannon on us . . . The fire was very brisk on both sides . . . We succeeded in silencing (so to say) the fire of their cannon with our musketry".[91]

Shaw's description of the battle mentions only two swivels, which is probably all the troops had time to set up.[92] It is very doubtful if there were any prepared gun emplacements or protected battery positions. The two swivels were probably mounted on wooden posts or blocks set in the open area between the stockade and the trenches. In addition to Shaw's reference, another participant, Major Stephen, reported that a section of the stockade was removed during the later stages of the battle so that swivel guns could be fired from within the stockade.[93]

On the day after the battle, according to Villier, "M. de Mercier caused the cannon to be broken, as also the one granted by the capitulation, the English not being able to take it away."[94] These "broken" (spiked?) guns must have been left lying about the site, and were probably among the very few things the Indians did not salvage, although Col. Burd reported seeing only two iron swivels when he passed there in 1759.

Except for the number of guns, all we can glean from the

records is that at least two were of iron, which we learn from Burd's accounts. Archaeological evidence, however, in the way of iron balls, furnishes a clue to the size of these swivels. Altogether, 12 iron balls were recovered in the various excavating activities, and they almost certainly were for use in Washington's nine swivel guns, since the French would certainly not have brought cannon all the way from Fort Duquesne.

Nine of the 12 balls were roughly 1.5 inches in diameter and weigh 7 ounces each. Three iron balls are a smaller size, about 7/8 of an inch in diameter, and weigh only 1¼ ounces. The guns for which these two sizes of balls were intended are difficult to determine, since the balls are badly rusted. The larger size was probably for ½ pounder guns. In addition to firing iron balls, "scatter" or "case" shot was also used in guns of this type. Such shot could have been either the larger musket balls, or the small pistol size.

Swivel guns of even the larger size could have been carried quite readily by packhorse, or in the wagons. Although such guns were sometimes mounted on galloper carriages, it is not likely that carriages were used in the 1754 expedition.

Such swivel guns were approximately 3 feet in length, with a breech diameter of between 5 and 6 inches. Several guns of this size were salvaged from British ships sunk in the York River at Yorktown during the Siege of 1781, and one, now in the Mariners' Museum at Newport News, is shown in Figure 27.

Governor Dinwiddie mentions other larger cannon in correspondence preceding Washington's expedition, but there is no evidence, documentary or archaeological, that this heavier armament ever reached Washington.[95]

Other Military Equipment

In addition to small arms and ammunition, there would have been many other types of military equipment, such as flags, drums, surgical implements, powder horns, tinder boxes, and cartridge boxes.[96] Only a single object was found in the excavating that related to such articles. This is a small brass knob (Figure 27), originally attached to a small case (tinder box or similar container) over which the lid strap was hooked. The case was apparently of wood, probably leather covered, since the end of the knob is threaded.

Horses and Wagons

It is quite clear from the records that there were both riding and packhorses at Great Meadows, and there were wagons even with Washington's first contingent. But though the horses were all killed during the battle, and the wagons left at the ruined fort, or burned, not a single fragment of harness, riding gear, or wagon hardware was found in the excavating. Some of the wrought iron nails and spikes recovered may have come from the wagons, but there is no certainty of this.

[89]Freeman, George Washington, I, 383.
[90]Fitzpatrick, Writings, I, 78.
[91]Sparks, Writings, II, 462.
[92]In his deposition (Appendix 4), Shaw made the following statement: "Our people having two Swivel Guns which were discharged at the same time".
[93]Freeman, George Washington, I, 409.
[94]Sparks, Writings, II, 462.

[95]In a letter to Col. Innes dated March 23, 1754, Dinwiddie wrote: "His M'y sent 30 Pcs Cannon, 4 Pounders, with all necessary Implem's. They are heavy, therefore have sent only ten to be carried in Waggons to the Ohio; if they be easily transported I shall send the other twenty". (Dinwiddie Papers, I, 126.) In a later letter to Gov. Glen of South Carolina, Dinwiddie states that these 4 pounders are mounted on "proper carriages", but he also adds that they have no "coe-horns, mortars, or shells". (ibid.; I, 129.) Later he writes again that the troops have no "cutlasses, mortars, granad shells, or coehorn" which are needed to capture Ft. Duquesne. (ibid., I, 159.)
[96]Called a "cartouche box" in contemporary records.

Tools and Implements

Since the expedition was primarily for the purpose of constructing roads, bridges, and fortifications, it would have been well equipped with tools needed for such projects. There would have been cutting, felling, and hewing axes, adzes, wedges for splitting logs, hammers and hatchets, shovels and spades, picks, and probably saws and other carpenter's tools. There would have been tools and parts for repairing wagons, shoeing horses, and for other routine work that would fall to the blacksmith. Strangely enough, not a single object or fragment suggestive of such equipment was found in the excavating, even though almost everything of this sort must have been left behind when the defeated army marched away on July 4. A great deal of the construction equipment, of course, would have been left at Gists' settlement when Washington and his men began their hasty retreat to Great Meadows.

Clothing and Uniforms

Some of the troops, certainly the South Carolina Company, had army uniforms. Of the durable remains one might expect to find from this source, such as buckles, buttons, and epaulets, the only objects found were three buttons (Figure 27). Two are of the composite metal and bone type, with only the convex brass portion remaining. They are both ¾ of an inch in diameter. One has a cast (self) shank, the other a riveted shank. The third button, also of brass, is an inch in diameter. It is the solid, convex type, with shank cast integrally with the body.

Personal Effects

A few odds-and-ends from the excavating cast an interesting light on the social and military attitudes of that day. In the face of shortages in provisions and munitions, it might seem slightly incongruous to find evidences of the "better life", in the way of a tea pot, tobacco pipes, and bottles for alcoholic beverages. We know from the records, of course, that a daily ration of rum was considered essential for all soldiers, and we should not be surprised in discovering that the officers, at least, had their afternoon tea, wine with their dinner, and a good smoke in the evening from their favorite "church wardens".[97]

A few scattered fragments of dark green bottle glass were found, apparently from one or two wine bottles typical of that period. Some of the fragments could be fitted together, and indicate a bottle of the type shown in Figure 28.

Several fragments of clay tobacco pipe stems were found, as well as a portion of a pipe bowl. They, too, are typical of the size and shape of the period. Tea-drinking is attested by the salt-glazed stoneware teapot lid (Figure 28), found during the 1931-1932 operations. An identical lid, with complete pot, is on display in the archaeological exhibit in the old Courthouse in Williamsburg.

Under the circumstances, it is not surprising that so little material of this sort was found. We can reasonably assume, however, that the men had various personal items, such as

[97] In reference to preparing for this expedition, Dinwiddie ordered that there should be one quart of rum for every four men per day. (Dinwiddie Papers, II, 121.) The main supply of rum was carried in casks, but bottle decanters were probably used to serve drinks to the officers.

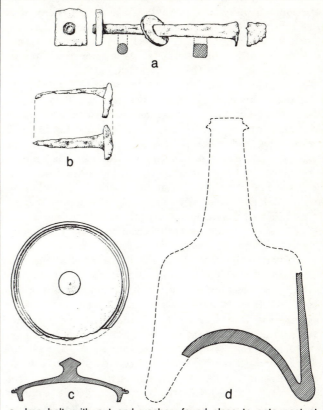

a. Iron bolt, with nut and washer, found close to gate post at entrance to stockade.
b. Typical iron spike.
c. Lid of salt-glazed tea pot. Identical specimens have been found at Colonial Williamsburg.
d. Portion of glass wine bottle. This shape is typical of bottles of the period.

FIGURE 28. Miscellaneous Objects Recovered in Excavations. (²/₃)

knives and spoons, cooking and eating utensils, musical instruments, and even dice for, after all, they were soldiers.

Indian Objects

Although Washington's Indian allies left him before the final show-down, we know there was a fairly large number of Indian warriors with the attacking French force. Presumably, they were mostly equipped with firearms, but it is conceivable that some had bows and arrows. The fact that the French were running short of ammunition before the fighting stopped would have been all the more reason for the Indians to have used arrows, provided they had any along.

One would expect, therefore, that at least a few arrowheads would have been found in the excavating. Actually, not a single point was recovered. A broken point is in the Tavern collection among the other objects said to have come from the fort site (Figure 27). If the Indians used bows and arrows, they evidently salvaged the arrows as thoroughly as they did the other usable objects left at the site after the battle.

CONCLUSIONS

The project started out as a half-hearted search for any remains that might have been left undisturbed from previous excavating and construction. If the earlier reconstruction, which by 1953 had fallen into partial decay, were to be rehabilitated, the least that could be done before any large sum was spent on the project was to make a cursory examination of the site. Actually, we very narrowly missed doing just that and nothing more.

There was just about so much a person could do with the available documentary evidence. Scholars of widely varying interests and abilities had analyzed this evidence off and on for over a century. After the first season's dig in 1953, however, we had a distinct advantage over previous students—we had some good *negative* evidence. The problem now took on a entirely different aspect. There are times when the situation calls for the archaeologist's particular approach, and Fort Necessity apparently was just that.

One thing an archaeologist acquires is a sleuthing instinct and a distrust of undemonstrated theories. He learns particularly to view the available evidence from every angle. In the modern vernacular, Fort Necessity had a lot of angles. The final result of viewing the evidence from the archaeologist's vantage point has been described in earlier sections of this report. In retrospect the outcome does not seem too startling. Nevertheless, it was exciting and undeniably satisfying.

Academically important as it is to be certain of basic facts when carrying out a historical reconstruction, possibly the major contribution of the Fort Necessity project is in its demonstration in methodology. Primarily, the project demonstrates two points quite forcibly. First, that in determining the original appearance of a structure which has been partially or wholly destroyed, documentary evidence of the sort available for Fort Necessity is susceptible of varied interpretation. No one person's interpretation should be accepted as final so long as there is any additional evidence obtainable, and certainly no interpretation should be accepted just because a reputable scholar presents it, even in published form.

Secondly, it demonstrates the importance in historical archaeology of securing the broadest and most comprehensive collaboration possible of relevant disciplines. Either the archaeologist must be a combined historian, architect, and military expert, as well as being familiar with many other pertinent specialties, or he must bring to bear on the problem the services of specialists. Obviously, the latter course is the only practicable one when dealing with the complex remains of modern civilization. The archaeologist who goes it alone on any such project will surely end up with an incorrect or, at best, an incomplete picture.

Except for details of the fort's construction, excavations at Fort Necessity produced no conspicuous results. Artifacts, normally the backbone of archaeology, were so scarce here that they tell very little. Their use in dating, usually of paramount importance, did not figure in this instance. True, we can say with considerable assurance that at least one person had his customary afternoon tea. We are also reasonably certain that some of the men smoked tobacco in clay pipes. But compared with all we do not know, this is not much. The fact is, a historian could probably reconstruct a fairly accurate picture of the life of the officers and troops by a sufficiently thorough study of contemporary records. In other words, the few objects found in the ground tell us practically nothing that we could not have deduced with a high degree of accuracy from conventional historical sources.

Undeniably, the objects recovered from the excavating have historical importance and add, even though relatively little, to the sum total of historical knowledge. They are possibly more valuable, however, in helping to picture Fort Necessity to the park visitor. They add reality and some measure of human interest to the colder facts found in historical documents.

In the main, therefore, the excavating revealed the correct picture of the physical structures involved; it prevented an entirely erroneous reconstruction from being perpetuated; and it furnished the evidence for a worthwhile educational exhibit that calls for a minimum of qualification.

RECONSTRUCTION OF FORT NECESSITY

Archaeology and Reconstruction

The responsibility of the archaeologist normally is assumed to end with a definitive report, based upon an analysis of excavated objects and field records, and conclusions drawn from this analysis. These conclusions, or interpretations, not only should include identification and dating of the objects and ruins, but even more important, the placing of the archaeological complex in its cultural, or historical setting. In other words, the archaeologist is expected to produce more than relics and statistical tabulations. He cannot stop even with identification and dating; he must produce "paper" historical reconstructions. To a degree, these reconstructions are guesswork, and that is why they are qualified with the convenient adjective "hypothetical". Of course, they are assumed to be sound, being based upon knowledge of the particular culture or historical situation involved, and upon experience in interpreting archaeological data. Then, too, the archaeologist must do more than just reconstruct; it is his added responsibility to weigh the soundness of his reconstruction and make his judgment in this respect clear in his report. This is important, for the reader, even though he is provided with every detail of the excavating, usually is not as qualified as the excavator and reporter to appraise the bases for interpretations.

At Fort Necessity, the so-called "reconstruction" went far beyond the usual archaeological requirements. In addition to the "paper" reconstruction, it was decided to reconstruct the structure physically, just as it probably looked on July 3, 1754. This decision was not arrived at, however, until sufficient evidence had been found to permit a reasonably authentic product. Lacking documentary evidence in the way of drawings or detailed written descriptions, the information had to come almost completely from the excavating.

The National Park Service, by policy and precedent, does not look with favor on reconstructions, particularly if the site or commemorated event can otherwise be interpreted with reasonable effectiveness. Two primary questions must always be answered in the affirmative before reconstruction is considered. First: Is reconstruction essential to adequate interpretation? Second: Is there sufficient information to permit an authentic reconstruction?

In the case of Fort Necessity, the answer to the first question seemed quite clearly to be in the affirmative. All above-ground traces of the original structure had been obliterated. Removal of the 1932 developments would have left nothing but a level field. True, the site could be marked with a monument or some commemorative feature and treated purely as a memorial. Such treatment had not seemed sufficient to the planners in 1931, nor did it to the National Park Service in 1953. Possibly the decision in the latter case was influenced by the earlier reconstruction, which, over the years, had become a landmark on the old National Road.

The Battle at Great Meadows is not one of the best known incidents in American history. It is not a Concord, a Valley Forge, or a Yorktown, as far as public knowledge and national lore are concerned. It has the makings of drama, but it has never been dramatized; certainly not to the extent that people would be drawn to the site just to stand on hallowed ground. There seemed to be a distinct need, therefore, to provide the visitor to Fort Necessity with some of the missing parts. (Figures 29 and 30).

That reconstruction as an interpretive need was called for at Fort Necessity was more or less taken for granted when the archaeological explorations were planned in 1952. The earlier reconstruction had been accepted, and what we were

concerned with primarily was to secure any information possible before the stockade was rehabilitated. It was not that everyone was completely happy with the earlier reconstruction. Some of the details were questioned, but basically it appeared to fit the evidence. As soon as it became apparent that a drastic revision in the existing structures was called for, actually involving complete rebuilding, an entirely different view was taken. Now the usual criteria were operative again; now we had to face the second and crucial test: Is there sufficient evidence to justify a reconstruction?

This called for extensive archaeological exploration. Results of these explorations satisfied reconstruction requirements. The earthworks could be rebuilt with reasonable

FIGURE 29. View of 1932 Stockade, Looking North from Entrance Walk, Showing Trench "A" Being Staked Preparatory to Start of 1952 Explorations.

FIGURE 30. View of Fort Necessity as Reconstructed in 1953 and 1954, Looking North from Same Position as Figure 29.

accuracy. All details of the stockade were known with the exception of its height, the precise location of portholes, and the design of the gate. Least of all was known about the storehouse. But all things considered, a reconstruction was thought to be both needed and within the bounds of acceptable authenticity. (Figures 31 and 32).

Limiting Factors

Every development designed for public use of necessity is affected by a great many factors—traditions, construction problems, visitor convenience and safety, maintenance costs, and many other practical considerations. Fort Necessi-

ty could not be constructed in a vacuum. Consequently, there had to be some compromises.

Soil conditions, as well as cost, prevented restoration of the original ground level. The anticipated tramping of many feet called for paved walks. The Run could not be restored to its original meandering course without inviting spring floods. The slopes of the earthworks had to be sodded for purely practical maintenance reasons. The logs had to be peeled so that they could be chemically treated. Sentiment and common sense called for replacing the bronze plaques. And so it went.

Basically, the final result is a reasonably authentic reproduction of the original. The visitor will probably not be as disturbed by the drinking fountain as he would be by the lack

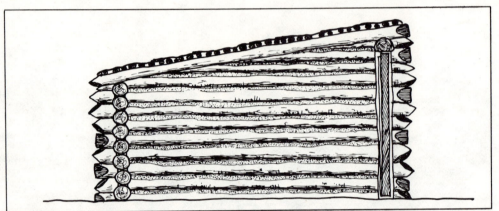

FIGURE 31   Possible Shed-Type Appearance of Original Log Storehouse. Public Use and Greater Permanency Required Better Construction and Higher Roof for Reconstructed Building.

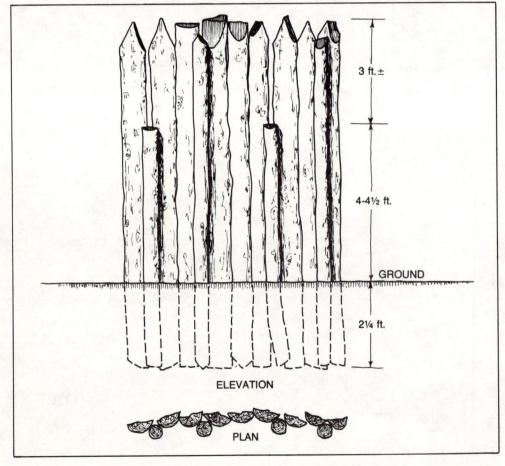

FIGURE 32.   Probable Construction of Original Stockade. Small Unsplit Filler Poles were Possibly Used More Frequently Than Shown in this Drawing.

of water if it were not available. The paved walks enable him to visit the site in any kind of weather. The purist—and there always are some—will be disturbed by some of these incongruities. In solving the public-use problem, however, some concessions have to be made. The aim at Fort Necessity was to concede no more than visitor use and certain practical limitations required. Primarily the objective was to enable 200,000 people every year to learn a little more about their country's history, to gain a little more respect and appreciation for their historical heritage, and to have one more experience worth talking about with the folks back home.

The Reconstruction

Although believed to be located correctly, all of the reconstructed features are approximately a foot above their original level. This was necessitated by the swampy terrain. Even if funds had been available to remove the foot of fill, placed in 1932, there were distinct reasons for leaving it. It not only makes the site accessible throughout the year, but it leaves a large portion of the original entrenchments undisturbed. This possibly has no real merit, but it makes one feel a little better not to have destroyed every vestige of evidence. After all, we were very glad that Hulbert in 1901 and Blackford in 1931 left something for us.

The entrenchments are probably fairly close to their original size and shape and certainly in their original location, even though the grassed slopes are an added feature. The inner slope of the parapet undoubtedly was a little steeper, and there may have been logs laid on it for added protection. Nevertheless, for all practical purposes, the restored entrenchments probably are fairly authentic.

The stockade could not have been very different from the reconstruction. There is no reason to believe that the posts were any higher than necessary to give protection from musket fire. The reconstructed height of seven and a half feet above the ground must be very close to the original height. The greatest departure from archaeological evidence was in peeling the logs, required for preservative treatment. (Figures 33 and 34).

The storehouse, on the other hand, is almost pure guesswork. All we really know is that there was a building inside the stockade. It probably was built of logs; it was said to have been roofed with bark and hides; and, according to one account, was 14 feet square. It very likely had a slightly sloping, shed roof, rather than the reconstructed gable roof (Figure 31). Since it was built primarily, if not solely, as a storehouse, the walls would have been as low as practicable, both to expedite construction and to make it less vulnerable in case of attack.

Such a building was not feasible in developing the site for visitor use. Protected space was needed for the attendant and for a few interpretive exhibits. A gable roof, therefore, was more suitable, and, after all, log structures of this design were common in that day—even more common, in fact, than those with low, shed roofs. As for the roof covering, a more waterproof and durable material than the original was required. The original must have been pretty much of a make-shift affair, with pieces of bark and hides laid over branches. In the reconstruction, a water-tight roof was first laid over the log rafters, with deer hides added to simulate the original.

The concessions to visitor comfort and the added interpretive devices, such as the bronze plaques and the exhibit panels, understandably interject an incongruous note and lessen the realism of the reconstruction. The one consolation, in addition to knowing that thousands of people will derive a great deal of pleasure from their visit to the site, is that all, or any part, can be done over at any time. All the available evidence is now in one place for everyone's use. Some day the logs of the present stockade will rot; another archaeologist may come along and question the reconstruction or the adequacy of the explorations. If he decides to explore a little further, he may find some additional evidence, and, if this evidence warrants, a different reconstruction will be conceived. Or possibly, by then, reconstructions will be out of style. (Figures 35 and 36).

FIGURE 33. Erecting Stockade and Log Cabin in 1954.

FIGURE 34. Erecting Section of Circular Stockade in 1954.

FIGURE 35. View of Fort Necessity as Reconstructed in 1954, Looking East.

FIGURE 36. View of Reconstructed Fort, Looking North. Mount Washington Tavern in Background.

APPENDIX 1

Villiers' Account of the Battle at Great Meadows

Description of the battle from the journal of Capt. Louis Coulon de Villiers, Commander of the French detachment. From the translation in Cleland, *George Washington in the Ohio Valley*, 108–111.

I sent scouts who were to go close to the camp; and twenty more to support them; and I advanced myself in order; when some of my people returned to tell me that we were discovered; and that the English approached in order of battle to attack us: as it was said they were close to me, I put my troops in order of battle, and in a manner suited to woods-fighting. It was not long before I perceived that my scouts had led me wrong; and I gave order to my troops to advance towards that side from which I apprehended an attack. As we were not acquainted with the ground, we presented our flank to the fort from whence they began to cannonade us: I perceived almost at the same time, to the right, the English coming towards us in order of battle. The Indians, and we also, set up the cry, and advanced to meet them: but they gave us no time to make our discharge: they filed off, and withdrew into an entrenchment which lay next to their fort. We then set ourselves about investing the fort: it was advantageously enough situated in a meadow, the wood of which was within musket shot of it. We came as close to them as it was possible, to the end that his Majesty's subjects might not be exposed without necessity: the fire was pretty brisk on both sides, and I repaired to the place which appeared most to favor a sally. We succeeded in silencing the fire of their cannon, I may say, with our small arms. It is true that the zeal of our Canadians and soldiers worried me, because I saw that we would in a little while be without

ammunition. Mr. Le Mercier proposed to me making arrangements to bolster our positions so as to confine the English in their fort and entirely prevent them from leaving. I ordered Mr. De Bailleul to assemble as many men as possible in order to help the quarter which would be attacked in case of a general sortie. At this time we distributed provisions, ammunition and goods, which encouraged the Indians and militiamen.

The enemy's fire began again at six o'clock, with more fury than ever, and lasted till eight o'clock. As we had spent our time all day drying things from the rain, the Detachment was very tired. The Indians had announced to me their departure on the next day. Rumor said that the beat of drums and the firing of cannon had been heard from a distance. I proposed to Mr. Le Mercier to offer to parlay with the English.

The 4th, at break of day, I sent a detachment to take possession of the fort; the garrison filed off, and the number of their dead and wounded raised compassion in me, notwithstanding my resentment of the manner in which they had made away with my brother.

The Indians, who had in every respect, complied with my desires, had laid claim to the pillage. I opposed it, but the consternation of the English was so great that they ran away and left behind them even their flag and a pair of their colors. I demolished their fort and Mr. Le Mercier caused their cannon to be destroyed together with the one which had been granted them by their capitulation, the English not being able to take it away.

I hastened away, after having first destroyed the casks of liquor, in order to prevent the disorders which they would have inevitably caused. One of my Indians took ten English and brought them to me; I sent them away by another . . .

I lost in this attack only two French and one (Indian), I had seventeen wounded, of whom two were Indians, exclusive of several wounds so slight as not to require the attention of the surgeon.

APPENDIX 2

Washington's Account of the Battle at Great Meadows

Shortly after Washington returned to Williamsburg and reported to Governor Dinwiddie, a full account of the battle, apparently furnished by Washington or taken from his official report, was published in the *Virginia Gazette*, July 19. The story later was printed, almost verbatim, in the *South Carolina Gazette*, August 22. The following is copied from the facsimile copy of the *Virginia Gazette*, published in 1932 by the Fort Necessity Chapter, Sons of the American Revolution.

Williamsburg, July 19

On Wednesday last arrived in Town, Colonel George Washington and Captain James Maccay, who gave the following Account to his Honour the Governor, of the late Action between them and the French, at the Great Meadows in the Western Parts of this Dominion.

The third of this Instant July, about 9 o'Clock, we received Intelligence that the French, having been reinforced with 700 Recruits, had left Monogehela, and were in full March with 900 Men to attack us. Upon this, as our Numbers were so unequal, (our whole Force not exceeding 300) we prepared for our Defence in the best Manner we could, by throwing up a small Intrenchment, which we had not Time to perfect, before our Centinel gave Notice, about Eleven o'Clock, of their Approach, by firing his Piece, which he did at the Enemy, and as we learned afterwards killed three of their Men, on which they began to fire upon us, at about 600 Yards Distance, but without any Effect: We immediately called all our Men to their Arms, and drew up in Order before our Trenches; but as we looked upon this distant Fire of the Enemy only as an Artifice to intimidate or draw our Fire from us, we waited their nearest Approach before we returned their Salute. They then advanced in a very irregular Manner to another Point of Woods, about 60 Yards off, and from thence made a second Discharge; upon which, finding they had no Intention of attacking us in the open Field, we retired into our Trenches, and still reserved our Fire; as we expected from their great Superiority of Numbers, that they would endeavor to force our Trenches; but finding they did not seem to intend this neither, the Colonel gave Orders to fire, which was done with great Alacrity and Undauntedness. We continued this unequal Fight, with an Enemy sheltered behind the Trees, ourselves without Shelter, in Trenches full of Water, in a settled Rain, and the Enemy galling us on all Sides incessantly from the Woods, till 8 o'Clock at Night, when the French called to Parley: From the great Improbability that such a vastly superior Force, and possessed of such an Advantage, would offer a Parley first, we suspected a Deceit, and therefore refused to consent that they should come among us; on which they desired us to send an Officer to them, and engaged their Parole for his Safety; we then sent Capt. Van Braam, and Mr. Peyronee, to receive their Proposals, which they did, and about Midnight we agreed that each Side should retire without Molestation, they back to their Fort at Monongehela, and we to Wills's Creek: That we should march away with all the Honours of War, and with all our Stores, Effects and Baggage. Accordingly the next Morning, with our Drums beating and our Colours flying, we began our March in good Order, with our Stores, &c. in Convoy; but we were interrupted by the Arrival of a Reinforcement of 100 Indians among the French, who were hardly restrained from attacking us, and did us considerable Damage by pilfering our Baggage. We then proceeded, but soon found it necessary to leave our Baggage and Stores; the great Scarcity of our Provisions obliged us to use the utmost Expedition, and having neither Waggons nor Horses to transport them. The Enemy had deprived us of all our Creatures; by killing, in the Beginning of the Engagement, our Horses, Cattle, and every living Thing they could, even to the very Dogs. The Number of the Killed on our Side was thirty, and seventy wounded; among the former was Lieutenant Mercier, of Captain Maccay's independant Company; a Gentleman of true military Worth, and whose Bravery would not permit him to retire, though dangerously wounded, till a second Shot disabled him, and a third put an End to his Life, as he was carrying to the Surgeon. Our Men behaved with singular Intrepidity, and we determined not to ask for Quarter but with our Bayonets screw'd, to sell our lives as dearly as possibly we could. From the Numbers of the Enemy, and our Situation, we could not hope for Victory; and from the Character of those we had to encounter, we expected no Mercy, but on Terms that we positively resolved not to submit to.

The Number killed and wounded of the Enemy is uncertain, but by the information given by some Dutch in their Service to their Countrymen in ours, we learn that it amounted to above three hundred; and we are induced to believe it must be very considerable, by their being busy all Night in burying their Dead, and yet many remained the next Day; and their Wounded we know was considerable, by one of our Men, who had been made Prisoner by them after signing the Articles, and who, on his Return told us, that he saw great Numbers much wounded and carried off upon Litters.

We were also told by some of their Indians after the action, that the French had an Officer of distinguishable Rank killed. Some considerable Blow they must have received to induce them to call first for a Parley, knowing, as they perfectly did, the Circumstances we were in.

APPENDIX 3

Governor Dinwiddie's Official Account of the Battle

Following is a portion of a letter from Governor Dinwiddie to the Lords of Trade, dated July 24, 1754 (*Official Records of Robert Dinwiddie*, I, 239–241).

A few Days ago arriv'd here Colo. W., Com'd'r of the Forces, rais'd in this Dom'n, and Capt. McKay, of the Ind't Compa. from So. Car., from our Camp at the Meadows, near the Ohio river, who gave the following melancholy Acc't of an Engagem't between our Forces and the French. On the 3d of this Mo. they had Intelligence y't the French were reinforc'd (at the Fort they took from Us, in May last, near the Ohio,) with 700 Men, and y't they were in full March with 900 Men to attack our small Camp, w'ch consisted of few more than 300 besides Officers. They imediately connected and prepared to make the best Defence their small Numbers W'd admit of, by throw'g up a small Intrenchm't, which they had not time to compleat, before their out Centry gave the Alarm, by firing his Gun, of the approach of the Enemy. Imediately they appear'd in Sight of our Camp, and fir'd at our People at a great Distance, w'ch did no harm. Our small Forces were drawn up in good Order to receive them before their Intrenchm'ts, but did not return their First Fire, reserving it till they came nigher. The enemy advanc'd irregularly within 60 Yards of our Forces, and y'n made a second Discharge, and observing they did not intend to attack them in open Field, they retir'd within their Trenches, and reserv'd their Fire, thinking, from their Numbers, they w'd force their Trenches, but finding they made no Attempt of this kind, the Colo. gave Orders to our People to fire on the Enemy, w'ch they did with great Briskness, and the officers declare y's Engagem't continue (d) from 11 O'Clock till 8 O'Clock at Night, they being without Shelter, rainy weather, and their Trenches to the knee in Water, whereas the French were shelter'd all round our Camp by Trees; from thence they gall'd our People all the Time as above . . . I beg leave to observe to Y'r L'ds. the Misfortunes attending thro' (the) Expedit'n.

APPENDIX 4

Deposition of John Shaw

On August 27, 1754, one John B. W. Shaw appeared before a committee headed by Governor James Glen of South Carolina and made an affidavit describing the battle at Great Meadows and events leading up to the engagement. The deposition recorded here was entered in the Journal of the Council of South Carolina, the original manuscript now being in the British Public Record Office. A photostatic copy was furnished by the South Carolina Archives Department. It is recorded here in full, since it has never before been published.

A very similar affidavit is also found in the records of the South Carolina Indian Affairs, photostatic copy of which was also furnished by the South Carolina Archives Department. Since both versions are almost identical, only the Journal manuscript is recorded here. Differences in the two are slight and of no consequence.

Nothing has been learned of the deponent. From his affidavit, it would appear that he was a member of Washington's original Virginia Regiment, although no John Shaw is found in the presumably complete muster roll prepared by Washington after the battle. In any event, Shaw's description checks so closely with other contemporary records that there can be little question that the deponent was an active member of the expedition.

The following is a full typescript of the Journal entry, with the exception of marginal notes. None of these is of particular interest with the exception of the first, which furnishes the date of the affidavit, reading in part: "Affidavit. Made before his Ex.^{cy} by John Shaw 27. Augt 1754".

His Excellency the Governor Communicated to the Board the following Affidavit of John Shaw concerning the Attempts of the French to Interrupt the Tranquillity of the Inhabitants of Virginia—

BEFORE me James Glen Esquire Governor and Comander in Chief in and over his Majesty's province of South Carolina Personally appeared John Shaw, who being duely Sworn on the Holy Evangelists, Made Oath, That he was born in the City of Dublin in the Kingdom of Ireland. That he is of the Age of Twenty Years and upwards that he has used the Seas Severall Years, That he was a Boy on Board his Majesty's Ship Expedition Captain Summers but was Discharged from her at the Breaking up of the late War, and has been Employed in the Merchant's Service in the Virginia Trade, That he was in Virginia when Proposals were made and published to give Encouragement for Settling some Lands on the Ohio, And that he was amongst many others that embraced the said Proposals And he Believes there might be 100 in all But it being found Necessary that some Forces should be raised, They were thrown into the Virginia Regiment as few or none would Inlist, and were called Volunteers. There were also Twenty two Gentlemen's Sons or thereabouts that made part of the said Regiment as Cadets, but he Believes they were to Receive no pay, But all the Volunteers who were to Settle the Lands were to have eight pence (per) Day Virginia Currency, but that he never Received one ffarthing tho' he was above five Months in the Service. That Col:^{o} Washington marched with the first Detachment of that Regiment over the Allegani Mountains some days before the Detachment that he belonged to Followed. That the Detachment the Deponent Belonged to Consisted but of Eighty Men, And when they were all Joined the whole Virginia Regiment Including Cadets and Volunteers did not amount to Two hundred Men. Four or five days the Virginia Regiment had been alltogether at a place called the Great Meadows. They were Joined by Captn. Mackay with the Independent Company from South Carolina making in the whole with the aforesaid Regiment a Body of near three hundred Men. That they were for severall days together without any other Provisions than a Quart of Indian Corn delivered to each man, and for three days with only one pound of Beef each without any Corn. That he has heard that the Half King had Sixty Indians with him who were in our Interest But that he never Saw above fforty. That he has been Informed by All the Men who belonged to the first Detachm.^{t} That a few days before the Second Joined them they had an Engagement with a party of French And the Account given to him was as follows. That an Indian and a White man having brought Col Washington Information that a party of ffrench consisting of ffive and thirty men were out scouting and lay about Six Miles off, upon which Col Washington with about Forty Men and Captn. Hogg with a party of fforty more, and the Half King with his Indians consisting of Thirteen, Immediately Sett out in Search of them, But having taken Different Roads Col:^{o} Washington with his Men and the Indians came first up with them, and found them encamped between two Hills. Being Early in the Morning Some were asleep, and some eating. But having heard a Noise they were Immediately in Great Confusion and Betook themselves to their Arms. And as he this Deponent has heard One of them ffired a Gun upon which Col Washington Gave the Word for All his Men to Fire. Severall of them being Killed; the Rest Betook themselves to fflight; But our Indians having gone round the ffrench, When they Saw them Immediately ffled Back to the English, and Delivered up their Arms desiring Quarter, which was accordingly promised them. Sometime after the Indians Came up, The Half King took his Tomahawk and Splitt the head of the ffrench Captain, having first asked if he was an Englishman And having been told that he was a ffrench Man, he then took out his Brains, and washed his hands with them, And then Scalped him—All this he has heard and never heard it Contradicted, But knows nothing of it from his own Knowledge. Only he has Seen the Bones of the ffrench Men who were killed in Number ab^t. 13 or 14, And the Head of one Stuck upon a Stick; for none of them were Buryed. And he has also heard that one of our Men was killed at that time.—

That Sometime after Captain Mackay had Joined the Virginia Regiment, Col Washington proposed to March to Attack the French Fort, and accordingly Marched with the Virginia Regiment to Clear the Roads leaving Captn. Mackay behind at the Great Meadows. That they Cleared the Roads about twelve Miles, having been on that Service about three days, and then News having been brought by Two Indians That the French having been Reinforced with a large Body of Men, Were coming to Attack them with Nine Hundred Men. Orders were immediately Sent to Recall that party And also that Captn. Mackay should Advance with his Company, Which he accordingly did: And having Joined them about two in the Morning, They Marched all back to the Great Meadows Burying in the Woods what part of their Ammunition they could not Carry with them. They Continued at the Great Meadows three days before the ffrench came to Attack them,—And in the Morning before the Engagem^t. they Endeavour'd to throw up a little Intrenchm^t. round them about two foot deep, But could not finish it, as the ffrench appeared betwixt Nine and ten in the Morning. We had Centinels placed out to Give Notice of of (sic) the Approach of the ffrench; one of which fired his Peice, and immediately after the ffrench Began to Fire, but being still at a considerable Distance, And did us no hurt. Our Men were drawn up before the ffrench, but did not ffire, The ffrench still keeping at a Distance; They then turned off to a point of Wood that lay very near our Men, Upon which Our Men went into their little Intrenchment—Upon which the French made a Second General Discharge But our Men having kept up their ffire, their Indians were thereby Encouraged to Advance out of the Wood, and Show themselves—pretty near where our Men lay, upon which Col^o. Washington Gave the Word to fire which was accordingly done, and many of the Indians were killed. Our people having two Swivel Guns which were discharged at the same time. After this neither French nor Indians appeared any more but kept behind Trees firing at our Men the best part of the Day. As our People did at them. There was At this place a Small Stocado Fort made in a Circular fform round a Small House that Stood in the Middle of it to keep our provisions and Ammunition in, And was Cover'd with Bark and some Skins, and might be about fourteen ffeet Square, And the Walls of the Fort might be eight ffeet Distance from the said House all Round. The ffrench were at that time so near that |Severall| of our people were wounded by the Splinters beat off by the Bulletts from the said House. At Night the ffrench Desired to Parley with our people, But Col^o. Washington refused. Imagining it might be some Deceit, however upon the Assurances given by the ffrench, That they would· Act honourably. Captn. Vanbram and Adjutant Pyronie were sent to them—And were told by them that they were to be Reinforced in the Morning by four hundred Indians who lay about twelve Miles off; And then it would not be in their Power to give them Quarters. Advised them therefore to Capitulate. That they should be permitted to Return Home with their Arms, And to Carry with them what Provisions and Ammunition they could Carry. But that they should Engage that none of them should be seen on the Waters of the Ohio for a Year and a day afterwards. And that if they Agree'd to these Terms They should Hoist no Colours the next Morning. This was . . accordingly Agree'd to and Signed by Col^o. Washington & Agree'd to by all the Officers, And accordingly next Morning We Hoisted no Colours. And as soon as it was day the French & their Indians came in a Body beating their Drum And formed themselves into two Ranks, That our People might pass through, Which they Accordingly did with their Drums beating, with their Arms and what provisions and Ammunition they could Carry. But we were Obliged to leave behind our Swivel Guns and some Arms which soon after were destroyed and broke to peices by their Indians. Such of our Men That were in that little Fort having Broke the Heads of the Powder Barrells and Strewn it about that it might be of no Service to the French.

We were also obliged to leave with them Captn. Vanbram

and Captn. Stobo as Hostages for the Delivery of the Twenty one prisoners that had been taken by Col^o. Washington as this Depon^t. has related above who were then at Williamsburgh—

That The French had been joined that Morning by above One hundred French Indians who could hardly be Restrained by them from falling on our People—

This Deponent has heard that some Dutch Men who were along with the French told some Dutch Men who were with us That they had lost three hundred Men, But does not know That of his own Knowledge, But Believes they lost a great many, As our people kept constantly firing at them the whole day. Of our Side there were Ten of the Carolina Company killed Of whom Lieutenant Mercier was one, And Twenty belonging to the Virginia Regiment. There were also a great many wounded whom our people carried with them the first day's March, But then were Obliged to Leave them & a party with them to take Care of them 'till Horses could be sent for them, but he has heard that seven of them Died the first Night—

This Deponent then Marched on with the Rest of our Men to Will's-Creek but were Obliged to leave all their Stores and Baggage behind them. At Wills-Creek Sixteen of the Volunteers of the Virginia Regiment went in a Body to Col^o. Washington telling him, that as they Came to Settle the Lands, Which now they had no more thoughts of doing, They were determined to Return home. Col^o. Washington endeavoured to perswade them to Stay, promising to procure them some Gratuity from the Government of Virginia for all their trouble and Losses, But he could not prevail with them, For they went off in a Body Soon after which he and Captn. Mackay set out for Williamsburgh And after he was gone the Men went off daily in Two's and Three's, so that he verily Believes there was full two thirds of them gone When he this Deponent came off—

Some of the Indians who were in our Interest some days before the Engagement under Pretence of making some Discovery went Towards the French Fort and Meeting a French party, Were told that if they would not fight against the English, they would Scalp them—Upon which they all turned to the French. The Half King however with their Women and Children in Number about Thirty Came with our people to Will's Creek. From which many of them Sett off For a place called Jemmy Arther in Pensilvania where they Intended to live for fear of being killed by the other Indians. All the Indians on the Ohio and in those parts being in the French Interest And this Deponent declares that there was not one Indian wth. our people in the Engagement. The two that brought the News of the approach of the ffrench having immediately Sett off after—delivering the above Intelligence 27 Augt. 1754   (Signed) John B W Shaw's Mark.

APPENDIX 5

Description of the Battle
Written by Washington in 1783

In the seventeen eighties a David Humphreys began assembling material for a life of Washington, and sent several pages of manuscript to Washington for review. The following is taken from the comments on this material that Washington sent Humphreys, dated by Fitzpatrick as October, 1783 (Fitzpatrick, *Writings*, XXIX, 40). Some minor inconsistencies with earlier records are not surprising. Washington admitted that his memory was not the best on many details, and prefaced his remarks to Humphreys as follows: "This is a task to which GW. feels himself very incompetent (with any degree of accuracy) from the badness of his memory, loss of Papers, mutilated state, in which those of that date were preserved ..." (Fitzpatrick, *Writings*, XXIX, 38).

About 9 Oclock on the 3d. of July the Enemy advanced with Shouts, and dismal Indian yells to our Intrenchments, but was opposed by so warm, spirited, and constant a fire, that to force the works in *that way* was abandoned by them; they then, from every little rising, tree, stump, Stone, and bush kept up a constant galding fire upon us; which was returned in the best manner we could till late in the Afternn. when their fell the most tremendous rain that can be conceived, filled our trenches with Water, Wet, not only the Ammunition in the Cartouch boxes and firelocks, but that which was in a small temporary Stockade in the middle of the Intrenchment called Fort Necessity erected for the sole purpose of its security, and that of the few stores we had; and left us nothing but a few (for all were not provided with them) Bayonets for defence. In this situation and *no* prospt. of bettering it terms of capitulation were offered to us by the enemy wch. with some alterations that were insisted upon were the more readily acceded to, as we had no Salt provisions, and but indifferently supplied with fresh; which, from the heat of the weather, would not keep; and because a full third of our numbers Officers as well as privates were, by this time, killed or wounded.

APPENDIX 6

Report of 1931 Explorations

Portion of report by Harry Blackford describing the archaeological explorations of 1931. The original report not being available, the following is a copy of the transcript made by Thomas L. Loy in 1935.

On August 4, 1931, the writer of this article made an attempt to verify the surveys of Mr. Lewis and Mr. McCracken, and on attempting to fit the Lewis survey to the existing mounds, found that Lewis had ignored the mound on the lines B-F of the appended plot of survey of Aug. 4th, 1931. The lines A-C and A-B agree very closely to the distances given by Mr. Lewis and the angle B-A-C checks the angle found by Mr. Lewis within 2½ degrees, which variation might easily be caused by taking different points on the mounds. Having thus proven Mr. Hulbert's statements that the Lewis survey would not fit the existing marks on the ground to our own satisfaction, we decided to accept the survey of his engineer, Mr. McCracken, until such times as excavations on the site would prove him right or wrong, and so proceeded to stake the fort as shown by lines A-B-F-G-C-A.

On November 17, 1931, at 7:40 an excavation for the reconstruction of Fort Necessity was started under direction of the writer. Operations were begun by first digging exploratory trenches at right angles to the existing embankments to determine, if possible, the location of the old stockade with reference to the embankments. No indications being found, work was started in digging a trench along the line C-A three feet wide and averaging in depth two and one-half feet, which depth reached hard pan in the form of hard yellow clay which showed no evidences of having ever been disturbed.

The first day the trench was completed from the point C to a point about twenty feet beyond A on the line A-B. The workmen were instructed to carefully examine and break up all excavated material in the hope that relics might be found of this historic battle. The first day's work netted four lead musket balls, of about one-half ounce size, heavily coated with oxide, these being uncovered at depths ranging from six to eighteen inches below the surface. The next day the trench was completed to the point F and seven more lead musket balls, all of one-half ounce size except one which weighed a shade over an ounce were found. At a point on the line B-F about three feet from B, the first indication of the old stockade was unearthed, it being a section of fairly solid heart wood eighteen inches long, three and one-half inches wide and two inches thick, badly pitted from the action of time. The bottom of this piece was almost in the center of the trench, about three feet under ground with the top inclined at an angle of about forty-five degrees towards the inside of the fort as though it had been pulled over in the demolition of the stockade.

From F, as there is no known description from which a definite location could be fixed on the ground, it was decided to follow the line F-G-C. This was carried out, without finding further indications until the intersection of line G-C with D-E was reached. At this point three large pieces of the stockade were uncovered at a depth of three feet. This depth is just water level of the branch of Big Meadow Run near this point and probably accounts for the fact that the timber here found had been preserved all these years. As the line of the stockade was plainly indicated by the three pieces unearthed, excavation was carefully extended on this line towards E, with the result that six more pieces were found, the last being at E. From here a trench towards F was started which resulted in finding three more pieces at a point five feet beyond E on the line E-F and another large piece which had just been missed while excavating along the line F-G. These pieces of stockade were all in an upright position and many showing ax marks where they had been pointed to aid in penetrating the ground. They varied in thickness from six inches to, in one case where the log had evidently been split in half, seventeen and one-half inches. The tops were typical of wood that has long been exposed to the action of water and time.

At a point four feet from E on the line E-F on the inside of the trench and two feet below the surface, six iron balls each one and one-half inches in diameter and weighing about one-half pound were dug up within the space of one cubic foot. These were, in all probability, ammunition for Washington's swivel guns. Seven lead musket balls, all of about one-half ounce size were also found on this line. At the point D, seven small pieces, indicating an angle in the line of the stockade, were found and all along the line D-C, which coincides very closely with Hulbert's line D-C, bark, pieces of rotten wood, which was in such a condition that it could not be preserved, were uncovered. These findings substantiated Mr. Hulbert's statement of finding bark on this line. Also, at various points along this line, pieces of charred wood and lumps of charcoal were excavated from a depth of about three feet, thus giving evidence to support the statement that the stockade had been burned. Ten feet beyond D on the line D-C, a large iron cannon ball, three inches in diameter and weighing three and one-half pounds, was found on the outside edge of the trench about twenty inches below the surface. Numerous lead balls of various size came to light on lines E-D and D-C, some of them weighing as much as one and one-half ounces.

While excavating for drain tile inside the lines of the fort, approximately two hundred lead shot, ranging in size from number eight to Buck shot, which looked as though they had been hurriedly made by pouring molten lead in a thin stream into cold water, were found, also numerous lead musket balls of one ounce size and the flint for a flint lock musket.

Three feet under ground and midway between E and D a small piece of straight grained wood, seven inches long and of one half inch diameter was uncovered. This could easily be a portion of either a wooden ram for the muzzle loading muskets or an Indian arrow shaft.

Summing up the evidence found by investigation of this site, we have: The embankments found on the lines C-A and A-B which were in evidence in 1816 as proved by the Lewis survey. The embankment on the line B-F which may have been, and probably was, visible at the time of Mr. Lewis' survey. This embankment is plainly joined to the one on the line A-B on the inside of the fort at the point B and in no possible way could it be construed as being thrown up in excavating a farm drain as some authorities have advocated. Besides, it is proven at B and at F by the finding of parts of the stockade. The lines F-E, E-D, and D-C are indisputable, as sufficient remains of the stockade were excavated to prove their location beyond a shadow of doubt.

REFERENCES

Note: The following references are limited to the sources referred to in this work.

ABRAHAM, J. W.
1932 "Redstone Old Fort and Fort Burd". *Fort Necessity and Historic Shrines of the Redstone Country*. Washington Bi-Centennial Issue 1732-1932. Fort Necessity Chapter, Pennsylvania Society of the Sons of the American Revolution. Uniontown, Pa.

ALBERT, GEORGE D., ED.
1896 *The Frontier Forts of Western Pennsylvania*. Report of the Commission to Locate the Site of Frontier Forts of Pennsylvania, Vol. I. State Printer of Pennsylvania.

BANISTER, JOHN, JR. to ROBERT BOLLING
Cited in *William and Mary College Quarterly*, old series, X, 104.

BLACKFORD, HARRY
1931 Record and Description of the Reconstruction of Fort Necessity. Typescript of unpublished manuscript report.

BROCK, R. A., ED.
1883 *The Official Records of Robert Dinwiddie, Lieutenant-Governor of the Colony of Virginia, 1751-1758. Now First Printed from the Manuscript in the Collections of the Virginia Historical Society. 2 vols.* Virginia Historical Society, Richmond. *Collections of the Virginia Historical Society*, New Series, Vol. III.

CLELAND, HUGH
1955 *George Washington in the Ohio Valley*. Pittsburgh.

COWAN, JOHN P.
1954-5 "George Washington at Fort Necessity". *The Western Pennsylvania Historical Magazine*, XXXVII, Nos. 3 and 4, 153-177.

FAYETTE COUNTY RECORDS
Deed Book 512, p. 480. Uniontown, Pa.

FITZPATRICK, JOHN C., ED.
1925 *The Diaries of George Washington*. 4 vols. Boston.

FITZPATRICK, JOHN C., ED.
1931-44 *The Writings of George Washington*. 39 vols. Washington.

FORT NECESSITY MEMORIAL ASSOCIATION
1931 *A Young Colonel from Virginia*. Uniontown, Pa.

FREEMAN, DOUGLAS S.
1948-51 *George Washington, A Biography*. 5 vols. New York.

HARRINGTON, J. C.
1955 "Archeology as an Auxiliary Science to American History". *American Anthropologist*, LVII, No. 6, Part 1, 1121-1130.

HARRINGTON, J. C.
1952 Preliminary Report, Archeological Explorations, Fort Necessity National Battlefield Site, August-September. National Park Service, Region One Office (September 22, 1952). Manuscript Report.

HARRINGTON, J. C.
1953 Report on 1952 Archeological Explorations at Fort Necessity National Battlefield Site. National Park Service, Region One Office. Manuscript Report.

HULBERT, ARCHER
1903 *Washington's Road*. Vol. 3 in Historic Highways of America Series. Cleveland.

LOWDERMILK, W. H.
1878 *History of Cumberland*. Washington.

PRUSSING, E. E.
1927 *The Estate of George Washington, Deceased*. Boston.

SALLEY, A. S.
1932 "The Independent Company from South Carolina at Great Meadows. *Bulletins of the Historical Commission of South Carolina No. 11.* Columbia, S. C.

SEARIGHT, THOMAS B.
1894 *The Old Pike: A History of the National Road*. Uniontown, Pa.

SHAW, JOHN B. W.
1754 Deposition Made before Governor James Glen of South Carolina on August 27, 1754. Original document in British Public Record Office; photostatic copy furnished by Historical Commission of South Carolina from microfilm negative.

SPARKS, JARED, ED.
1837 *The Writings of George Washington*. 12 vols. Boston.

THWAITES, R. G.
1904 *How George Rogers Clark Won the Northwest*. Chicago.

TILBERG, FREDERICK
1953 The Location and Structure of Fort Necessity and the Physical Features of Great Meadows. National Park Service, Gettysburg National Military Park. Manuscript Report.

TILBERG, FREDERICK
1953 "Washington's Stockade at Fort Necessity". *Pennsylvania History*, Vol. XX, No. 3. Pennsylvania Historical Association Quarterly Journal.

TILBERG, FREDERICK
1954 *Fort Necessity National Battlefield Site, Pennsylvania*. National Park Service Historical Handbook Series, No. 19. Washington.

UMBLE, R. E.
1932 "Mount Washington, Fort Necessity and Shrine". *Fort Necessity and Historic Shrines of the Redstone Country*. Washington Bi-Centennial Issue 1732-1932. Fort Necessity Chapter, Pennsylvania Society of the Sons of the American Revolution. Uniontown, Pa.

VEECH, JAMES
1910 *The Monongahela of Old*. Pittsburgh.

VIRGINIA GAZETTE
1932 Williamsburg, Va., July 19, 1754. Facsimile copy published by Fort Necessity Chapter, Sons of the American Revolution.

CHAPTER 20

The Archaeology of Nineteenth Century British Imperialism: An Australian Case Study

JIM ALLEN

In 1838 the British began their third attempt to settle north Australia. In the previous decade between 1824 and 1829 two abortive settlements had been established at Melville Island and Raffles Bay, in the vicinity of the Cobourg Peninsula, a small peninsula jutting into the Arafura Sea at the western end of Arnhem Land (See Figure 1).

These earlier settlements had been established primarily for commercial reasons, in an attempt to command some of the trade in the eastern end of the Indonesian archipelago. They were begun in high hopes, but visions of a second Singapore quickly faded. This was partly to do with the changing political situation during this decade and was also associated with the failure of the British in this area to trap any of the trepang (*bêche-de-mer*) harvest taken annually from the north Australian coast by fishermen from Macassar, and destined for China markets.

Despite these failures less than ten years later the British began another attempt in the same area setting up a tiny garrison on the site named Victoria in Port Essington, also on the Cobourg Peninsula.

THE POLITICAL BACKGROUND

Elsewhere I have argued that the overriding consid-

eration in both the establishment and maintenance of the settlement at Port Essington was that of maintaining sovereignty over the entire coastline and adjacent sea-lanes and that, as such, the settlement at Port Essington is to be seen as a successful strategic manœuvre rather than a failed attempt at colonization, despite the fact that the settlement was abandoned in 1849 (Allen 1972).

The Port Essington venture was essentially the brainchild of Sir John Barrow, Second Secretary at the Admiralty, who felt that it would be quite 'a most humiliating mortification to witness the tricoloured flag, or that of the Stripes and Stars waving on Dampier's Land' (Barrow to Glenelg, 13 December 1836. C.O. 201/256). At the Colonial Office James Stephen also shared this opinion and wrote of the 'paramount importance of retaining permanent possession of the entire coast of Australia' (Stephen to Wood Eyre, 16 May 1837. C.O. 201/264). The Port Essington venture was only hung upon the façade of commercial enterprise at the stage when the Colonial Office made overtures to the Treasury for the financial backing to establish Port Essington (Stephen to Spearman, 28 July 1837. C.O. 202/236). However, the Chancellor of the Exchequer refused to go to Parliament with the estimates for the proposed settlement (Barrow to Stephen, 18 January 1840. C.O. 201/302). Undeterred, the Admiralty proceeded with the project and in February 1838 H.M.S.

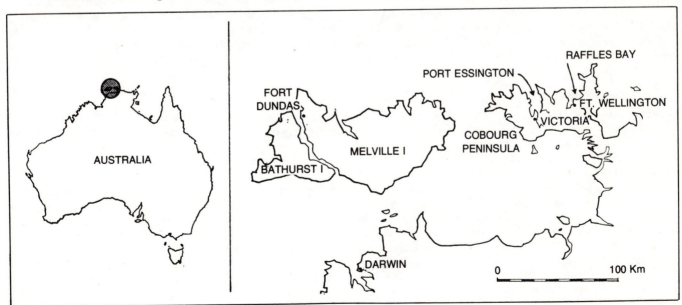

FIGURE 1. Map Showing the Location of the Settlement of Victoria, Port Essington, Together with the Earlier Settlements of Fort Dundas on Melville Island, and Fort Wellington in Raffles Bay.

Alligator under the command of Sir James J. Gordon Bremer, together with H.M.S. *Britomart* commanded by Captain Owen Stanley R.N., sailed from England bound for Sydney and north Australia with a party of Royal Marines.

The political and administrative history of Port Essington has been dealt with in depth elsewhere (Howard 1933; Graham 1967; Allen 1969; 1972) and will not be reviewed here. However, several points do need further discussion.

Firstly, it must be remembered that during its entire history the settlement at Port Essington was within the colony of New South Wales, and necessarily came under the jurisdiction of the colonial Governor in Sydney. In this sense Port Essington was very much a colony of Sydney which itself was a colony controlled by the Colonial Office in London. Hence the problems met with during the early part of Sydney's history in relationship to this extreme distance from the mother country were exaggerated in the case of Port Essington which was, by the most direct sea route, more than 4,000 kilometres from Sydney. Usually a request from Port Essington would be directed to the Governor in Sydney; if the matter was beyond his jurisdiction the letter would be enclosed in correspondence from the Governor to the Colonial Office in London. Since the actual control of Port Essington was in the hands of the Admiralty the letter would be forwarded on to the Admiralty for their opinion or decision, returned to the Colonial Office then back to Sydney and on to Port Essington. In this manner delays of eighteen months or more were common for simple administrative decisions.

Despite the large amount of documentary evidence which emphasizes the difficulties of distance and second and even third hand administration of Port Essington, the question of the immediate physical problems faced by the settlers and their solutions to them is one which has not been answered satisfactorily from this sort of evidence (e.g. Spillett 1972). It was mainly to this end that excavations were undertaken at the site between 1966 and 1968. The resulting picture derived from a combination of documentary and archaeological evidence has proved more satisfactory.

PERSONNEL

Throughout its existence Port Essington remained a tiny settlement manned almost entirely by Royal Marines. Unlike the earlier northern settlements, and most other colonial towns and hamlets in Australia, it was not supplied with convict labour, except for four months in late 1844 and early 1845.

Between 1838 and 1844 the permanent personnel at Port Essington consisted of 53 Marines, 3 Marine wives and 4 children, and 4 civilians in a semi-official capacity. When this garrison was relieved in 1844, 6 people had died and 19 others had been already discharged, mainly invalided. For the second half of the settlement's history the permanent personnel consisted of 66 Marines, 6 Marine wives and 5 children, and 1 civilian. Of these 78 only 43 still remained when finally relieved in 1849, 8 having previously been discharged (7 invalided), and 18 having had their deaths recorded. The remaining 9, since the records contain no reference to them, are also thought to have died (figures compiled from Spillet 1972: 178–85). Thus the death-rate ran at approximately 23% for the lifetime of the settlement, excluding deaths of ships' crew members in Port Essington which added seventeen to the total number.

Almost without exception deaths at Port Essington result-ed from malaria, the cause and transmission of which was unknown. The settlement remained free of fever for the first few years, but during the 1842–3 wet season, outbreaks were widespread and no one went unscathed. In August 1843 Jukes reported the outpost to be a garrison of 'yellow skeletons' (Browne 1871: 199). Despite the urgency of the situation it was seventeen months before the relief detachment arrived from the time of the initial communication (Parker to Admiralty, 18 June 1843. A.R.M.P.). Within twelve months every man in the new garrison had contracted malaria, and deaths occurred at regular intervals. During the wet season of 1848–9 the disease laid waste to the garrison in the worst epidemic experienced in the settlement. It seems probable that the nine marines of whom there is no record died during this period.

THE SITE

The Cobourg Peninsula is a relatively flat area, the outstanding topographical feature of which is the number of harbours and inlets which indent its coastline. The largest of these is Port Essington which has a mouth some 11 kilometres wide, and which extends 32 kilometres to its head. The harbour is divided naturally into inner and outer harbours by a narrow spit of land. The shoreline consists of dunes screened by mangrove mudflats or sandy beaches, although in places a low cliffline reveals the hinterland as open sclerophyll forest with pockets of monsoonal jungle. Being well within the tropical zone the area is hot and humid and averages 130 cm. of rain each year which falls within a wet season of October to April. Records kept during 1840 indicated an annual temperature range of 17° C–26° C minimum to 32° C–36° C maximum (Barrow to Stephen, 2 July 1841. C.O. 201/313).

The site of the settlement is on the western shore of the inner harbour on a plateau which is the highest area in Port Essington, and a classically defensive position, for which reason it was probably chosen (Earl 1863: 33). Yet no water was to be found in the immediate area, and garden soils were no better than at other locations about the harbour. Worse still the site was some 27 kilometres from the harbour mouth; the climate at this point was not relieved by coastal breezes, and passing ships, being under sail, might have to spend two or three days working in and out of the port. Gaps of up to eight months between ships visiting Port Essington were experienced for this reason.

In June 1840 and May 1841 earth tremors were noted in the settlement, but were inconsequential compared with the hurricane which struck the settlement in November 1839, smashing trees and houses and causing H.M.S. *Pelorus* at anchor nearby to run aground with the loss of eight lives (Allen 1969: 359–61).

Apart from crocodiles and poisonous snakes north Australia possessed no animals which the garrison might fear. However, rats attacked the gardens and cockroaches and flies continually spoiled food and stores. Sandflies and mosquitoes were sufficiently irritating to cause them, and the painful ulcers they induced, to be mentioned in despatches (Bremer to Beaufort, 7 December 1838. H.D.: B.798), while the green tree ants in their millions made clearing a slow and painful procedure.

However, it was the tiny termite *(Isoptera)* known popularly in Australia as the 'white ant' which provided the most concerted opposition to the British settlement, and even during its lifetime these creatures were victorious (see below).

ARCHITECTURE

The architectural history of Port Essington has proved an excellent reflector of the immediate difficulties faced by the British in northern Australia. By combining the documentary and archaeological evidence three distinct phases can be traced which emphasize the technological shortcomings of the garrison and the environmental pressures put upon it.

Phase I

Whilst in Sydney in 1838, the expedition took on board seven timber buildings prefabricated there at the direction of the Governor of New South Wales. These included a dwelling for the commandant, a dwelling for the officers, two barrack rooms, a kitchen, hospital and storehouse (Bremer to Admiralty, 16 September 1838. C.O. 201/286). In addition a prefabricated church provided by the Lord Bishop of Australia (Spillet 1972: 12) was also shipped to the settlement. Upon arrival in Port Essington, the garrison, assisted by the sailors aboard H.M.S. *Alligator,* H.M.S. *Britomart* and the supply ship *Drontes,* began the difficult task of clearing an area for the settlement. Bremer complained in a manner reminiscent of Sydney fifty years earlier, that the timber of the country defied the saws and tools which they had brought (Copies or Extracts: 9–10), but the archaeological evidence suggests that fire was also used to assist the clearing (Allen 1969: 7). Bremer had been instructed to erect any defensive earthworks which might be considered necessary (Adam and Parker to Stanley, 30 January 1838. Adm. 2/1965) and a simple ditch and bank enclosing an area of some 600 square metres (Allen 1969: 142–3) was probably thrown up at this time although it was not mentioned in despatches, and was probably never used.

During the first six months of the settlement all things prospered, and by April 1839 Bremer was able to report the completion of the pier, the hospital and officers' quarters, together with progress on the batteries and storehouse. In addition, the men were housed in '24 cottages and gardens, all comfortable' (Copies or Extracts: 11).

The area chosen for the settlement was strewn with ironstone boulders, and this stone was widely used although it was of such hardness that it proved difficult to work. Thus the pier had only the southern side of dressed masonry. A similar economy can be noted in regard to the prefabricated structures. Rather than face the arduous task of levelling extensive areas it was found more convenient to set these buildings on piles. The largest of these, Government House, was described as 18 feet by 40 feet and having a split shingle roof (Earl 1846: 88). This building, together with the ordnance store, was set on dwarf piles several feet from the ground, but the remaining prefabricated buildings were raised eight feet from the ground on timber piles (H.R.A., I, xxvi: 373–4). Accidentally the garrison had hit upon an effective method for controlling the inroads of the termites. Later, Captain John McArthur, who succeeded Bremer as commandant, was to note that 'had [these buildings] been fixed upon the ground in the usual manner, they must have been destroyed long since by vermin' (H.R.A., I, xxvi: 374). Also such a technique provided better ventilation, and when

later rediscovered in Queensland became a distinctive feature of Australian tropical architecture (Freeland 1968: 207).

Of the '24 cottages, all comfortable' description depends more heavily on archaeological evidence, and suggests anything but comfort. In the course of excavation, two floor mounds identified as single men's huts were examined. Each suggests a floor plan size of about 3 metres square which housed four men (Sweatman n.d., 2: 256), either completely bark-covered or with reed walls and a thatched roof which McArthur recorded as lasting two to three years (H.R.A., I, xxvi: 373–4), by which time the framework would be completely destroyed by termites. The archaeological evidence indicates that these huts were burnt and rebuilt on the same sites. Introduced red clay appears to have been first employed for flooring, but after this the stratigraphic evidence illustrates that successive layers of fine beach shell were laid down. This technique, which became traditional at Port Essington, clearly reflects the common use of mixed sand, lime and ashes in Britain at this time (Smith 1834: 22; C. B. Allen 1849–50: 41).

Phase II

The second phase of architectural expansion at Port Essington can be directly related to the hurricane which struck the settlement in November 1839. Of the more substantial structures, Government House was lifted from its piles and thrown 3 metres through the air; the church, only half completed, was totally demolished; many of the flimsy cottages were flattened (Spillett 1972: 56–63).

As a result of this devastation, building policy clearly altered. Although no experienced sawyer was amongst the garrison, the shortage of supplies from Sydney, particularly timber and nails, forced the garrison back on to its own resources. A primitive saw-pit was cut into a cliff-face, and the garrison learnt to produce battens and planking for the buildings. The blacksmiths made nails, pointed the mason's tools, and constructed iron-work for the buildings, which McArthur deemed necessary following the destruction caused by the hurricane (H.R.A., I, xxvi: 374).

The wreck of the *Pelorus* at this time proved beneficial for the settlement since although refloated it stayed at Port Essington throughout 1840. Its crew thus provided an additional supply of labour to assist with repairing the damage of the hurricane. More importantly one of its crew was by trade a brickmaker and was able to fill an important gap in the skills of the garrison. A good clay source had previously been located near the settlement, and this marine produced bricks using the traditional open topped wooden mould with a removable base. By modern standards these bricks were of poor quality, comprising 20% clay and 80% sand, tempered with ironstone nodules. They were not highly fired, and consequently were porous and soft. They were not frogged and were of irregular size, but they were a technological achievement in the settlement and McArthur was highly elated with their possibilities (Copies or Extracts: 29). However, when the *Pelorus* sailed in March 1841 the brickmaker left also, and none remaining could apparently emulate his skill. Thus the use of brick in the Port Essington archaeological record is a precise dating indicator. A mixture of clay and lime, manufactured from burning shells, was used to bond both bricks and masonry from this time onwards.

The major architectural change during this period was obviously made to prevent the possibility of future hurricane devastation. Government House was replaced on dwarf piers of stone. The quartermaster's store, which on its 8 feet wooden piles had survived the devastation, was now enclosed underneath with rough-hewn masonry built directly around the piles. This action proved a retrograde step because it assisted the photophobic termites and by 1848 this building had become so infested that it was no longer habitable (Brierly 1848: 14 November). McArthur noted that much additional storage space was achieved, but Earl Grey recognized that this action had accelerated the destruction of this and other buildings for the sake of additional accommodation (H.R.A., I, xxvi: 373–4).

The original hospital was completely dismantled and despite the labour involved the area was levelled and a lower storey of brick on solid stone foundations was constructed (Figure 2). The prefabricated wooden structure became an upper storey and the whole was converted to a store, while further north, another large area was levelled by the crew of the *Pelorus* and a larger hospital, the last prefabricated building to be brought to the settlement, was erected on low ironstone footings.

In external appearance, the hospital reflected the classic features of the nineteenth-century Australian farmhouse, with the broken-backed pitch of the roof spreading over a verandah on all sides, with each corner enclosed. The verandah, echoing its English antecedents, provided covered access as well as shade (Freeland 1968: 45–7). A small nearby structure was identified by excavation as a dispensary, built of stone and brick (Allen 1969: 370).

While these public buildings were relatively substantial and well built, the dwellings of the enlisted men continued to be the basic bark huts described above. During this period, however, cottages were also built for the few enlisted men who had brought their families with them to northern

Australia. Although slightly larger in size than the quarters for single men these were also built of bush materials, with 'little square holes for light and air, with little raised shutters like the ports of a vessel' (Brierly 1848: 14 November). The important addition to each of these cottages was that in each case the southern wall consisted of a semi-circular buttressed stone chimney, identified as the first examples of the distinctive Cornish round chimney located outside Cornwall (Allen 1967).

Five such chimneys standing in a line were recorded. Four of these were still complete, the fifth having been demolished by a falling tree. In each instance these chimneys were constructed of local stone with only the external faces shaped, and the internal walls coated with lime plaster. Bricks had been used to construct the arch above the fireplace, again offering a general date for their erection. Despite the general conformity of design, however, significant variations in construction methods were apparent, particularly in relation to the usage of timber which was reflected archaeologically as gaps in the stonework. By the analysis of these differences the chimneys were eventually seriated and fell into one group of three and one group of two, with one of the former group being considered transitional, and relevantly, this one was physically placed between the other four examples (Allen 1967; 1969: 47—56).

The detailed analysis of these structures indicates that their builder was less than proficient, but unwittingly he left evidence of both his own ingenuity and the general improvisation of the garrison. A pictorial representation of a similar round chimney at Glenelg in South Australia can be dated 1836–8 (Wallace n.d.) and may be related to the Port Essington examples, since additional Marines were taken by the expedition from that settlement in 1838 (Spillett 1972:

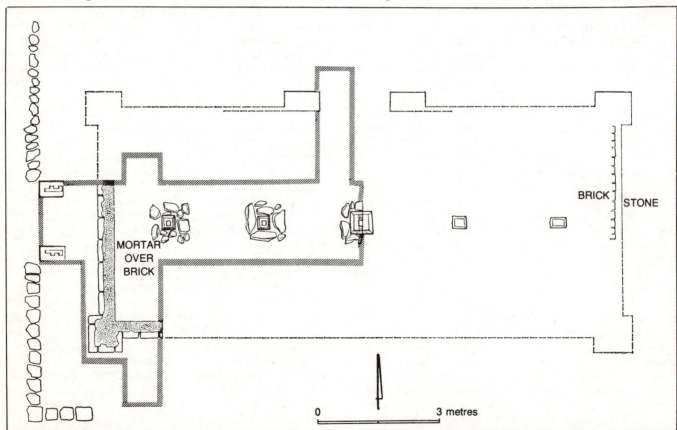

FIGURE 2. Ground Plan of the Original Hospital Building After its Rebuilding as a Store. The Shaded Outline is the Line of Excavation, and Shows the Internal Stone Bases Used for Supporting Timbers. Excavations Showed That This Building was Burnt and Reduced to Foundation Level Prior to Abandonment.

20). A neat confirmation of the archaeological division of these chimneys came later: up until 1844 there were only three wives in the settlement. When the detachment was replaced, six women came into the settlement (Spillett 1972: 179–84). One, the wife of the quartermaster, lived above the quartermaster's store, thus necessitating the construction of two additional family cottages. Some three weeks in November–December 1844 was spent in effecting the changeover of the garrison, and it was possibly during this time that the original builder supervised the construction of the new cottages. The improved construction of these within the general style of the earlier ones may either be thus attributed to experience of the deficiencies of the earlier ones, or more probably may reflect the presence at this time of a team of convict masons and builders at Port Essington, and more properly should be considered as part of the third phase of architecture in the settlement.

Leaving aside these two cottages, by the beginning of 1842 the modest architectural needs of the garrison had been sufficiently met. A stone magazine, sunk into the ground to minimize risks of explosion, and a blockhouse and breastworks had been completed on a prominent headland; the men were housed; there were sufficient storehouses; kilns for charcoal and lime manufacture; a smithy and bread oven had been constructed (Allen 1969: 371–2). The remains of all of these structures reflect the transposition of British prototypes into a technologically ill-equipped colony. The bread oven for example had been constructed in cemented rough-hewn masonry with timber supports at the corners. The interior had been filled with clay and rubble to a height of 90 cm. then a platform of squared stone blocks laid down, then the oven itself constructed of a masonry and brick arched vault. A fire inside the oven would heat the entire structure, the fire would then be raked out, the bread placed inside and the entrance blocked until the baking was completed.

Phase III

In January 1844 twenty picked convicts, masons and quarrymen, sailed from Sydney to construct a beacon at Raine Island in the Barrier Reef (Ritchie 1967: 300). Completing the work there in September they embarked in H.M.S. *Fly* and H.M.S. *Bramble* for Port Essington where they remained until the end of January 1845, while the two vessels journeyed to Sourabaya. While at Port Essington the skills of these men were put to good use. Some, it appears, were put to work constructing the two new family cottages (above) while others were employed constructing a beacon at the mouth of Port Essington (Allen 1969: 372—3).

Within the settlement itself the construction of the kitchen (Figure 3) which served the hospital may reasonably be attributed to the work of these masons. In striking contrast to other architecture in the settlement, this building bears all the aspects of professionalism. All corners, entrances, windows and the chimney were quoined in good quality masonry, and the walls, of rough-hewn stone, were well laid and even. The floor level was raised above the outside ground level, using stone doorsteps and an internal flooring of shell. On the insides of the door uprights the use of timber jambs is reflected in the cement, and cuttings in the stone also indicate the use of wooden lintels and window sills.

Apart from the fireplace wall the ground plan is symmetrical and the design was almost certainly adapted from, if not actually, a stock pattern, and Figure 3 shows a similar British design pattern for a dwelling for the 'labouring classes'. Here the description reads in part, 'the walls are proposed to be built entirely of rubble stone, and the corners, rebates, soles [sic] and lintels merely hammer dressed.... The floors to be elevated above the surface of the ground ... to be formed of a composition of lime, earth, and engine ashes.' In addition the window sashes were to be of wood and windows glazed, with hung doors and stone doorsteps (Smith 1834: 22).

During fieldwork three kilns were recorded in the settlement. Two of these were relatively small and could be attributed to Phase II architecture (Allen 1969: 138). The third kiln (Figure 4), however, is much larger and constructed of rough-hewn masonry in the shape of a truncated cone. Let into the side of a small cliff, the kiln, used for producing lime, would have been fed from the top. The action of the kiln would have been intermittent rather than continuous, and after each firing would have been emptied through the arched opening at the base. The expertise in the construction of this kiln points strongly to its having been built by the convict masons. Today it still stands intact and is a classic example of a pre-1850 British lime-kiln (Hudson 1965: 138).

Finally, the smithy was rebuilt at this time, with a fine stone chimney standing some 6 metres high, which has recently been demolished by a falling tree. The basic functional technology was reconstructed from the base (Allen 1969: 104–5), which incorporated blocks of coral conglomerate in its construction. This is the single example of non-local stone being used, and the nearest source of this material, near the harbour mouth, suggests that this stone was brought to the settlement after the beacon had been completed. This archaeological date accords well with a brief documentary reference which suggests a completion date of 1846 (H.R.A., I,xxvi: 374).

With the probable exception of several vaults in the cemetery, the smithy appears to be the last building constructed in the settlement. For the remaining three years the garrison, continuously weakened by malaria, struggled to maintain the status quo which they had established. By 1848, however, both the quartermaster's store and the blockhouse had been abandoned to the termites, and a late report urged that iron frameworks for houses should be sent 'as it has been found impossible to guard against the inroads of the white ants by any means that experience could suggest or ingenuity devise' (Stanley to Deas Thompson, 17 April 1849. D.H. SL.15f).

SUBSISTENCE

While Bremer's early despatches praised the fertility of the soil and reported success with citrus fruits, bananas, plantains, coconuts, sugar, rice and cotton (Copies or Extracts: 9), seasons and climate were never fully understood and subsequent reports indicate that agriculture never rose above subsistence levels and necessitated constant attention and hard work to achieve even this (Allen 1969: 375–80). Of the local land fauna the archaeological evidence suggests only kangaroo and occasional birds provided meat, and throughout the lifetime of the settlement the garrison depended on livestock introduced from the neighbouring islands or Sydney. Pigs, cattle, sheep and goats were continually supplied, despite staggering losses en route. For example, of one shipment of 45 cattle sent from Sydney, only 14 were landed, of which 2 died almost immediately. Once arrived the stock had to be hand-fed, since some of the local

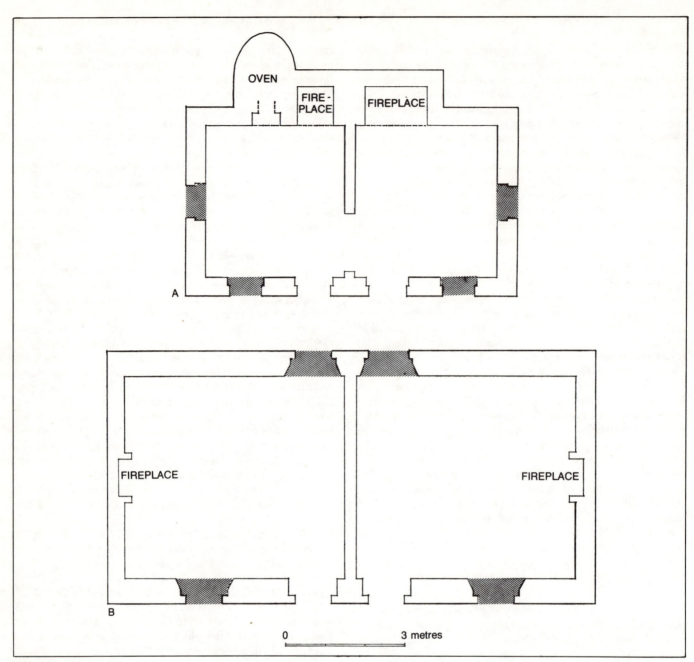

FIGURE 3. (A) Ground Plan of Hospital Kitchen. This was Presumably a Stock Pattern and May Be Compared with (B) which Shows a Similar Stock Pattern (after Smith 1834).

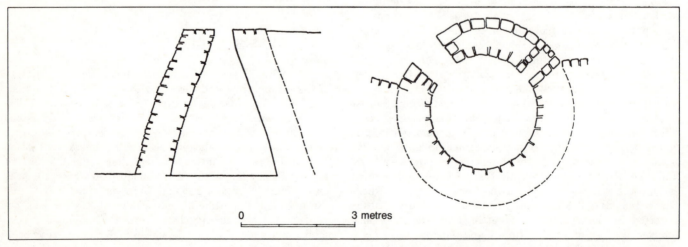

FIGURE 4. Plan of Lime-Kiln; Constructed into a Small Bank and Fed from above, It Is a Good Example of a Pre-1850 British Lime-Kiln.

144

flora proved poisonous, and since the task required more manpower than was available stock continually strayed and became wild (Copies or Extracts: 30–1). Sheep in particular were vulnerable in the tropical climate, and although this had been noted in the earlier settlements, they continued to be sent to Port Essington until 1849.

Unlike other Australian colonies the garrison at Port Essington lived harmoniously with the Aborigines. While this probably reflects the effects of earlier contact with both the British and the Macassan trepangers, and the garrison's own deliberate policy of non-violence, the small British population was insufficient to threaten the economic basis of Aboriginal life. Indeed, the Aborigines appear to have supplied the settlement with shellfish, turtle and the hearts of the cabbage tree palm (*S.M.H.* 21 June 1840), although they could not be induced to work in the settlement for more than a few days at a time. The Aborigines were eager for European goods, especially metal for fishing spears, clothing, which they traded into the interior, and tobacco. The excavation of two midden sites close to the settlement has shown that the Aborigines remained in close attendance to the settlement. Bottle glass, particularly the thickened bases, provided an alternate material to stone, of which there is little in the region of good quality for implement manufacture, and the analysis of glass artefacts (Figure 5) has demonstrated a systematic exploitation and modification of this material (Allen 1969: 216–43). However, the lasting legacy of European contact was, as in other places in Australia, disease, which reduced an estimated population on the Cobourg Peninsula of 200 in 1838 to 28 before the end of the century (Allen 1969: 399).

ARTEFACTS AND EXPORTATION TIME-LAG

Space does permit a review of the total artefactual information recovered from excavations at Port Essington. In general artefacts were almost all of British origin and reflected the military nature of the settlement. The quantity of South-east Asian ceramics did underline, however, the garrison's dependence on island goods and emphasizes the isolation of Port Essington from Sydney.

The somewhat surprising result of the analysis of European artefacts, however, was that they indicate a relatively short time-lag for their export to Australia. Amongst the ceramics the majority of items are of the glazed white clay variety commonly labelled 'china'. Decoration in this category is almost exclusively of transfer printed designs, of which the ubiquitous 'willow pattern' constitutes some 40%. Dating these wares has proved difficult, particularly given the small number of items bearing makers' names (Figure 6), but the literature does contain certain clues. For example, writing in 1829 Simeon Shaw noted the introduction of red, brown and green colours for printed decoration (Godden 1963: 149) and Honey places this innovation later, in the 1830s (Honey 1965: 224–5). By using both marked pieces and style innovations it has been possible to construct Figure 10, which indicates the relationship between the temporal span of the settlement, and manufacturing firms and style changes which are represented in the collection. It is of interest to note that multicolour printing of which there is a single example from Port Essington was not used commercially until the late 1840s (Godden 1963: 152). Few, if any, of the items appear to be made outside the Potteries region in

Staffordshire, and represent a typical collection of utilitarian wares which fit into a manufacturing time range of 1830–48, and possibly a shorter period still.

Amongst the large collection of bottle glass a number of seals were recovered. One group of seven seals is seen as having been attached to bottles which were government issue (Figure 5). One seal is inscribed 'G↑R'; two 'W↑R'; and the remaining four 'V↑R'. These are seen as referring to George IV, William IV and Victoria, and indicate one example pre-1830, two examples 1830–7, and four examples post-1837. If this small sample is representative of the many unsealed bottles (a minimum number count of eighty-five bases in the collection), there is again little time-lag in the passage of bottles to Port Essington.

A large collection of buttons and other insignia were recovered during excavations, most of which as expected relate to the Royal Marines. When presented to Professor Charles Thomas, Institute of Cornish Studies, he was able to conclude, without knowing the date of the settlement, 'I would guess that none of these items is earlier than *c.* 1830 and probably refer to military occupation between 1830 and 1860. If one had to pin it down, the earlier half of this period might be preferred' (Thomas, pers. comm.).

Finally, both gunflints and percussion caps were recovered from the excavations. Clarke (1935) dates the introduction of the latter to 1832 and notes that the sale of the last consignment of gunflints to the British Government took place in 1838. That both types of firearm were present in this isolated settlement indicates that the changeover was extremely rapid.

While the archaeological evidence does not lend itself to precise statements on exportation time-lag, when taken in conjunction with the general documentary evidence it is clear that technological invention in Britain took no significant time to reach its far-flung colonies. If the single sherd bearing multicoloured transfer printing can be taken as a valid guide, in some instances at least this lag was reduced to as little as two or three years, which was virtually the length of time needed to transport the goods.

CONCLUSIONS

By virtue of its late colonization, Australia provides an excellent area for examining problems of colonialism which seem likely to be universal to all periods, historic and prehistoric. The specific value of Port Essington is that it is an extreme example in most respects. Its environment was extremely foreign to the British, and the absence of labour, convict or indigenous, exaggerated this. Its isolation from the mother colony was extreme. The size of the garrison was so small as to be almost non-viable, and its technological skills so limited as to reflect continually the processes of improvisation rather than adaptation.

For the statesmen who manipulated the puppet-strings of Port Essington in another world, the settlement provided an important, if temporary, strategic dot on the Australian map. But for the unfortunates who manned the post, the immediate problems of daily survival continued uppermost.

Leadership within the settlement was at best uninspired and governed by the Books of Regulations and Revelation. Temporal relief in rum or gambling or fighting among the enlisted men was put down by imprisonment in irons on bread and water, and T. H. Huxley reported that although there were only five officers in the settlement, 'there is as

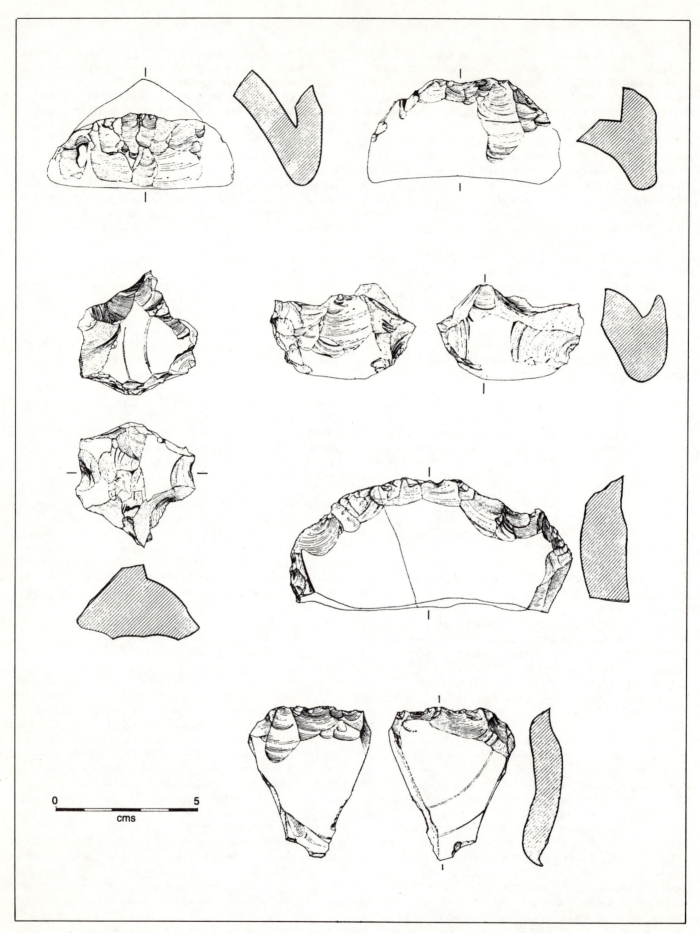

FIGURE 5. Aboriginal Artefacts Manufactured from Bottle Glass. The Heavy Profile Lines Indicate the Original Surfaces of the Bottles, and Demonstrate the Use of the Thickened Bases.

146

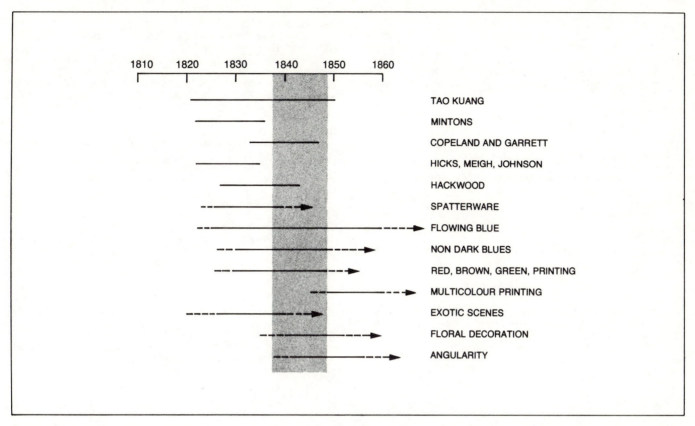

FIGURE 6.   The Relationship Between the Temporal Span of the Settlement (Shaded), and the Manufacturing Firms and Style Changes Represented in the Ceramic Collection.

much petty intrigue, caballing and mutual hatred as if it were the court of the Great Khan' (Huxley 1935: 149). Thus while the pomp and circumstance of the parade ground might have little application at Port Essington, since it was considered necessary for discipline, the Marines paraded in their red serge uniforms, while the termites unceremoniously attacked the sofa in Sir Gordon Bremer's tent, 'although I cause it to be moved every day' (Bremer to Beaufort, 7 December 1838. H.D. B.798).

The dearth of women at Port Essington also reflects in exaggerated fashion an Australian colonial problem, for in 1831 males outnumbered females in the country by more than 3 to 1 (Blainey 1966: 170) and men remained numerically greater in the country until 1916 (a year in which Australian men were occupied fighting a British war overseas). Harmonica reeds recovered during excavations bear testimony to the simple entertainments to be had living in the Australian bush, and the growth of Australian bush ballads, adapting the traditional songs of Britain, can be readily understood in conditions such as those at Port Essington. There can have been little relevance in the news that the Bishop of York had been thrown from a horse 'but was feeling better' (Brierly 1848: 16 November) in a settlement which years before had been so short of supplies that all the men were barefooted and dressed almost entirely in cotton cloth purchased from the Macassans (Allen 1969: 395). Above all, Port Essington is to be seen as a microcosmic example of the situation repeated a hundred times in the early history of Australia, and which moulded a new culture from the old—the small artificial male societies which gave rise to the Australian legends of sport, hard drinking and mateship (Blainey 1966: 170–2).

ACKNOWLEDGEMENT

I am grateful to Miss Winifred Mumford for the line drawings.

2.xii.1972

Department of Prehistory
Australian National University
Canberra

ABBREVIATIONS

Adm.	Admiralty Records in the Public Records Office, London.
A.R.M.P.	Archives of the Royal Marines, Portsmouth.
C.O.	Colonial Office Records in the Public Records Office, London.
Copies or Extracts	*Copies or Extracts of any Correspondences Relative to the Establishment at Port Essington.* London. 1843.
H.D.	Hydrographic Department, London. Correspondence.
H.R.A.	Historical Records of Australia.
S.M.H.	*Sydney Morning Herald.*

REFERENCES

ALLEN, C. B.
   1849–50 *Cottage building: or hints for improving the dwellings of the labouring classes.* London.

ALLEN, J.
1967 The Cornish round chimney in Australia. *Cornish Archaeology.* 6:68–73.

ALLEN, J.
1969 *Archaeology, and the history of Port Essington.* Ph.D. thesis, Dept. Prehistory, Australian National University, Canberra.

ALLEN, J.
1972 Port Essington: a successful limpet port? *Historical Studies.* 15:341–60.

BLAINEY, G.
1966 *The tyranny of distance.* Melbourne.

BRIERLY, O. W.
1848 *Journal with sketches, 1846–1849.* MS. Mitchell Library, Sydney.

BROWNE, C. A. (ed.).
1971 *Letters and extracts from the addresses and occasional writings of J. Beete Jukes.* London.

CLARKE, RAINBIRD
1935 The flint-knapping industry at Brandon. *Antiquity.* 9:38–56.

EARL, G. W.
1846 *Enterprise in tropical Australia.* London.

EARL, G. W.
1863 A handbook for colonists in tropical Australia. *Journal of the Indian Archipelago and Eastern Asia.* (n.s.)4:1–187.

FREELAND, J.
1968 *Architecture in Australia.* Melbourne.

GODDEN, G. A.
1963 *British pottery and porcelain, 1780–1850.* London.

GRAHAM, G. S.
1967 *Great Britain in the Indian Ocean.* Oxford.

HONEY, W. B.
1965 *English pottery and porcelain.* (5th edn). London.

HOWARD, D.
1933 The English activities on the north coast of Australia in the first half of the nineteenth century. *Proceedings of the Royal Geographical Society of Australasia, South Australian Branch.* 33:21–194.

HUDSON, K.
1965 *Industrial archaeology.* London.

HUXLEY, J. (ed.).
1935 *T. H. Huxley's diary of the voyage of H.M.S. Rattlesnake.* London.

RITCHIE, G. S.
1967 *The Admiralty chart.* London.

SMITH, G. S.
1834 *Essay on the construction of cottages suited for the dwellings of the labouring classes.* Glasgow.

SPILLETT, P. G.
1972 *Forsaken settlement.* Melbourne.

SWEATMAN, J.
n.d. *Journal of a surveying voyage to the N.E. Coast of Australia and Torres' Sts, in Her Maj. Schooner, Bramble, Lieut. C. B. Yule, Commander, 1842–47. 2.* MS. Mitchell Library, Sydney.

WALLACE, J.
n.d. *Journal kept on board H.M.S. Alligator.* MS. National Library of Australia, Canberra.

CHAPTER 21

Probate Inventories: An Evaluation from the Perspective of Zooarchaeology and Agricultural History at Mott Farm

JOANNE BOWEN

During the past two years, a number of students from Brown University have conducted an interdisciplinary research project to investigate the nature of over 250 years of life on a rural farmstead in Portsmouth, Rhode Island. Various projects have focused on architecture, social history, agricultural economics, and settlement patterns, with each centering research on the problem of integrating such sources as archaeology, architecture, zooarchaeology, and documentary evidence. The site is ideally suited for such a project, as the farm is essentially the same size as it was in the seventeenth century, except for 40 acres appropriated by the United States Navy in 1909. Originally granted to Adam Mott, Sr., in 1639, the farmstead remained virtually intact and in the hands of the same family until 1895, when it was sold to another family. As was common in New England, the Motts divided the land among sons, but in every case these portions were returned to the homestead within the next generation. Thus, unlike so many New England farms that underwent a number of divisions, this farmstead was distinctive in its cohesiveness.

Besides these well defined social limits, the physical limits of the farmstead proved equally well defined, as the tenant farmers, who occupied it after the Motts, left the fields, house, and outbuildings much as they were in the nineteenth century. This archaeological site has proved to be an excellent laboratory for first, the study of changing intrasite settlement patterns and space utilization within a rural farmstead, from its early development to the twentieth century; and secondly, the study of social relationships, economic behavior and farming practises as they have been maintained or changed through time. While seemingly narrow, this family centered research has proved itself to be productive, for we have been able to observe the family social unit within its larger community through a remarkably long time period that has seen much change. With this approach, it has been possible to grasp a measure of continuity in family and farm life within those changing social and economic patterns.

Drawing on both historical and archaeological sources and information from social and economic history, various town documents and Mott probate inventories have been used in conjunction with archaeological, zooarchaeological and architectural data in order to define the uses of animals in terms of agricultural economics and foodway patterns on a family farmstead. Historical sources, both primary and secondary, were consulted for data on the various uses of animals, agricultural and hunting practices, dietary prefer-

ences, and the adaptation of the English to the environment in the New World. Specific information on agriculture and animal husbandry for the Mott family was drawn from both documentary and archaeological sources; first from probate inventories of their personal estates that listed items associated with dairying and animal care, and farm animals owned by that individual at the time of their death, and then from data derived through the analysis of the faunal remains found in the excavation of the Mott farm.

From the various areas excavated during the 1973–74 field season, the fill from one cellar was chosen to analyze, for the date of the fill and documentation presented a tight social and chronological context. The cellar appears to have been rapidly filled in during the 1730's. Architectural dates established for a house that stood just south of the cellar seemed to confirm this interpretation which was based on artifacts found in the cellar fill, for its 1738 addition was constructed directly over a portion of the fill. One document, the probate inventory of Jacob Mott II, provided not only a close confirmation of this date, but also demonstrated a clear connection of the contents of the cellar fill with his family. The closeness of the fill and architectural dates, plus the fact that Jacob II took over the farm in 1736, suggested that upon his father's death, he decided to pull down the older structure, fill in the cellar, and build an addition on to the newer house. This close integration of data sources has produced a clear temporal and social context from which foodway patterns can be determined. And when combined with zooarchaeological data obtained from the bones excavated from the cellar and specific data on livestock holdings and items associated with animal use obtained from Jacob II's probate inventory of 1736, an unusually productive interpretation of agriculture, animal husbandry, and foodway patterns from the perspective of a family farmstead becomes possible.

This paper will first define the social and economic context of the site and then interpret the uses of domestic animals in light of the existing structure of the family farmstead in 1736. An emphasis will be placed on the kinds of agricultural information that can be generated from a probate inventory and on how this information can best be integrated with faunal analysis.

The interpretation of uses of animals on a rural farmstead required a refinement of the notion of a family farmstead. The same lands had been maintained within the family for over eight generations, but at times these lands had been divided into more than one farm (Figure 1). Thus the definition of the social and economic family unit was expanded to

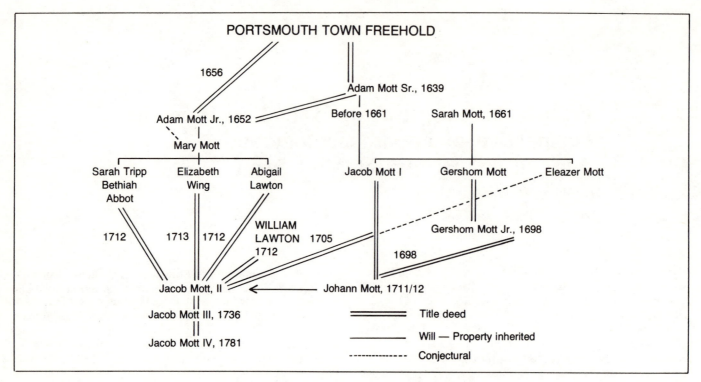

FIGURE 1. Mott Farm Owners 1639–1781.

consider not only one household, but several. These households formed an extended family of parents and siblings with their own established families living on separate portions of their father's lands. Philip Greven's work lends support to this approach when he comments on the structure of the colonial family:

> My own definition of the extended family equates it with a kinship network consisting for the most part of separate households. Throughout the colonial period in Andover, as probably elsewhere in the New England colonies and in England as well, the basic household most often was nuclear in structure. The principal variable, then, is not the structure of the household . . . but the structure and extent of the extended kin group . . . (Greven 1970:15–16).

Thus the approach used was that of focusing on succeeding generations of the Mott family, with the hope that changes in the family structure would become more evident. As well, it would give a better means to interpret what constituted the family farm and its patterns in economic trade, animal husbandry, and foodways for the 1730's.

If the principal variable of the family lies not in the household but in the structure of the kin group in a community, then the definition of the social and economic unit is dependent on being able to define inheritance as a means of passing land from generation to succeeding generation. Probate inventories, wills, land evidences, and vital records were examined to find patterns of inheritance, and how land had been used by parents for the purpose of providing for the settlement of their offspring.

It quickly became obvious that the process was one of partible inheritance, whereby virtually no man left their lands intact to any one son. Following this tradition of partible inheritance from the early settlement of a community, both Greven and Kenneth Lockridge have demonstrated the interrelationship between land and inheritance patterns. As long as sufficient amounts of land remained, more than one of a man's sons could expect to receive land (Lockridge 1968: 56–71; Greven 1970: 80–84). But, after several generations of land divisions, the average farm had insufficient amounts of acreage to withstand yet another division and the pattern of inheritance shifted to provide land to one son, forcing the others to emigrate or establish themselves in another occupation. In Dedham, Massachusetts, Lockridge has shown that from the 17th to the late 18th century, landholdings had undergone a division among sons with each succeeding generation, until the acreage had dropped from 100 to 200 acres to an average of 40 (Lockridge 1968: 65–71). By the fourth generation, the family structure had inevitably felt the consequences. The former tightly-knit system, where one or more sons established a household on a separate part of the original grant, changed to a more nuclear type, where only one household functioned independent of any other.

Patterns very similar to those defined by Greven and Lockridge emerge in following the Motts from generation to generation. These patterns show a relationship between land inheritance, family structure, and how the land belonging to the Mott family was both split and used by its various members through several generations. Three basic patterns can be traced: (1) a father might relinquish title to a part of his land to a son, (2) allow him to farm and live on a portion but withhold a title until his death, or (3) withhold any of these privileges until his death. Implications of any of these patterns are important in considering the homestead as a farm unit, for withholding all rights to the land would mean the farm remained a single unit. On the other hand, allowing a son to use or own land could mean independent farms within an extended family structure.

By the third generation of Motts the original grant had been split into as many as four holdings at one time, and into families that ranged from nuclear to extended households. Jacob II, in the third generation, had been given the southern half of his father's farm and the southern half of the house in 1705, six years before his father's death (Jacob Mott I to Jacob Mott II, August 28, 1705, Land Evidences 1/512).

While his father was still alive he lived in an extended household including his parents, wife, and seven children. Apparently father and son ran the farm jointly. Upon his mother's death he became the sole heir of his father's land. Soon thereafter he was able to purchase the remainder of the original grant that was a parcel held by his uncle, Adam, Jr. (William Lawton to Jacob Mott II, September 7, 1712, *Land Evidences* 2/41; Benjamin and Abigail M. Haviland to Jacob Mott II, May 18, 1713, *Land Evidences* 2/61; Matthew and Elisabeth M. Wing to Jacob Mott II, July 31, 1713, *Land Evidences* 2/68; Sarah Tripp and Bethyah Abbitt to Jacob Mott II, August 21, 1713, *Land Evidences* 2/76; Sarah Tripp and Bethyah Abbitt to Jacob Mott II and William Cogge-shall, August 21, 1713, *Land Evidences*, 2/77). Once again, the farmstead had become one social and economic unit. Moreover, Jacob II retained ownership of the entire property and withheld financial assistance toward the independence of his sons until his death in 1736 (Will of Jacob Mott II, dated March 5, 1729, proved March 14, 1736/37, *Portsmouth Town Records*, 3/182−185). Thus the Mott farm remained a single farmstead throughout the period of his control, with his son, Jacob III, and his wife and children remaining economically dependent on that farm. Not surprisingly, Jacob II's probate inventory appears to be a comparatively complete list of what was a working farm (Will of Jacob Mott II, dated March 5, 1729, proved March 14, 1736/37, *Portsmouth Town Records*, 3/182−185). With the well-defined social and physical limits of Jacob II's farmstead it would seem, then, that the use of his personal estate inventory in conjunction with faunal materials from the same time period should produce some stimulating ideas on animal husbandry, economic history, and foodways on the Mott farmstead.

THE ECONOMIC CONTEXT

The final choice of food to be consumed is influenced not only by culturally determined preferences and individual tastes but also by a number of economic factors. In establishing their community and producing sufficient quantities of food for their subsistence, they drew on the familiar common field system for maximum efficiency in the production of food. Within this system, colonists in at least the areas of Aquidneck Island and the Narragansett Bay quickly developed an economy and agricultural system that was not only an efficient and successful adaptation to Rhode Island's environment, but also successfully drew them into New England's trade economy. By 1641,

The first settlers—rich, middling, and poor—who located themselves on Aquidneck and adjacent islands of Narragansett Bay. . . . [had already established] a rural society characterized by a commercial agriculture . . . Those largely responsible for this development were wealthy 'farmer-merchants.' Assured of ample tracts of fertile land—with more easily available when they wanted them—these merchant-experimenters utilized the whole ecological scene for their own purposes and profit. They avoided the rigid conservatism of the small farmer and shifted from intensive mixed tillage emphasizing wheat to an extensive pastoral husbandry. From the aborigines they borrowed methods and plants freely; they exploited safe pastures on the islands; they made the several wooden by-products of forest clearing yield them profitable cargoes. But the real secret of their success was the grazing, breeding, and fattening of livestock to vend in distant markets and the growing of only such selected grains as they required for their own provisions and the feeding of their beasts . . . (Bridenbaugh 1974: 27−28).

An unlimited market was found in the Middle Colonies and West Indies, where the sugar cane plantation owners found it cheaper to import livestock—especially horses—salted beef, pork, and fish, and other food products than to raise them themselves. By 1690 Newport had become the center of this trade.

Although situated in a rural farming community, the Mott farm was close to Newport and within easy reach of the trading centers. Average farmers from this area who did not have large investments in trade managed to benefit and could produce a small surplus each year for sale to outsiders (Bridenbaugh 1974:21). From town records we know Jacob II was a farmer of some wealth and active in the community. A certain concern by the Motts for trade and commerce is indicated by the recovery of a box turtle of the southern variety found in the Caribbean from the cellar fill, for these turtles were imported from the West Indies and sold on the wharves in Newport (Dyer 1972: 63). If this trading interest is the case, then one should expect the animals the Motts raised and the food they consumed to reflect their interaction in the local economy in some way.

With the integration of data from the faunal remains and probate inventories, it becomes somewhat more feasible to postulate such a position for the Mott farmstead within the

Table 1. JACOB MOTT II   PROBATE INVENTORY

(Will of Jacob Mott II, dated March 5, 1729, proved
March 14, 1736/37, Portsmouth Town Records, 3/182−185)

Value Personal Estate L 672 8s. 6d.	March 14, 1736/37		
LIVESTOCK	L.	s.	d.
To Two Mares and the Half of Another	28	00	00
To Nine Cows and Heifers	81	00	00
To Five Two Years Old Neat Cattle	39	00	00
28^L: 10^s. To Four Yearling Neat Cattle 10^L: 10s.			
To Two Working Steyrs and a Bull	27	00	00
To Seventy Three Sheep and Lambs	70	00	00
To Ten Shoots 15^L. Geese Turkeys and Dunghill Fowls 4^L: 15^s	19	15	00
Total	264	15	00

larger Rhode Island and New England economy. To do this, however, one must first be able to delineate and separate the various uses of animals; establishing the fact that the Mott family raised and consumed a portion of their livestock, and produced a certain number for clothing, draft, and other purposes. Only then can one postulate the additional use for trade and get at their position in the local economy.

The comparison of differences in the percentages from the probate inventory listings and faunal analysis can at least help to identify uses other than food consumption. The bones from cows, pigs, and sheep all showed signs of butchering and many of the pig bones had been burned, so in a broad sense this body of archaeological data represents animals that had in the end been a part of the Motts' food consumption. The livestock listed in the inventory, on the other hand, includes animals intended for any number of uses. The relative frequencies of animals for the two sources vary considerably and the striking discrepancies can be explained in terms of uses other than food.

In order to be able to compare the livestock listed in the inventory to animals identified from the 1730 fill, data from both sources had to be ordered into similar categories. Thus, all livestock data from the inventory were grouped according to species, combining the different ages and sexes within each group (Table 1). Two groups were excluded, first the barnyard fowl as it lacked quantitative data and then the horse group as no horse had been identified in the faunal remains. Relative frequencies were then figured from the remaining groups; pig, cow, and sheep. From the archaeological sample which included a long list of identified species, only those animals which appeared on the inventory were selected, and percentages were figured for both groups.

FAUNAL ANALYSIS

Before presenting the analysis of this information, a brief presentation of the methods of faunal analysis is necessary, for the value in using faunal materials to interpret dietary and economic patterns is contingent on a proper understanding of that evidence. The method of a simple numerical count of bone fragments first identifies and quantifies fragments, and then percentages of the various specimens are figured on the basis of the total number of identified pieces. If these figures are left by themselves to represent the relative importance of different animals, one must assume that all individual bones of all species are equally affected in their initial treatment and survive equally well in different methods of cooking, soil preservation, and archaeological treatment. The method thus presents confused, undifferentiated natural and cultural variables. Specific patternings such as butchering, trade, and food consumption become lost, for differential butchering practices can produce many more fragments from a large animal such as a cow than from a smaller one. By merely relying on the percent of identified fragments, there is no way to determine how many actual animals are present, as one identified species represented by a large number of fragments may be only a few individuals, and another many individuals.

From his work on !Kung butchering practices, John Yellen has shown that the butchering of larger animals produces a proportionately larger number of fragments than for smaller animals. Once the soft spongy inner material of a bone has been exposed, the soft surface deteriorates rapidly, reducing the survival rate significantly. Bones from smaller animals, on the other hand, were more frequently discarded in a complete state. Consequently, the survival rate for these was much higher than for the larger animals (Yellen 1974: 55).

Another problem is that some species are more easily identified than others. Pig and sheep bones are close to each other in size, but often pig bones can be more easily identified from the fragments than sheep, as they have characteristic traits which distinguish them from sheep. These sheep bones, however, closely resemble other Artiodactyls, such as goat and deer, and often cannot be distinguished. In this case, sheep fragments would be under-represented in the relative frequencies of identified bones. If bone fragments are in poor condition, this problem in identification becomes even more pronounced. One solution, used in instances where positive identification was not possible, was to assign bone fragments to categories ordered by varying degrees of accuracy. If a bone closely resembled a species, but was in too poor a condition to be absolutely certain, they were assigned to a cf. or "compare" category. An example would be cf. *Sus scrofa* for a bone fragment that closely resembled the domestic pig. Another group, Sheep/ or /Goat, was formed to include those fragments which could not be distinguished between either sheep or goat. And finally, an Artiodactyla group was formed to include deer as well as sheep and goat.

One attempt to resolve the dilemma in the misrepresentation of animals has been to determine the minimum number of animals from the identified fragments. All fragments are first identified and then compared with each other to determine the number of individuals present in the sample. When used in conjunction with percents of identified fragments, the comparison of the two figures can be quite useful in determining first those species which have a relatively small number of fragments for the individuals and secondly those with a large number of fragments.

For the Mott farm faunal material, only the positively identified fragments were used initially to calculate the percentages of animals and determine the minimum number of individuals (Table 2). In order to solve the problem of the disproportionate identification of different species, the percentages of goat and deer bones in the site were calculated with the sheep, cow, and pig. They amounted to such minor proportions, that it was assumed that almost all the bones in the sheep/goat and Artiodactyla categories were actually sheep bones. The figures for these two categories were added to the sheep to see if the initial proportions would vary. Some significant changes in proportions resulted. The sheep figure of the identified fragments rose from 12 to 26%, a figure much closer to the percentage of the minimum number of sheep—24%. If the minimum number of individuals is a more reliable estimate of the actual animals present than a fragment count then those proportions of fragments based on the combined sheep group are more comparable to those based on the minimum number of individuals and a better estimate of the actual number of sheep present on the site. Consequently, comparing faunal remains with livestock listed in the probate, the set of figures for the combined sheep category will be used; first those based on the minimum number of individuals and second those based on the number of fragments. It is important to note, however, that the utility of this procedure would not hold in a situation where there were more equal proportions of either the sheep, goat, or deer.

Another method which is useful in indicating various uses

Table 2. JACOB MOTT II   1736 PROBATE: ARCHAEOLOGICAL SAMPLE

	Number of Individuals	%	Minimum Number of Individuals/cf.	%/cf.	Number of Identified Fragments/cf.	%/cf.
Equus caballus HORSE	2.5	—	—	—	—	—
Sus scrofa PIG	10	10	9/10	39/40	257/285	38/38
Bos taurus COW	21	20	9/9	39/36	351/373	51/50
Ovis aries SHEEP	73	70	5/6	22/24	75/92	11/12
	104	100	23/25	100/100	683/750	100/100

a

	Number of Identified Fragments/cf.	%/cf.		Number of Identified Fragments/cf.	%/cf.
Equus caballus HORSE	—	—	*Equus caballus* HORSE	—	—
Sus scrofa PIG	257/285	33/34	*Sus scrofa* PIG	257/285	31/32
Bos taurus COW	351/373	45/44	*Bos taurus* COW	351/373	43/42
Ovis aries SHEEP SHEEP/GOAT included	166/184	21/22	*Ovis aries* SHEEP, SHEEP/GOAT ARTIODACTYLA included	215/234	26/26
Capra hirca GOAT	1/4	.1/.8	*Capra hirca* GOAT	1/4	.1/.4
Odocoileus virginianus DEER	0/1	0/.1	*Odocoileus virginianus* DEER	0/1	0/.1
	775/847	100/100		824/897	100/100

b

a, percentages of identified faunal remains compared to 1736 probate.
b, percentages of identified faunal remains: Sheep, Sheep/Goat and Artiodactyla included with Sheep.

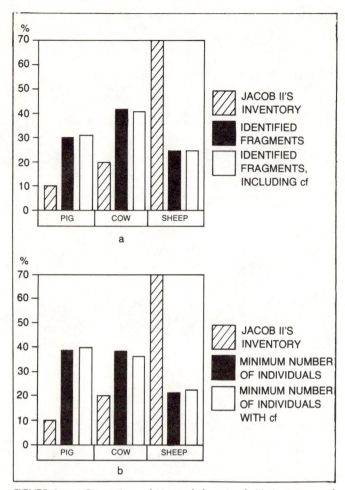

FIGURE 2. *a,* Comparison of Livestock from Jacob II's Inventory and Identified Fragments, Including Sheep/Goat and Artiodactyla Fragments with Sheep. *b,* Comparison of Livestock from Jacob II's Inventory and Minimum Number of Individuals from Faunal Remains.

of animals is to determine the age at death by noting the fused or unfused condition of the epiphyses of limb bones. The rate of fusion appears to remain relatively constant within a species and for some of the domestic animals the age of fusion for different bone elements has been analyzed (Silver 1970: 283–88). Though the exact age at which these bones fuse varies according to a number of factors including diet, climatic conditions, and breeds, it was assumed that the sequence of fusion has remained constant over time and a distribution of ages could be worked out by analyzing the percentages of fused and unfused bones. The distributions of ages for cow, sheep, and pig were determined using the fusion ages published by Silver and the method R. E. Chaplin used in *The Study of Animal Bones from Archaeological Sites* (Chaplin 1971: 128–33). The distribution of ages for sheep was then checked by using age data published in the 19th century and for an early maturing breed (Silver 1970: 283–88). In both cases, the distribution of ages remained essentially the same. Ages given in the text are those determined from Silver's data, but they should be taken only as a relative age, not the exact age.

With the integration of the archaeological figures with those established from the probate inventory, discrepancies between the two demonstrate different uses for the horse, cow, pig, and sheep (Figure 2). The most striking discrepancy between the two sources is found in the sheep (Figure 3). Sheep on Jacob's farm made up the largest portion of the animals listed in the inventory (70%), yet the smallest

portion of the archaeological remains (26%). It would seem reasonable to presume that sheep were mainly raised for purposes other than food. Bidwell and Falconer tell us that "Wool and not mutton was the object of sheep raising," and indeed it was a major concern to produce enough wool to provide clothing for one's family (Bidwell and Falconer 1925: 110).

Sheep raising was one of the most successful financial ventures in Rhode Island, especially on the island of Aquidneck. After 1660 a marked expansion began with a number of wealthy merchants possessing tremendous flocks, raised mostly for export purposes. By 1690 the flocks in the area where the Motts lived numbered 200,000 (Bridenbaugh 1974: 57). By the 1730's Rhode Island had become known as the main supplier of wool and sheep to Long Island and as far south as Delaware Bay. On a smaller scale, less wealthy farmers in Rhode Island took part in this livestock thoroughfare by selling their surplus to the wealthier merchants. Flocks weren't as large but towns encouraged it and by 1701 Portsmouth had reserved Hog Island, an island in Narragansett Bay that had long been used to graze livestock, for sheep only (Town Meeting June 18, 1701, *Town Meeting Book,* 1/11). Jacob's interest in this enterprise is evidenced by the fact that in 1714 he purchased two parcels of land situated on this island (William Anthony received 20 L from Jacob II for land on Hog Island, September 22, 1714, *Land Evidences,* 2/91).

Thus, the sheep were primarily raised to (1) provide wool for those living in the household, (2) raise a small surplus for the sale of wool, live sheep, and barreled mutton, and (3) consume a certain portion of the older animals. The determination that sheep were used towards ends other than food is supported by Jacob's inventory, where 18 yards of woolen

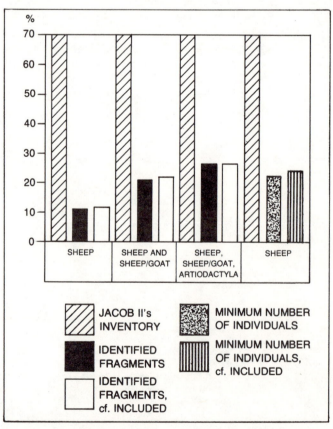

FIGURE 3. Comparison of Sheep from Jacob II's Inventory with Minimum Number of Individuals and Identified Sheep, Sheep/Goat, and Artiodactyla Fragments.

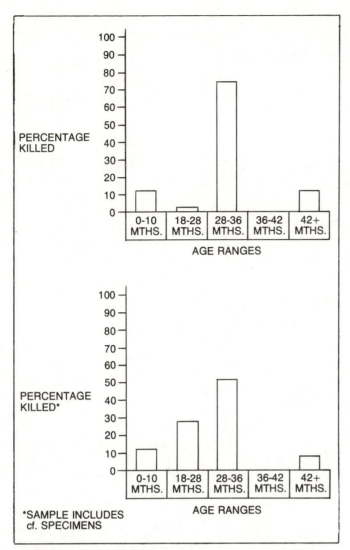

FIGURE 4. *Ovis Aries*, Age Ranges, Showing Percentage Killed in a Given Age Range.

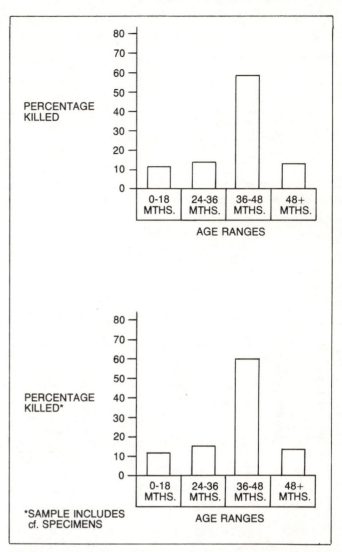

FIGURE 5. *Bos Taurus*, Age Ranges, Showing Percentage Killed in a Given Age Range.

drugget, 11 yards of blanketting, sheep's wool, and a loom are all listed (Will of Jacob Mott, II, dated March 5, 1729, proved March 14, 1736/37, *Portsmouth Town Records*, 3/182–185). Faunal analysis also supports this interpretation, for, of those identified, 86% were two years or older, and only 14% were under two years of age (Table 3; Figure 4).

It is somewhat comforting to note that horse remains were not found in the cellar fill, but were listed in Jacob's probate inventory. While oxen were used for the heavier work, horses were kept for light tasks, such as transportation, harrowing, or together with oxen for heavy work (Bidwell and Falconer 1925: 111). Horses were also an export item, and many were raised on Aquidneck for this purpose as early as 1647. Many of the smaller farmers must have owned a fair number, for during the latter part of the 17th century, the town of Portsmouth had found it necessary to restrict each household to pasturing one horse over a year on the common lands between April 1 and October 1 (Town Meeting, March 8, 1675, *Portsmouth Town Records*, 1/165). Jacob's inventory lists only 2½, an average number for the late 17th century, so it is not likely that he raised horses for export.

The data for cattle is more difficult to assess. In the probate inventory, cattle account for 20% of the animals listed, but for the faunal remains 36% in the minimum number of individuals and 42% in the fragment counts represent cattle. It would seem that cattle made up the major part of the

Motts' diet, for the amount of useable meat per animal is far more than for either the pig or sheep. In terms of pounds per animal, using 18th century figures, an average sized cow weighed 450 pounds dressed, while the sheep 50 and the pig 122 (Bidwell and Falconer 1925: 108–11). Based on these three figures, beef made up for 76% of the meat represented by the minimum number of individuals.

But the cattle were used by the Motts for other purposes, as the ages established from the faunal remains demonstrate (Table 4; Figure 5). Over 80% of those in the archaeological sample were older than three years and less than 20% were younger than three years. Oxen, of course, were used for draft purposes and milk cows to supply dairy products such as milk, cheese, and butter. These last two, in fact, are listed in Jacob's inventory. In the latter part of the 17th century, most farmers in New England kept from 1 to 5 cows. Jacob II, with his 21 animals probably kept more than needed for just his family's consumption and in all probability they were raised to first produce cheese, butter, salt beef, and other by-products for themselves and then a certain amount to sell to outsiders.

The pig data follows a very different pattern. The pig was cheap, easy to raise, fed on practically anything, matured quickly, and became a staple in the colonists' diet. Most families kept a number of them as a basic food source and even average farms produced enough to sell a small surplus

Table 3. OVIS ARIES

Age of Fusion—0 to 10 Months

				With cf. Specimens	
Bone and Epiphysis		*Fused*	*Not Fused*	*Fused*	*Not Fused*
Humerus—distal		7	0	7	0
Radius—proximal		4	1	4	1
Scapula		4	1	4	1
	Total	15	2	15	2
	Percentage of Age Range	88%	12%	88%	12%

Age of Fusion—18 to 28 Months

				With cf. Specimens	
Bone and Epiphysis		*Fused*	*Not Fused*	*Fused*	*Not Fused*
Tibia—distal		3	0	3	3
Metacarpal—distal		2	0	2	0
Metatarsal—distal		1	1	1	1
	Total	6	1	6	4
	Percentage of Age Range	86%	14%	60%	40%

Age of Fusion—28 to 36 Months

				With cf. Specimens	
Bone and Epiphysis		*Fused*	*Not Fused*	*Fused*	*Not Fused*
Femur—proximal		0	0	0	1
Radius—distal		1	7	1	7
Ulna—proximal		0	0	0	2
	Total	1	7	1	10
	Percentage of Age Range	12%	88%	9%	91%

Age of Fusion—36 to 42 Months

				With cf. Specimens	
Bone and Epiphysis		*Fused*	*Not Fused*	*Fused*	*Not Fused*
Tibia—proximal		1	0	2	1
Femur—distal		1	0	2	0
Humerus—proximal		0	1	0	1
	Total	2	1	4	2
	Percentage of Age Range	67%	33%	67%	33%

(Source of Fusion Ages: Silver 1969: 285–86; Chaplin 1970: 128–33)

Table 4. BOS TAURUS

Age of Fusion—0 to 18 Months

				With cf. Specimens	
Bone and Epiphysis		*Fused*	*Not Fused*	*Fused*	*Not Fused*
Scapula—distal		5	2	5	2
First Phalange		10	1	10	1
Humerus—distal		2	0	2	0
Radius—proximal		1	0	1	0
Second Phalange		3	0	3	0
	Total	21	3	21	3
	Percentage of Age Range	88%	12%	88%	12%

Table 4. (CONTINUED)

Age of Fusion—24 to 36 Months

				With cf. Specimens	
Bone and Epiphysis	*Fused*	*Not Fused*		*Fused*	*Not Fused*
Metacarpal—distal	11	3		11	3
Tibia—distal	2	2		2	2
Metatarsal—distal	3	1		3	1
Total	16	6		16	6
Percentage of Age Range	73%	27%		73%	27%

Age of Fusion—36 to 48 Months

				With cf. Specimens	
Bone and Epiphysis	*Fused*	*Not Fused*		*Fused*	*Not Fused*
Femur—proximal	1	6		1	6
Humerus—proximal	0	2		0	4
Radius—distal	1	2		1	2
Ulna—proximal	1	0		1	0
Femur—distal	1	7		1	7
Tibia—proximal	0	7		0	7
Total	4	24		4	26
Percentage of Age Range	14%	86%		13%	87%

(Source of Fusion Ages: Silver 1969: 285–86; Chaplin 1970: 128–33)

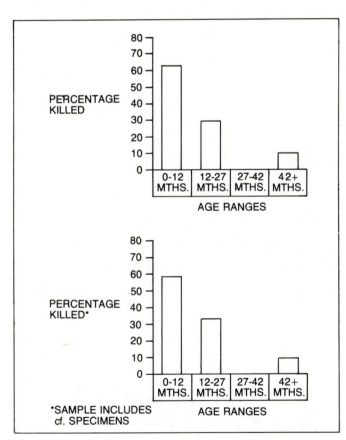

FIGURE 6. *Sus Scrofa,* Age Ranges, Showing Percentage Killed in a Given Age Range.

(Bidwell and Falconer 1925: 111; Bridenbaugh 1974:21). When the percentage of pig in the inventory is compared to the percentage of minimum number of individuals and number of identified fragments, it becomes apparent that the Motts raised the pig primarily as a food source. In the probate, pigs made up for only 10% of the total, but in the archaeological sample 32% for the fragment count and 40% for the minimum number of individuals.

The determination from the faunal material of the age at which the swine were killed supports this thesis that pigs were basically a food source; even if it was also an exported food item (Table 5; Figure 6). Of those animals in the sample, approximately 60% were under one year at the time they were killed and another 28% were under 2¼ years, making 88% less than 2¼ years old. Bidwell and Falconer claim that most pigs in the 17th and 18th century were killed before they reached 1½ years—a claim well substantiated by the Mott farm faunal materials (Bidwell and Falconer 1925: 111).

CONCLUSION

In conclusion, if used within a carefully defined social context, such as the Mott farmstead, the use of probate inventories in conjunction with data generated from faunal analysis can delineate various uses of domestic animals. Inventories can tell us that individuals had a certain number of each animal, but without faunal analysis we would never really be able to get at how the Motts and other farmers used animals. From town records we know Jacob was active in the community and that financially he was fairly well off, but it is impossible to say to what extent certain animals were used towards various ends. However, with discrepancies derived from the integration of faunal analysis and probate inventories, one can get a better idea of how Jacob's farmstead took part in the local economy. And with supportive data from the age at which animals were slaughtered, it becomes somewhat clearer that not only could these domestic animals serve basic food needs, but they could also provide for other needs.

However, one cannot go far with these inferences, and patterns born out in the archaeological record should only be

Table 5. SUS SCROFA

Age of Fusion—0 to 12 Months

	Fused	Not Fused	With cf. Specimens Fused	Not Fused
Bone and Epiphysis				
Second Phalange—proximal	7	9	7	9
Humerus—distal	1	4	1	4
Radius—proximal	2	2	3	2
Scapula—distal	1	3	2	3
Total	11	18	13	18
Percentage of Age Range	38%	62%	42%	58%

Age of Fusion—12 to 27 Months

	Fused	Not Fused	With cf. Specimens Fused	Not Fused
Bone and Epiphysis				
First Phalange—proximal	2	18	2	19
Metacarpals—distal	3	8	3	8
Tibia—distal	0	9	0	9
Metatarsal—distal	0	15	0	15
Total	5	50	5	51
Percentage of Age Range	9%	91%	9%	91%

Age of Fusion—27 to 42 Months

	Fused	Not Fused	With cf. Specimens Fused	Not Fused
Bone and Epiphysis				
Humerus—proximal	0	2	0	2
Radius—distal	0	5	0	5
Ulna—proximal	2	1	3	1
Femur—proximal	0	1	0	1
Tibia—proximal	0	0	0	1
Femur—distal	0	0	0	1
Total	2	9	3	11
Percentage of Age Range	18%	82%	21%	79%

(Source of Fusion Ages: Silver 1969: 285–86; Chaplin 1970: 128–33)

taken in the broadest sense. For example, specific uses, such as slaughtering cows or pigs to preserve the meat and sell it to traders, are impossible to distinguish from those slaughtered for their own use. The only way to achieve this would be to do a butchering study to see what was discarded and what preserved. Only then might one be able to see a lack of choice cuts in the discarded remains the archaeologist has to deal with and from there infer the sale of salted meat.

In defining foodways, the use of inventories cannot go beyond the domestic animals. It is here that faunal analysis becomes invaluable in delineating the broad outlines of the cultural screen that underlies the whole interrelated system of foodways. It is within these outlines that the selective use of wildlife becomes explainable.

REFERENCES

ANDERSON, JAY
1970 Scholarship on Comtemporary American Foodways. In *Reports from the First International Symposium for Ethnological Food Research*, edited by Nils-Arvid Bringeus and Gunter Wiegelmann. Lund.

ARNOLD, SAMUEL
1859 *History of the State of Rhode Island and Providence Plantations*. Vols. I and II, New York.

BAILYN, BERNARD
1955 *The New England Merchants in the Seventeenth Century*. Harper Torchbooks, New York.

BICKNELL, THOMAS WILLIAMS
1920 *The History of the State of Rhode Island and Providence Plantations*. American Historical Society, Inc., New York.

BIDWELL, PERCY WELLS and JOHN I. FALCONER
1925 *History of Agriculture in Northern United States, 1620–1860*. Carnegie Institute of Washington, Washington D.C.

BOESSNECK, J.
1970 Osteological Differences Between Sheep and Goats. In *Science in Archaeology*, edited by Don Brothwell and Eric Higgs. Praeger House Publishers, New York.

BRIDENBAUGH, CARL
1974 *Fat Mutton and Liberty of Conscience*. Brown University Press, Providence, Rhode Island.

CHAPLIN, RAYMOND E.
1971 *The Study of Animal Bones from Archaeological Sites*. Seminar Press, New York.

DEMOS, JOHN
1970 *A Little Commonwealth*. Oxford University Press, New York.

DUNTON, JOHN
1686 *Letters from New England*. Burt Franklin: Research & Source Work Series #131, New York.

DYER, CEIL
1972 *The Newport Cookbook*. Hawthorne Books, Inc., New York.

GREVEN, PHILLIP, JR.
1970 *Four Generations*. Cornell University Press, Ithaca.

HALL, E. RAYMOND and KEITH R. KELSON
  1959   *The Mammals of North America*. Vols. 1 and 2. The Ronald Press Company, New York.
HASKINS, GEORGE L.
  1969   The Beginnings of Partible Inheritance in the American Colonies. In *Essays in the History of Early American Law*, edited by David H. Flaherty. University of North Carolina Press, Chapel Hill.
LAND EVIDENCES
  Portsmouth Land Evidences. Bound documents held in the Office of the Town Clerk, Town Hall, Portsmouth, Rhode Island.
LOCKRIDGE, KENNETH
  1968   The Evolution of New England Society, 1620–1790. *Past and Present*, Vol. 39, pp. 62–80.
PORTSMOUTH TOWN RECORDS
  Portsmouth Town Records. Bound documents held in the Office of the Town Clerk, Town Hall, Portsmouth, Rhode Island.
RUTMAN, DARRET B.
  1963   Governor Winthrop's Garden Crop: The Significance of Agriculture in the Early Commerce of Massachusetts Bay. *William and Mary Quarterly*, 3rd Series, Vol. XX.
  1967   *Husbandmen of Plymouth*. Beacon Press, Boston.
SILVER, I. A.
  1970   The Aging of Domestic Animals. In *Science in Archaeology*, edited by Don Brothwell and Eric Higgs. Praeger Publishers, New York.
SISSON, S. and J. D. GROSSMAN
  1953   *Anatomy of the Domestic Animals*. W. B. Saunders Company, London.

TOWN MEETING BOOK
  Town Meeting Book. Bound documents held in the Office of the Town Clerk, Town Hall, Portsmouth, Rhode Island.
WALCOTT, ROBERT
  1936   Husbandry in Colonial New England. *New England Quarterly*, Vol. IX, pp. 218–52.
WOODWARD, CARL
  1971   *Plantations in Yankeeland*. Pequot Press Inc., Connecticut.
YELLEN, JOHN
  1974   Cultural Patternings in Faunal Remains: Evidence from the !Kung Bushmen. Unpublished manuscript.

ACKNOWLEDGEMENTS

I want to thank the many who worked on the Mott Farm project; James Deetz, Marley Brown, Joyce McKay, Steven Pendery, Laura Stopps, and Dell Upton. Also, I would like to thank Peter Schmidt and Douglas Anderson for their advice; and Stanley Olsen, John Sparling, and James Kelley for their patient guidance with the identification of the faunal remains.

CHAPTER 22

Archaeological Investigations at La Purísima Mission

JAMES F. DEETZ

PREFACE

The most recent excavation program at Mission La Purísima, Lompoc, California, is but one of a series of investigations which began in the 1930's and was continued from time to time in the period following the first extensive Civilian Conservation Corps program. As a result of this work, La Purísima may well be the most thoroughly studied mission in the State of California from an archaeological standpoint. This mission, constructed on its present site following the severe earthquake of 1812 which completely destroyed the first mission establishment, had fallen into near complete ruin when the Civilian Conservation Corps began to work on its restoration. While structures remain to be excavated, studied and restored, there exists today a graphic and impressive re-creation of early mission days at La Purísima.

The work described in this report was in most of its aspects a continuation of projects which had their initiation at some earlier point in time. The writer is extremely grateful to many people who made the results here reported possible through their truly devoted and conscientious efforts. Special appreciation is due to Mr. Arthur Sill, Head Ranger at La Purísima State Historical monument, and to Wayne Caldwell, also a ranger, for their very considerate assistance in every phase of the project. Donald Miller, William Allen and William Haney served capably as field assistants, and the following crew members performed their duties without complaint and with true enthusiasm: Diana Ausbury, John Bishop, Jo Ann Brady, M. D. Farmer, Martin Farrell, David Gabel, Robert Hoover, Richard Humphrey, Susan Kardas, Diane Lindros, Cheryl Miller, Bonnie Parker, Linda Pierce, Sid Riggs, Lana Spraker and Robert West. The laboratory was competently supervised by Catherine Gates, assisted by Barbara Spaulding. Special thanks are owed my wife, Jody, for her capable direction of one of the most important aspects of any field program, the purchase and preparation of food for an always hungry and properly appreciative crew. Richard Humphrey has done an excellent job of preparing the preliminary drawings and photographs for the report, and Sharon Arnold is to be commended for reducing pages of rough draft to neatly typed manuscript. Heinke Forfota recatalogued and properly stored the specimens in the Mission which were collected during Gabel's 1951 excavations. To all of these people, the writer acknowledges a debt of gratitude; whatever is of value in the following pages is largely the result of their efforts.

INTRODUCTION

This report details the results of archaeological excavations at La Purísima Mission (SBa-520) during the period from July 23 through September 7, 1962. Work was accomplished by two parties from the University of California, one under California State Contract # SPCF-065 and the other a student group enrolled in Anthropology 197, an upper division course in archaeological field method given by the Sociology-Anthropology Department of UCSB. Both groups were under the direction of Dr. James Deetz, Assistant Professor of Anthropology, UCSB, with the state contract group working under the immediate supervision of Mr. Donald Miller, Field Assistant.

Four major features were investigated: a tanning vat and accompanying pipeline and spring complex, the blacksmith shop, a segment of the Indian barracks and an extensive dumping area. In addition to this work, testing of a limited nature was undertaken in several areas and previously excavated collections were sorted, catalogued and placed in proper storage. All of these projects were a part of a list of desired investigations made following consultation between Mr. Arthur Sill, Head Ranger, La Purísima Mission State Historical Monument; Francis Riddell, Archaeologist, California State Beaches and Parks Division; and the writer in February, 1962.

Portions of the Indian barracks and blacksmith shop were excavated by the Civilian Conservation Corps project in the 1930's. In 1951, a party under the direction of Dr. Norman E. Gabel, then Assistant Professor of Anthropology, UCSB, excavated the northern section of the barracks (Gabel 1952). The portions of the barracks and blacksmith shop excavated during the 1962 season were located beneath now abandoned County Route 1, and were inaccessible until the present time.

The primary objective of this study was to provide as much information as possible to aid in the eventual restoration of the excavated structures, and to obtain a body of interpretive data which would assist in further clarification of our knowledge of life in the California Missions during the first part of the nineteenth century. As a result of this study, further insights into the acculturative process as it occurred among the Chumash Indians through missionization have been provided; several previously unknown items have also been added to our inventory of material culture of both Indian and Spaniard at La Purísima during its existence as a Franciscan frontier mission.

EXCAVATIONS

The Tanning Vats: Feature Two

While the export of hides formed the basis of the mission economy following the Mexican Revolution of 1810, hides prepared for export were not tanned at the missions, but simply scraped and dried. The only hides tanned were for domestic use, and at La Purísima probably did not number more than 100 a year at maximum. Several mission tanning vats are known, including those at San Gabriel, San Antonio and Santa Barbara.

Prior to the investigations herein described, the location of the vats at La Purísima was unknown, although a rectangular foundation north of the mission was thought to be the ruins of a small vat (Figure 1, Feature 2). A small portion of this ruin had been cleared in 1959, but work was stopped due to lack of proper supervision. When first relocated and photographed in the spring of 1962, only a small corner of the wall projected above the ground. The entire ruin was overgrown with a dense thicket of poison oak.

Before describing the excavation of the vats, a brief description of the hide tanning process as it was accomplished at the missions will aid in understanding the significance of the architecture and artifacts encountered. The hides were scraped clean of flesh and fat, and then soaked in slaked lime for a period of ten to fourteen days. This treatment loosened the hair to the point where it could be easily removed by beaming (removal of the hair with a type of scraping tool). The hides were then washed clean and placed in a tannic acid solution, where they remained for a period of time up to six months in length.

The tannic acid was derived from the ground bark of the tanbark oak (*Quercus densiflora*), and produced by alternating the hides with layers of milled bark and covering the hides and bark with water. For this purpose some type of vat was needed, and the typical mission vat was a rectangular masonry structure with a plaster floor. Since the hides remained in the tanning solution for long periods of time, easy access was not a necessary requisite for locating the vats. This aspect of the process plus the objectionable odor produced by the soaking hides made it feasible and even desirable to locate the vats at some distance from residential areas. After being soaked in the tanning solution, the hides were washed and oiled, and were then ready for use in the manufacture of leather goods of all types.

The vats at La Purísima Mission are located approximately one-quarter mile north of the mission buildings, on the opposite or east side of Purísima Canyon, in close proximity to the reservoirs (Figure 1). Here there was adequate water close at hand, and the distance was sufficient to remove the tanning operation from immediate contact with the living areas.

Excavation Technique. The La Purísima vats, designated as Feature 2, are similar in construction to those at other missions, and bear a close resemblance to those figured by Webb (1952:199) at San Gabriel Mission. The general plan is one of two separate compartments enclosed by a masonry wall. These compartments were designated Vat One and Vat Two (Figure 2). Both vats were covered by a layer of dark organically stained sand which sloped up from a small section of exposed floor in the southwest corner of Vat One to a depth of four feet at the northeast corner of Vat Two. A portion of Vat One was rapidly cleared using shovels in order to determine the limits of earlier excavations. A trench was then excavated along the longitudinal, north-south axis of the ruin, crossing both Vats One and Two. This trench exposed the footings of the dividing partition separating the vats, and the north wall base. The profile of this trench revealed a two zone fill, with the dark sand overlying a mass of rubble formed by the collapse of the upper portions of the outer walls and a part of the dividing partition. Excavation then proceeded according to these two zones, with provenience controlled horizontally to vat quadrants (NE, NW, SE, SW) and vertically to three zones, *fill, rubble* and *floor*. The overburden of sandy fill was removed by rapid shoveling after spot checks were made to determine its sterility; the rubble and floors were excavated by trowel. No screening was attempted.

Architecture. Excavation revealed a rectangular two compartment structure, with each compartment measuring 12.2 feet north-south and 13.4 feet east-west inside dimensions and enclosed by a wall 2.4 feet thick. The original height of these walls is difficult to determine, but probably did not exceed the highest portion of the remaining wall, which is five feet high. The outer walls are of lime mortared rubble, laid in alternate courses with rectangular floor tiles and slabs of local shale (Figure 3). The outer surface of these walls is covered with a layer of pink plaster. The dividing partition, of which only the lowermost tile footings remain, is formed of evenly laid floor tiles, a tile and a half or 1.8 feet in width. Whether this footing was surmounted by partial rubble construction similar to the outer walls is unknown, since the outer walls also have neatly laid floor tile footings, two full tile or 2.4 feet wide. The floors of the vats are of pink plaster overlying a two feet thick layer of roof tile fragments and lime mortar. The vats rest on the green clay subsoil of the site, and were probably constructed after a cut had been made in the hillside to achieve a solid base and a level floor.

A layer of lime ranging from 0.2 foot to 0.02 foot in thickness covered the floor of Vat One (Figure 3). Vat Two in marked contrast had no lime on the floor but showed the original pink plaster coating. This pink coating also could be seen in two places on the floor of Vat One where the lime layer had not completely covered the floor. On the basis of the difference between the two floors, Vat One is thought to have served as a dehairing vat, and Vat Two as a tanning vat. Samples of the plaster from both floors were submitted to Dr. John Bishop, Tidewater Oil Company, Los Angeles, for analysis in the hopes of finding traces of tannin in the floor of Vat Two. Although the results were negative, this does not detract from the functional identification of either vat, since tannic acid, being organic, would have long since disappeared due to leaching and some neutralization by the lime in the plaster. Bishop (personal communication) states:

A test for tannins with FeCl₃ was performed on both samples with negative results, although the test is very sensitive and reacted normally with a known sample. In my opinion, this should not be interpreted as proof that tanning had not been done at this location. Tannins are water soluble, and being organic, also decompose and oxidize with aging. In 130 years it is possible that all traces of tannin would have weathered away.

Concerning a sample of lime from the floor of Vat One, he says:

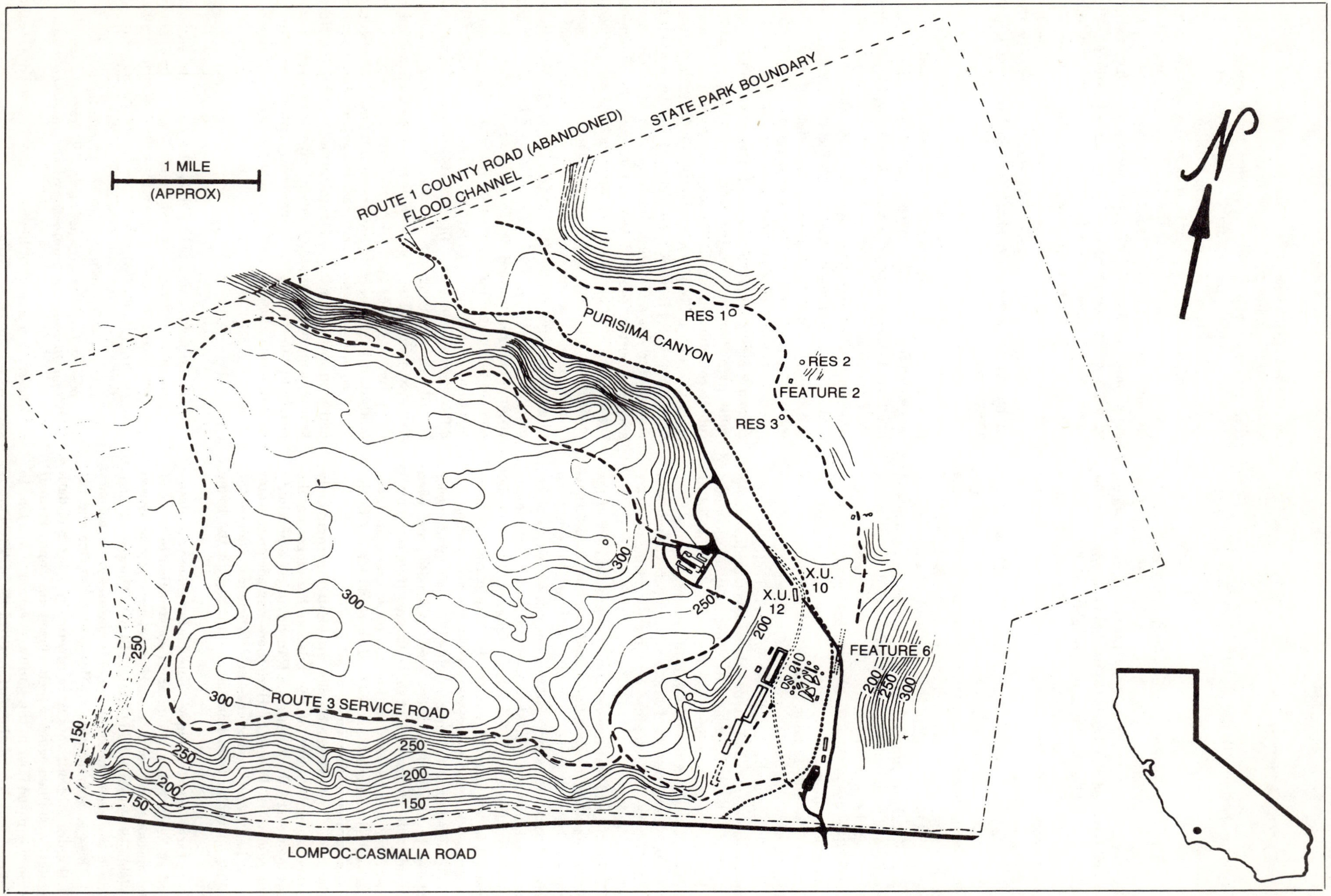

FIGURE 1. La Purísima Mission — Site SBa-520.

162

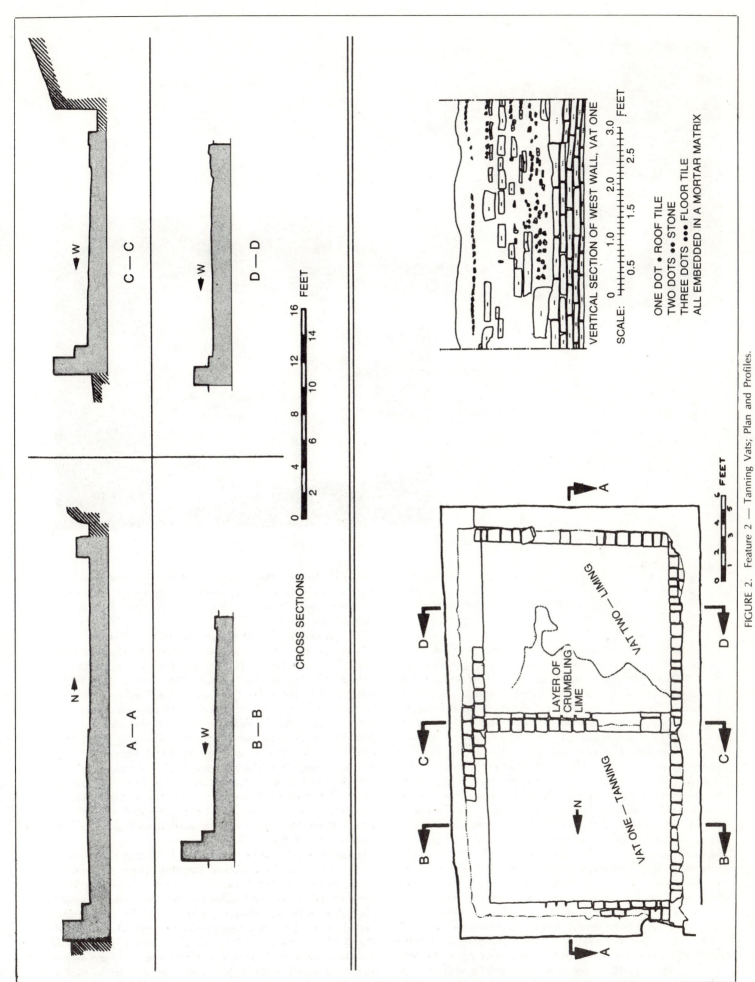

C—C

D—D

CROSS SECTIONS

A—A

B—B

N

W

W

W

0 2 4 6 8 10 12 14 16
FEET

VERTICAL SECTION OF WEST WALL, VAT ONE

SCALE: 0 0.5 1.0 1.5 2.0 2.5 3.0
FEET

ONE DOT • ROOF TILE
TWO DOTS •• STONE
THREE DOTS ••• FLOOR TILE
ALL EMBEDDED IN A MORTAR MATRIX

VAT TWO—LIMING

LAYER OF
CRUMBLING
LIME

VAT ONE—TANNING

N

A

B

C

D

A

B

C

D

0 1 2 3 4 5 6 FEET

FIGURE 2. Feature 2 — Tanning Vats; Plan and Profiles.

after stabilization

after excavation

FIGURE 3.   Feature 2 — Tanning Vats.

The light colored deposit assumed to be a lime residue does appear to be just that. It was almost completely dissolved by HC1 with CO₂ evolution typical of CaCO₃.

During stabilization and repair operations in fall of 1962, following the cessation of the archaeological program at the mission, park personnel uncovered a drain leading from Vat Two and an interconnecting line between Vats One and Two (Figure 3). The drain clearly served to remove water from the vats. The connection between the vats probably was used when the vats were emptied, since this would be a more efficient method than draining the vats individually. The alternative explanation, that water was normally channelled from Vat One to Vat Two as a part of the tanning process, seems unlikely in view of the difference in condition of the two floors. If it was customary to use water in Vat Two after it had been employed in Vat One, much more lime would have been deposited on the floor of Vat Two. On the other hand, if the connection functioned only at the time that the vats were fully drained, conditions such as those observed would prevail. Much water loss at the vats must have resulted from evaporation, yet there needed to be some means of emptying the vats quickly when necessary. The connection and drain would serve this purpose well.

No indications of a superstructure were observed. Webb (1952:193) refers to the construction of ramadas over the vats at San Antonio. It is possible that such a shelter was constructed over the La Purísima vats; investigations of the area surrounding the vats in an effort to locate post holes were severely hampered by the heavy growth of poison oak, the roots of which were thickly concentrated in the soft sand surrounding the ruin.

Artifacts.   The most common artifact from the vats is a beamer fashioned from a cow rib. These tools are scarcely identifiable as artifacts; they exhibit a high polish along one edge which does not extend more than 1/64 inch along the sides of the ribs away from the edge. Two complete rib beamers and fragments of three others were recovered (Figure 4, Items 2 and 3). All were in the rubble overlying the floor in the tanning vat (Vat Two). The only other bone artifact is the ulna of a small mammal which is highly polished along one surface and has the distal end coated with lime (Figure 4, Item 1). This implement was probably used in cleaning the lime from small creases in the dehaired hides. It is possible that Vat One originally contained a number of bone artifact which were subsequently dissolved by the lime solution on the floor.

In contrast to the bone tools, three of the four chert objects found came from the rubble of Vat One. Three of these are simple primary flakes of Monterey chert with no secondary working. The fourth resembles half of a side notched projectile point, with a well-worked notch on one side, and a slightly worn, smooth, unmodified edge along the side opposite the notch (Figure 4, Item 5). All four chert pieces could have been used in the removal of hair from the lime soaked hides; this seems best to explain their presence in the rubble. The only other artifactual material found in the vats was a fragment of thin flat greenish glass embedded in the lime on the floor of Vat One. The total lack of metal beaming tools is worthy of note.

The Pipelines: Features One and Five

A tanning vat must be supplied with water in which to soak the hides and tanbark and from which to prepare the lime solution for dehairing. This water supply need not be constant, yet it must be available in quantity when needed. Water was piped into the vats through two separate pipelines, with origins in two separate springs. The first of these lines, Feature One, had its origin in a live spring 18.5 feet to the east and 10.0 feet above the vat floor. This line is made of uncemented tile water pipe, each segment measuring 0.2 foot inside diameter, 0.04 foot thick and 0.8 foot long. The lower end of the line is badly broken, probably due to the hillside having slid downward to a degree following the abandonment of the vats. The inlet end is of floor tile set in mud, forming a small catch basin (Figure 5). Leading out of this basin to the south is another line, covered for approximately eight feet with curved roof tile. This tile covering would suggest that the second line had originally been laid on the surface, and was subsequently covered with sand. The second line extends 14 feet to the south, at which point it is broken,

and efforts made to relocate it were unsuccessful. In all probability, it had been removed at some time in the past, since a portion of Feature Five, the second pipeline, had been similarly obliterated in the same area.

The Feature Five pipeline is 234 feet long, of tile pipe identical to that of Feature One, leading from a spring southeast of the vats to the south wall of Vat One. Unlike Feature One, this pipeline is cemented at the joints, and in places near the vats had a thin layer of lime mortar underlying it along its course (Figure 6(a)). For the last fifteen feet prior to the point where the Feature Five pipeline empties into the vat, the pipe is missing, although the plaster footing remains. This seems to indicate an intentional removal of this portion of the lime which may also explain the missing sections of the second line of Feature One. The Feature Five line curves along the hillslope south and east of the vats, rising 4.6 feet before terminating in a live spring and inlet similar to that of Feature One (Figure 7). In this inlet, which also serves a second line which runs directly to a small reservoir to the west (Reservoir Three), was found a plug made from a piece of roof tile ground to fit the open end of the line (Figure 4, Item 4). Through the use of this plug, water could be diverted to either the vats or to the reservoir. Although a similar plug was not found at the Feature One inlet, it is probable that such a device was used to supply

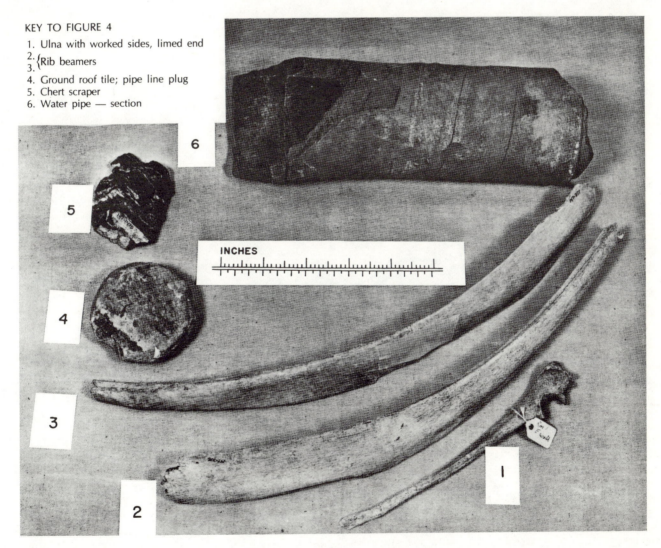

KEY TO FIGURE 4

1. Ulna with worked sides, limed end
2.
3. } Rib beamers
4. Ground roof tile; pipe line plug
5. Chert scraper
6. Water pipe — section

FIGURE 4. SBa-520: Artifacts from Feature 2.

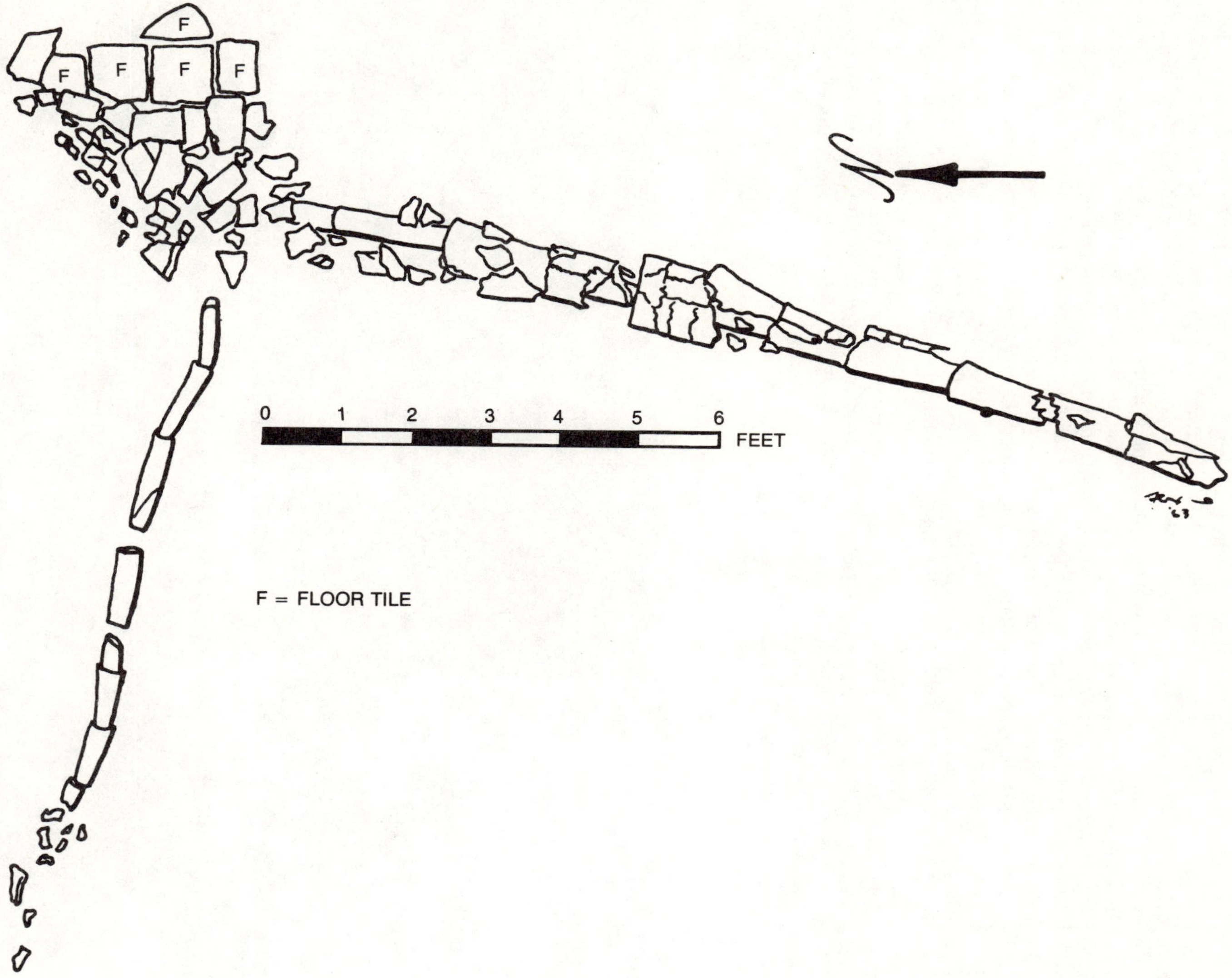

FIGURE 5. SBa-520: Feature 1 — Basin and Pipelines.

F = FLOOR TILE

FEET

0 1 2 3 4 5 6

FIGURE 6. Pipeline, Feature 5; Blacksmith Shop, X.U. 12.

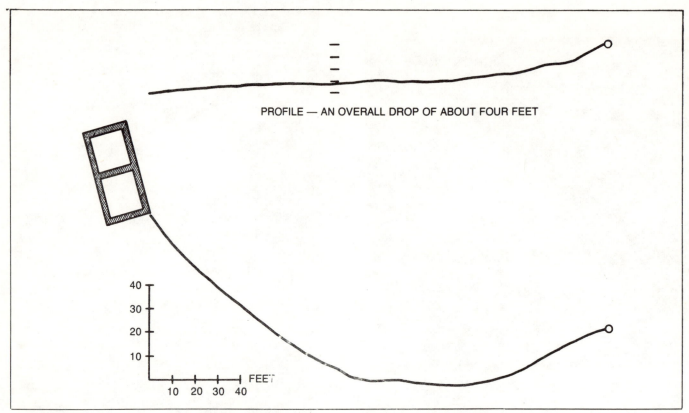

PROFILE — AN OVERALL DROP OF ABOUT FOUR FEET

FIGURE 7. SBa 520 Feature 5; Long Pipeline Plan and Profile.

water to the vats from the spring at that point. Since the tanning vats did not require a constant supply of water, and since springs cannot be turned on and off at will, some method was needed to divert the output of the springs to a storage facility when their water was not needed at the vats. Each line is one of two leading from a spring, the second line in each case leading to a reservoir. Although the second diversion line of Feature One was never followed to an end, the presence of a waterline junction box at the foot of the hill immediately below the vats and Feature One indicates that this line was probably directed to a reservoir. In the mud surrounding the spring at the south end of Feature Five were found two wood fragments which are probably contemporary with the construction and use of the inlet. One of these pieces is a sawed board 1.7 feet long, 0.4 foot wide and 0.08 foot thick. The other resembles one end of a wooden wool skein, and is 0.54 foot long, 0.13 foot wide and 0.03 foot thick. Their excellent state of preservation is probably due to the water-logged soil in which they were found.

Since the vats were served by two separate lines, three possibilities exist to explain this diversity. It is possible that both lines were used simultaneously in an effort to fill the vats with relative rapidity. However, it may be that the spring feeding the Feature One line was not dependable, and so the second line was brought in from a considerable distance to supplement the slow flow of the nearer spring. It is equally possible that the spring feeding the Feature One line dried to a point where the second line became an absolute necessity. The existence of the nearer spring was unknown prior to the excavation of the vats. It was not until a trench was cut into the inlet that this spring began to flow. Even then, the flow was meager and evaporated before reaching the vats over the tops of the exposed pipeline sections of Feature One. Since the winter of 1961–1962 was a relatively wet season in the local area, this rate of flow probably more closely approximates the peak rate during the

past century. In a drier year, this spring might not exist. By comparison, the spring feeding the Feature Five line is known by the park officials, and is kept covered and maintained as a perennial water source.

When the tanning vats were abandoned is unknown. It is reasonably certain that portions of the vat walls were removed for use in other construction. The east wall, which is located against the hillside, is missing down to the lowermost footings. It was first assumed that this wall had collapsed from pressure of sand sliding down the hillside. However, at one point on the inside wall of Vat Two, a portion of the floor plaster which originally had been lapped against the wall was still standing 0.2 foot high. A collapsed wall would have leveled such a plaster layer. The only way such a projection could have been left standing would be through a removal of the tile footing blocks from behind the plaster coating. Furthermore all of the east wall is leveled to the same point (floor level), unlike the south, west and north walls. Since this wall would have had the greatest water seepage exposure, due to its position against the hillside, and since roots would have grown into the cracks between the structural material in such a situation, it seems that the east wall was in an advanced state of disintegration while the other walls were still structurally sound, and therefore more easily used as a source of building blocks. The most probable manner of use would have been in the construction of a later structure somewhere in the immediate vicinity. The only such structure now known is the so-called Malo House, supposedly the property of Ramón Malo to whom a portion of the mission property was ceded in 1845. This building is mentioned in the conveyance of the property to J. S. Alemany, Bishop of Monterey, by the United States Government in 1874 as a house belonging to Ramón Malo. The Civilian Conservation Corps excavated this structure, having located it according to the original survey description (Engelhart 1932).

During the time in which the vats were being investigated,

a small excavation was made at the site of the Malo House, but only to an extent which would allow observation of the building materials used in the footings. A section of badly tumbled wall was exposed, constructed of rubble, including floor tiles of dimensions equal to those of both sizes used in the vats. While this does not provide absolute proof that a portion of the vat walls was incorporated in the foundations of the Malo House, it does provide a possible explanation of the final disposition of a portion of the east wall of the vats.

Conclusions—Tanning Vats and Pipelines. The vats, pipelines and associated artifacts provide us with a full picture of the tanning of hides at La Purísima Mission. The hides were probably transported in carretas, either directly from the abattoir after a preliminary defleshing, or from the warehouse. The remainder of the tanning process took place at the vats. Vat One was filled with lime and water in which the hides were soaked until the hair was loosened. Following this treatment, the dehairing was accomplished with cow-rib beamers and chert flakes. Since this labor undoubtedly was accomplished by the Indians, it is of interest to note that the tools used to remove the hair according to a recently learned European process were of bone and chert, materials already familiar to the Indians. Judging from the amount of metal artifacts elsewhere in the mission, iron tools for beaming were certainly available to the Indians, yet they chose to retain their older tool types. In the case of the beamers, however, the bone used was from an animal also unknown to the Indians prior to Spanish contact. The pattern here is one of blending of aboriginal and introduced elements which, in the case of the beamers, can be seen at the individual artifact level, with an aboriginal practice (beaming) being done as part of an introduced technology (tanning) with a tool made from material known and used aboriginally (bone) obtained from an animal introduced by the Europeans (cow).

At the foot of the slope on which the vats are located is a growth of Fuller's Teasel (*Dipsacus sylvestris*), a thistle-like plant of European introduction. The seed heads of this plant were used by the Mission Indians for carding and combing wool, and they would certainly have served well as hide scrapers. Since the teasel is uncommon south of Morro Bay, California, and since it does not volunteer freely in Santa Barbara County, it is likely that these plants grew here at the time the vats were in use, and thus they may have been used in the dehairing of soaked hides.

Following the removal of the hair and cleaning of the lime from the hides, they were placed in Vat Two, probably with alternating layers of milled tanbark, and allowed to cure for several months. Water for the vats was supplied by two springs, one a short distance to the east which flowed through a surface line, and one 234 feet to the southeast which flowed through a cemented subterranean line.

The Purísima vats differ from published descriptions of the vats at San Gabriel and San Antonio, in that the former combine both dehairing and tanning in the same structure, making use of contiguous tanks. They appear very similar to the Santa Barbara vats on the other hand, although excavation at Santa Barbara would be necessary to indicate the extent of similarities.

The Blacksmith Shop

The structure identified as the blacksmith shop was discovered in 1937 during a fence building operation along the western edge of now-abandoned County Route 1 to the State Historical Monument headquarters. It was one of the last structures examined by the Civilian Conservation Corps.

At the time of their investigation of this structure, those portions of the foundation not covered by the macadam were exposed, and the limits of the footings beneath the road were determined by augering through the road surface at several points. This procedure met with limited success; while it determined the northern limit of the smithy, it failed to provide a clear picture of the architecture of the unexcavated portion.

The structure is described in the Civilian Conservation Corps report as having two rooms, with the southern room slightly larger than the northern. The most significant feature located by the Civilian Conservation Corps during the excavation of the southern portion of the blacksmith shop was a forge in the southwest corner. This feature, herein designated Feature Seven, plus an abundance of iron and copper scraps and metal tools were decisive factors in the identification of the structure as the smithy. The Civilian Conservation Corps report does not indicate any specialized function for either of the two rooms discovered.

During the 1962 season, the remaining unexcavated portion of the smithy was excavated, having been made accessible at that time by the abandonment of the county road. The southern section was re-excavated and when all work was complete, the entire foundation had been exposed. Excavation revealed a three room structure seventy-six feet long and twenty feet wide at the base of the rather steep hill which forms the western wall of Purísima Canyon (Figure 1, X.U. 12; Figure 8; Figure 6(b)).

Excavation Technique. The smithy was excavated by a procedure somewhat different from that employed at the tanning vats and in the Indian barracks. The limits of the Civilian Conservation Corps excavations were shown on a drawing in the Civilian Conservation Corps report which served as a guide for the beginning of the exposure. The areas previously excavated by the Civilian Conservation Corps were cleared by tractor and cut down to a level approximately 0.5 foot above the footings. Shovels were then used to clear all of the previously excavated portion until a point was reached along the northern end of the excavation which was obviously undisturbed since the collapse of the building. This point was easily identified by the sudden increase in frequency and regularity of roof tiles, which covered the unexcavated sector completely, and which had been removed and not replaced by the Civilian Conservation Corps in the sections where they had worked. As was suspected, the entire southern sector had been excavated, and the unexcavated portions of the foundation were first encountered near the shoulder of the county road.

At the northern end of Room One, the southernmost room, an east-west trench was excavated at right angles to the long north-south axis of the structure. This trench served to determine the depth of the floor in the unexcavated portion, and also provided the excavators with a clear understanding of the extent and nature of the roof fall, and the nature of the boundary between sterile subsoil and the fill of the structure. A similar trench was excavated at the southern end of Room Three, the northernmost room.

Those areas which had not been exposed by the Civilian Conservation Corps were plotted into a grid network of five-foot-square units. This grid network was designated *Excavation Unit Twelve*, and individual squares were given coordinate designations within this unit in the usual fashion using a fixed datum. Several septa were left during the course of excavation as a control on vertical stratification. Vertical control of provenience was by visible zones, as follows:

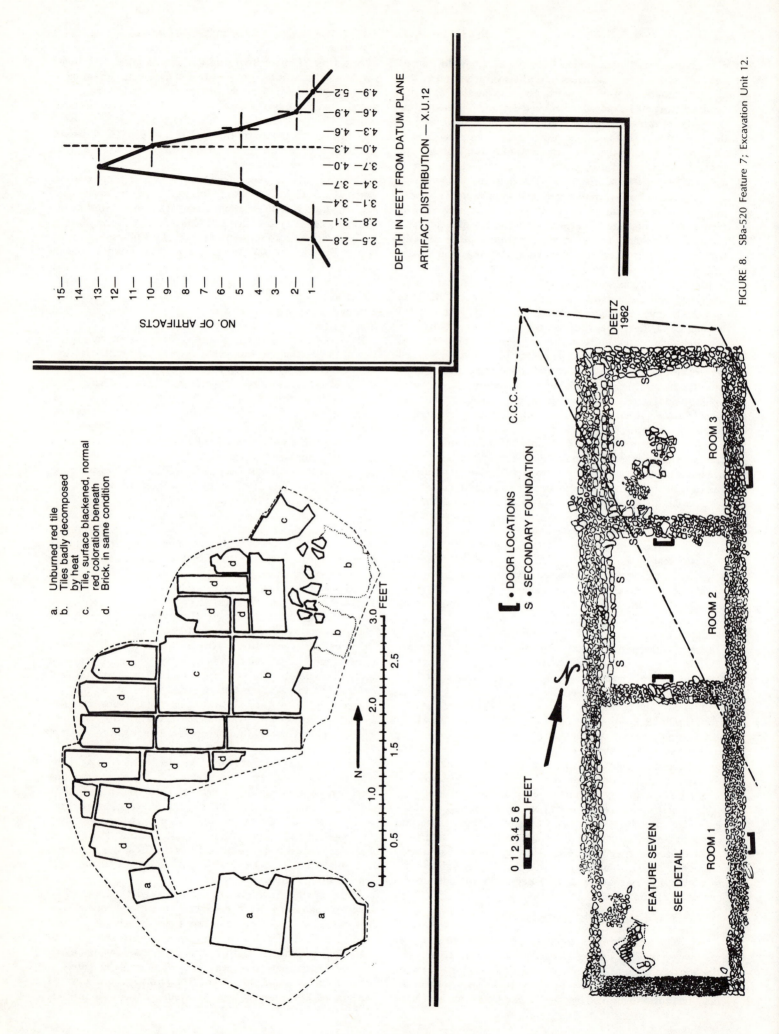

DEPTH IN FEET FROM DATUM PLANE

ARTIFACT DISTRIBUTION — X.U.12

NO. OF ARTIFACTS

a. Unburned red tile
b. Tiles badly decomposed by heat
c. Tile, surface blackened, normal red coloration beneath
d. Brick, in same condition

N

0 0.5 1.0 1.5 2.0 2.5 3.0
FEET

DEETZ 1962

C.C.C.

[• DOOR LOCATIONS
S • SECONDARY FOUNDATION

N

0 1 2 3 4 5 6 FEET

ROOM 3

ROOM 2

ROOM 1

FEATURE SEVEN

SEE DETAIL

FIGURE 8. SBa-520 Feature 7; Excavation Unit 12.

Surface to Tile, from ground surface to the top of the roof; *Tile*, the roof fall itself; and *Fill*, the material beneath the collapsed roof.

Since it was obvious quite early in the course of excavation that the floor was weakly defined, a datum plane was established over the entire structure, and all significant fill artifacts were recorded according to depth beneath this plane. This precaution was to be rewarding later in the definition of the floor level by the occurrence of artifacts in a well defined zone at the base of the fill.

Following the definition of three rooms in the structure, artifact lots were recombined from their discrete square proveniences to room lots, and subdivided according to stratigraphic zones. Appendix I provides a catalogue of the smithy artifacts according to room designation and vertical zone according to this procedure. While a grid was employed, each vertical zone as defined by visible strata was excavated as a unit; thus all of the collapsed roof was exposed, mapped, photographed and removed, and then excavation proceeded uniformly to the fill zone. Excavation of grid squares was by trowel; no screening was attempted.

Architecture. The La Purísima blacksmith shop was a typical tiled-roof adobe structure of the Mission Period. It is 76 feet long and 20 feet wide, based on measurements made on the stone footings. These footings are made of unmodified stone laid on the natural contour of the ground. The stones are extremely variable in size, ranging from 0.2 feet to 2.0 feet in diameter, with the larger stones usually located at the corners of the building. The smallest of the footing stones were used as a filling between the larger ones. Certain sections of the foundation are built of consistently larger stones, although there is no clear pattern of their use in these sections. The average size of stones used for the western and northern footings is somewhat larger than the mean size of all footing stones. Partition footings are made from stones smaller than those used in footings for exterior facing walls. The footings of the partitions are from 0.2 to 0.3 foot lower than the west wall at the point of intersection. This feature and the smaller size of the partition footing material suggests that the partitions were constructed following the construction of the exterior wall footings. While none of the foundation stones are cut or broken to fit in any way, it is obvious that a careful selection had been made for suitable cornerstones and for footing edges.

The footings are 2.4 feet wide and 1.0 foot deep. They serve to support rather massive adobe brick walls. Traces of the bricks used in the construction of the walls were found, and provide information on the dimensions and construction of the exterior walls and partitions. Discrete adobe bricks could be discerned in three locations: at the eastern ends of the room partitions and along the eastern wall of Room Two. These bricks measured 0.9 foot by 2.2 feet by 0.4 foot. Their long axes were aligned with the long axis of the building in those locations where they were observed. The bricks were laid in two parallel rows, with two widths (1.9 feet) forming the thickness of the walls. The initial course of bricks laid on the footings was leveled by varying the amount of mortar used between brick and footing stones. This leveling is the only evidence recovered to indicate the manner in which the builders compensated for natural variations in the site's contour. At the intersection of the Room Two-Three partition and the east wall, a basket hopper mortar and three animal ribs had been used as an aid in leveling the walls. These objects were directly incorporated in the initial course of bricks, underlying them and resting on the footings. Just

south of this point on the west wall were found two more long bones of a large sea mammal employed in an identical manner.

Four doors were located in the structure: one entering Room One from the east, one entering Room Three from the east, and one each leading from Room Two to Rooms Three and One (Figure 8). Room Two, the center room, apparently lacked a doorway leading to the outside. All four doorways were marked by threshold slabs, and the door leading from Room Three to the exterior was further defined by roof tiles which had fallen directly on the footing stones, since there were no wall bricks to deflect the falling roof tiles to the outside at this point (Figure 6(c)). No evidence of the location or number of windows was found.

The roof of the smithy was gabled, presumably with the main support beam located over the center axis of the foundation. Although no postholes were found in the floor of the structure, the roof may have been supported by separate posts upon which rested a ridge beam. It is equally possible that the partition walls and end walls were adequate to provide a bearing for the roof. The pattern formed by the tile as shown by the excavated roof fall suggests that the roofing material slid off in both directions, as it would in the case of a gabled roof. Those roof tiles found covering the floor would have fallen through the deteriorating roof.

Presumably, the smithy stood for a long interval of time prior to the total collapse of the roof and subsequent melting of the adobe walls. A zone of water-deposited sand between the base of the roof fall and the floor zone suggest periodic flooding of the structure, probably after it had been abandoned but before the roof caved in. Most of this earlier filling presumably came from the slope immediately to the west as a result of erosion during heavy rains. Later, after the building had collapsed, Purísima Creek became an important agent in the flooding of the valley. The removal of vegetative cover from the upper end of the Purísima Creek drainage led to its increased activity in the period following 1900, and the smithy ruin was covered with 3.5 feet of sterile sand. It is significant that a photograph taken in 1870 (Figure 9 (a)) does not show a stream bed in the area where Purísima Creek now runs.

The floor of the blacksmith shop was difficult to define. The most consistent indication of its location was provided by the distribution of artifacts beneath the tile zone. Most artifacts in this zone were clearly located in a stratum 0.5 foot thick. The flooding which took place at frequent intervals following the abandonment of the smithy would also have led to a dulling of the definition of the floor. The actual location of the floor is based, consequently, on artifact locations and observations made on the footing-floor relationship in other buildings in the mission complex. Figure 8 shows the distribution of artifacts in the smithy by depth. It can be seen that most objects occurred at the 4.0-foot level, and the likelihood is extremely great that this level indicates the floor surface.

Three separate features were recorded within the limits of the smithy excavations: a secondary foundation of Rooms Two and Three, the forge (Feature 7) previously excavated by the Civilian Conservation Corps (Figure 8; Figure 6(d)), and a concentration of green abalone shells (designated as Feature 4), just to the north of the foundation. The secondary foundation is located along the entire interior west wall of Rooms Two and Three, and extends for a short distance along both sides of the Room Two-Three partition and along the inside of the north wall of Room Three (Figure 8). It is probable that these additional footings represent buttressing

(a)

1870 — STANDING PORTION OF
INDIAN BARRACKS, FOREGROUND

(b)

VIEW IN 1962

(c)

1962 — INDIAN BARRACKS
AFTER EXCAVATION

FIGURE 9.   La Purísima — 1870 and 1962.

walls constructed in an effort to stabilize this portion of the west wall of the blacksmith shop. Since there is evidence of severe erosion of the west slope visible in trenches excavated along that side of the structure, it seems likely that flooding action during heavy rains resulted in a weakening of the west wall, and that an additional section had to be construct-

ed within the building to strengthen the walls against such erosive action. Remains of bricks defined along this wall are badly melted and slumped in marked contrast to the bricks defined on the east wall, which still have their outlines clearly preserved.

The large heap of green abalone shells located against the

north wall of the smithy probably represents the dumping of food remains in that location by the inhabitants of the structure. This dump serves to support the identification of Rooms Two and Three as a domestic unit attached to the shop to house the blacksmith and his family.

The forge is an elevated platform of tile and brick, badly burned over much of its surface, in the southwest corner of Room One (Figure 6(d)). Although in a rather poor state of preservation, having been excavated on two separate occasions, its identification as a forge seems reasonable in view of the evidence of extreme heat indicated by the tiles which form its upper surface. This forge probably was the location of an elevated bed of coals used for heating metals to a workable point, and perhaps also served as a working surface for certain operations.

Artifacts. The artifacts from the blacksmith shop are listed according to provenience in Appendix I. It can be seen that many of the objects from Room One indicate its specialized nature, and that Rooms Two and Three contain more objects which could be considered to be domestic and indicative of these rooms having served as a residence unit. Many of the artifact types from Room One were encountered in no other excavation during the 1962 season, whereas the majority of the Room Two-Three artifacts can be duplicated in the Indian barracks, also a residential unit. The smithy is also unique in the large quantities of slag fragments recovered from its fill; these lumps of fused silica and iron oxide would be expected in such a structure, and were found also in an adjacent dump (Excavation Unit Ten), but at no other location.

Conclusions—Blacksmith Shop. The functional identification of the three rooms in the blacksmith shop is reasonably simple, as indicated above. Room One, in which the forge was located, contained by far the heaviest concentration of scrap metal and tools which would likely have been in the shop, whether for use or repair. The absence of large artifacts connected with metal working might be explained by the fact that anvils, large hammers, quenching tanks and larger bars of iron, in addition to being virtually indestructible, would have been attractive to people who might have removed them from the ruin for later use elsewhere. This could have resulted from their being removed for use at other missions following the abandonment of the smithy, or their removal by parties unconnected with the mission in the period after abandonment of the entire mission complex by the Franciscans but prior to the collapse of the roof.

Rooms Two and Three could have been used as a residence unit, probably for the blacksmith. This conclusion is supported by the interior circulation between Rooms One and Two and Rooms Two and Three, and by the presence of milling equipment, china, and food refuse in these rooms. The dimensions of these rooms are not greatly different from those of the individual two-room residential units in the Indian barracks.

The archaeological evidence collected from the blacksmith shop excavations is clear in its implications, and supports the earlier Civilian Conservation Corps conclusion that this structure was in fact a blacksmith shop. Excavation in the northern half of this structure has provided further information regarding the architecture and has demonstrated the existence of a third room, unknown prior to this time. The identification of Rooms Two and Three as a residence unit is also new, and provides us with a clearer picture of this portion of the La Purísima Mission complex.

The Indian Barracks

The neophytes' residence at La Purísima Mission formed the major portion of two tiled-roof buildings, 532.5 feet in combined length, located on the opposite side of the mission quadrangle from the residence buildings, shops and church. These structures have been investigated twice in the past, first by the Civilian Conservation Corps, at which time all of the ruin south of the county road was excavated as well as a small portion north of the road, and later, in 1951, by the University of California, Santa Barbara, at which time the remaining 202.5 feet of the barracks north of the road was exposed. It was this latter investigation which demonstrated that the barracks actually occupied two separate buildings rather than one extremely long structure. The road covered a critical portion of the building, since at the point where the building encounters the shoulder of the road on the north side it is composed of contiguous two room apartment units, with an off-center partition dividing the rooms, and at the point where it emerges from beneath the road to the south, the structure is only one room in width with no partitioning. The 1962 excavation beneath the road revealed the point at which this architectural change takes place and the nature of the abutment between sections. Figure 10 shows the nature of this transition, and the portions of the barracks excavated by the three different parties.

Both the Civilian Conservation Corps and the University of California investigations showed the barracks to be composed of two-room apartments, with a doorway connecting the rooms, but probably lacking circulation between adjacent apartments. This plan is supported by photographs taken during the latter part of the nineteenth century which show a small portion of the barracks still standing. The section of the barracks which was the last to fall into complete ruin seems to have been located just north of the present county road (Figure 9(b)).

Excavation Technique. The entire barracks ruin beneath the road was designated Feature Six. Four complete rooms (two apartments) and portions of three other rooms were excavated. The rooms were excavated as units, with provenience controlled to location within the rooms horizontally and by visible stratigraphic zones vertically. These vertical zones were established by placing a test pit in the approximate center of each room. The room was then excavated to the floor in discrete strata, usually three in number, as follows: *Surface to Tile*, representing all material from above the collapsed roof; *Fill*, the material between the layer of roof tile and the floor, and the layers of tile itself; and *Floor*, artifacts found on the floor. In addition, certain artifacts found on the floors were pedestalled, mapped and photographed *in situ*. Sample screening with 1/8-inch mesh screens was accomplished on a random sample of all floor material and some fill material. This screening indicated that a negligible amount of material was being lost by the techniques employed, and that this amount was not commensurate with the amount of time required for screening.

Excavation technique varied according to stratigraphic zone. The material above the roof fall was summarily shoveled out, after being inspected for large objects. Large portions of this first zone were composed of road ballast and asphalt surfacing material. The tile zone and fill were shovel-shaved carefully or troweled. Floors were troweled in all instances.

In most rooms, the basal portions of the original adobe

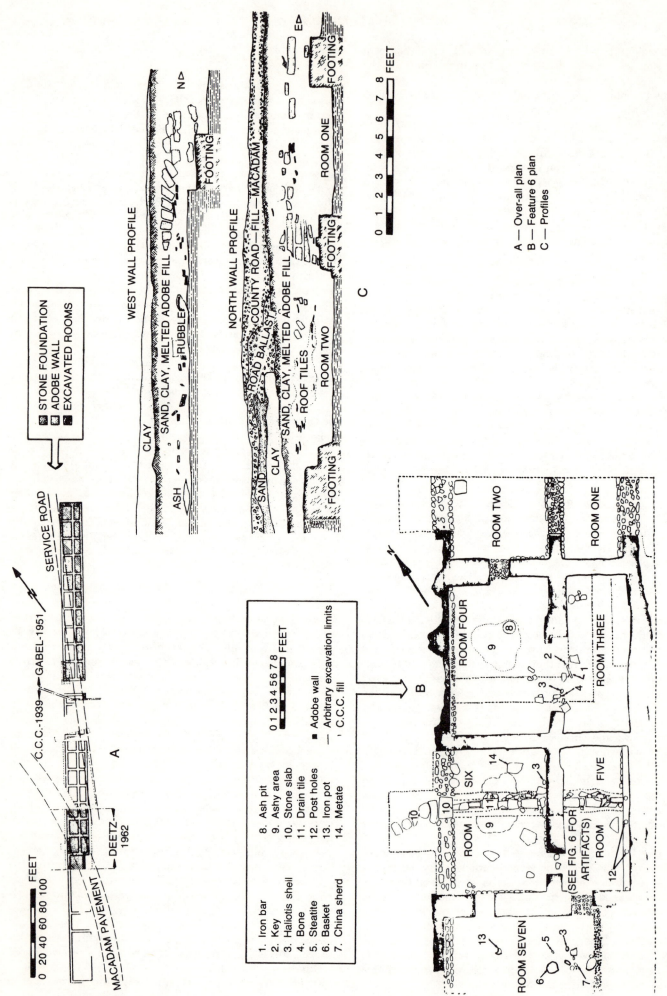

WEST WALL PROFILE

CLAY

SAND, CLAY, MELTED ADOBE FILL

RUBBLE

ASH

FOOTING

N△

NORTH WALL PROFILE

COUNTY ROAD—FILL—MACADAM

ROAD BALLAST

SAND, CLAY, MELTED ADOBE FILL

ROOF TILES

SAND

CLAY

FOOTING

ROOM ONE

ROOM TWO

FOOTING

E▷

0 1 2 3 4 5 6 7 8 FEET

C

STONE FOUNDATION
ADOBE WALL
EXCAVATED ROOMS

FEET
0 20 40 60 80 100

SERVICE ROAD

C.C.C.-1939

GABEL-1951

DEETZ-1962

MACADAM PAVEMENT

A

1. Iron bar
2. Key
3. Haliotis shell
4. Bone
5. Steatite
6. Basket
7. China sherd
8. Ash pit
9. Ashy area
10. Stone slab
11. Drain tile
12. Post holes
13. Iron pot
14. Metate

0 1 2 3 4 5 6 7 8 FEET

Adobe wall
Arbitrary excavation limits
C.C.C. fill

B

ROOM TWO

ROOM ONE

ROOM FOUR

ROOM THREE

ROOM SIX

ROOM FIVE

ROOM SEVEN

(SEE FIG. 6 FOR ARTIFACTS)

A — Over-all plan
B — Feature 6 plan
C — Profiles

FIGURE 10.   SBa-520: Indian Barracks.

174

brick walls remained. These walls stumps were defined and exposed including their junction with the stone wall footings. Along the west side of the ruin the road fill had cut so deeply that the adobe wall material had been removed by the construction of the road to the level of the footings. Here, only the footings were exposed.

In four rooms, there were double stratified floors separated by additional fill ranging from 0.2 to 1.5 feet in thickness. In these cases, the material from the two floors was separated, and the higher floor was exposed and recorded prior to removal and clearing of the second floor. In addition to the barracks structure, three other features within the barrack were recorded and will be described separately below.

Architecture. The portion of the barracks located beneath the road is identical in architectural plan to the segment north of the road, with adobe walls set on stone footings and roofed with tile. The footings are of small unshaped pieces of local sandstone set in adobe. Fragments of roof and floor tile were also used in the footings along the outer edges to make leveling more effective. The footings, where complete exposures were made (west wall and Room One-Two partition), are from 2.4 to 3.0 feet wide and 0.5 foot deep. No effort was made by the builders of the barracks to level these basement walls. The natural contour of the site was followed throughout, and leveling of the walls was achieved through variations in the thickness of the adobe bricks. The bases of the adobe walls could be defined clearly in the majority of cases with the exception of the west side of the ruin. The bricks used in constructing these walls are variable in their dimensions, but average approximately 2

feet in length, 0.7 foot in width and 0.5 foot in thickness, with a wide range of variation.

The floors of the room are quite variable in construction, and will be discussed at length in the treatment of individual rooms below. There was an adequate amount of broken roof tile in most of the rooms, indicating that there had been little or no removal of tiles following the abandonment of the barracks. As a result, the rooms were found to be very rich in artifact content, particularly Room Five, which is thought to have been a storeroom. The protective effect of the road which covered this portion of the barracks in later time may have contributed largely to the undisturbed nature of this segment of the structure.

The following discussion of individual rooms will be according to apartment units (Rooms One and Two, Three and Four, and Five and Six), and the section excavated, which was only one room wide (Room Seven). Architectural variations will be noted, and significant artifacts will be discussed. Appendix I provides a complete list of artifacts by provenience.

Rooms One and Two. Rooms One and Two were excavated in part by the Civilian Conservation Corps in their work north of the county road (Figure 11). The northern end of the 1962 excavations begins in the same rooms in which the Civilian Conservation Corps work was terminated. Since neither room was fully excavated, their length cannot be accurately determined.

Room One is the smaller of the two rooms, One and Two, which form a single apartment unit. Only the southern half of this room was excavated. Room One is 6.6 feet wide, this

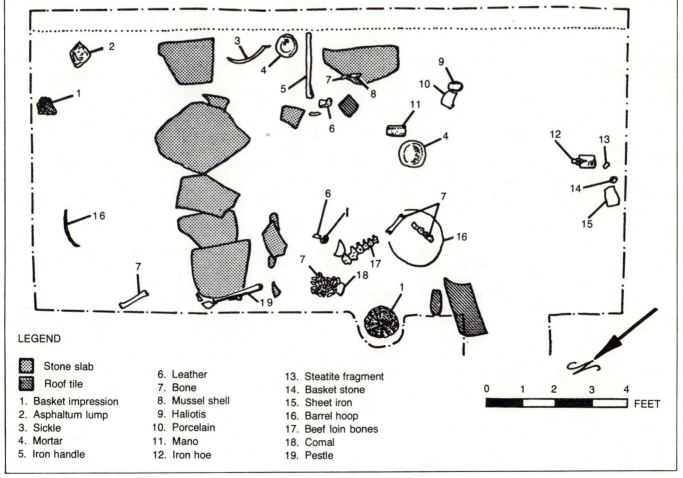

LEGEND

Stone slab
Roof tile

1. Basket impression
2. Asphaltum lump
3. Sickle
4. Mortar
5. Iron handle
6. Leather
7. Bone
8. Mussel shell
9. Haliotis
10. Porcelain
11. Mano
12. Iron hoe
13. Steatite fragment
14. Basket stone
15. Sheet iron
16. Barrel hoop
17. Beef loin bones
18. Comal
19. Pestle

0   1   2   3   4
FEET

FIGURE 11.   Feature 6 — Room Five Artifacts.

measurement being based on the distance between footings. The floor is reasonably level, and was covered with a thin layer of ash, charcoal and shell and bone fragments. The floor is located 1.0 foot below the top of the east wall footings and 0.5 foot below the top of the center footings. No evidence of a doorway between Rooms One and Two was preserved, although such evidence should have existed, since the adobe wall stumps were removed in the initial sectioning of these rooms. There was no evidence of a hearth in the excavated section of Room One. Neither Room One nor Room Two showed any evidence of floor superposition, such as was encountered in Rooms Three through Seven. The fallen tile in the exposed section of Room One was sparse, far less dense than in other rooms excavated. Whether the roof tiles slid to the outside of the structure when the walls collapsed or was removed by some other agency cannot be determined without further excavation to the east.

Rooms One and Two are located at the point of an initial section of the barracks structure made with a tractor and blade to the top of the roof fall. It was this cut which removed the adobe wall stumps from this section of the barracks, and a less precise definition of certain features in Rooms One and Two resulted.

Room Two, the larger of the Room One-Two complex, is 11.4 feet wide and of unknown length. The floor of this room was marked by a layer of ash, charcoal and shell and bone fragments, similar to that on the floor of Room One. This floor is level and 0.2 foot below the floor of Room One, 0.5 foot below the top of the center footings and 1.2 feet below the top of the west wall footings. Roof tile was thickly concentrated in a zone 1.0 foot above the floor of Room Two over the entire excavated area of that room (Figure 11). Eight feet from the southeast corner of Room Two, touching and level with the top of the west footings, is a large shale slab, almost square, measuring 1.4 feet on a side. This slab may mark the location of the entrance through the west wall, since it is in the same location on the west wall as are the doorways in the center walls of the other two room apartments, and since the 1870 photograph (Figure 9 (a)) shows exterior and interior doors to be aligned in the remaining portion of the barracks. While there was no evidence of a hearth in the floor of Room Two, ashes at floor level in the vertical face of the northern limits of excavation in the room might mark the location of such a feature. In comparison, Rooms Four and Six each have a hearth in their approximate centers.

In contrast to Room One, Room Two was quite rich in artifact content. This difference may relate in some way to the relative scarcity of roof tile in Room One, if the scarcity can be interpreted as evidence of burrowing into the room at some later date to remove anything of value.

The artifacts from Rooms One and Two represent a relatively normal sample of what would be expected in a neophyte residence on the basis of Gabel's 1951 excavation of twenty rooms representing ten two-room apartments (Appendix I). The material culture of the Indians residing in the barracks was a blend of Hispanic and aboriginal elements. Approximately three quarters of all objects recovered from Rooms One and Two are of Spanish introduction, and the remaining quarter of the assemblage represents items already in the aboriginal material culture inventory at the time of initial European contact, including comales, pestles, shell beads, baskets and arrowshaft straighteners. Particularly striking is the scarcity of chipped stone artifacts and of flakes resulting from the manufacture of such implements. Since there was probably an overabundance of meat as a result of the hide industry, it can be suggested that hunting was rapidly relegated to a minor role in the subsistence of these Indians. This change is clearly reflected in the extremely low chipped stone count from Rooms One and Two and the other rooms of the barracks. Since the Indian males were needed for work in the raising of crops and were trained to do other jobs within the mission complex, there was much less time to devote to hunting. The minor amount of stone working suggested by the few flakes recovered might have been devoted wholly to the manufacture of stone tools with which to accomplish certain introduced technologies, such as tanning, as evidenced by the chert hide scrapers recovered in the tanning vats. In marked contrast to the near absence of chipped stone materials is the abundance of aboriginal artifacts which are connected with the processing and preparation of vegetable foods. Mortars, pestles, comal fragments, plugged haliotis shells, basketry impressions, and Mexican manos and metate fragments all indicate the continuation of the aboriginal pattern of food preparation. This selective disappearance of various aspects of the aboriginal assemblage seems to relate to a differential in the degree of change of male and female tasks, with female duties remaining relatively unchanged. This pattern of acculturation will be discussed at greater length in the conclusion of this section.

On the basis of architectural features and artifact content, Rooms One and Two can be identified as forming one more residence apartment, identical in most ways to those previously excavated.

Rooms Three and Four. Rooms Three and Four were fully excavated and are identical in architectural plan and approximate dimensions to the other two room units in the barracks structure (Figure 6). Room Three is 7.6 feet wide and 18.8 feet long. Room Four is 12.0 feet wide and 18.8 feet long. In each room, there is a second floor stratified beneath the upper floor level. The upper floors are 0.5 foot above the top of the footings and are essentially level and in the same plane. Roof tile was solidly distributed over the floors and in the fill of each room, with the exception of an area in the northeast corner of Room Three which marked the location of a Civilian Conservation Corps test pit identifiable from the description in their report. The adobe walls could be identified on all sides, with the exception of the west wall of Room Four, and are preserved to approximately 1.0 foot in height on the east side, 1.2 feet along the center partition, and slope from 1.0 foot at the center of the north wall to only footings at the west wall. These walls are at least two feet thick, and were probably thicker, since slumped wall material had to be removed in order to reveal the seams between the bricks. The existence of these wall bases made it possible to locate an entryway between the rooms 2.4 feet north of the south cross wall and at least two feet wide. The footings extend across beneath this gap in the adobe bricks, but tile fragments on the floor in line with the wall (Figure 11) and the absence of adobe bricks at this point made it possible to locate the passageway. This location is in close agreement with the location of the passageways between rooms visible in the 1870 photograph of the remaining portion of the barracks. This passageway seems not to have had a door hung in it, since no hinges or other hardware were found, and there is no evidence of accommodations for a frame in the remaining portion of the center wall.

The adobe walls of both rooms still bear traces of lime whitewash in the form of a paper-thin layer of lime adhering to the bricks in several places, including the south inner face of the passageway. The upper floor of Room Three is plastered with lime in a layer 0.1 foot thick over its entire surface. It is this lime plaster which makes it possible to identify Room Three as a room tested by the Civilian Conservation Corps; an identification which is further supported by having located their test trench in the fill and through the floor of the room. The Civilian Conservation Corps report (Harwood 1939: 2) states that lime plaster was encountered on the floor of a room in which only a small test sounding was made. Their indication of the location of this trench, coupled with the definition of their pit and the plastered floor makes possible in turn an accurate connection between the Civilian Conservation Corps map and the 1962 excavations as shown in Figure 6.

Room Four, on the other hand, has a conventional dirt floor, similar to those in the other units of the barracks. This room also has a circular hearth of compacted ash, approximately six feet in diameter, in the upper floor. The plastering of the floor of Room Three and the whitewashing of the walls of both rooms in this unit has no counterpart in any of the other units in the barracks structure. Since only the 1962 excavations were able to define the adobe walls, due to the greater depth of the ruin at this point, other walls may have been whitewashed, but lime plastered floors in the other units would have been impossible to overlook, and none were recorded in this condition.

The lower floor of Room Three is one foot below the upper floor, and, unlike the latter, is of dirt thickly covered with ash, bone and shell fragments. Due to limitations of time, only a section of this lower floor was exposed. The lower floor of Room Four is also one foot below the upper floor, and, like the lower floor of Room Three, is of dirt but with far less refuse scattered on it. Consequently, it was much harder to define this floor, and in places it could not be accurately located. One curious aspect of the lower unit formed by the lower floor levels of these two rooms is the problem created by the footing of the partition wall, which would have projected half a foot above the floor, and would have necessitated stepping over when one passed from one room to another.

In the fill between the upper and lower floors of Room Three was found an intense concentration of bottle and porcelain sherds. These when reconstructed proved to be the remains of four porcelain vessels and five wine bottles (Figure 12). This sherd material was limited to a space of approximately one cubic foot, and many of the fragments had air spaces between them. They seem to have been buried intentionally, but for what purpose it is difficult to ascertain. The dirtfree spaces between the sherds suggests that they were buried in an unbroken condition, and were later fragmented by traffic over the upper floor surface. The lime plaster coating of the upper floor was unbroken in the area over the feature material, indicating a deposition either at the time of building up the floor or a later intentional burial of the objects and careful repair of the lime plaster.

The rich fill of these rooms produced an assemblage which is somewhat more specialized than that recovered from Rooms One and Two (Appendix I). This rather unusual group of artifacts, including a cello string, wine glass and wine bottles, fine porcelain, stirrup, and spur rowel, and the relative absence of distinctively aboriginal artifacts, coupled with the unique architectural features of whitewashed walls and plastered floor suggests that this apartment might have been occupied by a European, perhaps a military guard, rather than an Indian family. This possibility is further enhanced by the presence of a storeroom in the adjacent apartment (Room Five). In contrast to the relatively high number of aboriginal artifacts from Rooms One and Two, only 17 percent of the Room Three and Four artifacts are aboriginal, and many of these could have served either Indian or Spaniard equally well.

Except for the functional aspect of this apartment and its architectural peculiarities, it resembles others in the barracks. The only other unusual feature is the superimposition of floors, a trait shared with Rooms Five, Six and Seven. This stratification may have resulted from extensive rebuilding of this portion of the barracks. Rooms Five and Six also show evidence of later repair and rather extensive structural changes.

Rooms Five and Six. Rooms Five and Six form the southernmost of the three apartment units excavated during the 1962 season, and the southern limit of the two-room architectural plan. Room Seven, which abuts this apartment, is a single room occupying the entire width of the building (Figure 10). Rooms Five and Six are similar in dimensions to Rooms One and Two, and Rooms Three and Four, and to the other two-room apartment units in the barracks structure. Room Five is 7.9 feet wide and 16.9 feet long. Room Six is 11.2 feet wide and 16.9 feet long. Unlike the other two-room units however, the Room Five-Six unit is clearly of a specialized functional nature. The contents of Room Five clearly indicate its use as a storeroom, and Room Six shared in this function at least in part.

The floor of Room Five is double, having been built up by puddling adobe in a layer approximately 0.2 foot thick over the entire lower floor surface. The lower floor had a thin layer of ash and charcoal on its surface. The upper floor was marked only by a textural and color change in contrast to the overlying fill material. The floor of Room Six is also double, with a greater separation between floors than in Room Five. The upper floor, marked by a layer of bone fragments and ash, is 0.5 foot above the lower floor. The lower floor was also covered with ash and refuse fragments, and has a large circular hearth in its center. This hearth resembles the hearth in Room Four, and is 6.5 feet in diameter and 0.5 foot thick. No hearth was found in the upper floor of Room Six. The upper floors of both rooms were covered by a thick layer of broken roof tiles, and there was no evidence of burrowing through these tiles by parties in the past to gain access to the contents of the rooms. The fill of these rooms was extremely rich, and it seems probable that the total contents of both rooms at the time of the collapse of the roof were available to the 1962 excavators.

The walls of both rooms are very well preserved and of similar dimensions to those of Rooms Three and Four. As in the case of the latter rooms, individual bricks can be seen and have similar dimensions to others defined in this section of the barracks. A clearly defined doorway between Rooms Five and Six was located, 2.4 feet wide and 2.0 feet from the south crosswall. Like the passageway in Rooms Three and Four, this passageway was defined by an abrupt break in the bricks and by tiles resting on the floor in the wall line (Figure 10). Four post holes were encountered along the east wall of Room Five. One of these, located in the southeast corner of the room, still had wood fragments in it; the others were marked by a dark, loose fill. These post holes probably represent posts which were set in the east wall of Room Five to stabilize and repair this portion of the barracks.

The tentative identification of Room Five as a storeroom is based on the very diverse and rich contents recovered. Figure 11 shows the location of the number of objects which were

INCH

INCH

a

b

INCH

c

INCH

d

e

INCH

INCH

g

INCH

f

FIGURE 12.   Feature 6 — Artifacts from Room 3 (under floor).

178

FIGURE 13. Features 8 and 9.

mapped and photographed *in situ* on the floor of Room Five. Remains of five asphaltum-lined twined baskets were found at intervals along the west, south and east walls. Barrel hoops indicate the presence of barrels, although their contents cannot be determined. The most concentrated group of objects was designated Feature Eight (Figure 13(a)). This feature was located against the east wall just north of the passageway between Rooms Five and Six. The large basket visible in the left center of the photograph was in an excellent state of preservation. In front of this basket was a loin of beef, overlying a barrel hoop and the remains of a basket full of paired mussel shells. This second basket probably had a leather strap attached, fragments of which were recovered in the vicinity. A large pestle is also included in this group of artifacts. In addition of the Feature Eight concentration, the floor of Room Five also produced a large lump of unmodified asphaltum, the handle of an iron implement, perhaps a branding iron, a large Wedgewood Queensware bowl sherd, two basket hopper mortars, an iron hoe, leather fragments, a large Mexican mano fragment, and numerous other objects listed in Appendix I. The large number of objects in this room is strongly indicative of its use as a storeroom, since it could not have been employed as a living area with all of these objects in the locations in which they were found. Numbers of storage containers, such as barrels and baskets, and farming implements, such as the hoe and sickle, also suggest this use for Room Five.

The slabs designated S on Figure 11 are of local shale, and extend through the wall between Rooms Five and Six and into Room Six. These slabs served to cover and protect a drain, designated Feature Nine, which extends the full width of Rooms Five and Six and, after passing through the east exterior wall of Room Six, extends an undetermined distance to the east beyond the barracks structure. Various aspects of this drain are shown in Figure 13 (b, c and d). It is made of roof tiles laid with their concave surfaces facing; no mortar was employed in its construction. Some of the tiles used for this drain are of a type not encountered heretofore in excavations at La Purísima Mission. These unusual tiles have a constriction at one end, and are slightly larger than those tiles normally encountered. Whether they were made especially for use in the construction of this drain or represent a rare type of roof tile cannot be determined with any degree of certainty. Fragments of similar tiles were encountered in Room Six, but whether these fragments came from the drain or from the roof is not known. The purpose of the drain seems to have been to relieve flooding and water accumulation along the east exterior wall of Room Five. It was noted above that this wall of Room Five shows signs of having been stabilized by the insertion of posts flush with its interior walls. The ditch for the drain was excavated after the building had been completed, and probably after it had been in use for some time. This later construction is indicated by the condition of the area of the Room Five-Six partition wall, which had been removed to allow passage of the drain, and which had been badly patched after the tiles had been installed. The hearth in the lower floor of Room Six is cut through by the ditch for the drain, and the west exterior footings of Room Six have been modified to permit passage of the drain tiles. The second, upper floors of both Room Five and Room Six are flush with the slabs which cover the drain, and probably were built up higher to raise the floors of both rooms above the water seepage level. Since the lower floors of both rooms show evidence of domestic use in the form of ash and food remains, and since the upper floors were clearly lacking in such refuse, it is likely that the modification of this room complex from a former residence unit to a store-room took place at the time when the repairs were effected. The rebuilding of these two rooms probably took place at about the same time as the modification of Rooms Three, Four and Seven, and probably represents a late modification of the barracks structure.

Room Seven. Room Seven marks the transition from one architectural plan to another in the long southern unit of the barracks complex. The southern portion of this room was excavated by the Civilian Conservation Corps during their extensive program, but their progress northward was blocked by the county road. The nature of the abutment is reasonably clear from the plan recovered during the 1962 season. The width of the building is reduced from 25.8 feet (footing measurements) to 18.8 feet, a reduction of ten feet at the point where the two sections meet. There is no break in the structure, but rather a contiguous relationship between the two sections (Figure 10, Figure 9 (a)). Although the Civilian Conservation Corps identified the southern portion of this room as an infirmary, no evidence to support or to refute this identification was recovered in the northern section. The inside width of Room Seven is 17 feet. The wall on the west side of this room was so poorly preserved that it was necessary to excavate to the footings to define the room's precise limits. Roof tile was heavily concentrated over the entire floor area of the room. An opening in the wall between Room Seven and Room Six may indicate a passageway, although the evidence is not too clear. This opening may have been a later passageway cut between the rooms at the time of the reconstruction of this section of the barracks, following the abandonment of the Rooms Five and Six unit as a residential apartment.

Room Seven, like Rooms Three through Six, had a double floor. Definition of both floor levels was weak, although it was possible to follow the limits with care. The lower floor of Room Seven is approximately 0.8 foot below the upper; neither floor was marked by the presence of food remains as were the lower floors in the other stratified rooms.

The off-center central partition of the two room portions of the barracks probably served to support the central roof beam. The reduction in width of the building at the Room Seven point may well have resulted from the need to reduce the width of the roof when the center partition was removed. Twenty-eight feet is a large distance to span with a single roof, supported either by cross walls or by posts which support a beam. It is very likely that the width of the building had to be reduced in order to accommodate a different type of roof construction.

The artifacts from Room Seven provide no specific indication of its function. The second of two nearly complete baskets from the barracks was found on the upper floor near the west wall. Like the basket in Feature Eight, Room Five, this basket is an asphaltum-lined twined storage bottle. A

Artifact	Alamo Pintado	La Purísima
Chipped Stone, including waste flakes	654	10
Shell Beads	835	17
Ground Stone	99	12
Worked Bone	9	3
Steatite	14	25
Glass Beads	69	28
Basket Stones	65	5
Shell Ornaments	4	0
Glass	1	48
Wood Objects	1	0
Basket Impressions	6	32
Pottery		
Earthenware	3	9
Porcelain	0	50
Metal		
Iron	1	99
Copper	0	4
Brass	0	1
Bronze	0	1

rim sherd of Leeds china with a blue rippled edge and an asphaltum coating along the lip was found just west of the basket. Other noteworthy artifacts include half of a tripod iron pot, a plugged haliotis shell and a large stone pestle.

Conclusions

Indian Barracks. On the basis of the seven excavated rooms in the portion of the barracks which had long been covered by the county road, several significant conclusions can be drawn concerning the nature of the acculturative process as it occurred among the Purisimeño Chumash at La Purísima Mission. These observations are supplemented by previous work done in other sections of the barracks and elsewhere at the mission. While the decline of the Chumash under missionization was rapid, spectacular and complete, it should not be viewed as a uniform process. The culture probably disintegrated more rapidly in some aspects than in others, and the material remains give some glimpses of the differential operative between the various areas of cultural loss.

As is suggested above, there seems to have been at least a sexual differential in the degree of initial loss. The assemblage from the Indian barracks is indicative of a greater change in male roles than female. The absence of chipped stone, almost complete in the section excavated, indicates the probable disappearance of hunting, skin dressing with aboriginal equipment in the residences and weapon manufacture. On the other hand, the quantities of basketry, milling equipment, comales and other artifacts associated with food preparation which was the work of the female in the missions suggests a relatively minor degree of disruption of this aspect of aboriginal culture.

Particularly striking is a comparison between the assemblage from Rooms One through Seven and that from a historic Chumash village only twenty-five miles distant. This village, the Alamo Pintado site, is located in the Ynezeño area, near Los Olivos, California, at the foot of

Figueroa Mountain, at the southern limit of the San Rafael Mountain range. Excavations at this site in the summer of 1961 provide us with a clear picture of Chumash material culture in the interior as it was just prior to the establishment of the Mission at Santa Ynez and the construction of the new Purísima complex. Tabulated below are the assemblages from the Indian barracks and from Alamo Pintado, with quantities of each type of artifact indicated.

These tabulations are based on an area two hundred square feet in extent and 1.5 feet deep at the Alamo Pintado site, and only the material from the floor zone at the Indian barracks. While it is difficult to estimate the relative significance of the distributions from each site, it can be said that the barracks material in all probability represents the activities of fewer people than does the Alamo Pintado assemblage. Even with this qualification, striking differences are apparent between the two situations. Chipped stone, already commented on, is sixty times more common at Alamo Pintado. Even though this tabulation represents a concentration of activity three times as intense as in the excavated portion of the barracks, chipped stone frequencies are twenty times greater. Applying the same approximate three times reduction as a rough guide to achieving some type of rough comparability, it can be seen that shell bead differences are much greater than the differences between numbers of glass trade beads. It is interesting to note that in the adjacent dump, described in a later section of this study, shell beads were much more frequent than glass beads. The relationship is reversed in the barracks, with nearly twice as many glass beads as shell beads. While a much greater quantity of ground stone was recovered at Alamo Pintado, this difference between the two situations is not as great as it might first appear. The ground stone from the barracks is all in the form of finished, complete artifacts, while much of the ground stone from Alamo Pintado is in the form of small fragments, creating a misleading proportion. The greater quantities of steatite artifacts at the barracks are due largely to large numbers of comales and comal fragments. Basketry impressions were much more numerous in the barracks, while basket stones and asphaltum coated pebbles used in lining baskets were much rarer than at Alamo Pintado. This difference may reflect the normal location of basket lining activities, or it may indicate that most of the baskets were brought into the barracks from the villages when their owners came under the jurisdiction of the mission.

In fact, in view of the rather brief life expectancy of the Indians at the missions, it may well be that much of the aboriginal assemblage in the barracks was made elsewhere, and brought to the mission at the time when the Indians moved in. If this is the case, the difference in chipped stone frequencies would not be as significant as indicated by the relative figures, although the total absence of chipped stone tools in the barracks still contrasts sharply with the one hundred odd projectile points and several hundred chert scrapers from the Alamo Pintado site. The occurrence of quantities of metal and glass objects in the barracks ruin and the relative absence of this type of material from Alamo Pintado needs little comment, since in this instance a case of full substitution is involved rather than a modification of a pre-existing aboriginal material inventory.

The Indian barracks at the time of its fullest utilization could have accommodated only a relatively small portion of all of the Indians at the mission. Since there was a dormitory for unmarried girls, the barracks probably housed family units, married couples and small children. Whether unmarried males lived in the barracks until marriage or at some other location is not known. In any event, there must have been numbers of temporary, less substantial residences, probably in the vicinity of the barracks, which housed those Indians not living in the barracks.

It is probable that the barracks was abandoned from its northernmost limits southward, with the section excavated in 1962 being the longest and latest occupied. Evidence for this north-south abandonment is provided by the relationship between the dump (see The Dump: Excavation Unit Ten) and the barracks, and Gabel's description of the northernmost rooms having been used to dispose of large quantities of animal bone and other refuse. Examination of the collections made by the Gabel party indicates also that there was a greater concentration of chipped stone waste flakes, and some chert tools in the more northern sections of the barracks. This is in accord with the suggestion put forth here that stone chipping became a lost technology during the time the Indians resided in the barracks, and, as expected, the southernmost section, inhabited longest, has provided the smallest amounts of stone chipping evidence. Furthermore, the southernmost section of the two-room apartment type structure is the most extensively rebuilt. The modifications of the wall and floors of Room Five and the construction of the drain to remove standing water from behind the barracks by Room Five (the lowest point of the east wall), all indicate extensive reconstruction. Double floors were not noted by Gabel in any of the apartments in the northern building or apartment units. In all probability, at the time that the barracks were in full use, the dump (Excavation Unit Ten) was used by the residents of the barracks. Following the progressive abandonment of this portion of the quarters, the abandoned rooms seem to have been used for the disposal of debris. After all, this section would be closer than the dump and more easily reached from the southern end of the barracks. Finally, it is more logical to suppose that if any portion of the barracks were to be abandoned, it would be the northern section, since this portion is furthest removed from the remainder of the mission buildings, particularly the shops, chapel and other residents. It is probably not coincidental that the portion of the barracks still standing in 1870 is near the southern end, since this was probably the last to be inhabited.

If the reconstruction and raising of the floors in Rooms Three through Seven occurred near the end of the occupation of the barracks, and if the Room Five-Six storeroom was established at this time also, perhaps the movement of a soldier into the Room Three-Four apartment took place at this time, one of his duties being to guard the storeroom next door to his apartment.

The Dump: Excavation Unit Ten

An extensive dumping area located just east of the blacksmith shop (Figure 1, X. U. 10) was encountered during a sewer installation in 1961. During the summer of 1962, this feature was used to train students in basic excavation procedures, so the investigations were guided primarily by teaching needs. Consequently, this feature had not yet been fully excavated, and an extended definitive description of it is not yet possible. Further excavation is planned for the summer of 1964. Figures 14-16 show representative artifacts.

The dump was excavated according to a five-foot-square unit grid system, much in the manner employed at the

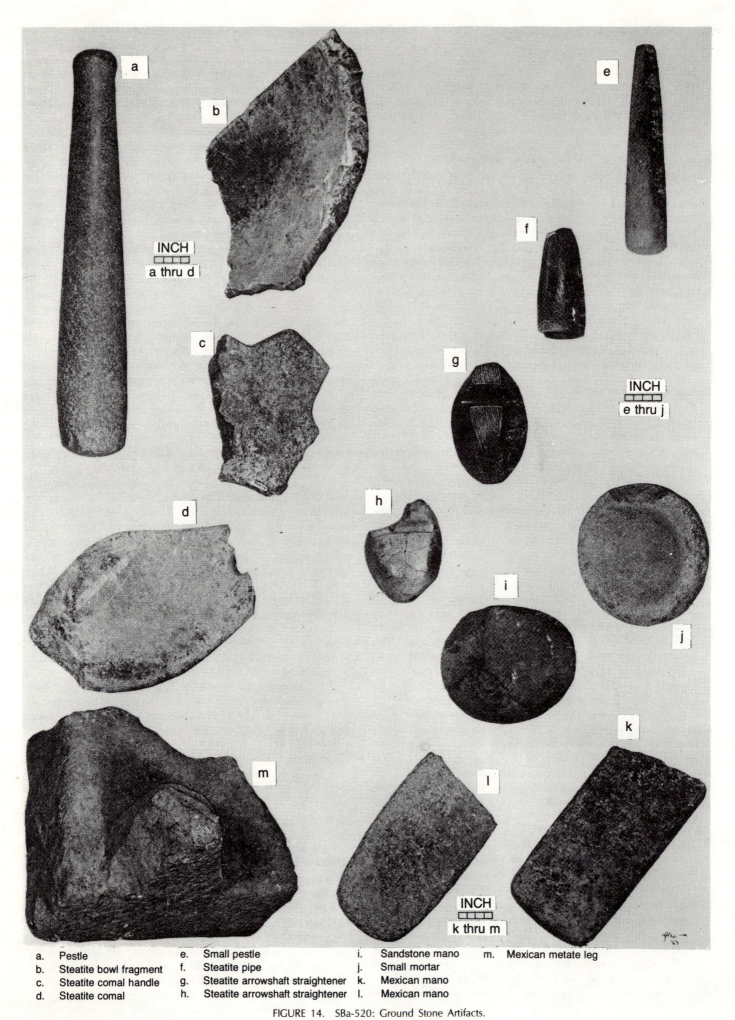

a. Pestle
b. Steatite bowl fragment
c. Steatite comal handle
d. Steatite comal
e. Small pestle
f. Steatite pipe
g. Steatite arrowshaft straightener
h. Steatite arrowshaft straightener
i. Sandstone mano
j. Small mortar
k. Mexican mano
l. Mexican mano
m. Mexican metate leg

FIGURE 14. SBa-520: Ground Stone Artifacts.

INCH
a thru g

INCH
i thru l

INCH
r thru u

INCH
m thru p

FIGURE 15. SBa-520; Pottery, Glass and Miscellaneous Artifacts (See Key on page 185).

183

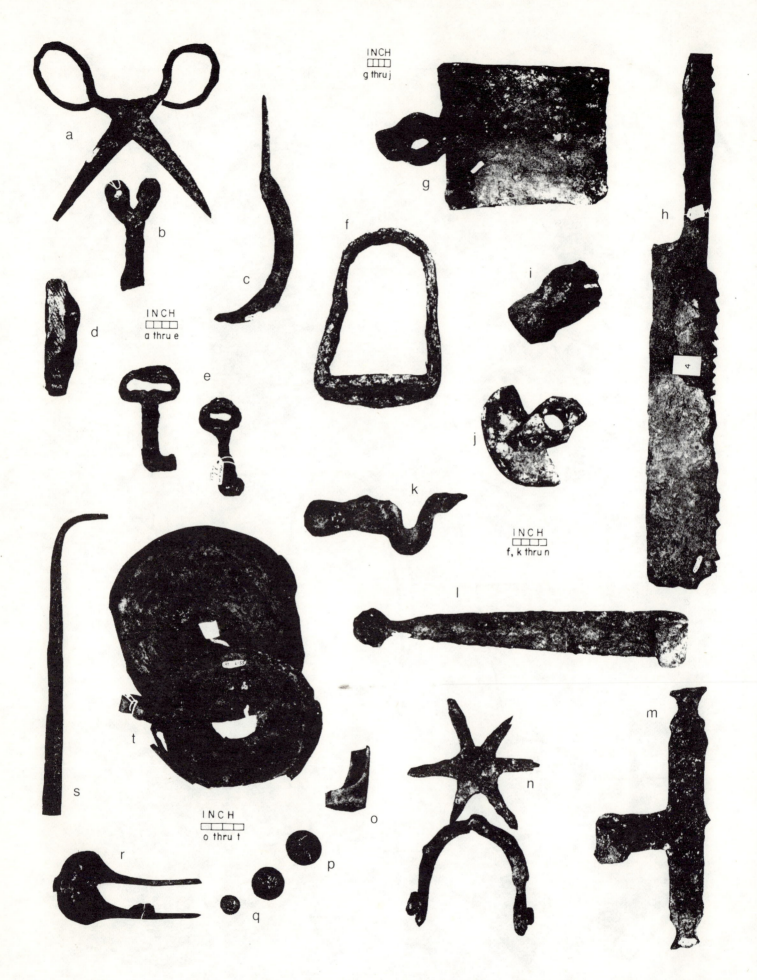

INCH
g thru j

INCH
a thru e

INCH
f, k thru n

INCH
o thru t

FIGURE 16.   SBa-520: Artifacts of Iron and Other Metals (See Key on page 185).

KEY TO FIGURE 15.

a. Cream-colored earthenware; Leeds blue rimmed
b. Bowl sherd; Wedgewood Queens Ware
c. Cream-colored earthenware; orange transfer print (inscription: ". . . RMY GIRL")
d. Cream-colored earthenware; Staffordshire purple transfer print
e. Cream-colored earthenware; Staffordshire black transfer print
f. Cream-colored earthenware; black and tan banded
g. Polychrome "Gaudy Dutch" pottery
h. Cream-colored earthenware; Staffordshire blue transfer print
i. Mexican lead glazed earthenware
j. Blue Canton Chinese porcelain
k. Mexican tin enameled earthenware ("Mexican Majolica")
l. Mission bowl base; unglazed coarse earthenware
m. Columella bead
n. Boar tusk pendant
o. Plugged abalone shell
p. Cello string
q. Wine glass base
r. Decanter stopper top
s. Glass beads
t. Small bottle
u. Drinking glass

KEY TO FIGURE 16.

a. Shears
b. Shears
c. Sickle blade
d. Jackknife
e. Keys
f. Stirrup
g. Square hoe
h. Saw
i. Axe head
j. Hoe
k. Half of a bit
l. Hinge
m. Hinge and portion of frame
n. Spur rowel; spur heel piece
o. Sword butt
p. 1782 Spanish coin
q. Phoenix buttons
r. Pistol butt
s. "Pipette"
t. Lamp — crushed

smithy. Overflow from Purísima Creek had deposited as much as two feet of sterile sand over the area in the period following the abandonment of the mission when the creek became quite active. The deposits extended approximately 35 feet in a north-south direction and at least 20 feet east-west. This overburden was removed. Stratigraphic levels were defined in the dump deposits and used as a guide to excavation. All units were screened to 1/8 inch.

The dump seems to have been used as a disposal area for the blacksmith shop, as indicated by the large amounts of slag recovered, and by the barracks during its earlier period of use. It is primarily characterized by very concentrated deposits of animal bone, slag, shell, potsherds, beads and ash in a layer which averages 1.5 feet in depth. The large amount of cattle remains indicates the probable consumption of beef in large quantities by the Indians and Europeans. While bones representing all parts of the cow were recovered, the presence of numerous articulated forequarters suggests that this part of the animal may have been disposed of intact, while the more meaty hindquarters were used as food. Articulated forequarters and large numbers of horn cores, but few skull parts, indicate the use of the dump as a disposal area for the abattoir. The custom of cooking the heads of cattle (Webb 1952:199) by burying them in a heated pit would account for the isolated horns. It would be far more efficient to remove the horns from the cow's head prior to burying it, thus necessitating a smaller pit for the operation.

Shell beads were approximately three times more numerous than glass beads in the dump. This ratio is the reverse of the situation in the Indian barracks, where glass beads were twice as numerous as those of shell. If the dump was used by the earlier inhabitants of the barracks, as the refuse in the northernmost rooms of the barracks suggests, this reversed ratio may reflect an increase in the use of glass beads in favor of shell beads through time; a trend to be expected.

Little more can be said concerning the dump at this point. Further investigations are planned for future field programs. When the recovered sample has reached a larger size, a more complete and definitive discussion of this feature will be possible. Appendix I gives the artifacts from the dump by type.

SUMMARY

In many ways, this report is a preliminary statement. The primary aim of the work accomplished under the contract was directed toward architectural data collection, and consequently this report is oriented in the direction of architectural reconstruction with final restoration as a desirable end result. Full faunal identifications, studies in depth of the ceramics recovered, and further interpretive study of the artifacts remain to be done, and will be accomplished in time. Most interpretive conclusions are given in the individual sections describing the various features investigated, so that further discussion at this point is unnecessary.

BIBLIOGRAPHY

Engelhard, Zephyrin Father
1932 *Mission La Conceptión Purísima de María Santísima.* Mission Santa Barbara, Santa Barbara.

Gabel, Norman E.
1952 Report on Archaeological Research, La Purísima Mission State Historical Monument. Manuscript on file at California State Division of Beaches and Parks, District 5 office, Goleta.

Harwood, Harvey R.
1937 Archaeological Report, January, 1937, La Purísima Camp SP–29. Manuscript on file at La Purísima State Historical Monument Headquarters, Lompoc.

1939 Archaeological Report on Structure Number 102 in *Archaeological Reports, Civilian Conservation Corps.* Manuscript on file at La Purísima State Historical Monument Headquarters, Lompoc.

Webb, Edith Buckland
1952 *Indian Life at the Old Mission.* Warren F. Lewis, Publisher, Los Angeles.

APPENDIX I: ARTIFACT INVENTORIES

SMITHY

Room One

2 iron spur rowels
1 piece of an iron door hinge
1 iron hammerhead

1 iron hook
1 iron pot
miscellaneous iron fragments
1 copper pipe
1 miscellaneous copper fragment
1 lump of slag

Some other pieces found are: lead bullets, 1 bullet mould, ornamental brass buttons, portions of metates, bones, and old hand made nails, all of which were probably left there from Mission days (Harwood 1937:3).

Room Two

Surface to Tile
1 iron nail
2 iron blades
1 branding iron
miscellaneous iron fragments
1 miscellaneous copper fragment
1 lump of slag
3 stone flakes
1 stone pestle fragment
1 comal
1 steatite bead
3 miscellaneous steatite fragments
8 glass beads
1 glass cup handle
9 pieces of glass
54 olivella shell beads
7 clam shell beads
3 pieces of porcelain
1 piece of lead glazed earthenware
charcoal
miscellaneous wood fragments

Tile to Floor
5 iron nails
miscellaneous iron fragments
2 miscellaneous copper fragments
2 stone flakes
1 stone pestle fragment
3 steatite comal fragments
1 glass bead
1 glass bottle base
7 pieces of glass
1 piece of porcelain
1 lump of asphalt
charcoal
2 miscellaneous wood fragments

Floor
1 iron axe head
1 iron key
1 iron wall bracket
1 iron tea kettle spout
1 iron buckle
1 iron mattock head
1 miscellaneous iron fragment
1 piece of a brass candle holder
1 steatite comal
1 steatite bowl fragment
1 comal fragment
1 miscellaneous steatite fragment
1 glass bead
1 glass bottle fragment
1 glass bottle base
miscellaneous pieces of glass
1 piece of white and grey cream colored earthenware
1 basket impression in asphalt
1 basket stone
1 bone button
1 leather fragment

Foundation
1 basket impression in asphalt

Room provenience only
1 piece of an iron door hinge

1 piece of an iron door latch
5 iron nails
1 iron spike
1 iron key
1 iron hinge
1 iron mattock head
1 iron sickle blade
miscellaneous iron fragments
1 copper button
2 miscellaneous copper fragments
1 glass head
2 pieces of glass
1 piece of unglazed earthenware
charcoal

Room Three

Surface to Tile
1 iron spike
3 iron nails
1 iron key
miscellaneous iron fragments
1 lump of slag
3 stone flakes
1 steatite bowl fragment
1 glass bead
1 glass bottle fragment
4 pieces of glass
3 pieces of white cream colored earthenware
1 piece of yellow glazed cream colored earthenware
1 piece of cream colored earthenware with blue transfer print

Tile to Floor
1 iron spike
1 iron spool
miscellaneous iron fragments
1 lump of slag
1 steatite comal
1 steatite bowl fragment
1 glass bottle fragment
1 piece of glass
2 lumps of asphalt

Floor
1 iron axe head
1 piece of copper sheeting
1 brass lid
1 pestle
2 steatite comal fragments
2 steatite bowl fragments
2 pieces of porcelain
1 piece of cream colored earthenware with blue transfer print

Room provenience only
1 iron door hinge
miscellaneous iron fragments
1 lump of slag
1 steatite comal fragment
1 glass bead
1 glass bottle fragment
4 pieces of glass
1 piece of white cream colored earthenware
1 piece of cream colored earthenware with blue transfer print
3 miscellaneous wood fragments

Provenience Unknown

1 iron hoe blade
1 iron heel fastening for spur
2 miscellaneous iron fragments
1 stone flake
2 Mexican metate fragments
3 basket hopper mortars
4 steatite comal fragments
1 piece of white cream colored earthenware
1 piece of cream colored earthenware with blue transfer (?)

FEATURE 6: INDIAN BARRACKS

Room One

Fill
2 iron wedges (?)
1 iron cleaver (?)
1 iron knife blade
1 iron spike
2 iron nails
1 brass door decoration
1 stone flake
1 mano
1 piece of bottle glass
4 pieces of glass
1 olivella shell bead
1 lump of asphalt
2 miscellaneous wood fragments
1 leather fragment

Floor
1 lump of slag
1 stone flake
miscellaneous pieces of glass
1 shell bead
2 pieces of lead glazed earthenware

Room Two

Fill
1 "S" shaped iron hook
1 pair of iron scissors
1 iron barrel hoop
1 iron axe head
1 iron nail
1 iron blade (?)
miscellaneous iron fragments
1 copper sword hilt
1 copper button
1 miscellaneous copper fragment
1 pestle fragment
8 steatite comal fragments
2 steatite bowl rims
3 miscellaneous steatite fragments
13 glass beads
3 bottle glass fragments
1 wine glass stem
miscellaneous pieces of glass
2 olivella shell lip disc beads
2 pieces of lead glazed earthenware
2 pieces of white cream colored earthenware
1 piece of cream colored earthenware — white with green rim
1 piece of cream colored earthenware
1 basket impression in asphalt
3 lumps of asphalt
1 basket stone
charcoal
miscellaneous wood fragments

Floor
1 miscellaneous iron fragment
3 glass beads
1 bottle glass fragment
1 piece of porcelain
1 piece of cream colored earthenware with blue transfer design
1 piece of white cream colored earthenware
2 pieces of lead glazed earthenware
1 leather fragment
1 boar's tusk pendant
1 arrowshaft straightener

Room Three

Surface to Tile
1 iron staple
2 iron nails
1 piece of iron barbed wire
1 bottle glass fragment
4 pieces of glass

1 piece of unglazed earthenware
1 piece of porcelain
1 piece of white cream colored earthenware
3 pieces of cream colored earthenware with black transfer print
1 basket stone
18 pieces of redwood post
1 license plate accessory tag

Fill
1 piece of an iron handle (?)
9 iron nails
4 miscellaneous iron fragments
1 bronze phoenix button
3 stone flakes
1 steatite bowl rim fragment
1 steatite bead
2 steatite comal fragments
5 bottle glass fragments
10 pieces of glass
3 pieces of lead glazed earthenware
3 pieces of unglazed earthenware
8 pieces of white cream colored earthenware
1 piece of cream colored earthenware with hand painted flowers
1 piece of cream colored earthenware with blue transfer print
1 piece of cream colored earthenware with black transfer design
1 piece of porcelain
2 basket impressions in asphalt
charcoal
1 miscellaneous wood fragment

Floor 1
5 iron nails
1 iron spike
1 iron spur
1 iron stirrup
1 iron knife blade
1 iron hoe
8 miscellaneous iron fragments
1 copper wedge
1 stone flake
1 basket hopper mortar
1 Mexican metate leg
5 bottle glass fragments
1 piece of glass
1 piece of porcelain
1 piece of unglazed earthenware
1 piece of cream colored earthenware with hand painted flowers
1 lump of asphalt
2 rocks coated with asphalt
1 cello string

Floor to Floor
miscellaneous iron fragments
1 stone flake
2 Mexican mano fragments
1 glass bead
3 pieces of glass
2 shell beads
2 pieces of porcelain
1 piece of unglazed earthenware
5 pieces of white glazed cream colored earthenware
1 Spanish apothecary jar
1 English bowl
1 English pitcher
1 Chinese chafing dish

Floor 2
4 olivella shell beads
4 pieces of canton ware porcelain
1 piece of cream colored earthenware with blue transfer

Room Provenience only
1 piece of porcelain

Room Four

Surface to Tile
9 iron nails
1 miscellaneous iron fragment

2 lumps of slag
1 stone flake
6 bottle glass fragments
7 pieces of glass
2 pieces of white cream colored earthenware
1 piece of white cream colored earthenware with blue edge
1 miscellaneous wood fragment
1 metal sphere

Fill

8 iron nails
1 iron spike
1 iron hook
7 miscellaneous iron fragments
1 miscellaneous copper fragment
1 bronze button
2 bottle glass fragments
9 pieces of glass
1 columella bead
3 pieces of white cream colored earthenware
2 pieces of white cream colored earthenware with blue transfer print
1 piece of white cream colored earthenware with blue rim
3 pieces of cream colored earthenware with orange transfer print
1 basket impression in asphalt
1 worked bone

Floor 1

3 iron nails
1 iron hoe
1 file shaped iron object
1 iron buckle
1 unidentified iron blade
9 miscellaneous iron fragments
1 copper ring
2 manos
1 Mexican mano
1 Mexican metate leg
1 pestle
1 pestle fragment
2 steatite comal fragments
1 miscellaneous steatite fragment
5 glass beads
1 bottle glass fragment
8 pieces of glass
1 columella bead
2 pieces of porcelain
6 pieces of white cream colored earthenware
1 piece of cream colored earthenware with lavender edge
2 pieces of cream colored earthenware with blue and white transfer print
2 pieces of cream colored earthenware with black and white transfer print
8 basket impressions in asphalt
1 lump of asphalt
2 worked ribs
1 water pipe
1 wheat kernel

Floor to Floor

half of a pair of iron scissors
1 stone flake
3 steatite comal fragments
1 steatite bowl fragment
2 miscellaneous steatite fragments
4 pieces of glass
1 piece of porcelain
1 piece of cream colored earthenware with blue transfer print
lumps of asphalt
1 piece of tile pipe

Room Five

Surface to Tile

1 piece of cream colored earthenware with hand painted floral design
2 pieces of cream colored earthenware with blue transfer print

Fill

2 iron nails
4 pieces of barrel hoop
1 pair of iron scissors
1 iron chain link
1 iron key
1 piece of an iron sickle blade
9 miscellaneous iron fragments
1 bronze phoenix button
1 stone flake
1 pestle
2 mortars
2 glass beads
1 bottle glass fragment
5 pieces of glass
2 olivella shell beads
1 piece of porcelain
2 pieces of white cream colored earthenware
1 piece of cream colored earthenware with blue transfer print
17 basket impressions in asphalt
1 lump of asphalt
2 pieces of roof tile
1 piece of a walnut shell
1 abalone shell filled with asphalt

Floor

1 iron nail
1 iron hoe
1 iron knife blade (?)
1 iron barrel hoop
1 square iron bar
1 iron sickle blade and handle
9 miscellaneous iron fragments
1 brass button
1 stone flake
1 Mexican style mano
1 miscellaneous steatite fragment
1 glass bead
2 bottle glass fragments
3 pieces of glass
1 piece of porcelain
2 pieces of cream colored earthenware — white
1 piece of cream colored earthenware with blue transfer print
basket impressions in asphalt
4 lumps of asphalt
1 basket stone
leather fragments

Floor 2

3 iron nails
1 iron spike
1 piece of iron barrel hoop
3 miscellaneous iron fragments
1 copper button
1 stone flake
2 steatite beads
1 steatite comal fragment
16 glass beads
1 glass handle
4 pieces of glass
8 olivella shell beads
1 piece of cream colored earthenware with blue and white transfer print
2 basket impressions in asphalt
1 lump of asphalt
1 leather fragment

Room Six

Surface to Tile

5 iron nails
1 iron spike
iron wire
4 miscellaneous iron fragments
1 lump of slag
3 miscellaneous steatite fragments
5 bottle glass fragments
1 piece of porcelain
2 pieces of white cream colored earthenware

3 basket impressions in asphalt
charcoal
1 piece of roof tile
1 water pipe
1 asphalt covered rock

Fill

2 iron nails
1 iron spike
1 iron rod
5 miscellaneous iron fragments
2 stone flakes
4 steatite comal fragments
3 steatite bowl fragments
5 miscellaneous steatite fragments
1 decanter top
7 bottle glass fragments
2 pieces of glass
2 lumps of asphalt
4 pieces of charcoal
2 metal coins or buttons (?)

Floor

5 iron nails
1 iron spike
1 iron hoe
1 iron wedge
1 iron ring
1 piece of iron wire
1 iron chain link
1 iron razor with carved bone handle
1 iron jack knife
1 iron door hinge
1 iron door hinge (?)
1 iron latch (?)
15 miscellaneous iron fragments
1 copper button
3 stone flakes
1 mano
1 ground stone bowl fragment
5 steatite comal fragments
4 steatite bowl fragments
1 steatite pipe
1 miscellaneous steatite fragment
5 glass beads
2 bottle glass fragments
5 pieces of glass
2 olivella shell beads
1 plugged abalone shell
2 pieces of porcelain
1 piece of white cream colored earthenware
1 piece of hand painted cream colored earthenware
1 basket impression in asphalt
12 lumps of asphalt
1 basket stone
1 leather fragment
1 drain tile
1 burned corn kernel
1 arrowshaft straightener

Room Seven

Surface to Tile

1 piece of horse's bit
1 copper screw eye (?)
2 bottle glass fragments
2 pieces of glass
2 pieces of porcelain
2 pieces of white cream colored earthenware
1 piece of white cream colored earthenware with blue edging
1 piece of white cream colored earthenware with blue transfer print
1 piece of white cream colored earthenware with yellow brown bands
1 piece of white cream colored earthenware with flower decoration
1 basket impression in asphalt
1 basket stone

Fill

3 iron nails
1 iron knife blade
1 iron blade (?)
4 miscellaneous iron fragments
3 stone flakes
2 steatite bowl fragments
4 miscellaneous steatite fragments
4 glass beads
3 bottle glass fragments
7 pieces of glass
1 piece of porcelain
5 pieces of white cream colored earthenware
1 piece of white cream colored earthenware with blue rim
1 piece of cream colored earthenware with red transfer print
1 piece of water pipe

Floor

1 iron nail
1 part of a pair of iron scissors
6 miscellaneous iron fragments
1 stone flake
1 pestle
2 steatite comal fragments
1 glass bead
2 bottle glass fragments
3 pieces of glass
1 piece of porcelain
1 piece of white cream colored earthenware
1 piece of white cream colored earthenware with blue rim
2 pieces of blue edged cream colored earthenware
1 piece of red cream colored earthenware with white transfer print
15 basket impressions in asphalt
1 basket stone

Feature 8

2 iron nails
3 pieces of iron barrel hoop
3 miscellaneous iron fragments
1 steatite comal
basket impressions in asphalt
leather fragments

Feature 9

1 iron nail
2 miscellaneous iron fragments
1 stone flake
1 steatite comal fragment
1 miscellaneous steatite fragment
1 bottle glass fragment
3 pieces of glass
1 piece of white cream colored earthenware with red transfer design
1 piece of tile drain plug

Provenience Unknown

11 iron nails
1 modern iron nail
3 square iron nails
1 iron spike
1 iron hammer head
1 iron horse's bit
1 iron wall fixture
miscellaneous iron fragments
1 copper 22 caliber shell casing
5 stone flakes
1 pestle fragment
1 hammerstone
1 miscellaneous piece of ground stone
2 steatite comal fragments
1 miscellaneous steatite fragment
9 bottle glass fragments
1 glass bottle stopper
53 pieces of glass
15 pieces of porcelain
7 pieces of white cream colored earthenware

1 piece of white cream colored earthenware with painted border
1 piece of red cream colored earthenware with white transfer
3 pieces of cream colored earthenware with blue and white flower transfer
1 piece of cream colored earthenware with brown, grey, and white bands
1 piece of cream colored earthenware with blue transfer print
5 pieces of lead glazed earthenware
2 pieces of unglazed earthenware
3 basket impressions in asphalt
2 lumps of asphalt
1 basket stone
miscellaneous wood fragments

Dump

13 iron nails
1 iron spike
2 iron eyes
miscellaneous iron fragents
1 copper button
1 copper wire
49 lumps of slag
32 stone flakes
2 Mexican mano fragments
1 mano fragment
1 miscellaneous fragment of ground stone
1 steatite coal fragment
1 piece of steatite pipe

14 miscellaneous steatite fragments
5 glass beads
5 bottle glass fragments
1 piece of glass with chips removed
18 pieces of glass
3 shell beads
36 olivella shell beads
8 clam shell beads
35 pieces of porcelain
2 pieces of porcelain with hand painted butterfly
16 pieces of white cream colored earthenware
1 piece of white cream colored earthenware with green rim
1 piece of white cream colored earthenware with blue edge
4 pieces of cream colored earthenware with blue transfer print
3 pieces of cream colored earthenware with flower design
1 piece of orange cream colored earthenware
1 piece of green glazed cream colored earthenware
32 pieces of unglazed earthenware
8 pieces of lead glazed earthenware
1 unglazed earthenware leg of vessel
1 unglazed earthenware leg of flat vessel
2 lumps of asphalt
2 basket stones
charcoal
1 bone awl
1 bone awl fragment
4 miscellaneous wood fragments
3 tile fragments

CHAPTER 23

Archaeology as the Science of Technology: Mormon Town Plans and Fences

MARK P. LEONE

For as long as archaeology has been practiced, archaeologists have been concerned with what the discipline is about. That is probably as it should be and, when compared with similar preoccupations in other disciplines, is not unusual. Whether long-standing concern with rationales is a uniquely American phenomenon is unclear, but not at all unclear is that American archaeologists have long been making public statements devoted to what makes them do what they do. Wissler, Taylor, Binford and almost every practitioner who has seriously lifted a spade has felt compelled to explain why he did so. The explanations occasionally are personal and idiosyncratic. More common is the usual explanation about wanting to know what the prehistoric past was all about. But in general, as Taylor showed in 1948 and as Binford demonstrated in 1968, there are really two or three basic aims that unify the whole of the archaeological subfield.

The first is history: culture history, culture-historical reconstruction, reconstruction of past lifeways, putting the flesh on the bones of the past, or discovering the Indian behind the artifact. This goal of archaeology deals with unique, particular, nonrepetitive events. It is history; it aims to do history. Dealing with this aim, Taylor distinguished between mere chronicle and social history (or functional history). The distinction issues from the observed discrepancy between announced archaeological goals and archaeological results. The former is what archaeologists can be observed to do and is chronicle; the latter—functional history—is an unrealized aim. This was Taylor's judgement and, as of 1948, there was no gainsaying him.

Two and a half decades later we are presented with several widely celebrated efforts at social or cultural history. They are not called that, to be sure. The new archaeology has given us consistent efforts to understand the social and economic organization of several extinct societies. That they are completely novel and innovative is beyond reasonable questioning at this late date. These studies (Binford, Deetz, Flannery, Hill, Longacre, and Whallon, for example) are based on the now widely understood effort to link archaeological contributions to anthropological theory, especially materialist evolutionary theory. The studies have not been assessed yet as a coherent body of contributions using the explicit goals that they themselves set out to achieve. Preliminary judgments offered in *New Perspectives in Archaeology* (Binford and Binford, 1968b:343–361) indicate happiness with the potential transformation archaeology is capable of, but some doubt about whether it can ever really be achieved. Two questions are posed by the commentators in *New Perspectives*. The first is traditional and wonders whether archaeologists will ever discover what questions cultural anthropologists think are significant. The second is a bit more implicit and wonders whether, because of the muteness of its data, archaeology is not permanently condemned to subordinate status in anthropology. This second question asks whether any of the primary models for comprehending cultural phenomena can spring from prehistoric data. This question has its traditional answers. To answer it, we should ask whether any recent pieces of archaeological research contribute new models to the domain of social organization. For instance, do we now know more about the general patterning of either the subsistence activities or the kinship systems of hunting-gathering or agricultural peoples? We may. On the other hand, we may simply have a bigger fund of data and problems than before. A clear answer to this question is not yet in hand. To see if recent archaeological work is really contributing in a primary way to cultural anthropology, we might choose to ask whether or not the models used by archaeologists are assessed as valid after being subjected to testing on the prehistoric record. That this question has no unambiguous answer is an index to the irrelevance of testing in the research design of most archaeologists.

The second aim of anthropological archaeology is harder to put into words. The ringing phrase of the 1960s is "culture process." The goal is a knowledge of the systematic ways in which cultures fit their subsystems together and how such articulated variables shift or change over time. Through the use of the strategy of cultural ecology, this goal of archaeology is aimed at establishing the principles of cultural evolution. Some excellent examples of scholarship are addressed to this aim. Adams (1966a), Binford (1968b), Flannery (1965), Murra (1968), and others have attempted to isolate the processes behind uniform sets of cultural events. In many ways these are the most recent and widely known contributions of archaeology to its parent discipline. It is important, nonetheless, to see that every one transgresses—really overcomes—the chief boundary around prehistoric archaeology. Researchers are not content to borrow bits and pieces of the present and, by analogy, apply them to the past; they borrow a model whole-hog out of the living (historic) present. In the work of Adams and Murra, both possess long chains of written records for the very periods with which they are concerned. Both are as deeply immersed in the written records of the periods surrounding the events they are trying to explain as they are with the archaeology of the problem. They are, in fact, doing a form of historical archaeology (Schuyler 1970). Binford and Flannery have used models from demography and plant genetics and applied them to the origins of domestication. While it is an exaggeration to say that those disciplines are the only sources of their respective inspiration, it is also an error to suppose that they picked up a model one place and plunked it down at another. The living ethnography of the Middle East, of hunters and gatherers, of pastoral nomads, and of Inca ethnohistory played an important role in formulating their models. Furthermore, the models were modified to fit prehistoric data. Leaving such qualifications aside for a moment, these archaeologists, in borrowing models, borrow the processes that link together a set of factors. They utilize in their own analysis a system (a set of understood interconnections) that is the product of an investigation that took place in the present. The present here may even be the ethnohistoric record, as is the case with Murra but, nonetheless, it is the present in the sense that it is living or was recorded while it was living. Such models are then fitted on the past and the goodness of fit is an index to their success as models.

Some assessment is needed about the scale of the contribution made by efforts at studying culture process. That cannot be done with any sophistication here. It may just be too early to do so anywhere. A few observations can be made without prejudice, however. Such contributions are rare. They are rare because few archaeologists comprehend the rationale of culture process and still fewer attempt to actualize it. They are also rare because to make such a contribution demands that the prehistoric data be tied to documents, or that the archaeologist must become familiar enough with another discipline to borrow from it in reasonably sophisticated ways. In sum, it is the muteness inherent in prehistoric data. When processualist-oriented archaeologists are successful, it is because they keyed into models that could be adjusted to fit the data they had in hand for their particular problem. In principle, this need not limit an archaeologist. But, in fact, few archaeologists deal comfortably with living or historic models, and few can take time to discover what other disciplines can contribute to their own range of problems. Where does this leave us?

There is a sense of incompleteness in archaeology. It may have always been there, but there is little doubt about its heightened presence at the moment. A reading of the present temper of our subdiscipline shows a growing (but undirected and unrealized) promise and a temper tied (in ways that should be specified better than has been done here) to the predicament related above. Thus, of the two goals of archaeology, the first—history, even social history—today leaves people with genuine doubts about its ultimate validity. The second—studies of cultural evolution—has seen well over a decade's worth of attempts with relatively few results and some staggering conceptual problems.

When archaeologists talk about their own field, they are myopic. After all, how do you obtain any kind of objective perspective on yourself—especially when you have never been trained to do ethnographic fieldwork, let alone intellectual history? Most people who have done the history of archaeology have generally been so unconscious that they have built their schemes around the public statements archaeologists made or, doing some fieldwork, they have contrasted different periods of research with an eye to the different kinds of empirical results produced. None has systematically contrasted the public pronouncements with the published results. But, more to the point, rarely has a historian of archaeology stepped aside to ask what are the patterns in American culture of which archaeology is a product. Every anthropologist, on the other hand, makes it a point in his professional teaching career to reveal to students

that they are the products of culture, that they, like all people, are molded by culture to behave the way they do, and that they behave neither randomly nor through the exercise of free will. Inevitably our subdiscipline is the product of and is subject to the same forces that we as individuals are. As Glyn Daniel (1962) has shown, archaeology is the product of a set of larger events: processes that are tied to the Industrial Revolution and half a dozen associated events. If we assume that archaeology was not created by mistake, then I think we must assume that there are some systematic reasons for its present activities. In the absence of an intellectual history of archaeology, it is appropriate to ask not what archaeologists say to themselves or to the public but, instead, what does the public do with archaeology? What does a nation that spends millions of dollars annually on archaeology get out of that investment? The answer to these questions could show us that there is more to archaeology than the two aims discussed. It is just too naïve to suppose that the return on the investment really takes the form of monographs, journal articles, and professional conventions. Even classroom teaching is not a sufficient return.

What the public gets out of archaeology is archaeology's third major, but unrecognized, rationale: the empirical substantiation of national mythology. Such a hypothesis deserves more careful scrutiny than it is possible to give here where it serves as a foil for a larger issue. There are two clusters of evidence that serve to illustrate some of the uses to which archaeology is being put. The first is exemplified by the reconstruction of colonial Williamsburg, the Mormon reconstruction of Nauvoo, and the Canadian reconstruction of the colonial French fortress of Louisbourg. Subsets of this genre are the great and popular archaeological national parks of the southwestern United States, typified by Mesa Verde. The genre is the three-dimensional reconstruction of past lifeways.

There isn't a soul who needs colonial Williamsburg identified for him. The role of archaeology in providing the endless accuracies that are said to be represented there is primary. Archaeology provides a level of credibility or probability—in short, believability—for all the uses Williamsburg was to be put (Cotter 1970).

The Mormon restoration of Nauvoo will be, as one journalist put it, the "Williamsburg of the West." Nauvoo, a city of 12,000–15,000 people in 1845 (then the largest city in Illinois), had been founded some 12 years earlier by the Mormons after they had been run out of Missouri. The Mormons completely abandoned the city in 1846–1847 after the death of their prophet at the hands of a mob in 1844. Nauvoo partly fell into ruins and partly was sacked by anti-Mormons; it was in a state not unlike Williamsburg before reconstruction was begun. The Mormons are spending a large amount of money to restore parts of Nauvoo. They are quite explicit about the potential usefulness of this reconstruction as a center for demonstrating their own history for the purpose of making converts. The excavation of Nauvoo is in the hands of competent archaeologists and there is no doubt that the effort at literal accuracy in recreating what the place looked like will be as fastidious as Williamsburg.

The same kind of instantaneous national monument (or monument to national culture) has been put together with the rebuilding of the royal French fortress at Louisbourg. This is an ongoing project as those at Williamsburg and Nauvoo and, because the installations are so massive, it will require decades to complete. This, of course, has the advantage of allowing the site to reflect the change that interpretations undergo. Dozens of archaeologists have been employed by the central Canadian government in the primary work needed to insure authenticity.

What are these sites all about and why do they rely as heavily as they seem to on archaeological techniques? All of the three-dimensional reconstructions that archaeology is responsible for are sets (or microenvironments). They are the literally reconstructed lifeway of an extinct epoch. The crucial factor is that you, the visitor, the living native from another culture, walk through the set and bring life to it with your own imagination, aided by the many sights, sounds, smells, feels, signs, labels, talks by local folk in eighteenth-century costumes, and your own textbook knowledge of American history. As visitor, you take all this folklore and all this symbol mongering and imagine yourself to be the native of Williamsburg or Mesa Verde and, as the anthropologist would say, attempt to get inside the heads of the original natives. And because the data are relatively mute and the colonial stones do not speak distinctly, they are then more easily made to give the messages of those who do the reconstructing. Modern America rebuilt Williamsburg: modern America and not the eighteenth century is the source of the message derived from Williamsburg. The tourist does not really become immersed in the real eighteenth century at all; he is spared the shock of the filth, degradation, and misery common to that era, and is led into a fake eighteenth century, a creation of the twentieth. While in this altered frame of mind he is faced with messages—the reinforcement of standard modern American values like those surrounding the myths of our own origin as a nation—that come out of today, not two centuries ago.

The archaeologically based set—the recreated stage—provides the empirical environment for the tourist to transport himself physically and mentally out of the immediate present. In that environment the tourist is told certain things. They may be things pertaining to the eighteenth century or to the way the twentieth century handles the eighteenth. At any rate, they are communicated with unusual effectiveness because of the environmental niche of extraordinary reality in which they are set. Because most of the original context of meaning surrounding the artifacts is gone, such extraordinary reality is far more easily produced by using archaeological materials. Meanings are notoriously difficult to recreate and recapture and, as a result, a new set of meanings—more accurately, a reinterpreted set of meanings—is readily imposed on the artifacts themselves. The meanings and interpretations that the visitor picks up are those created by administrators and technicians. Archaeologists usually play a small role in constructing these meanings and sometimes, because of their ability to read the archaeological record, they are in disagreement with the official version. For any disagreement to exist, the archaeological record has to be somewhat less than mute. I think we can admit that it is. But because it is so often difficult to read and because the reading is so often anemic, the record is more easily molded and distorted (or simply fleshed out) by official interpreters.

A caution is necessary: because what goes on in the minds of the visitors at an archaeological site is essentially a mystery and has never been the subject of ethnography, much of the above is hypothetical. But if any part of the argument seems plausible, then surely we should make every effort to get that ethnography done.

The messages communicated by sites like Williamsburg, Nauvoo, Mesa Verde, and the hundreds of national, state, and private parks that use archaeological materials are difficult to establish without doing the ethnography of specific sites. There is nothing mysterious about what they have to say; I think the sites should be seen as being straightforward in their goals. Listen to the guides, read the signs, and the messages are clear. As Voltaire has pointed out, "History is the lie commonly agreed on." Agreeing with the interpretation—his meaning of a lie—is implied by visiting the site. But the site (the environment) is especially effective because it is up to you, the visitor, to reach the message yourself by wandering through the setting, picking out in empirical detail how something you are looking at strikes you. History may be the commonly agreed-on lie but, for that common agreement to be sustained and realized in individuals, they must see it for themselves. They must decipher it for themselves, live in history, first-hand. This can be done by using artifacts that have no meaning in themselves apart from their archaeological context, no meaning that will contradict the one imposed on them by those responsible for the "authenticity" of the hundreds of colonial Williamsburgs throughout this country.

The ability of Americans to manage the past is probably not unique, but the extensive use to which we put the past may be. We certainly do not comprehend what happens to us as we are submerged in environments composed by prehistoric and historic archaeologists and the "interpreters" who reassemble the fragmentary archaeological record. We have no real idea that this use of archaeology educates (not just in the usual sense) and reinforces values we are not always consciously aware of. In that sense, either as archaeologists or as citizens, we are not aware that the ideas we propagate are those of our culture. Nor, as Marx has said that, "The ruling ideas are the ideas of the ruling class." As scientists we need to be more aware of what we have been doing, who our masters are, and whom we serve. We can properly be accused of being acolytes and prostitutes to our culture; so we will remain until we see our third role as archaeologists clearly and consciously.

We need to be aware that Mesa Verde and Williamsburg use archaeology for the same purpose, and that those two sites substantiate bits of our national mythology. There is absolutely nothing wrong with that in principle; however, you may agree or disagree with the factuality of the particular bit of mythology in any one case. But we should realize that all of these hundreds of sites are merely an example of how our culture manipulates history. Cultures have a set of techniques at their disposal to reconstruct history. We provide living fairy tales for every man—ourselves included—to participate in, not as spectators but as creators.

The uses of archaeology I have been suggesting are not exhausted by the movie-set dioramas just described. There are also films. They are the second cluster of evidence for archaeology's third role. Of the films, usually first produced as television programs based on prehistoric data, two come to mind. One is the CBS program on Stonehenge as an astronomical calculator, *The Mystery of Stonehenge*. The other is the equally well-known *Dr. Leakey and the Dawn of Man*. Both of these hour-long television programs, shown in prime evening time, used prehistoric archaeology as their basic data. One has to assume that there is something inherent in these topics for them to be exposed by sponsors to millions of Americans. I think the inherent interest of the data is clear enough and need not be argued over. Here, too, basically mute data are being interpreted within the framework of powerful ideas used in the service of living national cultures. Stonehenge is turned from a scene of romantic and misplaced

Druids into a massive computer invented by people living in a place directly ancestral to us. Stonehenge is putative Anglo-Saxon glory. It competes, we are urged to suppose, with the material from the eastern Mediterranean and Near East that for so long has been proclaimed the root of civilization.

I do not think the surface theme of *Dr. Leakey and the Dawn of Man* will lead us away from the central idea behind that film. The message is: everything changes and can be expected to continue changing because everything has always changed. After all, it is through evolution, or change, that we have come to occupy the present position of eminence we enjoy, and it might safely be reasoned that evolution is the key to the future well-being of us all, might it not? Here, in another medium, is archaeology and its data serving goals and ideas of which it is largely unaware. Thus the empirical base for human evolution falls into those ideas that belong today to the ruling elite (at least that part of it represented by northeast-coast television people and sponsors).

Certainly there is nothing wrong with this last use of archaeology. Indeed, none of the uses to which our subdiscipline is put seems objectively unworthy. Archaeology in the service of national goals hardly merits condemnation; in fact, it merits some celebration. We would, I think, be a good deal happier with our own work if we appreciated the high degree to which we did serve. What is unfortunate, however, is that archaeology as a subdiscipline is quite unaware of this last function. Its role in national myth substantiation is, it seems to me, quite inoffensive, but what is not inoffensive is the archaeologists' unawareness of this function. A distinction should be made between one of the uses of our discipline and the obligation its members have to participate in that use. Because substantiation is an end to which archaeology is put does not mean we, as archaeologists, must participate in it. Until we become aware that there is an activity we have the option of choosing or avoiding, we cannot even make the choice.

One of the early standard lessons one learns in archaeology is the relative muteness of archaeological data. That relativity is often assumed to be a function of the distance of the data from the present. The farther artifacts are removed from the present or from historical sources, the harder it is to figure out the function of the artifacts and, consequently, anything about the culture that produced them. Recently archaeologists have started with the reverse assumption: since an artifact is the product of a total cultural system, it is likely to present evidence about the perishable parts of the systems that created it (Binford 1962). The logic of that assumption cannot be denied. The positive effect it has had on the higher quality of archaeological analyses is there for the whole discipline to see.

However, one point common to all archaeology, new and more traditional (despite internal theoretical differences on the relative muteness of artifacts), is that all investigators assume that the job of archaeology is to deal with the past and to extrapolate from the artifacts to the subsystems that created them. Almost every archaeologist is concerned with the subsystems (usually the subsistence system) as they are reflected in the patterns of artifacts. The general assumption is that some subsystem, or factors found in several subsystems, are responsible in a positive, causal sense for the artifacts we dig up. The subsystems created and patterned artifacts as we see the remains in the archaeological record. The artifacts are regarded as indices to the systems of primary subsistence and exchange, of social relations, and of

beliefs that brought them into existence. However, the artifacts and pieces of technology are, in some sense, determined in form and distribution by other systems including the social and ideological structures.

Have we as archaeologists, and especially those of us interested in aspects of prehistoric social organization, allowed ourselves to fall into the error of idealism? We assume that since other systems created the system of patterned artifacts, those systems become recoverable through the artifacts. The error is not in attempting to recover extinct systems. But there is something incorrect for professed materialists—all new archaeologists and many more traditional ones—to use as a primary assumption the supposition that other systems, which are theoretically derivative, determine the system of technology. It is a perversion of materialism to have as our primary concern the use of artifacts to show how they reflect other parts of an extinct or historic system. Instead, we might consider asking how the system of artifacts, the primary and undestroyed system of technology, caused or determined the other systems to take shape. What is there about the system of technology that either facilitated or determined parts of the social or belief systems?

We have understood for some time the relationship between tool use and the development of the brain in human, biological evolution. We have understood for an even longer time the relationship between the use of machines in factories and forms of economic and social organization. Industrial sociology has contributed considerable knowledge to our understanding the relationship between using large, powerful, repetitive machines and assembly lines and the psychic and social problems they produce. Many sociologists have shown how the determinitive powers of technological devices—from cars to buildings—are used to influence our behavior. More recently, we have begun to be aware of the impact of all forms of media on us. All of this is so much sophisticated technological determinism and materialism, and it has told us important and remarkable things, things the Greeks did not see and things we never saw before at all.

Although it is argued that archaeology should concern itself with the relationship between technology and the rest of culture, it should also be pointed out that there is a discipline already doing just that. Historians of technology have devoted themselves to understanding technology in the context of culture: the Society for the History of Technology has published *Technology and Culture* since 1960. Then is the job of understanding already done? Not exactly. Historians of technology have been concerned with several central themes: the relationship of technology to science, engineering, and art; the nature of invention; and "how things are done and made" (Daniels 1970). This latter phrase is what most essays on the history of technology are about. This group of historical scholars has done critical work and considers itself allied to historical archaeology, as can be seen in articles that appear in *Technology and Culture*. There is much to praise in the accomplishments of historians of technology but, for obvious reasons, I am more interested in the shortcomings.

Labeling themselves "antiquarians of technology" (Daniels 1970: 2), the historians of technology have discovered that they are rarely concerned with technology as a social phenomenon. They usually deal with complex machines of the sort produced by the more recent phases of the Industrial Revolution. They are, as historians, concerned with the particular, not with the comparative nor with the general. They are not cross-cultural nor, as historians, are they concerned with applying the goals of science to the study of technology. As a consequence, they have left most technology, including simple machines, outside their domain and thus have deprived themselves of the temporal laboratory in which change could be examined. As technological determinists, most historians of technology have considered technology in and of itself, divorced from social and ideological concerns. They deal with the skyscraper in terms of structural steel and the revolving door; they are not concerned with the effects that such buildings have on culture. The historians of technology are uninterested in generalizing and are quite restricted in time. Furthermore, they have little training in handling social and cultural variables: the causal relationship between technology and the rest of culture does not really interest them.

Considering the state of the history of technology and the unconscious state of archaeology, neither discipline is concerned with how technology affects culture and how technology is manipulated by culture. These two concerns would seem to be appropriate domains for archaeology. We have seen the way archaeology is tied to the present. Not only are all of its models derived from the present but, more to the point here, one of archaeology's major roles is a function of how it is used in the present. Should not archaeology then study how it is used, how its data (i.e., material culture) are used by the present, and how material culture, when used, affects the culture doing the using? Archaeology could profitably study both the manipulation of material culture (why and how we do what we do with technology) and the manipulating that technology does on the rest of culture.

Archaeology is a product of the present; it is used by the present. Of course, it has other, better recognized uses, too. We should then study how material culture works in the present. "In other words archaeology *already* has more to do with the present than the past (cf. Fontana 1968), so why not *also move on a scholarly level* to catch up with what has already happened to the function of the field and *study technology in the present as well*" [Schuyler, personal communication]. Archaeologists would automatically contribute several dimensions to the work of the historians of technology. We would add a comparative and, hence, a more formally scientific approach; we would vastly increase the temporal depth of the field and; most important, we would be studying technology within the matrix of culture.

If such welding of archaeology's potential and the activity of historians of technology is plausible, then an example of how it might be done is in order. The example is drawn from my own work with Mormons and Mormon technology in Arizona and utilizes Mormon town plans and fences. In this space it is only possible to illustrate some of the points an archaeological analysis of material culture might cover.

In 1847 the first 10,000 Mormon settlers reached the area of Great Salt Lake in the Great Basin. They entered an area that had been passed through and over by people going to California and Oregon. Utah was sampled and rejected: the few attempts to explore and settle it found it a semiarid waste supporting what were considered to be poverty-stricken Utes, Paiutes, Shoshones, and other Great Basin groups. The Mormons, as everyone knows, settled the Great Basin successfully—so successfully, in fact, that by the early 1870s the valleys of central Utah were overpopulated. It was then that areas of the Great Basin peripheral to Utah were purposefully colonized by the Mormons. One such area was the drainage of the middle and upper Little Colorado River in eastern and central Arizona. A southern, semiarid extension

of the Colorado Plateau, the Little Colorado offers a more severe version of the environmental zones into which Mormons brought and perfected a technology.

The Little Colorado River had not been occupied by an extensive population since long-term prehistoric settlement ended in the fourteenth century of the present era. Since then the only Indians were small groups of Western Apaches wandering in from their home area to the west of the Little Colorado and occasional Navajos and Hopis passing through from their home areas to the north. There were some dispersed Anglos and more dispersed Mexicans. Into this environment moved Mormon colonists. The Mormons understood the harshness of the environment and they understood how marginal it was for farming. Mormon settlement pattern, broadly conceived, is directly related to the success of Mormon culture in settling this semiarid region. The pieces of technology articulated the religious culture with the environment with which it had to cope. The settlement plan was the conscious product of religion. The plan for laying out a town, called the Plat of the City of Zion, was drawn up by the Prophet Joseph Smith and came to have a status not unlike revelation. The settlement pattern determined some of the relations Mormons had with each other. It is those relations that helped form the basis for Mormon adaptive success. They saw their problem as setting up the kind of social and religious systems that would allow them to extract a living from harsh circumstances. This was done through the use of several pieces of technology, and those to be illustrated are the devices used to parcel out space. The way in which Mormons set up villages, farm sites, and house plans is closely tied to what they knew their social and religious systems would accomplish.

Some of the reasons for living in villages come directly from the Church leadership:

> In all cases in making new settlements the Saints should be advised to gather together in villages, as has been our custom from the time of our earliest settlement in these mountain valleys. The advantages of this plan, instead of carelessly scattering out over a wide extent of country, are many and obvious to all who have a desire to serve the Lord. By this means the people can retain their ecclesiastical organizations, have regular meetings of the quorums of the priesthood and establish and maintain Sunday schools, Improvement Associations, and Relief Societies. They can also cooperate for the good of all in financial and secular matters, in making ditches (for irrigation), fencing fields, building bridges, and other necessary improvements. Further than this they are a mutual protection and strength against horse and cattle thieves, land jumpers, etc., and against hostile Indians, should there be any, while their compact organization gives them many advantages of social and civil character which might be lost, misapplied or fritted away by spreading out so thinly that intercommunication is difficult, dangerous, inconvenient, or expensive [Fox 1932:93].

This letter from the Church First Presidency to the Freemont Stake in Utah specifies village life as opposed to scattered homesteading. It also specifies the effects of living in a village cluster. All forms of cooperation are facilitated. Farming, irrigation, exchange of essential scarce goods, schooling, worship, government, and Mormon endogamy were all facilitated through the village plan. But there is the reverse, too, of which the Mormons were well-aware. If proximity meant cooperation, it also meant a means to insure homogeneous behavior. Proximity allowed the continual contact that all village members were to have with each other. Such a system allowed public and neighborly sanctions to operate with greatest effectiveness. Although there was a hierarchy and a system of ecclesiastical courts, neither of these was the chief instrument for keeping social order; proximity was.

Initially Mormons were to be completely communal, sharing all property and living in common quarters. That failed during the Prophet Joseph's lifetime and failed again on the frontiers of Utah when it was tried a second time in the 1870s and 1880s. By holding all property in common, wealth was to be equalized. All were to have an equal amount, according to need. Equality in all earthly things was the stated goal of the Prophet's plan. When, after the sharing of one-tenth of one's annual increase was substituted for complete sharing of property, some means had to be found to guarantee that the resources available were evenly distributed. In an agrarian community, this was largely a matter of parceling out land. When a town was surveyed and plots were laid out,

> Every family was to receive a building lot in the city. In addition the farmers were to receive an allotment of land outside the city. The mechanic was to receive the necessary tools and materials for his trade, the teachers, writers, musicians were to have a home site and a license or appointment to serve the community according to their respective abilities. The town residents, of course, would participate in the production of the farmers through regular commercial channels or through the redistribution of the storehouse [Spencer 1937:103].

Furthermore, farming plots as well as house lots in the village "were distributed in the following manner: by ballot, each lot having been numbered previous . . . each man's name (who was) applying for a lot formed a ticket, which tickets were thrown together in a hat and shaken up together, then drawn out one by one . . . the first name drawn took the first lot . . . " [Ricks 1964:60]. Drawing land parcels by lot (distribution therefore being based on chance) guaranteed equal access to all land. Since land was usually sectioned according to quality, a man would be allotted proportionate shares of good and less good land. All of these niceties of distribution could only be realized if the land itself were subdivided before parceling out in a way that predetermined equality. That guarantee was provided by the Plat of the City of Zion.

The Plat was originally conceived by the Prophet Joseph in 1833, but it underwent several modifications as the Mormons moved west. The modifications were mainly in the size of the city. The key determinative feature was the equal size of all plots in the city. Furthermore, there was to be only one house to a plot. ". . . . the city (was to) be laid out in ten-acre squares, each divided into eight lots, ten by twenty rods; that streets be eight rods wide, and that houses be built one to a lot in the middle, as a precaution against fire, and twenty feet back from the line, to leave ample space for the planting of flower gardens" [Fox 1932:41].

In addition to the equal size of all lots in a town, the Plat, which was a grid, guaranteed equal access to irrigation water. The canals flowed down the streets on the side. A grid made water dispersal efficient by packing farm land in the village close, and choosing lots by chance meant that water rights could not provide a basis for social inequality. Land and water, the two key sources of wealth for farmers in a

semidesert, were distributed in equal amounts based on chance. Chance, when applied to land and water, could guarantee equal distribution only because a preexisting grid with equal divisions and equal access to water had subdivided those resources in the first place. The grid with equal-size rectangles was a piece of technology that enabled the principle of equality to be realized in land and water distribution. This, together with distribution based on chance—a practice deduced from the ideological notion of equality—made economic equality a reality. There is nothing inherent in a grid except its equal subdivisions that links it to equality in land access. But that trait, combined with the ideological goal of equality and the social device of drawing by lot for rights to land, did promote equality.

It was obvious to the leaders of the Mormon population, as to most other nineteenth-century utopian planners, that the way the physical environment was managed had direct effects on behavior. They believed that there were direct, causative effects. We, I think, are ready to accept the fact that at least there were enabling (or facilitating) effects. With a systematic view of mutual cause, it makes sense that a basic relationship should exist between technology and all subsystems. In the Mormon case, the strongest illustration of this relationship exists in the designs Joseph Smith did not choose for his people's city. He had several alternatives open to him in terms of the traditional ways frontier towns were designed (Reps 1969). In view of his decision to put his people in a town, as opposed to scattering them over the countryside in homesteads, the town could simply have been allowed to grow around some central intersection of one or two planned streets, the pattern closest to the early New England heritage Joseph Smith knew. Boston and the other cities of New England had only a planned main street or two and the city or town defined itself from these streets. That may have been the most natural and the easiest way to set up a new settlement. Main-street towns were a common frontier alternative: one long, central axis along which the principal buildings were erected with homes and secondary buildings scattered in a planless way behind this facade. This sort of town was located along a regional trade artery or crossroads. The utopian planners, on the other hand, offered several types of town plans. The star or circle plan focused on a central place and radiated all streets and lots out from that point. This graduates land in two ways. Lots are inherently unequal in size and are graduated more precisely from the central point. The star or circle could be transformed into a grid with ranked sets of concentric blocks spreading out from the center. Such blocks were of unequal size, and distance from the center was especially emphasized. This type of grid could vary street width and block size, thereby segregating neighbors and neighborhoods from each other. Grids may well be the logical way to set up instant towns on any frontier, but their properties vary widely and can be geared to accomplishing varied social purposes. The grid of Manhattan was geared maximally for land speculation (Reps 1969: 194–203). Long, narrow blocks, in contrast to a grid of equal-sized squares, hold more houses, waste less central space, force houses close to each other, and allow less freedom expressed in terms of unbuilt land.

Joseph Smith did not choose a grid with equal-sized squares by chance. The fact that he understood the physical properties of a technological device for subdividing space, as did all other utopian planners, is indisputable. Indisputable, too, is the fact that the piece of technology he chose facilitated and helped to realize the social and religious goals he was after. There is a nonarbitrary connection between equal-sized pieces of space available to farmers and egalitarianism. A lot of things have to be held equal for this to be true—such as quality of land—but one would never think the reverse to be true: that unequal distribution of land of equal quality would produce economic equality.

The Prophet Joseph built another guarantee of equality into the Plat of the City of Zion. The city was made up of large square blocks with wide streets between. Each block was subdivided into equal-size, rectangular house lots. To create the subdivision, an axis was drawn down the middle of the block. At right angles to this property line were drawn four or five other lines that divided up the block into smaller, equal rectangles. A house was to be centered in each rectangle facing the street. With such a setup, houses would be back-to-back facing in opposite directions. No houses would face out to the streets on two sides of the block. If every block were divided the same way, half the streets in the town would automatically be side streets, devoid of houses and inferior to the others. Furthermore, if every block were divided the same way, the front of every house would look into the front of every other house, optimizing visual contact but minimizing privacy. To correct both of these flaws, Joseph Smith alternated the central axis on every other block in the city. This reversed the direction of house lots in every other block.[1] It meant that every street had people facing it in equal numbers. It also meant that nobody looked into anybody else's front yard. It made all streets equal and simultaneously heightened the level of privacy.

Mormon settlers paid close attention to the allotment of land in a uniform way in a community. They paid equally close (but less conscious) attention to the layout of the house lot in a town. Mormons built an identifiable type of house all over the Great Basin and set up the large space around the house in a characteristic way. In addition to the house, the most noticeable artifact was the fence. There are a set of distinctive pieces of technology that set off a Mormon town from all others in the desert West. In addition to its grid settlement pattern are its broad streets lined with trees giving the town the appearance of an oasis, its two-story gabled brick and wood houses, its hay lifts or cranes pointing heavenward like so many mechanical steeples, and its fences. There are several types of fences. By far, the most common fences in a town are standard, average, picket fences. Outside the town in the fields, barbed wire strung between posts was typical. But there are remnants of fences made by fitting broken tree and shrub limbs against each other; these are called rip-rap fences. Wire and branches were not used in the town, however; there, picket fences predominated. Between the town and the fields, rows of lombardy poplars were planted. These stand like walls between the residential and farming areas and are one of the characteristic traits of all Great Basin Mormon towns. They, too, are a kind of fence.

Mormons built fences throughout the nineteenth century and, today, they continue to build fences, walls, partitions, and other separators. Historians have suggested that this is a carryover of the New England heritage Mormons brought with them across the Great Plains. That is probably true but does not tell us why, under such stressful conditions, Mormons continued and still continue to put up fences. They left other things behind, like the New England settlement pat-

tern, so why should they drag fences 2000 miles out of one environment into a completely different one? And, even more curiously, why should they continue to build them today?

Like any artifact, especially one for which we have the historic context, we can make fences tell us about the rest of the culture—in this case Mormon culture. As will become clear, that is not a dull business. But in addition to being the passive product of Mormon culture, fences are also a causative agent. When dealing with an object (a piece of technology) one needs to know what the forces are that bring it into being what causes it to be, what the object causes in its own right. I would like to make that analytical distinction to get at the difference between reconstructing a historical context—the usual business of prehistoric and historic archaeology—and doing an analysis of the determinative characteristics of technology. The second half of the distinction asks what using fences does to Mormon culture, as opposed to asking what can we learn about Mormon culture from their fences. The latter question is not significant, because you can learn more about almost any aspect of Mormon culture by sitting down in a library and reading about it . But no library has the answer to the question: What did Mormon fences enable Mormons to do? Even the Mormons do not have the whole answer.

Every house (indeed every building in a Mormon town, and every Mormon house in a Gentile town) had a fence around it. They still do. In the nineteenth century, picket fences were used. Picket fences were used around gardens and lawns and continue to be used in those contexts now throughout the Little Colorado River area. Wire and brush were used in the pastures outside the towns. Larger fields were surrounded not by fences but by hedgerows and rows of trees, including poplars. There was, in other words, a nonrandom pattern of fence use. The kind of fence used was decided by what was kept in or, as the case will show, what was kept out.

While the Little Colorado region as a whole contains a fair range of environmental variation in terms of flora and fauna, no one site contains such a range. The zones are very spread out and cannot be encompassed by any one farm, let alone something the size of a Mormon farm. Nonetheless, the Mormon settler operating under the ideal of self-sufficiency attempted to control a whole set of ranges of plants and animals in his allotted area. He had to keep horses and dairy cattle, and sheep and goats; he had to keep a supply of poultry for eggs and meat, an extensive kitchen garden, and an orchard. That is not very different from the standard American farmer, except that it had to be done on a single piece of land, in a town, and in an area that was a semidesert. The Mormon farmer had to reproduce in one fair-sized plot the varied environments that guaranteed the success of all the diverse living things he needed for survival. But he had a plot where not one of them lived naturally. He not only had to reproduce in his farm yard the niches available to him in the Great Basin, he had to create niches that did not exist for a thousand miles around. Once that was done, he then had to keep the competition between occupants of different niches apart. Browsers had to be kept out of the orchards and gardens, sheep and goats separate from horses and cattle, and natural predators from everything domesticated.

Fences created the boundaries between all the niches. In addition to the scarcity of water, which fences did not alleviate, one of the critical environmental hazards to plant life in central and northern Arizona is windblown soil particles. In this area very strong winds blow day and night from

---

[1] I am grateful to Hanno Weber for pointing out the implications of this innovation.

January to May. That is bad enough, but when, starting in the late 1880s, overgrazing removed the ground cover, the wind lifted the soil and sand grains and carried them away in large quantities. Because the particles picked up are naturally smaller than those that are larger and heavier, they fell between the larger soil particles when they were redeposited on the ground. The fine wind-borne sand seals the ground where it falls, with the result that air and water cannot penetrate down to plant roots, and seeds cannot break the seal to reach the surface. The amount of sand deposited in a five to six month season of wind storms would be enough to lower the capacity of a field. Picket fences, hedgerows, and rows of trees serve as windbreaks to protect the crops from the destructive capacity of the wind itself and to filter out the sand before it lands on cultivated areas. Picket fences, hedgerows, and rows of trees function the way snow fences do along highways. A solid wall of fencing could not withstand the velocity of the wind, yet enough of the force is broken by closely placed slats to protect whatever is on the other side, in addition to filtering out the wind-borne material. Hence, there are picket fences around crop-growing areas, along with hedgerows and tree lines. These were used as opposed to wire fences and tree limbs, which were cheaper and protected areas used for domestic animals.

Fences are an ecological necessity for any agrarian regime in the plateau country of Arizona. They separate competitive niches from each other and protect all artificially created niches from the universally destructive wind. The ecological functions of fences could be further specified, considering this region, but I think their primary role as a piece of enabling technology is established.

The determinative or causal aspects of technology are not limited to the subsistence system. We should assume that it is possible to show how aspects of social and ideological organization are influenced by technology, that is, how technology operates to shape these aspects. Here, too, Mormon fences serve quite well. Although streets and irrigation ditches separated blocks in a town from each other, fences provided the visible distinction between individual property holdings. They did this within a town and in the fields and ranges surrounding the town. The essential insight into the social functions of a fence is the tired but accurate line from Robert Frost: good fences make good neighbors. In a town where the social structure was based on equal property and close cooperation, and where order was maintained through everybody knowing everybody else's business, fences drew the literal line between closeness and privacy. Land was subdivided and allotted to guarantee equality, but town life among people who were supposed to be economic equals still had to solve the problem of privacy. The Mormons put people more closely together than any other Anglo group in the West but separated them by using fences. Just as the barnyard containing the many competitors necessary for life could only exist using fencing, so the propinquity of town life could only work by providing a degree of distance within the essential closeness. The neighborliness that expressed itself in watchfulness had a natural limit set to it. The spatial closeness that enabled cooperation and survival also needed fences, hedgerows, and trees to prevent the other kind of closeness that destroyed privacy and caused friction.

Fences, like house decorations, also were used to express status and, later, wealth differences. This seems to be a less important function. But the number of gates in a fence, like the number of doors in a house, indicated the number of wives in a man's household and hence his status. The Church maintained elaborate rules about the equivalent treatment due to a man's plural wives. If they were not given separate houses, they were to have separate and equal apartments in the same house. Separate meant, among other things, separate gates in the fencing. These have served as examples of how technological items served to accomplish some social tasks. Since the technological items also helped to shape parts of Mormon ideology, the following view of Mormon beliefs is appropriately considered.

The religious reasoning was as follows: God's elect, in these latter days, exist because they please God. The Lord suffers them to exist because they continue to please him. In all millennial movements the imminent Second Coming of Christ meant that a group, for whom he was explicitly to come, was to prepare the way for that coming. The preparation of that way was in the hands of those specially chosen by God for the task. The task was enormously difficult because it was two-sided. The earth had to be changed and prepared for its redemption by God's more recent elect. But the very process of preparation was a demonstration by his elect that they themselves were worthy of the Second Coming. For Mormons, the kingdom that was to be the theater for the Second Coming was founded in the 1820s when God directed his latter-day prophet—Joseph—to set up a church that was to be the major instrument insuring the apt preparing of the earth for Christ's early reappearance.

The process of redeeming the earth was carried out by an agrarian people and, as a result, or perhaps by design, actually involved making the earth bloom. When the Mormons reached the desert West, the redemption of the earth was to involve making the desert bloom like a rose. Just as the desert of the original Zion was made green under the ministration of God's elect, so the new Zion, also in a desert, was to be subject to an identical process. The original beauty of God's creation and the Garden of Eden was to be reestablished. A semblance of the divine was to be called back into existence. While the language was metaphorical, the redemption process involved the substantial reification of the metaphors. The land of the saints really was going to bloom and, by God, it did. And it bloomed because they used fences.

Picket fences, barbed-wire fences, hedgerows, lines of brush, and lines of trees were all fences. The saints also used other equipment to make agriculture in the desert work and some of it was even more important, such as irrigation. But without the repertory of fences and the way they were used, settlement would not have worked. The act of fence building was and remains part of the necessary landscaping of a house and farm; in fact, both living informants and statements from nineteenth-century journals say that a fence is an inherent part of the house itself. A building is not complete until it has a fence around it, holding it down. But the act of fence-building itself is not what was most crucial. What was crucial is what fence building allows a Mormon to accomplish. Building fences allows Mormons to do things. The ecological and subsistence accomplishments dependent on fences are clear; so are the social benefits. However, when a Mormon raises a garden or a lawn behind a fence, he has shown that he has subdued a piece of the earth and made a bit of the desert bloom. He has helped redeem the earth. Growing a garden or a lawn is a challenge that he has met. He has made something more beautiful, more orderly, and more refreshing; something neater, cleaner, and more desirable. He has created a semblance of the divine. By managing, manipulating, and grooming the earth, he has imitated God and proven that he is worthy: he is a saint. A Mormon who creates something green has shown his inner state. In this context, fences are valuable because of what they preserve behind them. What they preserve in addition to a subsistence base is a man's right to a place in the Kingdom of God. One local Mormon summed it up: "The state of a man's yard is the state of his religion." In this way, the enabling role of a system of technology operating within the sphere of religion is somewhat clearer. In a complementary way, it is also possible to see how something like fences, which have no obvious iconographic value, become religious artifacts.

Mormon fences, insofar as they are artifacts arranged in regular, predictable patterns surrounding the living spaces of the people, have a final dynamic and, if you will, determinative role. The whole living space of agrarian Mormons and of Mormons today in towns throughout the Great Basin is parceled out by fences. The Mormon's physical world is divided or compartmentalized by interior walled spaces, yards full of fences, and gridded towns with gridded fields. This is the cultural environment the Mormon was and is born into and raised in. He knows it all his life and it is reasonable to assume it has an effect on him: a cognitive effect. Such an environment is the product of ecological constraints but also is an explicit statement of some part of the religious system we have seen above. This environment is a result of the way Mormons have had to think about their world and of what the Mormon idea-system was and has become. If fences are a piece of enabling (even determinative) technology, then it is reasonable to suppose that the technology enables them to think in certain ways, as well as to grow crops in certain ways. As a result, this system of technology should have cognitive consequences. It ought to affect the way we think. The question is no sooner asked than answered, at least tentatively. One of the standard observations made about Mormons is that they see no contradictions between the literalism of their doctrine and a scientific world view. That Mormons have established a huge educational network and have produced many excellent scholars while supporting belief in a literal reading of the Bible, a belief in continual revelation and an imminent Second Coming, has puzzled more than one observer. That the problem of blacks is not a social or civil problem for them but a religious one only, illustrates the distinctions current Mormons make between levels of reality. And that most outside witnesses see contradictions where Mormons see harmony hardly needs to be emphasized. How then, at a general level, can one have literal religion and rather full participation in modern science? This puts the problem of compartmentalization in current context, but it was just as much a problem in the nineteenth century.

Mormons have lived by the Little Colorado for a century. They are still building fences. The materials are different now: cinderblocks, chain link fences with and without aluminum slats woven into them, and prefabricated wooden fences that are almost walls. Their yards are still subdivided very finely by using smaller, lower fences; plants; flowers; trees; vines; stones; and even prehistoric artifacts. The farmyards are now flower gardens. The manifest subsistence explanation for the fences has disappeared. It is still necessary to keep out the wind and wind-blown sand in order for anything to grow. And it is still crucial to demarcate the visibly redeemed land of the Saints from the rest. Furthermore, especially in towns where Mormons are not in a majority, Mormons draw a clear line between themselves and the others. If we look at the changes in fence use among Mormons in this one place in Arizona over 100 years, we see that the materials with which fences are constructed have completely changed, and we find that the barnyard ecology that required intricate fencing has completely disappeared and does not survive in the many present subdivisions of gardens. We also find a more immediate need to separate their pieces of Zion from the Gentile world and this sometimes requires walls instead of fences. Despite these changes in the material and distribution of these artifacts, we can see what no prehistorian could know and what no historian of technology would ask about: despite overwhelming changes in Mormon culture, there is an unchanged relationship between a key set of artifacts and a set of religious symbols. Fences still keep the same things in and keep the same things out. They keep out very literal things like wind and sand. They also keep out and keep separate less literal but no less powerful things like the Gentile world and internal categories that do not mix. Consequently, now, as in the nineteenth century, fences do the same things for Mormons, and Mormons do the same things with fences. The fences enable them to redeem the earth and manipulate and act out the categories used to deal with the world. Despite changes in form, there have been few changes in function.

Fences and their use, the way Mormons divide up the space that immediately surrounds them, are the concrete representations of the Mormons' many separate categories. Fences—and the compartments they create—reify and reinforce the noncomparable divisions Mormons (and Mormonism) use to understand the world. In this way, Mormons live in their categories. It is not just that Mormons and their religion created settlements and spatial subdivisions and made life work; Mormonism could not exist without the spatial representations and technological devices that allowed its population to exist. Here we see that mental processes are as much a product of the use of tools, as the way that the tools are used is a product of mental rules. And, as a result, we also see the incomplete understanding we have of the role of technology and an area that archaeologists may choose to give some thought to as well.

All of these data on Mormon town plans and fences demonstrate how thoroughly technology is embedded in the subsistence, social, and ideological systems of culture. Since this chapter has dealt with Mormon cultural subsystems (and the influence of technology on them), the shifting locus of cause can be more clearly seen. We can, for one thing, be sure that technology really did and does cause Mormons to do some things, and we can be just as sure that Mormons manipulated technology to accomplish some ideological principles. Cause works both ways, and by considering plural contexts we can assign it a locus, albeit a shifting one.

By taking technological determinism seriously, we can see the effect of artifacts on culture. We do more than "read" Mormon culture from their use of fences, which is what even the most sophisticated prehistoric archaeologists do in principle. Instead, we can begin to straighten out the determinative characteristics of technology.

Nothing has been said here about town plans and fences that is necessarily true outside of Mormonism. A comparative, generalizing study has not been done. Such an approach is clearly within the scope of this type of archaeology, although it is not within the scope of this chapter. There is a good literature within architecture (Reps 1969; Evans 1971a, 1971b) on the function of town plans, walls, and fences. There is also a superb literature on the technology used to divide space by other utopian groups in the nineteenth century. The work ranges very widely from analyses of

Jeremy Bentham's panopticon (Evans 1971a) to the panopticon's American derivative, the domestic octagon (Creese 1946) to the relationship between the American Shakers, famed for their furniture, and their precept: "Hands to work and hearts to God" (Andrews and Andrews 1966). Further, as archaeologists we already have a supporting competence in settlement pattern studies. That, with the concerns outlined in this chapter, constitutes a new problem with new ideas. Will we choose it?

ACKNOWLEDGEMENTS

The comments and suggestions of friends and colleagues have been very helpful in developing the ideas in this chapter. I thank Steve Barnett, David Crabb, Vincent Crapanzano, Hildred Geertz, Gilbert Kushner, Mary Miller, Peter Nowicki, Sherry Ortner, Peter Seitel, Martin Silverman, and Hanno Weber. I am particularly indebted to Robert Schuyler for clarifying several points regarding historic archaeology and its relationship to the rest of the field. Conversations with Richard Swiderski clarified many of the arguments on technology and behavior, and editing by Jeanette Mirsky has made the chapter significantly better.

REFERENCES

ADAMS, ROBERT MCCORMICK
1966 *The Evolution of Urban Society*. Aldine Publishing Company, Chicago.
ANDREWS, E. D. and F. ANDREWS
1966 *Religion in Wood: A Book of Shaker Furniture*. Indiana University Press, Bloomington.
BINFORD, LEWIS R.
1962 Archaeology as Anthropology. *American Antiquity* 28:217–225.
1968 Post-Pleistocene Adaptations. In *New Perspectives in Archeology*, Sally R. Binford and Lewis R. Binford, editors. Aldine Publishing Company, Chicago.
BINFORD, SALLY R. and LEWIS R. BINFORD
1968 *New Perspectives in Archeology*. Aldilne Publishing Company, Chicago.

COTTER, JOHN L.
1970 Colonial Williamsburg. *Technology and Culture* 11:3:417–427.
CREESE, WALTER
1946 Fowler and the Domestic Octagon. *The Art Bulletin* 28:2:89–102.
DANIELS, GEORGE H.
1970 The Big Questions in the History of Technology. *Technology and Culture* 11:1:1–21.
EVANS, ROBIN
1971a Bentham's Panopticon. An Incident in the Social History of Architecture. *Architectural Association Quarterly* April–June:21–37.
1971b The Rights of Retreat and the Rights of Exclusion: Notes Toward the Definition of Wall. *Architectural Design* 41:335–339.
FLANNERY, KENT V.
1965 The Ecology of Early Food Production in Mesopotamia. *Science* 147:1247–1256.
FONTANA, BERNARD L.
1968 A Reply to "Some Thoughts on Theory and Method in Historical Archaeology." *In* Historical Archaeology Forum-1968, Stanley South, editor. Box 1881, Raleigh, North Carolina.
FOX, FERAMORZ YOUNG
1932 *The Mormon Land System; a study of the settlement and utilization of land under the direction of the Mormon Church*. Ph.D. dissertation, Northwestern University, Evanston.
MURRA, JOHN V.
1968 An Aymara Kingdom in 1567. *Ethnohistory* 15:2:115–151.
REPS, JOHN W.
1969 *Town Planning in Frontier America*. Princeton University Press, Princeton.
RICKS, JOEL E.
1964 *Forms and Methods of Early Mormon Settlement in Utah and the Surrounding Region, 1847–1877*. Utah State University Press, Logan.
SCHUYLER, ROBERT L.
1970 Historical and Historic Sites Archaeology as Anthropology: Basic Definitions and Relationships. *Historical Archaeology* 4:83–89.
SPENCER, JOSEPH EARLE
1937 *The Middle Virgin River Valley, Utah: A Study in Culture Growth and Change*. Ph.D. dissertation, University of California, Berkeley.
TAYLOR, WALTER W.
1948 A Study of Archaeology. *Memoir No. 69. American Anthropologist*, Vol. 50, No. 3, Part 2. American Anthropological Assocation, Washington, D.C.

part 4

Theoretical Positions

INTRODUCTION

A comparison of the first and third sections of this volume shows that questions of semantics and disciplinary affiliations are not superficial. How a field is academically classified and socially organized will determine all of its facets from field operations to ultimate goals. Historical Archaeology in America would be a very different affair if most archaeologists in this country were art experts or historians rather than anthropologists.

In this section the theoretical disputes that underlie the labels of Part 1 and the substantive results of Part 3 are reviewed in seven well known selections. These papers represent the two sides—"historicalist" and anthropological—of a continuing debate. This division, however, is not complete. The positions advanced are frequently confused and oddly jumbled from author to author. In part this is because the questions under discussion are complex and are not limited to Historical Archaeology or even the broader fields of history and anthropology. Much of the confusion, nevertheless, is unique to this setting and arises from two sources.

The "historicalist" position is not representative of history as a discipline but rather derives more from the background of certain archaeologists. Some of the "historicalists", including Hume and Walker, are British archaeologists trained in a more humanistic and eclectic tradition, while others, such as Dollar, have been strongly influenced by the restoration-preservation theme and the extremely narrow view of history found in the National Park Service and other government agencies. On the anthropological side another factor is at work. Commencing in the early 1960's anthropological archaeology in America was altered, perhaps even transformed, by a paradigm revolution, the rise of the "new" or processual archaeology. Considering these two elements—the informal link of the "historicalists" to history and the internal strains among anthropological archaeologists—the reader should not be surprised by a debate that shifts alliances and positions from paragraph to paragraph.

When all the vituperativeness and rock (chipped?) throwing is eliminated the debate crystallizes around a few basic questions.

1. What are the primary divisions of scholarship?

Reality may be approached along several routes but many of these, especially mystical paths, are not based on empiricism and so are excluded from modern research. To a degree contemporary scholarship is structured into the triad of humanistic, scientific, and historical disciplines. The humanities are concerned with an emotional understanding and appreciation of reality, particularly human reality. In contrast history and science seek a non-emotional, impartial understanding. Of course these divisions are not absolute. All scientists, for example, are the product of their own historic period and culture. The differing orientations, at the same time, are real and meaningful.

Intrusion of this question into the "historicalist"-anthropological debate occurs in a somewhat anachronistic fashion because of the European background of some historical archaeologists. When Sir Mortimer Wheeler, the former doyen of British prehistorians, urges excavators to search for people rather than things he is not espousing cultural anthropology. Until quite recently much of English archaeology was field methodology with a humanistic coating. Thus when Hume places archaeology "with the arts" this decision is predicated on a misunderstanding of science, which Walker shares, and a humanistic perspective unacceptable to most social scientists and indeed many historians.

2. What is the relationship between history and science?

Binford's discussion is a good summation of this eternal debate. Some would dismiss the questions, as Walker does at certain points, but most philosophers of science and history agree that although both types of scholarship are empirically based (one is not subjective, the other objective), they are different in emphasis. The similarities and dissimilarities are real but not dichotomous. This relationship is not necessarily founded on the use or non-use of "empathic understanding" as that approach is characteristic of only some schools of historiography, particularly the works of Collingwood and Croce quoted by Walker. It is also not the "uniqueness thesis". The historian, unless he is in reality a social scientist as a few scholars in economic and social history are, is concerned with a particular, but not unique, topic as an end in itself. In contrast, the scientist is concerned with specific cases only as a step for creating broad generalizations or as a testing ground for hypotheses and hypothetical laws. By definition history is idiographic and science nomothetic. The historian may in a secondary fashion use generalizations, including covering laws, to create a better image and understanding of the past but he does not generate laws. The scientist may spend much of his time doing "history"; in fact, most ethnographies and site reports are histories, but it is not his primary purpose. The significant difference is not the degree of objectivity or the nature of the data (be they contemporary with the observer or removed by time or space), but orientation and end goals. The end products of historical research and scientific research are different and scholars in these two variants of knowledge will, or should, approach the same data from very different perspectives. Whether history or anthropology is the parent discipline for Historical Archaeology will most certainly have far reaching effects.

3. Is archaeology a technique or a discipline?

Ironically this question finds proponents at the extremes of the general debates holding similar views. Both Hume and Binford view archaeology as a set of techniques. Cleland and Fitting, on the other hand, more correctly realize that techniques do not exist in an intellectual vacuum and that all archaeologists must, at least implicitly, be something else—anthropologist, historian, art expert (humanist), or geologist. Perhaps Binford's point is that traditional prehistoric archaeology was not explicit concerning its theoretical foundations, which is true, but Hume's dispute with Webster is the more crucial issue. The two definitions are

> Webster—"the scientific study of material remains of past human life and activity"

> Hume—"the study of the material remains . . . in relationship to documentary history and the stratigraphy of the ground in which they are found."

Many archaeologists would disagree with Hume and find Webster's dictionary definition more current and anthropological. Material culture is the common denominator of all archaeologies. If the materials are above or below ground or even if, as with ethnoarchaeology, they are still "alive" is not the essential point. Archaeology is a subfield of anthropology not geology and the manner in which artifacts and garbage end up in the ground is of secondary importance. An attempt, as seen recently in "Behavioral Archaeology", to view archaeology as the study of the interaction of natural and cultural processes that create archaeological deposits and sites is a serious confusion of method and theory.

Since the disciplinary outcome of the "historicalist"-anthropological debate is already evident (and it must be kept in mind that some of these authors no longer subscribe to opinions expressed over a decade ago), a final question is what will be the impact of anthropology on the future development of Historical Archaeology. One stimulus is on the technical level. The methodology of Historical Archaeology is evolving away from the impressionistic, expertise-atmosphere of an earlier generation. More defined and quantified approaches are being introduced. Dollar's position in his 1967 paper is now invalid. South's "Mean Ceramic Formula" and related techniques demonstrate that historic assemblages are approachable with tools that are not qualitatively different from those used in other scientific endeavors. Another anthropological influence is seen in the expansion of research to include the reconstruction of past lifeways as well as culture history. Yet it must also be admitted that processual studies, the hallmark of science, exist in Historical Archaeology only on the polemic and not the operational level.

CHAPTER 24

The Why, What, and Who of Historical Archaeology

IVOR NOEL HUME

The sound of the bulldozer is loud in the land, and from Florida to Hawaii hardly a day passes without the earth's being torn and scarred by the jaws and wheels of progress. The carpet of the past is being rolled up behind us as we advance into the future, and before long when we look over our shoulders we shall see nothing but the mirror of ourselves. Thousands of miles of blacktopped roads and never-ending chains of cinder-block houses will stretch to the horizon with hardly a change of style or so much as a tree to break the monotony. One high-rise apartment building, one supermarket, one gas station will look exactly like another, and it will make little difference whether we are living in Smalltown, Minnesota, Virginia, or Oregon. Only the great cities will be different; they will rise above the rooftops as once the forests thrust upward amid the farmlands.

It has been estimated that in the next century the American population will increase by 800 million and that the East Coast will have become a vast concrete jungle stretching from Maine to Virginia. If you live in that section of the country you are probably already aware that the prophecy is quickly coming to pass. A few faltering steps have been taken to increase the number of state and national parks, but many of the proposals become bogged down in the mud of committees and many more are not voiced until it is too late to implement them. It is true that one of the "in" words of the 1960's has been "conservation," but largely in the context of natural resources and beautification. The conservation of the American past has received little attention.

One of the first questions we must ask ourselves is: "What is the American past, and is it worth bothering to conserve?"

The distinguished archaeologist Jaquetta Hawkes has written that archaeology gives a people a "sense of having roots," and this is indisputably true. It is why in Europe thousands of people from every walk of life spend their vacations working on their countries' archaeological sites. They do it in the United States too, from the White House downward, and the shades of countless Indians must scratch their heads in wonder as they watch their trash and bones being treated with a respect that their living descendants are denied. Expeditions are sponsored by universities, sites are protected by federal and state agencies, and across the land societies of amateur archaeologists devote themselves to the study of the American Indian. But do these worthy efforts contribute to our sense of having roots? I think not, for these are roots of a quite different tree, one that was cut down to make way for European seeds. The past that belongs to the vast majority of the American people began in the Spanish, French, and English settlements in the New World; this is where the history books commence, for these were the seeds out of which the culture of the United States has grown. It is the preservation and study of the relics of these beginnings that provide a "sense of having roots."

There is an even more important consideration, and it stems from the fact that there comes a time in the life of every nation when it can no longer put all its pride and enthusiasm into being young. It must then switch its approach to its people, and to the world at large, saying that it merits a place at the head of the table because of its wisdom born of long experience. It is not too long a step from there to a reliance on the deference due advanced age. Much is then made of tradition, pageantry, times remembered—in a word, history. This may not cut much ice among the world's new giants, the young, virile nations intent on taking our place, but it may be all that we have left. This generation's success, or lack of it, in the field of preservation and archaeology may have a very real influence on how this nation thinks of itself in the centuries ahead.

It can be argued, and frequently is, that the remains of America's colonial and Federal past are too recent to be worth studying. Antiquities, after all, must be ancient. It is one thing for the English to dig up their Roman remains, but quite another for Americans to give serious study to the relics of the English colonists of the seventeenth and eighteenth centuries. This is sheer nonsense, for three reasons: first, the past is worth studying as soon as it becomes in danger of being lost; second, the pasts of Roman Britain and colonial America are being destroyed at much the same rate; third, the relics of colonial America are to the United States what Roman remains are to Britain. Let us look at these reasons in more detail.

It is generally agreed that knowledge, any knowledge, is worth preserving. For centuries, astronomers studied the planets without expecting that there would be any immediate practical application for their deductions. Now, however, there is such a use. I believe we may equally contend that the study of the past can be just as worthwhile. It is true that the more remote the period the more aesthetically stimulating it becomes, and it would be fine if the remains of early America could be allowed to mature in the ground until they acquire the venerable patina of great antiquity. But the truth is that they cannot. They are being torn out by urban development, highway construction, reservoir building, reforestation, and by farming and natural erosion. It is a case of now or never. It is imperative that we realize that the techniques of archaeology can be usefully applied to any period, no matter how recent, if by digging something up we can learn more than is to be found in written records.

In this age of endless paperwork, it is often assumed that everything we do is fully documented and that we shall be remembered until Armageddon. It comes as something of a shock to discover that even if that day should occur in our lifetime, much of what we did and wrote in our youth will already have been forgotten. As we look back into the nineteenth century, visibility becomes increasingly poor. We see only the shadows of countless people who lived and died without their names surviving so much as a hundred years. Homes were built and destroyed, and so were the documents that identified the owners and their property. Fires, floods, the Civil War, neglect, and the unthinking and deliberate destruction of records have consigned thousands, even millions of Americans to oblivion. This becomes increasingly true as we go back into the colonial centuries.

Although the written word may not have endured, the material remains of the past often have survived. They are there, waiting to fill in the missing pages of history—provided that we can get to them in time.

My parallel between Roman Britain and colonial America is intended simply to give the latter the dignity that it is all too often denied. Yet there is more substance to it than a mere bracketing of labels; there is a close relationship between the benefits bestowed on Britain by the Roman conquest and those inherited by the United States from the era of English colonization. The major difference, of course, is that the Romans integrated the native population into the system and the English colonists were more interested in pushing the Indians out than in bringing them in. The Romans brought to Britain a mature civilization, a code of laws, a system of currency, a new language, new architecture, new styles of dress, new technology, new art, new methods of waging war, new pastimes, and new gods. All these the English brought to America, and most of them flourished and evolved into the way of life we enjoy today. These roots are therefore just as valuable to America as the remains of Roman frontier walls, fortresses, and villas are to the British.

I am not for a moment suggesting that there is a lack of popular enthusiasm for the memory of the American past or for the preservation of extant buildings. The millions of people who stream each year through restored Williamsburg and visit Mount Vernon, Monticello, Jamestown, Plimouth, Georgetown, and restored or reconstructed forts from St. Augustine to Michilimackinac, to mention but a handful, leave no doubt that the public is excited by a physical contact with history. However, it is a very limited interest, at least it has been until recently, the limitations being those that have long guided the popular press—a predilection for amazement at the first this or the largest that. It might be termed the Barnum and Bailey syndrome; to it should be added the "shrine" complex, which springs fully matured from a nationwide interest in kinship and the need to laud national heroes. These traits are thoroughly praiseworthy; without them many of the finest achievements in restoration and preservation would never have been started. But also because of them thousands of other buildings and sites have been neglected, mutilated, or lost. Because they did not belong to a national figure or were not the first or greatest of their kind, the preservation and historical organizations have been loath to take these ducklings to their ample bosoms.

The great majority of the historical sites that have been archaeologically explored in any depth have received attention not for the purpose of studying the past through its artifacts but as a prelude for restoration or reconstruction into a shrine, an exhibit, a tourist attraction. But, just as in Europe, the majority of excavated sites are not left open indefinitely or reconstructed into some semblance of what they were, so the time has come to think of American historical sites as being worthy of excavation simply to obtain information.

Unfortunately, thinking is not enough; agreement in principle must be transformed into dollars, money that may yield no dividends beyond a broadening of our knowledge of the American past. Of more immediate concern, however, is the problem of finding qualified people to undertake historical archaeology once we have agreed that it is worth the effort. But as a preamble to solving that problem, one must first ask the question: What is archaeology?

If we accept the Webster definition, archaeology is "the scientific study of the material remains of past human life and activity" and cites as examples "fossil relics, monuments, etc." It is not, I think, a very happy interpretation of the word. Quite apart from the fact that fossils are the province of geology rather than archaeology, the definition refers only to the study of the remains, a pursuit that could be applicable to anyone from a museum curator to a connoisseur of nineteenth-century chamberpots. The revered *Oxford English Dictionary* serves us no better; it too stresses the study of objects and points out that the word comes from the Greek ʼαρχαιολογία, meaning the study of ancient eras and their material relics, particularly those of prehistory. But as time changes, so do the meanings of words. It is, I believe, high time that the definition of archaeology be brought up to date, and if I may be permitted to aid the lexicographers, I would suggest that archaeology be described as the study of the material remains of both the remote and recent past in relationship to documentary history and the stratigraphy of the ground in which they are found.

This relationship between the layers of the soil and the objects they contain enables the archaeologist to extract from his site the all-important information of what happened, when, and (it is hoped) to whom. Thus, to extract this information the archaeologist must be competent to do two things: he must be able to take the ground apart in such a way that its secrets can be wrested from it, and he must be sufficiently versed in the history and objects of the appropriate period or culture to properly interpret the site he is destroying. I say "destroying," because archaeology is inherently destructive. Once something is dug up, it can never be put back exactly as it was. It is therefore our duty, even our sacred trust, to be sufficiently skilled and knowledgeable to extract every ounce of information that the ground has to tell us. Ideally, if we cannot in good conscience say this, we have no business digging. However, because historical archaeology is so young a discipline, there has to be a training ground and the novice must learn by experience, even if information is lost in the process.

Historical archaeological studies have been undertaken in the United States for at least thirty-five years, but until the 1950's they were bedeviled by the dictum that any "qualified" archaeologist is the right archaeologist to dig on historical sites. The fact that he happened to be qualified as an Egyptologist or a specialist in the Indian cultures of Central America made not the slightest difference. He knew how to dig a hole and pluck artifacts from the ground like plums from a cake, and that was all that mattered. Consequently, much of the early digging was done without an understanding of the complex stratigraphy to be found on most historical sites, or an ability to recognize and date the artifacts. Thus, although many of the early restorations and historical-site museums possess fine collections of artifacts recovered from neighborhood digging, they are hardly more meaningful than they would be if they had been salvaged from the city dump.

This lamentable situation still prevails in many quarters, from the federal government downward. Because practically all the professional excavators at work in the United States have been trained in schools of anthropology, an anthropologist is sought when a historical site is to be dug. This policy does neither the anthropologist nor the site the slightest justice, for neither can bring out the best in the other. Prehistoric archaeology differs from the historic primarily because the former must rely solely on the evidence of artifacts about which nothing is known except what prehistorians are capable of finding out. This is not so in historical archaeology, where there is documentary evidence to identify most of the relics. A fragment of pottery the size of a finger nail can be readily identified as to its composition, its approximate date of manufacture, and sometimes even its factory. We know how it was shipped to the colonies, how much it was worth, and an inventory may give us the name of its owner. This kind of information is all written down somewhere; all that is required of the archaeologist is the knowledge of how and where to look for it. This is the historian's approach; but it is frequently not that of the anthropologist, who takes the same piece of broken pottery and arrives at his conclusions by the same reasoning he applies to prehistoric artifacts. He tries to classify it on the basis of its appearance alone, devising collective categories for different types of ware. Such categories often have neither value nor meaning, for it is generally possible to find a book containing the necessary information, often including the potter's original name for his product.

I am not suggesting that anthropologists cannot be good historical archaeologists, only that initially they do not know the documentary sources essential to the study of historical artifacts. Why should they? They have been trained in a different field. Nevertheless, the fact that they do not realize how much is already known about the things they find naturally leads them to suppose that the artifacts cannot be accurately dated, and this in turn leads to another deadly error—failing to realize that the stratigraphy of the soil layers can also be accurately dated. Consequently, their methods of digging are often insufficiently refined to enable the artifacts to tell their story.

To a great extent the amateur antiquary is the custodian of our past, and this is as it should be. Professional archaeologists are few, and most of them are transients, moving to this site or that from a base at a university, museum, or government office. They are rarely long-time inhabitants of the areas in which they are digging and, while this is not particularly detrimental when dealing with prehistoric sites, it can be disastrous for the excavator of those of the historical period where a knowledge of local history is so important. But the amateur may devote his life to studying his neighborhood and so possesses knowledge that makes him a much more valuable asset than the hired professional.

As I stated in the introduction, there is a tendency for professionals in any sphere to look down their noses at amateurs, and the amateur archaeologist comes in for more than his share of disdain. It is a truism that the bad always attract more attention than the good, and the stories of "pot-hunters" who have looted and destroyed their (and often other people's) sites are legion, and long remembered. The amateurs' achievements, on the other hand, are all too often filed away in obscure journals and are either forgotten or become incorporated in some professional's magnum opus, with credits in very small print that nobody reads.

Archaeology involves digging in the ground for something informative and therefore valuable. This is not far removed from simply digging for valuables—treasure hunting. Indeed, the newspaper-reading public is conditioned to expect the archaeologist to recover treasures, and he makes headlines only when he does. For centuries antiquaries around the world have dug to learn and to possess, and it was out of private collections that public museums were born. There are still too few museums and too many private collectors, and the latter still exert a strong, though declining, influence on archaeological societies. Fortunately the societies are receiving transfusions of new blood as a general interest in the "science" of archaeology increases. Provided the newcomers are met by able tutors, there is great hope for the future. The problem, of course, is that prehistorians make up the hard core of most societies and the new members are naturally drawn in that direction. Nevertheless, it is important and encouraging that the nonprofessionals are developing a thoroughly professional attitude.

In the Webster definition, archaeology is called the "scientific study" of remains, and, in our anxiety to wrest archaeology away from the pot-hunters and dilettante collectors, we tend to overcompensate by elevating it to the ranks of the sciences. In truth it has no business there; its place is with the arts. The only skill that is peculiar to the archaeologist is his ability to study the artifacts in their relationship to the ground. That is what excavation is all about. But excavating is only a technique, and the excavator is, in theory, simply a technician who has mastered the art of taking the ground apart in such a way that it will give up its secrets. He is a detective, trained to expose the fingerprints of the past. He does not have to be a scientist (though his training as an anthropologist may make him one) to do a good job, but he must understand the contributions that such sciences as physics, microbiology, chemistry, botany, and computer mathematics can make to archaeological detection, dating, conservation, and interpretation. He must know when to call for the assistance of scientists.

The art or craft of digging can be readily learned by anyone, the only prerequisite being the possession of simple common sense—the ability to reason. This means that the mantle of the archaeologist can fit many shoulders. It can be worn equally effectively by social, architectural, and military historians, by students of technology, museum curators, and by intelligent collectors whose interest is as much in learning as in possessing. This young discipline needs the benefit of every knowledgeable pair of hands it can find, both professional and amateur. However, if we can accept the thesis that digging is so simple that it does not require a Ph.D. in anthropology to do it well, we must not be tricked into forgetting that there are two essential requirements, the abililty and experience to dig correctly and a *thorough knowledge of the history and objects of the period of the site being dug*.

The competent amateur excavator who happens to work in an iron foundry is likely to be much better equipped to interpret the remains of a seventeenth-century ironworks than a professional whose experience extended only to domestic sites. However, the ironworker would not be the right person to work on, say, the site of an eighteenth-century boatyard, while a shipbuilder would not be the best man to excavate the remains of an early Federal glass factory, though a glass collector might be.

The need for specialized knowledge is not confined to matters of technology; it extends to places and to periods. The excavator whose experience is confined to English colonial sites will be out of his depth if he tries to interpret those of Spanish origin. His knowledge of English architectural styles, English customs, English mercantile and social history will avail him little. His only asset would be his mastery of excavation techniques, and this would not be enough to see him through; for being unable to interpret what he found, he might just as well be blind. Similarly, the excavator who has worked only on English seventeenth-century colonial sites will find himself in difficulties if he transfers to a site dating from the Revolutionary period. The artifacts are still largely English, but the architecture, ceramics, glassware, weapons, and fashions in dress are different; so are trade regulations and restrictions that governed the presence or absence of certain items. Then, too, there are regional differences within a historical period that have nothing to do with nationalities but are geographic and social. In such an area as Tidewater Virginia where there is no natural rock, houses were built of brick or wood. Further inland, stone was readily obtainable and widely used; naturally it had a distinct bearing on architectural style and poses different problems for the archaeologist than the excavation of brick foundations. Social and economic factors created differences, making the frontier homestead an archaeological feature very different from a wealthy tobacco plantation house. It is essential that the excavator be aware of these characteristics and be able to read correctly the story that the ground has to tell him.

I am, of course, speaking now only of the director of an excavation; his assistants will learn from him. I freely admit that with our knowledge of historical sites and their artifacts still pathetically slender, the chances of finding an expert on the period and the region who is also a skilled excavator are somewhat remote. Many a restoration project has come to grief for this reason. Until such specialists are available, we must accept the fact that the best work will stem from a team effort. An excavator trained in the techniques of historical archaeology must be paired with the appropriate historian, technologist, student of ceramics, or possessor of whatever specialized knowledge the site demands. It is imperative that the "expert" be present on the site to feed the archaeologist his information minute by minute. It is no use sending around plans, photographs, or artifacts months later to see if someone can identify what has been found. Unless identifications and deductions are made while the excavation is in progress and open for study, it is impossible to know how to proceed, and without that information much time and money can be wasted digging in areas that are unimportant and failing to explore those that are. Besides, post-mortem conclusions will always be suspect. Archaeology requires that we see and understand, and it has been demonstrated time and again that what we do not understand we do not really see.

If, for example, we find a fragment of a much mutilated brick wall and know nothing of how brick walls were laid, we might deduce that it once extended for many feet in either direction. Yet the presence of a closer (the cut-down brick used by bricklayers in alternate courses to ensure that the courses are all the same length at the ends) would clearly demonstrate that the wall fragment was within a few inches of a corner—provided we recognized the closer for what it was. Then again the presence of a skinner's knife or a shaped bone used by pin makers would provide a clue to crafts once practiced on the site—provided we are capable of recognizing a skinner's knife or a pinner's bone when we find it.

Many amateur archaeological societies are now turning their attention to historical sites, but their members, while keenly interested, tend to sell themselves (and the past) short by saying that there is just too much to learn. "We know we don't know enough," they admit, "but where are we going to find experts in all these related subjects? We're just amateurs. We do the best we can." Remembering that without their efforts nothing would be done at all, there is no denying that the amateurs' contributions are eminently praiseworthy. But it is wrong to agree that they are doing the best they can. They are capable of much more.

The first step toward integrating the wide range of related subjects would be to divide the societies' membership into study groups. If, for example, a society plans to work on an English colonial tavern site, separate teams can usefully spend the preceding winter months exploring the history of ceramics, the evolution of bottles and table glass, the dating of tobacco pipes, tavern architecture, and, of course, the documentary history of the site.

In learning to identify and date artifacts (particularly ceramics and glass) there is no substitute for seeing and handling the objects. Such knowledge cannot be obtained from a book alone. But armed with the right books and artifacts from previous excavations, the basic information can be readily absorbed. I am not suggesting that one can become a ceramics expert by reading a couple of books and learning to differentiate between saltglaze and creamware. It is possible to devote a lifetime to English ceramics of the eighteenth century alone and still not know it all. In this, as in most other fields, the "instant expert" should be heard with caution, for the more one studies the more one finds there is to learn. Very few of us have the sort of photographic mind that can identify and date every fragment the instant it emerges from the ground. We simply possess a broad general knowledge coupled with the all-important asset of knowing which books to go to for the answers.

Historical research is just as much a part of historical archaeology as digging holes in the ground, and proficiency in it cannot come from reading a do-it-yourself handbook. Research, too, is based largely on knowing where to look for what. One can learn to read seventeenth- and eighteenth-century handwriting and interpret abbreviations without batting an eye, and one can know what contemporary newspapers, diaries, letter books, waste books, commonplace books, ledgers, insurance policies, court, tax, and church records are likely sources of information. But when we get down to work on a specific problem, we can get nowhere without being able to transfer these generalities into specific documents. This is where a close liaison with the local historical societies can be such an asset. Unfortunately, very few archaeological societies in the United States are affiliated with their historical counterparts, largely because the anthropologist in search of the prehistoric Indian had no need of the historian. The historian, on the other hand, generally dismissed the amateur archaeologist as a relic hunter with nothing to offer to history. Both were once right, but the advent of scholarly historical archaeological research has since made them wrong.

The professional historical archaeologist has realized from

the beginning his need of the historian, but the historian has been slow to reciprocate. His attitude has been that all he needs to know is to be found in his documents and that if it is not there, it is irreparably lost. He is only now beginning to realize his mistake and to see that excavation properly undertaken *can* fill in details missing from the written record and may even correct previous interpretations of it. There is no denying that to play the historian at his own game, the archaeologist must do his work supremely well. No matter how carefully he digs and how skillfully he interprets the evidence, he cannot hope to equal the historian who holds a document stating that the house he is excavating burned on January 27, 1734. The best he can hope to do (except in rare instances) will be to pin the fire to a decade. But what he *can* do is to show what was in the house at the time of its destruction and provide information as to its size and appearance—facts often available to the historian in no other way.

Digging in the documents and in the earth must be understood to be part of the same research and that one cannot do without the other. This fact was realized much earlier in Europe, and consequently many historical and archaeological societies operate and publish as one. But if there is to be progress, there must also be professionals. There are few university courses in historical archaeology, and most of them are treated as adjuncts of anthropology. So long as this approach continues, professional historians will have good cause for ignoring archaeology. It is imperative that historical archaeology be developed as a tool of the university history departments. The first major step in this direction was taken in 1966 by the state of Virginia when its general assembly authorized the establishing of a Research Center for Historical Archaeology on the campus of the College of William and Mary at Williamsburg, where it will work with both the history and anthropology departments.

Opportunities abound for properly trained historical archaeologists in the United States and Canada, and all over the globe. There are, in fact, many more jobs than acceptable applicants. Even some of the small emerging African nations are realizing that there is merit in preserving the relics of their colonial past and are calling on their erstwhile rulers for help in this work. At home, the urge to "restore" is taking firm hold on the minds of all manner of groups, from historical societies and garden clubs to Chambers of Commerce and industrial firms. They are aware that archaeology is involved, though they frequently do not appreciate its potential; nor can they until trained archaeologists are at hand to show them. Failure to understand what archaeology can do for them is particularly common among restoration architects who believe that its sole function is the exposing of buried foundations. Consequently, many architects advise their clients that they will conduct the archaeological studies themselves. This course has the advantage of enabling the architect to make sure that nothing is found that might interfere with his concept of the completed restoration!

There is no denying that the fruits of archaeology can be very bitter. Buildings associated with great names or events in history have been proved to date from a later period. Supposedly original features of handsome homes, such as wings and porches, have been revealed as much later additions, and in some cases supposed mansions were found to have been mere cottages. Conversely, the home sites of artisans and tradesmen, thought to have been meagerly furnished, were shown to have contained possessions as handsome as those in the homes of the nobility. In short, archaeology is no respecter of persons, conventions, or traditions. Furthermore, it often yields just enough of the truth to make it clear that our preconceived opinion was wrong, but insufficient to provide the full answer. For this reason the sponsors of a proposed restoration or reconstruction would be wise to complete their archaeological and historical studies before irrevocably committing themselves to their project. We must all surely agree that there can be no substitute for historical truth, even if the acceptance of it requires that we change our cherished concepts of the past. But if we do not seek it now, the opportunity will be lost and our misconceptions will be propagated until the end of time. The responsibility of this generation is to see that it is not allowed to happen.

CHAPTER 25

Historic Archaeology—Methods and Principles

IAIN C. WALKER

This paper is a discursive attempt to set down some of the writer's thoughts about North American archaeology based on over five years on this side of the Atlantic after being trained in Great Britain in prehistoric European archaeology. These thoughts are deliberately general but have a special reference to the field in which he now works in the New World, the excavation and interpretation of sites of post-Columbian European or European-derived occupation, and the study of associated material. If these ideas appear controversial they should at least stimulate further thoughts on archaeology.

The application of archaeology as a recognized method of adding to historical knowledge is very largely in its infancy in North America, and even more so in Great Britain. True, archaeology—in various standards of competence and incompetence—has been used on Classical and Near and Middle Eastern sites for 100 years or more, and the cultures excavated have been historical (in the sense of having a written past) or partly so. Yet as Gordon Childe once remarked (1956: 23–24), it was not until 1935 that classical archaeologists bothered to find what a Greek house of the Classical period really looked like. Until very recently Classical and Eastern archaeology has tended to be orientated very much towards "art and archaeology." With this as a background, it is not surprising that it has been said that the stratigraphy at Rome was worked out from excavations on the *limes* in Germany. In the same way, history, because of its plethora of written sources, has always tended to be considered self-sufficient in its approaches to each particular aspect of its field. A German Assyriologist, discussing Near Eastern excavation at the beginning of this century, felt obliged to ask rhetorically, "To what end this costly work of rummaging in mounds many thousand years old, of digging deep down into the earth in places where no gold or silver is to be found?" (Delitzsch 1903: 2–3), and an historic archaeologist today might find himself attempting to explain the same query from historians.

Historians in North America, if they think of American archaeologists at all, probably equate their work through anthropology to the sub-Freudian overtones of Margaret Mead's columns in *Redbook* and to the "Topless fad a healthy sign, says U.S. anthropologist" headline that reached newspapers recently. Archaeology is relatively young as a branch of academic enquiry, and not a few historians, it may be suspected, still find it difficult to believe that including archaeology among their research methods could add anything of value to historical study. Joan Evans, in fact, objects (1961: 152) to the use of the techniques of British archaeology in "historic and well-documented" medieval studies and would prefer the "more subtle, more aesthetic and more civilized methods of approach" of the art historian. She alleges the younger school of British medieval archaeologists to be more interested in "plans of cow-sheds and a series of sections of the rims of cooking pots." As an art historian herself her extreme view is probably not representative of historians at large, but the historian has still to appear who comprehends archaeological research sufficiently to incorporate its findings in any standard historical study. Dr. Evans's belief that medieval studies are historically well-documented indicates a total lack of comprehension of the breadth of historical studies: the art historian can tell us of the glories of English Gothic cathedrals, but nothing about the lives of the miserable peasants in their wattle-and-daub hovels who lived within sound of the cathedral bells. Similarly, an anthropologist entering the field of historic archaeology with no knowledge of historical methodology can naively assume that the historic period has been thoroughly researched by numerous historians.

Magazines such as *Antiques, The Connoiseur,* and *Country Life,* for example, have published articles for many years for the dilettanti on the fine glass and chinaware of gracious living over the last two or three centuries: by contrast, the Society for Post-Medieval Archaeology was founded only in 1967 by people interested in everyday material (the cow-sheds and cooking pots) from the second half of the fifteenth to the eighteenth century and in their archaeological context. The journal *Medieval Archaeology,* specializing in post-Roman material in Britain, is only a few years older. Similarly, people were interested in medieval castles and monasteries long before much thought was given to the study of the pottery found at such sites. This is but another aspect of what Fontana (1966) noted when he talked of people finding it difficult to accept nineteenth-century tin cans and nails as objects fit for study, or nineteenth-century trade catalogues a potential mine of information.

Work on medieval and even later periods in Great Britain has, of course, been done previously: the *Antiquaries Journal,* the *Journal of the British Archaeological Association* and the *Archaeological Journal* for example, have published numerous articles on work done on medieval sites, though not always concentrating on the pottery and other objects found. Nevertheless, it is only in recent years that there has been a conscious desire to form societies and arrange publications specializing in various aspects of archaeology in Britain of medieval and later periods. The recent emergence of industrial archaeology as a new field is similarly part of the marked rise in interest over the last few years in the archaeology—using the term in its widest sense—of the relatively recent past. Nobody in Great Britain, however, has yet produced the fascinating type of work on bottles, tin cans, and nails of the second half of last century done by Fontana at Johnny Ward's Ranch in Arizona (Fontana and Greenleaf 1962), by Brose at the Custer Road dump at Fort Mackinac, Michigan (Brose 1967), or by Durrenberger at Anderson's Mill in Texas (Durrenberger 1965). Indeed, the Society for Post-Medieval Archaeology appears to feel that once mass-production of pottery begins c. 1750 its interests should cease—to quote *1066 and All That*, "History comes to a."

With this in mind, it is clear that even in North America where interest in historic archaeology has existed appreciably longer than in Great Britain, few archaeologists now working on this period have received a formal, far less an academic, training in this field. As Fontana remarked during the panel discussion entitled "Who Shall Dig?" held during the Smithsonian Conference on the Role of Historic Archaeology, it is not so much a case of "who shall dig?" as "who is digging now?" The situation is similar to that in the field of prehistory in Britain during the 1920's and 1930's, when modern techniques and interpretation were being systematically evolved for the first time by people who grew up with the subject; the people of that period—Clark, Fox, Hawkes, Piggott, Wheeler—are now (or were—Fox died in 1967) the doyens of British prehistory and archaeology.

Thus, at present, people trained in other fields, or in other aspects of archaeology (such as the writer), have moved into the new and expanding field of historic archaeology, both in North America and Great Britain. There is nothing wrong with this: what is wrong is the idea that because a person is an "archaeologist" he can excavate any site. This point, with specific reference to historic archaeology in North America, was made more than ten years ago by J. C. Harrington (1955: 1125, 1126) in an excellent paper ignored by those at whom it was directed. If an archaeologist per se is only a technician (Taylor 1948: 43) then he is not an archaeologist: to maintain that because archaeology is a technique, an archaeologist is a technician is as much a solecism as to say allowance means permission. As Taylor appears to be appealing for archaeologists not to be merely technicians, he is confounding the issue by calling such people archaeologists in the first place.

It is quite possible to bring in a competent archaeologist, but one untrained on the particular type of site, and have him "dig" it (i.e., mechanically uncover it and mechanically record it) with some appearance of competence; the problem is how then to get him to interpret what he has uncovered. An archaeologist is no more merely a man who digs than is an historian merely a person who reads medieval manuscripts; an archaeologist is a man who interprets what he finds as a result of his excavation, and an historian is a man who interprets events in the light of his documentary research. Archaeology is the salvaging, with as few mistakes as possible, of as much information as possible while systematically destroying—by the very nature of its technique—the evidence. Far from being a science (using the word in its amorphous popular meaning as something accurate) it is one of the most subjective studies in the field of intellectual research. A person who claims that archaeology can be studied in some sort of intellectual vacuum, devoid of the contamination of knowledge from the vast variety of sources available from folklore to historical maps, is as unrealistic as would be an archaeologist who claimed that he never let the knowledge he had gained from previous excavations influence his approach to the next excavation.

The major difference between the Old and the New World

approaches to archaeology seems to the writer to be that while the latter is more concerned with classification and abstract concepts, the former is more concerned with "historical" interpretation of prehistoric material. It is perhaps partly for this reason that "historical" patterns in prehistory do not seem to be nearly as advanced here as those in Europe, and why in Britain and in modern Near and Middle Eastern excavations archaeology has come to mean much more than merely excavation. There is no cause for self-congratulation in the statement, approved of by Willey and Phillips (1958: 1–2, viii, 1962 ed), that American archaeology is anthropology or it is nothing. There is still less credit in asserting from this, as Willey and Phillips do, that "The American archaeologist, unless he thinks he can dispense with theory altogether, is therefore obliged to take a stand on some of the basic questions of general anthropological theory", and from this to take as read the assumption that anthropology is more science than history. Perhaps they should consider the assertion (quoted in Daniel 1967: 170) that anthropology must become history or become nothing. Childe (1956: 9), talking about European archaeology, and Mallowan (in Albright 1949: 6, 1960 ed) and Woolley (1930: 119, 1937 ed) discussing Near and Middle Eastern archaeology, have suggested that an archaeologist is in effect an historian. The problem as to whether archaeology belongs to history or to science is artificial, and in the last resort is answered largely as a matter of personal bias—Atkinson in fact (1962: 29) has suggested that it is a question that should never be asked at all. However, to continue to use historical metaphors, one might say that in the New World there is a positivistic (in the sense used to describe later nineteenth-century German and other historians) pigeon-holing approach, while Europe has been influenced by the *s'installer dans le mouvement* approach of the early twentieth-century French school, an approach which in France and with a number of art historians unfortunately became as irresponsible as the positivistic approach. Nevertheless it is the writer's contention that the British approach to archaeology has taken the best parts of the latter and fashioned them into a living study. In short, the British approach is integrated, the American is discrete. An example of American thinking can be seen in the review —by Lamberg-Karlowsky of Harvard—of Stuart Piggott's *Ancient Europe* (Lamberg-Karlowsky 1967: 117–8) where he complains that it is difficult to follow Piggott's discussion of the Neolithic and Bronze Ages because "he has abandoned structuring his discussion along the lines of the chronological systems devised by Montelius, Reinecke, and others." This is just a little like complaining that an historian has dealt with historic entities rather than confining himself to artificial chronological periods.

In too many schools of thought in America, archaeology tends to be reduced to methodism unrelated to practical considerations, to systems composed without regard to reality, to strategy rather than tactics. There seems to be an attitude that either archaeology is a science or it is nothing. This is analogous to the German positivists who replaced the word *Geschichte* with a new, improved, word, *Kulturwissenschaft*. The idea that science involves changeless and eternal reality is founded on an error in Greek philosophy, and is continued by those who seek comfort from chaos in self-devised order. However, no reputable modern scientist now looks for immutable laws. The so-called "scientific method" of last century, and the idea that reason alone is what advances science—or any other field of intellectual endeavour—is outmoded: scientific research, as has been pointed out by W. H. George *(The Scientist in Action: A Scientific Study of his Methods* [1936] quoted in Beveridge 1950: 138, 1961 ed), is an art, not a science. Over thirty years ago Cohen and Nagel, two Americans discussing scientific method, noted (1934: 396, 1936 ed) that there are absolutely no first principles in the sense of principles which had to be known prior to everything else. Empirical material, they noted, was what is alleged to be fact, and the selection, analysis, and interpretation of this material was done on the basis of the principles evolved. Cohen and Nagel thus stated scientific methodology to be "essentially circular." This has been more correctly put by E. H. Carr (1961: 30, 1964 ed) when he discussed history, and defined it as "a continuous process of interaction between the historian and his facts, an unending dialogue between the present and the past."

The fact that art historians make use of chemical analyses of paints or of X-rays to ascertain the authenticity of a painting does not make them scientists, nor does use of statistics or C-14 dating make an archaeologist a scientist. As the writer has remarked elsewhere (Walker 1965: 64), the uncritical use of statistics in any intellectual field reduces it to an automated absurdity, for the greatest tool of research is the mind of man. No real archaeologist would confuse the ends for the means, and there is a first-rate coverage of the ends through statistical means in Heizer and Cook's *The Application of Quantitative Methods in Archaeology,* but it is also possible (Spaulding in Heizer and Cook 1960: 89) to have a person who is in love with statistics for their own sake, and who as a result produces articles which are all but incomprehensible. Beveridge has pointed out (1950: 21–22, 105, 1961 ed) that the value of statistics is in testing hypotheses, not in initiating discovery: more discoveries have been made from an intensive study of very limited material than from statistics applied to large groups.

Yet the writer's impression is that time and again the so-called scientific basis of New World archaeology is vaunted because New World archaeologists (anthropologists) wish to emphasize that their approach has evolved a Linnaean classification and terminology, and does follow pure, objective, immutable laws, and is thus superior to the historical approach. One regrettable by-product of this mechanistic outlook in the New World is a desire to over-rationalize archaeology in an unnecessary attempt to justify it, and to disguise the obvious (and, one may suspect at times, the trite) under a cover of pseudo-technical verbiage. Thus, Walter Taylor (1948: 117): "The empirical form of an archaeological manifestation will be taken to mean the sum and arrangement of its component chemico-physical parts taken together with its empirical affinities; in other words that aspect of the phenomenon, whose expression can be observed directly and which, therefore, can be utilized as empirical data by the archeologist" or "[historiography] is projected contemporary thought about past actuality, integrated and synthesized into contexts in terms of cultural man and sequential time" (1948: 34–35). Do the phrases like "processual interpretation" or "cultural-historical integration" used and defined by Willey and Phillips (1958: part 1) contribute materially to our understanding of prehistory, and if indeed they do, why cannot simple English be used? What great unsung truths may lurk coyly behind such titles as "Archaeological Systematics and the Study of Cultural Process" (Binford 1965)? This approach leads to disintegration: one reason for the number of self-styled philosophers may be the lack of any truly great philosopher, but in the writer's opinion one major cause is the publish-or-perish attitude

which begets the principle that it is better to write rubbish than to write nothing at all. It also results in what G. H. Barraclough (1955: 16), talking of overspecialization, has described as "that devoted worship and admiring contemplation of its own navel which has made many otherwise not unsympathetic observers ask whether the measurable results justified the immeasurable expenditure of effort." Archaeology is a discipline, but it is not, in the vulgar sense, a science: archaeology is in fact a self-imposed discipline, which is precisely why it is so subjective.

An historian simply cannot "know" facts in an empirical sense of the word "know": empirical history does not exist. Precisely the same things may be said about an archaeological approach: the man who claims on the one hand that he knows what he is going to find, or on the other claims that by scrupulous recording of everything (whatever that means) and by packaging all the finds for their later study by experts (whoever they may be) a site can be adequately and responsibly excavated by a technically competent excavator (whatever that is) who knows nothing about the material he is finding should be run out of the profession under a close escort of tar and feathers. A. E. Housman (1921: 132), talking about textual criticism, noted that it deals not with mathematical exactitudes but with "the frailities and aberrations of the human mind, and of its insubordinate servants, the human fingers. It therefore is not susceptible of hard and fast rules. It would be easier if it were, and that is why people say that it is, or at least behave as though they thought it so." So too with archaeology. However much authorities in various fields may be asked to give detailed advice on material found by excavation, only the excavator with his frailities and aberrations can interpret the fluid and the variable as they occur: he, and he alone, must separate significant facts from accidental facts and he alone must stand or fall by his ability to interpret the site he is excavating. To compartmentalize research is to solidify the fluid and the variable. Knowledge must be related to experience as it is learned, not stored for some theoretical future union. To assert, for example, that excavation can be successfully accomplished when the basic research has not been done, or worse still, has been kept from the excavator in order not to "confuse" the "honesty" of his work is to insult and humiliate all those connected with the work, and to reduce the researcher to a mindless cog. Research cannot be done by half-a-dozen separated individuals and then allegedly synthesized by some master-brain. The idea that a person who has studied the nature of inference can judge the validity of an inference without having any special knowledge of the subject-matter may be a doctrine of Aristotle, but it is, as Collingwood emphasizes (1946: 233, 1961 ed), a delusion.

All people who study the past start from the point of view of the present. This point of view is valid to the historian—prehistorian, anthropologist, call him what you will—and to those whose environment is essentially similar to his, because unless he has a point of view from which to start, he can see nothing at all. Facts, therefore, like a diamond, have many facets: the diamond may be flawed, or may turn out to be glass. Only the continuous process of interaction between the historian and his facts and the unending dialogue between the present and the past establishes the ever-changing pattern of interrelated fact and interpretation that is history, prehistory, anthropology, science, or any other branch of learning.

If a person is unable to be intellectually honest in his approach, it is not the concept of integrated research that is at fault; it is merely that the person is incompetent. It is this very necessity to rely on the honesty of the excavator that can result in the prostitution of archaeology and the rape of a site when excavation is directed towards an ill-conceived or fundamentally improper end. The looting of a site to supply a museum or individual with spectacular exhibits, or the rebuilding of an inaccurate sham to impress unsuspecting tourists are two such misuses; and if an archaeologist is prepared to accept the condemnation of his peers he can do untold damage to the whole discipline of archaeology. The fact that archaeologists can, and do, resign when they feel their integrity has been compromised to an untenable degree is perhaps the only redeeming feature of such sordid situations. To be intellectually honest is not necessarily to be correct in one's interpretation: it is however, more important.

All of us tell our novice archaeological students to make certain they record everything when they are excavating, whether they understand everything or not: how many of us also tell them that you do not collect evidence independently of thinking, and that nothing is evidence except in relation to a definite question? An artefact only becomes historical evidence because we think of it as such. As Lord Acton, despite his positivistic beliefs, realized many years ago, one has to study problems, not periods. Hercule Poirot rightly belittled the omnivorous detective collecting uncritically everything that might eventually turn out to be a clue; not because clues should not be collected, but because collecting (pigeon-holing) or "preserving" (Taylor 1948: 191) *in itself* is not enough, as anyone will attest who has tried to understand the fieldnotes, however painstaking, of someone who did not understand what he was doing.

Discoveries rarely occur because data has been collected to such an extent that the generalization becomes a matter of logic (Beveridge 1950: 151, 1961 ed). As Housman pointed out (1905: 58; 1930: 105), evidence has to be weighed, not counted, and accuracy is a duty, not a virtue: in a study of the past, conscious accuracy is *only* a duty—interpretation and understanding are the virtues. Field assistants are not, as a rather inexperienced former colleague—British—believed, the eyes and hands of the archaeologist in charge: they are— or should be—part of his brain. As Leonard Woolley noted, (1930: 118–9, 1937 ed) no record can be exhaustive, and the excavator as he works is constantly open to subjective and intangible impressions which by no exact logical process result in theories. Only then is an excavator an archaeologist. Beveridge (1950: Chapter 7) notes the same applies in science: it is significance and consequence—interpretation in other words—which is important. Scientists cannot base ideas on reason alone, but must use inspiration—logic in fact can be an inhibiting factor in research. As the American anthropologist R. H. Thompson has observed (1958: 8), too often scholars have failed in their approach to a subject because they deliberately attempted to eliminate the influence of the subjective element.

Coming back to Taylor's work, if I interpret his definition of an archaeological manifestation correctly, he is trying to define a "fact": all intellectual work is based on facts, but facts are not immutable, so what is the "empirical data"— presumably such things as the size, shape and composition of a pot, and the number of pots found, and it may be debated whether even these are empirical. Empirical material, as Cohen and Nagel observed, is what is *alleged* to be fact. From this, as Beveridge has remarked (1950: 85, 1961 ed) theories can be deduced; all, some, or none of which may be true. Like

jesting Pilate who asked what was truth but would not wait for the answer, there are many who ask what a fact is but do wait for the answer. A scientist has defined a scientific truth as "a statement which has been publicly accepted by the experts" (Ziman in *The Listener*, 18th August 1960, quoted by Carr 1961: 61, 1964 ed). History is in fact a series of accepted judgements (Barraclough 1955: 14) and more than half a century ago the American historian, Carl Becker (1910: 528), suggested that historical facts only came into being when the historian created them. The selectiveness of the historian, and the "preposterous fallacy"—as E. H. Carr (1961: 12, 1964 ed) has described it—of historical fact existing as an objective and independent entity have been emphasized by Cohen and Nagel (1934: 324, 1936 ed), Collingwood (1946: 113, 248, 1961 ed) and Childe (1947: 22).

I presume Taylor is not trying to say by past actuality that the past is more objective—nearer to actuality—than the present just because it is past, but he does appear to be trying to find something absolute or empirical on which to base his thesis. But even if the shape, composition, and size of a pot are empirical in that sense—and I suggest they are not— then to quote Taylor himself at one point, so what? What he is trying to describe are axioms—things which we may assume and on which we base our deductions. To take one example, that a violent wave of destruction occurred in southern Palestine during the second half of the 13th century B.C. is, from excavation evidence from a number of sites, clear; that this was caused by the Israelite invasion is a reasonable deduction; that this was directed by God to fulfill his historical plan is an interpretation of faith not susceptible of historical testing (Wright 1957: 18, 1962 ed). The first statement may be regarded as a fact as defined above, but it in itself is based on a number of deductions and assumptions (cf. Becker 1910: 529). Evidence has had to be marshalled to sustain the dating, and also to maintain that the material found by excavation was not destroyed by earthquake or by a conflagration unrelated to an attack, or that it was not ashes taken from another context and dumped where found. The axiom, as near as one can reach into the sub-atomic structure of our fact, appears to be simply "here is a layer". Further archaeological work could alter both the first statement and the second deduction, as it has altered Garstang's identification of the walls he suggested fell before the Israelites at Jericho; ironically, it will not alter the third hypothesis which, though the most subjective, remains immutable. The objectivity Taylor implies by "past actuality" is nothing more than non-thinking. The layer which we decide is a destruction layer existed before excavation and was unknown—as soon as it becomes known, it becomes associated with thoughts and the result is historical facts. If Taylor meant this then he might have expressed himself in comprehendible terms and at rather less length.

It might be thought that Taylor would agree with these previous definitions of facts. He agrees that the positivistic approach does not ensure objectivity (1948: 34), that total history is impossible and that a conscious selection has to be made (29–30, 31, 35). He strongly contends that the insistence of archaeologists to have objective data (what he would call empirical data) for their cultural classification is a misconception of the nature of archaeological analysis, so that only by inference can the archaeologist reach "the realms of past actuality" (123–4, 140–2). Yet in his final summation, while he can say (p. 202) that archaeology must at least write history to justify itself as a social science (whatever precisely that means), he goes on to say that beyond this point (i.e., beyond history) archaeology recognizes "the personal inclinations of the individual", which implies that somewhere there is still an ultimate of archaeology which one must first define before descending to the headier levels of interpretation, opinion, and personal inclinations. The most important thing to know is not whether an historical statement—or an archaeological "fact"—is true or not, but what it means (Collingwood 1946: 260, 1961 ed). Thus archaeology rarely "proves" anything, its primary purpose is to discover not facts so much as facets.

Taylor seems to realize the value of the integrated approach as opposed to typological catalogues, for his last chapter (1948: 152–202) is entitled, not very euphoniously, "An Outline of Procedures for the Conjunctive Approach." (I assume conjunctive is a mistake for integrated.) However, his division of this approach into parts, to say nothing of his use of headings such as "Pre-local noncontemporaneous geographical data" for these parts, obscures the very point he is trying to make. Willey and Phillips (1958: Chapter 2) similarly get sidetracked into defining in vast detail artificial divisions before giving quite a readable prehistory of the Americas. At least, however, we have an admission from them that the "assumption of a more or less unvarying rate of cultural change in a spatial-temporal continuum has been overdone" in the past. Chapters II and III of *Archaeology and Its Problems* (de Laet 1957: 27–58) offer an explanation of the integrated approach far clearer and more precise, and in addition are written by an archaeologist talking from a wealth of practical experience, not a theoretician trying to fit his subject into readily definable classes. De Laet creates a living subject, Taylor kills the subject and dissects it to no clear gain. It is not a case of Taylor being wrong and de Laet right—inasmuch as this writer comprehends Taylor, he thinks Taylor is fundamentally trying to say much the same as he is—it is simply Taylor trying to rationalize something which cannot be reduced to simple equations while de Laet sees his subject as a living entity.

The writer of this article is subjective because he learned his subject in Great Britain where the product from archaeology, whether prehistoric or not, has always been regarded as an aspect of history, and from prehistorians who were imbued with the philosophic outlook of R. G. Collingwood; and unless someone can convince him to his own satisfaction that this outlook is invalid, he will hold to it. The point is, however, not whether this view is right or wrong (which would be a facile over-simplification in any case) but that this view is *no more* subjective than that of any other prehistorian and is more honest because the writer realizes it is subjective.

Taylor sounds like a propounder of theory and abstract logic, and his work appears as a laborious compendium—almost a delirium of sources—more of analysis than synthesis and without the benefit of personal practical archaeological experience. It took this writer half a dozen attempts at reading Taylor's turgid epic before he came to the conclusion that Taylor appeared to be advocating a movement away from what this writer thinks is still the basic outlook of American archaeology. However, he still feels so what. As the work stands, it is an undigested collection of largely unorganized and wholly unedited thoughts written in rank bad English. Obscure writing indicates confused thinking, and if this work was presented in this form to Harvard University as a Ph.D. thesis it is shocking that it was not sent back for reorganization and rewriting. In very few works

does the knowledge contained repay multiple readings and a translation into understandable English by a busy person, and Taylor's *Study of Archeology* is not one of them. As Thomas Huxley remarked of Cardinal Newman, "After an hour or two of him I began to lose sight of the distinction between truth and falsehood."

The Italian historian Croce (1915: 134, 1921 ed) pointed out that to understand the history of a prehistoric man we had to become in our own mind a prehistoric man: if we did not do that then the most we could do was simply to catalogue his remains. We all pay lip-service to understanding the past, but how many of us are content to make neat cataloguing systems and irrelevant chest-of-drawers categories in which to enclose man; or contrived designs with which to excavate his remains: do our models—in the technological sense—let us *understand* man? When Gordon Childe wrote *What Happened in History* (1942) and *History* (1947) he deliberately excluded almost all of what is normally thought of as history. He did so to emphasize that history is, so to speak, only the written extension of prehistory, for all that the evidence available to and the approach used by those studying prehistory and history differ (cf. Atkinson 1962: 8, 10). The study of the past, whether by history or prehistory, is part of a quest for heritage, as Cotter (1966) has pointed out—it should not be regarded as an opportunity to invent systems and terminologies and to marvel at one's skill in building elaborate and pretentious edifices. An artefact typology is a hypothesis which may or may not prove true and is occasioned by a lack of knowledge on a subject: it is the starting-point of a study, not the end result. It tends to presuppose a linear progression, features definable in exact terms, or aspects which really only exist because people want things to be neatly categorized. As knowledge progresses typologies become amorphous, just as the chronological systems of Reinecke and Montelius referred to earlier by Lamberg-Karlovsky have become.

But to return to the earlier remark about the need for an archaeologist to be able to interpret his findings, archaeology without interpretation makes nonsense of the profession, and it is for this reason that one may say with perfect correctness that it is better to leave a site undug than to dig it incompetently. If, as has been pointed out, history begins, not just yesterday, but today (Daniel 1963: 252), how can we justify the use of heavy earthmoving equipment to plough through "unwanted" occupation material covering two and a half centuries merely in order to expose structural remains—those that survive the process, that is—for reconstruction? One would think that such people had never heard of roofs collapsing into a building, leaving rafters and slate patterns vital for authentic restoration. Can we justify restoration work when what is built is predicated by cheapness of construction and ease of subsequent maintenance rather than authenticity? In too many cases there appears to be no realization that the primary responsibility of archaeology, as with all research, is to knowledge. Excavation by those unable to comprehend this basic fact is not only a waste of time and money, but of infinitely more importance, is a destruction of irreplaceable source material and the recording of distorted and worse-than-useless information, which in the final instance is worse than no recording at all. The writer does not subscribe to the extreme view that destruction of a site by a construction company is preferable to a few days' rush digging by an archaeologist, but the extreme limitations frequently imposed on using information gleaned under such conditions must be recognized, and to run a major long-term archaeological programme as though it were a salvage operation is utterly indefensible.

Unfortunately, few archaeologists are in the position of being able to specialize as much as they would like in their particular fields of interest. Government-employed archaeologists rarely have a say in what sites they excavate: Sir Lindsay Scott (Scott 1947: 184), one of the last of the gentleman amateur (sensu stricto) archaeologists in Britain, and a senior civil servant, talking of the problem of divided obligations in government archaeology, said "Archaeologists in the Public Service are not otherwise placed than other Civil Servants and owe an absolute allegiance to their administrative Chief, not to the learned Societies; their advice is tested by the overriding test of any government department, namely whether the minister could defend the decision in Parliament, and Parliament, in the fields on which government departments operate, is absolute." *The Times Educational Supplement* in London (20th May 1966: 1570), remarking on the Canadian government's decision to omit the word "victorious" from the epitaph on the new monument to General Wolfe at Quebec City (the former one having been blown up by French-speaking dissidents), asked if what it called this rewriting of history by the civil service might not eventually extend to, amongst other things, Britain requesting that George Washington be referred to simply as a gentleman rather than President of the United States of America, and describing William the Conqueror as "William, Duke of Normandy, soldier and surveyor." G. H. Smith (1958), discussing archaeological work by the United States National Park Service, noted that investigations tended to be more restricted in scope and significance and less concerned with how contributions could be made to the progress of knowledge at large, or even whether the archaeological profession was made aware (i.e., by publications) of what had been learned. These statements suggest that the framework within which a government-employed archaeologist is permitted to work professionally may differ from that available to archaeologists employed by other organizations.

In North America, where political patronage is not yet dead, an excavation may be authorized to employ the unemployed in the hope of catching votes or because local political pressure demands work done to boost the tourist industry. On the other hand, in both Great Britain and North America, more legitimate emergency work may be done because of impending road or reservoir construction. Britain probably has better laws both to protect sites and to prevent destruction before at least an emergency excavation has been done, and perhaps a more powerful public opinion on such matters, although recent legislation, both federal (1966) and state, suggests this discrepancy is being remedied in the United States. However, it would be foolish to maintain that the situation in Great Britain is by any means perfect, particularly where urban development is concerned. Thus governmental archaeologists—and this applies to both sides of the Atlantic—trained in one field have to undertake excavations of sites for which they may not be adequately trained. The excavation of a medieval castle in Britain may be entrusted to a Romano-British archaeologist because it is felt that Roman sites, whose excavation usually involves work on masonry structures, are vaguely analogous to medieval castles in construction. The writer knows of a nineteenth-century trading-post in Canada excavated in 1966 by a

prehistoric archaeologist who thought European clay pipe fragments were tubular beads.

But if we admit that ideally excavation of a site should be done only by those familiar with that type of site, we should also admit that at a practical level, particularly in any new and expanding field, the excavator is going to be largely self-taught and that in fact excavators are always going to discover the unexpected, like Fontana's mission station in Arizona turning out to be an 1850–1900 ranch. The success of this excavation lay in the ability of the excavator to address himself to the problems posed by hitherto largely unstudied artefacts. How well a person adapts when faced with this change from one type of site to another wholly unrelated depends not only on whether he is interested enough to transfer his studies from, say, beakers and bronze flat axes to clay pipes and tin cans, but also on whether his employer deems such a study relevant. Inasmuch as every site is to some degree unique, little comparative material may be available for study, but this does not absolve the archaeologist from the responsibility of becoming familiar with what there is to be known. Artefact study is, however, still regarded in some quarters as an esoteric pastime irrelevant to the job for which the employee is paid—publication of information is another field which may be regarded as an unnecessary expense and trouble.

It must also be admitted, however, that some American views on practical archaeological method are like anthropological philosophy, cluttered with irrelevant theory. Let us take one example from a standard textbook on method, which does contain useful information—*A Guide to Archaeological Field Methods*, which appears under the name, and therefore presumably with the approval, of R. F. Heizer. In the second edition of this work we are informed (Heizer 1950: 30) that while stratification may be visible in the walls of the excavation, "Any stratigraphy of artifact types and animal bones will appear after a study has been made and need not bother the excavator in the field," so dig out the occupation material, put it through a screen, and we can look at the takings in the evening. However, the editors of the third edition (Heizer 1958: 40–42) felt obliged to clarify their position, particularly with regard to Wheeler's sarcasms (1954: 70–71, 1956 ed), and explained that visible differences in stratigraphy are rare in California, but that in digging by 6- or 12-inch levels any stratification can be easily seen and the vertical location of any artefact is automatically known. However, "it is very important to watch for intrusive pits, for the fill of such disturbed areas will often date from a later time" (1958: 41). The earlier remarks about the excavator not needing to bother with the stratigraphic position of artefacts while in the field are quietly omitted. We are also told no archaeologist would quarrel with Wheeler's insistence on using visible stratification as the most accurate and meaningful method of recording data, and are quoted excavations by Strong and Corbett, and Strong and Evans, where the use of arbitrary levels obscures the context of material found. At Pachacamac, Strong and Corbett's report indicates that although "the sequence of pottery types is clear, a much more definitive and sharper difference would undoubtedly have been possible if the natural stratification had been properly utilized." We are also told, however, that most American archaeologists do not consider the arbitrary level method outworn, and are given an impressive list of references to excavations which were "successful" (on what criteria is not explained) and were done by excavating in arbitrary levels. Burial mounds are apparently still "particularly adaptable to trenching."

Of course British archaeologists quoted will excavate in arbitrary levels if no other method is applicable, and of course Childe can say a sequence of ceramic styles can be obtained by excavating in artificial levels—Strong and Corbett have proved that, and so did Flinders Petrie in 1890 at Lachish (Woolley 1930: 50–52, 1937 ed). However, it is quite clear from the context and illustrations, despite Heizer's attempts to suggest otherwise, that Wheeler was criticizing the use of arbitrary levels on complexly stratified, specifically Eastern, sites. Anyone can see that material in higher layers will be earlier than that in lower layers, as a general rule. If that were all that archaeology implied, then a programmed automation could do the work and churn out reports like cars from Detroit, so that all that an archaeologist would need to do would be to recall the one in four, or whatever proportion it is, cars for minor adjustments. Clearly the 1958 version of this section of the book is a poor attempt to accept both the common use of artificial levels and the better use of natural stratigraphy. A book which is being sold continent-wide cannot excuse its errors by saying that at least in California there is little visible stratigraphy, or that its use (as given on the back of the title page) is primarily for the Archaeological Survey and the Department of Anthropology of the University of California at Berkeley, or even (1958: 39) by saying that the essential rule about excavating is to use a system flexible enough to be adaptable.

One "scientific" aspect of archaeology which seems to be disregarded by far too many American excavators is neatness of excavation. It is not intended to labour the point, but it seems reasonable to suggest that the evidence recorded from excavations looking like Flanders fields will be poorer than evidence from an excavation whose trenches have cleanly-cut vertical sides. Further, an excavation run like a New Year's party is likely to be less successful than one run on well-organized lines. A tidy, organized, excavation is not necessarily a good one, but a good excavation has to be tidy and organized.

Historic archaeology in the New World is a field which is still in its formative stage. It is not too late to make it a field of distinction, independent of the confining bounds of anthropology-orientated theory. Presumably an anthropologist would not excavate a Roman site without first learning what such excavation involved—surely historic archaeology warrants the same courtesy. An excavator competent in one branch of archaeology is not competent in another branch simply by virtue of his former qualifications. When the Historic Site Archaeology Conference now held annually in the south-eastern United States was being mooted in 1960, John Goggin wanted to see a conference that would get down to practical problems such as artefact study (South 1964), and the papers given at these conferences indicate a successful adherence to this view. The Smithsonian Conference of 1966 referred to earlier was a success because it too avoided getting bogged down in aimless theory. To make a success, however, those who work in it must consider themselves not anthropologists, not archaeologists, but historical archaeologists.

BIBLIOGRAPHY

ALBRIGHT, W. F.
1949 *The Archaeology of Palestine*. 1960 ed. Penguin, Harmondsworth, England.

ATKINSON, R. J. C.
1962 *Archaeology, History and Science*. University of Wales Press, Cardiff.

BARRACLOUGH, G. H.
1955 *History in a Changing World*. Blackwell, Oxford.

BECKER, C.
1910 Detachment and the Writing of History, *The Atlantic Monthly*, Vol. CVI, pp. 524–36. Cambridge, Massachusetts.

BEVERIDGE, W. I. B.
1950 *The Art of Scientific Investigation*. 1961 ed. Mercury Books, London.

BINFORD, L. R.
1965 Archaeological Systematics and the Study of Cultural Process, *American Antiquity*, Vol. 31, No. 2, pt. 1, pp. 203–10. Salt Lake City.

BROSE, D. S.
1967 The Custer Road Dump Site: an Exercise in Victorian Archaeology, *The Michigan Archaeologist*, Vol. 13, No. 2, pp. 37–128. Ann Arbor.

CARR, E. H.
1961 *What is History?* 1964 ed. Penguin, Harmondsworth, England.

CHILDE, V. G.
1942 *What Happened in History*. 1964 ed. Penguin, Harmondsworth, England.
1947 *History*. Cobbett Press, Ltd., London. (Published in North America as *What is History?* Schuman, New York, 1953.)
1956 *A Short Introduction to Archaeology*. F. Muller, London.

COHEN, M. R., and NAGEL, E.
1934 *An Introduction to Logic and Scientific Method*. 1936 ed. Harcourt, Brace and Company, New York.

COLLINGWOOD, R. G.
1946 *The Idea of History*. 1961 ed. Oxford University Press, Oxford.

COTTER, J. L.
1966 Archaeology and the Quest for Heritage, *Eastern States Archeological Federation Bulletin*, No. 25, p. 13, Trenton.

CROCE, B.
1915 *Theory and History of Historiography*. English trans. 1921, Harrap, London. (Published in North America as *History, its Theory and Practice* (1960) Russell and Russell, New York.)

DANIEL, G. E.
1963 Editorial, *Antiquity*, Vol. XXXVII, pp. 251–5. Cambridge.
1967 Editorial, *Antiquity*, Vol. XLI, pp. 169–73. Cambridge.

DELITZSCH, F.
1903 *Babel and Bible*. Williams and Norgate, London.

DURRENBERGER, E. P.
1965 Anderson's Mill (41 TV 130): A Historic Site in Travis County, Texas, *Bulletin of the Texas Archeological Society*, Vol. 36, pp. 1–69. Austin.

EVANS, JOAN
1961 Anniversary Address, *Antiquaries Journal*, Vol. XLI, pp. 149–53. London.

FONTANA, B. F.
1966 "Historic Artifacts", unpublished paper given at the Smithsonian Conference on the Role of Historic Archaeology, Washington, 18th–20th April 1966.

FONTANA, B. F. and GREENLEAF, J. C.
1962 Johnny Ward's Ranch: A Study of Historic Archaeology, *The Kiva*, Vol. 26, No. 1–2. Tucson.

HARRINGTON, J. C.
1955 Archeology as an Auxiliary Science to American History, *American Anthropologist*, Vol. 57, No. 6, pt. 1. Menasha, Wisconsin.

HEIZER, R. F.
1950 *A Manual of Archaeological Field Methods*. (2nd rev. ed. 1950 of 1949 ed.) The National Press, Millbrae, California.
1958 *A Guide to Archaeological Field Methods*. (3rd rev. ed. 1958 of 1949 ed.) The National Press, Palo Alto, California.

HEIZER, R. F. and COOK, S. F. (EDITORS)
1960 *The Application of Quantitive Methods in Archaeology*. Quadrangle Books, Chicago.

HOUSMAN, A. E.
 1905 Preface to *Juvenal*, in *Selected Prose*, ed. J. Carter (1961) pp. 53–62. Cambridge University Press.
 1921 The Application of Thought to Textual Criticism, in *Selected Prose* (1961) pp. 131–50.
 1930 *M. Manilii Astronomicon Liber Qvintvs*. Privately printed.
LAET, S. J. DE
 1957 *Archaeology and its Problems*. Phoenix House, Ltd., London.
LAMBERG-KARLOVSKY, C. C.
 1967 Review of *Ancient Europe* (1965) by S. Piggott, in *American Antiquity*, Vol. 32, No. 1, pp. 117–8. Salt Lake City.
SCOTT, L.
 1947 Review of *Orkney and Shetland* (1946) published by the Royal Commission on Ancient Monuments, Scotland, in *Proceedings of the Prehistoric Society*, Vol. XIII (N.S.), pp. 183–4. Cambridge.
SMITH, G. H.
 1958 *Interpretive Values of Archeological Evidence*, in Papers given at the American Anthropological Association Symposium on the Role of Archeology in Historical Research, Washington, 22nd November 1958. Mimeographed by the National Park Service, Philadelphia.
SOUTH, S.
 1964 Preface to papers of Third and Fourth Annual Historic Site Archaeology Conferences, *Florida Anthropologist*, Vol. XVII, No. 2, p. 34. Tallahassee.
TAYLOR, W. W.
 1948 A Study of Archeology. *American Anthropologist*, Vol. 50, No. 3, pt. 2. Menasha, Wisconsin.
THOMPSON, R. H.
 1958 Modern Yucatecan Maca Pottery Making. *Memoirs of the Society for American Archaeology*, No. 15 (*American Antiquity*, Vol. XXIII, No. 4, pt. 2.) Salt Lake City.
WALKER, I. C.
 1965 Some thoughts on the Harrington and Binford Systems for Statistically Dating Clay Pipes, *Quarterly Bulletin, Archeological Society of Virginia*, Vol. 20, No. 2, p. 60–64. Charlottesville.
WHEELER, R. E. M.
 1954 *Archaeology from the Earth*. 1956 ed. Penguin, Harmondsworth, England.
WILLEY, G. R. and PHILLIPS, P.
 1958 *Method and Theory in American Archaeology*. 1962 ed. The University of Chicago Press, Chicago.
WOOLLEY, L.
 1930 *Digging up the Past*. 1937 ed. Penguin, Harmondsworth, England.
WRIGHT, G. E.
 1957 *Biblical Archaeology*. George Duckworth and Sons Ltd., London.

CHAPTER 26

Some Thoughts on Theory and Method in Historical Archaeology

CLYDE D. DOLLAR

The subject of my paper for this year's meeting falls in the category of 'new ideas'—or, more appropriately, I should say old ideas expressed in what is hoped to be a new way. As you can tell from the title of the paper, I am presenting these ideas in the form of 'thoughts' on the subject of theory and method in historical archaeology, rather than axioms or theorems, as I feel that the subject is just beginning to develop and will require the consideration and discussion of all of us before a body of method for historical archaeology begins to solidify.

Over the past eight years, I have become convinced that researchers in the field of historical archaeology are encountering problems the solutions to which seriously strain the ability of traditional anthropological methods to solve. I think it is time to give serious consideration to the recognition that there is a major difference in the concepts of methodology used in the excavation of a prehistoric site and those concepts necessary for use on an historical site. As I see it, the field of historical archaeology is coming of age as a distinct socio-scientific discipline (even duo-disciplinary in nature); we must, therefore, critically examine all aspects of the subject in order to arrive at valid new concepts for what is essentially a new discipline, and not necessarily borrow concepts and methodology wholesale from the existing body of anthropological thought. No doubt the argument whether the historical archaeologist is an historian with a shovel or an anthropologist with a history book will not be resolved by this paper—if indeed a resolution is required at this time. If anything, the argument will probably only intensify. So be it, but even this will afford an excellent opportunity (perhaps even a necessity) for the historical archaeologist to do serious reflecting on just who he/she is and what he/she is trying to do.

My paper will be divided into two major sections, the first part being a discussion of general concepts and limitations in the fields of history, archaeology, and anthropology, and the second being a presentation of ten theses for your consideration and discussion.

It has been said that the historian works primarily with 'words', the archaeologist works principally with 'things', and the anthropologist deals with 'culture'. While the situation is in reality considerably more complicated, this statement does define the three main areas in which these specialists do most of their research: 'words', meaning historical documents; 'things', meaning archaeologically obtained data and artifacts; and 'culture', meaning the observable characteristics of human existence. The three are manifestly interrelated and inseparable to a great degree, yet the laws, concepts, and research methodology pertaining to each are by no means directly substitutable for the others—just as the application of the laws of optics to research on the human eye does not fully explain the eye's functioning. Very frequently the differences in the research methods used in these fields (history, archaeology, and anthropology) are quite subtle, and being subtle, these differences are difficult to clearly define.

The historian is trained to seek out written documents covering the subject of his research, peruse these documents, and evaluate them for their validity and accuracy in relation to the context in which they were written. The very situation in which the historian works makes the obtaining of total historical objectivity an impossibility as he cannot escape his 'temporal present' entirely, and the historian who is sensitive to the responsibilities of his profession will readily admit this. We can no more objectively and fully 'know' what took place in the past any more than we can physically visit that past. The very act of interpreting a source creates a subjective atmosphere which, at best, can only be partially, never completely, clarified. St. Paul must have had the historian, as well as the theologian, in mind when he stated that "we see through a glass, darkly".

The historian, therefore, works in a subjective atmosphere while constantly attempting to achieve objective findings. As an aid in penetrating the inherent limitations of his 'temporally present conception of the past', the historian uses two main research methods or 'tools'. The first of these is the logical process of deductive reasoning, or, going from the general to the particular,[1] and the second is the application of tests for validity, or, the research processes of verification. Thus, the historical research framework is very legalistically and microscopically oriented, and verification of each step of the research process is a basic necessity if that research is to be considered valid and usable.

Before turning to the archaeologist and his sphere of activity in regard to 'things', perhaps I should state that my concept of 'archaeology' does not include the premise that the technique is the exclusive property of the anthropologist. Indeed, for specialists in Classical, Ancient Near Eastern, and European archaeology to have had advanced training along anthropological concepts is a definite rarity, and I am inclined to believe that the interchangeability of the words 'archaeology' and 'anthropology' which we so frequently practice in this country is the result of an association that, while having served its purpose in the past, is now somewhat outmoded. I conceive of archaeology as a field technique only,

---

[1]*This, of course, does not preclude inductive processes in historical methodology.*

a method of data control at a site, and within the framework of this conception, it is usable by a qualified researcher in any of the paleo-temporally oriented disciplines. During the past one hundred years or so, the field techniques of archaeology have been primarily used by anthropologists, and the character and interpretational aspects of its methods have been influenced quite naturally by this discipline. The paucity of temporal information at archaeologically investigated sites (almost without exception prehistoric in nature) has led to the development of statistical techniques centering around the use of cultural materials found at a given site as temporal indicators. Many of these statistical techniques involve the use of archaeologically obtained information translated into terms having a context removed from the physical matrix of the site itself, and while this practice has gained general acceptance throughout the field of anthropology for use at prehistoric sites, I question the validity of such techniques and data for applying to research at historic sites. This statistical usage I refer to as the 'extended' use of archaeological techniques, and I refer particularly to the practice of typology and seriation. Typology is defined as the process of arranging into groups those artifacts with a significant similarity of observable physical characteristics, and seriation is defined as the process of arranging these typological groups into certain patterns or orders in an attempt to determine temporal sequence or relationship. It has become a matter of increasing concern to me that these 'extended' uses of archaeological techniques do not seem to be able to produce totally distortion free information when tested at an historical site. The reasons for this, I believe, are inherent—but very subtle and profound—differences between the requirements for historical validity and the application of anthropologically influenced archaeological techniques at an historical site.

One of the reasons why 'extended' archaeological techniques are producing distorted and even erroneous data at historical sites is that the field techniques of archaeology are at best only a prolonged statistical sampling process of any given site, no matter how thoroughly the site is excavated. And historical sites have been almost invariably subjected to previous, extensive, and sometimes undiscernable, statistical samplings of various types, accidental or deliberate. In other words, field archaeology is only a statistical sampling of a statistical sample, and most generally not of the total population (statistically speaking).

Furthermore, the recovery of data from an archaeological site requires the researcher to make an interpretation based only on what can be physically seen and measured at any one time and place within and during the site's excavation (the keeping of extensive field notes notwithstanding). This situation cannot help but place the researcher in a subjective position in relation to the data being obtained. And the third, and perhaps most important reason why the use of 'extended' archaeological data does not seem to produce valid and usable historical information at an historical site is that such data, especially seriation information, is not subject to verification, and its use in the historical research process may introduce an invalid component upon which other hypotheses then will be constructed. The dangers in doing this are obvious.

In reality then, 'extended' archaeological data is constructed on the basis of a statistical sample arrived at through very subjective observation and is not inherently verifiable. This situation is somewhat comparable to typing and seriating the words of the King James english version of the Holy Bible in order to construct a hypothesis regarding the scholastic and intelligence qualifications of the original writers!

It is now time to discuss certain aspects of the anthropologist as he works with 'culture'. Anthropology has been defined as the study of Man, and 'culture' can be defined as the physical and observable expressions of the way Man lives. These are two meaningful and usable definitions within the framework of their specific discipline, and I have no quarrel with their formulation. However, I would point out that the study of Anthropology is, by its very definition, the study of Man as a collective entity, i.e., Man's various cultures are seen, and therefore defined, by the anthropologist primarily using those expressions of culture that are the most numerous and/or most frequent. Individual cultures have what can be termed a 'center' (*not* necessarily referring to a geographical location) which can be defined as those cultural expressions reflected by the most people participating in that culture in the most similar manner at the same time. This 'center' of culture is the most vivid and easily recognized expression of that culture, especially when studied on the prehistoric level. In addition, specific cultures have what can be termed 'peripheral areas' (again, not necessarily geographical in location), being very similar to what we might call 'country cousins' in relation to the cultural center. The cultural expressions of these peripheral areas differ from those of the center somewhat, but not necessarily greatly, and therefore are only infrequently recognized on a prehistoric level. And finally, specific cultures have what can be called 'variants' within their cultural complex, and these 'variants' can exist at any time or place within the cultural center or peripheral areas. These variants include the 'odd balls', the 'beatniks', those who don't exactly conform to the cultural center to a noticeable (and therefore bothersome) degree, as well as the thinkers, the explorers, and the inventors (those who will ultimately and profoundly influence the cultural expression of the surrounding cultural centers and peripheral areas). While these variants are sometimes difficult to overlook on a modern level, there does not seem to be any way to specifically recognize the existence of individual cultural variants on a prehistoric level through the use of archaeological techniques. Since the individual, or variant, exists only as a statistical expression within any general anthropological culture, the anthropologist uses archaeological techniques primarily as a means of further delineating the center and peripheral areas of the culture with which he is working. The variant of that culture simply does not exist for him because it cannot be recognized. His archaeological interpretations are therefore geared to the statistical definition of culture and he, over the years, has developed some very refined statistical tools, or, 'extended' uses of archaeology, to help understand his findings anthropologically. It would seem to me, therefore, that the study of anthropology, in general, is incapable of producing techniques for the recognition of either specific actions or single cultural contributions of any given individual within any given culture (the study of historical culture excepted). Anthropological thought, as it has grown over the years, is basically inductive and 'macroscopic' in that the aim is to construct generalities based on observed particulars, and the verification of such generalizations can only be inferential and circumstantial. Furthermore, the statistical processes of an anthropological nature do not possess the inherent characteristic of being verifiable on a level or scale smaller than the cultural peripheral area level. And, by the very nature of the thing itself, the study of an historical site involves intense encounters with individuals (who, on an individual basis cannot help but reflect pronounced cultural variants) and not anthropological culture on a center or peripheral area level. The anthropologist deals with 'people' and the historical archaeologist deals with a person or persons. 'People' have cultural expressions on a cultural center and peripheral area level; a 'person' is basically a cultural variant, and must therefore be dealt with historically and deductively.

I am not entirely suggesting that the historian, when he takes to the field to excavate an historical site, wears a white hat, and the anthropologist, when he takes his trowel to an historic site, wears a black one; the situation is not nearly so simple. Nor am I suggesting that the anthropologist is not equipped to make a noteworthy contribution to the understanding of history as a whole. I am suggesting, however, that when the anthropologist is faced with the task of excavating an historical site, he is in reality facing a whole new discipline the problems relative to which he is probably not initially trained to understand or surmount. Continued and persistent pursuit of historical sites by archaeologists using anthropological concepts, as I have outlined them in this paper, will, I firmly believe, lead to a growing body of 'generally' accurate historical knowledge that will in actuality contain distortions in the particular, or detailed, areas of historical information.

Increased public historical awareness and improved funds for doing historical research during the past decade have combined to progenate a situation wherein historical archaeology has become a 'fashionable' professional pursuit. Probably because of the current interchangeability of the words 'archaeologist' and 'anthropologist', those with archaeological experience have been approached by well-intentioned groups and individuals desiring historical site excavation and development.

Quite naturally, there seems to have developed a general agreement that 'an archaeologist is an archaeologist' regardless of the type of site being researched or the academic discipline forming the background of the researcher. As a result, we have seen a rash of anthropologically excavated historical sites, and in all kindness to my colleagues in the discipline of anthropology, some of the results have been anything but happy (and, lest I appear too presumptuous, let me state that I am only too aware of the fact that "pot can't call kettle black"). The field techniques of archaeology are, by their very nature, totally destructive, and it is therefore imperative that the researcher using archaeological techniques, be he historian or anthropologist, have firmly in mind the scope and limitations of the disciplinary concepts from which he draws his interpretation of data. As a step toward possible clarification, I would like to present ten theses to further define what I feel are certain major methods, techniques, and limitations of historical site archaeology.

THESIS NUMBER 1

Since the late 18th century, the number of different physical cultural expressions in the areas of artifact forms and variants within these forms has increased to the point where the complexity of the subject is almost beyond comprehension. This phenomenon has very important implications in the matter of using certain artifacts for specific dating purposes at an historical site. For example, there were in pre-Civil War America perhaps as many as 300 factories producing and marketing large quantities of cut metal nails. During the period from the Revolutionary War to the Civil War, probably dozens of patents[2] were secured for different manufacturing techniques in use at one or more factories at the same time. One such factory, the firm of Messrs. A Field & Sons at Tauton, Mass., is reported to have been making "about 1,000 different varieties" of nails a year during the early 1870's[3].

As for the subject of ceramics, which seems to be a favorite target for attempts at seriation, an equally complicated situation exists. In the Staffordshire district of England, from which the vast majority of pre-Civil War Americans obtained their dishes, probably more than 400 different potteries were operating during the 1820's to 1850's[4] and producing merchandise of a remarkable range and variety of forms—most of which was simply duplicated from one pottery to another. In other words, not only was there a great range and variety of form in early 19th century English ceramics (sherds of which are found in great numbers at American historical sites) but there was also a great number of different potteries and individual potters making essentially the same designs. As if this situation were not confused enough, I have been able to define at least five different variables in the manufacture of ceramics any one or all five of which could conceivably effect the observable physical characteristics of each and every ceramic sherd found at an historical site.

Also touching on the subject of ceramic dating is the problem of the dating of manufacturing technique improvements. For example, in 1829, there was a significant improvement made in the glazing and firing techniques of certain English wares. Unfortunately, we have no way at the present to know how many of the English potteries adopted these new techniques and how many continued the older processes and for how long. We probably never will entirely know much of this information as it was considered secret by the potters themselves, and therefore did not frequently reach the pages and reports of the primary source materials of the period.

[2]To list only a few: Thomas Clifford (received a patent for a nail making machine in 1790; Jeremiah Wilkinson (cut nail invention in 1776); Jacob Perkins (secured a patent on January 16, 1795, for a nail making machine able to produce 10,000 nails a day); Ezekiel Reed (invented a nail making machine in 1786, which, in 1815, was producing one hundred and fifty million tacks in one year); Jesse Reed (secured a patent on a machine that made tacks at the rate of 60,000 a day during 1807); Samuel Briggs (in August, 1797, received the first patent for a nail making machine issued by the United States); Thomas Perkins (in February, 1794 [I question the accuracy of this date] received a patent for a nail making machine); Samuel Rogers and Thomas Blanchard (received a patent for a nail making machine from the United States in 1817); David Fulson (received a patent for a nail making machine during 1789).

Major source of information: "The Great Industries of the United States: Being an Historical Summary of the Origin, Growth, and Perfection of the Chief Industrial Arts of this Country" by Horace Greeley, Leon Case, Edward Howland, John B. Gough, et. al., published by the J. B. Burr Publishing Co., Hartford, Conn., pp. 1069–1078). 1874.

[3]Ibid., p. 1077

[4]Major source of information: The Penny Magazine of the Society for the Diffusion of Useful Knowledge, Vol. I, #1, March 31, 1832 — #48, December 31, 1832; Vol. IV, #177, January 3, 1835 — #240, December, 1835; Vol. V, #241, January 2, 1836 — #305, December 31, 1836; published by the Society in London, New York, Boston, Philadelphia, and Baltimore.

THESIS NUMBER 2

While typological processes, in general, can be applied to any given body of historical site artifacts with a specified spatial and temporal limit (since this is only a grouping of artifacts based on similar or like observable physical characteristics, historical 'validity' as such is not a consideration), seriation processes, or the attempts to derive temporal data from within a typological pattern of historical site artifacts, have not as yet been proven to produce totally non-distorted historical data and therefore must not be used in the construction of historical hypotheses—unless of course, exteriorily known data can be used as corroborative evidence. I would cite two specific examples with which I am personally familiar. The first involves the archaeologically obtained buttons found during the excavation of the First Fort Smith (Arkansas) site by Mr. Jackson W. Moore, Jr., and myself during 1962/63. These buttons were typed and analyzed serially in several different ways, and the results of this seriation showed pronounced evidence sufficient to suggest that the greatest inhabitation concentration at this site occurred three years prior to the fort's having been built! In a similar example, the ceramics excavated at the Brigham Young House at Nauvoo, Illinois, (during the 1965 season) strongly indicated that the initial deposition of these artifacts occurred almost twenty years before Brigham Young arrived at Nauvoo and began the construction of his house. Clearly, something is wrong.

THESIS NUMBER 3

Every archaeologically recovered artifact from an historical site has two inherent dates: its date of manufacture and its date of deposition. On a prehistoric level, it is not possible to archaeologically distinguish between these two dates (dendrochronology being a possible exception). However, on an historical level, these two dates *must* be recognized as being an inherent and separate characteristic of the artifact itself, and therein lies the major challenge in the interpretation of historical site data, as well as the primary stumbling block for the construction of non-distorted seriations of historical site artifacts.

THESIS NUMBER 4

The date of manufacture for every archaeologically recovered artifact from an historical site implies two separate dates: an 'alpha' date and an 'omega' date. The 'alpha' date refers to the point in time at which that particular *style* of artifact (not a particular recovered artifact) began to be manufactured, and the 'omega' date refers to the point in time at which the manufacture of that particular style of artifact ceased. Somewhere between these two dates lies the date of manufacture of each specific artifact of a given style found at the historical site. More often than not, these 'bracketing' dates, (the 'alpha' and 'omega' dates) are very difficult to pin-point, and the finding of a certain type or style of artifact at an historical site is *not* valid historical proof that that certain type or style of artifact's dates of manufacture have any datable relationship to the site in question. It is a matter of no small wonder and frustration to me to

continue to discover more and more historical artifacts that do not as yet have an 'omega' date!

THESIS NUMBER 5

Every prehistorical and historical site has a 'provenience', meaning its definable relationship to a temporal scale. The 'provenience' of any given site can be defined as the period of time during which any significant cultural expression can be discerned. Within the provenience period of any historical site, at least two, possibly more, separate and yet related time periods must be delineated for the purposes of data interpretation. One of these periods (and not necessarily the earliest, depending on the site's history) is the 'historic' period, i.e., the period of cultural expression (and deposition) with which the historical archaeologist is most concerned from the standpoint of recovery of historical information. The other temporal period, which encompasses but does not include the historic period, can be termed the 'alter' (meaning 'other') period (and may even include the prehistoric period, if any) and this 'alter' period may then be further divided and defined if necessary for convenience purposes. The important aspect to keep in mind is that research (either historical or archaeological) must not be limited to only the 'historic' period of the site being investigated. For the First Fort Smith site, the dates of the historical period were 1817 through 1834 (the period during which troops physically occupied the buildings of the fort) and the provenience period of the site was from 1817 until 1958 (when the shanty town overlying the fort site was burned in preparation for the excavations; since that time, artifacts 'produced' at the site have been insignificant in both amount and historical value). The dates for the historical period at the Brigham Young House site were the period of Young's occupation of the structure (1839–1846); the dates of the provenience period for this site extend up to 1963 when the last occupant of the house vacated the premises. The dates of the historical period of the General Custer House site at Fort Abraham Lincoln, North Dakota, were from 1873, when the General and his wife moved into the newly constructed building, until late 1876, when the General's widow moved back to her family home in Ohio. The provenience dates of this site extend through 1894 when the local settlers dismantled the (by that time) abandoned buildings of the fort, including the Custer House. The recognition of these two separate but interrelated periods at an historical site by the historical archaeologist is vitally important to the validity of the archaeologically recovered historical data and artifacts from that site as it means that most, or all, of the recovered artifacts must be presented as having come from *both* the historical and provenience periods of the site being researched—unless the researcher can present valid proof of the fact that these artifacts can be assigned to *either* of these two periods.

THESIS NUMBER 6

Every archaeologically recovered artifact from an historical site has two definable locations in relation to the matrix of that site, and I call these the 'locative' characteristics of an artifact. The first of these locative characteristics is an artifact's vertical location in relation to the site's ground surface. The second is an artifact's horizontal location in relation to the artifacts and/or features surrounding it. It seems to be an almost universal characteristic of historical sites that the artifact assemblage is a thorough mixture of historical and alter period artifacts. Historical sites, as a general rule, are very shallow and have been subjected to rather long and sometimes intense occupation periods. This situation has frequently resulted in artifacts from widely separated time periods being deposited together in a very shallow and mixed stratum. Under these circumstances, any attempt by the researcher to make use of the depth of artifacts in order to arrive at relative dating usually dissolves into utter chaos. The same confused, and generally invalid, situation may not necessarily exist if the horizontal locative characteristics of these same artifacts are considered, and, since the vertical and horizontal locative characteristics of an artifact are separable as they are not necessarily temporally related, then this procedure is quite permissible. At the First Fort Smith site, the only historical site at which I have been able to actually test this thesis for applicability, it was found that the different classes of artifacts, when examined from the standpoint of their vertical locative characteristics, suggested badly distorted historical data, i.e., incorrect relative dates, erroneous periods of construction activity and occupation concentration, etc. On the other hand, these same classes of artifacts, when examined from the standpoint of their horizontal locative characteristics, suggested very useful and quite valid historical and architectural interpretations, i.e., areas within the site where specific building materials had been used, the manner in which certain structures were demolished, areas of specialized usage such as living and leisure areas, etc.

Several interesting speculations arise when examining the possible causes of this valid/invalid relationship between the horizontal and vertical locative characteristics of an historical site artifact. First, the phenomenon might be a product of the semantics of the situation, i.e., the vertical positioning of classes of artifacts can only be visually expressed using what are essentially statistical methods and histograms (the 'extended' usage of archaeological techniques), whereas the horizontal positioning of classes of artifacts can be visually presented to the researcher on a map showing direct relationship of artifact with artifact and with/to co-existent features. And thirdly, this phenomenon might be the result of what was purely an isolated research situation, and, especially in view of the fact that this thesis has been tested at only one site (the First Fort Smith site), I would advise considerable discussion, caution, and a great deal more testing before the precise formulation of this thesis is accepted.

THESIS NUMBER 7

And finally, as something of a summation of the above discussed six theses regarding artifact usage at historical sites, I would like to present the thesis that an archaeologically recovered artifact found on or in an historical site cannot be dated based only on the fact of its being found at that site, nor can an historical site be specifically dated by the artifacts found within the matrix of that site. It should be sufficiently clear by this time that variants in the manufacturing techniques of historical site artifacts totally destroy their value as specific dating tools for the historical archaeologist. If the historical sources do not supply specific dates for a site, then the techniques of field archaeology cannot (and must not) be trusted to accurately supply such dates.

THESIS NUMBER 8

Turning now from the usage of artifacts to a more wider view of the subject, I would state that historical archaeology must be architectural in orientation and reconstructive in both purpose and scope. With very few exceptions, historical archaeologists deal with areas that have been (or are) the sites of historical structures, as opposed to kill-sites, transient camps, caves, and other similar nonstructured prehistoric sites. More frequently than not, historical sites are (or were) multi-structured, as even the humblest log cabin had one or more outbuildings for domestic or livestock purposes (a 'cabin' is defined as a single-room structure and a 'house' is defined as a multi-room structure—both being used for dwellings). The purpose of historical archaeology must be to achieve, insofar as possible, the goal of complete understanding of the history of any given site, and the scope of such research must include the recovery of all evidence of historical cultural expression at that site, including all architectural evidence. This situation requires that the historical archaeologist be familiar with such architectural features as prepared foundations, footings, pylong, walks, fences, wells, balloon framing, floor joists, wall bonding, fireplaces, porches, lintels, stoops, basements, cellars, barns, chamfering, drip lines, and steps—to mention only a few. In addition, the historical archaeologist must also be well acquainted with the many ways in which building materials, such as wood, stone, brick, and mortar, can be used. And not only must he be familiar with these aspects of architecture but he must also be able to recognize traces of these features from archaeologically obtained evidence.

At the conclusion of the excavation and documentary research, the historical archaeologist should be able to present a thoroughly documented history of the site prior to its excavation, a lucid description of the archaeological work accomplished, and a synthesis of the results, and it is in this section of the report, i.e., the synthesis, that the reconstructive aspect of historical archaeology becomes most apparent. Ideally, when both the research and report are finished, the site can be theoretically (or actually) reconstructed to the desired historical appearance, and reconstruction is defined as the building from new of most or all parts of a vanished historical structure or complex of structures (not to be confused with less inclusive terms such as rebuild, remodel, develop, etc.). The final report should be of such a nature that a competent architect can take the findings and, with very little purely architectural interpolation, proceed with the actual reconstruction of the site. I would like to make it emphatically clear at this point that the reconstructive aspect of the research and report holds true for the historical archaeologist's work regardless of whether the site will ever be actually reconstructed.[5]

This is not the time to engage in a full scale discussion of the pros and cons of reconstruction, but I would like to make

[5]*Subsequent discussion of Thesis #8 by others called to my attention that I failed to make the meaning of this thesis clear. Please let me try again. In my opinion, the researcher is not only responsible for discovery, control, and identification of artifacts and other information at a site, but is also responsible for putting this information together in such a way that the structures become visible (insofar as the data permits) in the excavation report. In other words, the researcher must bring together what is available and give it three-dimensional meaning. This should be done regardless of whether the site's structure/s are to be reconstructed. BY NO MEANS am I suggesting in Thesis #8 that all sites and/or excavated structures should be reconstructed!! Dollar, Sept., 1977.*

a few brief observations on the subject. I would be (and on occasion have been) the first to advise against the actual reconstruction of historical sites. This recommendation is usually based on the premise that successful historical site development and interpretation is infrequently predicated on full reconstruction. In addition, historical reconstruction per se, unless grounded on a substantial funding basis, is all too often inadequate or unsatisfactory. However, it is disturbing to note the number of individuals (who may or may not be engaged in historical archaeology research) who chronically, and frequently without justification, deride any and all reconstructions of the historical sites or structures. I think that these people miss the entire point of historical archaeology, and I would advise them to do some very serious soul searching as to why they are involved in historical archaeology in the first place, if indeed they are.

In this reconstructive aspect, at least, the historical archaeologist takes on a far weightier and more encompassing responsibility than the anthropologist does in the excavation of a prehistoric site (I am certainly *not* suggesting that the one is more 'important' than the other). This increased responsibility and scope brings up the spectre of the length of time required to excavate and research historical sites. I would submit for your consideration that an incompletely excavated and researched historical site is far less desirable than no excavation or research at all. In my opinion, the reconstructive scope and purpose of this type of work requires a fully completed project, and I am highly opposed to the 'sampling' (not testing) of an historical site as this procedure introduces statistical unknowns into an already subjective situation. If an historical site is only 'sampled', and then all additional work neglected, or if a project is terminated prior to completion (such as the General Custer House site in North Dakota), then the validity of the results obtained is brought into serious jeopardy. An historical site can no more be halfway researched or excavated than can a structure be halfway built, and I think that is is high time that we stop using prehistoric site time/work experience factors to estimate the duration of an historical site excavation.

THESIS NUMBER 9

A considerable and basic dissimilarity exists between archaeological evidence for structures at an historical site and such evidence for structures at a prehistoric site. Historical structures, in almost all cases, were built according to patterns dictated by the thrusts, loadings, and stresses required to support the heavy building materials used in those structures, and herein lies the basic reason why the archaeological evidence differs from that of a prehistoric structure (the Meso-America and Mesa Verde/pueblo traditions excluded.

Other differences between these two types of archaeologically researched structures include the use of prepared foundations, commonly used units of measurement for building dimensions, structures of widely differing functions built in identical or very similar manners, and architectural features generally unique to historical building traditions and styles (such as porches, steps, wells, outhouses, cellars, and fireplace foundations, etc.). Since historical archaeology is reconstructive in purpose and scope, the researcher must determine both that such features exist at a site *and* their method of construction. It is a point worth very serious consideration that there are certain archaeological field techniques used to obtain information at a prehistoric site

which will actually obliterate vital architectural information when used at an historic site. For example, the practice of 'trenching along a wall line', i.e., excavating immediately adjacent and parallel to an historic foundation, will very probably destroy evidence for:

1. existence, depth, and configuration of a builder's trench,
2. original or historic ground surface, and
3. width of roof overhang (drip line).

Incorrect excavation of a fireplace platform (foundation) may result in the loss of evidence for:

1. possible indications of floor level and its type of construction,
2. room divider or wall location, and
3. estimated maximum height of chimney.

May I again point out that archaeology is a destructive process, and when doing historical archaeology, it is just as important to discover *how* the construction took place as it is to discover *that* it took place.

THESIS NUMBER 10

To 'identify' a site means to determine its temporal and cultural affinities, and to 'authenticate' a site means to trace the site's historical lineage to establish the authenticity of its historical association with specific individuals or groups. It is a function of historical archaeology to find (and present) evidence, develop hypotheses, and establish facts regarding both of these two aspects of site verification.

Site identification is a universal procedure common to all archaeological sites, historic or prehistoric, but site authentication is a verification function usually unique to historic sites. Unfortunately, site authentication is occasionally omitted in reports, but there are far too many myths, well intentioned but misplaced monuments, and outright pious frauds surrounding historical sites in general for the researcher to overlook the problem. The presence of an historical marker is at best only circumstantial evidence of a site's authenticity (the dignity and social position of the monument's sponsoring institution notwithstanding), and unless there is valid and usable historical evidence to prove the veracity of the monument's location, any previous historical identification of the site must be considered suspect. We are all no doubt familiar with 'humerous' tales on this subject, but when all of these tales are collected and considered, their numerical implications become much more sobering than funny. For the historical archaeologist to neglect the authentication of a site being excavated makes him a party to the possibility of another historical 'fraud', and this is a serious responsibility indeed.

Closely tied with problems of site verification is historical research necessary into the 'come-down' periods of the site— yet another activity unique to archaeology of historical sites. The tendency on the part of the researcher (and I know this from personal experience) is to unconsciously think in terms of the site's history as terminating with the close of the historical period being researched. It is almost axiomatic in site research that no site ever remains architecturally static once human occupation begins, and usually, the older a structure the greater will be the number and scope of these architectural changes. Therefore, the construction (or destruction) activity that occurred at the site between the end of the site's historical period and the end of the site's provenience period (what I refer to as a site's 'come-down' periods) frequently will be of major importance to the historical archaeologist as indications of this activity will be the first archaeological evidence encountered in a site's excavation. As a result, this 'come-down' evidence may go unrecognized or may even mask or confuse the archaeological evidence for the earlier periods of site occupation. It is in the unraveling of these 'come-down' periods that important architectural and cultural facets of the historical period of the site frequently can be discovered.

This concludes the presentation and discussion of the ten theses, and in closing, I would like to summarize the major points covered in this paper:

1. It is time to give serious thought to the recognition of historical archaeology as a distinct socio-scientific discipline with a methodology designed to cope with the unique problems encountered during the excavation of historical sites;

2. Two of the major research methods used by the historian are the logical processes of deduction and tests for validity, and both of these aspects must be a property of the research at an historical site if such research is to be legalistically and microscopically oriented, and therefore considered historically valid;

3. The techniques of archaeology (which are not the exclusive property of the discipline of anthropology) are field techniques only, and any 'extended' use of these techniques by the researcher is grounded on a statistical basis too far removed from the possibility of verification to be usable in historical research processes;

4. The concepts of anthropology are oriented toward macroscopic inductive processes and inferential verification, and training in this field frequently does not prepare the anthropologist to cope with the problems faced when researching an historical site;

5. The ten theses are as follows:
   - since the late 18th century (in America), the number of different physical cultural expressions in the areas of artifact forms and variants within these forms has increased to a point where the subject is extremely complex;
   - while typological processes, in general, can be applied to any given body of historical site artifacts with a specified spatial and temporal limit, seriation processes, or the attempts to derive temporal data from within a typological pattern of historical site artifacts, have not as yet been proven to produce totally non-distorted historical data, and therefore, must not be used alone in the construction of historical hypotheses;
   - every archaeologically recovered artifact from an historical site has two inherent dates: its date of manufacture and its date of deposition;
   - the date of manufacture for every archaeologically recovered artifact from an historical site implies two separate dates: an 'alpha' date and an 'omega' date;
   - within the provenience period of an historical site, at least two separate and related time periods must be delineated: the historical period and the 'alter' period;
   - every archaeologically recovered artifact from an historical site has two definable locations in relation to the matrix of the site (the 'locative' characteristics of an artifact): the vertical location and the horizontal location;
   - an archaeologically recovered artifact found on or in an historical site cannot be dated based only on the fact of its being found at that site, nor can an historical site be specifically dated by the artifacts found within the matrix of that site;
   - the discipline of historical archaeology must be architectural in orientation and reconstructive in both purpose and scope;
   - a considerable and basic dissimilarity exists between archaeological evidence for structures at an historical site and such evidence for structures at a prehistoric site, and certain archaeological field techniques, if used at an historical site, can actually destroy important historical evidence of an architectural nature;
   - it is a function of the historical archaeologist to find and present evidence, develop hypotheses, and establish facts regarding both site identification and site authentication.

CHAPTER 27

Binford, Science, and History: The Probabilistic Variability of Explicated Epistemology and Nomothetic Paradigms in Historical Archaeology

IAIN C. WALKER

"A paradigm, a paradigm, a most ingenious paradigm"

In his recent memoirs Binford describes himself as inviting students for relaxed discussions under his spreading trees and encouraging them to take him on in intellectual arguments (Binford 1972a: 450–51). This picture of benign scholarship does not wholly square with two equally-recent papers by Binford—his comments on South's "Evolution and Horizon as Revealed in Ceramic Analysis in Historical Archeology" (Binford 1972b) and his response to Hanson's criticisms of the Binford pipestem-dating formula (Binford 1972c)—and it is certain of the comments and concepts in these latter two papers and some of their relationships to the Binford memoirs and the so-called New Archaeology that will be discussed here.

If one word can sum up Binford's belief in what archaeology should be it would appear to be "scientific", and if another word can sum up his opinion of those archaeologists who are not of his persuasion it appears to be "historians". Thus faced with Hanson's criticisms (Hanson 1971) of his pipestem-dating formula (Maxwell and Binford 1961: 107–09; Binford 1962), Binford responds that Hanson's conjectures indicate

> . . . that I did not know how to calculate a regression, and secondly that I am unable to round numbers and correctly add, etc. This is the most patent kind of insult and, in addition, supplies us with a very nice example of the kind of methodological difference separating historians from scientists . . . A scientist being fully aware of the role of assumptions in any warranted argument is generally interested in their validity. Historians seems blissfully naive regarding their own thought processes and even defend this innocence by scorning theory and philosophical problems of epistemology (Walker 1970a). Hanson may well protest at this point that I too am making an assumption, that he is an historian. I don't know what his training has been but he behaves like one . . . Hanson should have written me regarding his questions about the data and my summary of it before engaging in "conjectural history" based on a false assumption . . . I hope that this exposition of tobacco pipe stems will help to demonstrate some of the differences between the approaches of scientists and those not so committed (Binford 1972c: 234–35, 251).

We thus have the essential difference, in Binford's mind at least, between scientists and historians. Historians suggest scientists might not always get their arithmetic correct, they scorn theory, and worst of all they do not write Binford for a personal explanation of what he really means before criticizing his publications. Apparently if we cannot understand what Binford says, the fault cannot be Binford's: it is merely our ignorance, caused by our naive, untheoretical, unphilosophical, and unepistemological education. *Also sprach* Binford! The scientificness of this approach escapes me, but then according to Binford I am an historian and therefore naive, untheoretical, unphilosophical, and unepistemological, so perhaps to the New Archaeology at any rate this approach is perfectly scientific.

Binford, however, is forced to admit that his presentation of his pipestem-dating formula was inadequate. The reasons apparently were that:

> At the time the formula was calculated it was done as a personal expedient for testing the validity of Harrington's observations. Later it became clear that it was of general utility. By that time I had misplaced the original data and it appears that at the present time the original data is no longer available . . . In fact, I am not sure that I even made any attempt to save it at the time I calculated the formula since I was toying with Harrington's observations simply to evaluate their utility as a possible research tool . . . Since there was a sub-rosa [sic] knowledge of my formula among historic sites archaeologists I orally reported on it . . . and a transcript of this report was published . . . (Binford 1972c: 235, 231).

This explanation of what really happened has all the hallmarks of being correct, for the two published accounts of the formula are from internal evidence just what Binford now says they were: the incidental inclusion of the formula in the Fort Michilimackinac report as it had been used at that site (Maxwell and Binford 1961: 107–09), and the oral presentation in 1960 and subsequent publication of a formula already known through the professional grapevine (Binford 1962). However, the Authorized Version implies a much more formal status for at least the latter presentation:

Archaeologists must explore the statistical and mathematical techniques available from other fields to increase their abilities in isolating and measuring relationships. This kind of searching is clearly demonstrated in my Kaolin pipe paper. Experimenting with statistical techniques has occupied much of my research time, and in some cases the results are clearly evident in my published papers (Binford 1972a: 330, cf 9).

There is no suggestion here that the formula was something Binford had been only "toying with", nor that its 1962 presentation was simply designed to formalize something already known informally in the field: further, despite Binford's quite valid observation (1972c: 248–50) that the cases of inaccuracy which will arise with his dating system are as important as the cases where the dating will be accurate, it is quite clear from the original presentations of the Binford formula that it *was* designed simply as a dating technique, unlike South's ceramics dating formula which was tied from the first to the equally-important, and interpretive, concept of cultural horizons. We are left to assume Binford's published presentation is an accurate, adequate, and of course scientific example of what archaeologists should be doing and on what Binford has been spending much of his research time. Until and unless the elusive Ur-Binford text turns up, however, we are forced to reply on an undocumented secondary account, which is hardly a shining example of accuracy, adequacy, or the scientific approach, unless I am missing something through being naive, untheoretical, unphilosophical, and unepistemological.

The key word which all of us working on pipe material and utilizing the Binford formula for the past dozen years have apparently overlooked, and on which we could have been enlightened if only we had written the guru and asked him what he really meant, is the word "original" in the statement "This I was able to do by using Harrington's original percentages and converting them to mean hole diameters for the given time period" (Binford 1962: 19; quoted in Binford 1972c: 235 with "original" underlined). This, we should all have known, refers not to the Harrington article (Harrington 1954) but to the original data from which Harrington derived the graphs in his article. Apparently a course in textual analysis and exegesis is necessary to interpret Binford's article. Are we *really* to believe this is a scientific presentation? The tone of Binford's attack on Hanson leaves no doubt that Binford realizes he has been caught with his tweed coat down and is mad about it.

Earlier I quoted Binford observing that "A scientist being fully aware of the role of assumptions in any warranted argument is generally interested in their validity" (Binford 1972c: 234). Having been dubbed an historian, and therefore presumably being unable to produce warranted arguments or consider evidence of validity, I may be being presumptuous, but let us examine some of Binford's assumptions on the subject of clay pipes. First, he says they are made of kaolin. They are not: they are made of ball-clay as I have stressed in three previous articles (Walker 1970c: 160; 1971a: 26; 1971c: 19). Like Binford I initially assumed they were made of kaolin—American archaeological literature still invariably so labels them—until I investigated pipe-manufacture; and had Binford been interested in pipes as socio-economic history rather than as merely a vehicle for toying around with some mathematics he too would no doubt have discovered this fact. Not perhaps an earth-shattering error, but one which should not have been made by a scientist.

Secondly, the inaccurate median date derived from the Binford formula for the Fort Michilimackinac occupation span is attributed to an increase in population in the later period of the fort and to "increased logistic efficiency" (sic—Binfordese for more supplies?). As a "scientist" Binford **has** no time for historical explanations, so the major historical event in the lifetime of the fort, its transfer in 1761 from the French to the British, is not even mentioned, and so the possibility of there being an historical or even political reason for an inaccurate date is utterly ignored—even though Harrington had noted (1954: 3) that Dutch pipes tended to have narrower stem bores than English pipes of comparable date and even though Omwake had identified Dutch pipes at Fort Michilimackinac (Maxwell and Binford 1961: 109). Indeed, a far more obvious historical event occurring about the time Binford says his formula ceases to be accurate is the American Revolution, which certainly caused both short-term and long-term disruption in established trade patterns—the cessation of trade in English Buckley earthenware, for example, and the appearance in Revolutionary contexts of French faience and Dutch pipes (Walker 1972a: 129 and refs.). Certainly first the Stamp Act troubles of 1765–66 and then the American Revolution practically killed the Bristol pipe industry, which did not begin to revive until the first decade of the nineteenth century (cf Walker 1972b: 11). All these factors, however, are connected with British political and economic history and therefore presumably ignored by Binford. That increases of population and an increased supply of pipes could effect the Binford data for a site is not denied, either for Fort Michilimackinac or anywhere else, but what Binford has done is to fall into the "fallacy of a single cause" (Beveridge 1950: 117, 1961 ed.).

Thirdly, regarding the breakdown in accuracy of his formula after ca. 1780, Binford states:

In the way of explanation it is quite obvious that with the influx of pipes manufactured in Montreal and at other seats of American [sic] pipemaking there is a corresponding re-occurrence of certain "early" styles, in addition to the appearance of a new style of elements. This break in the traditional direction of stylistic change is responsible, I feel quite sure, for the breakdown in the correlation after roughly 1780 (Binford 1962: 20).

As this explanation is so obvious to Binford presumably lesser researchers should have written him to obtain his evidence, for none is given here nor are footnotes cited (unless the evidence was in the missing text). His evidence for a Montreal pipe industry ca. 1780 would be particularly welcome, seeing that present available evidence shows the Montreal pipe industry to be wholly a phenomenon of the second half of the nineteenth century; the first known pipemaker there being recorded in 1847, the last in 1907, and the zenith of the trade being in the 1870's (Walker 1971c: 25). The only other North American pipemaking centre of any size known from present research is Detroit, where the industry came from Montreal in the late 1870's as the Montreal industry began to decline and where it too died out at the beginning of the twentieth century (Walker *loc. cit.*). The Glasgow pipe industry, which if Binford knew anything about pipes he would know was far more predominant in nineteenth-century North American markets than any native industry, only begins to achieve any importance in the early nineteenth century and present evidence does not suggest it was taking over the North American market before ca. 1840 (cf Walker 1971c: 23, 25).

If a change in source of supply is indeed responsible for the breakdown of the Binford formula the evidence is going to be forthcoming from identification of makers of marked pipes from datable contexts (or alternatively identification of datable regional pipe styles) and an examination of trade patterns, both of which approaches are straight history and neither of which needs to rely on the Binford formula for assistance. Thus, Liverpool-made pipes started appearing on North American sites from the 1760's into the early nineteenth century (paralleling a sudden expansion of the Liverpool pipe industry) while Bristol pipes had been declining in frequency on North American sites from the 1730's (cf Walker 1971c: 22–23; 1972b; 10–11). Professor Lehrer has suggested that with the New Maths (or Math) it is more important to understand what one is doing than to get the right answer (Lehrer 1965a): apparently with the New Archaeology it is not even important to understand what one is doing.

And still on Binford's alleged causes for the breakdown of his formula ca. 1780, one would like to know what he means by "the appearance of a new style of elements" and the "break in the traditional direction of stylistic change": to what "elements" is he referring, and what is the "traditional direction" which apparently breaks? Is he suggesting that a change in bore diameter is a stylistic change? Were all these points discussed in the lost text too?

And fourthly, though it appears not in Binford's comments on Hanson's criticisms but in his comments on South's paper (1972c: 249), we have an excellent example of the over-generalization far too common in the field, in this case resulting in a serious distortion of statements this writer made some years ago. Binford, talking about factors "which would tend to bias the pipes present in one area in favor of some manufacturers" [sic], says "I need only cite Walker's evidence for higher frequencies of Dutch-made pipes in the Northeast (Walker 1965)". What in fact Walker (1965) showed was that at *one* site in *eastern Canada* at *one* particular period of time within the lifetime of that site a sizeable number of Dutch-made pipes did occur and that at that one site the historical evidence—naive, untheoretical, etc., as it is—suggested the French occupation of that site was the source of that Dutch material and that this possibly was the cause of inaccurate Binford dates. Neither in my 1965 paper, nor in my detailed examination of pipes from certain areas at Louisbourg (Walker 1971b) of which the 1965 data was a part and with which Binford appears not to be familiar, do I make any suggestions whatsoever that on the basis of my work one can say there are "higher frequencies of Dutch made pipes in the Northeast". What Binford's statement here means is that any archaeologist working in the North-East who finds his Binford dates are inaccurate can say, and cite Binford's statement as proof, that the reason is the presence of Dutch pipes. From this of course one can then say there are Dutch pipes on the site even if one could no more identify a Dutch pipe from the literature than one could a checked stamped pot; in fact, one does not need to use such naive, untheoretical, etc., sources as history because Binford has "proved" the presence of Dutch pipes scientifically.

Binford says elsewhere (1972b: 122) that he believes historical interpretation "is dependent upon valid general propositions which can serve as pivotal points for interpretive arguments treating the specific facts of a specific case". A wide range of researchers, myself, South, philosophers of science like Hempel, physical anthropologists like Washburn, animal pathologists like Beveridge (Walker 1972a: 139 and refs.; South 1972: 79, 102 and refs.) agree that theories and hypotheses are invented to account for observed facts rather than derived from them, but the facts have to be observed and the theories and hypotheses made accountable. Binford's "valid general propositions" here are either whole-cloth fabrication—such as the explanations as to why the Binford formula breaks down towards the end of the eighteenth century—or one-swallow-makes-a-summer houses of cards such as the above remark on Dutch pipes in the North-East. For my part I specifically stated, after tentatively suggesting the substantial quantities of Dutch pipes in certain deposits at Louisbourg were the cause of inaccurate Binford dates, that "Further deposits containing large amounts of Dutch material would have to be analyzed before a definite statement could be made" (Walker 1971c: 119). Binford as in so many other cases where he makes dogmatic assertions on pipes, offers no original work of his own or even an adequate examination of others' work to suggest the single specific example I gave can be accepted as *a*, let alone *the*, reason for inaccurate Binford dates in the North-East. In theoretical discussion Binford can talk of hypotheses "which must be tested against independent data" (1972a: 93), but in practice he betrays a total inability to handle basic data. One can hardly have valid general propositions if one cannot handle the evidence which might validate them.

Further, in generalizing about the North-East—New York, New England, and the Atlantic Provinces—Binford is fatuously ignoring the very different historical backgrounds in these areas: Dutch pipes from sites in eastern Canada and other parts of the continent where there was French settlement in the eighteenth century do in fact appear on present evidence to indicate French occupation, but seventeenth-century Dutch pipes in New York and New Jersey certainly do not indicate French influence but reflect the Dutch occupation of that area. Dutch *eighteenth-century* pipes in northern New York state, however, could plausibly be associated with French influence. In New Jersey indeed, Dutch pipes in mid-seventeenth century contexts might at least as easily belong to its period as a Swedish colony, for the New Sweden Company in fitting out the settlement of the colony is known to have obtained Dutch pipes (quoted in Omwake n.d.: 8) and Dutch pipes were certainly common in Sweden in the seventeenth and eighteenth centuries (Puktörne 1968: *passim*). And to jump continents, Dutch pipes from West African historical sites need by no means indicate Dutch occupation or trade, for in 1719 it is noted (quoted in Donnan [ed.] 1930–35: II, 241–42, 1965 ed.) that though it was forbidden for English traders to obtain Dutch pipes for sale in England they were now permitted to buy them for trading on the African coast because Dutch pipes were cheaper than English. Thus Dutch pipes on West African sites can mean either English or Dutch trade, and indeed possibly French, Danish, Swedish, and Brandenburg trade as all these countries had posts at one time or another in West Africa and appear to have relied heavily on Dutch pipes. But all this requires a sound background in historical evidence, and all Binford has is his desk calculator (Binford 1972a: 9, 188), to which, Linus-like, he seems inseparably linked. If Binford thinks it funny that Griffin was hailed in 1938 as a master of statistical technique when all he had done was count something (Binford 1972a: 3) is it any less funny that Binford is hailed a generation later as the father of the New Archaeology because he uses an adding machine?

It is a supreme irony that Binford can quote Washburn's

remarks about the need to get beyond mere accurate description (Binford 1972a: 99, also quoted in South 1972: 79) yet fails to meet the required scientific scholarship necessary to present his data so that it can be meaningfully used in this fashion. Again, in generalizing as to the cause of Dutch pipes in north-eastern North America Binford falls into the fallacy of a single cause, and he compounds this with two other unscientific errors. First, he ignores the fact that experimental results are valid only for the precise conditions under which the experiments are conducted and that hypotheses are true only for the particular circumstances prevailing in these experiments. Secondly, he forgets that generalizations can never be proved and are accepted in practice only after all attempts to disprove them fail (Beveridge 1950: 88, 1961 ed.), something which Binford conspicuously fails to do here as elsewhere, despite his urging that "Anthropologists smugly displaying their scorn of historians must stop working as historians and start working as scientists to meet the need for valid general propositions" (Binford 1972b: 122). The physiologist Claude Bernard could have been thinking of Binford when he said "Men who have excessive faith in their theories or ideas are not only ill-prepared for making discoveries; they also make poor observations" (quoted in Beveridge 1950: 49, 1961 ed.).

At best, the Binford formula correctly used would give a date differing from that expected (if the context had known, and accurate, historical dates) which would tell the archaeologist to examine his pipes to see if he had some "non-standard" material, and if so describe this material; the historical approach, based on a knowledge of pipes, would be to examine the pipes, recognize some were Dutch, and offer an historical reason for their presence. Neither of these last two stages could be achieved by a Binford archaeologist unfamiliar with the historical evidence, however, and as that archaeologist, being unfamiliar with pipes, would be unable to give an adequate description of his pipes, let alone discern which were "non-standard" (Walker 1972a: 142–43), one can see no advantage, but rather several disadvantages, in using the Binford approach rather than the historical approach. Only the historical approach provides identification and interpretation. The only claim to advantage of the Binford approach is that one can get away, to a limited degree, with pure ignorance.

Until those involved in historical archaeology realize that the Aristotelian belief that someone who has studied the nature of inference can judge the validity of inference without any special knowledge of the subject-matter is wrong and put study of cultural remains and their contexts *before* philosophical interpretation they are going to remain nothing better than technicians, which is what Binford and others like him are (cf Walker 1972a: 140–41, 142–43, 145–46, 146–47). Because of this preoccupation with doing things backwards, the Maxwell and Binford report on the 1959 season at Fort Michilimackinac (Maxwell and Binford 1961) is useless as a provider of information on the material culture of an eighteenth-century frontier post with first French and then British occupation. South emphasizes in the strongest terms in his "Evolution and Horizon . . . " paper the need for an adequate knowledge of ceramics on the part of the archaeologist if his ceramic dating formula is to be meaningful:

> . . . the degree of refinement of the model is dependent upon the degree of sophistication of the archaeologist's ceramic knowledge . . . For the formula to be used, therefore, a knowledge of ceramic types is necessary,

> which can be learned from the many references available. This reference work must be combined with a familiarity with the archaeological specimens. A knowledge of the ceramic type attributes cannot be overemphasized for there are far too many meaningless descriptions appearing in the historic site literature now in spite of the availability of numerous excellent sources to act as guides for learning (South 1972: 80, 86).

yet Binford entirely ignores this vital basic point in his comments on South's paper. To the extent that only the archaeologist excavating the site can interpret what he is excavating R. H. Thompson is correct when he provocatively states:

> The individual investigator with his unique combination of interpretive skills provides the only possible means for the reconstruction of the cultural context of an archaeological collection. The final judgment of any archaeologist's cultural reconstructions must therefore be based on an appraisal of his professional competence, and particularly the quality of the subjective contribution to that competence (R. H. Thompson 1956: 331).

A simple, well-illustrated, corpus of the ceramics from Fort Michilimackinac instead of the offered hodgepodge of inaccurate and meaningless terminology would have been ten times as valuable as comments on vectors of skewing or the results of chi-square tests. As it is, if the data so scientifically analysed at Fort Michilimackinac was based on the farcical sub-categorizing indicated in the section on ceramics in the Fort Michilimackinac report (Maxwell and Binford 1961: 94–95) with its groupings such as "white-glazed delft" and "tin-glazed delft" then Binford was skewing nonsense and chi-squaring rubbish; and it is a mercy for historical archaeology that since his Fort Michilimackinac days Binford has not been engaged in that field (Binford 1972c: 231). Binford sub-titles his comments on South's paper "A Step Toward the Development of Archaeological Science" (Binford 1972b: 117): how would he know if the paper were scientific?—his lack of knowledge on historical ceramics would prevent his ever being able to use it.

If Griffin, according to Binford, has never gone beyond the study of artefacts it is no better that Binford attempts to do so *without* first studying artefacts. Certainly if one never goes beyond using artefacts to date a site little of the potential of archaeology has been realized, but if one insists on interpretive speculations without first having settled the essentials of the site such as its date then one cannot complain if people ask why (cf Binford 1972a: 10–11). As Beveridge points out, more discoveries have come from intense observation of very limited material than from statistics applied to very large groups: the value of the latter lies mainly in testing hypotheses arising from the former (Beveridge 1950: 105, 21, 1961 ed.). Darwin, who is commonly accepted as a scientist, maintained "I must begin with a good body of facts, and not from any principle, in which I always suspect some fallacy" (quoted in Beveridge 1950: 85, 1961 ed.). Binford, however, insists in going at it backwards—for he clearly knows nothing about pipes or any other historical artefacts—and thus comes up with absurdities. For similar reasons I have criticized several "scientific" approaches to historical artefact analysis (Walker 1972a: 140–43): it would be a major advance in the field of historical archaeology if those moving into it knew something about the data whereof they spoke.

But, it might be argued, such criticism of Binford based on detailed knowledge of a small and specialized field is unfair in that it obscures the usefulness of Binford's concepts even if they do not fit the particular evidence of a specific situation. There is some truth to this—a common tendency among historians reviewing Toynbee was to praise him for his breadth of concepts then pan him for all the errors of fact made in that part in which the reviewer was an expert, and more recently Clarke's *Analytical Archaeology* has received similar criticisms—so we can examine Binford's comments on South's "Evolution and Horizon . . ." paper to see whether they exhibit a more scientific approach. Alas, this does not appear to be the case. Binford starts out:

> *Stanley South's paper is excellent. It argues a closely reasoned justification for the development of a research tool which when properly applied should be of great value to historical archaeology (Binford 1972b: 117).*

He then goes on to discuss the recent exchanges in the field of historical archaeology theory stimulated by the 1967 South Forum when Clyde Dollar's "Some Thoughts on Theory and Method in Historical Archaeology" (Dollar 1968a) was presented. Binford's comments, mainly directed against the alleged shortcomings of historians and historical research, continue for six and a half pages and are then tied into two pages of general comments on South's paper. For obvious reasons, I would be the last to criticize papers in the South Fora for their rhapsodic nature: indeed, the most stimulating thing about these Fora is that one can—preferably using the theme paper as a basis—get well beyond the mundane book-review sort of critique; but the Forum contributor has some responsibility to analyse critically the concepts of the pivotal paper, and simply to say as here that South's paper is "excellent" and "closely reasoned" is not only naive, unthe-oretical, unphilosophical, and unepistemological but grossly unscientific. Once again—Thus spoke Binford! Where is the rigorous scientific method, the objective quantification of evidence, the explicated epistemology and nomothetic paradigms of the New Archaeology? The best, and by far the most incisive, appraisal of South's paper was L. M. Stone's five pages (1972): could not Binford, co-founder and father-figure of the New Archaeology, have given us such an old-fashioned display of simple logic?—it would not even have needed a knowledge of historical ceramics in this case, so Binford would not have been disadvantaged.

The simple fact of the matter is that historical archaeology by definition relies on historical interpretation for explanation. As Dollar put it a few years ago, "the name of the game is History, and if you have not played it according to its rules, then you have played in vain" (Dollar 1968b: 188). To fall back on facile generalization such as "logistic efficiency" and "the traditional direction of stylistic change" as explanations when historical evidence can offer far more precise and concrete suggestions is to betray an utter ignorance of the field of history and how its evidence can be used.

That such blissful ignorance is widespread is suggested by more than one study in the field of historical archaeology by anthropologists. Cleland's worthwhile study of faunal remains from Fort Michilimackinac (Cleland 1971a) correctly suggests that the difference between the British dietary pattern and that of the French can be plausibly explained by the former having superior naval power and a more active colonial policy, thus permitting a much better supply system; but the historical generalities in the conclusions read rather like a Rule Britannia interpretation of Noël Coward Englishmen transporting British culture overseas and establishing some corner of a foreign field that would be forever England. In fact, this caricature of British imperialism and its attendant Ryder Haggard and *Sanders of the River* folklore—from which Cleland appears to have derived his model—is one of the later nineteenth century and has nothing to do with events 100 years earlier at Fort Michilimackinac. It is naive, if not actually untheoretical, etc., to deduce from the evidence that the French displayed no tendencies to maintain or imitate the traditions of their native land while the British did; the evidence suggests simply that the British were able to but that the French had fewer opportunities to. (On the matter of mastering historical data one might point out that *crêpes suzette* [Cleland 1971a: 18] would not have been known to Frenchmen of any class at this time: like British imperialism, they are nineteenth century in date [Hale *et al* 1968: 727]. Tracing the origins of *coq au vin* [Cleland *loc. cit.*] proved difficult: one source [Oliver 1967: 148] appears to indicate that *coq au vin* is also less than 100 years old and that the use of wine in this fashion only became important from the beginning of the nineteenth century; the *Larousse gastronomique* [Montagné and Gottschalk 1938: s.v. Coq] quotes only "*une recette ancienne*", while Fisher's *The Cookery of Provincial France* suggests it is a traditional Burgundian dish [Fisher 1968: 24, 119–22]. It may be suspected that cooking flesh with wine must have been known from time immemorial in wine-growing areas; in any event *coq au vin* is not *haute cuisine*, as the Cleland reference implies, but *cuisine bourgeoise*.)

The idea of history as "specific things and events ordered in time" (Cleland and Fitting 1968: 132) or some similar piece of jargon is one which appears to be standard among anthropologists. Leslie White, whose ideas Cleland and Fitting paraphrase, commences his paper "History, Evolutionism, and Functionalism: Three Types of Interpretation of Culture":

> *There is a widely held view in contemporary anthropology according to which there are two, and only two, kinds of interpretative studies of culture: the "historical" and the "scientific". Historical studies, according to this view, are those which deal with chronological sequences of unique events (White 1945: 221)*

and while he goes on to expound his belief that there are not two but three kinds of interpretative studies of culture his definition of history does not change:

> *. . . the temporal process [is] a chronological sequence of unique events, the study of which is history; . . . the historic process deals with events determined by specific time and space coördinates, in short with unique events (White 1945: 222, 230).*

This is, as we shall see, an outdated concept of history, and it is undoubtedly this which contributes much of the confusion to the field. The result is a straw man: history is only specific things and events ordered in time and how much more lofty and cosmic a field of endeavour is anthropology, the study of man. And so it is, given the above definition of history; but as that definition of history is about as realistic as one portraying anthropologists as individuals studying nothing but the sex-lives of modern primitives the whole comparison falls to pieces.

Paul Chace, in his interesting paper "The Chinese Horizon

in America: the Archaeology of Railroad Camps" given at the autumn 1972 meeting of the Council for Northeast Historical Archaeology at Oneonta, New York State, prefaced his talk by stressing that history was only specific things and events etc., but that his study exemplified the anthropological approach; however, he then went on to use precisely the same sources and give the same analysis as any competent historian would have done. As for visiting the sites of railway camps, which it might be argued constituted a different approach to that which an historian might use, the book *History on the Ground*—which contains the comment that a good pair of boots are part of the minimum equipment of an historian in the field (Beresford 1957: 249, 1971 ed.)—was written by an economic historian nearly 20 years ago; and Beresford is only one modern representative of a British tradition of field archaeologists and historians which goes back to the fifteenth century and includes such observers as William Camden who in the 1594 edition of his *Britannia* noted, identified, and correctly explained crop-marks (quoted in Ashbee 1972: 42).

Again, Dethlefsen and Deetz in their equally-interesting study of Massachusetts tombstones (Dethlefsen and Deetz 1966) stress the anthropological nature of their work when in fact they are studying social, economic, religious, and art history, plus historical geography and some industrial archaeology—all aspects of the field of history. The appearance of a so-called Doppler effect in plotting rates of stylistic change (Deetz and Dethlefsen 1965) hardly converts the study to a science.

Binford in his comments on South's paper is much exercised about the "uniqueness" of historical events, which is what he apparently feels causes the innate inferiority of history compared to anthropology (Binford 1972b: *passim*). Of course historical events are specific (*not* unique, a term grossly misused in this context), and so are archaeological sites: so what? It is from these specific pieces of data that history is written. History, as I noted in discussing South's paper and elsewhere, is the interpretation of whole series of interrelated events, their causes, and their effects (Walker 1972a: 145; cf 1970a; 64[1]; 1968a: 27). The modern American historian Wish agrees, commenting that the nineteenth-century "scientific" approach to history was fruitless because:

> Literally taken, the idea that history consisted of wholly unique facts made even history itself impossible, for at the core of historiography was the idea of change and development—a process assuming some continuity, direction, and meaning. Aristotle had long ago exposed the fallacy of uniqueness by demanding a context of classification to make each fact meaningful. Uniqueness was a half-truth useful for the unimaginative (Wish 1960: 160–61).

I suggest historians will be as surprised as scientists—which latter point will be discussed later—to find Hempel suggesting that it is still "a rather widely held opinion that history, in contradistinction to the so-called physical sciences, is concerned with the description of particular events in the past rather than with the search for general laws which

might govern these events" (1965b: 231). Historians most certainly look for useful generalizations to further their research, though like modern scientists they no longer look for "laws" in the nineteenth-century positivist sense of that term. Almost half a century ago, Trevelyan, one of the great historians of his time, pointed out that historians do not just collect facts—they think about them (Trevelyan 1927: 26). One of the leading historians of the present day, Christopher Hill, talking of the complexities of the English Civil War, said:

> One easy refuge is to say that it is all so complex that no interpretation at all is possible. The historian can only record the multifarious things that happened, but must not attempt to make sense of them. I believe this is to abdicate the historian's function (Hill 1958: 38, 1968 ed.)

and elsewhere he commences a standard textbook in the seventeenth century:

> History is not a narrative of events. The historian's difficult task is to explain what happened (Hill 1961: 13, 1969 ed.).

Even Binford admits this, preferring to concentrate (Binford 1972b: 117, 118, 119) on what he conceives—with the aid of some sadly outmoded ideas as to how historical evidence is examined quoted from Hempel (1965b) and Dray (1957) (neither of whom is an historian) and from an article by Joynt and Rescher (1961) which flogs a dead issue in terms of an outmoded nineteenth-century conception of science and some hangovers from an equally outdated concept of history—to be the inferior methodology of historians. The idea that history is only collecting unique facts is utter rubbish, and either a red herring used by some anthropologists to extol their own field as some superior ultimate plateau of knowledge or the reflection of an outmoded and inadequate training in history.[2]

Collingwood saw the distinction between history and data-collecting thus:

> We preserve these relics, hoping that in the future they may become what now they are not, namely historical evidence . . . This task of keeping relics against the time when they become material for history is the task of pure scholars, archivists, and antiquaries. Just as the antiquary keeps implements and pots in his museum without necessarily constructing history from them, and as the archivist in the same way keeps public documents, so the pure scholar edits and emends and reprints texts of, for example, ancient philosophy without necessarily understanding the philosophical ideas they express, and therefore without being able to reconstruct the history of philosophy.
> This work of scholarship is often taken for history

---

[1] *In the 1970a: 64 reference—middle paragraph—a proof-reading error on my part prevented the removal of the phrase "—they do not . . . some lofty summit." which, as the astute reader will have observed, contradicts both the general tenor of that paragraph and the second paragraph on the following page.*

[2] *There is an interesting discussion of historical evidence in Winks's "Introduction" to the collection of extracts entitled* The Historian as Detective: Essays on Evidence *(1969), a book well worth reading, though its title will doubtless confirm in Binford's mind that historians, like Braidwood, believe their field to be "like a detective story, full of mystery and romance" (Binford 1972a: 11). An excellent example of the complexities of historical evidence, though unfortunately the footnotes and references have been omitted in the extracting, is* The Origins of the English Civil War: Conspiracy, Crusade, or Class Conflict? *(1960) ed. P.A.M. Taylor, 16 extracts from 13 writers on the English Civil War covering seventeenth-, nineteenth-, and twentieth-century views.*

itself; and as so taken becomes a special type of pseudo-history, which Croce calls philological history. As thus misconceived, history consists of transcribing, translating, and compiling. Such work is useful, but it is not history; there is no criticism, no interpretation, no reliving of past experience in one's own mind. It is mere learning or scholarship (Collingwood 1946: 203–04, 1961 ed.).

Elton writing in the *New Cambridge Modern History* puts it more tersely:

The attraction of the sweeping and enlightening generalisation, however dangerous, is legitimate; what distinguishes the historian from the collector of historic facts is generalisation—preferably successful generalisation (Elton 1958: 20)

and Carr is terser still: "It is nonsense to say that generalization is foreign to history; history thrives on generalizations" (Carr 1961: 64, 1964 ed.). Depending on one's definitions and inclinations, indeed, one could extol history as the superior field and relegate anthropology to the status of data collecting: some years ago I cited (against Willey and Phillips's dictum that American archaeology is anthropology or it is nothing) the view that anthropology has to become history or become nothing (quoted in Walker 1968a: 25), and Bibby in an entirely offhand remark observes that "so long as changes cannot be detected within a period as long as that intervening between the Pilgrim Fathers and our own day, then we are not writing history but only anthropology" (Bibby 1961: 274).

Binford's own view of history appears to be curiously superficial. He remarks (1972b: 119) that Dollar and I take a stand championed by what he calls the German School of the second half of last century. The term "German School" is bad, for there was a whole variety of German thought last century on history: what Binford is referring to is what is usually called the *Geschichtsphilosophie* school, which dates in fact to the last decade of the nineteenth century, and as Binford notes evolved the concepts of nomothetic science (science in the common meaning of the word, which had as its purpose the formulation of general laws and was the theory of knowledge) and idiographic science (history, which was the description of individual facts and was the theory of value). This philosophy, first put forward in 1894 by Windelbrand, was systematized two years later by Rickert, who saw two distinctions between science and history where Windelbrand had suggested only one. These distinctions, Rickert maintained, were between generalizing and individualizing thought and between valuing and non-valuing thought. From this, he produced four types of science: non-valuing and generalizing (pure natural science), non-valuing and individualizing (quasi-historical sciences of nature such as geology), valuing and generalizing (quasi-scientific sciences of history such as sociology), and valuing and individualizing (history proper). Obviously as Windelbrand defined history as the theory of value (as opposed to science, which was the theory of knowledge), the logical conclusion would be that history is not knowledge (Collingwood 1946: 165–70, 1961 ed.).

I cannot speak for Dollar, but I feel mildly surprised at being assigned to this sort of "general stance"—only mildly, however, for it is clear that in spite of some citing from works on the philosophy of history, Binford knows little history and therefore cannot analyse historical thoughts. So far as historical thought in Britain is concerned, these German philo-

sophic historians were, as Carr has noted (1961: 20, 1964 ed.), ignored. They may, however, have had some influence in North America—Binford asserts the idiographic approach has "recently" been reconsidered by historians (Binford 1972b: 119), by which he possibly means American historians—for the "individualizing" concept has obvious affinities to the "uniqueness" concepts anthropologists have of history while the "theory of value" concept of history closely corresponds to Cleland and Fitting's "low level" concept of history (Cleland and Fitting 1968: *passim*); and certainly the Cleland and Fitting chart showing history as temporal particularizing and anthropology as temporal generalizing (Cleland and Fitting 1968: 132) has close connections with Rickert's concept. Where this leaves Binford is somewhat unclear, unless possibly hoist with his own petard, for he and Cleland, both New Archaeologists, fit very much better into the philosophy they disparage than do I.[3]

The only reason I can see Binford might assign those disagreeing with him to the *Geschichtsphilosophie* school is that this school arose in opposition to, though deriving from and coloured by, the German positivist school which some years ago I suggested formed the basis for American anthropological thought and with which I specifically contrasted my views (Walker 1968a: 25). This school with its pseudo-scientific "objective" approach *wie es eigentlich gewesen*—simply to show how it really was—and its desire to frame laws was only the New History[4] of its day, complete with pseudo-scientific terminology such as *Kulturwissenschaft* (culture-science) for *Geschichte* (history) and like the New Archaeology "designed . . . to save historians from the tiresome obligation to think for themselves" (Carr 1961: 9, 1964 ed.). Historians went through their New Archaeology phase three generations ago, and in finally rejecting it, moved to a far more realistic level of history and interpretation.

Where the *Geschichtsphilosophie* school erred was in starting with the positivist principle that natural science was the only true form of knowledge—just as the New Archaeologist believes that unless archaeology can be made a "science" it is meaningless—when in fact such as assumption is nonsense. Collingwood attacked this assumption by asserting "facts" meant quite different things to a scientist from what they meant to an historian: "In science . . . facts are empirical facts, facts perceived as they occur", whereas in history a fact was "arrived at inferentially by a process of interpreting data according to a complicated set of rules and assumptions" (Collingwood 1946: 133, 1961 ed.); but one might argue from more recent philosophic thoughts on the meaning of science (e.g. Beveridge 1950; 1961 ed.) and in particular from a famous Cambridge physicist's definition of a scientific truth

---

[3] *I do not believe it is by any means so certain that even American historians have only "recently" begun to consider the limitations of idiographic history, whatever Binford may take Joynt and Rescher's article to imply. As early as 1910 Carl Becker, a very eminent American historian, rejected Rickert's philosophy (Becker 1910: 531–32); and I do not find evidence of* Geschichtsphilosophie *outlook in the works of any of the American historians whose work is discussed by Wish (1960). The concepts of history suggested by the definitions advanced by Binford and by Cleland and Fitting are hopelessly inadequate for a field whose complexity has to be tackled in books, not in glib one-sentence definitions. History cannot be adequately defined in the abstract, and when it is examined in the flesh it becomes clear its writers have an infinite variety and gradation of views in practice. Wish's survey of American historiography presents a very readable account of this complexity.*

[4] *The term New History is used here simply as a parallel to Binford's term New Archaeology; it does not refer to the American New History of Robinson, Beard, Becker, and others.*

as "a statement which has been publicly accepted by the experts" (J. Ziman, quoted in Carr 1961: 61, 1964 ed.), that scientists have come closer to the philosophy of post-positivist historians. As Carr puts it: "The historian has some excuse for feeling himself more at home in the world of science today than he could have a hundred years ago", for physicists now study events, not facts, and scientific laws in the eighteenth- and nineteenth-century sense of these terms are an outmoded concept (Carr 1961: 57–59, 1964 ed. and chapter 3 *passim*).

Binford, in a summary statement made in 1968 about the aims of the New Archaeology states:

> We seek to replace these inadequate propositions [*the old principles of interpretation, allegedly mainly intuition and inference*] by laws that are validated in the context of the epistemology of science, so that we may gain an accurate knowledge of the past (Binford 1972a: 121).

Such a positivistic view of science, far from being new, is as old and as outmoded as that of positivistic history: no less a figure than Max Planck argued strongly against it (Planck 1932: Chapter II, cf pp. 34–35). The physicist J. Robert Oppenheimer wrote "The ineluctable element of chance introduced into twentieth century physics heralds the end of the Newtonian paradigm of certain predictions of the future from the knowledge of the present" (quoted in Yankelovich and Barrett 1970: 208). As Beveridge points out (1950: 62, 1961 ed.), the teleological view that scientists should wonder "how" and not "why" is rejected by present-day science. Cohen and Nagel, two American philosophers on scientific method, noted that scientists "obtain evidence for principles by appealing to empirical material, to what is alleged to be 'fact'; and we select, analyse, and interpret empirical material on the basis of principles" (Cohen and Nagel 1934: 396, 1936 ed.): in other words, discoveries and new knowledge come not from establishing precise and universal laws but by forming hypotheses from available evidence which open the way to further inquiries and fresh discoveries. Binford's view represents the later Victorian optimism of Darwin and Huxley, or as a theological historian has put it, the "faith in science as a redemptive instrument guaranteeing progress in human affairs" (Farmer 1964: 181). By a curious irony Binford's definition of the "New" Archaeology now sounds like the conservative and reactionary elements of current politics and society:

> The marked tendency has been to consign whatever is not fully and articulately available in the waking consciousness for empirical or mathematical manipulation to a purely negative catch-all category (in effect, the cultural garbage can) called the "unconscious" or the "irrational" or the "mystical" or the "purely subjective" (T. Roszak, The Making of a Counter-Culture, quoted in Smith 1972: 286).

Yet this philosophy has clearly been followed by exponents of the New Archaeology, including those in historical archaeology: Cleland and Fitting offer (1968: 130–131) a concise positivist statement about their biggest problem, the "mystique of expertise":

> Thus specialists can distinguish German from Dutch earthenware on the basis of "experience" or "feel" but are reluctant to set forth specific criteria. We expect

these criteria are either nonexistent or are <u>undefinable, untestable, and therefore indefensible</u> (*emphasis mine*).

This appears to be the archaeological equivalent of the McNamara fallacy, explicated thus by Daniel Yankelovitch, who as head of a social research firm may know something about quantification:

> The first step is to measure whatever can be easily measured. This is okay so far as it goes. The second step is to disregard that which can't be measured or give it an arbitrary quantitative value. This is artificial and misleading. The third step is to presume that what can't be measured easily really isn't very important. This is blindness. The fourth step is to say that what can't be easily measured really doesn't exist. This is suicide (quoted in Smith loc. cit.).

In 1967 Binford, discussing his ideas on the role of analogy, declared (1972a: 48–49) that his procedure was:

> ... appropriate in the context of a positivistic philosophy of anthropology and archaeology. It denies categorically the assertion of antipositivists that the final judgment of archaeological reconstruction must be based on an appraisal of the professional competence of the archaeologist ([R. H.] Thompson 1956: 311). The final judgment of the archaeological reconstruction presented here must rest with the testing through subsidiary hypotheses drawn deductively.

This is straight Hempel (the "positivistic philosophy" Binford refers to is neo-positivism, not the Comteian positivism of last century in which as noted above North American anthropologists still misguidedly think historians are enmeshed); but Hempel also observes (1966: 15) that "The transition from data to theory requires creative imagination"—which certainly includes intuition. Further, Hempel talks of the transition *from* data *to* theory, and notes the importance of an "antecedent knowledge of specific facts" (1965a: 5) and a "thorough familiarity with current knowledge in the field" (1966: 15). Therefore when he maintains (1965a: 6) that "What determines the soundness of a hypothesis is not the way it is arrived at (it may even have been suggested by a dream or a hallucination), but the way it stands up when tested" one can assume that he did not mean the dream or hallucination part to be taken as literally as Binford appears to have done with for example his general propositions regarding pipes, that he expected the person propounding the hypothesis had a knowledge of the subject-matter, and that he supposed those testing the hypothesis deductively would be able to correctly judge the results of the tests.

In fact, both deductive and inductive reasoning are used by scientists but neither is sufficient, either alone or in partnership; Binford's conceptions appear to be based on a lack of appreciation of the complexities and limitations of inductive and deductive logic examined for example by Salmon (1973), though a year later Binford is admitting (1972a: 118) that "we must continually work back and forth ... between the contexts of proposition formulation (induction) and proposition testing (deduction)" and a year later again was saying that "scientific method proceeds in the context of complementary inductive-deductive methods" (1972a: 112–13), so that he now appears to unwittingly agree with Cohen and Nagel's description of scientific method noted above and with E. H.

Carr's definition of history (1961: 30, 1961 ed.) as a continuous process of interaction between the historian and his facts.

Deductive reasoning can lead to no major advances in science, for no new generalizations can come from applying a general principle to particular instances. Inductive reasoning, on the other hand, while more productive because from it one can derive new theories, is less trustworthy because one can often derive several theories by it, only some or even none of which may be true (Beveridge 1950: 84–85, 1961 ed.). Further, as regards deductive logic, there is the danger of falling into the "fallacy of affirming the consequent" (Salmon 1973: 77)—that is, of arguing backwards from the truth of the conclusion to that of the premise—a fallacy which Binford on the evidence of his statement that "The final judgment of the archaeological reconstruction . . . must rest with testing through subsidiary hypotheses drawn deductively" appears in danger of committing. The so-called "scientific method" which would have us believe that reason is the main or even the only means by which science advances was the conception of certain logicians of last century who had little real understanding of research: "taste . . . and the important roles of chance and intuition" form the basis for most scientific breakthroughs, and "Only the technicalities of research are 'scientific'" (Beveridge 1950: 137, 138, 1961 ed.). The anthropologist Levi-Strauss is essentially correct when he says that:

> The principle underlying a classification can never be postulated in advance. It can only be discovered a posteriori . . . by experience (quoted in Yankelovich and Barrett 1970: 402).

Where Binford and other North American anthropologists err is that they have ideas on history and science which are half a century out of date.

Collingwood (1946: 126, 1961 ed.) defines positivism as "philosophy acting in the service of natural science". As indicated above, historical positivists conceived natural science as comprising two parts: first, ascertaining facts and secondly, forming laws. The former were ascertainable through perception by the senses, the latter were framed through generalizing from the former by induction. Sociology was systemized by Comte as a sort of super-history to discover in true positivistic style the causal connections among these facts, the facts being supplied to the sociologist by the historian, and it is presumably from this that the idea originates (still widely believed among American anthropologists) that history is only raw data and specific things to be transmuted by the superior science of anthropology. The view of White in his paper "History, Evolutionism, and Functionalism" cited earlier certainly fits into this pattern in every way, and in his account of the history of thought on the two or three types of interpretation of culture he takes this definition well back into the nineteenth century and cites E. B. Tyler as endeavouring "to trace a chronological sequence of unique events, to reconstruct history" (White 1945: 224). Tyler, however, was writing in the heyday of positivism, from which these ideas clearly come. Even more revealing is a passage from White's *The Pattern of Culture* quoted by Binford (1972a: 105) where White quotes the Second Law of Thermodynamics—that matter is becoming less organized and energy more uniformally diffuse—and contrasts this to "living material systems" where:

> . . . the direction of the cosmic process is reversed . . . Biological evolution is simply an expression of the thermodynamic process that moves in the direction opposite to that specified for the cosmos as a whole.

This use of scientific laws is pure positivism; indeed Wish notes the use by the American positivist historian Henry Adams (1838–1918) of just this particular law (Wish 1960: 175–77). As Binford's philosophy owes a great deal to White (Binford 1972a: 341, 7–8), though unfortunately his writing style does not, it seems clear this is where Binford derives much of his determination to find laws. Winks (1969: 487–88) rather cynically describes the difference between the historical and sociological approach thus:

> Recently a graduate student in sociology defended to me a project I regarded as worthless—since he proposed to prove something historians had proved long ago—on the ground that while historians had to justify their existence by producing new data, sociologists justified theirs by testing their methodologies. This is, one hopes, not the whole of the truth, but it is a little part of it, for many social scientists seem to enjoy disputatious inquiries into their own methodologies without ever getting around to the delicate task of applying these methods to anything that ten sane men would regard as important. They enjoy packing their bags for trips they have no intention of taking, as one of their number has remarked. . . .

A rather similar situation prevails in present-day psychology and psychoanalysis, two equally positivist-derived fields, according to Yankelovich and Barrett (1970: 6–8 and *passim*): as they put it (p. 217), "The ghost of Newton, having suffered at the hands of modern physicists, has taken full revenge within the sciences of man."

Where historical positivism fell apart was in searching for facts, for it turned out there was no end to facts, so that in an endless quest for objective data historical positivism made historians encyclopedia-compilers, degenerated into sheer antiquarianism, and finally sank in a sea of facts. Lord Acton, writing about his teacher Döllinger, said on one occasion that "it was given to him to form his philosophy of history on the largest induction ever available to man" and on another that Döllinger "would not write with imperfect materials, and to him the materials were always imperfect" (quoted in Carr 1961: 15 and n.1, 1964 ed.). One practitioner went so far as to define the approach of the scientific historian thus: "If a certain philosophy emerges from this scientific history it must be permitted to emerge naturally, of own accord, all but independently of the will of the historian" (Fustel de Coulanges, quoted in Becker 1932: 232–33).

"What had gone wrong", as Carr (1961: 15–16, 1964 ed.) says, "was the belief in this untiring and unending accumulation of hard facts as the foundation of history, the belief that facts speak for themselves and that we cannot have too many facts". Beveridge points to the same misconception in science, observing that "it is a common error among philosophers and writers of books on the scientific method to believe that discoveries are made by the systematic accumulation of data until the generalisation is a matter of plain logic, whereas in fact this is true in probably a minority of cases" (1950: 151, 1961 ed.). Objective history, as the American historian James Harvey Robinson used to say (Wish 1960: 269), had become history without an object. As Carl Becker put it, the philosophy of the scientific historian was:

> . . . that by not taking thought a cubit could be added to his stature . . . surely the most romantic species of

realism yet invented, the oddest attempt ever made to get something for nothing! (Becker 1932: 233).

This is precisely what South (1972: 86, 102) and this writer (Walker 1972a: 139 and refs.) have castigated as an all-too-prevailing outlook in historical archaeology. Even Binford agrees that "Facts do not speak for themselves" (Binford 1972b: 120), and here he is curiously near the relativism of Becker who in 1932 noted that "Left to themselves facts do not speak; left to themselves they do not exist, not really, since for all practical purposes there is no fact until someone affirms it" (Becker 1932: 233) and who 22 years earlier (1910: 528) indicated that "The 'facts' of history do not exist for any historian until he creates them, and into every fact that he creates some part of his individual experience must enter". Like the positivist historians, far too many anthropologically-trained historical archaeologists have become bogged down in searching—usually by typologies, seriation, and statistical analyses—for objective "facts". The only difference seems to be that whereas the legacy of positivism was "a combination of unprecedented mastery over small-scale problems with unprecedented weakness in dealing with large-scale problems" (Collingwood 1946: 131–32, 1961 ed.) technicians in historical archaeology have so far not even been able to establish the least mastery of small-scale problems, such as artefacts (Walker 1972a: 139–44). The New Archaeologist, however, philosophizes as to how his data should be and how it should be found but without having mastered the essentials of interpreting the data from which he would indeed be able to draw inferences. He knows the price of everything and the value of nothing. History, to quote Carr again, "is a continuous process of interaction between the historian and his facts, an unending dialogue between the present and the past . . . the two processes of what economists call 'input' and 'output' go on simultaneously and are, in practice, parts of a single process" (Carr 1961: 30, 28, 1964 ed.). It is about time historical archaeologists started doing history.

Because of his nineteenth-century beliefs in the scientific-ness of facts, Binford is obsessed with the superior quality of anthropological evidence because it can be quantified or otherwise scientifically and objectively studied. In particular he worries lest I and other historians[5] contaminate the pure science of archaeological research with such subjective approaches as "intuitive tests of plausibility, internal consistency, or critical evaluation of the accuracy of the facts cited" (Binford 1972b: 120). Apparently, according to Binford, I have no philosophical beliefs, so I cannot make deductions because deductions are made from propositions which specify relationships between things and events, and conclusions are warranted only to the degree that their relevance to such propositions can be established and the conclusions justified logically. Once again we have an anthropological red her-

ring: apparently anyone whose philosophical beliefs differ from Binford's has no philosophical beliefs. This seems to be one of the more whimsical cornerstones of the New Archaeology, for Binford repeats it again with specific reference to me when belabouring Hanson for criticizing the methodology of his pipestem dating formula (Binford 1972c: 234) and Cleland and Fitting took precisely the same line a few years ago because I said much the same things about anthropology when commenting on Dollar's paper as I am saying now (Cleland and Fitting 1968: 126, cf Walker 1970a: 62). If I happen to think the philosophy of Binford, Cleland, *et al* is a collection of bankrupt ephemera I can see they will object, but to argue that I am a- or anti-theoretical because I disagree with their philosophy seems to indicate they have an impoverished philosophy in the first place. At least I do not believe I have ever deliberately destroyed evidence because I was unable to comprehend it and so disbelieved in its possible usefulness (Binford 1972a: 130–31). Similarly, if indeed Leslie White did say that Boas was muddle-headed and that his writings were like the Bible, wherein one could find anything one liked (Binford 1972a: 7–8), I do not see the relevance of the implied corollary that nothing in Boas or the Bible is worthwhile. Bacon noted that one should "Read not to contradict and confute, nor to believe and take for granted . . . but to weigh and consider" (quoted in Beveridge 1951: 3, 1961 ed.). One should remember the dictum of Housman:

A scholar who means to build himself a monument must spend much of his life in acquiring knowledge which for its own sake is not worth having and in reading books which do not in themselves deserve to be read; at illa iacent multa et praeclara relicta *(Carter [ed.] 1961: 159).*

The limitedness of outlook arising from preoccupation with a "scientific" approach is illustrated by the opening two sentences in Deetz's *Invitation to Archaeology* and the extensive footnote appended thereto. Anyone who thinks there is only one real archaeology—anthropological archaeology—and that classical archaeology is only concerned with art of the Mediterranean world (Deetz 1967: 3 and n. 1) has such a limited idea of what archaeology is, to say nothing of what the nature of evidence is, that it is hardly worth trying to correct his outlook. Archaeology, as I have noted before, is a grossly inexact field of research, at least as much so as documentary research, a field with whose evidence historical archaeologists have equally to struggle (Walker 1970b: 106). Archaeology has indeed been said to be "at best, the delicate balance of probabilities" (A. L. F. Rivet, quoted in Thomas 1973: 8). Noël Hume's "Creamware to Pearlware: A Williamsburg Perspective" (Noël Hume 1972) provides an excellent coverage of the conflicting vagaries of inadequate data which faces an historical archaeologist dealing with material represented in archaeological, documentary, and museum sources. Both history and archaeology rely a great deal on tests of plausibility and internal consistency and on critical evaluation of the accuracy of the fact cited, and the material which Binford and the New Archaeology so zealously quantify to prove the scientificness of their field is usually based on just such subjective and incomplete data.

As for the use of intuition, which so bothers Binford as being unscientific, problem-solving intuition plays a very important part in scientific discovery. Beveridge devotes a whole chapter to it (1950: chapter 6, 1961 ed.) and elsewhere (pp. 55, 57) quotes Planck and Einstein as stressing its

[5] *As the Bellman said, what I tell you three times is true: I would have hoped that having already specifically indicated on two occasions, both in papers from which Binford quotes, that my formal training was in a field other than history (Walker 1968a: 23, 1970a: 63) people would remember this. Presumably I am an historian to Binford either because he uses the term intuitively—as an insult—or as an anthropological generalization—based on inadequately tested assumptions to fit general propositions which can serve as pivotal points for interpretive arguments treating the specific facts of a specific case. Possibly I have not insulted as many historians as anthropologists, but I have no starry-eyed beliefs about the nature of historical evidence particularly when it has been applied to the field of historical archaeology (cf Walker 1968a: 23, 1968b: 120; 1970b: 100; 1972a: 145).*

importance. Newton, the inventor of scientific laws, is supposed to have said "No great discovery is ever made without a bold guess" (quoted in Beveridge 1950: 149). Even Binford would be hard put to prove Newton, Planck, and Einstein were unscientific.

The intuition of identification, which is perhaps to what Binford objects, is equally valid both in general living and in research. As Hercule Poirot put it:

> ... *what is often called an intuition is really* an impression based on logical deduction and experience. *When an expert feels there is something wrong about a picture or a piece of furniture or the signature on a cheque he is really basing that feeling on a host of small signs and details. He has no need to go into them minutely—his experience obviates that—the net result is* the definite impression that something is wrong. *But it is not a guess, it is an impression based on experience (Christie 1936: 171, 1941 ed.).*

In a specifically archaeological context it has been concisely summed up by R. H. Thompson as "the combination of the investigator's anthropological background or training in fact and theory, his archaeological experience which is often called familiarity with the material, and his intellectual capacity" (R. H. Thompson 1956: 328).

When Binford worked in forestry and wildlife conservation I very much doubt that every time he referred to an oak or an elm—or even to a chinquapin oak or a wych elm—he felt obliged to prove his identification. His identifications must have been intuitive, based on his expert knowledge of trees: he abstracted from his experience, his "familiarity with the material". Yet when an archaeologist with similar expert knowledge of artefacts makes identifications, those who, as Housman once put it, read too little and attend too little to what they do read and crown these defects "with an amazing and calamitous propensity for reckless assertion" (Carter [ed.] 1961: 91), rise up in protest, preferring not to be biased by any knowledge of the field (Cleland and Fitting 1968: 130–31). Cleland and Fitting admit (1968: 132) that "Higher level analysis can only be as good as the data produced [from excavation and artefact analysis] allows", but in practice they show little practical ability to handle the basic data in historical archaeology. There is no contradiction between Housman emending lines from Classical verse by combining a meticulous mastery of language and a first-hand knowledge of how poets express themselves to produce readings some of which were confirmed from manuscripts discovered only after his death (Wilson 1952: 76, 1962 ed.) and the theme in his 1911 Cambridge Inaugural Lecture that subjective impressions based on taste are a dangerous basis on which to emend an author's text particularly when the author wrote in a dead language and lived 2,000 years ago: textual criticism has to be based scientifically on observed or observable fact, and when science has done its best, art takes over, in the form of judgements within the limits prescribed by science in the preliminary analysis (Gow 1936: 34–35). As Beveridge says above, "Only the technicalities of research are 'scientific'".

Plausibility, internal consistency, and critical evaluation of the accuracy of the facts cited are equally important to scientists. Beveridge quotes (1950: 103, 1961 ed.) a director of Medical Sciences for the Rockefeller Foundation as saying:

> *Most of the knowledge and much of the genius of the research worker lie behind his selection of what is worth observing. It is a crucial choice, often determining the success or failure of months of work, often differentiating the brilliant discoverer from the ... plodder.*

In South's paper, for example, claimed as noted above by Binford as "excellent" and "closely reasoned", intuitive decisions have been reached as to the validity of using mid-range dates, critical evaluations have been made in identifying the ceramics involved, and the internal consistency of Noël Hume's work has been assumed.

Binford's rejection of such "unscientific" reasoning presumably goes back to his unhappy studenthood, when he found artefacts did not speak to him as they did to Griffin (Binford 1972a: 4–6). There are, however, possible reasons for Binford's failure to understand other than these forms of reasoning being wrong, one being that Griffin did not adequately explain on what he based his deductions from the artefact, another being that he did but Binford was unable to follow it. More subtle, but more probable, is the likelihood that some of Griffin's conclusions were right, some wrong, some had varying degrees of right or at least probability, and some were possible but unprovable: such complexity might well confuse someone who wanted to have a "scientific" approach which would give definite yes and no answers. "Learning", as an Oxford don of last century put it, "is a peculiar compound of memory, imagination, scientific habit, [and] accurate observation" (quoted in Sparrow 1956: 7). If my particular approach is "empathic", and if empathy is "unscientific" (Binford 1972b: 118)— a term which Binford persistently equates to "inferior"—I remain unrepentant: "dead archaeology is the driest dust that blows" (Wheeler 1954: 13, 1956 ed.). Whatever model we use, it is one we have invented, and as Fowler puts it, talking of the English pre-Roman Iron Age:

> ... *what worried Joe Celt was not whether he was conforming to the La Tène III norm or producing enough artefacts for statistical analysis but whether the spring would dry up this year, whether he could push his field further into the woods, or whether his feckless neighbour at Dindum was going to curb his pyromania these coming winter nights (Fowler 1969: 124).*

We are studying people, and anything else is a waste of time. Hill has remarked that:

> *Recorded history is like a photograph of an iceberg: it deals only with what is visible above the surface ... in commending the actions of men of the seventeenth century, as we should, in noting the very real constitutional, economic, and intellectual advances, let us also remember how much of the lives of how many men and women is utterly unknown to us (Hill 1961: 264, 266, 1969 ed.).*

Hill has perhaps done more to illuminate the lives and thoughts of ordinary people in England in the seventeenth century than any other historian; archaeology, when it excavates the residences of those of various social classes or better yet when it tackles whole villages as part of a coordinated interdisciplinary study sheds illumination on the lives and sometimes even the thoughts of ordinary people— this is why *Here Lies Virginia* (Noël Hume 1963) is so successful as "an archaeologist's view of colonial life and history", to quote its subtitle.

The other use of historical archaeology is in economic history: distribution of artefacts leads to generalizations about trade patterns which are simply the opposite side of the coin seen in studies of trade records and port books by economic historians. Hudson's Bay Company records show that the East London clay pipe manufacturing firm of Ford of Stepney, known on other evidence to have been in business 1823–1909, held a monopoly to supply pipes to the Hudson's Bay Company from 1831 to at least 1870 (later Hudson's Bay Company records have not yet been studied): so far, all Ford of Stepney pipes found archaeologically in North America appear either to come from Hudson's Bay Company posts or from sites, such as native sites, convincingly shown to be near or within the trading area of a Hudson's Bay Company post. None to my knowledge has so far occurred on any other type of site, from which we may generalize validly that in the light of present knowledge Ford of Stepney pipes if found in North America indicate Hudson's Bay Company trade. London trade directories list Ford as an exporter 1856–77 and 1880–1909: is this an inaccurate reference only to his Hudson's Bay Company contracts or did he export to a widespread market despite the apparent lack of his products in North America outside Hudson's Bay Company posts? The latter seems likely, for probable Ford pipes have been found in Australia and on Ascension Island (Walker MS). When one know one's data there is no lack of valid generalizations even if tomorrow's data modifies or ultimately negates those generalizations and produces new ones.

It is perfectly possible for historians to be as rigorous and scientific in examining their evidence as it is for scientists with theirs—indeed one of the most rigorous examinations of historical evidence I know, and one which is far more scientific than anything Binford has ever written, is Oscar Cullmann's study of the apostle Peter (Cullmann 1952, 1960 ed.), a book which the author incidentally describes in the foreword to the first edition as *ein Beitrag zur Geschichtswissenschaft*—a contribution to the science of history. Another example from the same field is G. M. Styler's analysis of the priority of Mark among the gospels (Styler 1962) (not that either example is by any means the last word in its argument: Carl Becker noted that "In the history of history a myth is a once valid but now discarded version of the human story, as our now valid versions will in due course be relegated to the category of discarded myths" [Becker 1932: 231] and as Christopher Hill has said "all accepted truths, just because they are accepted, tend to become lies" [Hill 1965: ix, 1972 ed.]; and this is every whit as applicable to the hard sciences as to the traditional arts). If we write history to the greater glory of God and because we enjoy it (Winks [ed.] 1969: xxiii) who is to say this is wrong, and if we seek to learn from the past one can note the words of the American historian Allan Nevins, who said that every generation must rewrite its own history because each generation wishes to draw from the past meanings that will help bring some order into the chaos of the present (quoted in Winks *op. cit.* 273).

Certainly the fact that anthropologists apply mathematical techniques to their study does not entitle them to call their field a science: does the application of statistics to the book of Isaiah (Radday 1970) or to the Pauline epistles (Morton and McLeman 1966) make theology a science or the X-ray examination of the Ghent Altarpiece (Coremans [ed.] 1953) make art history a science? Or, to descend to the commonplace, does calling the general dimensions of an artefact "metric attributes" (Cleland 1971b: 86) add to our information? Radday is very careful to insist his examination

of Isaiah results in no more than probabilities, and there are still reasoned objections to a multi-authorship of Isaiah. Indeed, Radday indicates his main aim was to objectivize the controversy "by strict quantification which does not allow any personal convictions, religious prejudice, or literary taste to influence conclusions" (1970: 73); but even this overstates the case, for however strict the quantification it does not in itself remove the biases noted.

The assumption that "scientific proof" is obtained by this sort of approach is one of the more spectacular pieces of idiocy now in vogue among some archaeologists. Earlier, I quoted Binford saying the original use of his pipestem formula was "for testing the validity of Harrington's observations": the Binford formula does nothing of the kind, it merely expresses Harrington's observations differently. Again, as noted earlier, Binford hails South's "Evolution and Horizon . . . " paper as "A Step Toward the Development of Archaeological Science": at that point I observed that Binford was in no position to judge whether South's paper is scientific or not, but what is it in the paper that makes Binford maintain (intuitively, one supposes, since he offers no explication) it *is* scientific? Presumably the use of a mathematical formula makes it so, yet as L. M. Stone points out (1972: 180), the formula *has* to work given its straightforward statistical nature, provided Noël Hume's identifications and dating of historical ceramics are correct. In other words, it is a clear example of the limits of deductive reasoning. Several years ago Cleland and Fitting indicated they felt Noël Hume's work to be "low level" (Cleland and Fitting 1968: *passim*); now Fitting retracts this opinion because "South has demonstrated beyond question the value of Noël Hume's work as a starting point for other types of analysis" (Fitting 1972: 158). Apparently South's formula is felt to prove the validity of Noël Hume's work, a patently absurd conclusion. Noël Hume's work, moreover (Noël Hume 1970), certainly involves tests of plausibility, internal consistency, critical evaluation of facts cited, intuition, and all the other techniques rejected by the New Archaeology; so where does this leave its practitioners? Once again, caught in their own devices, for they have committed the unscientific error of not checking their primary sources (which they surely would have pronounced unscientific and inadequate) before extolling the virtues of their secondary application. Further, they unwittingly underscore the limitations of deductive reasoning, the introduction of which Binford notes (1972a: 89–91) as a keystone of the New Archaeology.

What is particularly regrettable about Binford's lack of rigour is that others are falling into the same pit by blindly following his unsubstantiated claims. Thus Carrillo claims that Binford and South have taken "data previously compiled [by Harrington and Noël Hume] and have transformed it to construct testable mathematically controlled models structured within a general scientific paradigm" (1973: 1) and that his own statistical examination of bottles is "a mathematically testable model" because "the results obtained by dating [from Noël Hume's bottle typology] are visual and subjective, and cannot be tested for reliability" (1973: 4). As a matter of historical accuracy it was Harrington who applied a mathematical model to pipestem fragments, not Binford, who as noted above only re-expressed Harrington's data in a different form; and in fact of all the mathematical models noted here only Harrington's has any independent validity, because Harrington used statistics correctly—to test a hypothesis by a method allowing comprehension of data in the mass. Pipestems, unlike ceramics and bottles, are not (unless, obviously, they carry makers or other identifiable marks) generally datable: Harrington's process was to get samples from various differently dated contexts and examine them for significant change, and from this to extend the graphed changes to sites not readily datable; the South and Carrillo formulae, on the other hand, take dated material and simply express the date in another form.[6] They provide neither proof nor reliability, because they add no new evidence or independent data to the material being examined. Further, Carrillo's decisions as to what measurements he should use to determine evidence for chronological change, to say nothing of more subtle decisions as to precisely where on an object measurements should be taken for that particular dimension, are in themselves "visual and subjective, and cannot be tested for reliability". We are, if we follow the quest for "mathematically testable models" along these lines, in very great danger of ending up working completely in circles: the loss of innocence is one thing (Clarke 1973), but the loss of sense is another.

A problem nowhere tackled by Binford is why the existence of "laws that are validated in the context of the epistemology of science" (Binford 1972a: 121) are a legitimate assumption in the study of the past and therefore ultimately findable in the first place, and why archaeology should be forced to be a science. Are these intuitive assumptions? Hanson (1972: 255–56) comments here:

> Finally, Binford and others have set out to make archaeology a science. Archaeology is no more a science than medicine. No amount of statistical manipulation or reams of historical documentation can alter the archaeological record. In the end we must either interpret this record in the light of our manipulations and/or documentation or we must use our manipulations and/or documentation to support our interpretation of the record. The difference between the "new" and the "old" archaeology is simply a matter of whether the end justifies the means or the means justifies the ends. The only room for improvement is the technology by which the archaeological record is gathered so that it can be better utilized no matter which course is chosen.

When Binford talks of steps towards an "archaeological science" he thinks in terms of his validated laws; when Seminar Press talk of "archaeological science" they are thinking in terms of support science, as their series "Studies in Archaeological Science" shows, comprising as it does the titles *The Study of Animal Bones from Archaeological Sites; Methods of Physical Examination in Archaeology; Land Snails in Archaeology;* and *Ancient Skins, Parchments and Leathers.* As M. S. Tite puts it in the second of these books, "in spite of the increased range of data made available, the archaeologist should still remain in full control of the final co-ordination and interpretation of this accumulated data and it is at this fundamental stage that the subject retains its humanistic aspects" (Tite 1972: 5).

It is when Binford misunderstands the nature of science and then extols his methodology as "superior" to others and tries to fit his particular field of interest to that "superior" methodology that the situation becomes ridiculous. G. K. Chesterton said that when he became a Roman Catholic it was like leaning up against a brick wall: this does not entitle one to presume the ways of Rome are "superior" to those of other religious groups, it only means that the ways of Rome were to Chesterton emotionally satisfying. The same feeling occurs among historians who have moved away from laws (in the Binfordian sense) they feel to be restrictive to their research: those who gave up Marxist beliefs noted that "When we lose the comfortable formulas that have hitherto been our guides amid the complexities of existence . . . we feel like drowning in an ocean of facts until we find a new foothold or learn to swim" (Werner Sombart, quoted in Carr 1961: 60, 1964 ed.). Binford and the New Archaeology apparently feel that validation in the context of the epistemology of science (albeit an outmoded epistemology) provide them with their brick wall and emotional satisfaction, but it does not entitle them to set up as latter-day Jesuits—there are, after all, many mansions.

Moreover, Binford and others appear to assume that "science" is a monolithic structure, but such is not the case. Mathematics and chemistry, for example, use different principles of reasoning. Collingwood noted that:

> . . . anything that is a science at all must be more than merely a science, it must be a science of some special kind. A body of knowledge is never merely organized, it is always organized in some particular way.

Meteorology, he noted, was organized by collecting observations concerned with events of a certain kind which the scientist can watch happen though he cannot produce them at will; in chemistry scientists not only observe events as they happen but can make them happen under strictly controlled conditions; in other fields scientists do not observe events at all but make certain assumptions and proceed with the utmost exactitude to argue out their consequences (Collingwood 1946: 249, 1961 ed.). Each field of research is autonomous: "The way in which knowledge is related to the grounds upon which it is based is in fact not one and the same for all kinds of knowledge" (Collingwood 1946: 253, 1961 ed.). As the physicist Werner Heisenberg puts it, any truly distinct field of enquiry calls for its own basic postulates which can never be borrowed from another field (quoted in Yankelovich and Barrett 1970: 229). Archaeology is basically only a set of techniques used to produce evidence about man's past and thus add to his knowledge of history: it has nothing to do with "science" except that it can and does fruitfully use scientific techniques to augment its accumulation of data. Tricking out archaeology in the garments of science—and the cast-off nineteenth-century garments of science at that—no more makes archaeology a science than did dressing up convert Gilbert's ape into Darwinian man.

Talking of the stock market, one writer has noted that "Unlike chemical formulas, investment formulas, if they become widely accepted, tend to self destruct by distorting the very environment from which they are derived" (quoted in Smith 1972: 233): this is what Hill meant when he said all

[6]It is true that one could argue that because Carrillo is using bottles bearing specific dates and extending his findings to bottles with no dates that he is working in a manner similar to Harrington; but this would be misleading, for it would be ridiculous to suppose each dated bottle represents that year's specific style (even if the date given is assumed to closely relate to date of manufacture, something which might be queried). The most these single dates give is an approximation of date of manufacture (more specifically, a presumed terminus post quem) and thus an idea of when the shape was in use. This sort of evidence, together with that of material from datable stratified deposits, gives usable date ranges for various bottle-shapes. The resulting typology was published by Noël Hume a dozen years ago (Noël Hume 1961) and it is this rather than the later but much briefer discussion by Noël Hume in his A Guide to Artifacts of Colonial America (1970) used by Carrillo which should be used as a primary guide to dating bottles.

accepted truths, just because they are accepted, tend to become lies; and this was why Carr noted that historians emerging from the comforting "laws" of Marxist theory felt like drowning in a sea of facts until they readjusted their thinking.

Generalization, on the other hand, as we have seen, is a valid and fruitful means of furthering historical research— the difference between generalizations and "laws" in the study of the past is that the latter restrict development because they are in fact not laws: they are only generalizations artificially given the status of laws by those proposing them and they inhibit research because their originators imply that laws, being laws, can only be broken by fools, knaves, or charlatans and at the risk of scorn and censure by all established scholars. As Carr points out, nobody today would call Weber's thesis about the relationship of Protestantism and capitalism a "law", though it might have been so classified at an earlier period; and Marx's dictum that the hand-mill gives a society with a feudal lord and the steam-mill a society with an industrial capitalist is not a "law" either, even if Marx would probably have claimed it was: both generalizations, however, are fruitful hypotheses "pointing the way to further enquiry and fresh understanding" and "indispensable tools of thought" (Carr 1961: 60, 1964 ed.).

Even as hypotheses, however, Binford's "laws" fail to point the way to further enquiry and fresh understanding, for at least so far as historical archaeology is concerned Binford's valid general propositions can be seen to be invalid by anyone who knows his data, which latter knowledge as indicated earlier is one conspicuously lacking among most of those applying preconceived "laws" to historical archaeology. Here lack of historical understanding (or to be fair, a belief that historical understanding is unnecessary) is the problem. Historical data is far too complex to admit of the facile approach advocated by Binford: it is not a case of one piece of historical evidence being right and another wrong—it is a case of handling evidence from which one may be able to postulate several divergent interpretations. Verification is conducted on many planes, and its technique is not fixed (Barzun and Graff in Winks [ed.] 1960: 216). Psychoanalysts working away from the dead end of false categorization have asked the question "*What* experiences interact with *what* innate variables and universals at *what* time leading to *what* behaviors?" (John Benjamin quoted in Yankelovich and Barrett 1970: 405), an approach of which most modern historians would approve, echoing as it does Carr's definition of history cited above. Even Binford admits he had to learn data (1972a: 12, 132)—unfortunately he and others appear never to have tried to master historical data before entering the field of historical archaeology.

It might be instructive to find out what researchers in the hard sciences feel about the quest for "scientificness" in anthropology and archaeology. Certainly, hard scientists in Canada do not appear to consider anthropologists to be scientists, for in 1969 they let it be known that anthropologists would no longer be eligible for grants from the National Research Council of Canada, the federal government's scientific body, and suggested anthropologists address themselves to the Canada Council, the federal government's body for the arts, instead.

One cannot entirely disagree with scientists who feel this way when one reads of misuse by archaeologists of scientific terms such as feedback. Flannery's use of the concept of positive feedback, even metaphorically, is only partially correct; and his summary of its application to the development of agriculture in Meso-America shows he is confusing feedback with simple development.

> *Starting with what may have been (initially) accidental deviations in the system, a positive feedback network was established which eventually made maize cultivation the most profitable single subsistence activity in Mesoamerica. The more widespread maize cultivation, the more opportunities for favorable crosses and back-crosses; the more favorable genetic changes, the greater the yield; the greater the yield, the higher the population, and hence the more intensive cultivation. There can be little doubt that pressures for more intensive cultivation were instrumental in perfecting early water-control systems, like well-irrigation and canal-irrigation [references]. This positive feedback system, therefore, was still increasing at the time of the Spanish Conquest (Flannery 1968: 80).*

The initial steps, that of maize being cultivated on a more widespread basis and thus becoming more open to crossing and back-crossing, hence genetic improvements and from this greater yield, is—possibly—acceptable as being metaphorically speaking feedback; however, the effect on population, hence increased agriculture and more sophisticated agricultural techniques, is technological development, not feedback. In fact, Flannery's concept is not different from Childe's concept of the Neolithic Revolution in the Middle East and Europe. With the misuse of the terms positive and negative feedback in that well-known science the advertising business—feedback to mean customer reaction, positive being favourable, negative unfavourable—and their consequent popularization it is hardly surprising everyone who is not a scientist misuses them: Binford for example uses feedback in a vague way to mean reaction (Binford 1972a: 63, 324–25).

Even within the soft sciences objections have been raised about archaeologists lifting terminology from these fields to bolster their theory: geographers, for example, have protested "the indiscriminate application of principles and techniques derived from studies in contemporary geography to historical situations" by writers such as Clarke (Baker, Hamshere, and Langton 1970: 21 and n. 37).

It is difficult to avoid the conclusion that the new jargon is, to misquote Milton, but old archaeology writ large (and in the case of Watson [1972: 210] spelt wrongly). Despite Binford's denial of this, and his attempted justification of the New Archaeology on outmoded concepts of nineteenth-century scientific philosophy quoted earlier, Jennings is essentially correct in being cynical about the newness of the New Archaeology (quoted in Binford 1972a: 120). As another writer has observed (Hogarth 1972: 301, 303), New Archaeology is merely Newspeak Archaeology—the operation of simultaneous location determinative, detectional and status-analytical programs relative to primary source data retrieval contributive to reconstructive syntheses of pre-current sociocultural entities is still fieldwork—and new only to those unfamiliar with the old. The meta-language of explanation too often takes us backwards, not forwards: commenting on the abuse of language in psychoanalysis and citing the sentence "There are two techniques of restoring a feeling of being loved (of increasing the libidinal cathexis of the self)" the analyst and philosopher H. J. Home observes: "The first part . . . seems to me perfectly comprehensible; the second part is, I believe, meaningless" (quoted in Yankelovich and Barrett 1970: 279). Researchers, even social scientists, have an obligation to make their arguments comprehensible, and to quote Professor Lehrer again, if a person cannot communicate the very least he can do is to shut up (Lehrer 1965b). Among the origins of Newspeak Archaeology, Hogarth suggests (1972: 302), is the system of education common in North America where children instead of receiving the immediate benefit of the knowledge of their elders are encouraged to "discover" things for themselves, which while a valuable exercise as one of a general range of educational techniques runs the risk when elevated to a "method" of allowing the child to believe he has discovered for all mankind.

This analysis would certainly agree with my comments (Walker 1972a: 145–46) on the recent "discovery" that literary sources, defined for the occasion as analogues, are useful for dating archaeological material from historical sites. It would also explain some of the more idiosyncratic differences adduced by Binford as separating the Old and New Archaeologies: in his "Smudge Pits and Hide Smoking: the Use of Analogy in Archaeological Reasoning" (in Binford 1972a: 33–51), for example, we are told in a singularly tedious and laboured fashion that analogies are not always correct just because they seem plausible and that most archaeologists until Binford have not been rigorous enough in considering their analogical evidence; elsewhere we are informed that large complicated sites are difficult to understand and that from this one may generalize that it is better to excavate little simple ones first—apparently the Old Archaeology judged the importance of sites on the amount of artefacts which could be discovered—(Binford 1972a: 130); most archaeologists until Binford were apparently committed to inductive reasoning only, hence their limited understanding until Binford introduced deductive reasoning (Binford 1972a: 48–49, 89–91, 111, 133); before Binford invented scientific archaeology all we had were appraisals of the professional competence of the archaeologist (pp. 48, 87, 117), ad hominem arguments, common sense, conjecture, hunch (p. 99), inference and intuition (pp. 120–121). The mind boggles at what new revolutionary and scientific discovery Binford will hurl next against the cracking bastions of traditionalist archaeology: is his assertion of "higher frequencies of Dutch pipes in the Northeast" discussed above an example of the new art of deductive reasoning? One is reminded of the comment on Freud, that what was new in his writings was of doubtful validity and what was valid was not new.

As for Binford's ideas about history, if he really does believe that history is specific things and events ordered in time, and that historians are naive, untheoretical, unphilosophical, and unepistemological, we can only shake our heads and reluctantly conclude that Braidwood was in 1964, and still is, correct (Binford 1972a: 11). If Binford is really interested in how historians work I suggest the following reading list, to be taken in the order given: E. H. Carr's *What is History?* (1961, 1964 ed.); C. Becker's "Detachment and the Writing of History" (1910) and "Everyman his own Historian" (1932); R. G. Collingwood's *The Idea of History* (1946, 1961 ed.); R. W. Wink's *The Historian as Detective: Essays on Evidence* (1969): R. Wish's *The American Historian: A Social-Intellectual History of the Writing of the American Past* (1960); P. A. M. Taylor's *The Origins of the English Civil War: Conspiracy, Crusade, or Class Conflict?* (1960); Christopher Hill's *The Century of Revolution, 1603–1714* (1961, 1969 ed.), *Intellectual Origins of the English Revolution* (1964, 1972 ed.), *Puritanism and Revolution* (1958, 1968

ed.), and *Society and Puritanism in Pre-Revolutionary England* (1964, 1969 ed.); E. P. Thompson's *The Making of the English Working Class* (1963, 1968 ed.); K. S. Inglis's *Churches and the Working Classes in Victorian England* (1963); and Oscar Cullman's *Peter: Disciple, Apostle, Martyr* (2nd ed. trans. 1962); and after he has considered these he may turn to the rigorous discipline of literary criticism as exemplified by A. E. Housman's Classical studies—*A. E. Housman: Selected Prose* (Carter [ed.] 1961)—and thence—in view of his professed attraction to scientific method—to W. I. B. Beveridge's *The Art of Scientific Investigation* (1950, 1961 ed.).

Until then, while it would be unrealistic to ask Binford to return to his first field of forestry and wildlife conservation he might at least have the good grace to stay out of historical archaeology—a field about which he has amply demonstrated he knows nothing—until such time as he has demonstrated some ability to comprehend historical evidence.

REFERENCES

ASHBEE, P.
1972 Field Archaeology and Its Development, Chapter II in P. J. Fowler (ed.) *Archaeology and the Landscape*. Baker, London.

BAKER, A. R. H., HAMSHERE, J. D., and LANGTON, J.
1970 Introduction, in A. R. H. Baker, J. D. Hamshere and J. Langton (eds.) *Geographical Interpretations of Historical Sources*. David and Charles, Newton Abbot.

BECKER, C.
1910 Detachment and the Writing of History, *The Atlantic Monthly* Vol. CVI, No. 4 (October, 1910) pp. 524–536.
1932 Everyman His Own Historian, *The American Historical Review* Vol. XXXVII, No. 2 (January, 1932) pp. 221–236.

BERESFORD, M.
1957 *History on the Ground*, 1971 ed. Methuen, London.

BEVERIDGE, W. I. B.
1950 *The Art of Scientific Investigation*, 1961 ed. Mercury Books, London.

BIBBY, G.
1961 *Four Thousand Years Ago: A Panorama of Life in the Second Millenium B. C.* Collins, London.

BINFORD, L. R.
1962 A New Method of Calculating Dates from Kaolin Pipe Stem Fragments, *Southeastern Archaeological Conference News Letter*, Vol. 9, No. 1 (June, 1962) (Papers presented at the First and Second Conferences on Historic Site Archaeology). Cambridge, Massachusetts.
1972a *An Archaeological Perspective*. Seminar Press, New York and London.
1972b "Evolution and Horizon as Revealed in Ceramic Analysis in Historical Archaeology"—A Step Toward the Development of Archaeological Science, *The Conference on Historic Site Archaeology Papers 1971*, Vol. 6 (1972) pp. 117–126.
1972c The 'Binford' Pipe Stem Formula: A Return from the Grave, *ibid.* pp. 230–253.

CARR, E. H.
1961 *What is History?*, 1964 ed. Penguin, Harmondsworth, Middlesex.

CARRILLO, R. F.
1973 English Wine Bottles as Revealed by a Preliminary Probability and Statistical Study: A Further Approach to Evolution and Horizon in Historical Archaeology. *Research Manuscript Series*, No. 35. Institute of Archaeology and Anthropology, University of South Carolina, Columbia. This paper was subsequently republished in a somewhat different form but without substantial alteration of the contents as "English Wine Bottles as Revealed by a Statistical Study: A Further Approach to Evolution and Horizon in Historical Archeology" in *The Conference on Historic Site Archaeology Papers 1972* Vol. 7 (1974) 290–317.

CARTER, J. (ed.)
1961 *A. E. Housman: Selected Prose.* Cambridge University Press.

CHRISTIE, AGATHA
1936 *The A. B. C. Murders*, 1941 ed. Pocket Books, New York.

CLARKE, D.
1973 Archaeology: The Loss of Innocence, *Antiquity*, Vol. XLVII, No. 185 (March, 1973) pp. 6–18.

CLELAND, C. E.
1971a Comparison of the Faunal Remains From French and British Refuse Pits at Michilimackinac: A Study in Changing Subsistence Patterns, *Canadian Historic Sites: Occasional Papers in Archaeology and History*, No. 3 (1971) pp. 7–23.
1971b Smoking Pipes, Chapter 10 in C. E. Cleland (ed.) *The Lasanan Site: An Historic Burial Locality in Mackinac County, Michigan* (Publications of the Museum, Michigan State University, Anthropological Series, Vol. 1, No. 1). East Lansing.

CLELAND, C. E. and FITTING, J. E.
1968 The Crisis of Identity: Theory in Historic Sites Archaeology. *The Conference on Historic Site Archaeology Papers, 1967.* Vol. 2 pt. 2 (1968) pp. 124–138.

COHEN, M. R. and NAGEL, E.
1934 *An Introduction to Logic and Scientific Method*, 1936 ed. Harcourt Brace, New York.

COLLINGWOOD, R. G.
1946 *The Idea of History, 1961 ed.* Oxford University Press.

COREMANS, P.
1953 *L'agneau mystique au laboratoire* (Les primitifs flamands III, Contributions à l'étude des primitifs flamands, 2). De Sikkel, Antwerp.

CULLMANN, O.
1952 *Petrus: Jünger, Apostel, Märtyrer*, 2nd ed. 1960. Zwingli, Zürich and Stuttgart; trans. by F. V. Filsom as *Peter: Disciple, Apostle, Martyr*, 1962. SCM Press, London.

DEETZ, J.
1967 *Invitation to Archaeology.* Natural History Press, Garden City, New York.

DEETZ, J. and DETHLEFSEN, E.
1965 The Doppler Effect and Archaeology: A Consideration of the Spatial Aspects of Seriation. *Southwestern Journal of Anthropology* Vol. 21, No. 3 (Autumn, 1965) pp. 196–206.

DETHLEFSEN, E. and DEETZ, J.
1966 Death's Heads, Cherubs, and Willow Trees: Experimental Archaeology in Colonial Cemeteries, *American Antiquity*, Vol. 31, No. 4 (April, 1966) pp. 502–510.

DOLLAR, C.
1968a Some Thoughts on Theory and Method in Historical Archaeology, *The Conference on Historic Site Archaeology Papers 1967*, Vol. 2, pt. 2 (1968) pp. 3–30.
1968b Epilogue, *Ibid.* pp. 184–188.

DONNAN, ELIZABETH (ed.)
1930–35 *Documents Illustrative of the History of the Slave Trade to America*, 4 vols. Carnegie Institute of Washington Publication 409 (reprinted 1965 by Octagon Books, New York).

DRAY, W.
1957 *Laws and Explanation in History.* Oxford University Press.

ELTON, G. R.
1958 Introduction: The Age of the Reformation, Chapter 1 in G. R. Elton (ed.) *The New Cambridge Modern History: Volume II The Reformation.* Cambridge University Press.

FARMER, W. R.
1964 *The Synoptic Problem: A Critical Analysis.* Macmillan, New York.

FISHER, W. F. K. *et al*
1968 *The Cooking of Provincial France.* Time-Life Books, New York.

FITTING, J. E.
1972 Evolution, Statistics and Historic Ceramics, *The Conference on Historic Sites Archaeology Papers 1971*, Vol. 6 (1972) pp. 158–163.

FLANNERY, K. V.
1968 Archeological Systems Theory and Early Mesoamerica. In: *Anthropological Archeology in the Americas*, pp. 67–87. The Anthropological Society of Washington, Washington, D.C.

FOWLER, P. J.
1969 Fyfield Down 1959–68, *Current Archaeology* No. 16 (September, 1969) pp. 124–129. London.

GOW, A. S. F.
1936 *A. E. Housman: A Sketch.* Cambridge University Press.

HALE, W. H. *et al*
1968 *The Horizon Cookbook and Illustrated History of Eating and Drinking Through the Ages.* American Heritage Publishing Co., place of publication not given.

HANSON, L. H., JR.
1971 Kaolin Pipe Stems—Boring in on a Fallacy, *The Conference on Historic Site Archaeology Papers 1969*, Vol. 4 (1971) pp. 2–15.
1972 A Few Cents More, *op. cit. 1971*, Vol. 6 (1972) pp. 254–257.

HARRINGTON, J. C.
1954 Dating Stem Fragments of Seventeenth and Eighteenth Century Clay Tobacco Pipes, *Quarterly Bulletin, Archeological Society of Virginia*, Vol. 9 No. 4 (September, 1954) 5 pages.

HEMPEL, C. G.
1965a Studies in the Logic of Confirmation. In: *Aspects of Scientific Explanation and Other Essays in the Philosophy of Science* pp. 3–51. Free Press, New York.
1965b The Function of General Laws in History. In: *op. cit.* pp. 231–243.
1966 *Philosophy of Natural Science.* Prentice-Hall, Englewood Cliffs, New Jersey.

HILL, J. E. C.
1958 *Puritanism and Revolution.* 1968 ed. Panther, London.
1961 *The Century of Revolution, 1603–1714.* 1969 ed. Sphere Books, London.
1964 *Society and Puritanism in Pre-Revolutionary England.* 1969 ed. Panther, London.
1965 *Intellectual Origins of the English Revolution.* 1972 ed. Panther, London.

HOGARTH, A. C.
1972 Common Sense in Archaeology, *Antiquity*, Vol. XLVI, No. 184 (December, 1972) pp. 301–304.

INGLIS, K. S.
1963 *Churches and the Working Classes in Victorian England.* Routledge and Kegan Paul, London.

JOYNT, C. B. and RESCHER, N.
1961 The Problem of Uniqueness in History, *History and Theory*, Vol. 1 No. II (1961) pp. 150–162.

LEHRER, T.
1965a New Math. In: *That Was the Year That Was.* Reprise Records, Montreal.
1965b Who's Next. In: *op. cit.*

MAXWELL, M. S., and BINFORD, L. H. [sic—L. R.]
1961 Excavations at Fort Michilimackinac, Mackinac City, Michigan: 1959 Season *(Publications of the Museum, Michigan State University Cultural Series*, Vol. 1, No. 1). East Lansing.

MONTAGNE, P. IN COLLABORATION WITH GOTTSCHALK
1938 *Larousse gastronomique.* Larousse, Paris.

MORTON, A. Q., and McLEMAN, J.
1966 *Paul, the Man and the Myth.* Hodder and Stoughton, London.

NOËL, HUME, I.
1961 The Glass Wine Bottle in Colonial Virginia, *Journal of Glass Studies*, Vol. III (1961) pp. 91–117.
1963 *Here Lies Virginia.* Knopf, New York.
1970 *A Guide to Artifacts of Colonial America.* Knopf, New York.
1972 Creamware to Pearlware: A Williamsburg Perspective. In: *Winterthur Conference Report 1972: Ceramics in America*, pp. 217–254. Henry Francis du Pont Winterthur Museum, Winterthur, Delaware.

OLIVER, R.
1967 *The French at Table*, trans. by C. Durrell. The Wine and Food Society, London.

OMWAKE, H. G.
n.d. Dating Fleur-de-Lis White Kaolin Pipes. Manuscript from author.

PLANCK, M.
1932 *Where is Science Going?*, trans. and biographical note by J. Murphy, prologue by A. Einstein. Norton, New York.

PUKTORNE, T.
1968 Tobakspipor från Gouda och Varberg, *Varberg Museums Arsbok 1968*, pp. 61–82. Varberg, Sweden.

RADDAY, Y. T.
1970 Isaiah and the Computer: A Preliminary Report, *Computers and the Humanities*, Vol. 5 No. 2 (December, 1970) pp. 65–73. Flushing, New York State.

SALMON, W. C.
1973 Confirmation, *Scientific American*, Vol. 228, No. 5 (May, 1973) pp. 75–83, 120.

SMITH, ADAM (pseud.)
1972 *Supermoney*. Random House, New York.

SOUTH, S.
1972 Evolution and Horizon as Revealed in Ceramic Analysis in Historical Archeology, *The Conference on Historic Site Archaeology Papers 1971*, Vol. 6 (1972) pp. 71–116.

SPARROW, J.
1956 Introduction. In: *A. E. Housman: Collected Poems*. Penguin, Harmondsworth, Middlesex.

STONE, L. M.
1972 Comments on Stanley South's 'Evolution and Horizon as Revealed in Ceramic Analysis in Historical Archeology', *The Conference on Historic Site Archaeology Papers 1971*, Vol. 6 (1972) pp. 179–184.

STYLER, G. M.
1962 The Priority of Mark, Excursus IV. In: C. F. D. Moule's *The Birth of the New Testament*. Black, London.

TAYLOR, P. A. M. (ed.)
1960 *The Origins of the English Civil War: Conspiracy, Crusade, or Class Conflict?* Heath, Boston, Massachusetts.

THOMAS, A. C.
1973 Irish Colonists in South-West Britain, *World Archaeology* Vol. 5, No. 1 (June, 1973) pp. 5–13.

THOMPSON, E. P.
1963 *The Making of the English Working Class*, 1968 ed. Penguin, Harmondsworth, Middlesex.

THOMPSON, R. H.
1956 The Subjective Element in Archaeological Inference, *Southwestern Journal of Anthropology*, Vol. 12, No. 3 (Autumn, 1956) pp. 327–332.

TITE, M. S.
1972 *Methods of Physical Examination in Archaeology*. Seminar Press, London.

TREVELYAN, G. M.
1927 *The Present Position of History*. Longmans Green, London.

WALKER, I. C.
1965 Some Thoughts on the Harrington and Binford Systems for Statistically Dating Clay Pipes, *Quarterly Bulletin, Archeological Society of Virginia*. Vol. 20, No. 2 (December, 1965) pp. 60–64.
1968a Historic Archaeology—Methods and Principles, *Historical Archaeology* 1967 [Vol. 1] pp. 23–24.
1968b Comments on Clyde Dollar's 'Some Thoughts on Theory and Method in Historical Archaeology', *The Conference on Historic Site Archaeology Papers 1967*, Vol. 2, pt. 2 (1968) pp. 105–123.
1970a The Crisis of Identity—History and Anthropology, *Op. cit. 1968*, Vol. 3 (1970) pp. 62–69.
1970b Comments on Garry Wheeler Stone's 'Ceramics in Suffolk County, Massachusetts, Inventories 1680–1775', *Ibid.* pp. 99–111.
1970c Dating and the Clay Pipes From the Galphin Trading Post at Silver Bluff, South Carolina, *The Florida Anthropologist*, Vol. 23, No. 4 (December, 1970) pp. 159–162.
1971a Note on the Bethabara, North Carolina, Tobacco Pipes, *The Conference on Historic Site Archaeology Papers 1969*, Vol. 4 (1971) pp. 26–36.
1971b An Archaeological Study of Clay Pipes From the King's Bastion, Fortress of Louisbourg, *Canadian Historic Sites: Occasional Papers in Archaeology and History*, No. 2 (1971) pp. 55–122.
1971c Nineteenth Century Clay Pipes in Canada, *Ontario Archaeology* Publication, No. 16 (1971) pp. 19–35. [This appeared with a disastrous set of printer's errors because no proofs were sent; it must be read in conjunction with the corrections and additions noted in *Arch Notes: Monthly Newsletter of The Ontario Archaeological Society*, No. 72–3 (March, 1972) pp. 8–11.]
1972a Comments on Stanley South's 'Evolution and Horizon as Revealed in Ceramic Analysis in Historical Archeology', *The Conference on Historic Site Archaeology Papers 1971*, Vol. 6 (1972) pp. 127–157.
1972b *The Bristol Clay Tobacco-Pipe Industry*. City Museum, Bristol (bears date 1971).
MS Aspects of the Clay Tobacco-Pipe Industry From the Point of View of the Manufacturing Techniques and the Changing Patterns of Trade and Smoking, and with Particular Reference to the Industry in Bristol, Ph.D. Thesis at present in progress for the University of Bath, England. [This work has since been published in a partly revised and updated form as *Clay Tobacco-Pipes, with Particular Reference to the Bristol Industry*, Number 11 in the series *History and Archaeology* published by the Department of Indian and Northern Affairs, Ottawa.]

WATSON, R. A.
1972 The 'New Archeology' of the 1960's, *Antiquity*, Vol. XLVI, No. 183 (September, 1972) pp. 210–215.

WHEELER, R. E. M.
1954 *Archaeology From the Earth*, 1956 ed. Penguin, Harmondsworth, Middlesex.

WHITE, L. A.
1945 History, Evolutionism, and Functionalism: Three Types of Interpretation of Culture, *Southwestern Journal of Anthropology*, Vol. 1, No. 2 (Summer, 1945) pp. 221–248.

WILSON, E.
1952 A. E. Housman. In: *The Triple Thinkers*, 1962 ed. Penguin, Harmondsworth, Middlesex.

WINKS, R. W. (ed.)
1969 *The Historian as Detective: Essays on Evidence*. Harper and Row, New York.

WISH, H.
1960 *The American Historian: A Social-Intellectual History of the Writing of the American Past*. Oxford University Press, New York.

YANKELOVICH, D. and BARRETT, W.
1970 *Ego and Instinct: The Psychoanalytic View of Human Nature—Revisited*. Random House, New York.

CHAPTER 28

A Reply to "Some Thoughts on Theory and Method in Historical Archaeology"

BERNARD L. FONTANA

"Critical acumen is exerted in vain to uncover the past; the *past* cannot be *presented*; we cannot know what we are not. But one veil hangs over past, present, and future, and it is the province of the historian to find out, not what was, but what is" (Stapleton 1960: 7)

This maxim propounded by Henry David Thoreau might with profit be engraved on the wooden handles of archaeologists' shovels. If the sole aim of our endeavors is to bring back an extinct past, our efforts shall indeed be in vain. The bed in which George Washington slept shall never again contain his bones; the noise of the shot heard 'round the world has long since parted irredeemably for the realm of silence.

Whatever else might be said about restorations is that they *are* restorations. They are not recreations of the life of some remote time; rather are they the modern and sometimes distorted reflections of the physical trappings with which someone's forebears surrounded themselves. When a lad has been at work in a colonial-style printing shop for eight months learning to set old-style font by hand, and he proudly explains to me he is still an apprentice but that he looks forward to becoming a journeyman, I presume it means he has worked for the corporation for two-thirds of a year and has yet to get his first raise. I further presume that even as a master printer the present-day demand for his hard-earned talents shall always be limited. He is very much in danger, in fact, of becoming a company man. Surely it was different with his 18-century counterpart. Come to think of it, he has no 18th-century counterpart. The 18th-century printer was not a product of restoration.

Or let us consider Brigham Young's house. Whatever purposes it served that mighty Morman it shall nevermore serve. Let each square cut or hand-wrought nail be carefully pounded in place; let the structure's footings stand where they stood more than a century ago; and set the table with dishes identical to those whose pieces were thrown into Brigham's well. This will not bring the religion of Latter Day Saints back toward its beginnings; this will not effect the politics of 19th-century Nauvoo or rekindle the harsh judgments of Nauvoo's neighbors. It becomes instead a modern monument, however faithfully restored, which pleases Elders of the 20th-century church, which attracts tourists, and which stands to remind the modern Morman concerning some of his origins.

Lest anyone think I am being cynical, let it be understood that I am second to no one in my admiration for and love of restorations—and the more accurately restored the better. I think that such restorations serve a variety of very important present-day functions: economic, social, educational, personal, and, in some cases, religious. Let us not, however, delude ourselves into thinking that because we have copied a building, a ship, or a whole town we have somehow brought the dead back to life. An archaeologist is not Jesus; Old Sturbridge is not Lazarus.

If anything divides archaeologists into classes it relates but little to their academic training as anthropologists or as historians. Far more basic is the question, "Are we interested primarily in human beings or in things? Are we people oriented or object oriented?" Among the ranks of anthropologists, especially among those who have specialized in archaeology, we find practitioners of both leanings, even as we do among historians. All of us have known academicians with an antiquarian turn of mind. These are the chaps who pester us at cocktail parties, answering questions no one has asked or is likely ever to ask.

I cannot agree that "historical archaeology must be architectural in orientation and reconstructive in both purpose and scope." This view is so narrow that certainly it rankles anyone who has ever spaded a trash mound, cleaned out an ancient privy, salvaged the sawed bones of animal remains from a field where they were thrown, dug a cemetery, gathered tin cans from a cave where a prospector slept, or dived beneath icy waters to regain the cargo spilled by *voyageurs* at a portage of some Michigan river. What architecture? What kind of reconstruction? Nor are these sites the "very few exceptions."

Let us consider instead that the orientation of archaeology, historical or otherwise, be humanistic. Let restoration be on this basis; let us only then take up the matter of architecture should it be appropriate. "Nothing," says Thoreau again, "so restores and humanizes antiquity and makes it blithe as the discovery of some natural sympathy between it and the present. Why is it that there is something melancholy in antiquity? We forget that it had any other future than our present. As if it were not as near to *the* future as ourselves. "... The heavens stood over the heads of our ancestors as near as to us" (Stapleton 1960: 8)

As for the exposition of anthropological, historical, and archaeological concepts, theories, methodology, and methods in "Some Thoughts on Theory and Method in Historical Archaeology," there is nothing to be said concerning it in a short reply that will help. When the statements are not in error, confused, obscure, or ambiguous, they are either unduly contentious or painfully obvious. It is clear, in any case, that the attack is launched from a platform of ignorance rather than of knowledge. It is also launched in an aura of blind devotion to the written word. Is a documentary reference *per se* better evidence than that afforded by other kinds of data? I have heard it remarked that literary historians seated atop an exploding volcano would not be inclined to believe it was happening until someone committed the event to paper for them. A few of the remarks in the essay under consideration come precariously close to exemplifying that uncomfortable position.

The advancement of the causes of historical archaeology, whatever these may be to different people, will not be promoted by ill-considered debates between historians and anthropologists or by accusations that others are doing mayhem to their sites because of their departmental brand of training. We are joined together in the early growth of an exciting venture. Let us move ahead with the biblical aphorism in mind: "Old things are passed away; behold, all things are become new" (II Corinthians 5:17).

REFERENCE

STAPLETON, LAURENCE
1960 *H. D. Thoreau: A Writer's Journal.* Dover Publications, Inc., New York.

CHAPTER 29

The Crisis of Identity: Theory in Historic Sites Archaeology

CHARLES E. CLELAND and JAMES E. FITTING

Archaeological method must not merely be technically excellent; it must express good archaeological theory. Good archaeological theory demands a conjunction of methods, conjoined on a rational basis of good logic. History and Science have not to be segregated, but identified together.

Charles Frances Christopher Hawkes
1954

The Society for Historical Archaeology was organized in Dallas, Texas in January of 1967. While those assembled agreed on the need of such a society, not all were in accord on its direction. Some alterations in the proposed statement of purposes were strictly political; Noël-Hume's suggested name for the society was accepted because of his concern for what "politicians" think. The real crisis came when the problem of defining historic sites archaeology arose. An attempt was made to accept what seemed to us a very narrow, self-limiting, self defeating definition. This definition which was drafted by Larrabee, Cotter and Noël-Hume proposed that "Historical archaeology is the application of archaeological method to the study of History." After a very narrow vote of 32 to 30, the matter was wisely dropped and the problem of definition was left to the individual members.

While the Society for Historical Archaeology avoided imposing limitation on itself in open meeting, a number of its more vocal members have recently made statements which are as self-limiting and self destructive as those initially proposed at the Dallas meeting. It is the attitude taken by such scholars as Noël-Hume (1961), Walker (1967) and more recently Dollar, (this volume) that we view with alarm and dismay. We believe that such a rigid position will severely limit the potential contributions of historical sites archaeology.

The crisis of identity in historic sites archaeology is not unexpected. When several disciplines approach a new body of data, there will undoubtedly be a confusion of paradigmatic theories developed in these different disciplines. Questions dealing with the application of theory developed on one set of data to a new set may be logically raised. The question of whether anthropological theory, developed from the study of primitive cultures, is applicable to contemporary society was raised by Leslie White in his presidential address to the American Anthropological Association in 1964 (White 1965) and has been the subject of a major review article by Leo Despres (1968). The question recently asked is not how do anthropologists dealing with complex societies differ from sociologists, economists and political scientists but rather if they differ at all. The answer has been a resounding yes and

the contribution of anthropological theory to the study of complex societies has been demonstrated to be complimentary to, not mutually exclusive of, the bodies of theory which define other disciplines.

This crisis parallels that which is faced by historic sites archaeology today. Historic sites produce a body of data which may be studied in a number of ways and these approaches are also complimentary. To define historic sites archaeology as "a technique of history" or as a separate field of study to itself is to actually limit the extent of its importance.

Where the authors dealing with historic sites mentioned above have seen fit to identify their academic backgrounds it has been, in every case, history. In contrast the senior author's initial training was in the biological science with later specialization in cultural ecology. The junior author was a communications research student who shifted to a social science program. Our unified approach is through anthropological theory which we have adopted through choice, not by default.

We are very much aware of the differences in the theories of different disciplines and are equally aware that no discipline can exist without theory. Even Walker's (1968) denial of the need of theory has a theoretical base which he either does not realize or can not accept because of his antitheoretical stance.

Walker's article needs special mention since he makes some points which are well taken. However, he is not the first archaeologist to find Taylor illogical or Binford incomprehensible. It is unfortunate that he either was not aware of, or did not see fit to cite, any of the dozen or more better sources for anthropological theory in archaeology.

The paper by Dollar presents a somewhat different problem. The arguments which we find objectionable are as follows:

1. Historic sites archaeology should be a distinct discipline with its special methodology designed to deal with its unique problems.
2. The artifacts collected from historic sites are the result of industrial processes and are therefore so complex that the analysis of these artifacts can not be based on an objective appraisal of their attributes.
3. The research techniques and methodology employed by specialists engaging in historic site research, principally historians and anthropologists, are so distinctive that they are incompatible.

It is unfortunate but these three suppositions have gained wide acceptance among a large body of scholars engaged in historic sites research and are frequently stated in a circular self supporting argument which can be entered at the point best suited to the bias of the particular observer. Thus, Noël Hume (1961: 256) views anthropology as the poison in the pudding.

> *Colonial sites do not, as a rule, commend themselves to most amateur archaeologist or state archaeological societies. The former often fall into two classes, pot hunters and anthropologists, the latter being most interested in the broad culture trends that are to be gleaned from archaeology.*

He goes on to brilliantly observe that an anthropologist who digs a colonial farm site will write that the artifacts he finds indicate a barn-like cultural orientation (which is what would be expected if a barn were being excavated). Walker (1967: 32) supports Noël-Hume's distrust for anthropology and adds that it's not too late to save historical archaeology from "the confining bounds of anthropology-oriented theory."

From such a base these "colonial archaeologists" seem to argue as follows: Historic sites archaeology is a specialized field of history, while the proper realm of anthropology is prehistory. Because complex historical sites offer different problems than simple prehistoric sites the former sites must be worked by archaeologists who have developed special technical skills designed to meet unique problems of complex artifact assemblages. The very complexity of artifact assemblages can be understood only through an intimate knowledge of a particular historic period and not by objective analysis of attributes. As a result, historic sites archaeology should be a tool of history distinct from anthropology. This argument exactly parallels our introductory comments concerning the Anthropology of complex societies. Anthropologists who study complex societies are historians. The anthropologists who study complex societies, however, can benefit from both the sociologist and the historian and the historian and sociologist can benefit from each other.

The argument can also be entered from the point of view that historic sites archaeology is fundamentally different from other types of archaeology and should therefore be constituted as a distinct discipline. For example, Dollar informs us that "It is time to give serious thought to the recognition of historical archaeology as a socio-scientific discipline with a methodology designed to cope with the unique problems encountered during the excavation of historical sites." (Dollar, this volume). Harrington (1952: 343) agrees stating:

> *I think it proper to say that excavation in this field constitutes a new kind of archaeology, on a par with classical archaeology, American prehistoric archaeology or paleolithic archaeology. Historic sites archaeology involves a distinctive kind of site, develops a distinctive approach, both in field techniques and manner of interpretation, and produces characteristic conclusions and results.*

Such arguments again provide entree into the argument that since historic sites differ in kind, they require techniques different from those applied by other archaeologists. These new methods must recognize the complexity of historic sites and historic artifact assemblages, a complexity which can not be rendered intelligible by traditional anthropological or historical methods. They would argue that the development of new methods can only be accomplished by the establishment of a new and different historic sites field.

Finally, the complexity argument has frequently been evoked by those engaged in historic sites archaeology. Thus, Dollar informs us that "It should be sufficiently clear by this time that variants in the manufacturing techniques of historical sites artifacts totally destroy their value as specific dating tools for the historical archaeologists." Elsewhere Dollar, as well as many others have noted that because a particular category of artifacts were manufactured in hundreds of different factories that it is impossible to observe discrete attributes which could possibly lead to more definitive categorization. Similarly it has been argued that such "complex" artifacts are not amenable to statistical manipulation.

This argument again leads easily into the logical vortex which we have already described. The adoption of this type of theoretical position represents more than a harmless personal bias bred by disposition or training. It, in fact, determines the type of field works, description and analysis which historic sites archaeologists perform. More important, perhaps, this position can determine what kind of a field historic sites archaeology will be; will it be self-contained and self-limiting or will it make substantial contributions to the study of the natural and social sciences.

The adoption of the theoretical stance which has been described above seems to us to have led to a number of unfortunate and wholly disadvantageous attitudes, methods and conclusions on the part of many historic sites archaeologists. While we don't intend to engage in wholesale refutation of the group, we find the following trends to by and large characterize historic sites archaeology.

1. The excavation of sites by professional scholars who lack experience in archaeological field methodology. These are primarily historians and "specialist" in various artifact classes, people with interest in art history and architecture or salvage divers.
2. The excavation of historic sites with the notion that excavation is a simple technical process which may be carried out in a theoretical vacuum partitioned from its analytical or laboratory phase and terminated short of the integrative or synthetic phase.
3. The analysis of excavation material from a historical bias. The result is dull, unimaginative reports which contribute little or nothing to our understanding of history, cultural phenomena or anything else. These reports become in essence long lists and descriptions of artifacts and excavated building features.
4. The reluctance to adopt a classification process based on the discrete attributes of artifacts and to use sophisticated analytical techniques in classification has led to the appearance of a cult based on the "mystique of expertise." Thus, specialists can distinguish German from Dutch earthenware on the basis of "experience" or "feel" but are reluctant to set forth specific criteria. We expect that these criteria are either nonexistent or are undefinable, untestable, and, therefore, indefensible. The results of this cult is a huge group of specialists, oriented either temporarily (18th Century Colonial), regionally (Great Lakes fur trade) or most frequently topically (weapons, glass or ceramics).
5. The financial support of restoration programs at historic sites has produced a carnival atmosphere which is hardly conducive to genuine research. Research activities are often seen as peripheral to other activities such as providing evidence for building restoration or entertainment for tourists. As a result, the relatively minor, and certainly preliminary, field phase and analysis of structural evidence is given precedence over solid long term research.

The continuation of these trends will see historic sites archaeology develop as an unimaginative hobby characterized by low level research undertaken by poorly trained technicians who are aided and abetted by hordes of specialists who are, in essence, academic antique collectors.

As an alternative we argue that historic sites archaeology is not a different kind of archaeology but a field which requires the cooperation of a number of sub-disciplines. We argue that the field and laboratory methodology employed by historic sites archaeologists should be objective and rigorous and finally that anthropological and historic phases of research are not only compatible but are complementary and necessary in the understanding of any particular site.

We have thus far presented what we believe are the most prevalent and damaging trends in historic sites archaeology. These are for the most part based on a misunderstanding of the relationship between history, anthropology and archaeology.

Some years ago White (1945) presented a very instructive matrix to illustrate the differences in temporal and conceptual perspectives which produce differences in the theoretical ordering of natural phenomena. The matrix shown below is a modification of White's matrix to fit the situation under discussion.

	Temporal	Non-temporal
Particularizing	History	Field Work (Excavation & Artifact Analysis)
Generalizing	Anthropology	Structural-Functional (Sociological) Interpretations

Here we see the major conceptions of primary concern to historic sites archaeology. Field work is done in a non-temporal particularizing framework. In historical archaeology this is field excavation and simple laboratory description. All too often historic sites archaeology does not get beyond this point. The non-temporal particularizing frame, however, is basic for all types of scientific research in which things or events are observed within some context to produce basic data. Higher level analysis can only be as good as the data produced at this level allows.

The data may then be ordered in this paradigmatic form in three ways; temporal-generalizing, non-temporal-generalizing, and temporal-particularizing. The latter is history (specific things and events ordered in time) while the non-temporal generalizing frame provides sociological and social anthropological conclusions and the temporal-generalizing frame provides the basis for cultural anthropological interpretations. It is important to note that the same data produced by field and low level (laboratory) research can be interpreted in Historical, Sociological and Anthropological frames of reference. Most of the confusion over the role of history, anthropology and archaeology in historic sites archaeology has been the result of confusing these frames. The difference between archaeology and anthropology, or prehistoric archaeology and anthropology, or even the differences between history and historic sites archaeology have been clouded by the lack of reference to such a paradigmatic framework.

Harrington received some criticism when he wrote that excavations on historic sites contributed considerable historical data but results in relatively little history (Harrington 1955: 1124). Here Harrington was correctly recognizing the distinction between a non-temporal-particularizing and a temporal-particularizing frame of reference. Archaeology is definitely not, as Judson put it (1961: 410), ". . . a historic subject which reconstructs history from objects."

Once the above distinctions are clear, it is possible to proceed to a consideration of the methods used in the excavation of materials. It is our contention that historic sites do not constitute a unique phenomena in this regard, that they are no simpler or no more complex than at least some prehistoric sites and that they require no field techniques that may not be applied on other sites (see Powell 1967: 36 for a similar position). Thus, the central question becomes not who excavates but how well they excavate. We recognize that prior knowledge of historic records and documents is as important to the proper excavation of historic sites as the ability to distinguish between trench fill and potholes. Any technically competent archaeologist who has thoroughly researched the history of a site is qualified to dig, any historian who is thoroughly versed in history but lacks competence in archaeological field procedure is no more qualified than an archaeologist who is ignorant of a site's history.

The analysis of excavated materials is not unrelated to the way in which field excavation is undertaken. The computer programers adage, "garbage in-garbage out," sums up this point of view. Excavations designed simply to collect a sample of artifacts no matter how excellent in execution will not produce meaningful data. Excavations must be problem-oriented and oriented at a high level—locating a specific building known to have existed on a site is not high level imaginative research (see Harrington 1955: 1121 and 1126). Designing field research to generate data which can produce significant statements about technology, style, or function in a social, political or ideological context is a worthy goal of field research.

Laboratory analysis of excavated materials must be more than a descriptive process in which each specimen is intimately described (see Noël-Hume 1966a, 1966b). Instead, description should lead to well-defined classificatory systems which account for variation in terms of stylistic, functional or structural realities (see Witthoft 1968: 12−49, South 1967: 33−59, Marwitt 1967: 19−26 and Brose 1967). Such systems do not take refuge in expertise and therefore may run the risk of revision and obsolescence, yet they provide a systematic and useful framework for spatial and temporal comparison. The analysis of historic artifacts must be based on the quantification of empirical data.

Finally we come to the interpretation of excavated material. It has been noted that this may be undertaken in either an historic (temporal-particularizing), a sociological (non-temporal-generalizing) or anthropological (temporal-generalizing) context. An excellent site report *must* contain all of these and must be based on excellent analysis and excavation (non-temporal-particularizing). While it is a foregone conclusion that a historic site must be interpreted in the context of the international, national and local events taking place at the time the site was occupied, we see a stubborn resistance to any interpretation which is thought to be sociological or anthropological. Despite persistent urging principally by Foley (1967a: 43 and 1967a: 66) and some imaginative and useful cultural interpretations (Binford 1962, Dethlefsen and Deetz 1966, Brose 1967), few anthropological interpretations have been attempted for historic sites. Nonetheless, historic sites are potentially well suited for sociological and anthropological interpretation. We would, for instance, expect that our knowledge of 18th and 19th Century trade, transportation, social stratification, political spheres, craft specialization, and acculturation of native peoples could be tremendously enhanced by data from historic sites of this period. These and many other problems which involve the cultures represented by historic sites should be of tremendous interest to historic site archaeologists. While such problems cannot be studied without regard to historical data, neither can historic sites archaeologists who continue to ignore these problems expect to fully understand historic sites. We submit that historic sites archaeology can make but few contributions to history but tremendous contributions to other fields of study.

To use part of Walker's (1967: 32) recent statement, "Historic archaeology in the New World is a field which is still in its formative stage. It is not too late to make it a field of distinction . . . " Rather than freeing ourselves from "the confining bonds of anthropological theory" as Walker suggests, we appeal for objectivity, quantification and the unbiased use of *both* anthropological and historical methodology and add a plea for more thoughtful orientation rather than a conscious limitation to low levels of interpretation as Noël-Hume, Walker, Dollar and others seem to advocate.

REFERENCES

BINFORD, LEWIS R.
1962 A Discussion of the Contrasts in the Development of the Settlement at Fort Michilimackinac under British and French Rule. *Southeastern Archaeological Conference Newsletter*. Vol. 9, No. 1: 50–52.

BROSE, DAVID S.
1967 The Custer Road Dump Site: An Exercise in Victorian Archaeology. *The Michigan Archaeologist*. Vol. 13, No. 2:37–128.

DESPRES, LEO A.
1968 Anthropological Theory, Cultural Pluralism and the Study of Complex Societies. *Current Anthropology*, Vol. 9, No. 1, pp. 3–26. Chicago.

DETHLEFSEN, EDWIN and JAMES DEETZ
1966 Death's Heads, Cherubs and Willow Trees: Experimental Archaeology in Colonial Cemeteries. *American Antiquity*, Vol. 31, No. 4: 502–510.

FOLEY, VINCENT P.
1967a Status and Progress Report on the 18th Century Bethlehem, Pennsylvania Historic Site Project. *Conference on Historic Sites Archaeology Papers 1965–1966.* Vol. 1:66–73.

1967b Pre-1800 Historic Sites-Urban. *Historical Archaeology 1967:* 43–46.

HARRINGTON, J. C.
1955 Archaeology as an Auxiliary Science to American History. *American Anthropologist*. Vol. 57, No. 6, Pt. 1: 1121–1130.

HAWKES, CHRISTOPHER
1954 Archaeological Theory and Method: Some Suggestions from the Old World. *American Anthropologist*. Vol. 56: 155–168.

JUDSON, SHELDON
1961 Archaeology and the Natural Sciences. *American Scientist*. Vol. 49, No. 3: 410–414.

MARWITT, RENEE H.
1967 Punch Card Design for Ceramic Analysis. *The Conference on Historic Site Archaeology Papers 1965–1966*. Vol. 1: 19–26.

NOËL-HUME, IVOR
1961 Preservation of English and Colonial American Sites. *Archaeology*, Vol. 14, No. 4: 250–260.

1966a Excavations at Tutter's Neck in James City County, Virginia, 1960–1961. *Contributions from The Museum of History and Technology: Paper 53:* 31–72.

1966b Excavations at Clay Bank in Gloucester County, Virginia, 1962–1963. *Contributions from the Museum of History and Technology: Paper 52:* 3–28.

POWELL, BRUCE B.
1967 Excavation Accompanying Building Restoration. *Historical Archaeology 1967:* 36–38.

SOUTH, STANLEY
1967 The Ceramic Forms of the Potter Gottfried Aust at Bethabara, North Carolina, 1755–1771. *The Conference on Historic Site Archaeology Papers 1965–1966*, Vol. 1: 33–52.

WALKER, IAIN C.
1967 Historic Archaeology-Methods and Principles. *Historical Archaeology 1967*, 23: 34.

WHITE, LESLIE A.
1945 History, Evolutionism and Functionalism: Three types of Interpretation of Culture. *Southwestern Journal of Anthropology*, Vol. 1, 11. 221–248.

1965 Anthropology 1964: Retrospect and Prospect. *American Anthropologist*. Vol. 67, pp. 629–637.

WITTHOFT, JOHN
1966 A History of Gunflints. *Pennsylvania Archaeologist*. Vol. 36, No. 1–2. 12–49.

CHAPTER 30

"Evolution and Horizon as Revealed in Ceramic Analysis in Historical Archaeology": A Step Toward the Development of Archaeological Science

LEWIS R. BINFORD

In a recent series of exchanges, numbers of historical sites archaeologists have expressed their views regarding the field and its current development. A wide variety of opinion has been expressed and clearly some tempers have been aroused.

Since this debate has been largely stimulated by Clyde Dollar's (1968) paper, I will attempt to make a few points germane to his discussion, the implications of which I feel have not been fully explored by his critics.

I will try to summarize these points as I see them:

1. Researchers in the field of historical archaeology are encountering problems, the solutions to which seriously strain the ability of traditional anthropological methods to solve (Dollar 1968:4).
2. The historian uses two main research methods or "tools." The first of these is the logical process of deductive reasoning, or going from the general to the particular, and the second is the application of tests for validity or the research processes of verification (Dollar 1968: 11).

I feel that Dollar is correct in these assertions and in general his sketch parallels the analysis frequently made by philosophers of science regarding historical methods.

> It is a rather widely held opinion that history, in contradistinction to the so-called physical sciences, is concerned with the description of particular events of the past rather than with the search for general laws which might govern those events (Hempel 1965: 231).

One might reasonably ask: Where does the historian obtain the general propositions which, as Dollar points out, permit him to proceed from the general to the particular?

> ... in history no less than in any other branch of empirical inquiry, scientific explanation can be achieved only by means of suitable general hypotheses, or by theories, which are bodies of systematically related hypotheses. This thesis is clearly in contrast with the familiar view that genuine explanation in history is obtained by the method which characteristically distinguishes the social from the natural sciences, namely the method of empathic understanding: The historian, we are told, imagines himself in the place of the persons involved in the events which he wants to explain; he tries to realize as completely as possible the circumstances under which they acted and the motives which influenced their actions; and by this imaginary self-identification with his heroes, he arrives at an

understanding and thus at an adequate explanation of the events with which he is concerned (Hempel 1965: 239–240).

Dollar himself is silent on this issue but Walker, with whom Dollar clearly identifies (Dollar 1968a: 139), provides us with a classical statement of the method "of empathic understanding."

> ... We cannot understand the history of prehistoric man unless we become in our own mind a prehistoric man—so also with historic man. Each site excavated is individual to some degree, and the product of individuals (Walker 1968: 119).

This procedure seems to be justified by the advocates of historical methodology as an appeal to the "uniqueness thesis" which is widely held by historians. It has been stated this way:

> History is different in that it seeks to describe and explain what actually happened in all its concrete detail. It therefore follows a priori that since laws govern classes or types of things, and historical events are unique, it is not possible for the historian to explain his subject-matter by means of covering laws. If he is to understand at all, it will have to be by some kind of special insight into particular connections (Dray 1957: 45).

That this seems to be an adequate summary of Dollar's and Walker's views is best demonstrated by their words:

> It would seem to me, therefore, that the study of anthropology in general, is incapable of producing techniques for the recognition of either specific actions or single cultural contributions of any given individual within any given culture (Dollar 1968: 10–11).

> ... anthropological studies tend to formalize generalizations which are difficult to prove ... to make conclusions which may be valid as generalizations; but being generalizations, are often inapplicable to single instances (Walker 1968: 108).

While Dollar characterizes himself as a "differing dragon" (Dollar 1968b: 156), the general stance of both Dollar and

Walker was championed in history during the last half of the nineteenth century by what is frequently referred to as the "German School." Proponents differentiated between those subjects which were considered amenable to the idiographic method, e.g., exploring particular connections. Nomethetic approaches were used where establishing generalizations was a goal. This idiographic approach in history has recently come under scrutiny by historians themselves. In an interesting study, Joynt and Rescher (1961) conclude that the uniqueness thesis cannot be sustained either through logic or an appeal to the actual activities of historians. Since all events may from one perspective be considered unique there is, therefore, no essential difference between the historical and natural sciences deriving from the character of their data. Distinction only arises by choosing to treat events as unique. One may choose to use events or facts as members of a type or class with the aim of establishing generalizations and propositions of law-like validity. Such a choice is not dictated by the character of the data.

Inspection of the works of historians demonstrates their dependence upon categories, classes, and generalizations:

> *It is clear that the historian in effect reverses the means-end relationship between fact and theory that we find in science. For the historian is interested in generalizations and does concern himself with them. But he does so not because generalizations constitute the aim and objective of his discipline, but because they help him illuminate the particular facts with which he deals (Joynt and Rescher 1961: 153).*

The essentially dependent character of historians for the propositions which serve as links in their interpretative arguments is well stated by Ernest Nagel.

> *There is an important asymmetry between theoretical (or generalizing) science and history. A theoretical discipline like physics seeks to establish both general and singular statements, and in order to do so physicists employ previously assumed statements of both types. Historians, on the other hand, aim to assert warranted singular statements about the occurrence and the inter-relations of specific actions and other particular occurrences. However, although this task can be achieved only by assuming and using general laws, historians do not regard it as part of their aim to establish such laws (Nagel 1961: 550).*

That this is the general stance of those who recommend to us "the stiffening discipline of historical philosophy" (Walker 1968: 108) is well demonstrated in the following statement by Walker (1970: 67).

> *. . . I suggest that the end result is of more importance than the abstract theory woven in an attempt to find that end result; If Cleland and Fitting . . . . can re-create the past from an excavated site in a way which enables us to see, however dimly, how people lived and worked, then provided their conclusions are legitimate deductions from the evidence available their philosophical beliefs are not of the first importance.*

This comment presents us with some interesting notions. For instance, how does one deduce conclusions from available evidence? Deductions are made from propositions which specify relationships between things and events. Conclusions regarding observations are warranted to the degree that their relevance to such propositions can be established and the conclusions regarding specific cases are justified logically. Surely if one is to work deductively then one has some interest in the validity of the propositions from which deductions are drawn. One wonders, in the absence of concern for philosophical "beliefs," what criteria Walker might use to determine whether an archaeologist's conclusions "are legitimate deductions from the evidence." I fear that Walker's criteria would be intuitive tests of plausibility, internal consistency, or critical evaluation of the accuracy of the facts cited. For the scientist there are other major concerns: the validity of the assumptions regarding man, of the character of the archaeological record, of the past, of contingencies believed to affect man's behavior, etc. These are assumptions which we must all use in order to interpret the data of archaeology. Facts do not speak for themselves.

Dollar points out that many general propositions current in anthropology appear vastly inadequate when adopted for use by historians. In this position I would agree with Dollar. Anthropologists have not addressed themselves to the job of making explicit and testing the validity of the law-like propositions which they have expounded. For instance, Dollar points out the failure and lack of retrodictive accuracy when using seriation techniques as they have frequently been employed by anthropologists. He equates seriation with a dating technique. This has clearly been done by archaeologists working with prehistoric materials, but the utility of the technique, *qua* technique, need not be equated with some individual's excesses. Seriation is simply an arranging of samples or items in a series with regard to some specified criterion. As generally used, samples or populations are arranged in series with regard to some measure of similarity between the samples. As outlined this is purely descriptive procedure. Dollar seems to object to the proposition that all observed variability is referable to cultural change or differentiation, an assumption which must be made if a scale of differences is equated with time. I think that Dollar would find very few anthropologists anxious to defend that proposition, and in fact the heyday of seriation used in this manner has been over in American archaeology for at least ten years.

This does not mean that seriation as a technique is not still being widely employed: it is. As archaeologists, our job is the explanation of observed similarities and differences in the archaeological record, and seriation techniques are very useful in evaluating such differences and similarities. This is not to say that in many cases similarities and differences as measured by seriation techniques do not demonstrate significant temporal patterning: they do. By discouraging the use of "extended anthropological techniques" Dollar is not just complaining about the utility of some of the anthropologists' general propositions, he is advocating a historical approach and asserting anew the "uniqueness thesis," i.e., that historic sites are unique, and are therefore not appropriately investigated as cases in the testing of propositions of potential general validity. Strangely, he inveighs against formal descriptions of artifacts, statistical techniques, etc., though these approaches are completely consistent with traditional historical approaches.

The debate largely boils down to an attempt on the part of Dollar to set forth the "uniqueness thesis" as the justification for adopting a set of goals commensurate with traditional historical perspectives. His concern is with specific events, dates, and actions of individuals summarized in the pursuit of reconstruction. Dollar offers further justification through a criticism of the accomplishments of "generalizing anthropology," which are set forth as a contrastive set of "failures," which he sees as further support for "uniqueness" claims and for the dismissal of generalizing propositions in historic sites archaeology.

The "uniqueness" position is invalid as a justification for pursuing idiographic goals. All events or facts may be viewed as unique, or one may choose to treat them as cases in the context of generalizing propositions. The character of the data is never a justification for the limited pursuit of limited goals. Similarly the failure of attempts to treat events and specific observations in a generalizing framework is not sufficient justification for abandoning generalizing goals.

Reliable historical interpretation and hence reconstruction of life ways, etc., is dependent upon valid general propositions which can serve as the pivotal points for interpretive arguments treating the specific facts of a specific case. In order to increase our powers of historical interpretation, making use of archaeological facts, progress is needed on two fronts:

1. An active attempt to explicitly state and test the validity of high level generalizations regarding
   a. the processes responsible for the formation of the archaeological record, and
   b. the processes responsible for bringing about changes and maintaining diversity in the life ways of peoples.
2. An active attempt to increase the accuracy with which we observe and describe the facts of the archaeological record.

What is needed to increase our abilities in historical reconstruction is the development of a science of archaeology. Anthropologists smugly displaying their scorn of historians must stop working as historians and start working as scientists to meet the need for valid general propositions.

Another note, however, seems to dominate the discussion and this is the note I find disturbing. I am not disturbed that historians find anthropological generalizations inadequate: they generally are. I am not disturbed that in the absence of a sound scientific basis for the interpretation of specific historical events that some should be pragmatic and follow an eclectic procedure. I am disturbed with what appears to be a commitment to the maintenance of this state of affairs. Dollar seemingly wants to become more restrictive in the degree that we investigate the archaeological record itself and decries the use of statistical procedures when they do not yield "accurate" results. Walker, although less radical, appears to be saying that an explicit concern with science is not necessary since the expedient positions forced on historians in the absence of sound scientific understanding are in fact desirable:

> ... the suggestion that anthropology must become history or become nothing is not just a smart remark to Willey and Phillips: it is the statement of what I conceive to be the goal of all those who study man and his past, a conclusion to which Boas came in 1932 (Walker 1970: 65).

I would amend this position in the following way: anthropology must become a science before it can adequately serve to enhance our historical understanding of man and his past. I suggest to historians, anthropologists, and interested bystanders alike, that insofar as we agree that our goals in historical sites archaeology are historical understanding of the events and the people which were responsible for the production of the archaeological record, such understanding will not be forthcoming until a science of archaeology is developed. Rejection of the pursuit of scientific or nomothetic understanding because of failures in this direction within the field of anthropology, or a commitment to particularistic approaches in the absence of such understanding is counterproductive. Historic sites archaeologists should actively engage in nomothetic studies aimed at the specification of general propositions amenable to testing regarding (a) the processes responsible for the formation of the archaeological record and (b) the processes responsible for change and diversification in human lifeways. Success along these lines will lead to a greater success in the understanding and reconstruction of specific events and specific historical facts.

Historic sites work seems to me to be particularly suited to this type of development since many conditions of the past are known through written documentation. We are, therefore, in a more informed position to test the validity of generalizing propositions than many prehistoric archaeologists working in a much less informed domain.

How does all this discussion relate to the paper presented by Stanley South? I think it is germane in a number of ways. South's paper is a fine example of the development of a research tool making claims of general utility. South has summarized a series of median dates for the periods of production of a selected control group of ceramic types. He proposes that the arithmetic mean of these dates, for examples of the types found in archaeological contexts, when weighted individually by the numbers of each type found will yield the best estimate of the median date of the elapsed time during which the archaeological sample was accumulated. This suggestion assumes that the maximum production of any given ceramic form will be in essential identity with the median date of that form's production history.

In the context of the current debate I anticipate a number of potential responses to these suggestions. I fear that many will view South's proposal in a limited perspective seeing it only as a *dating technique*. Some will almost certainly offer numerous arguments as to why, as a dating technique, it cannot be valid. In such arguments the most common citation will be to conditions in the past which when operative would tend to result in inaccurate dates. Others will take the position that the inaccuracy is not tolerable in the context of their specific historic needs and therefore dismiss the research tool as irrelevant to their interests. Still others may well conclude that the procedure is too time-consuming when they can date their sites more accurately with other means.

I will try to treat each of these anticipated responses in the context of my analysis of the current debate in the field.

The first response, that of offering many reasons why the proposal cannot work, is not a sufficient justification for an archaeological scientist to reject the proposal. South offers a general proposition and a demonstration that at least in the context of the materials used it does work. The scientist could only take the enumeration of reasons why it shouldn't work as a challenge. The exploration of the organizational relationships between differential production, the logistics of differential distribution and the differential utilization of products, and their final loss to the system as potential contributors to variability in the archaeological record are essential kinds of knowledge for the accurate interpretation of archaeological variability. South's methods when used in conjunction with others provide us with an interesting tool for the initiation of such studies aimed at the understanding of processes which were certainly operative with regard to the above mentioned factors. The fact that South's proposal seems to yield consistently reliable results needs to be explained. Similarly, cases of demonstrated inaccuracy demand explanation.

The second response, that of dismissing the methods because the levels of inaccuracy as a dating technique are unacceptable, betray a naive notion regarding the character of the archaeological record. The only accurate dating techniques which the archaeologist might develop for treating unknown materials are those which are dependent upon the operation of processes independent of the operation of cultural processes. Leaving aside for a moment the levels of accuracy problem it should be clear that Carbon 14, dendrochronology, and all other such techniques are dependent upon the operation of regular processes in the past, independent of the operation of cultural processes. We may make use of knowledge of such processes for dating by the demonstration of correlations or associations with materials relevant to cultural processes. Any technique of dating which is based on cultural materials may exhibit regular trends temporally, but it is always dependent for its accuracy on the stability of certain relationships in the organization of cultural dynamics. When we can demonstrate the accuracy of such a temporal trend in cultural materials we have isolated a phenomenon which once again demands that we seek an understanding. How general is its reliability, how variable is its accuracy, what were the determinants operative to produce variable accuracy, etc., are the questions we want to answer. If we understand these things, we would be both learning more about the past and increasing the utility of our original observations as a dating technique which could be utilized with confidence within stated ranges of accuracy. The persons who dismiss South's technique and view it simply as a dating technique of questionable utility are relinquishing their scientific role in favor of ignorance regarding the character of cultural processes operative in the past.

The response that South's procedure is too time-consuming and that other more reliable means of dating materials may be available is taking a very short sighted view of the field. More reliable dating means places such a researcher in the position of contributing some of the most important information to investigations into the character of the organizational relationships obtained in the past. Such persons are in a position to evaluate the accuracy of the procedure and hence the degree that the relationships in the past which resulted in the regular trend were truly stable, fluctuating, or affected periodically by other unknown sets of variables.

Thus I suggest that in the context of scientific development there are no foreseeable justifications for not using South's procedure, for dismissing it, or for giving precedence to other procedures. Scientific understanding is necessarily a cumulative process, particularly insofar as it is dependent upon a broad-scale comparative strategy. The scientist must frequently engage in work which is not directly productive of results in the context of his limited immediate goals. We must all be aware of the need to accumulate documented case material and well-described situations as a prerequisite to rewarding comparative studies. I sincerely hope that the suggestions of Dollar do not influence the field of historic sites archaeology. Since it is a relatively new field, the documented basis for productive comparative studies is not yet available in spite of the number of sites which have been excavated. To dismiss the application of "extended anthropological techniques" insures that such a basic corpus of data usable in the context of a controlled procedure will never accumulate. I urge historic sites archaeologists to use the technique, whether they agree with it or not, since the only way of gaining sufficient knowledge for evaluating their skepticism is to have available a broad comparative body of data for evaluation in the context of scientific methods.

BIBLIOGRAPHY

DOLLAR, CLYDE D.
1968 Some Thoughts on Theory and Method in Historical Archaeology. *The Conference on Historic Site Archaeology Papers, 1967* 2, Part 2:3–30. Stanley South (ed.).
1968a Reply to Cleland and Fitting. *The Conference on Historic Site Archaeology Papers, 1967* 2, Part 2:139–141. Stanley South (ed.).
1968b Reply to Vincent P. Foley. *The Conference on Historic Site Archaeology Papers, 1967* 2, Part 2:142–157 (footnotes). Stanley South (ed.).

DRAY, W. H.
1957 *Laws and Explanation in History,* Oxford.

HEMPEL, CARL G.
1965 *Aspects of Scientific Explanation*, The Free Press, New York.

JOYNT, C. G. and N. RESCHER
1961 The Problem of Uniqueness in History. *History and Theory* 1:150–162.

NAGEL, ERNEST
1961 *The Structure of Science*, Harcourt, Brace and World, New York.

WALKER, IAIN C.
1968 Comment on Clyde Dollar's 'Some Thoughts on Theory and Method in Historical Archaeology.' *The Conference on Historic Site Archaeology Papers, 1967* 2, Part 2:105–123. Stanley South (ed.).
1970 The Crisis of Identity—History and Anthropology. *The Conference on Historic Site Archaeology Papers, 1968* 3, Part 1 and 2:62–69. Stanley South (ed.). The Institute of Archeology and Anthropology, University of South Carolina.

Future Trends

INTRODUCTION

Archaeological investigations of historic periods in America, and by implication in Africa, Oceania, Latin America, and parts of Asia, are on the verge of a major quantitative and qualitative expansion. Entirely new topics of research, as seen in the study of ethnicity and industrial urbanism, are being added to a continuing emphasis on traditional fort, mission, and colonial sites. Equally important is the growth in the variety and sophistication of methods and theoretical models. In large part these new horizons, which are only in an embryonic state, stem from anthropology. The five selections in Part 5 highlight these future anthropological trends as they cluster in two principal areas.

Structural-Functional Trend

In the 1950's the functionalistic school of social anthropology had a delayed impact on prehistoric archaeology. Works by Americans like W. W. Taylor proffered a "conjunctive" (read functionalism) approach that shifted concentration from limited culture historical comparisons and chronology to the spatial distribution, quantification, and context of artifacts as a basis for reconstructing past lifeways. It was not until the 1960's that computer technology made this paradigm significant, if not dominant, in the field. An even greater delay is detected in reference to Historical Archaeology and it is only now that some excavators are trying to compare, quantify, and culturally interpret historical assemblages by focusing on context. Stanley South's *Method and Theory in Historical Archaeology* (1977), from which the essay on "Exploring Analytical Techniques" is taken, is the first major opus in this new tradition.

Evolutionary-Processual Trend

At the core of anthropology, and one of its hallmarks as a science, is the cross-cultural comparative method. Only by contrasting clearly separate cultural patterns is it possible to delineate recurrent, processual variables from the background noise of unique and secondary events. The rich but mainly unrealized potential of historic sites for comparative studies has been discussed by a few writers (see Chapter 8), but it is only now that a methodology and theoretical orientation are being adopted that will make comparisons operational.

Meaningful evolutionary comparisons must crosscut cultural stage boundaries. Either an immediate succession of cultures in the same area (the basis of Binford's paper), qualitatively different cultural stages in the same area over greater lengths of time (as with Deetz' interpretation of material culture in New England between 1620 and 1830), or geographically and temporally isolated case studies must be used. Two of the most promising topics for such projects in the immediate future are English-French-Spanish contrasts, particularly in the Great Lakes region and what was formerly northern New Spain, and more restricted comparisons of the English colonies in Tidewater Maryland (St. Mary's City) and New England (Plimouth Plantation). Differing environments, aboriginal cultures, and a plantation versus farmer-merchant society are significant differences against a general Angloamerican commonality.

A Prospective Statement on Historical Archaeology

Historical Archaeology is now a recognized field of scholarship that has made impressive progress during the last decade. Nevertheless, almost none of these advances have been processual in nature. Better chronological control, more detailed knowledge of specific artifact categories, and in a few instances better defined images of the past are significant achievements but historical archaeologists must also consider a different range of methodological problems if there is to be a transition to theoretically oriented research. The most fundamental problem in methodology continues to go almost unrecognized—the nature and interrelationship between archaeological and documentary data. Only this relationship (which, of course, is indirectly related to cultural complexity) differentiates prehistoric from Historical Archaeology. What is an artifact? What is a document? What kinds of information do they, or do they not, convey? How are the approaches of the historian and the archaeologist similar and how are they different? Artifacts and documents are, in part, qualitatively different types of cultural products and the failure to recognize this differential has eviscerated Historical Archaeology and limited it to a kind of prehistoric archaeology of complex societies. When it is recognized that historical archaeologists are able to directly reconstruct images of the past with full *etic* (behavior) and *emic* (beliefs) aspects, an accomplishment impossible for the prehistorian, then an entire range of new methodological problems intrinsic to the discipline will be evident. How can the products of past human behavior and past human beliefs about that behavior be unified. Is it a matter of simply using one as a mirror for the other, or is a much more complex dialectical process involved?

Assuming historical archaeologists finally start to do complete Historical Archaeology, and except for a few scholars like Deetz and Henry Glassie (both idealists), most of us have yet to stop being transposed prehistorians, then and only then will Historical Archaeology be able to approach theoretical problems and produce anything of unique merit from either an anthropological or historical perspective.

The subject matter of Historical Archaeology, as practiced in America, is the point by point parallel to current developments in social anthropology and linguistics that are establishing cultural anthropology as a truly holistic field. Urban anthropology, modernization studies, and the investigation of state formation and pluralistic societies in the Third World are all parts of a research expansion that has not abandoned the traditional subjects of primitive and complex but non-civilized cultures but rather has reached out to incorporate new areas, especially the modern world. In the historian's sense the modern world is only 400 to 500 years old. Its roots lie in Medieval and Renaissance Europe although its effects are now worldwide. Post-Medieval Archaeology, Historic Sites Archaeology, and Industrial Archaeology (and some aspects of ethnoarchaeology) are the study of specific segments of the evolutionary process that created contemporary society, segments that are identical to the new research topics of other anthropologists.

Most developmental schemes propose a minimum of four stages in the evolution of culture. The first two, the initiation of culture as a phenomenon and its transformation when new sources of energy were discovered in the Neolithic, are primarily the concern of the prehistorian (and ethnographer and ethnohistorian), but the later two great transformations—the emergence of civilization and its elaboration when different sources of energy were again discovered in the Industrial Revolution—are in part or totally subjects for the historical archaeologist. Research on the rise of both civilization and the modern world that combines archaeological and documentary data can make a contribution that is simultaneously different from but complimentary with the findings of the historian and non-anthropological social scientist. A series of prerequisite steps are necessary, however, if Historical Archaeology is to make either a substantive or theoretical contribution:

1. the methodological significance of the artifact-document nexus must be recognized,
2. realization that all specializations within Historical Archaeology, ranging from Classical to Industrial Archaeology, are methodologically one discipline,
3. an equal and secondary recognition that the specific subjects of these subfields are not similar because of the qualitative nature of cultural evolution, and
4. utilization of a broad, cross-cultural approach to search for underlying patterns and explanations for these patterns.

At the end of this logical sequence the historical archaeologist will be operating as an anthropologist, but an anthropologist who will possess a new and uniquely rich data base compared to that of the historian, social anthropologist, or his prehistoric colleagues.

CHAPTER 31

Exploring Analytical Techniques

STANLEY SOUTH

EXAMINING THE *KITCHEN* ARTIFACT PATTERNS

After almost a half-century of various kinds of digging on historic sites, justified by varying rationales, there are as a result certain questions that can be answered. Unfortunately, there are other problems that are no nearer a solution now than before all this activity began. Some artifact types have been described and some classes have been established. Artifact types can sometimes be placed in a chronological framework relative to a manufacture period for those types. As a result, historical archaeologists are anxious to pass this information on to others less informed, and reports of excavations on historic sites emphasize the chronological placement of the relics recovered, too often ending with that.

Some other questions that can be answered by the historical archaeologist are: Was this a pottery making site? Was this a glasshouse site? Was this a printshop? Was this a blacksmith shop? Was this an iron foundry? The historical archaeologist's "skill" at interpreting the remains from the past allows him to identify, for example, the kilns, wasters, furnaces and slag, printer's type and crucibles as the by-products of such specialized past activities. He can also interpret the function of wells, privies, smokehouses, fireplaces, and springhouses.

Questions he cannot so readily answer after a half-century of effort are: Were women present on this site? Was this a domestic or a military occupation? Was a battle fought on this site? Was this a trading post or a frontier home? Was this a tavern or the governor's home? What impact on the archaeological record did women and children have? Can we tell from the archaeological record whether the occupants of the site were participants in a German-American cultural system or a British-American system? Does this collection of artifacts represent the cultural by-products of activity by slaves, or by the master of the plantation? Was this ruin once the home of a wealthy gentleman planter or his servant? Is this ruin a typical mid-eighteenth-century dwelling, and if not, in what way is it different from the multitude of other domestic dwellings of the period? What does this difference mean when interpreted in the cultural system of which it was once a part? Does the increase in tailoring objects from 5% in one ruin to 13% in another indicate that one was a domestic dwelling while the other was a tailor shop? The list could be made even more lengthy, but the point we are making is that if we are to make more progress in the next half-century than we did in the last there must be a fundamental, revolutionary change in thinking, design, and method in historical archaeology. The change should be aimed toward answering these elementary questions. In asking the question the revolution has begun.

We must begin asking what to some may seem to be impertinent, irrelevant questions in order that pertinent and relevant answers can emerge. Once the questions are asked, methods relevant to them must be developed for collecting the appropriate data. This chapter will explore only a few of the methodological tools being developed toward answering such questions. I will examine artifact classes in the *Kitchen* group and derive from them a Kitchen Artifact Pattern. In a similar manner, I will explore the classes of artifacts by deriving simple ratios for pattern recognition. Finally, I will provide an example of pattern recognition using probate inventories, and will compare these to pattern in the archaeological record.

Artifact Class Pattern

In the same manner that the Carolina and Frontier Patterns were derived, the individual artifact groups can be broken down into their constituent classes to allow for comparison and isolation of variables on the class level. The *Kitchen* artifact group will be used here as an example of this procedure to point the way toward the delineation of specifically sensitive pattern on the artifact class level. The relationship of Kitchen Artifact Classes from several sites is seen in Table 1.

The remarkable similarity of the percentage for Ceramics is seen for the domestic sites, with the relationship between Ceramics and Wine Bottle classes indicating patterning within the grouped sites (Table 1). The grouped sites can be compared by determining the mean for each artifact class to reveal Kitchen Artifact Class Patterns (Table 2).

The ratio between Ceramics and Wine Bottle classes is the most critical for determining the variation in these types of sites. If these patterns were based on 15 or 20 sites, their predictive value would be far firmer than is now the case. However, the domestic group of four sites is extremely regular and should prove a good pattern for comparison of the ratios of these eight artifact classes with new site data.

The Signal Hill ruins have three classes of artifacts missing from the tabulation, those missing probably having been counted under other classificatory headings. This results in a higher ratio of Ceramics than would likely be the case had these three classes of artifacts been included as separate units. It is suspected that if this were done, the Signal Hill data would fall far closer to the Domestic mean, rather than "distorted" as it appears here.

The artifact classes reveal a greater sensitivity to variability than do the groups when classes are missing from the

253

Table 1. THE RELATIONSHIP OF KITCHEN ARTIFACT CLASSES FROM SEVERAL SITES

Domestic Sites

Class	Brunswick (S25) Count	%	Brunswick (S10) Count	%	Brunswick (S7) Count	%	Cambridge (96) Count	%
1. Ceramics	16,288	72.5	4618	68.0	2521	68.1	8751	68.1
2. Wine Bottle	3895	17.3	1753	25.8	841	22.7	2123	16.5
3. Case Bottle	445	2.0	29	.4	56	1.5	201	1.6
4. Tumbler	768	3.4	100	1.5	190	5.1	714	5.6
5. Pharmaceutical	473	2.1	45	.7	35	1.0	873	6.8
6. Glassware	431	1.9	191	2.8	38	0	57	.4
7. Tableware	122	.5	35	.5	11	.3	116	.9
8. Kitchenware	57	.3	24	.3	10	.3	19	.1
Total	22,479	100.0	6795	100.0	3702	100.0	12,854	100.0

Distorted Domestic Sites (from lack of complete data)

Class	Signal Hill (4) Count	%	Signal Hill (9) Count	%
1. Ceramics	2548	79.9	4715	81.3
2. Wine Bottle	439	13.8	689	11.9
3. Case Bottle	0	0	0	0
4. Tumbler	0	0	0	0
5. Pharmaceutical	65	2.0	190	3.3
6. Glassware	131	4.1	191	3.3
7. Tableware	5	.2	10	.2
8. Kitchenware	0	0	0	0
Total	3188	100.0	5795	100.0

Revolutionary War Military

Class	Ft. Moultrie (A) Count	%	Ft. Moultrie (B) Count	%
1. Ceramics	1217	29.1	269	22.3
2. Wine Bottle	2213	52.9	754	62.4
3. Case Bottle	363	8.7	51	4.2
4. Tumbler	114	2.7	30	2.5
5. Pharmaceutical	261	6.2	87	7.2
6. Glassware	3	.1	10	.8
7. Tableware	10	.2	4	.3
8. Kitchenware	4	.1	3	.3
Total	4185	100.0	1208	100.0

Frontier Sites

Class	Ft. Ligonier (FL) (distorted) Count	%	Ft. Prince George (FPG) Count	%	Spaldings Store (SS) Count	%
1. Ceramics	3170	57.0	764	45.5	2796	48.3
2. Wine Bottle	1894	34.0	624	37.2	1516	26.2
3. Case Bottle	0	0	139	8.3	896	15.5
4. Tumbler	0	0	32	1.9	0	0
5. Pharmaceutical	0	0	75	4.4	504	8.7
6. Glassware	395	7.1	1	.1	12	.2
7. Tableware	85	1.5	6	.3	7	.1
8. Kitchenware	22	.4	38	2.3	58	1.0
Total	5566	100.0	1679	100.0	5789	100.0

tabulation. In cases where there has been a tendency of the archaeologist to lump artifacts under catchall classes such as "Miscellaneous Glass," "Miscellaneous Hardware," "Miscellaneous Iron," and "Miscellaneous Artifacts," the group level of comparison allows such lumping to be accommodated far better than does the more specific class level of comparison we are concerned with here.

The high ratio of Wine Bottle to Ceramics at Fort Moultrie, seen in Table 2, was identified in the last chapter as the variable contrasting Fort Moultrie with the domestic and frontier groups of sites. Whether this phenomenon will be seen to represent pattern on military sites of the Revolutionary War period generally will have to await other data designed to answer this question through quantification.

A detailed discussion of the variability in all classes will not be undertaken here, but the Case Bottle Class 3, which has a mean of 1.4% on the domestic sites but jumps to 6.5% and 7.9% on military and frontier sites, is certainly a significant difference reflecting frontier and/or military contrast in activity. This could well be the result of the ease of transporting such square bottles in cases (thus the name Case Bottle) to frontier locations in contrast to transporting the round Wine Bottles to such remote areas.

Pharmaceutical type bottles also show a decided increase on military and frontier sites, possibly reflecting a greater need for, and use of, medicines in frontier situations as opposed to domestic life. As limited as this data base is, the patterns revealed are provocative of postulates directed at further pattern recognition, and explanation of the patterning through hypotheses focused on the past cultural system. Further pattern can be abstracted by isolating variables through comparison of simple ratios.

ISOLATING VARIABLES THROUGH COMPARISON OF SIMPLE RATIOS

The Ceramic Ratio

The ceramic ratio is determined by subtracting the total for ceramics from the entire artifact count for the site, and dividing the ceramics by the resulting artifact total. The resulting ceramic ratios for eleven sites can then be grouped by similar ratios into three site groups: domestic sites, Signal Hill, Newfoundland, sites, and military-frontier sites as shown in Table 3.

The implication here is that domestic site ceramic ratios may be expected to fall within the .44 to .79 range, with

military-frontier sites in the .11 to .25 range when the ceramic ratio is used as an index.

The Signal Hill sites pose a problem in that they are clearly on the opposite end of the scale from the military-frontier sites, yet Signal Hill was a nineteenth-century military site. This being the case it is suspected that the Signal Hill ceramic ratio of 1.00 may well foretell this ratio as an index for nineteenth-century military sites. In order to test this proposition comparable data from nineteenth-century military sites can be compared using the ceramic ratio as an index. With the great interest in such sites in the western states, such comparative data should be available from those archaeologists willing to undertake the basic task of quantitative analysis of data recovered under controlled conditions.

The Colono-Indian Pottery Ratio

In the above examination of the ceramic ratio from various sites, the Fort Prince George, S.C., site adjusted total was used, as was that for the Brunswick S25 for tailoring, and the Fort Moultrie collections for Colono-Indian pottery (Noël Hume 1962; South 1974). The Fort Prince George adjustment was necessary owing to the presence of 2583 Cherokee Indian pottery fragments recovered along with the other artifacts of European and Indian origin. The pottery was not, strictly speaking, Colono-Indian, but complicated stamped and plain wares of the eighteenth century, another reason for eliminating them from our model. The presence of Cherokee Indian pottery is no surprise since the fort was designed to protect and encourage trade with this nation.

With these facts in mind it should be interesting to see what the ceramic ratio for Fort Prince George would be if this Colono-Indian Class 36 were transferred to Class 1 (Ceramics) and added to that total. This would be done under the assumption that in situations where Colono-Indian pottery is present on a site, it reflects a need not otherwise met and a high percentage of Indian or Colono-Indian pottery might be assumed to reveal not only Indian contact but kitchen-related activity along with other ceramics. The best expression of this variability is seen in the Colono-Indian Pottery ratio.

Before comparing these ratios, we will add the Ceramics and Colono-Indian totals for Fort Prince George to see what the resulting ratio reveals in relation to the ratios for the other types of sites. The 2583 Cherokee sherds added to the 764 sherds of European origin at Fort Prince George results

Table 2. THE KITCHEN ARTIFACT CLASS PATTERNS

Artifact class	Domestic (S25, S10, S7, 96)	Distorted Domestic (Signal Hill 4, 9)	Revolutionary War military (Ft. Moultrie)	Frontier (FL, FPG, SS)
1. Ceramics	69.2	80.6	25.7	50.3
2. Wine Bottle	20.6	12.9	57.7	32.5
3. Case Bottle	1.4	0	6.5	7.9
4. Tumbler	3.9	0	2.6	.6
5. Pharmaceutical	2.6	2.6	6.7	4.4
6. Glassware	1.5	3.7	.4	2.5
7. Tableware	.5	.2	.2	.6
8. Kitchenware	.3	0	.2	1.2
Total	100.0	100.0	100.0	100.0

Table 3. THE CERAMIC RATIOS FOR 11 SITES

Site	Ceramics	÷	Adjusted total less Ceramics	=	Ceramic ratio	=	Resulting site grouping
Brunswick S25	16,288	÷	20,477	=	.79		
Brunswick S10	4618	÷	8500	=	.54		
Brunswick S7	2521	÷	5662	=	.44	=	Domestic sites
Cambridge 96	8751	÷	11,129	=	.79		
Signal Hill 4	2548	÷	2497	=	1.02		
Signal Hill 9	4715	÷	4733	=	1.00	=	Signal Hill sites
Ft. Moultrie A	1217	÷	4885	=	.25		
Ft. Moultrie B	269	÷	1476	=	.18		
Ft. Ligonier	3170	÷	18,608	=	.17	=	Military-Frontier sites
Ft. Prince George	764	÷	6624	=	.11		
Spalding's Store	2796	÷	13,974	=	.20		

in a ceramic ratio of .50. When we compare this with the ratios for ceramics from the other sites we find that it falls easily within the range for the domestic sites (Table 3). Using the ceramic ratio (including Cherokee pottery) as the only criterion results in the classification of Fort Prince George as a Carolina Pattern site, not a Frontier Pattern site. In other words, the shortage of European ceramics at Fort Prince George on the Carolina frontier appears to have been compensated for by utilization of Cherokee pottery.

This situation reveals the wisdom of placing Colono-Indian pottery as a class within the *Activities* group rather than with European ceramics as a separate class under the *Kitchen* group. It is best to classify the Fort Prince George site by means of the Frontier Pattern as a frontier site, *then* examine the Colono-Indian to European ceramics ratio by the means used here. This procedure allows this variable to be isolated, helping us to understand the relationship between Indians and colonists through the archaeological record.

In this same regard, the Fort Ligonier site should be examined for the relationship revealed by the archaeological record between the Indians and the occupants of the fort. The Indian objects recovered from Fort Ligonier are prehistoric and unrelated to the historic occupation of the site (Grimm 1970: 170). Therefore, no Colono-Indian ratio can be determined. When we ask why this contrast to the Fort Prince George site existed (at the same time period) we are struck by the fact that historical control data indicate a friendly trade relationship at Fort Prince George, whereas Fort Ligonier functioned entirely as an anti-Indian stronghold (Combes n.d.; Grimm 1970).

In view of this fact, the dramatic contrast between the Cherokee pottery at Fort Prince George and the absence of contemporary Indian pottery at Fort Ligonier is most interesting. The archaeological data alone would suggest trade and contact with Indians at Fort Prince George and the absence of behavior reflecting such friendly relations and culture contact at Fort Ligonier. This is exactly what the historical documents suggest was the case.

Before examining the manner in which the Colono-Indian Pottery Ratio Index separates the various sites with which we are concerned, a comment on the Fort Moultrie middens should be made. Colono-Indian pottery was one of the classes used to adjust these site totals, since a considerable quantity of this ware was recovered from both the British and American occupations (South 1974). When we add the Colono-Indian pottery totals to the ceramic totals for Fort Moultrie,

we find that the resulting ratios are .38 for the American midden at the site (A), and .28 for the British midden (B). These increased ratios do not have the dramatic impact seen at Fort Prince George but do raise the American midden ratio to within a few points of the lowest ratio in the domestic group of sites. Again, the need not met by European ceramics at Fort Moultrie was apparently being filled, or was being attempted to be filled, by Indian ceramics. The presence of Colono-Indian pottery in such large quantities at Fort Moultrie (about 40% of all ceramics) has been interpreted as resulting from behavior of enlisted men, whose usual equipment was not ceramics, but wooden bowls and/or tin cups and plates, the officers being the carriers of ceramics in the latest fashion from Europe (South 1974; Ferguson 1975). Both the British and Americans had Indians with them at Fort Moultrie. By subtracting Colono-Indian pottery from the total artifact count from various sites, the Colono-Indian pottery ratio is determined as shown in Table 4.

This Colono-Indian pottery Ratio has divided the sites into three groups, those domestic sites having a small amount of Indian pottery, those frontier and domestic as well as nineteenth-century military sites having no Indian pottery, and those frontier sites having far more Indian contact, as suggested by the contrasting ratios of Colono-Indian Pottery. These ratios may well serve as indices for determining the relative degree of friendly Indian contact as revealed by the single variable Colono-Indian Pottery or pottery contemporary with the site being studied. As we have seen suggested by the contrasting data from Fort Ligonier and Fort Prince George, basic policy regarding trade as opposed to warfare may be reflected in the behavioral by-product Colono-Indian pottery and/or contemporary Indian pottery recovered from historic sites.

The Military Ratio

The artifact class most sensitive to determining the difference between a military and a domestic or nonmilitary frontier site is Class 42, Military Objects. This class is composed of military insignia, artillery objects, swords, bayonets, etc. As we have seen, the *Arms* group of artifact classes, which includes musket balls, gunflints, gunparts, etc., can be used to distinguish frontier-military sites from trading posts and domestic sites, but it did not distinguish

Table 4. COLONO-INDIAN POTTERY RATIOS FOR 11 SITES

Site	Colono-Indian Pottery	÷	Total artifacts less Colono-Ind.	=	Colono-Ind. ratio	
Brunswick S25	231	÷	36,534	=	.006	Some Indian contact on domestic sites
Brunswick S7	12	÷	8171	=	.001	
Cambridge 96	62	÷	19,818	=	.003	
Brunswick S10	0	÷	13,118	=	0	No Indian contact revealed
Signal Hill 4	0	÷	5045	=	0	
Signal Hill 9	0	÷	9448	=	0	
Ft. Ligonier	0	÷	21,778	=	0	
Ft. Moultrie A	617	÷	6346	=	.10	Frontier sites with far greater Indian contact than domestic sites
Ft. Moultrie B	141	÷	1981	=	.07	
Ft. Prince George	2583	÷	7388	=	.35	
Spalding's Store	167	÷	16,603	=	.01	

Table 5. THE MILITARY OBJECT RATIO FOR 11 SITES

Site	Military objects	÷	Adjusted total less military	=	Military ratio	Resulting site grouping
Brunswick S25	0	÷	36,765	=	0	No military activity revealed on domestic sites
Brunswick S10	0	÷	13,118	=	0	
Brunswick S7	0	÷	8183	=	0	
Cambridge 96	0	÷	19,880	=	0	
Signal Hill 4	70	÷	5038	=	.01	Military activity revealed on all known military sites
Signal Hill 9	9	÷	9439	=	.0009	
Ft. Moultrie A	5	÷	6097	=	.0008	
Ft. Moultrie B	1	÷	1744	=	.0006	
Ft. Ligonier	170	÷	21,608	=	.008	
Ft. Prince George	4	÷	7384	=	.005	
Spalding's Store	0	÷	16,770	=	0	No military activity revealed on trading post site

between these and the military sites at Fort Moultrie and Signal Hill. Using the Military Object Class 42, a military ratio can be seen as in Table 5.

This military ratio for Class 42 appears to be a positive index for identification of a military versus a nonmilitary site, in spite of the small ratios involved. This variable is far more critical in this respect than the *Arms* group, which includes items used both in a military and a nonmilitary context.

The Nail Ratio

In the previous chapter we examined the nails and found that a high ratio can be expected on frontier sites compared with domestic sites, and the details of that procedure will not be repeated here. However, the implications of a nail increase on frontier sites call for explanatory postulates. The domestic sites involved in this study all represent considerable periods of occupation, around 50 years in most cases, whereas the frontier sites, mostly forts, represent less than a decade. There was a greater period of time for generalization and integration of activity by-products on domestic sites as opposed to frontier sites, which might well be a major factor in pattern variability between domestic and frontier sites.

What we may be seeing, therefore, is the result of a great amount of construction activity in a relatively small area

(inside the walls of a fort), thus concentrating the architectural by-products within narrow spatial bounds. Add to this a short occupation period in which by-products of activities can accumulate in this small area. Add to this the likelihood that in frontier-military situations, midden would not be allowed to accumulate indiscriminately around the structures inside the fort. Add to this the fact that in domestic situations such as Brunswick Town, no such military prohibition existed. The result may be that the archaeologically revealed record might well show a high nail ratio in relation to other artifacts.

We have listed these postulates in the framework of an assumption, that we can historically demonstrate that the sites from which the pattern was derived are frontier sites. However, the contrast in the inverse ratio between *Kitchen* and *Architecture* group artifacts seen on domestic and frontier sites may not be due to the domestic versus the frontier type of site at all. This contrast might well be the result of the variable of time of occupation, suggested as a postulate in the earlier discussion. This postulate could be tested by excavation of historically documented structures known to have been occupied for a short time. The results might reveal patterning such as that seen at the Brunswick S7 ruin, with a high *Architecture* to *Kitchen* artifact ratio. Such testing should help to reveal the extent to which time was a critical variable in the differences in pattern we are seeing between frontier and domestic sites of the same time period. The goal of such studies is, of course, to isolate the variables responsible for the patterning we delineate in the static archaeological record. In so doing, we gain a better understanding of cultural processes and how they work.

An artifact class relating to *Architecture* is Construction Tools in Class 31. An increase in these on frontier sites might be expected to parallel an increase in nails, because increased architectural activity ratios might well be accompanied by an increase in breakage and loss of tools relating to construction.

The Construction Tool Ratio

Although small numbers are involved in the Construction Tool Class 31, the ratios may still be expected to reflect variation in behavior on domestic versus frontier sites, where behavior might well be expected to vary. The Signal Hill site did not include a classification allowing separation of construction tools, so comparison could not be made with that site. The average ratio for the four domestic sites at Brunswick and Cambridge can be compared with the average for the two military frontier sites, Fort Ligonier and Fort Prince George. The frontier average for Construction Tools, Class 31, was four times that of the domestic sites, a ratio increase paralleling that for nails on the frontier. This parallel increase in these artifact classes relating to construction activity certainly warrants attention when comparative studies of historic site data from comparable sites are undertaken.

The Wine Bottle Ratio

The wine bottle ratios were also examined in the past chapter, and contrasted with nails and ceramics. The ratio of wine bottles to other artifacts was seen to be quite stable for domestic and frontier sites, but increased considerably on the Fort Moultrie site. As was suggested earlier, this may reflect the increase in use of bottled spirits during the Revolutionary War period compared with the use from barrels. The closeness to the source of supply may also be involved. An obvious first attempt at interpretation may be the postulate eventually demonstrated to be the case, namely, that both the British and Americans drank a lot at Fort Moultrie. The contrast at Fort Moultrie is certainly fascinating, but equally significant is the stability of the wine bottle ratio across the domestic and frontier sites. Further pattern recognition such as demonstrated here can contribute to answering these questions.

Explanation of the variability we are examining in this chapter must come through testing of hypotheses directed at behavioral variability, such as implied by the postulate stated above that "soldiers drank a lot." If this is indeed found to be the behavioral cause of the increase in the wine bottle ratio on military sites of the Revolutionary War period, then we have still to ask why. We still must cross the "why threshold" of the hypothetico-deductive method to enter the theory building arena. Hypotheses directed at explanation of this phenomenon would question the role of the male on the frontier; the role-specific, ego-indulgent activity in military behavior contrasted with multiple options of domestic life. These would need to be examined in a context of the logistics of distribution on the colonial frontier.

Questions such as these can be asked through the hypothetico-deductive method of science as pattern, such as we have been concerned with in this book, is being delineated from the archaeological record. Our primary concern here has been to demonstrate the tools the archaeologist has at his disposal for exploring the statics of the archaeological record for abstracting the dynamics of past cultural systems represented by that record. A vital part of that tool kit is the conceptual theory set the archaeologist carries with him throughout the archaeological process. Without this he may find himself particularistically involved with mere things, a collector of relics from the past rather than a manipulator of ideas about man's past and his unique attribute, culture, its dynamic processes and how they work.

The Bone Ratio as an Indicator of Adjacent and Peripheral Secondary Midden

Analysis of archaeological bone from historic sites can determine which animals were being utilized, which imported, which obtained locally, and which used for specific behavioral functions such as button making. We concentrate here on the fragments of bone "garbage" discarded on historic sites. We assume bone discard behavior can be monitored by ranking pieces of refuse on an "odorimetric" scale. For example, those odorous remains of refuse, such as bone, would be discarded farther from the structure whereas those less odorous items such as a broken plate, dish, or sweepings from the floor would be thrown nearby, beside the back door or off the end of the porch, front or back, to become scattered throughout the yard by pigs, dogs, chickens, and children. Under these conditions, a higher ratio of bone to artifacts thrown from the house would be found at a distance peripheral to the structure, whereas that refuse thrown adjacent to the house would have a low bone-to-artifact ratio.

The midden-filled cellar hole at Cambridge at Ninety Six, S.C., is an example of what we have termed a peripheral secondary midden, the refuse having been thrown there by someone living nearby, not by the occupants of the structure represented by the cellar. A fort moat would be a good example of peripheral midden since a moat filled with refuse is an obvious result of behavior designed to remove such trash from the immediate vicinity of the occupied area of the fort. It is expected that artifacts recovered from inside a fort will reveal a far lower bone-to-artifact ratio than midden thrown into the moat, where a high bone-to-artifact ratio would result from attempts to get the refuse beyond the occupied area as far as possible without going too far out of one's way.

The refuse allowed to accumulate inside a military fort would be relatively slight compared to that likely to be found in the moat, and within this accumulation the ratio of bone to artifacts would be small. These factors, as has been pointed out before, may well result in an inversion of the frequencies of the *Kitchen* and *Architecture* artifact groups if only the inside of the fort is excavated. A similar situation may be expected at domestic sites where middens adjacent to dwellings would be expected to have a low bone content compared with those peripheral middens farther from the house, in a gully, a marsh, or abandoned well, privy, or cellar hole.

To test these postulates, we can examine the bone ratio from the ruins used in this study (Table 6).

Table 6. THE BONE RATIO

Site		Bone fragments	Adjusted total less bone	Bone ratio	
	Ft. Ligonier	44,547	21,778	2.04	High bone ratio indicating a *peripheral* secondary midden is involved (Range: .36 to 2.04)
	Ft. Prince George	2644	7388	.36	
	Ft. Moultrie A	4057	6102	.66	
	Ft. Moultrie B	1020	1745	.58	
	Spalding's Store	8214	16,770	.49	
	Cambridge 96	11,187	19,880	.56	
	Brunswick S25	5497	36,765	.15	Low bone ratio indicating an *adjacent* secondary midden is involved. (Range: .03 to .17)
	Brunswick S10	519	13,118	.04	
	Brunswick S7	222	8183	.03	
Sq. 1–8	Brunswick S25 Front Yard	66	1110	.06	
Sq. 16–18	Brunswick S25 Rear Yard	2265	13,570	.17	
Sq. 22–26	Brunswick S25 Inside Ruin	526	7220	.07	
Sq. 21–25	Brunswick S7 Front Yard	2	1181	.002	Extremely low bone ratio indicating adjacent secondary midden; parallels a decrease in *Kitchen* artifacts. (Reflecting special antirefuse disposal behavior around this structure.) (Range .002 to .02)
Sq. 7–14	Brunswick S7 Rear Yard	51	4047	.01	
Sq. 11	Brunswick S7 Midden Area	16	915	.02	

The highest bone ratios are seen for the frontier and fort sites, as well as the Cambridge 96 cellar hole. All three domestic Brunswick Town, N.C., ruins have lower bone ratios than any of the frontier or military sites. The Brunswick (S25) Tailor Shop ruin also has a low bone ratio in all three areas examined. The midden area behind the tailor shop, however, has a slightly higher ratio than that inside or in front of the structure, due perhaps to the "over-the-wall" situation seen at this structure, allowing some peripheral midden to be thrown outside the lot over the lot wall. This still does not bring the bone ratio high enough to match those high peripheral ratios seen on the frontier and military sites, or at the Cambridge 96 cellar.

The Brunswick S7 ruin, which revealed so low a percentage of *Kitchen* artifacts compared with the *Architecture* group was of interest in that it was hypothesized that this was the result of special antirefuse disposal behavior around this ruin, and a very low adjacent secondary midden ratio would support this interpretation. The ratios seen at the Brunswick S7 ruin are indeed the lowest for any site in this study, indicating a different behavioral patterning was probably involved at this structure, producing this effect on the archaeological record.

The low bone ratio at the Brunswick Town ruins certainly indicates that the artifact-loaded peripheral middens were never excavated at these structures, probably having been thrown over the high bank across the street from the ruins. Using this ratio the archaeologist may well judge whether he has located and excavated the major secondary midden represented by the high bone ratio peripheral midden. This ratio may well be used in cases where test squares are used to attempt to locate the architectural area of an historical ruin. Those test squares having peripheral ratios might be those containing the best representative collection of artifacts from the site, but the architectural remains of the structure itself should be found in those areas having an adjacent bone ratio.

Although the bone variability allows the identification of an adjacent as opposed to a peripheral secondary midden deposit, it is anticipated that the number of classes of artifacts reflected in either type of deposit would remain relatively the same. This is based on the assumption that over a period of years there will be a blending effect to erase all but the most dramatic differences in by-product clusters reflecting specialized activity areas; thus most artifact types and classes will eventually be found distributed around the structure through this generalizing process of refuse disposal. If this is the case the same general number of artifact classes should be found in peripheral deposits as found in adjacent areas. The average number of artifact classes for the adjacent midden sites is 32.25, whereas that for the peripheral midden sites is 33.50, revealing that bone is apparently the primary variable for distinguishing an adjacent from a peripheral midden deposit.

Summary of Ratio Comparison

Some of the many possibilities of isolating variables on historic sites have been explored here through the use of simple comparison of artifact ratios. The broad base for such comparison lies in the Carolina Pattern and the Frontier Pattern, but examination of specific behavioral variability reflected in artifacts is most effectively seen on the level of artifact class ratios, some of which we have examined here. Any artifact class tabulated in the manner done here can be examined for information it may contain relative to identifying and understanding variability and regularity in the archaeological record.

Other classes of artifacts not examined here can be explored for clues to past human behavior, such as Toys, Class 33, a class recovered from all sites except two, representing domestic, military, frontier and trading post sites. This class could be considered as indicating the presence of women and children, but is this a valid assumption? Why are "whizzers," Jew's-harps, and marbles frequently found on military camp sites of both the British and American Revolutionary War forces (Calver and Bolton 1970)? Do these artifacts represent children, and thereby women, or do these items merely reflect the youth of some of the soldiers on both sides during the Revolution? It very well may reflect behavior among adults at that time period; behavior no longer practiced among adults today. Marbles, or taws, for instance, may have evolved from a game played by adults and children to a game played primarily by children, and today, to a game played by hardly anyone. The forms of the game, no doubt, have changed considerably, many varieties being known to most people only a few years ago but unrecognized by children of today.

Questions such as these call for coordinated research between the historical archaeologist, the historian, the folklorist, and the social historian for effective interpretation of the information revealed by the archaeologist. The groups and classes used here dictate to a degree the results of our comparisons, and we realize that ratio comparisons on the artifact type and attribute level will be more sensitive yet in answering some questions. Quantification studies based on them should be used to gain a greater command of the broader patterns revealed at the group and class level.

In working with folklore specialists, social historians, and other specialists we may find that in order to understand a past cultural system, the classification of marbles, Jew's-harps, and "whizzers" as artifacts in a class called "Toys" is not acceptable procedure. This may become apparent *if* we learn that in the eighteenth century "whizzers" were used for gambling, marbles for witchcraft ceremonies, and Jew's-harps for making music and thus better classified under "recreation," "religion," and "musical instruments." The point is that classification may vary with the questions being asked, because many artifacts functioned in different ways in different contexts in past cultural systems.

SUMMARIZING VIEWPOINT— THE FLAX HACKLE EXAMPLE

The many contexts within the cultural system in which a single artifact can occur are well illustrated by the case of the lowly flax hackle. The hackle was an instrument made of a number of sharp headless nails fastened through a tin-wrapped board. It was used to comb flax fibers in preparation for spinning into linen yarn. It functions in the "technomic" sense as an instrument for combing flax, or for combing hair for making wigs (Binford 1962: 219; South 1968: 224). It is seen by the archaeologist as a rusting pile of what appears to be headless nails. If he is unfamiliar with the hackle he may well identify the remains as a pile of headless nails. When the hackle was an artifact in the "systemic context" (Schiffer 1972), it had the initials of a betrothed couple and their betrothal date, as well as a decorative tulip shaped by nail holes punched into the tin band around the wooden base. In the historian's eyes, surviving examples of this type are documents subject to genealogical search to establish the name the initials represent. As a betrothal gift, however, the hackle symbolized the fulcrum in the balance of labor involved in producing clothing for the family, the man growing, retting, and breaking the flax to the point where the fibers were combed. Then the woman took over, combing, spinning, weaving, and sewing until a garment was complete. This symbolic connotation of the cooperative division of labor between the sexes had the hackle functioning as a "socio-technic" object in the system, "articulating individuals one with another into cohesive groups capable of efficiently maintaining themselves and . . . manipulating the technology (Binford 1962: 219)." In the

betrothal ceremony focused on the hackle, and in its symbolic context, it is an "ideo-technic" artifact symbolizing "the ideological rationalizations for the social system and . . . [providing] the symbolic milieu in which individuals are enculturated, a necessity if they are to take their place as functional participants in the social system (Binford 1962: 219–220)."

In the antique store the hackle becomes a piece of merchandise to be sold because it is "old." In this context it takes on new symbolism, one in which the mere fact of age is important, both to the seller and to the buyer. In this "relic merchandising" or business context, the past "technomic," "socio-technic," or "ideo-technic" functions of the hackle are irrelevant; it is primarily seen as a curiosity, and as merchandise. However in this latter context the hackle is still a part of a system, but with changed symbolic meaning. As a museum object it functions in an educational context, serving to recall to mind the "technomic" function it once served in the past, and if the curator is perceptive, its past symbolic and betrothal gift aspects may be emphasized, in order to effect a "confrontation with the past." (See Figure 1)

The woman using a modern version of a hackle in a fashionable wig shop to comb swatches of hair has no knowledge that she is using the same instrument and making the same motions as those used in preparing flax. In the art museum, hung by the original hole used to fasten it to a bench and festooned with a complex hanging of macramé, the hackle becomes part of a work of art to be admired for its role in a composition having nostalgic overtones. When the show is over, a visit to the artist's shop finds him combing flax with the hackle part of his masterpiece having been caught up in a national "return to the soil" movement involving the replication of the entire flax growing, retting, breaking, combing, spinning, weaving, and sewing process. In this renaissance the hackle again takes on the same literal "technomic" function, but now after 200 years the system is different, the reasons for the function are different, and the complex of performance variables is different, even though the task performance is the same. The hackle continues to function in the system, however, in whatever context the imagination of man can dream up.

To return to the archaeologist who found the pile of what he cataloged as a set of headless nails, what can he interpret from the data he has unearthed? First, he must identify the

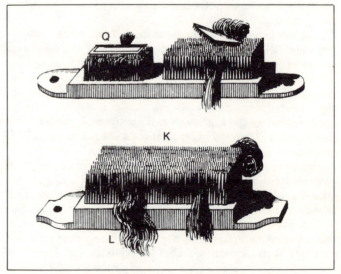

FIGURE 1. Hackles are Used to Comb Flax for Linen and Hair for Wigs.

"nails" as a hackle. The task facing him now in regard to interpreting the hackle in terms of the past cultural system is the same that faces him for virtually all of the artifacts he uncovers. He could tack onto his report the story just related from the "vast corpus of material already published on the subject," as Noël Hume has urged us to do, and thus attempt to arrive at a "confrontation with the past." In so doing he makes his report a clothes horse of history draped with a few archaeological specifics (Noël Hume 1968: 104).

His alternative is to view the hackle as a contribution toward understanding culture process. His careful study of associations relating to the hackle may reveal the pointed iron spindle and other artifacts associated with spinning and weaving flax into linen. In this context he is addressing himself to the functional associations on the "technomic" level. He must look beyond his ruin, however, to find the broader answers he is seeking. In doing this he may find that more hackles in archaeological context have been reported from Pennsylvania than any other area, in association with artifact frequencies fitting the "Pennsylvania German Colonial Artifact Pattern" (yet to be developed). He may discover that a secondary concentration of hackles in archaeological context has been reported from Virginia and North Carolina Piedmont. From these quantification-distribution comparisons he is now about ready to suggest what is beginning to appear as a correlation with historical data relating to a German-American migration out of Pennsylvania into the Carolinas. He may then suggest that if this proposition is true, there may be a correlation between the soils, temperature, and rainfall, in relation to the requirements for successful flax growing, and the archaeological data he has at his command. He may also suggest that in areas where soils are poor, such as coastal zones, no hackles would be expected, and available data from Brunswick Town and other colonial sites in this zone could be used to support such a postulate, no hackles having been found on such sites. By now it may have become apparent that hackles are to be recovered on German-American sites identified by the Pennsylvania Pattern, but not found associated with sites fitting the Carolina Pattern. At this point prediction might be made with considerable expectation that examination of empirical data will verify expectations and validate the postulates upon which predictions were stated. The pattern recognized, questions of causal processes can be asked.

Assuming that this hypothetical projection of pattern relating to flax hackles is demonstrated, and assuming that similar patterning of other artifacts indicating a high degree of self-sufficiency in German-American settlements during colonial times is also demonstrated, such a situation could likely be expressed as a "law." The testing of the "law" through new data collection would follow, and finally the threshold of the hypothetico-deductive method would be crossed by asking why the pattern was as it was observed to be. The hypotheses would be directed at examining the German-American colonial idea of encouraging self-sufficiency, and the British-American colonial idea of discouraging self-sufficiency, as well as propositions examining the British-American and the German-American distributive systems for supplying the American colonies. Other hypotheses might examine the tulip motif found on flax hackles, locally made pottery, and many other objects in the German-American areas. These hypotheses might ask:

1. Why does the tulip appear on German-American artifacts?
2. What is the relationship between the concept of self-reliance and the tulip motif?
3. What is the relationship between the tulip motif and the five doctrines of Calvinism affirmed at the Synod of Dort in 1618–1619 held by the Reformed Church of Netherlands, each of which began with a letter in the word "tulip"[1] (Hall 1965; Kingdon 1973)?
4. Did the "tulipomania" of 1638 relate to the Reformed Church doctrines affirmed in 1618 (Evans 1931: 79)?
5. Is there a connection between the attitude of self-sufficiency reflected by the artifacts from German-American communities and the individualistic philosophy fostered by Calvinist doctrine as opposed to the more conservative, authoritarian-based principles of Lutheranism? Is the tulip primarily a Calvinist-based motif?
6. What laws, relating to motifs such as the tulip and its connection to religious ideology, can be formulated from such motif patterns derived from historic site archaeology?
7. What hypotheses can we deduce for explaining pattern based on the knowledge gained from such a tulip motif study?
8. Can the laws derived from such a combined archaeology and archival study be projected through hypotheses and testing for explanation of prehistoric motifs?

Such hypotheses, once stated in the hypothetico-deductive framework, would be tested with new data. The intent here is not to go through such a procedure, but merely to cite an example of how such historic site data can be dealt with for arriving at some degree of understanding of past cultural processes. The flax hackle is only one of the many artifacts that could be similarly dealt with.

Thus through continuous observation, analysis, synthesis, questioning, and testing through the scientific cycle, the archaeologist can arrive at laws relating to culture process as seen through data from sites of the historic period. In the case of the flax hackle, a great deal depends on establishing whether flax hackles are objects to be found more in one area than in another, and this can be done only through an awareness of the problems raised by each class of data, artifacts, architecture, features, frequencies, and associations. Such an approach demands a similar frame of reference for revealing culture process to be used by archaeologists excavating historic sites in America, so that comparable data can be made available. With each archaeologist excavating his site as though it were a particularistic, unique phenomenon, this visionary projection appears, at times, as a remote dream. However, processual archaeology has its dreamers, its missionaries, and its prophets. For the most effective pursuit of laws of culture process that directed past human behavior, everyone must get into the act.

The significant point here is that the archaeologist must work with the record remaining from the complex social system that produced that record, and a first step toward understanding something about the laws under which that system operated comes with an understanding of the pattern in the data at hand, be it flax hackles or Jew's-harps. That pattern will be revealed through quantification analysis, regardless of the classificatory system used as a tool to abstract the pattern from the data. In other words, horseshoes could be combined with ceramics in a study designed to reveal pattern, and pattern would be revealed.

If consistent covariation exists between this horseshoe-ceramic class and a class made up of wine bottles and nails, then it matters not what the archaeologist's preconceived notions are about the relationship between ceramics, horseshoes, wine bottles, and nails; the reality of the pattern and the predictive value of this knowledge is what is archaeologi-

---

[1] *Theocentrism, Unconditional predestination, Limited atonement, Irrestibility of Grace, Perseverance of the saints.*

cally important. By examining other variables such as floor space, relative position of various buildings on the site, the source of water, the relationship of high ground to marsh, the location of the kitchen, barn, roads, and the refuse disposal practices of the occupants, the archaeologist may discover other covariables. With this information he may begin to understand the pattern in terms of his site. When he expands his view to other sites and other areas, again looking for regularity and variability, he may begin to address himself to the system of which his site is a part. This approach removes the archaeologist's preconceptions as to the meaning inherent in the artifacts themselves and directs him toward ascertaining their relevance in a broader context.

Quantification analyses of archaeological data can be done on the level of the group, the class, the type, or on specific attributes in order to determine pattern reflective of past human behavior. This can be done under almost any classificatory scheme toward discovering pattern reflecting culture process. Historical archaeologists have leaned on historical data to allow them to interpret the "true" meaning of "whizzers," marbles, and Jew's-harps, when the meaning lies in the questions he asks and in the relevance of the data he collects toward answering these questions. If classifying ceramics and horseshoes in the same artifact class is relevant to the question being asked, then the archaeologist by all means should do this to get at answers. He should not imply, however, that his classification is the end result being sought in archaeology (Stone 1974), when it is merely a convenience toward asking specific questions of the data. If we merely classify attributes, types, classes, and groups without a research design justifying such a procedure, then we are merely placing artifacts into pigeon holes.

As we learn more about the patterning in the archaeological record, and the processes that caused this patterning, we will certainly revise our classification schemes. We will be asking questions relating to the critical variables responsible for trade, status, the expanding frontier, socio-economic level, national and ethnic origins, plantation economy, the industrial revolution, and changing life styles.

The analyses such as we have conducted here are certainly only a beginning, raising as many new questions as providing answers to other ones, but questions are the beginning of the scientific cycle. For instance, examining the relationship between seventeenth-century settlement along major river systems as revealed by maps of the period, and the points at which the deep water channel touches high ground, in relation to the class status of individuals located at such points, is certainly worthwhile. Questions regarding population studies of historic sites from artifacts recovered in relation to the square footage excavated could be asked by using historical data indicating the number of occupants in a structure for a known period of time; excavation of the ruin would yield artifacts recovered from known square footage areas, and from these data eventual per-capita-per-year-per-square-foot indices could be developed from which predictions could be made. Testing and continual evaluating of variables would eventually produce a body of reliable data.

Perhaps these are audacious and impertinent questions, but merely to continue to insist, as some have done in the past, that answers to such questions are impossible to abstract from historic sites through archaeological procedures is counterproductive. Isolating variables as we have done here, in order to understand the processes reflected by human behavior through the archaeological record, is a first step in archaeological analysis. Historical archaeology is caught in the wave of an archaeological revolution in theory, method, and research design leading toward archaeological science. Archaeologists must either ride the crest of the scientific wave or "wipe out," falling victim to the internalized, particularistic undertow.

EXPLORING INVENTORY PATTERN FOR COMPARISON WITH ARCHAEOLOGICAL PATTERN

In deriving the Carolina and Frontier Patterns the archaeological record has been used. The question arises as to the relationship between the archaeological patterns and historical inventories of past household goods. It should be clear from the summary presented in the previous section that analysis of archaeological patterning is not done with the view of satisfying our preconceptions about past cultures by imposing our expectations, as programmed into us by our own culture, on the data.

The recognition of pattern in the archaeological record is certainly not a process designed to allow us to reconstruct past inventories. It does behoove us, however, to have an understanding of the relative degree to which the archaeological record represents, even in a gross manner, an inventory of the system of which it was once a part. Ceramics and wine bottles in their fragmentary state constitute the major artifacts, along with nails, used on British colonial sites examined in this study. Silver forks, gold coins, and pewter objects are seldom seen on archaeological sites, yet we know from surviving documents that such objects were indeed a part of the British colonial system. These highly curated objects, when inventoried by the participants in the culture, would certainly represent a ratio different from the one for fragments of the same objects in an archaeological context.

In this section, Carolina inventories for the same time period as that represented by the Carolina Pattern will be used to derive an Inventory Pattern. The differences between these patterns will be examined for developing transformation indices that will allow a statement to be made contrasting what *was* there in the system to what *is* there in the archaeological context.

This goal could best be accomplished with the help of a computer. A data base exists in the form of probate records providing inventories for many areas during the past 300 years. Studies are under way toward programming such data into computer banks for use in asking many questions. However, this study will be designed primarily to be compatible with the archaeological patterns we have examined so that a direction can be explored, rather than to present a definitive pattern based on such a project as that outlined earlier.

The Method of Abstracting the Inventory Pattern

The *North Carolina Wills and Inventories* volume by Grimes (1912) was used as a source for the eighteenth-century inventories used in this study. The first 25 pages of the "Inventories" section (pp. 469–494) were used to obtain a sample of wills for North Carolina. A seventeenth-century inventory from South Carolina was also used (Salley 1944:

25), which was made when John Foster and Capt. Thomas Gray dissolved their partnership in a store in 1672, at Charles Towne, S.C. A Maryland inventory of Thomas Jenings (South 1967) was also used in comparison with the Carolina data.

In tabulating the objects listed in the inventories, items likely to leave no archaeological record, such as books, cloth, clothing, table cloths, napkins, chairs, tables, salt, and grain were not listed. Those items of furniture listed as having drawers were counted as a single item under the assumption that the drawer might well have brass hardware. Objects clearly capable of leaving an archaeological record were tabulated, such as pewter plates, basins, dishes, bottles, forks, spoons, knives, tongs, hammers, hinges, kettles, spits, andirons, and pothooks. No consideration in this study was given to the value of the estate being inventoried, nor was any attempt made to evaluate the social status of the individuals involved, their economic level, or profession. Our primary concern was with a tabulation of objects within the artifact classes used in developing the Carolina Pattern.

Questions of socio-economic level, etc., can well be asked using inventories from individuals for whom historical data are available in order to determine which artifact variables covary with the known information. Such studies constructed on inventories from a wide area, using selected classes of individuals based on controlled attributes for selection, should provide information of value in comparison with artifact inventory profiles constructed from archaeological excavations. Such studies should be based on a close parallel between the types of data listed in the inventory and that from the archaeological context. The critical factor in such comparisons will be the transformation of pattern from the archaeological record to the systemic inventory. The exploration of this factor is the purpose of the following study.

The 13 inventories chosen for comparison were used in the Hierarchical Clustering Program of the OSIRIS statistical package in order to arrive at a computer clustering of the inventories based on the frequency relationships between the 41 classes of artifacts. The results of this clustering are seen in Figure 2. Six inventories are seen to cluster at the .94 level of significance, and these were chosen for illustration.

A second cluster at the .71 level is seen for the inventories of Richard Eagles (a Cape Fear landowner), Governor Arthur Dobbs (Royal Governor of North Carolina), and Dr. John Eustace (Figure 2). In examining these three inventories for clues as to why they differ from other inventories, joining with the primary cluster at a level of only .39, we see that the *Clothing* group for Dr. Eagles is unusually high (Table 7) because of 480 mohair buttons, that Governor Dobbs' *Personal* group is extremely high because of 230 gold and silver coins, and that Dr. John Eustice's *Activities* group is high due to 73 surgical tools.

If we had a sample of inventories numbering in the hundreds, for which historical research had provided data for division of the inventories into postulated status groupings before such a cluster analysis was conducted, differences and clusterings such as we see here would allow the abstraction of pattern having status predictive value. In the case of these three inventories, we do not know what the relationship between these men might have been relative to status within the system, but it is interesting to note that merely in the titles of the men accompanying the inventories we have clues to the socio-economic level for at least two of the individuals involved. However, individuals in the .94 cluster may well have had equal status within the Carolina colonial system with which we are concerned. We will ignore these questions for the moment since our problem does not involve status but rather the determination of an Inventory Pattern based on the mean of the six inventories correlating at the .94 proximity level, for use in comparison with the Carolina Artifact Pattern.

Two inventories are dramatically contrastive with the others, and these are the two seventeenth-century examples (Figure 2). These examples suggest that if we had available many seventeenth-century inventories, a radically different pattern might be revealed to contrast with that cluster of eighteenth-century inventories at the .94 level. Identification of such pattern by those having access to seventeenth-century data should be undertaken.

The Eighteenth-Century Inventory Plan

The artifact counts and percentage relationships for the eight artifact groups in our classification are seen in Table 7 for the six inventories we will use for constructing the Inventory Pattern. In addition to these eight artifact groups, we have added a pewter class to illustrate the many classes of material objects that were in the cultural system but seldom in any numbers in archaeological contexts. When we derive the mean for each of the percentages for each artifact group, the resulting Inventory Pattern is seen in Table 8.

It is interesting to note that the percentage relationship of the *Kitchen* group of artifact classes is very close in both the archaeological and the inventory means. Groups such as the *Architecture* group however, reveal a contrast because the

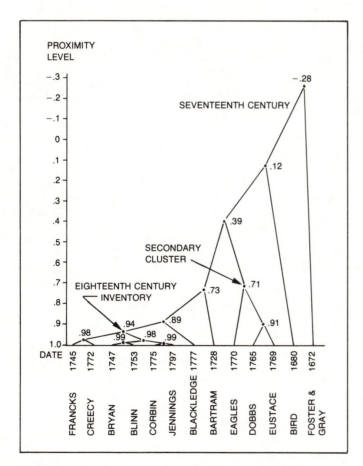

FIGURE 2. Probate Inventory Cluster Analysis.

Table 7. EIGHTEENTH-CENTURY PROBATE INVENTORIES CLUSTERING AT THE .94 PROMIXITY LEVEL[a]

Artifact group	Martin Francks 1745		Levy Creecy 1772		William Bryan 1747	
	Count	%	Count	%	Count	%
Kitchen	208	49.8	225	52.3	251	62.7
Architecture	0	0	0	0	0	0
Furniture	5	1.2	8	1.6	5	1.3
Arms	4	.9	4	.8	12	3.0
Clothing	2	.5	8	1.6	0	0
Personal	8	1.9	6	1.2	7	1.8
Tobacco Pipes	0	0	0	0	0	0
Activities	118	27.8	158	32.5	93	23.2
Pewter	80	18.8	49	10.0	32	8.0
Totals	425	99.9	488	100.0	400	100.0

Artifact group	Daniel Blinn 1753		Mrs. Jean Corbin 1775		Thomas Jenings 1797	
	Count	%	Count	%	Count	%
Kitchen	175	59.9	298	60.7	470	63.8
Architecture	0	0	0	0	0	0
Furniture	5	1.7	4	.8	13	1.8
Arms	3	1.0	4	.8	7	.9
Clothing	4	1.4	2	.4	0	0
Personal	5	1.7	16	3.3	35	4.7
Tobacco Pipes	0	0	0	0	0	0
Activities	68	23.3	156	31.8	188	25.5
Pewter	32	11.0	11	2.2	24	3.3
Totals	292	100.0	491	100.0	737	100.0

	Richard Eagles 1770		Gov. Arthur Dobbs 1765	
	Count	%	Count	%
Kitchen	1285	42.8	549	62.0
Architecture	522	17.4	0	0
Furniture	11	.4	14	1.6
Arms	160	5.3	0	0
Clothing	608 (480 mohair buttons)	20.3	7	.8
Personal	80 (62 coins)	2.7	245 (230 coins)	27.7
Tobacco Pipes	0	0	0	0
Activities	310	10.3	38	4.2
Pewter	26	.8	33	3.7
Total	3002	100.0	886	100.0

	Dr. John Eustace 1769	
	Count	%
Kitchen	558	84.5
Architecture	0	0
Furniture	6	.9
Arms	7	1.0
Clothing	1	.2
Personal	15	2.3
Tobacco Pipes	0	0
Activities	73 (surgical tools)	11.1
Pewter	0	0
Total	660	100.0

[a]The inventories used here are from Grimes 1912, pages: Francks, 494; Creecy, 481; Bryan, 480; Blinn, 476; Corbin, 482; Eagles, 486; Dobbs, 484; Eustace, 490. The Jenings inventory is from South 1967, p. 203.

inventories don't mention these construction-related artifact classes. The *Activities* group is also much higher in the Inventory Pattern than in the Carolina Pattern as is the *Personal* group. The Pewter class is represented by a percentage of 8.9 in the inventories, but is absent from the archaeological pattern. The higher percentages seen in the Inventory Pattern are thought to reflect the curation of these objects in the cultural system, resulting in their appearing in higher frequencies in the inventory than in the archaeological context.

The absence of artifacts from the inventories that are found in considerable quantities in the archaeological context, such as *Architecture* and *Tobacco Pipe* artifacts, reflects the fact that nails, window glass, and tobacco pipes were not considered a part of the inventory, except perhaps in unusual cases not seen in these six examples.

If we can consider, for purposes of illustration, that the Inventory Pattern is reflective of the patterning seen in the cultural system, and the ratio between the percentages for the Inventory Pattern and the Carolina Pattern mirrors a degree of curation, then it would be possible to construct a curation-transformation ratio from this information. This step might allow a statement to be made about the historical inventory represented by an archaeological artifact collection on the basis of the ratio difference between the Inventory Pattern and the Carolina Artifact Pattern. The application of the curation-transformation ratio to archaeological data (Cambridge 96) for deriving an interpreted historical inventory is shown in Table 9.

This curation-transformation ratio procedure has been used to express the artifacts from the Cambridge 96 ruin in terms of the Inventory Pattern to produce an interpreted Cambridge historical inventory percentage profile. This percentage profile inventory is not intended to represent a literal inventory of the goods from the occupants of the home from which the Cambridge midden was thrown. Rather, it is an interpretive tool intended to make the archaeologist aware of the fact that the 25% of all artifacts he recovered from the ruin he excavated, represented by the *Architecture* group, were not likely to have been included in inventories. He should also be aware of the fact that the archaeologically revealed .5% of all artifacts, represented by the *Personal* group, was likely to represent 5.8% in inventories of material culture make by those participants in the system represented by the archaeological record. This percentage is a figure 12 times (curation-transformation ratio) that seen in the ar-

Table 8. INVENTORY PATTERN FROM SIX INVENTORIES OF THE EIGHTEENTH CENTURY COMPARED WITH THE CAROLINA PATTERN

	Mean %	Range	Carolina Artifact Pattern
Kitchen	58.2	49.8–63.8	63.1
Architecture	0		25.5
Furniture	1.4	.8– 1.8	.2
Arms	1.2	.8– 3.0	.5
Clothing	.6	0– 1.6	3.0
Personal	2.4	1.2– 4.7	.2
Tobacco Pipes	0		5.8
Activities	27.3	23.2–32.5	1.7
(Pewter)	8.9	2.2–18.8	0
	100.0		100.0

chaeological record. Similarly the *Activities* group artifacts are mentioned in inventories 16 times more frequently than the fragmentary remains of such activities in the archaeological record.

These contrasts relate to the degree of curation of personal items such as watches, gold, and silver and to the fact that once architectural hardware becomes a part of a structure, its frequency ratios to other artifacts is far more likely to be revealed by the archaeologist than by a study of the inventories. Tobacco pipes leave a far more impressive record in archaeological context than in the lists provided by those participants in the past cultural system who were listing only those things that had particular significance to them from an inventory point of view. Use of the curation-transformation ratio tool suggested here should help in attempts to discover laws governing behavior in past cultural systems.

In this study, we have compared whole objects on the one hand with fragments on the other, a procedure that makes absolutely no difference when our primary purpose is to compare these kinds of data sets. The archaeologist happens to work with fragments; the compiler of inventories is tabulating whole objects. Both types of data are material remains of past cultural systems. Inventory records are highly fickle due to the many variables involved in compiling the inventories, but regularities can be discovered that are pertinent to the analyses that archaeologists are making, provided

Table 9. APPLICATION OF THE CURATION-TRANSFORMATION RATIO TO DATA FROM CAMBRIDGE, 96, S.C.

Artifact group	Inventory pattern mean	÷	Carolina Pattern	=	Curation-Transformation ratio	×	Cambridge 96 count	=	Ratio-Adjusted Cambridge count	Interpreted historical inventory for Cambridge	Cambridge artifact % profile for comparison
Kitchen	58.2	÷	63.1	=	.9	×	12,854	=	11,569	52.2	64.6
Architecture	0(.1)*	÷	25.5	=	.004	×	5006	=	20	.09	25.2
Furniture	1.4	÷	.2	=	7.0	×	35	=	245	1.1	.2
Arms	1.2	÷	.5	=	2.4	×	27	=	65	.3	.1
Clothing	.6	÷	3.0	=	.2	×	1069	=	214	1.0	5.4
Personal	2.4	÷	.2	=	12.0	×	108	=	1296	5.8	.5
Tobacco Pipes	0(.1)*	÷	5.8	=	.017	×	349	=	6	.02	1.8
Activities	27.3	÷	1.7	=	16.0	×	432	=	6912	31.2	2.2
(Pewter)	8.9	÷	0	=	8.9	×	0	=	(1809)**	8.2	0
	100.0		100.0				19,880		22,136	99.9	100.0

*Insert .1 when zero
**When artifact count equals zero, insert the appropriate percentage (8.9) of the total ratio-adjusted count (20,327 × .089 = 1809)

inventory studies are designed to answer the kinds of questions archaeologists are asking. Too often there is a wide gap separating the studies being done by those dealing with probate records and those quantification studies being carried out by archaeologists looking for laws of culture process. Both types of data are rich sources for deriving pattern in the reconstruction of past cultural systems. Too often the probate records are used merely as a means for answering historical questions. Archaeologists are beginning to utilize historical documents from the point of view of abstracting data similar to that recovered from the earth in the form of fragments. Both records are fragmentary, but both can yield complementary data sets for discovering laws directing human behavior.

REFERENCES

BINFORD, LEWIS R.
  1962 Archaeology as Anthropology. *American Antiquity* **28** (No. 2):217–225.
CALVER, WILLIAM LOUIS, and REGINALD PELHAM BOLTON
  1970 *History written with pick and shovel.* New York: The New York Historical Society.
COMBES, JOHN D.
  n.d. The Archaeology at Fort Prince George. Manuscript in preparation. Institute of Archaeology and Anthropology, University of South Carolina, Columbia.
EVANS, JOAN
  1931 *Pattern.* Oxford: Oxford University Press.
FERGUSON, LELAND G.
  1975 Analysis of Ceramic Materials from Fort Watson, December 1780–April 1781. *The Conference on Historic Site Archaeology Papers 1973* **8**. Institute of Archaeology and Anthropology, University of South Carolina, Columbia.

GRIMES, J. BRYAN (EDITOR)
  1912 *North Carolina wills and inventories.* Raleigh, N.C.: Edwards and Broughton.
GRIMM, JACOB L.
  1970 Archaeological Investigation of Fort Ligonier 1960–1965. *Annals of Carnegie Museum 42,* Pittsburgh.
HALL, BASIL
  1965 Synod of Dort. *Encyclopaedia Britannica* **7**:p. 600. Chicago: Encyclopaedia Britannica.
KINGDON, ROBERT M.
  1973 Determinism in theology: Predestination. In *Dictionary of the history of ideas,* edited by Philip P. Wiener, New York: Scribner's.
NOËL HUME, IVOR
  1962 An Indian Ware of the Colonial Period. *Quarterly Bulletin* **17**, No. 1, Charlottesville: Archaeological Society of Virginia.
  1968 Historical Archaeology in America. *Post-Medieval Archaeology* **1**:104–105.
SALLEY, A.S. (EDITOR)
  1944 *Records of the Secretary of the Province and the Register of the Province of South Carolina 1671–1675.* Columbia: Historical Commission of South Carolina.
SCHIFFER, MICHAEL B.
  1972 Archaeological Context and Systemic Context. *American Antiquity* **37**:156–165.
SOUTH, STANLEY A.
  1967 The Paca House, Annapolis, Maryland. Prepared for Contract Archaeology, Inc. On file at Historic Annapolic, Inc. Alexandria, Virginia.
  1968 The Lowly Flax Hackle. *Antiques* **94** (No. 2):224–227.
  1974 Palmetto Parapets. *Anthropological Studies No. 1.* Institute of Archaeology and Anthropology, University of South Carolina, Columbia.
STONE, LYLE M.
  1974 Fort Michilimackinac 1715–1781. *Publications of the Museum.* East Lansing: Michigan State University.

CHAPTER 32

A Discussion of the Contrasts in the Developments of the Settlement at Fort Michilimackinac Under British and French Rule

LEWIS R. BINFORD

I would like to begin this rather brief comparison between the British and French occupations at Fort Michilimackinac with something of a statement of the history of the occupation itself. The French were the first settlers at the site, the actual date of initial settlement is in dispute, but sometime between 1705 and 1720 a French settlement was established at Michilimackinac. By 1720 we have a reference to its existence, so it was established prior to 1720. The primary function of the early settlement was not to house troops, but simply to serve as the hub for extensive fur trading activities with the Indians. It was a fortified settlement. Slightly after 1720 it did house a few militiamen; however, it was not a major military garrison under the French. The Fort remained under French rule until the end of the French and Indian war.

The British occupied the fort in 1760. In 1761 the British garrison was massacred there by the local Indian groups participating in Pontiac's uprising. It was not until '63 that it was reoccupied by British troops. In '63 a much different development began in terms of the settlement itself. The British moved in with garrison troops and throughout the period of British occupancy the number of troops in garrison increased. By the end of the British occupation (1781) there was a large garrison and the function of the site had changed from that of a fortified settlement to a strict military post. This we know from documentary data. We also know that the nature of the internal social organization of the settlement changed radically throughout the period. By the late British period we had a very definite and marked ranking of sub-groups among the people occupying the site. There were the commandant and certain officers and wealthy traders composing the highest status group, minor officers, enlisted men, civilian traders and camp followers all following with decreasing status. Such ranking was not characteristic of populations inhabiting the site during the French period, particularly during the early years. If we assume that as anthropologists one of our major aims in research is the explanation and explication of cultural differences and similarities, we are in an excellent position to make the maximum use of status, functional specificity, style change, logistical changes, etc. as explanatory hypotheses for observed differences in artifact distributions, formal differences and structural associations. This site provides an excellent methodological "laboratory case" for the analysis and interpretation of archaeological data.

Now to some of the differences and similarities which exist between the French and British materials at the fort. For the French period, our sample is restricted to what appears to be civilian housing. We have no identified French institutional buildings. Thus, when comparing French with British materials, we can exclude the known British institutional buildings. We have six civilian houses and the Commanding Officer's house of the late British period, but this happens to be status row. We know from the documents that the houses in this particular row housed the most wealthy traders and the high status officers so that the observed differences between French housing and British housing may be explicable in terms of the differential status of the occupants. Keeping this in mind, I will mention some of the major differences between these houses. The French houses, most of which were destroyed around 1734, are architecturally fascinating. You never know what to expect when you start on a new one in that each is different, although there are certain common patterns of construction. The north walls are generally vertical pickets with a daub plaster cover; similarly, south walls are generally of this construction. East and west walls may be constructed of small pickets two or three inches in diameter set in a different type of wall trench. In cases where we had a burnt structure, the latter type of wall was covered with elm bark siding. The floors in these houses were equally diverse, and in a single structure there may be several flooring techniques used. Adjacent to the hearth there may be a clay base with split white cedar puncheons, while back from the hearth area the flooring may be wooden planks on squared sills. In areas where sill and board construction was used there also tends to be the location of sub-floor storage basements. These are normally from three to four feet deep and five feet long, constructed with small vertical pickets and backed with elm bark. These houses yield no evidence of the use of plaster, brick construction, or shingles. Stone construction is normally restricted to the fire chambers of the fireplaces. Above the smoke chamber, construction was normally of stick framing with mud daub cover. Roofing was probably of elm bark. This is a rough picture of the civilian houses of the early French period, roughly 1720–1734.

The next group of houses to be considered was built by the French in the late 1740's and incorporates a number of new architectural features. These houses were rebuilt several times and were occupied in the late British period. They were stacked log exterior walls built on corner rock pilasters. They had fireplaces that tended to be of the earlier type but larger. Plank flooring was the only form used. Roofs were of split shingles and basements tended to be better constructed and larger. Hardware and structural fixtures were more elaborate including such items as door knockers, etc. Associated with these later houses are many more items manufactured in Europe which are the functional equivalents of locally made forms during the early period. These observations suggest a much higher level of logistic efficiency for the later period.

British institutional buildings are entirely different from anything else on the site. They have stone foundations, very massive back to back fireplaces, and brick construction. These were stacked log structures with many more windows and a different kind of window glass than was used in earlier buildings. There was obviously no lack of nails when these buildings were constructed, a situation we can infer for the early period, in that few are found.

A fascinating area of study besides the differences in institutional buildings versus habitational units in terms of architecture, etc. is the differential composition of materials associated with various civilian houses. With certain late houses are found such items as signets, handles from delicate boxes and writing cases, gold gilt pen knives, brass door knockers, ivory billiard balls and fine pewter. Such items certainly suggest high status, wealth, and access to the logistics network. In the way of contrast another house may have many awls, scraps from the manufacture of trade goods from sheet brass, tinkling cones, cubes of vermillion, and gun parts, all items suggestive of a very different status and way of life when contrasted with the former assemblage.

Ceramics tell a story which is not solely related to changing styles in Europe. Sherds from early contexts are few and then largely tableware as opposed to utilitarian bowls, etc. similar to the large quantities of "rough" ware found at such sites as Jamestown and Williamsburg. More cups, and "assessory" vessel forms occur in the early period with less items such as plates and bowls. No doubt most of the tableware utilized daily was locally made from wood. By the late period this situation had changed. A greater diversity in vessel form is obvious. Plates, bowls, creamers, teapots, cups and even an occasional decorative piece are part of the late assemblage.

I would like to conclude this very brief exposure to the materials from Michilimackinac by saying that in addition to the fascinating interpretative problems with regard to changing logistics, population density, functions of the site and social complexity with which we are attempting to cope, we are analyzing the materials from the fort in a detailed and completely formal frame of reference so that this material can provide a chronological control sequence for the Great Lakes area during the early historic period. It is hoped that the report which Moreau Maxwell and I are currently working on will provide such a framework together with the distributional, associational and functional analysis in something of an exercise in interpretative methodology.

CHAPTER 33

The Spoken Word, the Written Word, Observed Behavior and Preserved Behavior: The Contexts Available to the Archaeologist

ROBERT L. SCHUYLER

In a paper presented at the Sixteenth Annual Conference on Historic Site Archaeology, and published in that volume, Clyde Dollar has criticised the published research of several historical archaeologists. In general he proposes that historical archaeology has been artificially limited in its contribution to general scholarship because of the unwillingness or inability of its practitioners to undertake accurate, primary documentary research. More specifically he criticizes, among other projects, my research at Sandy Ground (Schuyler 1974) on the basis of what he conceives as a faulty outline of that community's history. He uses a specific source, the Federal Census (1830, 1850, 1860, and 1870), in an attempt to prove that most of the basic conclusions concerning the formation and nature of Sandy Ground are erroneous. In this reply I will take the opportunity to discuss some general points and then, in a second part, I will show that Dollar's criticisms are meaningless from the perspective of either a historian or scientist.

PART I

Scholars concerned with Man may approach their subject matter from one of two perspectives. They may base their investigations on direct or indirect observation of human behavior (an *etic* analysis) or they may concentrate on the views and beliefs that the subjects hold concerning their own behavior (an *emic* analysis). An individual study may be purely emic or purely etic or involve elements of both approaches. Access to emic or etic information, however, is strongly influenced by the context in which the data are found. If the researcher is contemporary with the situation he is studying he may directly observe human beings, their behavior, artifacts (in the broadest sense), and the use of artifacts. He also has direct access to the beliefs of his subjects through participant observation or the more focused use of informants and questionnaires. If the researcher is investigating a past situation he may gain indirect insight into human behavior as it is preserved in the archaeological record, documents, and human memory.

Although studies of past events may involve an ethnographic dimension, normally the data are limited to three contexts.[1]

Archaeological Context

Archaeological data present the researcher with one of the strongest lines of evidence for reconstructing past human behavior. Archaeology is the principal source when it stands alone as it does for the totality of prehistory and for the numerous prehistoric interludes within the historic period. Whether it is a "dark age", an undocumented frontier situation, or a non-historic enclave as seen in the life of the slave and peasant, archaeology is a major bridge across the lacunae in the historical record. More importantly archaeology continues to provide significant information even when its findings are paralleled by a complete written record. This fact has not been convincingly demonstrated on the substantive level until very recently. Projects, such as the study of the Mott farmstead (Brown 1976) and its work on faunal analysis (Bowen 1975) and family history, clearly answer the question so often asked of the historic archaeologist—Why dig things up when written sources are available?

For all its strengths, however, the archaeological record is uncommunicative in regard to an entire range of data. A purely prehistoric assemblage can provide direct and ample information on all aspects of culture provided the analysis is etic in orientation. Artifacts do not speak. Artifacts provide no information on the emic level. The emic aspect is present but unless there is documentation or a "direct historical/ general ethnographic analogy" it is uninterpretable. Even a cursory examination of Olmec art, for example, reveals a combination of symbols (were-baby, clefted head, fangs and snarling mouth) that are obviously part of the iconography of an archetypal Mesoamerican religion. What set of beliefs and values produced and gave meaning to these traits is lost unless some direct tie to the present, such as Furst (1972) assumes in his shaman-jaguar interpretation based on ethnographic analogy, is found. Psycho-ceramics (Emerson 1974) and speculations aside, totally prehistoric materials are mute.

Documentary Context

Documents can be the basis for either an etic or emic analysis, although they have almost never been used for the latter by historical archaeologists. Historical writings may record human behavior in the form of observations of human actions or statistical data. They also, of course, contain the values and beliefs of those writing the records and those written about thus giving direct access to the emic level. Nevertheless, this availability of the emic dimension is both the greatest strength and the greatest weakness of the document. As all documents were written by one or more persons, and not left inadvertently and directly as a result of human behavior, their emic aspect also erects a screen between the researcher and direct access to preserved human behavior. I once heard a colleague in historical archaeology say (he had been drinking) that the only thing a document proves is its own existence. Such a view is too extreme as there are methods of internal and comparative contextual analysis for evaluating documents, but it does emphasize the emic nature of written records.

Robert McC. Adams (1974) has lately offered an innovative interpretation of the nature of Mesopotamian society that relates to this problem. Adams proposes that the primary archives of Mesopotamia were produced by an urban elite with a strong commitment to and bias for city life. Thus the traditional reconstruction of the ancient Near East by historians is based on sources that distort what is a much more complex situation. The city was only one segment of an urban-village-nomad network within which even the city dweller did not necessarily lose his ability to return to a non-urban orientation when events called for such a "devolution". Yet only one segment of the continuum appears in the records.

Even in the most focused and systematic form of document, such as the questionnaire that underlies a census tract, the emic aspect is all pervading and dominant.

Oral History Context

Oral history is a bridge between documentary history and ethnography. Human memory preserves both emic and etic information but it also structures the data by placing a series of barriers between the past and the investigator. The emic aspect is intensified with oral sources because although beliefs about past behavior may survive, the behavior itself is not directly approachable. Just as the beliefs of a person recording events as they unfold always distort the past, consciously or unconsciously, so do the beliefs of a person undergoing an interview distort past behavior and concepts. In fact, there may be more than one screen erected; the original psychological and cultural blinders in force in the past and the present beliefs of the informant. However, the desire to rewrite one's past, along with the simple fallibility of human memory, is counterbalanced because oral history does present an opportunity to understand the cultural matrix of the informant and to cross-examine the sources to a degree that is usually impossible with written sources.

Oral history has been a part of general historiography since Herodotus and Thucydides interviewed survivors of the Persian and Peloponnesian Wars but it has probably, at least until recently (cf. Montell 1970, especially Preface), seen a greater development in anthropology. Cultural anthropological techniques, particularly the "new ethnography", depend on living informants and so naturally relate to oral history. Indeed, much of our knowledge of traditional American Indian and African cultures is based on such "memory ethnography". Questions concerning the differences between documentary and oral sources and their analysis are crucial and cause oral history to overlap as much with ethnography as with historiography.

PART II

Differing accounts of the history of Sandy Ground as offered in my original article and by Dollar in his critique are the product of two factors. First, although Dollar seems unaware of it, each account is in the main drawn from two different contexts—oral history and documentary history. Second, Dollar's account is grounded on a failure to recognize the nature and complexity of primary, written sources.

As most readers will only have a passing interest in the details of the history of Sandy Ground, I have relegated some of the data pertinent to a complete evaluation of Dollar's interpretations to a series of footnotes. The more general points will be briefly covered in this section and I ask the reader to keep in mind that my statements are in response to Dollar. I am not offering a documentary historical synthesis for Sandy Ground and so will limit my critique to the sources used by Dollar and not use other census schedules, state or local censuses, or the many other archival records.

Preliminary and Final Reports

Unfortunately Dollar opens his review with a misunderstanding of the nature of my paper on Sandy Ground. He views it as a final report when it is obviously a preliminary, programmatic statement which discusses the research design for Sandy Ground, the potential range of data, and presents some initial findings on the origins of one artifact category (glass containers) from a single excavated feature. The historical outline presented is drawn from the work of Dr. Mina Wilkins (1943a, b, c, d, e; 1972) and is in the main based on oral history. Her study is the *only* historical synthesis presently available for Sandy Ground.

Primary and Secondary Sources

Dollar's major criticism is that my paper is based on historical "writings" (i.e. secondary sources) rather than historical "records" (i.e. primary sources). In his comments Dollar seems to limit primary sources to documents thus excluding oral history. There is clear reference in my paper not only to Wilkins' historical synthesis but also to her original field notes and a recent interview with her. Texts or notes based on interviews, although different from some types of documents, are also primary sources. In fact, the method of interviewing that Wilkins used usually produces more extensive and reliable data than the type of interview on which a census is grounded. I will return to this point in Part III of this paper.

Use and Misuse of Primary Sources

After misinterpreting the nature of my article and arbitrarily limiting "records" to written sources, Dollar then uses such a source to criticise my presentation of Wilkins' historical outline. Although it is clearly stated in my paper that documentary research was being developed (Schuyler 1974: 43) this fact is ignored as is the specific reference to the availability of census data (Schuyler 1974: 22). Local historians on Staten Island are examining the census schedules, as well as other archival sources, on Sandy Ground. They recognize the obvious fact, however, that specific historic facts cannot be taken at face value nor removed from context.

Dollar in his survey of the censuses does not seem to be aware of the complexity of written sources. He directly offers a "reading" of the census tracts from which he draws several conclusions. The questions around which these conclusions center are legitimate points of debate but Dollar's interpretations are meaningless. He does not realize that it is necessary to evaluate specific primary sources, that the data contained in such a source must be analysed not "read", and that historical facts cannot stand in isolation from some meaningful context.

Although Dollar discusses several minor points his major conclusions consist of four basic statements that contradict my presentation of Wilkins' findings on Sandy Ground.

1. Sandy Ground is not a product of a planned migration from Maryland.[2]

Basis. Dollar grounds this inference on a comparison of the proportion of Marylanders to the total Black population of southwestern Staten Island.

Fundamental Error. Notwithstanding the fact that Dollar recognizes that Sandy Ground is located *in* Westfield he ignores this relationship in his calculations and inadvertently shifts the focus from Sandy Ground to a larger, arbitrary unit (see Figure 1). It is true that the census data are organized into the four traditional regions ("townships") that divided Staten Island during the 19th century. Westfield is one of these divisions. It is not possible or permissible, however, to use the Westfield data as a unit in reference to Sandy Ground. The majority of the Blacks in Westfield, with a few exceptions, were not involved in either the foundation or later history of Sandy Ground. To conclude that people giving Maryland as their state of origin only approximate "22% of the total Black population" in 1830 or that "barely 12% of the total Black community" were involved in oystering in 1870 are misleading and in fact meaningless statements. It would make as much sense to compare the proportions of Blacks of a Maryland origin with the total White population of Westfield, or all of Staten Island for that matter. There is no evidence of a Black "community" corresponding to the boundaries of Westfield and to assume that all Blacks in an arbitrary geographic section are equivalent units (which can be added, subtracted, or divided) is a blatant example of racistic thinking. Many of the Blacks in Westfield had a different origin than the Sandy Grounders, a different social relationship with the general Staten Island population, a different economic orientation (e.g. servants resident with wealthy White families), different church affiliation, and different, if any, relationships to the Sandy Ground community itself.[3]

Evaluation and Conclusion. Dollar may not be familiar with local Staten Island history but there is no excuse for this error. A perusal of any good 19th century map that carries the regional divisions shows Westfield covering most of southwestern Staten Island and including a number of towns (Rossville, Princes Bay, Tottenville), small settlements (Sandy Ground or Woodrow being one), and scattered farms. The problem of differentiating the residents of Sandy Ground from the total population is a difficult and crucial task.[4] It cannot be ignored or glossed over. Documents must be analysed not "read".

2. Sandy Ground was not, at least as late as 1870, a discernible community. Although there are some occupational clusterings, Blacks were scattered and/or intermixed with Whites.

Fundamental Error. Again the confusion between Sandy Ground and Westfield invalidates Dollar's conclusion but he compounds this error with a second oversight of equal magnitude. In his inferences on the degree of concentration or scatter for Westfield Blacks he clearly assumes that he has direct access to such patterings in the census data. This is not true. The censuses do not present a verbal map of human settlement, rather they contain an indirect and very nebulous presentation of residence patterns. Individual entries are organized on the basis of the order in which the individual dwellings and families were visited and it is not immediately clear how the census enumerator covered a given area. Using other sources (documents and oral accounts), in conjunction with the censuses, it is clear that Sandy Ground exists as a racially mixed but nucleated settlement in both the 1870 and 1860 censuses. However, the total settlement cluster of Sandy Ground is partially masked and artificially scattered by the manner in which the census was compiled. This factor is probably the most difficult to control in using the tracts but cross-reference to maps, other documents, and oral accounts *partially* solve it. Tentatively I suggest that what occurred was that the census taker did not cover a given settlement as a unit but rather ran several transects through an area. If, for example, the person was moving up Bloomingdale Road (N−S), a main thoroughfare for Sandy Ground, he might also cover Harris Lane, a dirt side street that was a deadend, but would not necessarily turn off on Woodrow Road (W−E) or Sharrots Road (E−W). Rather he or she would probably continue down Bloomingdale directly into Rossville thus passing outside of Sandy Ground proper. Such probable routes become evident only after examining local maps or by walking the area as I did frequently during the archaeological survey during 1971, 1972, and 1973.

Again, documents must be analysed not recited.

Evaluation. It would seem self evident that human settlement spread along roads is lineal in its pattern and not random or equidistant. This situation in turn should alert the researcher to the creation of a very complex and confusing arrangement if a house by house survey is the basis of recorded information. Which way did the person walk, when and why did he or she turn off on a new road, and what was a "natural unit" for completion? Dollar ignores all such complexities because he suffers from the blinders of a ruling hypothesis; that is, he is so committed to disproving Wilkins' conclusion that he starts to simplify and force the data into the direction of the "right" answer.

Conclusion. Settlement pattern as preserved in the censuses is the most complex and difficult problem encountered in the analysis of these data. Although there are maps dating from the 1850's these seem to be incomplete and later maps, at least until the appearance of detailed atlases after the turn of the century, are only slightly modified copies of these originals. Nevertheless using maps and other sources (e.g. gravestone inscriptions) it is clear that Sandy Ground existed and does exist today.

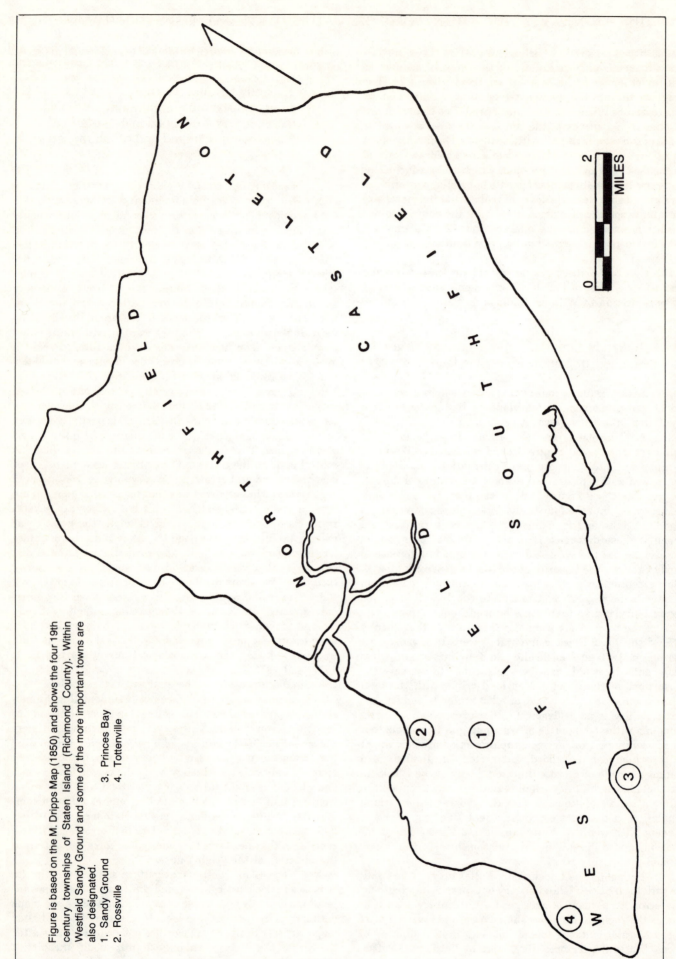

Figure is based on the M. Dripps Map (1850) and shows the four 19th century townships of Staten Island (Richmond County). Within Westfield Sandy Ground and some of the more important towns are also designated.

1. Sandy Ground
2. Rossville
3. Princes Bay
4. Tottenville

FIGURE 1.   Map Showing the Relationship Between Westfield and Sandy Ground.

272

It has geographical and social integrity. It is clustered in a specific area and although, as I originally pointed out (Schuyler 1974: 20), it was always intermixed with White dwellings, there are visible breaks between Sandy Ground and adjacent nucleated areas in Rossville, Pleasant Plains-Princes Bay, the new suburban housing development, and Charleston (see Figures 1 and 2b in Schuyler 1974). Socially it did and still does center on the Black church. It is and was a small community and it is here that Dollar also errs. He does not have the prerogative of determining proper demographic size for a community or to use this device to "define" it out of existence.

Historically, if one analyzes the census data, the existence of Sandy Ground is demonstrated by the patternings of the 1870 and 1860 censuses.[5] It is not clearly delineated in the 1850 census and there could be several reasons for this situation.[6]

3. Sandy Ground was not economically focused on oystering; indeed most Blacks in the area were in other trades.

Basis. Dollar compares the occupational status of all Blacks for each decade between 1850 and 1870 and finds that only a minority are in oystering.

Errors. Again the fundamental error of confusing the units of study invalidates his conclusion. It is true that a detailed study of the economy of Sandy Ground in 1870, for example, might show a greater division of income sources than the oral history would imply. At the same time, such a diversity would not necessarily contradict the claim that the economic focus of the community was oystering. Before its economic diversity in the 19th century can be understood there are several problems with the census data that have to be recognized.

When the perspective is shifted from Westfield to Sandy Ground there is a concentration on oystering although other occupations are also involved.[7] One problem is that it is not clear if the terms "boatman", "oysterman", and "laborer" are mutually exclusive categories. If younger males from Sandy Ground worked on a White oyster boat would they be "oystermen" or "laborers"? If sons worked, perhaps only part time, for a father or other relative on an oyster boat how would they be classified in the census?

Conclusion. Oral history repeatedly pictures Sandy Ground as an "oystering town". It is possible that such an image would not correspond with a tabulation of the total sources of income at a given point in time. Such a finding would not mean that the oystering image is false; in fact, many of the specific opportunities in such economic diversity might be indirect spin-offs of oystering (e.g. the Bishop blacksmith shop). The documents do not at this stage of analysis contradict the reconstruction based on oral history.

4. The inhabitants of Sandy Ground did not have a high standard of living and their standard lowered through the 19th century.

Basis. Dollar primarily supports this inference with an examination of "real estate" figures from the various tracts.

Error. Residents in Sandy Ground, as I pointed out, owned small units of land because they were not farmers.

Their specialized horticultural activity involved backyard gardening not farming. Therefore it is not surprising that their "real estate" valuation would be less than that of Staten Islanders involved in farming and certain other occupations. The "real estate" figures in isolation mean nothing; they will only be given pertinence, if at all, by detailed comparative studies.

Evaluation and Comment. Part of this problem is created by my use of the vague phrase "high standard of living". I did not mean to imply, nor does the oral history suggest, that the inhabitants of Sandy Ground were wealthy. In no sense are they to be classified with the minority of wealthy White oystermen who built mansions on Richmond Terrace on the northern end of the island. After the initial settling-in period, however, Sandy Ground was a stable and economically successful community until after the turn of the century. Its inhabitants owned their own houses and had steady, if varied, sources of income. In a few cases they owned boats and had manipulative amounts of capital.

All of the points Dollar attempts but fails to make are legitimate questions, but questions for which answers based on documentary research are not yet available. Dollar's ersatz research only confuses the situation because of his naivete concerning historiography.

PART III

If one source enables a scholar to gain direct access to past events while another by its nature offers only indirect access to the same events, it would seem that a reconstruction based on the former would be stronger by definition. Most documents give us direct insight into emic phenomena and indirect views of behavior (etic), while oral history removes both types of phenomena a step further from the investigator. As has been shown, however, it is not only the intrinsic nature of the written account compared to the verbal account but also the individual features of the specific item and the manner in which it is analysed that determines its worth.

Both documentary and oral history are similar in that they, unlike the archaeological record, do not directly preserve the remains of human behavior. They are different in that the recording of past events in documents may be contemporary with the event (an "eyewitness account")

	ETIC (Behavior)	EMIC (Concepts)
Archaeological Context	Directly Available	Present But Not Available
Historical Context	Indirectly Available	Directly Available
Oral History Context	Indirectly Available	Indirectly Available
Ethnographic Context	Directly Available	Directly Available

FIGURE 2. Various Contexts Within Which Data Are Available to the Historical Archaeologist.

while it is not when only the memory of events is preserved. Many documents, of course, also involve a memory factor in that they were written after the event, sometimes years later. The true contemporary document is a rarity among archival sources. A census is one of the exceptions and when properly utilized is a significant source of information.

An Isolated Document

The accuracy of primary, written sources is very difficult to evaluate except when independent sources of information, usually other documents, exist. Unless a document can be placed in a general historical *context* it must be used with extreme caution. Although Dollar compares censuses from different decades, he treats them as isolates removing them from any meaningful context. The only prepared context, that of oral history, he only uses in a negative manner. This approach forces him to accept the census "facts" as self validating. Such an oversight is not allowable. In fact, the specific nature of a census more than counterbalances the fact that it is coeval with the information it contains. If such data are used for broad, regional studies, as the cliometric historians have recently done for slavery, certain sources of error may not be statistically significant, but if the focus is on a local sequence of events these flaws are accentuated.

What is a census? Census schedules, at least the variety used by Dollar, are an attempt to collect quantified data by asking informants a set of standard questions. Anthropologists have learned that the questionnaire is probably the most misleading technique for collecting ethnographic data because the specificity and rigidity of the format distort the information obtained. Frequently the results have more to do with the people drawing up the questions than with the people being questioned. An additional factor concerns the conditions under which the questionnaire is administered. Who is the census enumerator? Today there is usually an attempt to use local people whenever possible, and it is known that one member of Sandy Ground did census tracts in the 20th century, but the 19th century circumstances are not clear. If a person was from Rossville or Tottenville or was White or Black could be important influences on the results obtained. Another problem is the possibility that the terms used in the censuses after 1850 did not carry the same meaning for enumerators separated by at least a decade. Historians working with censuses for the antebellum South have encountered similar problems (Bonner 1974: 36).

Dollar opens his discussion of the censuses with a rather amusing statement:

> Beginning with the 1850 census . . . it is possible to determine (for Sandy Ground and Westfield) the name of every person who lived there, the age, sex, and race of those persons, the profession or trade of every male over 16, the value of their real estate, the place of birth, marriage and education information, and whether they were deaf, dumb, blind, insane, idiotic, pauper, or a convict.

How many people are going to list the number of "insane" or "convict" members of their families for a census taker? Even if the enumerator is a local person and knows the real situation would he or she record it? Is it surprising to discover that these columns are almost uniformly blank on the census forms. All such categories prove is that they were of interest to the bureaucrats that composed the census.

Selecting a less obvious but perhaps more pertinent category, is it clear that people would give their correct place of birth? Why not? If in 1850, for example, some of the Marylanders then residing in Sandy Ground were squatting on land, as the land records seem to indicate, would they give their place of birth which might draw the attention of Staten Island officials or would they simply say New York? Indeed if they could avoid being covered by the census survey, which might not be too difficult if the enumerator was a White outsider, that might be an even simpler solution to this problem. Whether such behavior occurred or not is unknown but some of the Marylanders that oral history and other written sources would place at Sandy Ground in 1850 are not listed in the census.

As a final example there is the category of "personal estate". This column is frequently left blank but when figures are given, such as $100 for John Holmes or $400 for R. Langdon in 1860, what do they mean? Is "personal estate" the value of a person's material possessions, a potential annual income, the amount of savings or cash on hand, or some combination of these sums? What did the term mean to the person being questioned or the person asking the question? How would you answer it today? More importantly did this category, or the other phrases, consistently carry the same meaning from enumerator to enumerator or from census to census?

A Historical Synthesis

Dollar avoids problems of internal analysis by ignoring the need for a general documentary context which might alert the researcher to such distortions. Nowhere is this lack clearer than with the very foundation of his critique—primary versus secondary sources. He does not comprehend that Wilkins' synthesis for Sandy Ground, which is a secondary source, is stronger and more meaningful than an isolated series of "facts". Her image of Sandy Ground is based on a careful internal study and evaluation of primary oral sources and then an interpretation of these data.[8]

An examination of Wilkins' (1943 c, d, e) original notes and an interview with her (1972) show that she used adequate field techniques. She did not enter the community via a formal institution; in fact, she avoided the church since the minister was an outsider. After another investigator had attempted a study of Sandy Ground and failed, Wilkins simply walked in, found a child hanging clothes and was thus passed from family to family. Although she was White, she was also a Virginian and her background created an excellent rapport which lasted long after her study. She interviewed over 30 people and had six key informants making it possible for her to cross-check statements and reinvestigate nebulous or contradictory points. She also used written sources (censuses, land, probate, and church records) to check certain ranges of data.

A documentary synthesis equivalent to Wilkins' oral history might well produce a different and more detailed picture of Sandy Ground but Dollar does not offer such a synthesis and it does not yet exist. When it is produced by historians who understand primary documentation I predict that it may contain useful insights and data not available in the oral record but unless there are internal records such as diaries and letters, and these have not been found, it will not match the oral reconstruction of the culture history of the community.

Historical research must be based on primary sources but *raw data* can not be substituted for historiography. It is the secondary, scholarly analysis ("historical writings") that gives meaning to primary sources, not the reverse.

CONCLUSION

In an earlier presentation at the Conference on Historic Site Archaeology Dollar (1968) offered "Some Thoughts on Theory and Method in Historical Archaeology" and was severely criticised by several scholars for his misuse and misunderstanding of anthropological and archaeological concepts and terminology. Some commentators (Williams 1968) simply dismissed Dollar's paper because it displayed an acute lack of familiarity with their field. Nevertheless, when I reviewed that discussion I attempted to be fair by not dwelling on these failings but rather by tring to understand and evaluate the basic issues being debated (Schuyler 1970: 229–231). I shall take the same approach here.

Dollar's principal point seems to be that historical archaeology is being ignored by other fields, especially by professional historians, because historical archaeologists have failed to undertake accurate or extensive documentary research. This interpretation is incorrect. It is quite evident, especially is a particularistic, fact-oriented Dollarian version of historiography is espoused, that historical archaeologists are aware of primary documents and use them extensively and successfully to answer *specific* historic questions. A number of writers (e.g. Griffin 1958; Schuyler 1972) have discussed the desirability of shifting the focus from specific to broader problems and cultural reconstructions. Even if such an expansion occurred and historical archaeologists were to produce historical synthesis ("culture history" or "reconstructions of past lifeways") this shift would not necessarily draw the attention of historians. Successful endeavors in documentary history would only result in the generation of good local history and there are hundreds, if not thousands, of academic and regional historians already producing similar monographs.

Historical archaeology, with a few outstanding exceptions, has fallen short of its potential because of a set of more complex problems. Archaeologists have not fully recognized that there are several ranges of data which exist in related but different contexts and they have failed to consider the differences of these contexts, their interrelationships, and their potential unification into final, more replete reconstructions. Because of this oversight they have yet to even convincingly demonstrate the unique strengths of the context peculiar to their field—the archaeological record.

In Part II, I listed these contexts and reviewed their strengths and weaknesses but when their interrelationship is seen in the form of a table (Figure 2) the potential for historical archaeology is emphasized. It is only when the context of archaeological data is contrasted with other sources which deal with past events that its unique ability to serve as the basis for an etic analysis becomes clear. Several factors including the manner in which historical archaeology developed in America, limitations arising from an association with the restoration movement, and the short-term, limited nature of most historical excavations, have masked what should have been an obvious strength. However, if the etic-advantage of archaeology is recognized, such a realiza-

tion would not differentiate historical from prehistoric archaeology. It is only when documents (written records or oral accounts) appear that a fuller and different type of archaeology is possible. Yet most historical archaeologists use documents and other non-archaeological data to solve specific or at best etic-oriented problems ignoring the emic potential of archival, oral, or ethnographic contexts. As scholars who were formerly limited to etic data archaeologists tend to approach documents in a fashion that abridges much of the "historical" aspect of historical archaeology. They interdigitate artifacts and documents to get a more complete picture of past *behavior* or use them separately to get two varieties of the same etic view. Historical archaeology will emerge as a significant field only when it is realized that two contexts, which in part are qualitatively different, may be combined to form a superior cultural reconstruction. This possibility has been discussed by a number of scholars, although usually with an emphasis on the etic-etic potential, and I have recently (Schuyler and Mills 1976) explored a site by heuristically treating each context as a separate entity. Unfortunately the lack of extensive excavations and the specialized nature of the site, an 18th–20th century sawmill, limited the results.

Only one archaeologist, in the traditional sense of the word, has attempted the type of synthesis I am proposing. Deetz has combined archaeological data (gravestones, ceramics, and architecture) with an emic image provided by written sources to create a fascinating, if somewhat impressionistic, "cognitive historical model for American material culture" between 1620 and 1835 in New England (Deetz 1974).

What is an artifact? What is a document? Some consider the answers to these questions to be self evident. I do not. When an understanding of the various available contexts and their interrelationships is achieved and when this achievement is placed into a comparative, cross-cultural perspective, then the field of historical archaeology will draw the attention of both historians and scientists.

NOTES

[1] *The boundaries between archaeological, documentary, oral historic, and ethnographic sources are not absolute. A document, for example, is also an artifact and may be treated as such with chemical, C-14, and other tests. Certain documents are also more closely associated with artifacts on an interpretative as well as a technical level. Photographs are a good example. Although most illustrations may be viewed as typical documents (i.e. strongly emic in origin and nature), the invention of the camera added a mechanical element which directly preserves human behavior. Yet it should not be forgotten that even a photograph has to be "taken" and this process involves an emic screening process (see Adams 1975; Schuyler and Mills 1976).*

[2] *Sandy Ground did not have an 1820's origin, as Dollar states, although its ultimate roots may have that time depth in both the Delmarva and metropolitan New York areas. According to oral history the migration started in the 1830's and 1840's; in fact, the known arrival dates for specific families are in the late 1840's. By 1852 the movement had been extensive enough for the establishment of the local Black church.*

[3] *An examination of the 1820 and 1830 censuses, which bracket emancipation on Staten Island, show that a large population of Blacks, over a hundred, were already resident in Westfield before the formation of Sandy Ground. Many of these were slaves and after emancipation some set up their own homes or may have left the area but a number seem to continue as servants living with White families. With a few possible exceptions these Blacks had no connection with Sandy Ground. (See the map in Fogel and Engerman (1974: 45) for an impression of the place of Staten Island within what was in 1790 a heavy zone for slavery in the Northeast).*

[4]*There is strong evidence for a migratory origin for Sandy Ground in the 1860 census. This movement involved not only the families from Snowhill but also, as oral history relates, a broader oystering zone on both sides of the Delmarva Peninsula. Snow Hill is on the Atlantic side but oystering also extended into the Chesapeake Bay bordering on parts of Virginia as well as Maryland. Oral history refers to connections between Maryland and Virginia Blacks, such as with the Cooley family, and this relationship is also supported by the censuses. In 1860 sixteen families (41 individuals) in Westfield (the separation of Sandy Ground and non-Sandy Ground families in the documents is still incomplete at this stage of research) had a Maryland origin and Virginia has the second highest number of non-metropolitan origins (16 individuals).*

Joseph Bishop, who is interestingly listed as a "laborer" although his presence at Sandy Ground was a product of his ties to the oyster trade, is married to a Virginia woman and three of his five children were born in Maryland. There are two other Maryland-Virginia marriages similar to that of the Bishops and the Purnell family has a male member (brother?) from Virginia.

Another aspect of the formation of Sandy Ground is that even in the metropolitan area a migration is involved. Some Blacks moved from New York and New Jersey into the area probably as a result of their contacts through the oyster trade. Except for a few families, perhaps the Jackson and Henry, most Sandy Grounders were migrants and the initial core was from Maryland and adjacent areas.

[5]*In 1860 Sandy Ground existed as a community but is dispersed in the census probably for the reasons given in the text. For example, but order of visitation the enumerator is in Sandy Ground in the 1450's (1451, 1453, 1454) with the Bishop and Robbins families, which are probably on Woodrow, a side road. Again in the 1470's and 1480's (Stephens, Purnell, and Landin families), Sandy Ground families appear, but the main cluster is in the 1490's (1490, 1491, 1496, 1497, 1498, 1499, and 1500) with a number of Snowhill families prominent. These patterns are repeated in the 1870 census.*

[6]*A few Maryland families (e.g. Stephens) and non-Maryland but later Sandy Ground residents (e.g. the Henry family) appear in the 1850 census but Sandy Ground is not discernible as a settlement. Oral history would place more Maryland families in the area by this period and this seeming conflict may be explained by a number of factors: (1) the Marylanders were not covered by the census (see the discussion on this possibility in the text; also quote under note 8), (2) the formation of the community is slightly later than oral history would imply, (3) the Marylanders are on Staten Island but outside of Westfield. Oral history, however, does not support this last proposition.*

[7]*There is an association between Marylanders and the terms "oysterman" and "laborer" as against "farm laborer". In the 1860 census the Bishops (1451, 1454, 1498) are called laborers but they were tied into the oyster trade. Other families even more deeply involved in oystering (e.g. the Purnells) also fall under the "laborer" category. Another example of this problem is the Landin brothers. After Robert and Dawson Landin became owners of the "Fannie Fern" (1870's?) they employed ten men in oystering (Wilkins 1943 e: 24). How would their "crew" be classified in a census? Although sons may well have been farmed out as general laborers or even agricultural workers, I suspect that the term "laborer" may also cover working on an oyster boat.*

In the 1870 census the correlation between Marylanders, or other known Sandy Grounders, and oystering is more pronounced (especially the families listed under 724, 725, 727, 729, 730, 731, and 732).

[8]*Oral historical research is continuing at Sandy Ground but almost the entire generation that Wilkins interviewed, and which had at least indirect ties into the oystering period, is gone. However, there is another oral account of Sandy Ground that was collected in the period Wilkins was at work. In 1947 Joseph Mitchell followed Wilkins' lead into Sandy Ground to collect background materials for his book, The Bottom of the Harbor. His published account reads like a text; in fact, too much like a text as it is clearly a reconstruction of the actual interview. Recently part of Mitchell's (1973) original notes have become available and these give a firmer idea of his field methods. He briefly interviewed some of the people Wilkins worked with but his main "text" is that of George H. Hunter who was 87 in 1947. He was an outsider having arrived in Sandy Ground in the 1880's. His statements (Mitchell 1959: 108–110) confirm those collected by Wilkins but tend to give greater emphasis to the early, hard years during the founding of Sandy Ground:*

I wasn't born in Sandy Ground myself, 'he continued.' I came here when I was a boy. My mother and my stepfather brought me here. Two or three of the original men from Snow Hill were still around then, and I knew them. They were old, old men. They were as old as I am now. And the widows of several others were still around. Two of those old widows lived near us, and they used to come to see my mother and sit by the kitchen range and talk and talk, and I used to like to listen to them. The main thing they talked about was the early days in Sandy Ground—how poor everybody had been, and how hard everybody had had to work, the men and the women. The men all worked by the day for the white oystermen in Prince's Bay. They went out in skiffs and anchored over the beds and stood up in the skiffs from sunup to sundown, raking oysters off the bottom with big old claw-toothed rakes that were made of iron and weighted fourteen pounds and had handles on them twenty-four feet long. The women all washed. They washed for white women in Prince's Bay and Rossville and Tottenville. And there wasn't a real house in the whole of Sandy Ground. Most of the families lived in one room shacks with lean-tos for the children. In the summer, they ate what they grew in their gardens. In the winter they ate oysters until they couldn't stand the sight of them.

When I came here, early in the eighteen-eighties, that had all changed. By that time, Sandy Ground was really quite a prosperous little place. Most of the men were still breaking their backs raking oysters by the day, but several of them had saved their money and worked up to where they owned and operated good-sized oyster sloops and didn't take orders from anybody. Old Mr. Dawson Landin was the first to own a sloop. He owned a forty-footer named the Pacific. He was the richest man in the settlement, and he took the lead in everything. Still and all, people liked him and looked up to him; most of us called him Uncle Daws. His brother, Robert Landin, owned a thirty-footer named the Independence, *and Mr. Robert's son-in-law, Francis Henry, also owned a thirty-footer. His was named the* Fanny Fern. *And a few others owned sloops ... In those days, the oyster business used oak baskets by the thousands, and some of the Sandy Ground men had got to be good basket-makers ... Also, several of the men had become blacksmiths. They made oyster rakes and repaired them, and did all kinds of ironwork for the boats ...*

An interesting footnote in Hunter's recollection is that men used to appreciate the privacy of the cemetery lot for drinking. By the 1940's this lot was overgrown, implying it had been kept up previously, and the drinkers added broken bottles to the debris. Both these facts would mitigate against one of the explanations for the broken artifact-grave pattern I originally reported (Schuyler 1974), although I do not recall broken bottle glass as being the main item around the graves. What is needed is a detailed study of the cemetery to see if different graves (sex, age, and status) are associated with particular items.

ACKNOWLEDGEMENTS

I would like to thank Gail Schneider of the Staten Island Institute of Arts and Sciences for providing access to the original notes of Minna Wilkins and Joseph Mitchell. William Askins (CCNY) drew the map for Figure 1.

BIBLIOGRAPHY

ADAMS, ROBERT McC.
1974   The Mesopotamian Social Landscape: A View from the Frontier. Chapter 1 in *Reconstructing Complex Societies*, Ed. Charlotte B. Moore. Supplement to the Bulletin of the American Schools of Oriental Research No. 20. Boston.

ADAMS, WILLIAM H.
1975   "Power Structure Bias in the Archaeology of Complex Societies." Paper presented at the Eighth Annual Meeting of the Society for Historical Archaeology, Charleston, South Carolina.

BONNER, JAMES C.
1974   Profile of a Late Antebellum Community. In *Plantation, Town, and Country*, pp. 29–49, Eds. Elinor Miller and Eugene D. Genovese. Urbana: University of Illinois Press.

BOWEN, JOANNE
1975   Probate Inventories: an Evaluation from the Perspective of Zooarchaeology and Agricultural History at Mott Farm. *Historical Archaeology*, Vol. 9, pp. 11–25.

BROWN, MARLEY III
1976   "Archaeology and Social History: the Mott Farm Project in Interdisciplinary Historical Archaeology", *Abstracts*, p.8, Papers presented at the Ninth Annual Meeting of the Society for Historical Archaeology, Philadelphia, Pennsylvania.

DEETZ, JAMES
1974   A Comparative Historical Model for American Material Culture: 1620–1835. Chapter 2 in *Reconstructing Complex Societies*, Ed. Charlotte B. Moore. Supplement to the Bulletin of the American Schools of Oriental Research No. 20. Boston.

DOLLAR, CLYDE
1968   Some Thoughts on Theory and Method in Historical Archaeology. In "Historical Archaeology Forum on Theory and Method in Historical Archaeology." *Papers of the Conference on Historic Site Archaeology*, Vol. 2, Pt. 2, pp. 3–34, Ed. Stanley South. Raleigh, North Carolina.

EMERSON, J. NORMAN
1974   Intuitive Archaeology: a Psychic Approach. *Proceedings of the Annual Eastern States Archaeological Federation Meetings*, Vol. 33, p. 13.

FOGEL, ROBERT W. and STANLEY L. ENGERMAN
1974   *Time on the Cross*. Boston: Little, Brown, and Company.

FURST, PETER T.
1972   The Olmec Were-Jaguar Motif in the Light of Ethnographic Reality. Chapter 29 in *Contemporary Archaeology*, Ed. Mark P. Leone. Carbondale: Southern Illinois University Press.

GRIFFIN, JOHN W.
1958   End Products of Historic Site Archaeology. In *Symposium on the Role of Archaeology in Historical Research*, Ed. John L. Cotter. Presented at the American Anthropological Association Meetings, Washington, D.C.

MITCHELL, JOSEPH
1959   *The Bottom of the Harbor*. Boston: Little, Brown and Company.
1973   *U 489 Documents* (Notes of Joseph Mitchell's field work in Sandy Ground, 1947). Ms. pp. 1–19. Staten Island Institute of Arts and Sciences, New York.

MONTELL, WILLIAM L.
1970   *The Saga of Coe Ridge*. New York: Harper & Row.

SCHUYLER, ROBERT L.
1970   Review of *Papers of the Conference of Historic Site Archaeology* (Vol. 2, Pt. 2). *American Antiquity*, vol. 35, No. 2, pp. 229–231.
1972   Historical and Historic Sites Archaeology as Anthropology: Basic Definitions and Relationships. Chapter 13 in *Contemporary Archaeology*, Ed. Mark P. Leone. Carbondale: Southern Illinois University Press.
1974   Sandy Ground: Archaeological Sampling in Black Community in Metropolitan New York. In "Archaeology of Black Settlements". *Papers of the Conference on Historic Site Archaeology*, Vol. 7, Pt. 2, pp. 13–51. Ed. Stanley South. Columbia, South Carolina.

SCHUYLER, ROBERT L. and CHRISTOPHER MILLS
1976   The Supply Mill on Content Brook: an Example of the Investigation of Recent Historic Sites. *Journal of Field Archaeology*, Vol. 3, No. 1, pp. 61–95.

UNITED STATES CENSUSES
1820   *Fourth Census of the U.S.*, State of New York, County of Richmond, Township of Westfield, U.S. National Archives (New York Public Library), M 33, Roll 65.
1830   *Fifth Census of the U.S.*, State of New York, County of Richmond, Town of Westfield, U.S. National Archives (New York Public Library), M 19, Reel 106.
1840   *Sixth Census of the U.S.*, State of New York, County of Richmond, Township of Westfield, U.S. National Archives (New York Public Library), M T-5, Roll 104.
1850   *Seventh Census of the U.S.*, State of New York, County of Richmond, Township of Westfield, U.S. National Archives (New York Public Library), M 432, Roll 233.
1860   *Eighth Census of the U.S.*, State of New York, County of Richmond, Township of Westfield, U.S. National Archives (New York Public Library), M T-7, Roll 188.
1870   *Ninth Census of the U.S.*, State of New York, County of Richmond, Township of Westfield, U.S. National Archives (New York Public Library), M 102, Roll 188.

WILKINS, MINNA C.
1943a   Sandy Ground: A Tiny Racial Island. *The Staten Island Historian*, Vol. 6, No. 1, pp. 1–3; 7. Staten Island Historical Society, Richmondtown, Staten Island.
1943b   Sandy Ground: A Tiny Racial Island: Part Two. *The Staten Island Historian*, Vol. 6, No. 4, pp. 25–26; 31–32.
1943c   Field Notes on Sandy Ground Research, *Notebook* A, Ms. on file with the Staten Island Historical Society, Richmondtown, Staten Island.
1943d   Field Notes on Sandy Ground Research, *Notebook* B, Ms. on file with the Staten Island Historical Society, Richmondtown, Staten Island.
1943e   Field Notes on Sandy Ground Research, *On Cards*, Ms. on file with the Staten Island Historical Society, Richmondtown, Staten Island.
1972   Interview with the author. Ms. notes on file with the Staten Island Historical Society, Richmondtown, Staten Island.

WILLIAMS, STEPHEN
1968   Forum Comments. In "Historical Archaeology Forum on Theory and Method in Historical Archaeology." *Papers of Conference on Historic Sites Archaeology*, Vol. 2, Pt. 2, p. 73. Ed. Stanley South. Raleigh, North Carolina.

CHAPTER 34

The Use of Oral and Documentary Sources in Historical Archaeology: Ethnohistory at the Mott Farm

MARLEY BROWN

In a recent summary of the potential contributions which "ethnoarchaeology" can make to model-building and explanation in archaeology, Michael Stanislawski defines this field of study as

> the direct observation ... of the form, manufacture, distribution, meaning, and use of artifacts and their institutional setting and social unit correlates among living, non-industrial peoples (1973:8).

While this definition is suitable for archaeologists interested solely in bettering their understanding of prehistoric sociocultural systems, through the use of analogy and the direct historical approach, it ignores the fact that historical archaeologists also stand to benefit from the ethnographic investigation of material culture. Studies of the behavioral and cognitive dimensions of material objects should not be restricted to non-industrial contexts, if indeed such situations actually exist today. Rather, the scope of what has been called "ethnoarchaeology" should be expanded to include all ethnographic research concerned with material culture. In fact, the term "ethnoarchaeology" itself might be profitably discarded in favor of a broadened view of archaeology as a discipline. As James Deetz has argued:

> ... a coherent and unified body of subject matter entirely appropriate to the archaeologist is the study of the material aspects of culture in their behavioral context, regardless of provenience (1970:123).

In this expanded, ethnographic sense, archaeological fieldwork should involve not only the observation of actual behavior and the investigation of cognitive domains, but the eliciting of information about past behavior as well. In other words, provision should be made within archaeology for the oral history and folklore of material culture, particularly in the context of modern, industrial societies. It is the aim of this paper to provide some examples of how fieldwork in oral history and oral tradition which concentrates on material culture can contribute to a program of interdisciplinary historical archaeology. In addition, some ideas will be offered regarding the relationship between archaeological data from above and below the ground, and how the two might be connected in the study of British colonialism in the New World.

INTERDISCIPLINARY RESEARCH AT MOTT FARM

During the summer of 1973, a team of Brown University graduate students in anthropology and American civilization initiated a project which combines the disciplines of archaeology, folklore, architectural history, social history, and economic history, in the investigation of three centuries of life on a rural farmstead located in Portsmouth, Rhode Island. The general problem guiding research concerns the nature of interplay among the following sources:

1. archaeological data and information gathered through oral history and the study of folk material culture;
2. archaeological data and documentary evidence; and
3. documentary evidence and the data provided by the folklore and oral history studies.

The site in question, known as the Mott Farm, is ideally suited to such a research strategy for several reasons. First of all, the farmstead's acreage has remained remarkably intact since the original grant of land to Adam Mott, one of the founders of Portsmouth. An Englishman from Cambridgeshire, Mott settled in Rhode Island in 1638 after a four year stay in Hingham, Massachusetts. The Portsmouth grant, made to him in 1639, consisted of approximately 145 acres running in a narrow strip from Narragansett Bay on the west to a highway on the east which has connected Portsmouth with Newport, Rhode Island, since the early seventeenth century. Although some 40 acres were appropriated by the United States Navy in 1909, the major portion of the farm has been held together so that today its boundaries are essentially what they were in 1640. Ownership of the property passed from the Mott family in 1895 but has remained in the family of its present owner since that date. Under these owners the land has been rented and there appears to have been only minimal alteration of the farm since they acquired title. One of the chief aims of oral history research has been to document more fully the exact nature of occupation and use of the farmstead during the period 1895 to 1969.

In addition to the farm's preservation of an early seventeenth century settlement pattern, the site itself contained until the winter of 1973 a standing house which, in its earliest part, dates to the third quarter of the seventeenth century. This original wing is a two-story timber-framed

278

structure built on a one-room floor plan with a second-story overhang or jetty on the east end, and a stone chimney on the west. At right angles to the original are two additions dating to the first and second quarters of the eighteenth century. In the vicinity of the house are late nineteenth and early twentieth century outbuildings, including two barns and a privy. At least one of these structures rests on foundations which appear to date to the late eighteenth century. Spread over the rest of the property are stone walls which in some cases likely reflect Colonial field divisions. The house and the structures in the surrounding area, as well as those recovered by excavation, provide an excellent body of evidence for the study of changing intra-site settlement patterns and space utilization over a period of three hundred years.

A final advantage of the Mott Farm for an interdisciplinary approach is the wealth of primary historical sources available for the town of Portsmouth and the quantity of documentary material pertaining specifically to the Mott family, including probate, tax, and court records. A large part of the project has been devoted to analyzing the relationship between these primary sources and the evidence revealed by excavation and oral history/folk material culture studies.

With respect to the role of archaeology in the social history of the farmstead, the goal has been to coordinate feature-oriented excavation with research into the architecture of the standing house and the documentary data regarding the Motts and their social position within the Portsmouth community. Analysis in this context has been focussed on the problem of correlating specific family habitations with discrete archaeological features such as trash pits and living surfaces.

The economic history of the farmstead has been pursued through a detailed analysis of faunal and floral remains from the site, accompanied by an evaluation of documentary evidence relating to livestock practices and other agricultural activities and their position within the economic structure of the surrounding community.

While the approaches just outlined have been oriented to the period of Mott family residence on the site, it was also necessary to find out what had happened on the farm after their departure. Although documentary information is available for the period 1895 to 1969, it was felt that in light of recent demonstrations of the accuracy of oral history, such as that provided by Montell (1970), research in this area might afford a valuable supplement to the records. Fieldwork in oral history would also provide an opportunity for experiments involving the participation of the farm's former tenants in excavation strategy.

ORAL HISTORY AT MOTT FARM: DATA COLLECTION

With the assistance of Henry Glassie, a folklorist specializing in material culture studies (e.g., Glassie 1969), a preliminary research strategy was formulated incorporating the investigation of both the farmstead's use by former residents and its position within the oral tradition of the Portsmouth area. Students participating in a summer field school in historical archaeology held at the site were given a thorough orientation by Glassie and then sent out into the community in search of informants. It did not take long to locate a number of individuals who had spent anywhere from one to thirty years on the site. These people became the central figures in the oral history project, but many other informants were questioned as well in order to establish a comparative frame for evaluating the developments taking place on the Mott Farm over the last century.

Very soon after fieldwork began it became apparent that the occupation of the farm by successive generations of the Mott family for over two hundred and fifty years had given way to an entirely different pattern in the twentieth century. Although the farmstead was still the scene of family life, it had become the site of a rural tenement for Portuguese immigrants. Very soon after they acquired the property in 1895, the new owners leased it to one "broker" family, which in turn rented out space in the house to other Portuguese families. During the crowded years of the twenties, as many as four families resided in the first and second stories of the house, while "greenhorns," single men who had just arrived in Portsmouth, were boarded in the attic, sometimes as many as a dozen at a time. The flow of population through the site during the first three decades of this century was rapid, and many informants who had lived on the farm were there only as infants and toddlers. Fortunately, members of three families have been able to provide relatively specific information about their lives on Mott Farm. It should be mentioned that even though the majority of informants were able to recall many pleasant times on the site, the general quality of life there was not what most of them had in mind when they left the Azores for America. Problems with the landlord, and economic and social discrimination within the community of Portsmouth, clearly were factors in the high turn-over of renters at the farm.

During the course of their stay on the site, families shared the house and land with others that came and went in rapid succession. Because of the degree of mobility characterizing many of these families, and the age of individuals at the time of their residence on the farm, many informants had difficulty pinning down exactly when they were there. It is, however, possible to arrive at a fairly accurate chronology by comparing their respective accounts. The three families referred to above occupied the farm during the following periods: 1909–1924, 1934–1947, and 1947–1969.

Interviewing of the former residents was organized by an interest in the following subjects: Portuguese immigration to the Portsmouth area in the early part of this century, the general living and working conditions for Portuguese entering the community, and life on Mott Farm during the informant's time there. This latter category was broken down into more specific topics for consideration in interviews. The majority relate to the use of the site by the family in question. With regard to land utilization and subsistence activities, informants were asked about the crops grown and livestock raised, the procedures followed, and the ultimate disposition of farm products. Included here is information concerning the use of outbuildings and changes made to them, and the kind of equipment employed in farming. The main purpose of this line of investigation has been to reconstruct the general pattern of economic activity at Mott Farm over the past eighty years, as well as to establish the position of the farmstead within the wider economic network of the community during the same period. This information can then serve as a baseline from which to pursue the agricultural history of the farm during the seventeenth, eighteenth, and nineteenth centuries, a baseline which permits a more accurate assessment of the changes that have occurred.

Oral history research concerning the house has sought to determine how rooms were used, what interior remodelling had been done, and how, if at all, the frame and exterior of the structure had been altered. An attempt was made to elicit specific information about the scheduling and location of domestic activities within and around the house, the placement, use, and meaning of household furnishings, and the pattern of refuse disposal. For the areas immediately adjoining the house, the strategy has been to find out from informants the location of activity areas, and the spatial position and function of structures no longer standing when excavation began. It was hoped that through this approach it would be possible to at least partially piece together the structural layout of the farmstead during each period of occupation covered by the informants. These reconstructions could then be tested by excavation, and the accuracy of informant recollections measured. At the same time, provision was made for the use of informants to test the archaeologist's inferences concerning features located without their assistance.

Although it was possible to realize some of these objectives, the inability of former occupants to recall detailed aspects of their domestic and farmyard activities proved a major shortcoming. These memory lapses are understandable, given the highly routinized, even unconscious nature of much of the behavior involved. Nevertheless, they do pose a very serious problem, not only at Mott Farm, but in any ethnographic context where fieldworkers seek memory data regarding material culture. Depending on the situation, other factors can also hamper ethnographic research in this area including the age of informants, the length of time separating the behavior and accounts of it, and the scope and tempo of intervening social and economic change.

Because of the absence of a strong tradition tying the renters to the Mott Farm, the oral history project encountered obstacles which are perhaps unique to this site. Chief among these is the temporary nature of many of the occupations. The Farm was perceived by the majority of residents as simply a way station along the road to a better life, resulting in a minimal commitment to the site on their part. The owners demonstrated even less interest in the farmstead, except as a source of a rather small yearly income. This neglect has, in some ways, been a blessing to the archaeologist, as it is the major contributor to the Mott Farm's time-capsule-like appearance. Likewise, however, it has complicated efforts to reconstruct the site's use over the past century.

Of all the factors influencing the quality of data gathered in the interviews, perhaps the most significant involves the circumstances in which the informants were questioned. At least this is a variable that can be dealt with directly by the researcher. The plan initially followed in the oral history project consisted of two basic steps. After contact was established by phone, a team of two fieldworkers would make a preliminary visit to the home of the informant, at which time the aims of the study were explained and a general rapport hopefully established. This was followed by an invitation to visit the site in the company of the same two interviewers. On the occasion of the actual visit, informants were shown through the house and surrounding area, and questioned about various aspects of their domestic and agricultural activities. The assumption was that seeing their former home and being allowed to survey it at their own pace would contribute positively to their recollection efforts. Unfortunately, this strategy was only partially successful. Instead of having their memories jarred into action by the sight of the farm and house, many of the informants often seemed overwhelmed by the amount of perceptual input they had to process. In other cases, returning to the site did bring back memories, but those of emotional significance to them, the room where a loved one had died, the location of a once beautiful garden, and so forth, rather than recollections of immediate value to the archaeologist.

To compensate for possible distractions created by the abrupt return of informants to the farm after absences of, in some cases, 40 to 50 years, a revised interviewing format was needed, one which introduced former residents back to the scene more gradually. In his monograph on visual anthropology, John Collier points out that photo-interviews can often stimulate informants' memories and direct the pattern of their response in a way not possible with verbal techniques (1967:48). His discussion suggests an approach which might yield more satisfactory results than those obtained this past summer. Instead of returning informants to the site immediately upon establishing contact with them, a session in their homes using photographs of the house and adjacent grounds might give them an opportunity to organize their recollections without the distractions created by the farm's present condition. The family occupying the site during the period 1947 to 1969 happened to possess a collection of photographs showing the farm as far back as the late twenties. In the course of looking through the pictures with family members, many of Collier's observations about the value of photo-interviewing were borne out. The photographs did provide a focus for the interviewing and allowed the informants to react to individual pictures and questions concerning them in a more systematic and seemingly objective manner than that characterizing their responses during visits to the site. In any case, further work in the oral history of material culture at Mott Farm will be conducted with a revised interviewing schedule, incorporating the use of photographs of the farmstead as a step preceding the actual tour of the property.

Even though the recovery of information did not measure up to initial expectations, some informants did become actively involved in the excavation procedure. Their participation came in two forms: they attempted to place the location and describe the form of earlier outbuildings, and they tried to identify and date some of the features encountered in test excavations. The search for two features in particular, the privy used at the turn of the century, and the Mott Family cemetery, was guided by informants' recollections. Unfortunately, test excavations were inconclusive in both cases, although a number of possible locations were ruled out along the way. The privy search did literally become a process of elimination, which only began to show promise at the end of the summer. Late in the field season, an informant who had not previously been consulted pointed out that the privy in question had not stood over by a certain big tree, as another had indicated, but was instead to be found underneath the back dirt pile. The fact that people could not agree on where they had gone to the bathroom over the span of several years underscores the sort of problems encountered in this kind of research.

Hunting for the cemetery was perhaps even more frustrating than looking for the privy. Informants not only disagreed among themselves as to where they had seen gravestones standing, they often contradicted their own earlier testimonies. The location and excavation of the Mott Family plot is important to the project since it can provide demographic evidence not available in documentary sources. Hopefully, many of the individuals recovered can be identified by comparing the data on sex, age, and cause of death derived from skeletal analysis with a list of Motts known to have been buried on the farm. This information can then be evaluated in terms of the demographic profile of Portsmouth as a whole, drawn up from a survey of the town's other cemeteries, as well as from extant vital records in the courthouse. At present, a likely spot for the cemetery has been discovered, but not with the assistance of informants.

Even though the overall contribution of informants was disappointing, they were useful in the interpretation of a structure situated just below the surface in an area to the north of the house. Excavation revealed a set of large foundation stones in the shape of a rectangle, measuring approximately nine feet by thirty feet. The foundation cut into a living surface dating to the eighteenth century (ca. 1740 to 1775). Testing on the west side of the foundation turned up four large post molds, also intrusive into the eighteenth century living surface. These contained fragments of hard white ware and glass dating to the third quarter of the nineteenth century. While it is possible to date the foundation to the late nineteenth century, other aspects of the building's history were unclear, including how long it had stood, why it was built, and how it was used. Several former occupants of the farm, now in their late sixties and early seventies, could recall the building while it was still standing. Although the general method of construction was clear, two dry-laid stone walls supporting some sort of framed roof, informants were able to fill in some of the details of how the structure had been used in their day, and how and why it had been torn down. One man, whose father had used it, made a rough sketch of the building, which indicated that it had a wooden peaked roof, doors on either end, and no windows. He also recalled that his father had used the structure as a woodshed. This functional attribution was tested archaeologically, and received confirmation when the excavation of the floor revealed layers of rotted wood several inches thick over much of the area. The building was eventually torn down in the thirties because it was considered a safety hazard by the family in residence at the time. The walls were dismantled completely, and one by one the large slate chunks were loaded onto a horse drawn cart and hauled up the driveway to be used as underpavement for the road into the farm. This task occupied a father and son, laboring in their spare time at the end of the normal day's farm work, nearly a year to complete.

In addition to the help outlined above, informants have contributed a number of insights into the nature of garbage at Mott Farm. During the years the farm was rented out to Portuguese families, refuse disposal was a relatively simple matter. All garbage of interest to the pigs was set aside, and the remainder, mostly metal and glass waste, was thrown over the other side of a nearby stone wall. While the far side of many of the walls within reasonable walking distance of the house exhibit some refuse build-up, the bulk of trash has piled up in a small walled-in enclosure to the rear of the house. Artifacts jumbled together in this dump range from late nineteenth century bottles to late sixties Right Guard spray cans and BSA parts. Most of the site's former tenants remember contributing to it, and for this reason, the dump has definite experimental potential. With the cooperation of informants it should be possible to identify many of the discarded objects, as well as determine how they were used and where they were stored. Going over a lot of old trash, however, is not appealing to everyone, least of all those

responsible for it. Getting informants to spend the time necessary for such a project has proven to be very difficult. Nevertheless, the dump project will be pursued again in the coming field season.

Another of the dump's advantages is the possibility it holds for an archaeological definition of ethnicity. This feature is unquestionably the result of the site's occupancy by Portuguese immigrants, who were, for the most part, only minimally acculturated when they lived there. As Collier, among others, has observed, household furnishings can reflect ethnic identity or affinity (1967:79). With this in mind, a comparison of the Mott Farm dump with those situated on other farms in the Portsmouth area, known to have been occupied by families of non-Portuguese ancestry, might reveal differences in the assemblages related to ethnic identification. There are, of course, several social and economic factors which must be controlled, but this can be done by consulting documents and archaeological informants. This aspect of research will also be continued during the coming field season.

ETHNOGRAPHIC AND ARCHAEOLOGICAL MODELS AT MOTT FARM

Turning now to a consideration of possible strategies for connecting archaeological and ethnographic studies of material culture, work in two areas is brought to mind. Both Collier, in his discussion of "computing the cultural inventory," and Ruesch and Kees, in their treatment of "object language" (1972:89–158), engage in a kind of analysis which is highly compatible with the interests of archaeology. Their interpretations of the functions of the material environment in modern society are based on a premise familiar to all archaeologists, that a person's possessions can reflect not only his social and economic position, but his value-system and world-view as well.

Another line of research joining ethnography and archaeology in a meaningful way is the study of folk life and its material products. A comprehensive survey of this field can be found in the section devoted to material culture contained in the recent collection on folklore and folklife edited by Dorson (1972). Folk material culture studies that are most relevant to the Mott Farm project are those of Glassie (1969), Barley (1961), and others on the architecture of farm buildings and the structure of farm lay-outs, and those concerned with the role of material objects in traditional foodways (Anderson 1971). Although these analyses are based mainly on ethnographic and historical sources, their perspective is profitably combined with traditional archaeological data, as Deetz clearly demonstrates in his interpretation of the place of ceramics within Plymouth Colony foodways during the period 1620 to 1835 (Deetz 1973).

Of these above approaches, however, the most directly applicable to the Mott Farm case is Collier's cultural inventory analysis. The method he employs is the photographic survey of family households, selected with a specific set of problems in mind. To date, the most extensive study using this technique concerns the degree to which the adjustment of American Indian families to urban life is observable in their home furnishings (1967:81–104). Even though Collier places more emphasis on the relationship between material culture and values than would most archaeologists, his interpretive framework also includes categories of behavior familiar to archaeology (1967:79–81). His photographs do have many advantages over archaeological evidence, especially the detailed record they provide of the location and arrangement of household possessions. In practice, however, Collier's analysis depends as much on the fact that certain objects are present within a household, as it does on their spatial arrangement. His approach is, therefore, applicable to archaeological features such as trash pits and dumps, which are lacking in precise spatial control. The Mott Farm site is particularly suited to cultural inventory analysis because the features encountered there can be correlated with specific family habitations. Instead of the synchronic comparisons employed by Collier, the possessions of successive generations of the same family can be compared in order to document their changing lifeways.

An example of this kind of interpretation is the case of Jacob Mott III, whose family lived on the farm from 1736 to 1781. To the rear and north of the house a refuse layer was discovered which corresponds almost exactly to the duration of his occupancy (ca. 1740–1775). The assemblage recovered from this feature contains a very high proportion of fine imported ceramics, including wares of the Whieldon-type, Jackfield-type, fine English Brown and White Salt-glazed stoneware, and Chinese export porcelain, in vessel forms belonging to tea sets (teapots, cups, bowls, and saucers). At the same time, the study of the standing house indicates that the main room of the early eighteenth century wing underwent interior renovation at approximately 1765. New mouldings were added around the walls and fireplace of what was then the parlor in an attempt to visually raise the height of the ceiling. The mouldings and mantle-piece were executed in a late Georgian style that was reaching its peak of popularity at the time. Recent papers on the role of ceramics within Plymouth Colony households (Deetz 1973; Brown 1973) have shown that a relationship does exist between the possession of certain ceramic wares and social status. Similar evidence has come from inventory studies of eighteenth century houses in Boston and Providence (Stone 1968; Teller 1968; Cummings 1964). Combining these sets of data, it can be postulated that the family of Jacob Mott III was striving to become fashionable in at least one aspect of their material life-style, and that this is part of a broader claim on their part to a social standing not held by the preceding Mott Family, that of Jacob Mott II, who lived on the site from 1712 to 1736.

This inference can be translated into a number of propositions for testing in an independent source, documentary material regarding the two Mott families in question, and their relationships in the community of Portsmouth. If Jacob the Third was really more of a social climber than his father had been then this difference should be evident in the behavior other than acquiring certain ceramic wares and displaying them in a remodelled parlor. In the same way that Collier checked many of his interpretations by interviewing the owners of the houses he photographed, this explanation based on archaeological evidence can be evaluated in light of documentary information. It can be argued that if the interpretations concerning social status is accurate, there should be a corresponding change in the degree to which the two Jacob Motts participated in certain community activities of a prestigious nature. There should also be a difference in the content of their inventories, and perhaps even a different pattern exhibited by the marriage choices of their offspring. A preliminary search of some documentary sources reveals

that Jacob Mott III was definitely more active than his father in town and state politics. This finding does not confirm any hypotheses, but it does lend support to the interpretation. It can be further strengthened by other documentary research on the economic and social positions of the two men in the community.

It should be mentioned that the existence of the personal estate inventories for members of the Mott Family, and for most of the communities in New England and other English colonial areas, is another reason why the cultural inventory approach is so well suited to the historical archaeology of Colonial America. These records provide detailed accounting of peoples' possessions at the time of their death, usually included the value of the inventoried estate, and often are organized in a room-by-room fashion which provides valuable information regarding the spatial arrangement of households and their interior furnishings. In fact, these documents duplicate in written form much of what Collier attempts to record on film. The use of personal estate inventories in conjunction with the analysis of tightly dated trash pits, dumps, and cellar fills can produce stimulating explanations of the role of material objects in the behavioral dimensions of past cultural systems. This approach can be applied either diachronically within one Colonial community (Deetz 1973; Brown 1973), or both synchronically and diachronically in comparisons of different Colonial regions. The potential of household inventories in this latter case is especially great. Even without actual artifactual data it is possible to compare, for example, inventories from southern New England communities with those from settlements in the Tidewater region, or with English settlements in the Carribean, such as Barbados, in order to bring out differences in the patterning of material culture. These differences can then be analyzed in terms of how they relate to the process of adaptation of English Colonial societies to various regional environments.

One final point which should be stressed in this discussion of ethnographic approaches like Collier's and their application to archaeological and ethnohistorical data is that they are equally valid for both industrial and non-industrial contexts. Industrial refers here to those situations where the manufacture and availability of artifacts is not under the direct control of those using them. The emphasis of cultural inventory analysis is placed on how material objects are incorporated into larger complexes of patterned use and meaning, and what this says about the world-view and values of the people involved. This process of incorporation goes on in all societies, regardless of whether or not the individual objects themselves were produced there. In a recent report on ethnographic work in southwestern Alaska, Ackerman discusses the cultural inventory approach and its value for the study of spatial organization in modern Eskimo houses and how the patterns revealed by such an analysis might reflect traditional "object-orientations" (1970:37–41). In a similar vein, Deetz has suggested that the pattern of food consumption characterizing most American households today is a hold-over from an artifact usage introduced into this country during the late eighteenth century, and furthermore, that this pattern of consumption was just one aspect of a whole style of ordering the material environment which he identifies as belonging to the "Georgian mind-set" (1973:30–32).

Although the examples mentioned above are still at a speculative stage, they do draw attention to the potential existing in the ethnographic and ethnohistorical study of patterning in material objects considered as the expression of traditional cognitive styles. What has been referred to here as the cultural inventory approach, incorporating ethnographic observation, oral histories, and documentary source materials, holds considerable promise for archaeologists who want to contribute to anthropological theory. Not only do studies of this kind deal with dimensions of behavior of obvious interest to even the most symbolically oriented of cultural anthropologists, they also focus on processes of continuity and change which are usually neglected by cultural materialists. Finally, the cultural inventory approach can serve to generate hypotheses about the symbolic nature of material environments which may then be tested in more traditional archaeological contexts.

REFERENCES

ACKERMAN, R. E.
  1970 Archaeoethnology, ethnoarchaeology, and the problems of past cultural patterning. In *Ethnohistory in Southwestern Alaska and the Southern Yukon*, pp. 11–47. Edited by Margaret Lantis. Lexington, University of Kentucky Press.
ANDERSON, JAY
  1971 "A Solid Sufficiency: An Ethnography of Yeoman Foodways in Stuart England." Ph.D. Dissertation, University of Pennsylvania, Philadelphia.
BARLEY, M. V.
  1961 *The English farmhouse and cottage*. London, Routledge and Kegan Paul.
BROWN, MARLEY R.
  1973 Ceramics from Plymouth, 1621–1800: The documentary record. In *Ceramics in America*, pp. 41–74. Edited by Ian Quimby. Charlottesville, The University of Virginia Press.

COLLIER, JOHN, JR.
  1967 *Visual anthropology: Photography as a research method*. New York, Holt, Rinehart, and Winston.
CUMMINGS, ABBOTT LOWELL
  1964 *Rural household inventories, 1675–1775*. Boston, Society for the Preservation of New England Antiquities.
DEETZ, JAMES J. F.
  1970 Archaeology as a social science. *Current directions in Anthropology*, pp. 115–125. Washington, American Anthropological Association.
  1973 Ceramics from Plymouth, 1620–1835: The archaeological evidence. In *Ceramics in America*, pp. 15–40. Edited by Ian Quimby. Charlottesville, the University of Virginia Press.
DORSON, RICHARD M. ED.
  1972 *Folklore and folklife: An introduction*. Chicago, The University of Chicago Press.
GLASSIE, HENRY
  1969 *Pattern in the material folk culture of the Eastern United States*. Philadelphia, The University of Pennsylvania Press.
MONTELL, WILLIAM
  1970 *The saga of Coe Ridge*. Knoxville, The University of Tennessee Press.
RUESCH, JURGEN and WELDON KEES
  1973 *Nonverbal communication*. Berkeley, University of California Press.
STANISLAWSKI, MICHAEL B.
  1973 "The Relationships of Ethno-archaeology, Traditional, and Systems Archaeology." Paper delivered at the American Anthropological Association Annual Meeting.
STONE, GARY WHEELER
  1970 "Ceramics in Suffolk County, Massachusetts, Inventories, 1680–1775." *The Conference on Historic Sites Archaeology Papers*, Vol. 2, pp. 73–90.
TELLER, BARBARA
  1968 Ceramics in Providence, 1750–1800. *Antiques*, Vol. 94, pp. 570–577.

CHAPTER 35

A Cognitive Historical Model for American Material Culture: 1620–1835

JAMES F. DEETZ

I should like to present briefly some rather exciting developments in our project in historical archaeology primarily in the old Plimoth Colony area, where we have been working periodically for about 10 years. And what I would like to attempt here is the development of what might be thought of as an explanatory model which uses material culture to indicate and reflect the non-material dimensions of human behavior, by emphasizing my concern with the cognitive dimension of culture. I realize this borders perilously on paleopsychology, and it might be argued as impossible, particularly in data which are not accompanied by written or historical materials. However, ours is, and therefore we can formulate such things. I offer it not so much as a great hope, but rather as a caveat that maybe there are things in our data which we are not aware of, if for no other reason, than because we do not have the kinds of control which enable us to see them.

I would suppose that there is a cognitive dimension even in the simplest of societies, which has some effect, however small, on the way their material assemblages manifest themselves either to the ethnographer or archaeologist. But I think in most instances at the somewhat more simple end of the cultural complexity scale (in terms of socio-economics) this tended to become buried in more imperative aspects of culture. Subsistence being fairly urgent, there is not that number of alternatives available to a culture for it to employ one or another. Thus, if in fact this is even partly so, one could suggest that the cognitive dimension of material culture assemblages may become more visible, more explicit, and may tend to surface to a greater degree as one moves up the scale of complexity. Therefore, I think it is appropriate in a colloquium on complex societies to raise this point and to illustrate it with a society which fits this description. I might point out that it is an empire, the British, but that it is also a frontier; and it is certain that the material culture of a frontier society differs at least in the form of archaeological remains from that of the parent culture which gave it birth.

My insights are based on the work of Henry Glassie, a folklorist trained at the University of Indiana, with a strong cultural, geographical, and structural anthropology background. Basically, the model here is one which considers certain aspects of general culture in space and time. It is a formulation of what happened in Plimoth particularly between 1635, when our documentary data begins and our archaeology effectively starts, and ca. 1835. The description of this period was first read at a conference at Winterthur in Delaware in 1972.

While it is quite possible that every English colony estab-

lished during the 1st half of the 17th century would have passed through broadly similar changes in the cultural systems involved, this model here applies only to New England, Massachusetts Bay, and the Plimoth colonies. And it argues for three sequential cultural types or configurations, one following the other and each somewhat different from the other. The initial system in Massachusetts was that brought to the New World by Englishmen, and it most closely conformed to that which they practiced in their former homes. Since the population of early Massachusetts, particularly Plimoth, was not representative of contemporary English society in its entirety, their culture was also not totally representative. The life ways which were transported to New England in the early 17th century were basically those of the less prosperous steward, yeoman, and husbandman. Deeply rooted in an earlier medieval tradition, the culture of the Puritan separatist colonist was conservative, potentially self-sufficient, and heavily shaped by religious attitude. Once established in the New World, this system underwent minor modification as a result of a somewhat different environment, but it continued relatively unchanged for a generation. This period I would date ca. 1620–1660.

The Puritan Revolution led to a dramatic reduction in immigration during the 1640's, creating depressed economic conditions, a shortage of imported goods, and a cultural isolation which led to a slow but steady divergence from the earlier yeoman life ways. This divergence was reinforced by the increased presence of individuals who had been born in the New World. From this semi-isolated society, a distinctive Anglo-American culture emerged; one probably less English than before, and less than it would become by the eve of the American Revolution. This second cultural system, ca. 1660–1760, was a typical folk culture marked by strong conservatism, resistance to change, and regional variation. So strong was the conservative nature of this early folk culture that it continued relatively unchanged in the more isolated rural areas of New England until well past the middle of the 18th century.

The impact of the Renaissance in the form of the Georgian tradition was felt at different times in 18th century colonial America; earlier in the metropolitan centers - ca. 1700; later in the deep countryside - ca. 1760. And while buildings in the Georgian style began about the turn of the century in the more elite sectors of the society, for the purposes of the model in question the key element is that time when those cultural changes which the term "Georgian" denotes have an effect on the majority of society. Henry Glassie has argued that "Georgian" is far more than a stylistic category. Indeed, it can even apply to a distinctive Anglo-American mind set, characterized by symmetrical cognitive structures, homogeneity in the material culture, a progressive and innovative world view, and an insistence on order and balance that permeates all aspects of life from the decorative arts to the organization of space by society. Glassie has demonstrated elegantly how this particular cognitive system can affect everything from farm layout to carved chests. In these aspects, it contrasts sharply with the earlier medieval tradition. As opposed to the 18th century, I would suggest here that the yeoman and husbandman culture of New England in the 17th century was far more medieval than it was anything else. By the term "medieval" I mean a culture that was far more heterogeneous and asymmetrical in its cognitive aspects and conservative outlook. Another way of viewing it would be as an organic vs. mechanical system.

The impact of the Georgian world view on the older medieval-derived New England folk culture led to a third cultural system, which can be viewed as the first popular culture to appear in America. Only by the latter half of the 18th century did this new popular culture affect the majority of the population, particularly away from the cities. And only then did the regional boundaries begin to dissolve and the overall rate of cultural change begin to accelerate. Since the immediate origin of this new popular culture was England, as society felt its effects it became re-Anglicized. Therefore the vector of cultural change in New England can be thought of as a broad sweeping arc diverging from its English parent in the early 17th century and curving back to unite with it under the influence of new life styles appearing in the mid-18th century and beyond. By the turn of the 19th century even the most remote areas of New England were in this new cultural system which extended unbroken over all of Anglo-America. In archaeological terms, this period can be viewed as the first true horizon in American history.

Now then, that is essentially the model, in rather brief terms. The questions remain: is this model to be found in the data? Is there any kind of fit with the data? Can any manifestation of this model be picked up in the various material culture categories with which we, as archaeologists, function? I would suggest an affirmative answer, and I will confine my comments to three categories: ceramics, gravestones, and architecture, to demonstrate how this model can be seen to fit and does reflect these changes in these areas of material culture.

From 1631 on, probate inventories (recording everything in everyone's house and often prices and in what room objects were found) combined with archaeology are helpful in the analysis of the ceramics. There are very few in number and type from the first period; so few that when we dug the first site which was representative of this period, we thought we had missed the site entirely. The historical records indicate that at this particular time and in this particular class, ceramics played an exceedingly minor role, being related primarily to dairying activities. They simply were not involved that much in food preparation or food consumption.

In the second period, in sites which we have excavated and also from the probate inventories, ceramics tend to increase radically. They diversify in numbers and forms, and large numbers of rather fine imported types appear in the area for the first time. They seem to have occupied a larger position in the total, what we call, food ways pattern of the culture. However, they were not doing it the same way they were in England. In England individual plates were already beginning to be used as well as individualizing drinking containers. On the other hand, in New England the comparative rarity and elegance of the plates indicate that they were used in what Lewis Binford would call a socio-technical function exclusively. They were hung on the wall for decorative purposes; they were not used for eating. They were a kind of poor man's pewter and pewter was a kind of middle-class man's silver.

There was a surge of undecorated types through the 1640's and into the 1650's, an occurrence which, following Ivor Noël-Hume, just might relate to the Puritan attitude toward decorative elaboration. We know they passed laws in Massachusetts Bay establishing what one could wear and how short one's hair had to be cut. Even though there was no legislation regulating what kind of plates one had, there may have been a certain set of attitudes generated on behalf of the population which would lead them to bring in essentially plain undecorated forms. However, we must keep in mind that plain forms were being made in England at that time, and that certainly had an effect.

Basically, in this second period, we see greater diversity in ceramics used differently from the way they were being used in England. But still, according to Glassie's model and the one I have developed from it in a randomized, non-structured way, the food was not consumed from individual pieces; communal containers seemed to be the rule. This is seen not only in the inventories, but again is explained by the archaeological assemblages that we have recovered from farm sites through this period. Thus it seems to fit the suggestion that we are still dealing with the medieval cognitive map here, but that the manner in which the ceramics are being used in New England differs from that of old.

We excavated a series of trash pits which are very tightly dated to the third period, from ca. 1760 on. The ceramic inventory was radically different from anything that had come before. The most striking contrast seen in this later assemblage when compared to the earlier one, is the preponderance of plates and chamber pots. Not only were plates more common, but for the first time they belonged to matched sets. Matched sets had been produced in England for about 100 years before, but they did not appear in the New World until about 1760. More puzzling of course is the large number of chamber pots, which constitute the most common shape in the collection. Two trash pits yielded 28 chamber pots, yet there was a total of 4 chamber pots from 5 farms in the 17th century. Clearly this is a difference, but what does it mean?

Glassie's argument that the Georgian mind set was marked by bilateral symmetry which can be seen in e.g. architecture, furniture decoration, gravestone design, and farm layout is an excellent example of anthropological structural analysis of American cultural materials. The structure which he posits for the Georgian-derived cognitive system stems from the concept of an ordered universe, which in turn is an attribute of the new scientific natural philosophy of the 18th century. A reasonable suggestion might be that such a world view could lead to a great concern for an ordered fit between man and the physical world of his making. Thus they altered the medieval asymmetrical relationship between individuals and their material culture. A new, one man, one plate, one chamber pot relationship may have been operative. And indeed, it was one in which not only were the members of a social group rigorously accommodated by their artifacts, but in matched sets.

One could raise the question of how many people there

were involved, but I don't think that is a valid consideration since this is not an issue of ecology or adaptation but one of cognitive differences—partly due to man's urban-made rationality. Therefore, I think it raises certain concerns about the use of certain bodies of data for things such as population estimates.

One also might say that the people were too poor to afford these things. It is very common to find a man with 50–100 acres of cultivation who didn't even own a bedstead. And this, of course, pertains to the way the culture weights value. The source of supply was at hand in nearby Boston, and we know that some people were obtaining it. In Plimoth one finds that a merchant who was poorer than a yeoman farmer might have had much more matched, structured material culture sets than the yeoman farmer. The farmer still had his mind made up according to the older, medieval ancestry, and the merchant was more cosmopolitan and a part of a different social class.

Gravestones fit this model beautifully. The earliest ones, up to ca. 1660, are not decorated at all, but they are very competently executed. It makes sense if one takes into consideration a pure Puritan aversion to decoration. From ca. 1660 to 1760 there is a bewildering regional diversification of strange inexplicable forms. And then ca. 1760 suddenly there is a profusion of cherubs with a much greater effort to copy other carvers in a very slavish way, whereas earlier there is a freedom of creativity. Even the symbolism is relevant here, in that the cherub is far more fitting with a Renaissance-derived tradition while the death's head and its derivatives better fit the medieval pattern.

Third, in architecture, the best example of the earliest houses is the Fairbanks House in Dedham. It is a medieval, lopsided building with curved wind braces and wings sticking out in every direction. But by about 1660, a regional diversification in architecture began in this country which does not compare to anything in contemporary England. This continued again through the relevant period. The Cape Cod salt box with central chimney, surviving clear into the early 19th century, is a very nice example of just this pattern. But the Georgian house style is one which is radically different and exhibits the same horizontal tendencies.

As Glassie has pointed out (personal communication), when one walks into a pre-Georgian medieval-derived house, one walks right into the middle of the whole seething range of activities from childbearing to cooking, homecraft, and sleeping, all happening in one hall. When one walks into the door of a Georgian house, one sees doors. And when one walks through those doors, one is very likely to see even more doors before getting to the final activity that is going on. This again is bilaterality of the Georgian plan, this ordered, logical symmetry which seems to have come in at this time and is not evident in the earlier period. People would even gingerbread their older houses to make them look stylish on the outside, although they could not remodel totally. Thus it appears that the concern about privacy and individuality reflected in the architectural form of a Georgian house may in fact be definitely related to ceramic diversification and gravestone formality. The evidence suggests that these things fit together in a recognizable form and pattern.